CIPS Study Matters

Level 4

Foundation Diploma in Purchasing and Supply

Measuring Purchasing Performance

Second Edition

Bryan Jones and John Oliver
Supply Chain Projects Ltd

THE
CHARTERED INSTITUTE OF
PURCHASING & SUPPLY®

Published by

The Chartered Institute of Purchasing and Supply
Easton House, Easton on the Hill, Stamford, Lincolnshire PE9 3NZ
Tel: +44 (0) 1780 756 777
Fax: +44 (0) 1780 751 610
Email: info@cips.org
Website: http://www.cips.org

First published June 2006
Second edition published June 2009

While every effort has been made to ensure that references to websites are correct at time of going to press, the world wide web is a constantly changing environment and CIPS cannot accept any responsibility for any changes to addresses.

CIPS acknowledges product, service and company names referred to in this publication, many of which are trade names, service marks, trademarks or registered trademarks.

CIPS, The Chartered Institute of Purchasing & Supply and its logo are all trademarks of the Chartered Institute of Purchasing & Supply.

Technical reviewer: Anne Ball, University of Derby

Instructional design and publishing project management by Wordhouse Ltd, Reading, UK

Content management system, instructional editing and pre-press by Echelon Learning Ltd, London, UK

Index prepared by Indexing Specialists (UK) Ltd, Hove, UK

ISBN 978-1-86124-179-5

Contents

Introduction

This course book has been designed to assist you in studying for the CIPS Measuring Purchasing Performance unit in the Level 4 Foundation Diploma in Purchasing and Supply. The book covers all topics in the official CIPS unit content document, as illustrated in the table beginning on page xi.

Increasingly both public and private sector organisations are taking advantage of the gains good purchasing can bring in terms of improved service and product quality and contribution to the bottom line. Within such organisations there is generally a recognition that good purchasing does not 'just happen' and that there are many factors which need to come together for the best results to be obtained. Such organisations also recognise that, as with most aspects of business, purchasing performance needs to be measured if it is to be fully recognised and understood.

Whilst there can be many facets in the measurement of purchasing performance, this course book views some of the key basic issues from three perspectives.

Firstly we consider the measurement of procurement as a business function – how effective is it on behalf of the business or organisation in which it operates? This is particularly important because it affects the overall profile of procurement and the way the function is perceived by its stakeholders. This is an area of increasing interest to authors and researchers with a growing body of literature available to students.

Secondly we move away from the business contribution to consider the performance of suppliers. It is often said that purchasing is 'only as good as its suppliers', and there is much truth in this as supplier performance plays a major part in forming the opinions of users of procurement services. For this reason, and because there are many practical activities which can be involved, there is plenty of information available in this area for students to access.

Lastly we consider the performance of the buyers. In our opinion this area is overlooked in many books and publications, and indeed there is some 'blurring' between the procurement and human resources approaches. However it is critical for the success of procurement that staff performance is measured *and* that the information is used to train and develop buyers to meet organisational expectations.

Performance measurement is a complex and involving subject – we hope you will enjoy this course book.

How to use this book

The course book will take you step by step through the unit content in a series of carefully planned 'study sessions' and provides you with learning activities, self-assessment questions and revision questions to help you master the subject matter. The guide should help you organise and carry out your studies in a methodical, logical and effective way, but if you have your own study preferences you will find it a flexible resource too.

Before you begin using this course book, make sure you are familiar with any advice provided by CIPS on such things as study skills, revision techniques or support and how to handle formal assessments.

If you are on a taught course, it will be up to your tutor to explain how to use the book – when to read the study sessions, when to tackle the activities and questions, and so on.

If you are on a self-study course, or studying independently, you can use the course book in the following way:

- Scan the whole book to get a feel for the nature and content of the subject matter.
- Plan your overall study schedule so that you allow enough time to complete all 20 study sessions well before your examinations – in other words, leaving plenty of time for revision.
- For each session, set aside enough time for reading the text, tackling all the learning activities and self-assessment questions, and the revision question at the end of the session, and for the suggested further reading. Guidance on roughly how long you should set aside for studying each session is given at the beginning of the session.

Now let's take a look at the structure and content of the individual study sessions.

Overview of the study sessions

The course book breaks the content down into 20 sessions, which vary from three to six or seven hours' duration each. However, we are not advising you to study for this sort of time without a break! The sessions are simply a convenient way of breaking the syllabus into manageable chunks. Most people would try to study one or two sessions a week, taking one or two breaks within each session. You will quickly find out what suits you best.

Each session begins with a brief **introduction** which sets out the areas of the syllabus being covered and explains, if necessary, how the session fits in with the topics that come before and after.

After the introduction there is a statement of the **session learning objectives**. The objectives are designed to help you understand exactly what you should be able to do after you've studied the session. You might find it helpful to tick them off as you progress through the session. You will also find them useful during revision. There is one session learning objective for each numbered subsection of the session.

After this, there is a brief section reproducing the learning objectives and indicative content from the official **unit content document**. This will help you to understand exactly which part of the syllabus you are studying in the current session.

Following this, there are **prior knowledge** and **resources** sections if necessary. These will let you know if there are any topics you need to be familiar with before tackling each particular session, or any special resources you might need, such as a calculator or graph paper.

Then the main part of the study session begins, with the first of the numbered main subsections. At regular intervals in each study session, we have provided you with **learning activities**, which are designed to get you actively involved in the learning process. You should always try to complete the activities – usually on a separate sheet of your own paper – before reading on. You will learn much more effectively if you are actively involved in doing something as you study, rather than just passively reading the text in front of you. The feedback or answers to the activities are provided at the end of the session. Do not be tempted to skip the activity.

We also provide a number of **self-assessment questions** in each study session. These are to help you to decide for yourself whether or not you have achieved the learning objectives set out at the beginning of the session. As with the activities, you should always tackle them – usually on a separate sheet of paper. Don't be tempted to skip them. The feedback or answers are again at the end of the session. If you still do not understand a topic having attempted the self-assessment question, always try to re-read the relevant passages in the textbook readings or session, or follow the advice on further reading at the end of the session. If this still doesn't work, you should contact the CIPS Membership and Qualification Advice team.

For most of the learning activities and self-assessment questions you will need to use separate sheets of paper for your answers or responses. Some of the activities or questions require you to complete a table or form, in which case you could write your response in the course book itself, or photocopy the page.

At the end of the session are three final sections.

The first is the **summary**. Use it to remind yourself or check off what you have just studied, or later on during revision.

Then follows the **suggested further reading** section. This section, if it appears, contains recommendations for further reading which you can follow up if you would like to read alternative treatments of the topics. If for any reason you are having difficulty understanding the course book on a particular topic, try one of the alternative treatments recommended. If you are keen to read around and beyond the syllabus, to help you pick up extra points in the examination for example, you may like to try some of the additional readings recommended. If this section does not appear at the end of a session, it usually means that further reading for the session topics is not necessary.

At the end of the session we direct you to a **revision question**, which you will find in a separate section at the end of the course book. Feedback on the questions is also given.

Reading lists

CIPS produces an official reading list, which recommends essential and desirable texts for augmenting your studies. This reading list is available on the CIPS website or from the CIPS Bookshop. This course book is one of the essential texts for this unit. In this section we describe the main characteristics of the other essential text for this unit, which you are strongly urged to buy and use throughout your course.

The other essential text is:

The Performance Prism by Andy Neely, Chris Adams, Mike Kennerley (0-273-65334-2, 1ˢᵗ edition, 2002, Pearson).

This is a comprehensive and interesting book on performance management in general, and its approach is very much based on the need to understand the performance required by different stakeholders before deciding on the measures and systems to be put in place.

Its approach can therefore be said to be 'top down', making it particularly relevant to the first part of this course book, though there are useful sections on suppliers and alliances and employee relationships which relate to the rest of the course book.

This is *not* a purchasing book as such and students will need to consider how best to apply it to the specifics of procurement, whilst bearing in mind that the book argues in favour of taking a holistic rather than a fragmented approach.

Second edition amendments

As a result of the amendments to the learning objectives and statements of practice, several alterations have been made to this course book.

In section 10.3, two new paragraphs describe the balanced scorecard concept and the plan–do–check–act (PDCA) cycle and their relevance to purchasing performance.

In learning activity 2.4, the balance sheet and profit and loss account in figure 12.8 has been updated and amended. A new section, 12.5, has been added to study session 12, to describe the nature of cashflow analysis and why it is important in the supplier appraisal process.

In section 13.2, two additional bullet points have been inserted to describe the importance of a supplier's research and development activity and cultural adaptation on the part of the supplier.

Finally, at the end of section 15.6, a paragraph has been inserted on the nature of personality profiling and how it can be used to measure and improve individual purchasing performance.

Unit content coverage

In this section we reproduce the whole of the official CIPS unit content document for this unit. The overall unit characteristics and statements of practice for the unit are given first. Then, in the table that follows, the learning objectives and indicative content are given in the left hand column. In the right hand column are the study sessions in which you will find coverage of the various topics.

Unit characteristics

This unit is designed to help students to measure the effectiveness of the supply chain and its contribution to the competitiveness of the organisation.

By the end of this unit, students will be able to apply a range of measurement techniques in order to monitor the performance of suppliers at organisational, functional and individual levels, how they perform financially versus target, compliance to contract and specification, and potential risks that they may present. Students will also understand how the performance of purchasing departments and individual buyers can be measured and how targets for improvement can be formulated.

Statements of practice

On completion of this unit, students should be able to:

- Explain how measuring performance in supply chain activities fits into the overall management process of an organisation
- Evaluate the benefits of implementing a well-structured approach to measuring organisational, functional and individual performance
- Categorise types of performance measures that are available to supply chain managers
- Appraise measures that can be used to improve supplier performance
- Employ accounting techniques and ratios to measure suppliers' efficiency
- Evaluate targets as a means of improving the performance of the purchasing function and individual buyers.

Learning objectives and indicative content

1.0 **Measuring the performance of the purchasing and supply function (Weighting 40%)**

1.1 Evaluate the role and importance of measuring performance.   Study session 1
- Its relationship to the organisation's management decision-making process
- Its link to the organisation's mission and strategic goals and objectives

- The contribution made to the process of continuous improvement and continuity of supply
- The importance of performance measurement for control purposes
- Its role in the purchasing management process
- The advantages and disadvantages of performance measurement for the purchasing function

1.2 Explain the benefits of value added solutions.   Study session 2
- Savings resulting from improved performance
- Reducing inventory costs and administration
- Extending payment and warranty terms
- Using consignment stock
- Improving operational efficiency

1.3 Identify and explain the information required to perform   Study session 4
purchasing activities and how to measure purchasing
performance.
- Departmental versus strategic goals of the organisation
- Resource requirements
- Costing, pricing, inventory management
- Supplier and vendor information
- Product and service specifications

1.4 Analyse the types and categories of key performance measures   Study session 3
available to organisations.
- Contributions to profitability – savings, service and inventory
- Basic workload control
- Infrastructure and competency

1.5 Analyse and explain the methods that an organisation's   Study session 5
purchasing and supply function can use to manage and reduce
inventory costs.
- Economy: achieving best value for money. Managing the cost of the supply operation
- Efficiency: use of appropriate inventory management systems and techniques
- Effectiveness: level of service provided by the inventory function to its end users

1.6 Analyse and explain how the use of information technology   Study session 6
may help in the acquisition of purchase and supply performance
data.
- The use of appropriate management information systems to collect data for stock control and costs
- Databases for recording and storing supplier and vendor information
- Stock movement and monitoring systems, including point-of-sale data capture and delivery details
- Statistical database for quality monitoring purposes

2.0 **Measuring the performance of the supplier (Weighting 30%)**
2.1 Analyse key areas associated with supplier selection.   Study session 8
- The key stages in the buying process
- The variables considered when making the purchasing decision

- Cost of initial purchasing measure
- Ongoing levels of performance in carrying out the service: quality, after-sales service, price, consistency of performance

3.0 Measuring the performance of the buyer (Weighting 30%)

3.1 Define and explain the benefits of a well-managed and structured approach to measuring an individual's performance.
    Study session 15
- Investors in People (IIP) guidelines and structure
- Performance against target assessments
- Planning for improvements
- Using personality profiling to ensure that purchasing staff are appropriate to their role

3.2 Explain how appraisal and evaluation techniques can be employed to measure and improve performance.
    Study session 17
- Periodic reviews
- Informal and formal appraisals

3.3 Analyse and explain how individual components of a purchasing role link to the overall objectives of the organisation.
    Study session 16
- Contribution of individuals to an organisation's profitability
- Management of basic workload
- Development of purchasing infrastructure

3.4 Analyse and explain how an individual's knowledge, expertise and skills can be developed to the benefit of both that individual and the organisation.
    Study session 15
- Individual benefits: level of responsibility, job satisfaction, career progression, skills development
- Organisational benefits: better-trained workforce
- Improved productivity and profitability
- Competitive advantages

3.5 Evaluate and explain the use of a range of techniques to analyse the training needs of individual buyers.
    Study session 18
- Job profiles
- Key objectives
- Performance measures
- Appraisals

3.6 Explain how to measure individual performance against pre-set targets.
    Study session 19
- Cost reduction
- Profitability
- Productivity

3.7 Compare the relative performance measures of the buyer with those of his or her respective suppliers.
    Study session 20
- Key measures of supplier performance: competency, commitment, capacity, control
- Key measures of buyer performance: skill and knowledge, plus contribution to an organisation's goals and targets

Study session 1

Introduction to performance management in purchasing and supply

Introduction

This course book – *Measuring Purchasing Performance* – is divided into three parts:

- measuring the performance of the purchasing and supply function (sessions 1–6)
- measuring the performance of the supplier (sessions 7–14)
- measuring the performance of the buyer (sessions 15–20).

The whole course book will review all aspects of performance management for procurement professionals working in any business sector or organisation.

Performance management is not just the prerogative of large corporations; it is equally important for enterprises of all size and structure.

There are 20 study sessions in this course book. This first session lays the foundation stone for the subject.

> 'If you can't measure it, you can't manage it.'
>
> **This business axiom implies that performance measurement is critical to core business activities. This principle is valid for all organisations.**

Session learning objectives

After completing this session you should be able to:

1.1 State the principles of performance management in corporate business operations.
1.2 Explain how performance management is undertaken within purchasing and supply operations.
1.3 Explain how costs are identified and built up in business processes, from the acquisition of goods and services to added value, and to final delivery to customers.
1.4 Give examples of how performance measures are used as part of the wider principle of continuous improvement in business.
1.5 Assess how performance management is linked to the need for continuity of supply in a business operation.
1.6 Demonstrate the importance of effective supply chain performance management within the management of a successful operation.

Unit content coverage

This study session covers the following topics from the official CIPS unit content document:

Statements of practice

- Explain how measuring performance in supply chain activities fits into the overall management process of an organisation.
- Evaluate the benefits of implementing a well-structured approach to measuring organisational, functional and individual performance.

Learning objective

1.1 Evaluate the role and importance of measuring performance.
- Its relationship to the organisation's management decision-making process
- Its link to the organisation's mission and strategic goals and objectives
- The contribution made to the process of continuous improvement and continuity of supply
- The importance of performance management for control purposes
- Its role in the purchasing management process
- The advantages and disadvantages of performance measurement for the purchasing function

Prior knowledge

You should have some general knowledge of the supply chain process, and the basics of costs involved in managing a business operation and the goods and services used. You also need to have some financial/value analytical skills.

Resources

No specific resources are required, but it will be useful to be or to have been involved in some aspects of performance monitoring. This might be either in a general business operating environment or more specifically in measuring or monitoring purchasing-related issues. If not, you may find it useful to discuss this issue with other students or colleagues, or with a manager.

Timing

You should set aside about 6 hours to read and complete this session, including learning activities, self-assessment questions, the suggested further reading (if any) and the revision question.

1.1 The importance of performance management in business

Organisations in all sectors take many forms and functions, but they all have a common need to manage their business needs efficiently and effectively in line with their stated business objectives.

Most businesses set out a business plan, which begins with both a mission statement and a vision statement, and then set out a plan of how the business will be managed over time. Business management matters are led by strategic plans, which are delivered by tactical and operational methods. Management is then effected by implementing the longer-term strategy, executing medium-term tactical management, and directing the day-to-day operational processes.

Most organisations have a planned management structure that includes some, if not all, of the following interrelated management functions:

- finance
- human resources
- design
- production/service operations
- marketing
- purchasing
- administration.

Whatever the size of the business, success is judged by the result of the whole organisation's performance, and each element depends on all the others for corporate success. This first study session takes an overview of how the organisation is judged as a whole; in subsequent sessions we shall then move on to focus on how purchasing management plays its part in this corporate result.

In the opening sentence of this session we used the terms 'effectively' and 'efficiently' in describing how the achievement of business objectives is assessed. In considering performance management we need to understand the meaning of both effectiveness and efficiency before we move on to consider performance measurement in subsequent study sessions:

- **Effectiveness** is measured by the extent to which stakeholders' or customers' requirements are met over time.
- **Efficiency** is measured in terms of how economically the organisation's resources are utilised in providing a given level of stakeholder/customer satisfaction.

These two terms identify the dimensions of performance measurement for corporate managers in general, and for purchasing managers in particular.

The selected performance indicators are called **key performance indicators** (KPIs).

You can view performance management in terms of a process diagram, as illustrated in figure 1.1.

Figure 1.1: Purchasing performance management within the organisation

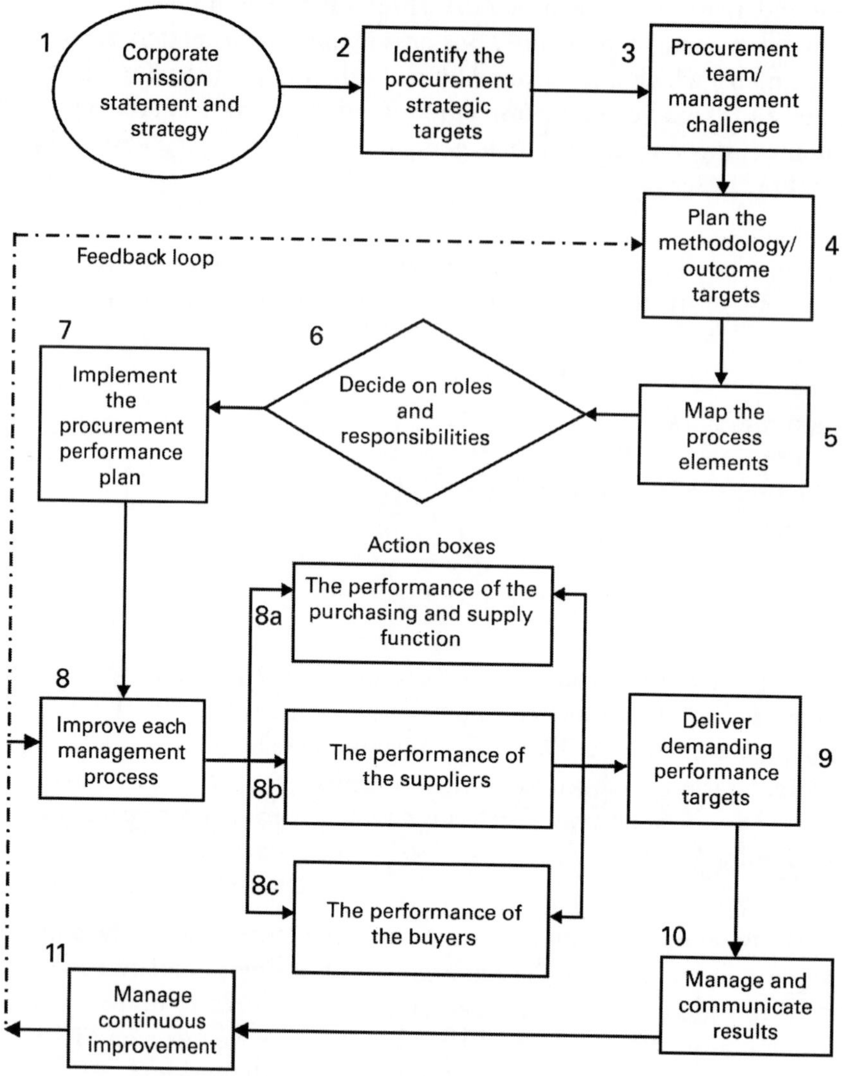

The numbered boxes in this diagram set out the key steps in purchasing performance management within corporate strategy:

1   The business management team or board establish the organisation's mission statement.
2   They then establish the purchasing function's strategic targets.
3   The procurement management team accept the challenge.
4   The purchasing manager or managers decide on their methodology and targets.
5   The manager or management team map out their plan.
6   Decision point: who does what?
7   Start the implementation plan.
8   Start the action plan: subdivide it into purchasing function performance, suppliers' performance, and buyers' performance.
9   Deliver the KPIs.
10   Communicate the KPIs.
11   Manage continuous improvement of the KPIs.

See also the dotted feedback loop: repeat the process as necessary.

1

Learning activity 1.1

Based on your organisation or experience, review the process diagram above and create a KPI checklist of purchasing points that you recommend should be measured in the action boxes 8a, 8b and 8c.

Feedback on page 14

Now tackle the following self-assessment question.

Self-assessment question 1.1

Based on the list you created in learning activity 1.1 above, categorise the performance indicators (KPIs) that you identified for your organisation to achieve operational and/or business success under the following three headings:

1   Strategic performance measures (longer-term senior management targets and issues)
2   Tactical performance measures (medium-term executive/supervisory management performance issues)
3   Operational performance measures (shorter-term process/transactional data and issues).

Feedback on page 15

1.2   Introduction to performance management in general and purchasing and supply in particular

Purchasing is an important function in any management team. Depending on the nature of the business, a significant percentage of turnover is spent through purchasing.

In this course book you will be focusing on purchasing, but the wider term **supply chain management** is implied in many cases. Supply chain management covers the whole process of managing goods and services into, through and out from the business. Supply chain management can and does have a direct effect on the profitability and performance of the business. The supply chain management functions interface both with the external environment and with internal management and processes. They fall into three supply chain or logistics categories:

- inbound supply issues
- intra-site management
- outbound delivery of goods and services to stakeholders or customers.

The broad process flow can be illustrated as in figure 1.2.

5

1

Figure 1.2: Supply chain performance measurement processes

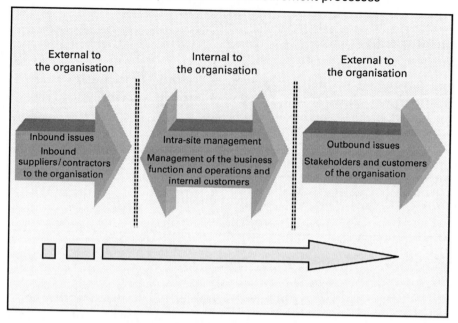

Learning activity 1.2

Reflect on your business or work experience to develop a list of the most effective points or issues that can be used to measure purchasing performance within the wider supply chain.

Feedback on page 15

Now tackle the following self-assessment question.

Self-assessment question 1.2

Based on what you have read so far and/or your commercial experience, list *five* different measures of purchasing performance for your business/organisation, and rank them in order of importance.

Feedback on page 16

1.3 Introduction to cost management in organisations and the link with purchasing performance

Financial management, budgeting, cost management and accounting procedures are fundamental to organisations, irrespective of their size or the market sector they are in. Private sector organisations measure percentage profitability and return on capital employed (ROCE) as key financial indicators. Public sector organisations have strict budgets, but usually measure service levels delivered as performance indicators. All organisations – private and public – need to manage their costs in order to achieve their strategic targets.

Products and services are costed and sold to consumers. The main elements of building a commercial cost model are labour, materials, overheads and profit. Public bodies and not-for-profit organisations (NPOs) may not make a profit as such, but they usually have to recover their service costs within their budget limits. However, whether you are a buyer for a private or a public organisation, you need to know how costs are accumulated, how they are accounted for, and how prices are determined.

There is not always a direct relationship between the cost of an item or service and the price you pay. There are many other market factors, some of which can be quantified and valued objectively, such as money, time, and level of quality. Other issues are more subjective: service quality, artistic or aesthetic value, business relationships and similar qualitative issues.

There is an old adage: 'There are some people who know the cost of everything but the value of nothing.' In commercial purchasing we *do* need to know the costs and, where appropriate, how they are made up, but in some cases market or category knowledge is equally important.

The measurement of purchasing performance, then, is a skill that requires us to consider both objective information and subjective opinion.

Mini case study: Cost analysis

You are managing a contract to supply office desks. The current price is £269 per desk. You request a cost analysis from your regular supplier, who replies with the information shown in figure 1.3.

Figure 1.3: Mini case study

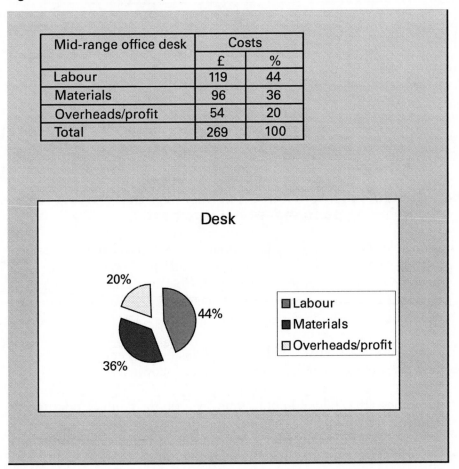

Mid-range office desk	Costs	
	£	%
Labour	119	44
Materials	96	36
Overheads/profit	54	20
Total	269	100

You now have some better cost information about the product you are purchasing. You can see where the costs occur, and can use this information for a variety of purchasing purposes: comparison, price monitoring over time, and so on.

Obviously the costs for different goods and services will vary greatly. Some are labour-intensive, some are dominated by the price of materials, and some carry different overhead or profit levels. The main point here is that, by having a more detailed cost analysis, a buyer has better information to link to performance management tasks.

You will have the opportunity to develop the principles of cost and price analysis further in study session 4.

Learning activity 1.3

Explain how costs are identified and built up for a product or service with which you are familiar.

Feedback on page 16

Now tackle the following self-assessment question.

Self-assessment question 1.3

You wish to find out more about the cost of items you buy. Draft a table or form for your suppliers to complete when they next quote a price for goods or services.

Feedback on page 16

1.4 Continuous improvement in business, and the link with purchasing performance management

The principle of **continuous improvement** is common to many successful business operations where there is an ongoing culture of developing and improving processes and products over time. Continuous improvement organisations foster improvements in product quality, which often produce simultaneous reductions in costs.

Various quality 'gurus' have developed the principles of continuous improvement, and some milestones include the following:

- Demming (1982): his 14 points, moving from the product 'price tag' to a total cost philosophy
- Ishikawa (1985): quality circles and continuous improvement principles
- Taguchi (1986): improvement by statistical process control (SPC).

The Japanese philosophy of continuous improvement has developed as part of both just-in-time (JIT) and the more recent lean supply culture in industry.

In both research and development and, later, the production environment the learning curve principle will apply. When a new product is developed, the prototype and early product runs will take longer to make than subsequent runs. Manufacturing tasks are performed more quickly with each subsequent repetition (up to a certain limit). Therefore the process labour costs will reduce as we 'learn'. This is one practical example of continuous improvement in production management operations.

The Japanese word *kaizen* means 'improvement'. Kaizen strategy calls for everyone linked to the organisation to make never-ending efforts to improve – managers, workers, suppliers, stakeholders and customers alike.

Based on this philosophy we shall now focus on the contribution that purchasing performance measurement can make to the wider process of continuous improvement.

Purchasing can ensure improvements at all stages in the supply chain. Here are some examples:

- managing the quality and service delivery of inbound supplies
- ensuring continuity of supplies to the organisation by means of best purchasing practice tactics
- ensuring selection of the best suppliers for the business
- reviewing the transactional processes in purchasing (i.e. the many transactions that take place in the supply chain)
- ensuring adequate stockholding where appropriate
- managing the purchasing process to best effect
- managing cost reductions as suppliers make 'learning curve' savings
- feeding back vendor performance rating to existing suppliers
- ensuring that outbound processes and services satisfy customer needs.

No doubt you could add to this list based on your own experience or business needs. The main point here is that you need to recognise how we in purchasing can be proactive in the process of managing continuous improvement, whatever our role and responsibility.

Look back at the process diagram in figure 1.1. Point 11 in the diagram marks the continuous improvement point of review. This is where you can identify opportunities and follow the feedback loop to undertake continuous improvement in purchasing performance.

Learning activity 1.4

Identify three ways in which you can achieve continuous improvement gains over time with a supply partner.

Feedback on page 16

Now tackle the following self-assessment question.

Self-assessment question 1.4

Explain the process of continuous improvement with respect to the concept of the learning curve.

Feedback on page 17

1.5 Continuity of supply, and the link to measuring purchasing performance

One of the buyer's most important roles for his or her organisation is to ensure **continuity of supply** – the availability of materials or services to the organisation when they are needed.

Figure 1.4 illustrates several 'core tasks' that are the role and responsibility of purchasing in the business. They involve short-, medium- and longer-term actions incorporated in the purchasing strategic plan.

Figure 1.4: Purchasing: the key tasks within a business or organisation

You may need to refer to this diagram several times as you progress through this course book. Depending on the nature of the organisation you may need to consider other tasks, but this model summarises the core tasks for a purchasing manager.

Ensuring continuity of supply to the organisation is shown as one of the core tasks, along with the need to produce verified performance indicators.

Most organisations need some form of goods or services to run their business – raw materials, components, consumables, equipment, repairs and maintenance, wholesale/retail stock etc, depending on the business needs. Without these basics businesses could not continue, but that does not mean that purchasing should obtain them at any price. Purchasing's role is to manage the supply inputs regularly and consistently over time to meet the business's needs. The measurement of this core task must provide a meaningful indicator of purchasing performance.

Continuity of supply can be achieved in many ways; some of them are listed below (you should remember, however, that buyers must consider the cost–benefit consequences of each action relevant to their particular organisational and financial needs):

- multi-source supplies
- single-source agreements
- developing a strategic partnership
- managing stock and stockholding
- market research and knowledge
- collaboration/cooperative strategies.

These opportunities offer different benefits in the short, medium and longer term. They can be used independently, or together; they are not mutually exclusive.

Having made operational choices, managers can then measure the outcomes and the performance indicators, which are thus a measure of the success or failure of the strategy or tactic adopted.

The measurement of supply continuity outputs would address such issues as:

- customer service/product delivery performance
- number of production line hold-ups due to non-supply
- the cost of holding stock as 'insurance'
- the cost of being without supplies
- the acquisition costs of obtaining supplies.

Learning activity 1.5

Supply continuity is an important core activity. However, we have emphasised the need to be aware of cost–benefit issues. Purchasing costs money; holding stock costs money. Organisations can choose to have more or less of each.

Using these two terms create a list of costs that you would include under these two headings:

1   What is the cost of acquiring goods and services?
2   How much does it cost to hold inventory/stock?

Feedback on page 17

Now tackle the following self-assessment question.

Self-assessment question 1.5

What are the costs of non-supply of goods and services to your business operation?

Feedback on page 17

1.6 The importance of measuring purchasing and supply chain performance in public and private sector organisations

So far in this first study session we have introduced the wider context of performance management in general and the measurement of purchasing performance in particular.

The holistic concept of measuring purchasing performance was illustrated in the steps of the process flow diagram in figure 1.1. This diagram included three action boxes:

- 8a The performance of the purchasing and supply function
- 8b The performance of suppliers
- 8c The performance of buyers.

You will see that these purchasing actions are preceded by planning and policy actions. When the performance in boxes 8a, 8b and 8c is measured, the flow diagram shows that the next step is to communicate the results and then link them to the process of continuous improvement within the business.

In an organisation that has chosen to manage performance across all three functions – supply, suppliers and buyers – each departmental area of operation would be managing its own set of action boxes in order to make its input to the corporate performance objectives. Thus the individual departments or functions work as a team in achieving the corporate performance goals.

Purchasing plays a key role in this corporate process, and in task 6 of figure 1.1 the purchasing team players agree their roles and responsibilities linked to the purchasing targets.

We have now introduced the main elements of purchasing performance management. As you worked through each of these you had an opportunity to identify some specific purchasing performance measures.

You now need to start on your own path to continuous improvement by looking back over your work and improving the outputs, aiming at effective and efficient measurements of purchasing performance.

In the spirit of continuous improvement you will develop your skill and understanding further as you work through the course book.

We now focus on the way in which purchasing has a direct effect on all organisations, even though they may measure their performance in different ways:

- private sector businesses: company profits, ROCE, value for money (VFM), cost reduction, reduced stockholding, customer service
- public sector/NPOs: service to users, utilisation of funds, profitability, response and service times, stock availability.

We can classify measurable improvements linked to purchasing under various headings:

- cost reduction
- service improvement
- continuous improvement progress
- improved/reduced stockholding
- improved quality outputs
- improved delivery/schedules
- improves process control/systems
- reduced transaction costs
- improved supplier base management
- improved communications
- measures specific to the organisation.

We can view the above issues as long-, medium- or short-term indicators: the strategic or longer-term issues measured over 1–4 years, tactical or medium-term issues measured over 1–2 years, and the shorter-term transaction/operational issues measured over 6–12 months. Each may also be part of a wider continuous improvement development programme within the organisation. Each is important to the organisation plan in general and to purchasing management in particular.

Having discussed the theory you now need to put purchasing performance management into practice by using your own skill and judgement in selecting practical measures that will contribute to your organisation's success.

Learning activity 1.6

Develop a checklist of purchasing performance indicators at the strategic, tactical and operational levels that could be applied to a chosen working environment.

Feedback on page 18

Now tackle the following self-assessment question.

Self-assessment question 1.6

For a given operational environment select the four best practice purchasing performance indicators.

Feedback on page 18

Revision question

Now try the revision question for this session on page 331.

Summary

This session opened with the wider corporate view of performance measurement within the whole organisation, and showed where the purchasing role fits into that process.

The session then developed the issue of performance management elements, cost and price management, links to continuous improvement, and the importance of continuity of supply to all organisations. Each of these is equally relevant in any business sector, whether public or private.

The final section developed the many and various opportunities to measure performance, and encouraged students to relate the theory they are studying to practical situations in their own experience.

Suggested further reading

Students will find Neely et al (2002) particularly useful supplementary reading, providing a higher level overview relevant to study sessions 1 to 6. Lysons and Farrington (2006) provides excellent and detailed information on strategy and strategic procurement theories, and chapter 9 of Poister (2003) provides a perspective on how to apply measures at a strategic level, all of which is also relevant to these six sessions.

For this session in particular students will find more information about the works and theories of the quality 'gurus' (Deming, Ishkawa and Taguchi) in Lysons and Farrington (2006), chapter 9, pages 271–2.

Feedback on learning activities and self-assessment questions

Feedback on learning activity 1.1

The purpose of this activity was to set the scene for the course book by first understanding that purchasing is an important part of any management team, in terms of its contribution to success as measured by the achievement of agreed targets set in the business plan.

You should have identified a minimum of three KPIs for each action box.

8a KPIs related to the management and organisation of the purchasing function.

For example, the KPI process time for processing a customer requisition to order:

KPI versus actual over the last quarter.

8b KPIs related to performance of suppliers selected by the purchasing managers

For example, the published performance levels for a category of suppliers:

- KPI: delivery performance of top five suppliers last quarter.

8c KPIs related to personal performance of buyers in the organisation

For example, the savings target versus actual.

- KPI: target for a buyer group over the last quarter.

Any of these examples can be expanded. For example, a KPI developed under 8b could be fleshed out in detail for a specific supplier:

- Delivery performance for a specific product from key supplier ABC Ltd.
- Target: 95% of 'on-time' deliveries as per dates agreed.
- Measured: monthly, giving percentage result and variance from target.
- Feedback and actions: on results and variance.

Feedback on self-assessment question 1.1

There is no right or wrong answer here. This is your list, and the object of the question was for you to understand the differences in timescale and actions related to business strategy management, tactical management targets and process/transactional issues that exist in any organisation.

Feedback on learning activity 1.2

We can generate a useful general management checklist for this type of question by asking the questions How? What? Where? Why? and When?

At this stage you are being asked to decide 'where' and 'what' to measure on the basis of information given to you up to this point.

As you progress you will be more selective in your answers, but you should have identified some performance indicator suggestions for each of the three stages in the flow diagram.

Generic examples might include the following:

- inbound: supplier delivery/quality KPIs
- intra-site: stock and warehouse management KPIs
- outbound: transport and distribution KPIs.

Feedback on self-assessment question 1.2

As we have seen, there are many issues and actions that can be measured, and which you might have listed. The point of this question is to develop your skill and judgement in assessing which measures are the most useful and relevant to meet your success criteria.

The purpose of ranking them in order of importance is to show that you must be selective in deciding on the indicators and on how you will measure them for best effect.

Feedback on learning activity 1.3

The purpose of this activity was for you to understand the elements of cost for goods and services supplied, and how they are broadly classified in a cost accounting price build-up format.

You should have chosen a product or service that you offer or consume, and have should have researched the basis of the main cost headers that we introduced above.

You may have accurate cost analysis data, or you may have made a reasonably informed judgement on the item or service that you have chosen.

You should have subdivided the costs into labour, materials, overhead and profit, and have calculated the percentage make-up of the total you pay.

Feedback on self-assessment question 1.3

You need to undertake this activity selectively for key items only, and not for everything you buy. Table 1.1 shows the basic data we would expect you to include on such a form.

Table 1.1 Cost information

Product	Cost	Percentage %
....		
Labour costs		
Material costs		
Overheads		
Profit		
Selling price/total		

Feedback on learning activity 1.4

This activity takes you to the beginning of the supply chain – inbound – where buyers agree the purchase of goods, stock, services etc The use of the term 'supply partner' implies the existence of a longer-term relationship with a vendor. If both parties – buyer and supplier – wish to maintain that relationship, it is in both their interests to work together and follow a continuous improvement strategy by:

- the buyer giving clear and timely notice of needs
- the seller being open with cost information
- the buyer reducing transactional costs to a minimum and paying suppliers on time
- the seller passing on process/manufacturing improvement costs as the learning curve effect progresses
- the seller looking for cost reductions or service improvements that have mutual value for the relationship.

These are just some of the ways you can achieve continuous improvement gains in purchasing management. How did your list of three ways compare?

Feedback on self-assessment question 1.4

As you have read in this session, a basic form of continuous improvement is linked to the management theory of the learning curve.

Most people improve their skill or competence when undertaking the same task after several repetitions. In a manufacturing context we can negotiate cost reductions as the workforce make improvements in manufacturing time or associated costs, including:

- improved speed and efficiency in producing the product
- less scrap generated
- improved process controls/methods
- investment in capital equipment to speed up the process for longer runs.

Feedback on learning activity 1.5

It is important to ensuring continuity of supply, but there are cost–benefit limits in achieving this objective.

By listing the costs under each heading you will now be in a position to review the balance between costs and benefits. We shall develop these issues further as we progress through this course book.

Feedback on self-assessment question 1.5

The cost of not having goods and or services when they are needed can far outweigh the cost of acquiring or of holding stock. For example:

- In a retail situation customers will migrate away from stores that do not have the range or depth of stock they are looking for.
- In a manufacturing operation a production line can be halted for the lack of a key component. Just-in-time can become 'just-too-late'.

You will no doubt be able to add other examples based on your own experience.

Feedback on learning activity 1.6

This activity develops from the concluding paragraph of this study session. There is no right or wrong answer, but rather your own informed view of how to put theory into practice in your own organisation so that you can relate the study material to practical situations.

Feedback on self-assessment question 1.6

This question adds value to learning activity 1.6, in which you developed a list of performance indicators.

In any business you have to prioritise time and effort. This question requires you to do this by ranking the issues in order of importance and then listing the top four: that is, those that you would act on first for best effect.

As an example, consider an answer for a private sector wholesale business that supplies and distributes engineering tools. What KPIs would senior managers be most interested in?

- stock availability: linked to stock/stores management
- market price: linked to buyers' performance
- delivery service: linked to stock distribution management
- gross/net profit: linked to overall business costs and profitability
- customer service: customers' views/loyalty.

Adding value to the business

Introduction

When we buy goods or services there is a usually an actual monetary cost, but 'value' is more subjective. Quality, on-time delivery or service, or indeed a better discount or a reduced cost – these and other factors all add value to a transaction. In a manufacturing operation the business can add further value in the production process.

A purchasing manager's task is twofold:

1   to establish a competitive cost
2   to gain added value or business benefits for the process through good purchasing/commercial management.

'Some people know the cost of everything and the value of nothing.'

In daily life and in business operations we all want value for money – but what *is* value? By understanding what value is we can then develop the principle of added value, and how we can achieve it.

Session learning objectives

After completing this session you should be able to:

2.1   State the principle of added value with respect to the role of purchasing and supply in a business operation, and describe how it can be measured.
2.2   Give examples of added value opportunities that purchasing and supply managers can offer to a business.
2.3   Assess the added value opportunities afforded by improved performance in purchasing and supply, and describe how these can be measured.
2.4   Assess the added value opportunities afforded by reducing inventory costs and administration and the use of consignment stocks in purchasing and supply, and describe how these can be measured.
2.5   Assess the added value opportunities afforded by purchasing and supply managers negotiating improved procurement and contract terms with suppliers, and describe how these can be measured.
2.6   Assess the added value opportunities afforded by improving operational efficiency in purchasing and supply, and describe how these can be measured.

Unit content coverage

This study session covers the following topics from the official CIPS unit content document:

Statements of practice

• Evaluate the benefits of implementing a well-structured approach to measuring organisational, functional and individual performance.

2

- Categorise types of performance measures that are available to supply chain managers.
- Appraise measures that can be used to improve supplier performance.

Learning objective

1.2 Explain the benefits of value added solutions.
- Savings resulting from improved performance
- Reducing inventory costs and administration
- Extending payment and warranty terms
- Using consignment stock
- Improving operational efficiency

Prior knowledge

You should have a basic understanding of the business concept of adding value in a business operation. From this basis of knowledge, the study session develops the concept with respect to purchasing and supply at the strategic, tactical and operational levels of management.

Resources

No specific resources are required for this session.

In order to apply the concepts described, it would be useful to have access to some cost information on goods or services you are or have been involved with. However, we do give examples if no direct information is available.

Timing

You should set aside about 5 hours to read and complete this session, including learning activities, self-assessment questions, the suggested further reading (if any) and the revision question.

2.1 Added value performance management in corporate business operations: general principles

One definition of **added value** could be the achievement of equivalent financial savings or benefits that are not based on a movement in unit price only.

The monetary benefits of added value are sometimes estimated subjectively, because by their nature they will often be less tangible than a specific price benefit, which is more easily quantified.

The wider corporate principle of the **value chain** was illustrated by Michael Porter in his classic model (figure 2.1). It shows how margin is created as functions add value, which is created by process flow both through primary activities and through associated 'support' activities. The resulting 'margin' is a direct function of how well these primary and secondary activities are managed.

Figure 2.1: The value chain: creating and sustaining superior performance

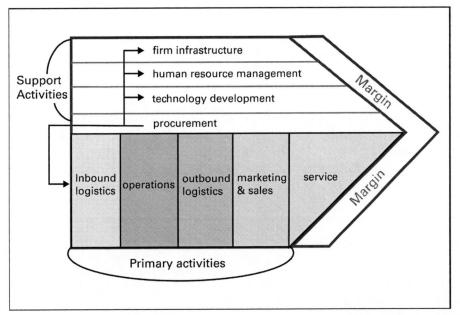

Source: Porter (1985)

Each function or activity is part of the corporate management, and either contributes to or diminishes the operating margin. Thus the members of the corporate management team all have a role and responsibility in generating the business margin.

In this model we see that Porter listed procurement as a support activity, which then feeds into the primary added value processes that feed forward to the business/profit margin.

You can see that procurement can and does have a direct effect on the value added business margin with each of the functions within the primary value-adding activities illustrated in figure 2.1.

Learning activity 2.1

Based on your experience, and on the definition of added value given above, create a list of opportunities where purchasing and supply managers can achieve added value for the business operation.

Feedback on page 30

Now tackle the following self-assessment question.

2

Self-assessment question 2.1

Describe the relationship between performance measurement and performance management.

Feedback on page 30

2.2 Added value opportunities

We now move from the general corporate added value to the specific contribution that can be made via the purchasing function. The Porter model is based on a manufacturing or process type of operation, but of course there are similar value-adding opportunities within public service and NPO organisations.

Learning activity 2.2

Develop a flow diagram of a typical supply chain, and annotate sequential points where value added opportunities can occur.

Feedback on page 31

Examples of purchasing-related savings that can contribute to the corporate value added chain include:

- eliminating or changing the initial requirement specified by the end user or customer
- changing the product/service specification or standard
- substituting lower-cost items – links to value analysis techniques
- extended payment terms
- extended warranty terms
- reducing stock or using a consignment stock facility
- improved operational efficiency – links to learning curve theory
- lower administration costs
- lower transactional costs.

There may be other opportunities within different organisations – some general, some specific to the organisation.

As some of these procurement issues are subjective rather than quantifiable, added value savings or benefits can be more difficult to substantiate and audit, but they are no less important to the organisation.

To summarise, the performance targets can be said to fall under the following headings:

- the same goods or services for lower cost, or
- the same costs but improved goods or services, or

- both lower costs and improved goods or services – the ultimate target!

Figure 2.2: A supply chain flow model from suppliers to customers

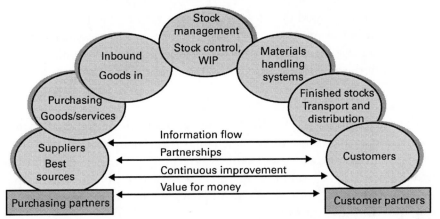

Source: Supply Chain Projects Ltd

Self-assessment question 2.2

Based on figure 2.2, give one example of an added value measure that a purchasing and supply manager can achieve at each main stage of the supply chain: that is, inbound, intra-site, and outbound.

Feedback on page 31

2.3 Measuring value added performance achieved by purchasing and supply

Having established some added value opportunities offered by improved purchasing and supply performance, we now need to consider how they can best be measured.

Setting, achieving, reporting on, and constantly revising purchasing and supply performance measures help the department improve its strategic position in the organisation.

Organisations may be at different points in their business evolution. If an organisation is just beginning, the 'best' performance measurements will depend on where the purchasing and supply department is in the development of the organisation and its supply base.

For a young or newly formed purchasing and supply department, the focus may be on cost reduction, supply base reduction, and service-level measurements.

As purchasing and supply departments mature, so do performance measures, to match and service more advanced relationships between the purchasing organisation and its key suppliers.

In section 2.1 we looked at the broad principles of what purchasing and supply managers can offer to the business. We shall now focus on specific

2

tasks that are the role and responsibility of the buyer, and on how these can be measured.

The term 'buyer' is a broad one: it covers the sourcing of goods and establishing prices and subsequent placing of orders to meet business needs. This role embodies a front-end supply chain process, and is the point of contact and interface between the organisation and the external supply market.

There are various titles for the jobs that involve work within the purchasing and supply function at this part of the chain, including order clerk, buyer, purchasing manager, procurement officer, agreements manager, and contract manager. All work within an organisation and are responsible for soliciting information and prices from potential suppliers in a market sector and entering into contracts for supply.

Thus if the job is to buy goods and services to meet the needs of the next step of the supply chain (figure 2.2), we can measure efficiency and effectiveness in various ways. To take the buyer as an example:

- Efficiency:
    - actual costs of the buying process
    - buyers' cost per order, or per pound or euro spent
    - the cost of acquisition
    - savings achieved
    - added value gained
    - cycle times (network flow)
    - use of information technology
    - organisational structure
    - supplier management
    - work force assessment.
- Effectiveness:
    - customer service levels
    - goods/services within budget
    - quality levels
    - goods and services reach customers on time
    - service delivery to customers
    - improved relationships
    - impact on capital efficiency, asset management and profits.

Having read the efficiency and effectiveness issues in this list you should now be in a position to review your organisation's needs and add points relative to your own operation. When this is done you are ready to begin or revamp your purchasing and supply department's purchasing performance measures.

What is the first step in achieving this? If there is one consistent piece of advice, it is to make sure your purchasing performance measures reflect your own organisation's goals. Most purchasing and supply professionals start with the 'macro' goals and work down. Little value is found in a measure developed by a purchasing department if the measurement does not follow the stated organisation's wider goals.

Learning activity 2.3

Write a report on the merits of a bonus payment system based on measurable savings achieved by purchasing managers.

Feedback on page 31

Now tackle the following self-assessment question.

Self-assessment question 2.3

List three added value opportunities that you would recommend for a middle manager to take in order to improve his or her performance and contribution to the organisation. Write a short note on each.

Feedback on page 32

2.4 Adding value by reducing inventory costs and administration and using consignment stocks

Not all organisations hold stock; indeed, with the development of materials requirements planning (MRP) and the just-in-time philosophy (JIT), the holding of stock has been dramatically reduced in process and manufacturing industries. But there are still many other businesses and organisations that trade or rely on stockholding to achieve their business needs. The important point here is that stock has value, but also carries costs. Organisations need to identify where those costs lie in order to make a value judgement on the need to have or hold stock.

In the broadest terms stock is an asset; accountants include it as part of working capital on the balance sheet. Cash is the most liquid asset a business can have; although stock is an asset, it is not 'liquid' until it is sold. Excess stock ties up cash and reduces liquidity. Insufficient stock may reduce levels of service to customers (whether internal or external). So how much stock do we need to hold?

Study session 5 will analyse these cost–benefit issues in detail; at this point you need to understand the basic issues relating to added value within the broader supply chain.

Look again at figure 2.2. The centre link in the chain refers to stock management, stock control and work in progress (WIP). At these points in the chain goods have arrived in, perhaps as raw materials, or stock items, or components or sub-assemblies.

In a business operation some of the costs of stock are operational: those costs that accrue as part of the stockholding and handling process.

2

A second category of costs are financial: the costs of financing the acquisition of stock from working capital. These costs are linked to bank interest rates.

Still other costs are described as **opportunity costs**. This is an economics term. It means, with respect to stock, that we have an opportunity to invest our working capital in business stock or elsewhere. That decision can be based on a financial cost–benefit analysis: which is the best opportunity to utilise the money/working capital for a business.

In a manufacturing organisation business stock aggregates up as work in progress towards finished goods stock. There are process costs along the chain: buying the goods, handling the stock, assembling and moving the stock, and finally issuing and despatching the finished stock produced.

In wholesale, retail and service operations the goods are not processed as such. Bulk stock arrives and is stored, and then sales unit items are issued to users or customers.

In several industries, including retailing and manufacturing, buyers use consignment stock to reduce inventory costs. Where demand is independent but usage is regular, stock is delivered 'on consignment' to the point of use. As the need or sale arises, stock is issued and paid for when used. This has the benefit of stock availability and reduced cashflow for the buyer. There are still administrative and physical storage costs associated with the consignment stock, but the principle has worked well in many retail and maintenance operations.

Having identified where costs can accrue in managing inventory, you can see there are many opportunities for purchasing managers to reduce those costs.

Learning activity 2.4

Draw a process diagram showing how cost accrues to stock items as they pass through a stores/stock control system.

Feedback on page 33

Now tackle the following self-assessment question.

Self-assessment question 2.4

What do you understand by the term 'opportunity cost' with respect to stock held by a business organisation?

Feedback on page 33

2.5 Added value opportunities of negotiating: improved procurement and contract terms with suppliers

The quality of the agreements that buyers enter into with their suppliers can make a contribution to added value. The terms and conditions (T&Cs) of the agreement or contract can and will have an effect on the price.

The general concept here is the **total cost of acquisition** (TCA) and the wider concept of **total cost of ownership** (TCO): that is, not just how much the item or service costs but rather what its corporate life costs are, as set out in the cost equation (figure 2.4).

Figure 2.4: The cost equation

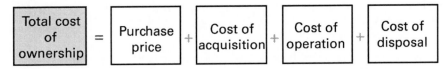

In this section we focus on the buying TCA/TCO in general, and in particular on how a buyer can add value by improving the T&Cs of the agreement.

Most agreements are covered by general terms of trade linked, where applicable, to express product or service conditions.

A buyer may have the opportunity to apply leverage to a proposed or negotiated deal based on various circumstances and needs.

Some negotiations result in objective, quantitative reductions: price, time, trade discount percentage, settlement discount. Some negotiations result in more subjective improvements or values: better quality, improved service, or extra warranty.

Other savings can accrue from reduced transaction costs of buying: fewer orders, call-off orders, procurement card usage, reduced transaction time, streamlined processing/systems resulting in reduced administration costs.

In summary, buyers can add value based on their skill and competence in both the TCA and TCO issues concerning the acquisition of goods and services by obtaining cost reductions or service improvements linked to negotiation of the commercial T&Cs of the agreement or contract.

Learning activity 2.5

Prepare a brief set of discussion points to be discussed at a planned negotiation meeting with a supplier.

Feedback on page 33

Now tackle the following self-assessment question.

2

Self-assessment question 2.5

How would you assess the effectiveness of a business negotiation meeting with a supplier?

Feedback on page 34

2.6 Adding value by improving operational efficiency

A key element in the cost of acquisition of goods and services is the actual cost of buying itself. The buying costs include:

the wages and salaries of buyers and purchasing staff
the cost of office premises and support costs
the cost of systems – both paper-based and IT/IS.

Operational efficiency is based on:

- HR factors: buyers' personal and or professional competence – skill, knowledge, experience, qualifications and attitude
- system and process factors: purchasing procedures, strategy, tactics, transactions, relationships, business IT systems and communications.

The operation of a buying person or team costs money and time, and as in all investment there is in effect a cost–benefit decision to be made. But if we assume that we have an existing team of buyers, then we need to measure their operational efficiency based on quantifiable volumes and values.

The principles set out here are developed in more detail in subsequent sessions, but at this point you need to consider issues based on:

- the volume of purchasing work
- the value of purchasing work.

The first step is to understand the current 'where are we now?' issues in order to establish a baseline for both the volume and value of work undertaken.

We can then go on to assess how buyers can improve their working operation, in both effectiveness and efficiency terms.

- The volume of work. This will include:
    - the numbers of orders placed over time
    - the number of items/services undertaken
    - the number of queries dealt with – how well the buying process works.
- The value of work. This will include:
    - the monetary value of those orders
    - the transactional costs involved – enquiries, evaluation, meetings etc
    - the savings made against budget.

The key question is: how are the volume and value of work managed by buyers? The answer to this question will vary from business to business, depending on the type of operation, its size and its complexity. For example, in a small business, is buying done by one person or several? Is buying general, or based on commodity knowledge or skill?

In a larger operation, with several geographic locations, is buying centralised at one site, or undertaken at every site?

There are many operational business buying combinations for managing the purchasing process, and they all have their respective advantages and disadvantages in terms of cost and efficiency. Your job is to be aware of the opportunities and then to assess how to evaluate both the purchasing efficiency and the effectiveness of the chosen application of the resources available to provide service and add value to the business.

Learning activity 2.6

List the advantages and disadvantages of a central purchasing operation for a UK manufacturer that has three separate production sites in the north, centre and south of the country.

Feedback on page 34

Now tackle the final self-assessment question in this study session.

Self-assessment question 2.6

Describe, in terms of added value, the operational efficiency advantages of having a fully integrated IT/IS system for an organisation.

(Fully integrated IT/IS systems are known as **enterprise resource planning (ERP)** systems; examples include SAP and Oracle.)

Feedback on page 35

Revision question

Now try the revision question for this session on page 331.

Summary

Added value is an important business and management concept. In this session you were introduced to Porter's value chain, which illustrates the contribution to margin made by the various business activities. In this session we have focused, in particular, on how the purchasing function can add value and create margin.

Value can be added both to manufactured goods and to services provided in any business sector. We considered each part of the supply chain, and reviewed the various ways in which value is added along it.

We then moved on to the wider consideration of how the concept of added value can be measured to ensure efficiency and effectiveness in parallel with continuous improvement targets.

Suggested further reading

Students can find more detail of the works of Michael Porter, particularly the concept of 'the value chain', in Lysons and Farrington (2006), chapter 3, pages 101–2.

Feedback on learning activities and self-assessment questions

Feedback on learning activity 2.1

The purpose of this activity is for you to recognise where value can be added. Using the Porter's value chain concept illustrated in figure 2.1 you can focus on the opportunities where purchasing and supply's value added inputs correlate to the wider supply chain or logistics concepts or terms noted in the diagram.

You could classify your list of purchasing and supply opportunities against each of the primary activities in the model, and decide on appropriate KPIs as follows:

- Inbound logistics: costs of acquisition, costs of bringing goods in, handling inbound goods.
- Operations: availability and costs of goods to the operations, manufacturing or process functions.
- Outbound logistics: costs of packing, picking and moving finished goods outbound to the customer.
- Marketing and sales: working with this function on product development and on products as they progress through their marketing life cycle.
- Service: costs of services that relate directly to the added value production process.

Feedback on self-assessment question 2.1

You identified some specific procurement measurement opportunities in learning activity 2.1. This question asks you to build on this by giving some examples of how to manage the process of reporting and achieving the chosen performance measures.

This relates to the opening statement in the previous study session: 'If you can't measure it, you can't manage it.' Having chosen some performance measures, how do you manage purchasing performance?

To help answer this, look back to figure 1.1. It shows that, once the agreed measurements are chosen, you should set demanding performance targets (process point 9) and then manage and communicate the results (process point 10).

Feedback on learning activity 2.2

Figure 2.2 is one representation of a supply chain flow model. The chain link elements overlap as the process flows from beginning to end.

The first link of the chain represents the upstream or inbound flow of goods or services into an organisation as they are sourced and bought by purchasing managers.

As these goods enter the process they are managed as stock and/or converted into products. Purchasing and materials managers have further opportunities to create added value within each link of the chain.

As goods are taken from stock and sold, or complete their process of manufacture, they move downstream into the outbound distribution chain, where purchasing managers can add further value.

Finally, as goods arrive at the end user or customer, purchasing managers can make further outbound added value contributions.

So we can see that a supply chain is only as strong as its weakest link. The purchasing manager's role is to ensure strength in every link of the chain.

In order to maximise the added value opportunities the four supply chain cross-links in the figure must also be robust:

- information flow
- partnerships
- continuous improvement
- value for money (VFM) criteria.

Feedback on self-assessment question 2.2

- Inbound. A key measurable here is supplier performance.
- Intra-site. In manufacturing or process operations this is where the materials are converted into assemblies and products. At this stage there are many performance measures. One key measurable here is inventory management.
- Outbound. At this end of the chain purchasing managers interface with distribution management. There are several outbound measures that fall under the general heading of distribution resource planning (DRP) performance management.

Feedback on learning activity 2.3

Most frontline sales staff have the opportunity to earn bonus based on sales success, in terms of value and/or volume. Is there an equal case for offering an incentive to buyers?

There is no single right or wrong answer, but – as for most questions of this nature – you could list points for and against in order to develop your understanding.

2

Consider the following points, which you might include in your report.

There is a basic difference here between public sector and private sector organisations. In the private sector the key driver is return on capital invested (ROCI), as measured in terms of profitability and shareholder value. In the public sector the key driver is service delivery. There is no profit as such; any savings or added value gains allow more of the budget to be spent on service delivery opportunity.

Thus the payment of a bonus – in cash terms at least – becomes a problem in the public sector for reasons of public accountability, because payment to one group may reflect and include the effort of others.

There are of course many ways in which value added savings are rewarded, rather than payment of a bonus as such: they include professional and job motivation linked to the organisation's vision and values, which ensure that buyers do contribute to the process. In effect the organisation receives the bonus of value contributed by the whole management team, including purchasing managers.

Feedback on self-assessment question 2.3

In most management organisations there are three broad levels of management:

- senior managers: the board, making strategic long-term decisions
- middle managers: aware of the business strategy, and tactically exercising management control of medium-term management operations
- supervision and operational workforce employees: undertaking the volume of transactional and operational work on a shorter-term timescale.

This self-assessment question focuses on the middle managers in the business. A purchasing manager within this group would have many opportunities to obtain and retain added value and set appropriate KPIs based on:

- understanding the purchasing issues set out in the strategic business plan
- setting up a purchasing business plan to manage his or her own area of responsibility
- identifying those medium-term tactical tasks that purchasing can undertake.

A list of tactical management issues might include:

- market analysis, knowledge and information sources
- understanding the demand for goods and services in the business operation
- source management of new and existing suppliers
- ensuring that robust procedures and processes exist to manage purchasing
- utilising the best available IT systems to support purchasing.

Your answer could have included three points from the above summary, with notes on how you would measure them.

Feedback on learning activity 2.4

Figure 2.3 shows a cut-away view of a typical industrial stores. The key costs associated with holding stock are annotated alongside.

Figure 2.3

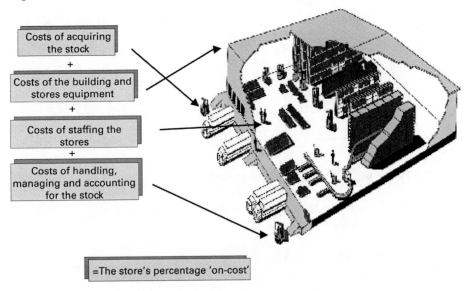

Costs of acquiring the stock
+
Costs of the building and stores equipment
+
Costs of staffing the stores
+
Costs of handling, managing and accounting for the stock

=The store's percentage 'on-cost'

Feedback on self-assessment question 2.4

In this section you were introduced to the term 'opportunity cost' with respect to stockholding. You were told that stock is valued as part of a company's working capital, and thus the more stock you hold the more cash is tied up.

Your answer should consider the cost–benefit opportunity decisions to be considered for holding stock, based on such questions as:

* How much cash should be tied up in stock?
* What is the cost of not having stock – lost sales or delayed production time?
* How else could working capital be used in the business – equipment, staff, systems?
* Could you obtain a better return on business cash from any other investment?

The opportunity cost of stock is based on these and similar business opportunity assessments.

Feedback on learning activity 2.5

Preparation for any negotiation is always based on good planning and market knowledge. In this section we are concerned with issues of added value accruing from better T&Cs obtained by the buyer from a supplier.

This learning activity is a broadly based task, which will vary from case to case. However, a general list of discussion points would include those set out in table 2.1.

Table 2.1

T&C discussion point	Opportunity
Purchase price	Can it be reduced?
Current discount structure	Can this be improved, based on this deal or on longer-term commitment?
Settlement terms	Can these be extended in the buyer's favour without increasing the price?
Warranty terms	Can we obtain a longer warranty on parts and labour at no extra cost?
Quality/service	Can we have better quality/service for the same price?
Transaction and administration costs	Can the number of paper/electronic transactions be reduced?

Feedback on self-assessment question 2.5

You would be able to do this by measuring the 'before' and 'after' values of the price or deal agreed.

- Some of these values are objective, eg actual price reductions.
- Some are subjective, eg better quality for the same price.

You would need to quantify and add up the objective values, and agree a notional value to the business for the subjective vales.

Feedback on learning activity 2.6

This learning activity is designed for you to assess the organisational aspect of purchasing operational efficiency in a larger business. The discussion about centralising or decentralising operations often arises in business. A basic list could include some of the following points:

Advantages of centralisation:

- Buyers can aggregate demand for maximum leverage with suppliers.
- Buyers may specialise in commodity sectors.
- Buyers can cover each other more effectively over time.
- Fewer orders are placed, resulting in improved control over costs and budgets.
- Administration costs are reduced.

Disadvantages of centralisation:

- It may take longer to process orders centrally.
- Buying staff may not understand local management or production needs.
- Buyers are not part of the respective regional management team.
- Buyers don't know the local market or suppliers as well.
- There is some duplication of costs of buying and administration.

Feedback on self-assessment question 2.6

This question looks at the value of IT/IS processes used to support buying and thus improve that particular aspect of operational efficiency.

Most organisations need an IT system to support their purchasing managers. There are many good stand-alone systems that can achieve this. The purpose of this question was not to identify this need, but to describe how this can be improved by the use of ERP systems.

Enterprise resource planning (ERP) systems integrate all data management and information systems for the whole organisation: finance, HR, marketing, production and administration. The key point is the word 'integrate': all the systems draw on a central database and cross-communicate one with another.

For example, in a manufacturing environment the buyer can interface with production needs, and check supplier payments, goods received, stock positions and supplier history, all on the one system, thus improving purchasing efficiency and the effectiveness of data/information transfer.

2

2

Study session 3
Categories of performance measurement

Introduction

Having established the importance of performance measurement within business in general and in purchasing operations in particular, we now need some quantitative and qualitative markers. These are the **key performance indicators** (KPIs).

In purchasing, both efficiency measures and effectiveness measures are critical to long-term success. Purchasers should be careful to not confuse the two concepts, and to balance the energies devoted to each.

These approaches are useful in assessing not only purchasing, but also the entire supply chain. As chains become more sophisticated and complex, new and more bespoke means of measuring performance need to be devised and implemented.

The management guru Peter Drucker stated: 'In comparing efficiency and effectiveness it is more important to do the right things (improve effectiveness) than to do things right (improve efficiency).

'Thus, if an organization is doing the right things wrong (that is, is effective but not efficient), it can outperform organizations that are doing the wrong things right (that is, are efficient but not effective).'

There is no one best set of solutions for performance measurement in purchasing, but there is no better endeavour on which to expend purchasing efforts and resources than working to strengthen the skills, techniques and perspectives used to enhance overall professional performance. We therefore need a wide cross-section of key performance indicators (KPIs) to measure progress.

This study session sets out the main groups of purchasing KPIs that will achieve this objective. We also consider the 'how, why, which, when and where' questions for selecting appropriate measures for short-, medium- and long-term objectives.

Session learning objectives

After completing this session you should be able to:

3.1 Describe how purchasing and supply expertise can contribute to KPIs for a corporate business team.
3.2 List the main categories of KPI within a purchasing and supply management operational department.
3.3 Define the most appropriate KPIs that will contribute to profitability with respect to cost savings, services and inventory management.

3.4 Define the most appropriate KPIs that will contribute to profitability with respect to basic workload control within a purchasing operation.

3.5 Define the most appropriate KPIs that will contribute to profitability with respect to purchasing infrastructure and organisation.

3.6 Define which purchasing and supply competences are required to contribute effectively to profitability.

Unit content coverage

This study session covers the following topics from the official CIPS unit content document:

Statements of practice

- Categorise types of performance measures that are available to supply chain managers.
- Appraise measures that can be used to improve supplier performance.
- Evaluate targets as a means of improving the performance of the purchasing function and individual buyers.

Learning objective

1.4 Analyse the types and categories of key performance measures available to organisations.
- Contributions to profitability – savings, service and inventory
- Basic workload control
- Infrastructure and competency

Prior knowledge

You need to have completed study sessions 1 and 2.

Resources

No specific resources are required for this session.

Timing

You should set aside about 5.25 hours to read and complete this session, including learning activities, self-assessment questions, the suggested further reading (if any) and the revision question.

3.1 How do purchasing and supply managers contribute to the KPI targets set by corporate management?

Corporate management structures and business plans vary with the nature of the business, but in a general manufacturing organisation the functional and business planning structure may well be set out as in figure 3.1.

Figure 3.1: Purchasing within a corporate business planning and management structure

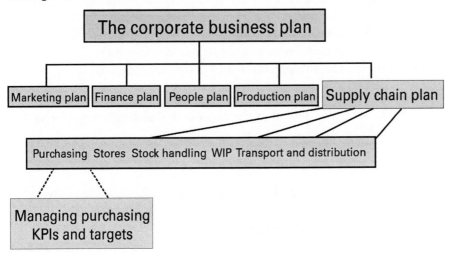

Each department and functional unit has its own business plan, which feeds upwards to the corporate business plan as set out by the strategic management team.

The strategic management team set the vision and values, and incorporate these and other management issues in the corporate business plan. The operational and functional department managers then generate their own business plans as part of the team, and set their respective KPIs and targets as their contribution to the corporate plan.

Before progressing further, tackle this learning activity.

Learning activity 3.1

Create a list of KPIs for a business operation at the strategic level.

Feedback on page 51

In figure 3.1 you can see that the purchasing managers are contributing to the supply chain plan. Purchasing is one of the five departments that are managing their respective departmental business plans.

Before we discuss the detail of how purchasing can contribute to the corporate planning structure, we need to reflect on some of the basic issues and terminology that are used in performance measurement and the links to the continuous improvement process.

Careful selection of performance measures is vital if we are to achieve meaningful outcomes. Figure 3.1 reminds us how important it is to link all departments to the corporate objectives and planned outcomes.

When selecting categories for performance measurement it is important to consider the following questions, in terms of both the efficiency and the effectiveness of the outcome.

- Why are we measuring this?
- What are we trying to achieve?

3

- What is our core business product or service?
- Who are our key customers – both internal and external?
- Who are our key suppliers?
- How and when do we obtain and disclose the performance KPI results?
- Do we have robust processes to support our core business?
- Do we have excellent information and communication channels?

Once we have answered these basic questions we can use the following six-point guide, which will assist in the process of selecting categories for performance measurement.

Performance measures should:

1 *Be reliable*. Basic data is gathered from robust, reliable and consistent information sources. The best sources come from established quality data, which is updated regularly as part of the day-to-day business transaction process.

2 *Be meaningful*. The KPI is relevant; it is the 'right' measure, which has meaning for and value to you and others. It must be clear to recipients, and not be chosen just because it is easy to obtain, or to 'make weight' in a list of KPIs.

3 *Be focused*. The measures should be focused on the core business or operational issues, not just on interesting facts. A focused measure measures only what we planned to measure.

4 *Be fair and balanced*. The KPIs should reflect your operation in all respects, not just the parts that make the organisation 'look good'. Aim to select a good balance of objective and subjective issues in the selected KPIs.

5 *Be capable of change and improvement*. Continuous improvement leads to change. Can your selected KPI adapt to change too?

6 *Manage the target*. The objective is not just to hit a target but rather to improve the output within agreed timescales. Individual 'quantum' measurements could just be manipulated – eg how many orders are placed per month. For example, a buyer might simply place more one-line orders so that a numerical target was achieved.

The process of selecting categories for performance measurement indicators requires a considerable investment of time at all management levels.

How can we judge whether the chosen measures are going to meet the targets set?

Targets are quantified objectives, set by management, to be attained at a future date. The setting of targets is an important part of a measurement process. The target is the objective and the measurement tells us how fast or well we are approaching that objective.

Targets may take various forms. For example:

- A simple yes/no target: Did we do that?
- An achievement target: Did we increase sales by x%?
- A reduction target: Did we reduce the number of queries/complaints by y%?
- An outcome target: Did the project complete to time/budget?
- A quality target: Did we improve quality/service over time?

3

One of the management tools that can be used to judge the quality of targets is to apply the **SMART** criteria. SMART is an acronym that crops up in many areas of general management. We can apply this general management tool to the selection of categories for performance measurement:

- S = specific (specific, clear unambiguous easily understood)
- M = measurable (being capable of reasonable measurement)
- A = achievable (a target that can reasonably be achieved)
- R = relevant (to the core business or service)
- T = timed (should have an agreed timescale).

Self-assessment question 3.1

The management board of Alltrading UK plc set a corporate target of a 5% growth in sales over the last financial year as part of its annual business plan.

You have the task of assessing this particular corporate target by using the SMART criteria. Complete table 3.1 with your comments on each SMART element of this target.

Table 3.1

SMART criteria review Alltrading UK plc	The corporate target of a 5% growth in sales over the last financial year
S Specific	
M Measurable	
A Achievable	
R Relevant	
T Timed	

Feedback on page 51

3.2 How do purchasing and supply managers select and set KPIs for their core: business operation?

We can now move from general, corporate management issues to the specific selection of categories of performance measurement for purchasing managers.

The main criteria for effectiveness and efficiency still apply at this level, and we can use the six-point selection guide and SMART assessment tools here too.

Referring back to figure 3.1, we are now focusing on the supply chain plan. The supply chain manager will be concerned with all elements of the supply chain: inbound, intra-site and outbound.

3

In this section we shall focus on the front – upstream – element of the supply chain, and specifically on purchasing management's input.

At this point the purchasing role is to interface with external suppliers and internal customers or user departments. (See also figure 2.2.) In basic terms, purchasing managers receive instructions on supply needs from users, source supply, and raise orders for goods and services.

Having revisited these basic core tasks for purchasing managers, we can now consider the selection of appropriate purchasing KPIs.

For the purposes of this selection process we shall be considering various purchasing roles:

- order placing
- spot purchasing
- creating agreements
- setting up contracts
- managing longer-term agreements.

These tasks and terms are not mutually exclusive, and often overlap, depending on role and job title. The work may be undertaken with the purchasing department at the strategic, tactical or transactional level.

In order to select KPIs in purchasing we need to develop this range of work tasks. See table 3.3.

Table 3.3 Categories of performance measurement

Purchasing business planning headers	Typical purchasing business plan tasks	General purchasing KPI headers
Strategic	Working with key stakeholders/users	Managing the supplier base
	Managing key suppliers	Managing long-term relationships
	Developing internal and external relationships	Managing cost reduction plan
	Establishing long-term agreements/ partnerships	Undertaking purchasing research
Tactical	Obtaining/evaluating quotes, proposals bids	Planning medium-term supply/service delivery
	Managing general suppliers	Managing current supplier relationships
	Working with operational departments	Interfacing customer needs with supply market
Transactional	Obtaining and checking prices	Number of orders to place per week/ month
	Placing stock and non-stock orders	Number of queries raised per week
	Managing data input process	

Learning activity 3.2

From your knowledge or experience create a list of three specific KPIs for a manager operating at the middle management/tactical level in a purchasing team.

Feedback on page 52

Now go on to tackle self-assessment question 3.2 below. Completing these two tasks will enable you to apply this knowledge in various practical situations.

Self-assessment question 3.2

Draft up a simple process diagram to show the key steps in selecting a purchasing and supply KPI.

Feedback on page 52

3.3 Purchasing's contribution to improved service and the bottom-line profit

Purchasing managers are responsible for various costs within a business, and the management of these costs has a direct effect on the business in terms of profitability and/or customer service delivery.

Goods and services fall into various categories of purchasing management. Some of the main groupings are:

- raw materials
- components and sub-assemblies
- repair and maintenance items
- capital equipment
- stock and non-stock
- service contracts
- facilities management contracts.

In a private sector business the cost-of-sales items have a direct impact on trading accounts and the bottom-line profit and loss account. The amount of stock held is part of the company balance sheet, and excess stock can affect liquidity ratios.

In public sector organisations and NPOs there is no profit as such, but the general supplies – goods and services purchased with the budget – have a direct effect on service provision opportunity.

Thus in all sectors of an economy and for all organisations, whether large or small, purchasing has a direct effect on outputs and on financial and service performance. Buyers are not alone in this role, but they are key team players in this area of cost management and subsequent performance.

In this section we shall review the selection of KPIs for one of the most important buyer contributions to profit: materials cost saving. By understanding the principles here, buyers can identify cost analysis data and develop similar models for other areas of the supply chain, such as service contract management, stores and inventory management, or distribution.

Each of these supply chain headings will be developed later in this course text. Our objective here is to explain the importance of the principles by using the example of materials cost savings, and thus show how purchasing managers can have an effect on other supply-chain-related business outcomes.

Materials cost savings

In basic terms the measure is: how much can we save on cost from some agreed base? That base may be the last price paid, the budgeted price, or an estimated target cost. All these cost bases are linked to price movement over time.

For example, we can claim a cost saving if we pay the same price now that we paid, say, 12 months ago. If inflation increased prices in the market by 2.5% in the last year, then if we pay the same price there is an effective saving of at least the 2.5% expected inflation increase. The guide here is to track prices and aim to be equal to or lower than the tracked increase.

There are many cost-saving opportunities and techniques open to buyers, and we can apply them as appropriate within a supply market. In terms of measuring performance it is important to establish a base price, track market movements, buy items, and then measure the differential.

The savings described above are based on single event or spot purchases. There are many other opportunities for buyers to contribute to profit or service improvement. The principles of total cost of acquisition (TCA) and total cost of ownership (TCO) were introduced in study session 2. By applying purchasing skills and tactics the buyer will also contribute to these evaluations; however, the calculations are more detailed, and the profit impact may take time to be assessed.

The effect on profitability can be illustrated by some basic calculations. Consider the basic profit and loss account shown in table 3.4.

Table 3.4

		£000s	%		£'000	%
				Sales	325.0	100.0
Less cost of sales	Labour	149	51.0			
	Materials	109	37.3			
	Overheads	34	11.6			
	Total	292	100.0	Costs	292.0	89.8
				Profit	33.0	10.2

Here the profit on sales turnover is £33,000 (10.2%) where the cost of sales is £292,000. The materials element of the cost of sales is £109,000 (37.3%)

Now consider the following example (table 3.5)

Table 3.5

		£'000	%		£'000	%
				Sales	325.0	100.0
Less cost of sales	Labour	149	52.0			
	Materials	**103.55**	**36.1**			
	Overheads	34	11.9			
	Totals	286.55	100.0	Costs	286.6	88.2
				Profit	38.5	**11.8**

Here the purchasing manager has been able to reduce the material costs to £103,550: a reduction of 5%. This saving has a direct effect on the profit, which is now £38,500: in percentage terms +1.6% extra profit for this business.

Learning activity 3.3

Prepare a plan of action to achieve direct cost savings/service improvements in a business operation and set achievable targets that can be measured over time.

Feedback on page 52

Now tackle the following self-assessment question.

Self-assessment question 3.3

Take an example from your own organisation/experience. What is the effect on the bottom-line profit achieved by a direct material cost saving?

Feedback on page 53

3.4 Selecting KPIs to measure management of departmental purchasing process and supply chain costs

Within a typical management structure (figure 3.1) each departmental business plan will be underpinned by a robust process of system and control. These processes will link to the basic business transactions and will be managed at that level. Middle and senior managers will manage the medium-term and longer-term tactics and strategy associated with the transactions and data that are created.

There are several processes within the supply chain:

- purchasing
- stores and inventory management
- links to added value manufacturing (production management, MRP, JIT options)

- storage and delivery of finished goods
- customer relationships.

In this study session we shall now focus on the purchasing process, but the principles of process review linked to improvement management would follow a similar pattern if we were reviewing any of the other direct or indirect supply chain processes mentioned above.

Figure 3.3 is a flow diagram showing the detailed links associated with the purchasing process within most organisations, both public and private. Each link is reviewed and assessed in order to develop the strength of the whole chain.

Figure 3.3: The purchasing process links

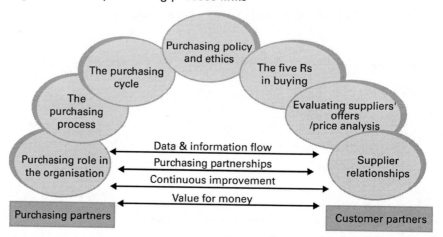

Source: Supply Chain Projects Ltd

This simple diagram covers the key process points involved in managing purchasing. The total cost of acquisition (TCA) and total cost of ownership (TCO) include the costs involved in purchasing the goods and services that are needed by an organisation.

Once again we see that the terms 'efficiency' and 'effectiveness' describe measures of how well the process is managed and delivered to users.

In order to review how efficient and effective this process is, we need first to understand the elements of the process and be capable of undertaking a benchmark comparison with industrial or professional 'best practice'. On the basis that any process is capable of some improvement, this task becomes an ongoing need if the principle of continuous improvement is to be effected.

The basic best practice tests of this process flow diagram include the following:

- Is the role of purchasing clearly set out and understood?
- Is there a purchasing manual or process flow chart of how a buyer is expected to work?
- Does the manual follow clear sequential steps that should be followed?
- Are purchasing policy and ethics standards set out in the corporate business plan?
- Are all purchasing basics understood (the 5Rs: right place, right price, right quality, right quantity and right time)?

- Do staff know and understand the bid evaluation and contract award criteria?
- Do we 'manage' customers, both internal and external?
- Do we have robust IT systems?

The efficiency and effectiveness of the purchasing process are thus functions of all these elements. Once purchasing managers have studied their own system, the continuous improvement process requires them to periodically address and re-address these questions, and then set targets and select measures to review and improve the purchasing process.

Learning activity 3.4

Prepare a plan of action to achieve measurable savings and/or process improvements by re-engineering the operational management and processes in purchasing and supply.

Feedback on page 53

Now tackle self-assessment question 3.4 below to develop your skill in this area.

Self-assessment question 3.4

List three methods for improving departmental acquisition costs by reviewing purchasing and supply transactions and process time.

Feedback on page 54

3.5 Selecting KPIs that link to the purchasing infrastructure within an organisation

Where does purchasing sit in the business infrastructure? In figure 3.1 we showed a typical structure for the supply chain and purchasing in a single-site organisation. In larger organisations the structure can be much more complicated, with, for example:

- several sites in one country
- several sites in several countries
- head office in one country with operational or retail divisions in other countries
- manufacturing subsidiaries or supply partners in various places
- companies with stock and distribution
- companies without stock.

This is just a representative selection of business infrastructures; you may recognise others. The question is: where does purchasing fit best in the infrastructure in terms of efficiency and effectiveness?

3

As in many similar business situations, there is no single answer, but managers aim to review the costs and benefits and come to a view. This section therefore sets out some of the possible options, and describes how purchasing can fit into the infrastructure.

First, how is purchasing organised itself? Here are some options:

- central purchasing departments
- decentralised purchasing – full delegation to operational divisions or subsidiaries
- centre-led action networks (CLAN) – a combination of centrally led management with agreed delegation of category or common needs being undertaken within divisions.
- category purchasing – specialist buyers for specific categories of goods and services
- consortium purchasing – mainly public service for operations with similar non-competing services, eg university or local government consortiums
- cooperative purchasing between groups with similar needs.

Each of these options has advantages and disadvantages, and carries costs and benefits in its application.

The purchasing infrastructure can also be influenced by the location of the supply market, but this factor is of less importance in the modern world of high-speed communications, logistics supply and distribution operations.

The decision on purchasing infrastructure is a strategic one. Setting up and commissioning a purchasing infrastructure is a medium- to long-term decision, and will have a direct effect on costs, and on operational effectiveness and efficiency. In any organisation the decision needs to be carefully considered at senior management/board level, and the costs and benefits of 'commercial risk' need to be fully reviewed. There is never one single best solution, but rather what works best for a particular organisation and its needs. Having taken the decision within a strategic life cycle the effects can have long-term consequences for a business or service organisation.

Learning activity 3.5

Look at the structure of an existing purchasing and supply operation, and list three issues that you would recommend for review in order to reduce transactional purchasing costs.

Directly following this learning activity try self-assessment question 3.5 below to link these issues. By doing this you develop your skill of applying theory to practice.

Feedback on page 54

Now tackle the following self-assessment question.

Self-assessment question 3.5

How would you improve the purchasing and supply infrastructure in an organisation that was expanding from one operational division to three sites?

Feedback on page 55

3.6 Purchasing competence and the link to business objectives

Competence in any field is important, but competence does not mean you have to 'know all' before acting. For example, a newly qualified lawyer may not be competent to handle a complex litigation because of his or her lack of courtroom experience or skills. Competence is acquired and developed over time, and through real situations.

Competence is measured by several elements, including skill, experience, knowledge and attitude, and when combined with a qualification will have best effect.

Many leading businesspeople have achieved much without all of the perceived competence elements; however, a balanced selection of each marks out progressive degrees of competence linked to business or organisational needs.

Some learning may major on academic knowledge alone, whereas other learning requires a wider basis of practical skill and experience: for example, NVQs are based on this latter format.

Competence to work in an environment is important, but in many situations individuals need only agreed levels of competence, whether implied or evidenced. In the context of this study session the issue is: what categories and measures are relevant to the competence of purchasing staff who need to achieve business deliverables?

In many organisations purchasing is delegated with budgetary control to staff and managers who may be full-time or only part-time purchasing people. Managers may have purchasing responsibilities as part of other roles, or they may move into purchasing from other disciplines.

The key to managing this situation is to look at the competences required and then assess the 'gaps'. Based on this assessment, the organisation should decide its purchasing competence needs and assess and train staff up to that level, by facilitating training or skill development to develop the required competences.

The measures can be objective or subjective.

- Objective:
  - Based on an agreed set of competences, how many 'gaps' are there to be filled?

- What is the timescale to achieve the competence level, by individual, team or category?
- Are there measurable improvements?
- Subjective:
  - How well is the person doing?
  - How is the mentoring and/or training programme progressing?
  - Are teamwork and/or business relationships improving?

Learning activity 3.6

Review a purchasing and supply job description and identify four key competences that the post-holder would need.

Feedback on page 55

Now tackle the following self-assessment question:

Self-assessment question 3.6

Create a list of the purchasing competences that will have the most effect on business profitability. Rank your list in order of priority for your organisation.

Feedback on page 55

Revision question

Now try the revision question for this session on page 332.

Summary

This study session was concerned with categories of performance measures and their selection in a purchasing environment.

It reviewed how purchasing fits into an organisation management planning structure and thus how it can first support the business planning corporate aims and then manage its own agreed plan.

In order to do this various categories of purchasing KPIs were discussed, and how these achievements contribute to business mission, vision values and financial targets.

In undertaking this form of review you were reminded that such an assessment was judged at three levels or over timescales. The categories of measures and results selected can be grouped in various formats or models, but the common theme would be to analyse them as:

- short-term transactional measures
- medium-term tactical measures
- longer-term strategic measures.

At every level there should be selection tests based on the six-point guide to selecting performance measures.

Suggested further reading

In this session we have referred extensively to the theories of Peter Drucker, one of America's leading authors on management and business. Students wishing for an overview of his work could do worse than read Drucker (2003) which contains much of his best work. Any good on-line bookshops will have details of his work. Drucker is also quoted in Neely et al (2002) on pages 24 and 190.

Feedback on learning activities and self-assessment questions

Feedback on learning activity 3.1

You should be thinking at the corporate level, and, with reference to figure 3.1, have selected KPIs linked to the main business plan. Strategic KPIs are part of an organisation's long-term planning, and when deciding on this set of performance measures managers should be sure that they can access the relevant data as and when they need it.

Suitable strategic KPIs would include:

- profitability
- return on investment
- cashflow
- customer service levels
- sales growth
- production/productivity levels
- performance against budget
- cost management
- HR targets
- R&D developments.

This list of KPIs reflects corporate targets and key departmental targets within set time periods.

Feedback on self-assessment question 3.1

See table 3.2.

Table 3.2

SMART Criteria review Alltrading UK plc	A corporate target of a 5% growth in sales over the last financial year
S Specific	Yes, the target was specific in specifying all sales/turnover generated by the company in one financial year.
M Measurable	Yes, it is measurable from prime documents. Sales money value is an objective measurement.

(continued on next page)

Table 3.2 *(continued)*

SMART Criteria review Alltrading UK plc	A corporate target of a 5% growth in sales over the last financial year
A Achievable	This depends on the market in which the business is operating. In general terms a 5% target is a realistic positive target.
R Relevant	The measure is relevant to the core business of a trading company.
T Timed	Yes there was a clear timed element – one full financial year.

Feedback on learning activity 3.2

The list will vary according to your experience, or the business area you choose. However, you should have referred to table 3.3 and developed your specific KPI list from this guideline.

Feedback on self-assessment question 3.2

Based on the study session so far, your flowchart should have included the elements shown in figure 3.2.

Figure 3.2

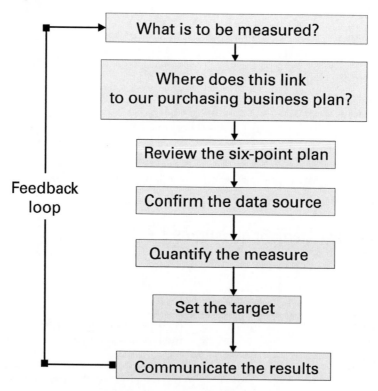

Feedback on learning activity 3.3

A basic action plan should identify the action, the target date, the person responsible for delivering the action, and the timescale. See table 3.4.

Table 3.6

Buyer action plan		
Subject: Materials cost reduction		
Issue	**Description and details**	**Action list and results**
		Dates and times
Product or service		
Present cost		
Target saving		
By when		
By whom		

Feedback on self-assessment question 3.3

On the basis that you have some information on the price of the item or service selected, you can create a simple cost analysis before and after the purchasing action and calculate what the materials cost was as a percentage before and after cost reduction, and thus estimate the percentage contribution to profit.

Feedback on learning activity 3.4

We introduced a basic action plan in learning activity 3.3. This activity requires you to produce a more detailed version of an action plan that should be capable of application to any aspect of the process. For the purposes of illustration we have chosen an operational aspect of basic purchasing: obtaining an outside supplier's quotations or bid price for an internal customer.

The performance measure may be to calculate internal response time to obtain priced quotations for internal customers, and to measure how those customers perceived the quality of that service.

In basic terms the efficiency and effectiveness can be measured as follows.

- Efficiency: How long did it take?
- Effectiveness: Did it meet all the customer needs?

See table 3.7.

Table 3.7

Action plan: Review of a purchasing process	Process element: Obtaining an outside suppliers quotations/ bids price for an internal customer	Action	
Efficiency: How long did it take this time?	A time measure in days	By whom	By when

(continued on next page)

Table 3.7 *(continued)*

Action plan: Review of a purchasing process	Process element: Obtaining an outside suppliers quotations/ bids price for an internal customer	Action	
		Can the process be improved to do the job in less time?	Target date for improvement
Effectiveness: Did it meet all the customer's needs?	Did the customer consider that purchasing obtained VFM?	How could we obtain better VFM?	
Linked issues	Number of quotes obtained		Target date for improvement
	Delivery times offered		
	Quality measures/standard		

Feedback on self-assessment question 3.4

'Time is money', so process time improvement can be achieved by streamlining the task process time to be more efficient.

You could have selected any of the process steps from figure 3.3 and illustrated or suggested improvements in transactional time, procurement methods and general time management issues, which will in effect manage TCA purchasing costs.

Specific techniques could be:

- measuring the number of transactions
- measuring the volume and value of purchase order transactions in a set time period
- measuring the average time taken to process transactions, say on a weekly basis.

By managing TCA, purchasing managers contribute further to business benefits of cost reduction, efficiency and effectiveness.

Feedback on learning activity 3.5

This activity is part of a strategic review, but you were asked to focus on one area of cost management – transactional costs.

The first task is to quantify the transactions and their costs. These fall into three broad categories:

- inbound transactional costs: number of quotes/orders/supplier queries etc
- intra-site transactional costs: number of goods in, stores movements, inventory transactions

• outbound transactional costs: picking, issue, distribution, customer transactions.

The second part of the activity would be a discussion and review of the number, size and value of transactions, and a debate as to whether some aspect of purchasing organisation and/or methodology would lead to fewer transactions or reduced operational costs. You should use the text and content of this session to lead your thoughts and suggestions in answering this question relative to a chosen organisation.

Feedback on self-assessment question 3.5

Based on the text you may want to consider the following options:

• Retain full central purchasing control.
• Delegate all budgets to each site and allow them to operate as independent self-managing units and cost/profit centres
• Agree categories of supply management and location within the new three-division structure

There may be other relevant options based on supply sources, logistics infrastructure or divisional needs that could form part of your answer.

Feedback on learning activity 3.6

Taking a basic purchasing job description involving process and practice, you could have selected the following.

• What skills are required to do this job?
• What knowledge or experience is needed to do the job?
• What targets must be achieved (volume, value)?
• What – if any – are the recognised qualifications to do this job?

Your task would then be to review the 'gap' between the ideal and the actual competence and close the 'gap'.

Feedback on self-assessment question 3.6

The question focuses on competences that have an effect on business profitability.

The yardstick is: which purchasing actions will improve bottom-line profit? As we have seen in this study session, these can include:

• Objective measures (quantitative):
    • cost reduction
    • improved quality at no additional cost
    • better delivery
    • reduced stockholding
    • improved efficiency
    • fewer complaints.
• Subjective measures (qualitative):
    • better business relationships
    • better customer service

3

- more long-term agreements
- better process management and teamwork
- improved assertiveness/confidence
- better use of IT.

The second part of the question is designed to put theory into practice. The basic list is, in effect, a professional best practice list, but the issues will have different values for each organisation. Your task is to prioritise such a best practice list into a practical solution for your particular needs.

Study session 4
Cost and price measures

Introduction

- Just what is a price?
- When do we need to know about cost elements?
- How are costs and prices determined?
- In business, just what do we need to know about cost and price in order to improve our purchasing performance?

> The cost is not always a function of the price; price is not always based on cost.

'I am always very fearful of markets and very respectful of them, and I intend to watch them closely.' (Dr Alan Greenspan, Chairman of the United States Federal Reserve Board, on his appointment to that office)

One of the basics of economics is the **law of supply and demand**, which states that, in a perfect marketplace, price will be a direct function of supply. So how are costs and prices related in other markets?

Many international commodities are traded, with price being a function of supply. Following this economic rule, if we have a bumper wheat harvest the price of grain in a free market will fall, whereas in a poor-yield year the price will rise. In both cases it probably costs the same to grow and harvest the grain, but the price is different because of economic laws of supply and demand.

There are other examples. For instance, in the world of fashion, a sought-after garment or brand may cost thousands of pounds. The actual materials and labour are only a small percentage of the cost, so why do some people pay so much? Here we see the subjective value of brand, design, limited availability and current fashion, where price has almost no relationship to product production costs.

In manufacturing and service provision costs are more closely related to price. There are, of course, many other factors, but if we know the process costs we can start to correlate the price in a more commercial way.

Purchasing managers therefore need to understand costs and prices, and how they are related in business.

In this session we shall focus on issues of commercial pricing strategy, and on how an understanding of this can contribute to both profit and service delivery. Commercial pricing strategy is linked to the supply of goods and services. A key element of the measurement of purchasing performance is thus a function of the management of both cost and price.

Session learning objectives

After completing this session you should be able to:

4.1 Describe the market forces that determine a price within a market.

4

4.2 Define, in cost accountancy terms, the main elements in building up the costs of a product or service.

4.3 Analyse the cost information provided for a given product into the main percentages, and illustrate this in a graphical format.

4.4 Undertake a detailed cost breakdown example as part of a negotiation with a supplier claiming a price increase due to an annual increase in labour costs.

4.5 Give examples of cost elements that are not subject to increase over time for a given product.

Unit content coverage

This study session covers the following topics from the official CIPS unit content document:

Statements of practice

- Categorise types of performance measures that are available to supply chain managers.
- Employ accounting techniques and ratios to measure suppliers' efficiency.
- Evaluate targets as a means of improving the performance of the purchasing function and individual buyers.

Learning objective

1.3 Identify and explain the information required to perform purchasing activities and how to measure purchasing performance.
- Departmental versus strategic goals of the organisation
- Resource requirements
- Costing, pricing, inventory management
- Supplier and vendor information
- Product and service specifications

Prior knowledge

You need to have completed study sessions 1, 2 and 3.

Resources

No specific resources are required for this session.

Timing

You should set aside about 5 hours to read and complete this session, including learning activities, self-assessment questions, the suggested further reading (if any) and the revision question.

4.1 The bigger picture: costs and forces that determine a price within a market

Before we look at the issues of commercial pricing strategy we need to think about the terms 'cost' and 'price'.

As we stated in the introduction, these two terms have different meanings. In order to measure purchasing performance we need to look further at each term, if cost or price is to be used as a measurement criterion:

- **Cost** is the total of the various individual costs involved in making a product or providing a service.
- **Price** is the sum for which the product or service can be sold in its market. It is almost certainly *not* the cost.

First, consider the many factors that a supplier may review when setting a commercial price. In manufacturing or service delivery a cost accountant would work with internal information from marketing, process/production, purchasing and others, while also being aware of relevant economic and market issues. Business traders will need to know their markets and customers in order to make their decisions. There is no single formula or method, but some of the main issues in this information-gathering/decision process are listed in table 4.1.

Table 4.1 Commercial pricing strategy checklist

Economic and marketing pressures (local, national or international)	Management and cost accounting information-gathering and decisions options
Market competition Supply and demand Value to customer Profit opportunity	Basic costs Direct labour costs to make the product Direct material costs for the product Fixed overheads for the business Profit margin
Price elasticity Market segmentation Market forces Alternatives available Possible new entrants to this market	Cost comparison/benchmarking Profit target/return/mark-up Contracting price format: fixed price, target price, cost plus, etc
Volume – size of run – order Time period of production/order/contract Buyer power Seller power	Price calculations Cost/capital/tooling apportionment policy Traditional overhead apportionment Activity-based costing (ABC) cost apportionment of overheads Cost/volume profit calculations Breakeven price/marginal costing Accounting procedures Finance legislation/tax rules

In many cases a buyer just needs to establish a selling price and compare this with other prices for similar specifications (**price analysis**). In manufacturing and more complex goods and service contracts, which may run over longer time periods, it is important to understand the cost base of the item (**cost analysis**).

From this understanding, purchasing performance can be measured relative to cost/price movements in a market.

Learning activity 4.1

Read the financial sections of the business press or professional periodicals and identify the major commodity prices or labour rates that will directly affect your business or operation.

Feedback on page 68

Now go on to tackle the following self-assessment question.

Self-assessment question 4.1

Based on your selection of commodities from learning activity 4.1 above, create a graph illustrating the price movements of these commodities over the last 24 months.

Feedback on page 68

4.2 Basic cost analysis: how costs are allocated and accounted for in a commercial organisation?

In many businesses, prices are built up by aggregating various categories of cost and then setting a selling price. You need to understand the basic principles of this part of cost accountancy, and how purchasing contributes to the process.

In the commercial pricing strategy checklist in table 4.1 there are two column headings:

- economic and marketing pressures
- management and cost accounting information-gathering and decision options.

As a purchasing manager you may be involved at two levels:

- providing cost information to your own cost accountants as part of setting a selling price for your goods and services
- requesting cost information from a supplier so that you have a cost analysis of the goods or services you wish to purchase.

In either case you need to understand the basis of costs. Using the principle of **cost price analysis** (CPA) a cost breakdown can be divided into cost centre categories. The usual main headers are: labour, materials, overheads and profit. These headers are grouped as variable and fixed costs, as listed below and illustrated in figure 4.1.

Variable production costs for the product or service:

- direct cost of raw materials/components
- direct cost of production (production managers/supervisors/labour)
- direct manufacturing consumption costs, eg power/energy
- fixed business/indirect overhead costs and profit for the business operation.

Indirect business overheads:

- indirect general management/staff/labour
- profit and margin amount/percentage.

The exact allocation of costs into cost centres is based on accounting best practice and principles, but for the purposes of this study session these are the main groups.

Figure 4.1: fixed and variable costs

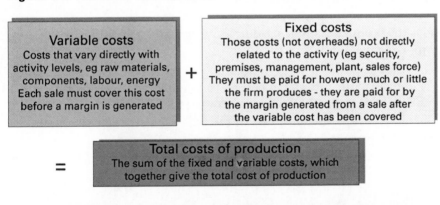

Learning activity 4.2

Choose a product or service with which you are familiar and analyse all the elements of cost that make up the total.

When you have done this, move straight on to self-assessment question 4.2 below.

Feedback on page 68

Now go on to tackle the following self-assessment question.

4

What is the difference between the direct costs and indirect overhead costs of a product or service?

Feedback on page 69

4.3 Introduction to cost price analysis: how are variable costs managed?

Undertaking this class of analysis will give you a clearer perspective on what is, otherwise, purely numerical information on the final selling price.

The direct or variable costs are the cost centre data on the actual cost of sales/production of a specific product or service. They are the direct costs to make the item or deliver the service: thus the more we make or do, the more direct costs we incur. The main elements of cost are the actual labour, the materials, and any direct overhead costs that are consumed.

Consider the product example used in learning activity 4.2 above – the rotary mowing machine.

- The direct labour is the time needed to manufacture and assemble the machine, charged at the respective pay rates.
- The materials specified or listed in the bill of materials are the direct material costs.
- The production manager's/supervisor's time allocated to make this item is part of this direct overhead cost.

There are allocation decisions to be made here. For example, if a supervisor is responsible for more than one product, how is the cost of his or her time allocated? We need not go into this in detail; suffice it to say that we are interested in the principle of the main cost centres, and are aware that certain allocated costs need clarification.

The value of this class of information for the measurement of purchasing performance is that, if we are aware of these more detailed costs, then:

- we can make more informed purchasing decisions, and
- manage and measure any price or rate movements over time more accurately for each element of cost.

For example, say you are the buyer of components for the rotary mower considered in learning activity 4.2 above. The engine is made mainly of aluminium alloy and steel. It would be useful for you to solicit the original base price, with cost analysis details, so that when prices or rates move, you can be in a better position to negotiate with a long-term supplier on any selling price review or variation requests.

By knowing the cost of sales in terms of labour and materials you can ensure that any price increase negotiations are within benchmark limits, as indicated by analysis of independent government indexes of labour in the industry or published price movements for material base costs.

The measurement opportunity is to maintain and retain prices/costs from suppliers that continue to give you competitive advantage at any point in time.

By having detailed cost price analysis and access to independent comparators, your purchasing 'price paid' performance can be measured more accurately and more fairly.

4

Learning activity 4.3

Based on the rotary mower example in learning activity 4.2 above, create a pie chart showing the main direct cost elements.

When you have completed this, develop your skill by doing self-assessment question 4.3 below.

Feedback on page 69

Now tackle the following self-assessment question.

Self-assessment question 4.3

You are the buyer at Motor Mowers UK Ltd. You plan to purchase a 9hp petrol mower engine for one of your products, and request a quotation from Alloy Engines UK Ltd.

The engine selling price is quoted at £94.00. You also request a cost analysis breakdown on this price. The details of the cost analysis are as given in table 4.5.

Table 4.5

Cost centre	Amount
Direct labour costs	£42.0
Direct materials	£31.0
Direct overheads	£12.0
Profit	£9.0
Selling price	£94.0

Calculate the four cost centres as percentages of the total selling price, and create a pie chart to illustrate your result.

Feedback on page 70

4.4 Using cost analysis and measuring your purchasing performance

Developing cost information, or requesting it, as part of establishing a selling price has several added value opportunities for purchasing managers. The evaluation and awarding of contracts is a complex process of assessment and decision, and cost information is a key part of that process. Depending on the industry, and on the time period of a project or contract, there can be many changes or variations during its life. For example:

- changes in costs/price over time
- changes in specification or quality levels
- redesign over time
- additions or removal of work over time
- variations to the work.

Change and change management are a part of business life. Purchasing managers need to respond to change on an ongoing basis.

The opportunity to manage costs can be measured as part of a purchasing manager's contribution to profit. The principle here is that every pound saved by buyers for the same specification goods or services from suppliers has a direct effect on profit. A £1 reduction in cost can be equal to or greater than a £4 increase in sales turnover. Many organisations recognise this, and treat purchasing departments as profit centres, based on this principle.

Buyers cannot just keep obtaining price reductions; no one is just going to supply on a regular basis at or below their own cost. The measurement criterion is to set an opening or target price, and then aim to achieve or improve on this. Very often these measures are on a portfolio basis rather than a single-item basis; with this methodology a measure for a sector can be compared over time.

Certain industries, such as construction or electrical/mechanical engineering, have had processes linked with variation and change included with their contracts. For example:

- The Institution of Civil Engineers (ICE) Institution of Civil Engineers: http://www.ice.org.uk developed the New Engineering Contract (NEC) in 1993. This has now been updated as the Engineering and Construction Contract (ECC) for the industry. The ICE also offers advice on application and conciliation of contract adjustment issues.
- The British Electrotechnical and Allied Manufacturers' Association (BEAMA) British Electrotechnical and Allied Manufacturers' Association: http://www.beama.org.uk has developed the BEAMA Contract Price Adjustment Clause and Formulae, the BEAMA Labour and Material Cost Indices, and the BEAMA Contract Price Adjustment Advisory Service.

These two industrial examples are excellent best practice processes and methodologies based on the principles of cost price analysis of work.

At a more basic level we can use cost price analysis data to manage and measure performance. Price increases are inevitable over time, but the skill is to manage the changes so that you maintain and retain the competitive position you achieved when you first awarded the order or contract.

In order to achieve this you need base cost information and data on price and rate movements over time. You can then use these to check your position over time for the goods and services in question.

Learning activity 4.4

You work for Alloy Engines UK Ltd, and you have been supplying engines to Motor Mowers UK Ltd for one year. This was the first year of a four-year supply contract. You are reviewing the selling price of the 9 hp petrol engine.

The costs a year ago were quoted as shown in table 4.7.

Table 4.7

Cost centre	Amount
Direct labour costs	£42.0
Direct materials	£31.0
Direct overheads	£12.0
Profit	£9.0
Selling price	£94.0

Your agreement with Motor Mowers UK Ltd is that you can request an increase on direct labour and materials, but your overhead and profit percentages are fixed.

- Labour: During the last 12 months the engineering labour index for your industry has moved up by an increase of 2.8%.
- Materials: The main items have moved over the same period by an average of 3.6%.

Calculate a new selling price for the 9hp petrol engine

Feedback on page 71

Now go on to tackle this self-assessment question.

Self-assessment question 4.4

List the main issues when dealing with price increase requests from suppliers. What and how would you measure in terms of purchasing performance?

Feedback on page 71

4.5   How are fixed costs managed?

In section 4.1 we listed the main cost elements that make up a commercial selling price.

In this section we are focusing on overhead costs.

In business there are certain costs that have to be covered independent of production activity or saleable services. These **overhead costs** include:

- premises costs
- administration costs
- management functions, such as finance, human resources
- health and safety
- security
- facilities management services, such as cleaning and catering.

All these are needed if there is to be production or service provision, but most are not directly related to the cost analysis of specific products or services.

In considering these fixed costs, we need to ask:

- Are the fixed costs completely independent of the cost of sales?
- How are these overheads allocated into the selling price?

Some fixed costs may clearly be shared: for example, there may be a security cost for the premises. However, let us consider the example of security further:

- There may be some aspects of security that are clearly part of the production cost, and so can be allocated as a 'direct overhead' and therefore part of the selling price.
- Some security may be only part of a direct overhead cost, and thus may be described and allocated as a semi-variable cost.
- Other security costs are completely unrelated to the product or service, and so come under general business overheads.

Each of these points links to best practice accounting policy, tax financial rules or accounting processes, and will vary according to the situation.

In basic terms the fixed overheads can be allocated from a single central cost centre and charged back to the selling price costs in a equal spread over all activities. Alternatively the principle of **activity-based costing** (ABC) can be used. This is an approach that recognises that not all activities and processes consume or utilise the same amount of resources. Activity-based costing is an allocation approach that uses multiple cost centres with different cost drivers linked to business activity, rather than a single, central cost centre.

All overhead costs will eventually be reflected in the selling price, but if you are a buyer it is in your interest to be sure that you pick up only those overhead costs that are fair and relevant to your product or service.

Cost price analysis facilitates this information for the key goods and service items you purchase. Thus an understanding of the principles of their allocation is a useful part of measurement and tracking. This clearly links to performance measurement processes.

Learning activity 4.5

Using the example of the motor mower manufacturer, identify from the following list of costs which elements are indirect fixed cost items:

- the wages of the production workers
- the head office power costs
- the paint for the machines
- the office cleaning costs
- the maintenance costs for the assembly line
- the canteen costs
- the cost of the outsourced engines for assembly
- the payroll costs
- the health and safety manager's costs
- the sales manager's salary.

Feedback on page 71

Now tackle the final self-assessment question in this session.

Self-assessment question 4.5

Give True or False responses to the following statements.

1   Direct labour costs are fixed costs. TRUE/FALSE
2   Premises costs are fixed costs. TRUE/FALSE
3   ABC overhead apportionment allocates all costs equally. TRUE/FALSE
4   Bill of materials (BOM) components are variable costs. TRUE/FALSE

Feedback on page 72

Revision question

Now try the revision question for this session on page 332.

Summary

Purchasing managers are concerned with the 5 Rs: right price, right place, right time, right quality, and right quantity.

Each element of the 5 Rs can be measured. One of the basic measures is price. In this session you looked at this term, and considered the definitions of price and cost.

Detailed cost analysis is valuable information to a professional buyer. Although price is only one criterion of a purchasing decision, the more information we have on price the better we can use that as part of the evaluation process. Later on we can measure how prices have moved over time and thus ensure that we continue to get value for money over longer-term deals/contracts.

The elements of cost price analysis (CPA) were covered and discussed. CPA puts you, as a buyer, in a position to monitor and use measurement processes to best advantage for your organisation.

Suggested further reading

Useful websites to support references in this session are those of the Institute of Civil Engineers http://www.ice.org.uk, and the British Electro-technical and Allied Manufacturers Association (BEAMA) http://www.beama.org.uk.

Feedback on learning activities and self-assessment questions

Feedback on learning activity 4.1

Many financial and professional publications contain commodity prices and indexed price movements over time.

Thus if you are purchasing, for example, goods containing copper you need to know the London Metal Exchange (LME) published price for copper so that you can 'track and trace' the raw material cost that makes up part of this item's price. Financial newspapers usually publish commodity prices in their business analysis sections.

Similarly, government departments maintain details of labour wage or pay rates in many categories, so if you know the category you can 'track and trace' cost movements of the direct labour costs included in items you are buying.

Based on this data a buyer can set cost and price performance measures that can be compared with agreed independent commodity/labour benchmarks.

For further information see UK National Statistics online at UK National Statistics: http://www.statistics.gov.uk.

Feedback on self-assessment question 4.1

A good working example is a commodity metal, such as copper.

Your answer should be a clear analysis of the data you collected and keyed into a spreadsheet, and should include the visual illustration of a graph of copper price movements over time.

Feedback on learning activity 4.2

Consider, for example, an item such as a commercial rotary motor mower selling for £250.00. The analysis of cost data could look like this (see table 4.2, table 4.3 and figure 4.2).

Table 4.2

Cost centre	Cost (£)	(%)
Direct labour	79.00	52.7
Raw materials and components	49.00	32.7
Direct overheads	22.00	14.6
Total cost of sales	**150.00**	**100.0**

Table 4.3

	£	%
Sales price	250.00	100.0
Less costs	150.00	60.0
Operating margin and profit	100.00	40.0

Figure 4.2

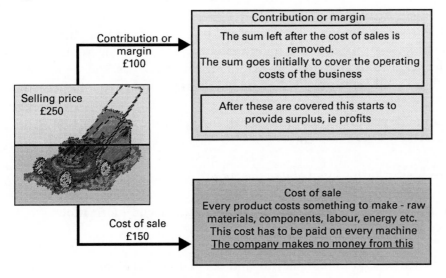

Feedback on self-assessment question 4.2

Direct costs are those costs directly allocated to the cost of production and sales, including labour, materials and any direct overhead costs. These costs are 'variable' in direct proportion to the quantity produced.

Indirect or fixed costs accrue in managing and operating a business and its general overhead costs. These costs are mainly independent of the quantity produced.

Feedback on learning activity 4.3

The cost of sales data in learning activity 4.2 was as shown in table 4.4.

Table 4.4

	£	%
Direct labour	79.00	52.7
Raw materials and components	49.00	32.7
Direct overheads	22.00	14.6

Figure 4.3 shows this data plotted as a pie chart.

Figure 4.3

Rotary mower

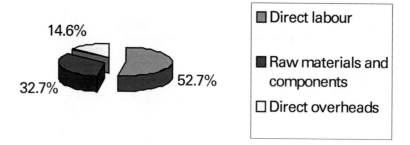

14.6%

32.7%

52.7%

- ◼ Direct labour
- ◼ Raw materials and components
- ☐ Direct overheads

Feedback on self-assessment question 4.3

On the basis that this type of purchase will be based on a longer-term supply relationship, you may continue to buy engines from Alloy Engines UK for, say, the next two to four years. By requesting a cost analysis, and seeing this in both cost and percentage terms, you have better purchasing information.

You can now measure their costs and percentages at the bid evaluation stage before making a commitment.

On the basis that this supplier was the chosen source, you are now in a position to 'track and trace' the main cost elements over time. In addition you can measure any price increases against independent information sources in the future.

The calculation is given in table 4.6, and the graphical analysis is shown in figure 4.4.

Table 4.6

	£	%
Labour	42.00	44.7
Materials	31.00	33.0
Direct overheads	12.00	12.8
Profit	9.00	9.6
Opening base price	94.00	100.0

Figure 4.4: Cost price analysis, 9 hp petrol engine

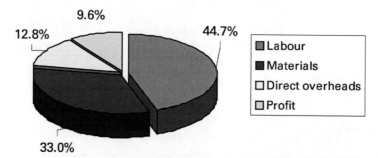

9.6%

12.8%

44.7%

33.0%

- ◼ Labour
- ◼ Materials
- ☐ Direct overheads
- ☐ Profit

Feedback on learning activity 4.4

The new selling price is now £97.00, based on the opening price 12 months ago, and:

- 2.8% increase in labour costs
- 3.6% increase in materials costs.

The direct overhead and profit margin percentages are fixed at 12.8% and 9.6% of the new selling price respectively.

The calculation is as shown in table 4.8.

Table 4.8

	Index price movement (%)	New cost (£)	(%)
Direct labour	2.8	43.20	44.5
Direct materials	3.6	32.10	33.1
Direct overheads	pro rata	12.40	12.8
Profit	pro rata	9.30	9.6
Total		**97.00**	**100.0**

Feedback on self-assessment question 4.4

- Review purchasing processes in terms of the use and application of cost price analysis.
- Make sure that key suppliers and products have cost price analysis information.
- Calculate the expected increases yourself.
- Challenge and check the suppliers' claims.
- Make sure claims are on variable direct cost elements only.
- Look for alternatives to an increase: order volume discounts, learning curve effect, value analysis reductions, no cost service/quality improvements.
- Aim to negotiate in any event.
- Target at equal or less than the indexed increases you have calculated: that is, maintain competitive advantage.
- Measure your result against the set target.

Feedback on learning activity 4.5

See table 4.9.

Table 4.9

Cost	Comment
The wages of the production workers	A direct variable cost. The more mowers made, the more labour is needed
The head office power costs	An indirect fixed cost overhead, which could be allocated as an evenly spread central cost, or by ABC allocation
The paint for the machines	A direct variable cost. The more mowers made, the more paint is needed

(continued on next page)

Table 4.9 *(continued)*

Cost	Comment
The office cleaning costs	An indirect fixed cost overhead
The maintenance costs for the assembly line	A direct fixed cost overhead for product production
The canteen costs	A fixed cost overhead
The cost of the outsourced engines for assembly	A direct variable cost. The more mowers made, the more engines are needed
The payroll costs	A fixed cost overhead, which could be allocated as an evenly spread central cost or by ABC allocation
The health and safety manager's costs	On the assumption that this person covers other products, a fixed cost overhead, which could be allocated as an evenly spread central cost or by ABC allocation
The sales manager's salary	On the assumption that this person covers other products, a fixed cost overhead, which could be allocated as an evenly spread central cost or by ABC allocation

Feedback on self-assessment question 4.5

1   FALSE. The direct labour time is a function of producing the goods or service. The more made, the more labour is needed.
2   TRUE. They are not directly related to the manufacture of specific goods or services.
3   FALSE. ABC allocates in proportion to the activity related to specific goods or services.
4   TRUE. The BOM items are a list of components necessary to manufacture an item. The more items made, the more components are needed.

Study session 5
Inventory management measures

Introduction

- Stock costs money. How much?
- Is it wrong to hold stock?
- What is the real cost of holding stock?

How do we find out the answers to these and other questions about our business stock?

Stock is a valuable asset, but it can be a sinking liability. The existence of stock is reassuring to those who are relaxed about planning their requirements sufficiently in advance of the need, and to those who take its availability for granted. Unfortunately, the premium for holding stock is too high to be complacent about it. The annual cost is typically between 25p and 40p in the £ of its value, and for some items – of low unit value but relatively bulky – it can work out to be much more.

The ideal would be to hold no stock at all and to be able to call on the supplier to provide items when the end user or customer needs them. In practice this approach is unlikely to be realistic, because administrative and usage level timings will require some stock to be held for operational reasons.

The aim must therefore be to reduce stockholding to the minimum level compatible with operational requirements and cost-effectiveness, and to set our performance indicators accordingly. These indicators are consistent with the other study session topics and include all three factors:

- economy: the added value/value for money (VFM) in holding stock
- efficiency: how well we manage the stock
- effectiveness: the stock availability 'service level' that we offer to users or customers.

In other words, is the cost of operating our stockholding as low as it can be while still providing the level of service that the end user or customer requires and minimising our investment in the goods stored?

Stock is part of business working capital in a balance sheet along with cash and other liquid assets. The more stock we hold, the more working capital is tied up.

In distributive trades we rely on those businesses that hold stock in wholesale and retail operations. However, most manufacturing businesses want to eliminate stock and become just-in-time operations.

In any situation, why are some businesses better than others at managing their stock and providing excellent customer service levels?

Session learning objectives

After completing this session you should be able to:

5.1 Assess the advantages and disadvantages of holding stock in a business operation.

5.2 State the main elements of cost that will accrue in the operation of a stores operation.

5.3 Show diagrammatically how costs are allocated into subgroups of inventory-holding costs.

5.4 Summarise the key performance indicators for a stores operation carrying inventory for a manufacturing operation.

5.5 Evaluate how a manager would review the performance indicators linked to inventory held in terms of economy, efficiency and effectiveness.

Unit content coverage

This study session covers the following topics from the official CIPS unit content document:

Statements of practice

- Categorise types of performance measures that are available to supply chain managers.
- Employ accounting techniques and ratios to measure suppliers' efficiency.
- Evaluate targets as a means of improving the performance of the purchasing function and individual buyers.

Learning objective

1.5 Analyse and explain the methods that an organisation's purchasing and supply function can use to manage and reduce inventory costs.
  - Economy: achieving best value for money. Managing the cost of the supply operation
  - Efficiency: use of appropriate inventory management systems and techniques
  - Effectiveness: level of service provided by the inventory function to its end users

Prior knowledge

There are no specific prerequisites other than to understand where stock and inventory fit within a supply chain.

Resources

No specific resources are required for this session.

Timing

You should set aside about 4.25 hours to read and complete this session, including learning activities, self-assessment questions, the suggested further reading (if any) and the revision question.

5

5.1 Stock: its place and value in business operations

Stock is part of most commercial operations, and is listed in the main financial record – the balance sheet. Stock is part of working capital, and is valued as part of the assets.

Once a business buys stock from liquid assets (cash or bank) it remains a semi-liquid asset till it is used or sold. Stock is held for different reasons in various levels of business operation. There are three generic business operation levels, as shown in figure 5.1:

- primary industry: raw materials and resources
- secondary operations: value-adding businesses
- tertiary operations: retail, wholesale and services.

Figure 5.1: The three levels of business operation

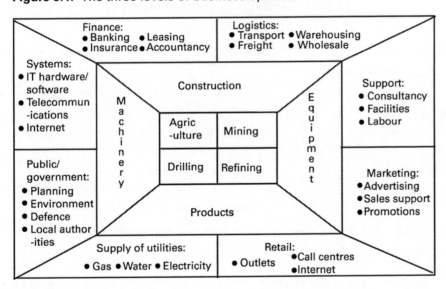

Stock is held in all sectors, but for differing reasons. Table 5.1 provides a brief summary of the sort of stock that would be held or used at each of the three levels.

There are many reasons for holding – or not holding – stock (figure 5.2). The performance measure has to reflect the value to a business that stock offers.

Table 5.1 Types of stockholding

Stock held at each operation	Classification of stock
Primary industry: raw materials and resources Secondary operations: value-adding businesses	MRO spares, bulk stock for sale Raw materials and components inbound Added value – work in progress stocks, MRO stock
Tertiary operations: retail, wholesale and services	Finished goods stock for sale Trading stock inbound, wholesale/retail Administrative and service stock Stock for service delivery

Figure 5.2: Factors affecting the need to hold stock

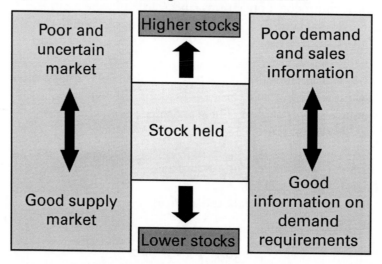

Learning activity 5.1

Using a manufacturing company as an example, design a questionnaire or checklist of information that will be of use in discussing with management how much stock should be held.

Feedback on page 84

Now you have completed this activity, try the following self-assessment question.

Self-assessment question 5.1

Which of the following will be needed to calculate the value of stock used in one year?

1 The part number.
2 The purchase price of the item.

(continued on next page)

Self-assessment question 5.1 *(continued)*
3   The name of the supplier.
4   The annual consumption.
5   The lead time for delivery.
6   The safety stock level.

Feedback on page 84

5.2   The cost of holding stock

Before we consider the cost of holding stock we need to consider the drivers behind stockholding policy:

- Finance managers want low stockholding to give better utilisation of financial resources.
- Production managers want stock availability to meet production plans.
- Marketing managers want to be able to sell based on low lead times for ex-stock products. Out-of-stock products lose sales too.
- Customers want quick delivery ex-stock.
- Buyers may get better deals for larger quantities.

As you can see, there are many push–pull drivers impinging on the supply chain managers in this sector of the cycle.

The business case for holding stock must take several cost centres into account, but the two main issues are:

- financial opportunity cost
- physical opportunity cost.

We introduced the economics concept of opportunity cost in study session 2. It is the opportunity of having (or not having) something – in this case stock. Before you can measure performance you need to know the basis of this cost.

Figure 5.3 summarises these two cost issues, which aggregate to a **total opportunity cost** – in effect the cost of holding stock for a business operation.

Figure 5.3: The real cost of holding stock

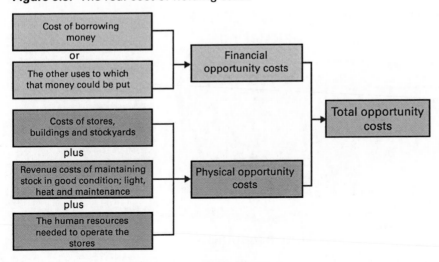

Learning activity 5.2

Reflect on our motor mower manufacturer Rotary Mowers UK Ltd, and the issues noted in figure 5.3.

Where would you obtain the key information that would allow you to calculate the total opportunity cost of stock held in such a business?

Feedback on page 85

Now you have completed this activity, try the following self-assessment question.

Self-assessment question 5.2

Which of the following costs are *not* part of the cost of holding stock?

1 The rent of the stores building.
2 The shareholders' dividend.
3 The cost of a bank loan.
4 The delivery time of goods into stock.
5 The Warehouse manager's salary.
6 The payroll costs.

Feedback on page 85

5.3 Building up the stockholding cost base and identifying links to performance management

We illustrated the concept of total opportunity cost in figure 5.3. You now need to relate these cost centres to your area of operation.

Figure 5.4 summarises the key operational processes involved in stock flow, movement, control and management. Stockholding costs aggregate along the process flow: each stage of the process can be measured and then its performance can be managed.

Figure 5.4: Stock flow

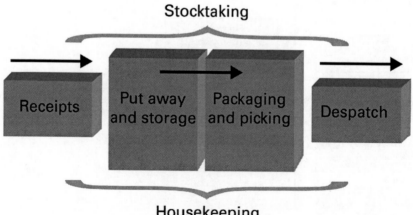

Learning activity 5.3

Develop a cost model for an area of business activity with which you are familiar. List the main costs of operating and managing inventory.

Feedback on page 85

5

Now you have completed this activity, try the following self-assessment question.

Self-assessment question 5.3

A business had a stock turnover of £350,000 in its last financial year. The bank loan allocated to fund the average stock value was £1,000 per month. The physical/service operating costs for the stores were £21,000. The HR costs were £43,000.

What is the gross percentage cost of stockholding for this business?

Feedback on page 86

5.4 Stores and inventory key performance indicators

On the basis that appropriate stock is essential for selective business needs, how will the stores and stock availability service be measured?

A stores/inventory manager would develop a set of operating indicators based on cost and customer service.

These key performance indicators (KPIs) would be equally useful to both internal and external customers, and could form part of staff incentive productivity bonus payments.

The KPIs would reflect the operational issues in running the stores, in holding stock, and the service offered.

In the introduction to this study session we referred to three factors linked to stockholding costs and measures:

- economy
- efficiency
- effectiveness.

Using this introductory framework, how would more detailed KPIs be set and managed?

Financial KPIs (linked to economy issues)

- Purchasing costs.
- Stores holding on-cost percentage calculated, then tracked over time.
- Sub-analysis of stores on-costs, split between operations and HR staffing.
- Stock turnover rate.
- Average stock value amount.
- Stock losses: depreciation, obsolescence etc.

Operational KPIs (linked to efficiency issues)

- How much stock to hold (range and depth of stock).
- The methods and management of the stock.
- Pareto, 80:20 or ABC analysis.

Stores/stock service delivery (linked to effectiveness issues)

Service level is based on the percentage of orders fulfilled on first request.

- Benchmark:
    - High range: 95–98% service level
    - Medium range: 91–95% service level
    - Low range: < 90% service level.
- Stock damage/obsolescence rates.
- Staff pick/put away rates.
- Maintenance percentages.
- The cost–benefit analysis of improving service levels.

Choosing your measures: converting the theory into best practice

The above headers are not mutually exclusive, and will vary from sector to sector, but they do form the basis for applied development to your organisation.

The principle here is to identify what measures are useful and then to track and trace them over time in order to effect continuous improvement in this part of the supply chain.

Practical examples

In large warehouse operations, where the number of individual items stored may run into many thousands, it is impractical to consider each item individually. There are various techniques that can be used to make the task more manageable. For example, the **Pareto rule** or 80:20 analysis can be a useful tool. The Pareto rule suggests that 80% of the value of the stockholding will be in the top 20% of the individual items.

Using this technique, individual stock items should be analysed to establish their total value over a 12-month period (ie annual usage × purchase price) and ranked according to the highest value. See figure 5.5.

Figure 5.5: The Pareto curve

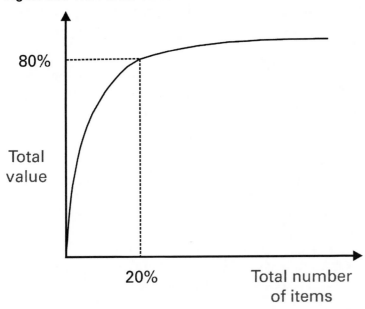

Focus should then be given to the top 20% of items, as they will account for approximately 80% of the total value of the stock during a year.

Another technique widely used is called **ABC analysis**. ABC is calculated in a similar way to Pareto but uses three or more categories of stock based on an item's turnover/usage in the stores rather than its value. See the example in table 5.5.

Table 5.5 ABC tabulation

Item	Movement	Turnover p.a.	Issues
Class A	Fast	7–10	70%
Class B	Medium	2–6	20%
Class C	Slow	< 2	10%
Class D	No movement		Scrap?

Stock turnover (which is generally calculated by dividing the total turnover – usually for a year – by the average stock value – for example, £100m turnover divided by average stock value of £7m equals 14.2 stock turn) is an important indicator, and is often used to describe stores performance. Increases in stores turnover rates indicate an improvement throughout the whole of the inventory management process

Learning activity 5.4

Create a customer survey questionnaire designed to rate the service performance of stock availability from a store.

Feedback on page 86

Now you have completed this activity, try the following self-assessment question.

Self-assessment question 5.4

1   Which of the following would be the best measure of a stores' service level?
A the percentage of items that are damaged in a period
B the percentage of days' absence of staff
C the percentage of items picked on first request
D the percentage of interest charged on stock.

2   Which of the following is the best definition of a stores' stock range?
A the lead time taken to deliver goods
B the variety of stock items available
C the level of safety stock held
D the brand name list of stock items.

3   Rotary Mowers UK Ltd has classified its stock based on the usage of items in the stores. This technique and measure is known as:
A Pareto analysis.
B ABC analysis.
C stocktaking analysis.
D pick time analysis.

Feedback on page 86

5.5   Managing inventory KPIs within the wider supply chain

This section turns theory into continuous improvement practice by managing the outputs in terms of cost and service indicators.

The key issue is how the KPIs are used to manage cost and service stores and stock indicators.

As in other aspects of performance measurement it is important to select the measures and targets carefully.

In this highly transactional part of the supply, where there is a large volume of data, managers need to identify the best KPIs to manage cost and service if they are to maintain and retain competitive edge via continuous improvement.

In this section you need to focus on the management of this objective: the service provision of stock to users.

The performance management process is thus customer driven, first in establishing both targets and KPIs, and then in reporting the results in a clear and practical format for all those persons concerned:

*   Senior managers will be looking at longer-term trends in order to develop strategic planning decisions and/or stock investment plans based on the data.
*   Operational managers need KPI information to plan workload and service delivery outputs in the medium term.

- Operative/workforce staff need to be aware of their operational efficiency and effectiveness outputs at the transactional, week-to-week level.

Learning activity 5.5

Taking a work example within your own experience, complete a template that will track a set of stores and inventory management KPIs at operational management level over time.

Feedback on page 86

Now tackle the final self-assessment question in this session.

Self-assessment question 5.5

Draft a report to management to communicate the performance of inventory management in the business.

Feedback on page 87

Revision question

Now try the revision question for this session on page 332.

Summary

The inventory management process and measures are an important element of the supply chain. Stock is an important part of the chain but the fundamental question is: how much stock do we need, and when do we need it. The traditional answer was to have stock in a store, but this is only one solution. In manufacturing and many service-based organisations just-in-time logistics solutions offer better solutions. In either case the 'just too late' outcome is to be avoided.

This session looked at the need for stock, at what it costs to hold stock, and at how we measure how well supply chain managers are delivering stock needs.

On the basis that many industries need stock we reviewed how best to measure the inventory management process to ensure that the lowest cost option consistent with service needs is achieved.

This balance is achieved in a variety of ways, and the session closed with suggestions as to how managers at all levels can simultaneously deliver the targets of low costs and high service levels.

Feedback on learning activities and self-assessment questions

Feedback on learning activity 5.1

Taking the example from study session 4 of a rotary mower manufactured by Rotary Mowers UK Ltd, we can use a single bought-in component such as a spark plug to develop a typical list. See table 5.2.

Table 5.2 Stockholding review data sheet

Component	Volume, value or data
Spark plug: 1 per machine	

Usage:
- original equipment needs (OE)
- spares sales (aftermarket)
- consumption history
- production plan
- forecast production/sales needs

Product:
- pack size
- price
- lead time

Supplier:
- current supplier
- alternative suppliers

Stock history:
- turnover
- value
- forecasts
- service level indicator

Stock levels:
- EOQ
- minimum stock
- maximum stock
- average stock
- safety stock

Other business issues

Feedback on self-assessment question 5.1

See table 5.3.

Table 5.3

1. The part number	Nominal information only for identification
2. The purchase price of the item	Yes. This is the basic unit cost
3. The name of the supplier	No. Not relevant to this answer

(continued on next page)

Table 5.3 *(continued)*

4. The annual consumption	Yes. Annual consumption × purchase price gives annual turnover value of a stock item
5. The lead time for delivery	No. This is the time it takes to deliver the goods from placing an order with a supplier
6. The safety stock level	No. This is a stock level minimum, which is set as a safety against stock-out

Feedback on learning activity 5.2

See table 5.4.

Table 5.4 Rotary Mowers UK Ltd: cost of holding stock

Financial opportunity costs	
Cost of borrowing money	The rate of borrowing money to buy stock. This percentage is a function of bank rate and business creditworthiness
or	
The other uses to which the money could have been put	What could the same money be invested in that would give a better return?
Physical opportunity costs	
Cost of stores buildings and stockyards	The rent, rates, costs, capital equipment, maintenance etc of and within the stores building
plus	
Revenue costs of maintaining stock in good condition. stores operating costs	The revenue costs light, heat, admin, IT costs of the stores building
plus	
The human resources costs to operate the stores	Staffing costs: management, supervision, workforce. Direct pay and employment costs.

Feedback on self-assessment question 5.2

1 Yes. Part of physical opportunity costs.
2 No. Not part of the cost of holding stock.
3 Yes. Part of the financial opportunity costs.
4 No. Not part of the cost of holding stock.
5 Yes. Part of the HR physical opportunity costs.
6 No. Not part of the cost of holding stock, although there is an indirect overhead chargeback cost for this service.

Feedback on learning activity 5.3

Your list will vary depending on which business sector you operate in. The three main sectors are:

- Primary industry. Mining/agriculture: raw materials and resources.
- Secondary operations. Manufacturing/assembly: value-adding businesses.
- Tertiary operations. Retail, wholesale and services.

Your list must include cost centres for both financial and physical opportunity costs. In order to calculate the percentage on costs you need to aggregate these costs and calculate them as a percentage of annual stock turnover value to get a figure for your industry.

Feedback on self-assessment question 5.3

The total costs are:

Bank interest	£12,000
Operational costs	£21,000
HR costs	£43,000
Total costs	£76,000

$$\text{Stores gross stockholding percentage} = \frac{\text{Total costs}}{\text{Stock turnover}}$$
$$= \frac{76,000}{350,000}$$
$$= 21.7\%$$

(Note that we have used the term 'gross stockholding' here. In reality there may be other amounts and adjustments, such as damaged stock, obsolescent stock, or stock adjustments, which may be used in a more detailed analysis.)

Feedback on learning activity 5.4

A customer survey needs to be industry/service specific for the customers in question. However, the following checklist is a basis for development for your industry.

- Range: Does the stores carry an adequate range of items?
- Depth: Does the stores carry sufficient stock to meet your needs?
- Service: Is the service adequate for your needs?
- Cost: In your view, is the cost of stock as charged out within your expectation/budget?
- Continuous improvement: How could range, depth or service be improved for you?

Your survey should remind customers that although range, depth and service can always be increased or improved there is a cost for this. What we are looking for in the responses is thus a customer/service balance of real needs at an acceptable cost.

Feedback on self-assessment question 5.4

Answers

1   C
2   B
3   B

Feedback on learning activity 5.5

Such a template will vary with the selected industry and management level.

This activity focuses on mid managers/supervisors, and a suggested template is shown in table 5.6. However, you should be able to develop similar templates at any level or for any industrial sector.

Table 5.6 Stores KPIs for operation managers

Broad category	General header example	Action/continuous improvement
Economy	Stores on-cost percentage	Identify variances, and manage within target budget
		Liaise with other supply chain managers/ stakeholders
Efficiency	Stores pick rates	Identify variances and manage process
	Stores space utilisation	Review process as required
		Train as necessary
		Review technology
Effectiveness	Stores service level to customers	Identify variances and trace negative factors

Feedback on self-assessment question 5.5

Your management report would be based on a template process, as illustrated in learning activity 5.5. It would include most of the following headers:

- Current results
- Track of results over time
- Analysis of trend
- Actions on variance
- Opportunities for improvement
- Any review of process
- Actions taken.

5

IT and data management

'Information is power.'

Introduction

How can you use the wide range of information available to measure purchasing performance and demonstrate continuous improvement to others?

You will recall from the unit content and the course introduction that this unit, *Measuring Purchasing Performance*, is based on three distinct categories of supply chain management:

6

- measuring and evaluating the performance of the purchasing and supply function (40% course content)
- measuring and evaluating the performance of the supplier (30% course content)
- measuring and evaluating the performance of the buyer (30% course content).

This study session introduces the way in which IT systems and information processes collect and subsequently report management information that can be used to measure performance in each of these three categories. In later study sessions these principles will enable you to add value to the opportunities to measure the various aspects of performance in all three categories.

Session learning objectives

After completing this session you should be able to:

6.1 State how IT systems are used in business operations in general, and where purchasing and supply systems support the process in particular.
6.2 Define the main elements of a purchasing and supply IT system.
6.3 Summarise the issues that, if measured, would add value to the management of purchasing and supply.
6.4 Summarise the issues that, if measured, would add value to the management of suppliers within an organisation.
6.5 Appraise how developments in IT technology can assist purchasing and supply managers in both current performance and future continuous improvement issues.
6.6 Formulate a set of performance indicators that would help a purchasing manager to reduce costs and/or improve service delivery.

Unit content coverage

This study session covers the following topics from the official CIPS unit content document:

Statements of practice

- Categorise types of performance measures that are available to supply chain managers.
- Appraise measures that can be used to improve supplier performance.
- Evaluate targets as a means of improving the performance of the purchasing function and individual buyers.

Learning objective

1.6 Analyse and explain how the use of information technology may help in the acquisition of purchase and supply performance data.
   - The use of appropriate management information systems to collect data for stock control and costs
   - Databases for recording and storing supplier and vendor information
   - Stock movement and monitoring systems, including point-of-sale data capture and delivery details
   - Statistical database for quality monitoring purposes

Prior knowledge

You will need a general knowledge of generic and certain bespoke IT systems and applications.

Resources

No specific resources are required for this session.

Timing

You should set aside about 5.25 hours to read and complete this session, including learning activities, self-assessment questions, the suggested further reading (if any) and the revision question.

6.1 Information systems in business, and the links with supply chain systems used to measure performance

Information is a key tool in achieving stated business goals and objectives. CEOs and strategic managers in most organisations see information as power, and thus as a valuable business asset. In the context of this study session you need to understand how information can support and develop the various links within the supply chain in particular, and the wider business goals and objectives in general.

Most managers want their enterprises to be more 'intelligent', meaning that they are able to react and plan by using information effectively. However, it is a challenge to define and characterise what an **intelligent enterprise** looks like.

Opinions vary widely on this, because all companies and organisations use information technology (IT) and use information systems (IS) differently. Organisations are at varying levels of IT/IS evolution and maturity, and at the same time the technology continues to move forward. The key to using information successfully is not necessarily how far the organisation has *evolved*, but how it is *evolving*.

The intelligent enterprise shows sound judgement and rationality in planning a practical approach to delivering solutions that meet the long-term information needs of the organisation.

This does not mean that the intelligent enterprise has all the latest and greatest technology; rather it means that it exploits information to establish and maintain the strategic vision, and then applies it in an effective manner.

The intelligent enterprise achieves its strategic and tactical objectives through information use. In private sector businesses this is to done to attain financial targets and maintain sustainable competitive advantage. In NPO and service sector organisations the mission is to attain service delivery within budget and VFM criteria. This can be achieved with simple or complex technology, from an SME to a corporate organisation.

As an organisation moves along the evolutionary process, it expands its capability for delivering increased business value via information. Understanding how to evolve to an intelligent enterprise means the organisation has to comprehend the steps along the way.

Organisations need to recognise where they are and why, and then understand how to move to the next level. These steps are best classified into the following five levels:

- Level 1: Operate.
- Level 2: Consolidate.
- Level 3: Integrate.
- Level 4: Optimise.
- Level 5: Innovate.

These five steps along the IT/IS evolutionary road, and some milestone issues, are illustrated in figure 6.1.

Figure 6.1: Evolving information systems

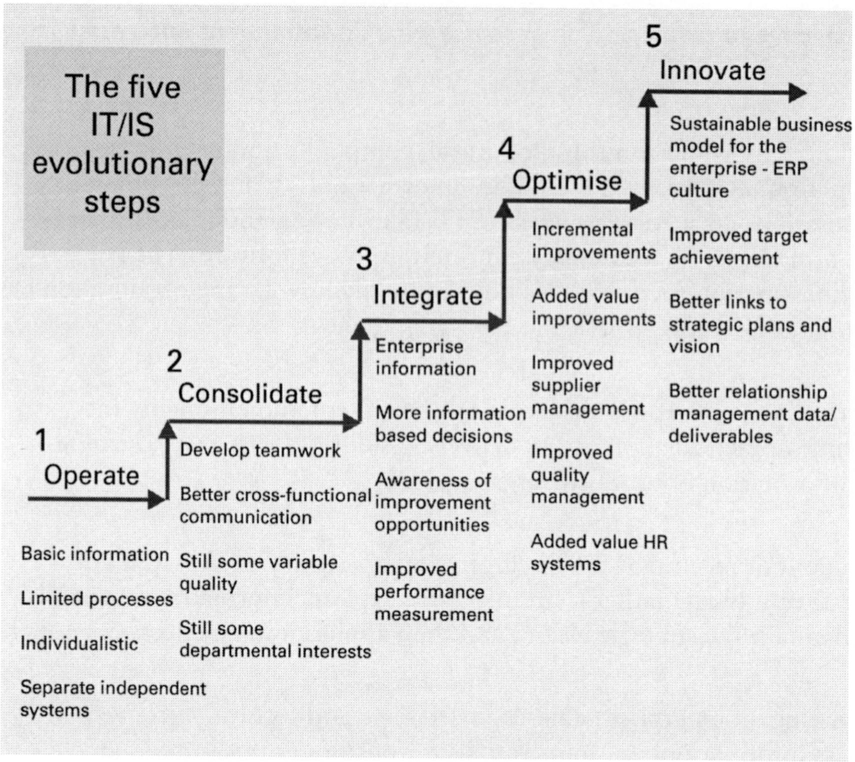

The five IT/IS evolutionary steps

5 Innovate
- Sustainable business model for the enterprise - ERP culture
- Improved target achievement
- Better links to strategic plans and vision
- Better relationship management data/ deliverables

4 Optimise
- Incremental improvements
- Added value improvements
- Improved supplier management
- Improved quality management
- Added value HR systems

3 Integrate
- Enterprise information
- More information based decisions
- Awareness of improvement opportunities
- Improved performance measurement

2 Consolidate
- Develop teamwork
- Better cross-functional communication
- Still some variable quality
- Still some departmental interests

1 Operate
- Basic information
- Limited processes
- Individualistic
- Separate independent systems

Having discussed the wider issues of IT/IS within an organisation, we now need to reflect on how to use information for the purposes of performance management in a variety of business and service sectors.

One of the first issues is to differentiate between data and information. Recall the old saying 'We can't see the wood for the trees.' Managers are often in this position: surrounded with data but having little information to work with.

In basic terms data is a set of facts or transactions. The skill of information reporting is to select the data for sorting and aggregation into meaningful sets and reports.

Selecting the data from robust sources/transactions is the basis of analysis. The aim should be to use existing data and then report selected trends, milestones, results from this. One common error is to create new data input to achieve this; best practice reporting relies on using existing transactional sources entered as part of daily operational transactions and then utilising that for information purposes.

Within supply chains there are several typical data sources. Figure 6.2 illustrates the main groupings that can be identified in most systems. These facilitate supply chain information and report sets that are the basis for performance measurement, and will also interface with corporate information needs.

Figure 6.2: Typical supply chain databases and outputs

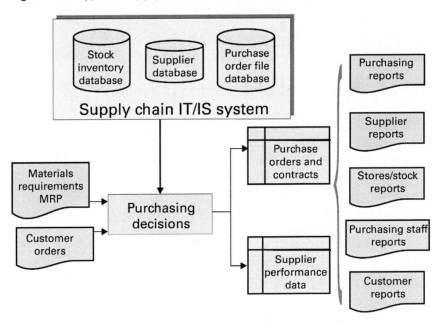

6

Learning activity 6.1

Describe the main elements of a corporate business IT system and the links to the supply chain process and systems.

Feedback on page 102

Now go on to tackle the following self-assessment question.

Self-assessment question 6.1

1   In the supply chain system, purchasing transactional data is input:
     A by finance in entering a budget cost centre value.
     B by buyers in raising purchase orders.
     C by buyers in entering quotation information.
     D by production in recording volume produced.
2   In a manufacturing company, the transactions on which a stores parts stock report is based are:
     A the volume and value of sales to customers.
     B the volume and value of supply chain distribution costs.
     C the volume and value of production stock items.
     D the volume and value of finished goods.
3   An information system that integrates with other corporate systems is known as:
     A a materials requirements planning (MRP) system.
     B a distribution requirements planning (DRP) system.
     C a purchasing management system.

(continued on next page)

Self-assessment question 6.1 *(continued)*

D An enterprise resource planning (ERP) system.

Feedback on page 102

6.2   The key elements of a purchasing IT system

Purchasing and supply systems can be either stand-alone or part of a corporate package. In either case, how do managers get the most from the system?

At this point we are not concerned what business sector is being served or whether or not the system should be stand-alone. For information, most larger systems now operate in a 'procure to pay' environment linked to e-procurement and web links.

The basic purposes of a purchasing system are to:

- receive or identify and log customer demands or requirements
- identify a source of supply to specification
- ensure audit processes and authority
- enable a buyer to agree a price and terms for supply
- raise an order or contract for delivery from a supplier
- ensure that goods are delivered to that order requirement
- generate the order or contract as a prime document in the payment process
- produce procurement reports.

The assessment and evaluation of existing or planned purchasing systems should relate to these basic purposes. However, if a buyer is involved in specifying an upgrade or a new system, there are several other costs and measures that should be considered:

- IT software licence fees
- database integration costs – set-up and or integration with existing systems
- installation costs
- training costs, both at set-up and ongoing
- usage costs, including software maintenance and upgrade time and costs.

In terms of the above processes, what outputs should be measured from a purchasing system in addition to ensuring good process control?

- the management of a rationalised supplier base
- the opportunities from using leveraged buying power
- the opportunity to reduce purchasing transactional costs.

These three headers are intentionally broad. The operational details will vary according to the business sector in which a buyer works, and the IT environment of the organisation. However, the purchasing performance measures and targets can be related to these three key headers in most situations. You will develop the added value and purchasing measurement opportunities offered via IT systems in more detail later in this session.

Learning activity 6.2

Create a process/flow diagram of a purchasing and supply IT system, and note the corporate interfaces.

Feedback on page 103

Having completed this, now try the following self-assessment question.

6

Self-assessment question 6.2

List at least five reports that a buyer could generate and use at the transactional level as a basis for measuring aspects of purchasing performance over time.

Feedback on page 103

6.3 The added value issues and linked performance indicators for managing the purchasing function

In any IT system there is a high volume of data. Managers must be able to select, classify and create useful reports to support their professional or management skills.

In section 6.2 we reviewed the added value of an IT system in purchasing management, and the self-assessment question required you to elaborate on how purchasing performance measures can be identified from data available.

In these next three sections of this session you will categorise those opportunities in line with the unit content, setting the scene for their further development later in this course book:

- performance management of purchasing
- performance management of suppliers
- performance management of buyers.

The final section will review the specific opportunities for saving costs and adding value that are offered to purchasing by IT/IS systems.

Learning activity 6.3

In self-assessment question 6.2 above you developed a list of basic transactional reports concerned with the management of purchasing.

(continued on next page)

Learning activity 6.3 (continued)
Based on your own experience, rank the top five in order of priority, and briefly explain your reasoning.

Feedback on page 103

In any business, each department has to perform efficiently and effectively. The purchasing function is a cost to the business in providing the service of obtaining goods and services required. You therefore need to manage this cost as part of purchasing performance management.

The cost of purchasing is an element in the concept of the total cost of acquisition (TCA) and/or the wider concept, the total cost of ownership (TCO), which we introduced in study session 2.

In some organisations purchasing is set up as a cost centre or profit centre linked to production costs or business profit margins. In other organisations the purchasing department staff and operating budgets are just part of a departmental, operational or corporate budget, and are not specifically identified. But however the cost accountants set up the details, purchasing managers need to be able to manage their 'business'.

In managing the purchasing business there are various aspects to be considered: process and procedures, professional practice and methods, and HR costs. The application and operation of IT systems form part of that management process.

Performance measurement of the purchasing function can be either objective or subjective:

- Objective measures involve measurable quantity or values, such as money, time, or rates.
- Subjective measures involve more qualitative or service value measurements, such as customer surveys, personal assessment or value judgement opinions.

In the measurement process both formats can be used independently or jointly. You will see examples of both in this course book, and will no doubt be aware of specific examples in your own organisation or experience.

To summarise, purchasing performance management will draw on a wide range of facts, opinions and information in assessing its effectiveness and efficiency as a service provider within a commercial, service or manufacturing operation. IT systems can support, facilitate, log, track, trace and collate such information, but success is not guaranteed by merely having the latest state-of-the-art system.

Self-assessment question 6.3

Give True or False responses to the following statements.

1   The measurement of a category of spend by purchasing is a subjective measure. TRUE/FALSE

(continued on next page)

2 Purchasing can have a direct effect on the gross profit of a business. TRUE/FALSE

3 The cost of the purchasing function is part of the total cost of acquisition for an organisation. TRUE/FALSE

4 A purchasing department can operate as a profit centre in a business. TRUE/FALSE

Feedback on page 104

6.4 The added value issues and processes in managing the performance of suppliers

6

Most organisations have too many suppliers. How do we manage the supplier base for best performance?

Consider the following questions, which purchasing managers should review on a regular basis:

- How many suppliers does our business organisation have?
- How many suppliers does our business organisation need?
- How do we manage the selection of potential new suppliers?

The management of the supplier base is just as important as the management of the performance of suppliers currently being used.

In most organisations there are too many suppliers. The purchase ledger is full of suppliers who are seldom used. Suppliers who supply the same goods or services are listed, and others are left on the lists with minimal annual spend amounts. There are of course some positive reasons for having more than one supplier for some goods or services, but the issue in this section is how well we manage our supplier base.

Learning activity 6.4

Undertake a review of your own organisation's list of suppliers. Categorise them by annual spend value.

Feedback on page 104

Having considered the supplier base, it is equally important to consider how we manage those suppliers with whom we have current agreements or contracts to supply goods and services.

Purchasing managers can use their IT/IS systems to facilitate the management of the performance of current suppliers:

- How do we manage the relationship with current suppliers of goods and services?
- How do we manage the performance of these existing suppliers?

Later sessions of this course book cover the detail of these and other processes. In this session we are looking at the way in which IT/IS systems can collect data and consolidate information into performance management reports for transactional, operational and strategic management purposes.

The important word here is 'manage'. On the basis that we must manage business resources, our suppliers and their performance are key to success or failure. Therefore the management of suppliers must be a proactive role for purchasing managers.

As in all aspects of management there are different priorities of need and action: short-term transactional matters, medium-term operational/tactical issues and long-term strategic policy.

6

Self-assessment question 6.4

Draft a management report on the current supplier base list in a commercial or service operation.

Feedback on page 105

6.5 The added value issues and processes in managing the performance of buyers

Having considered how purchasing IT systems can assist in managing the purchasing function and the supplier base, we now move forward to issues concerned with the purchasing people.

The people who work in purchasing and the associated supply chain functions are the key human resource of the service. Therefore performance management of these human resources is a vital link in the chain of purchasing performance management.

In considering this aspect of performance management there are several criteria to take into account. There are many possible headers, but the following list covers most general areas that can be measured in the context of purchasing performance management:

- the purchasing/supply management competence requirement
- the person
- the post
- the customer service.

The general term 'competence' is used in many aspects of commercial and academic assessment. Competence is generally a measure of several factors, including skill, experience, knowledge, qualifications and attitude.

Competence attributes are acquired over time, and can be assessed and graded according to the needs of a job or certain standards. The elements of competence are not necessarily equal or mutually exclusive.

In terms of purchasing, for example, there are a set of national competence standards aligned to NVQ qualifications. However, not having a qualification, skills or certain knowledge does not necessarily mean that a person does not have competence to do a job. It is all a matter of judgement, linked to the other criterion of needs.

The needs of a purchasing job will be based on a person specification and a job description, written to meet the needs of the job and service required.

In terms of service, our purchasing customers are those people who use the purchasing or supply chain service. Later sessions of this course book will develop these assessment processes and measurement opportunities. In this session we need to focus on how purchasing IT systems will facilitate the purchasing HR measurement process.

Data records will link with corporate HR information, but the purchasing manager needs to provide and have access to this resource in order to undertake performance measurement processes.

The prime documents are the person specification and job description. Based on this, the purchasing manager can measure a person according to the criteria for and needs of the job. This can be by formal assessment or by informal interview. Many organisations undertake an annual review with managers and staff, and this can form part of that process.

A positive review will identify aspects of competence or gaps, with actions to support staff in whatever needs are identified, such as training, mentoring, coaching, or customer service advice. In some cases formal competence assessment is linked to grades and pay, and is seen to be progressive. IT systems can be used to track and trace HR information and link this with performance measurement targets.

Staff development of IT skills, in particular, is part of the general purchasing competence assessment process. Figure 6.1 highlighted the continuous development of IT systems. As purchasing systems evolve there is a specific need to ensure continuous professional development (CPD) in this area of purchasing management.

Staff may need to develop their skills on generic systems, such as Microsoft Office, or in using bespoke software. In both cases there is also a need to interface to web developments such as e-commerce, e-tendering, e-auctions, business interfaces (eg business to government, B2G), and ERP systems. Part of the process of competence review and measurement is clearly linked to the performance of these tasks too.

Learning activity 6.5

List four recent developments that you have researched on IT/IS systems or web information opportunities.

Feedback on page 105

Now go straight on to the following self-assessment question.

Self-assessment question 6.5

Rank the list in learning activity 6.5 above in order of importance as it would apply to your business.

Feedback on page 105

6.6 Best practice: which KPIs will help supply chain managers reduce cost and improve service?

Having considered how IT systems can support the management of the purchasing function, its suppliers and the purchasing staff, we move on to business values and outline how IT systems can reduce cost or improve service – or preferably both.

All supply chain managers must manage costs, manage the supplier base, and deliver measurable contributions and business benefits.

In terms of the issues in this course book we can review cost reduction and service improvement under various supply chain headers, as follows.

Purchasing:

1   interactive cost price analysis (CPA) for goods and services
2   a proactive approach to market knowledge and supplier source management
3   a strategic approach to supplier management of goods and services
4   negotiation at every stage in supply chain and contract management – the contribution to the bottom line
5   improving purchasing customer service, both perceived and actual.

Inventory, warehouse and distribution management:

6   managing the flow of goods in the supply chain via IT systems
7   standardisation and variety reduction in the supply chain
8   improving stores/inventory users customer service, both perceived and actual.

On this basis, how can IT systems support the purchasing performance measurement process?

There is usually an abundance of data and information to draw from. In selecting which ones to use, the keys are relevance and value. Setting KPIs and targets is an important task, and will involve time and effort, so their selection is critical.

The first step is to refer back to the issues introduced in study session 1 – the links to an organisation's mission and values – and ensure that the main performance indicators are in line with these.

Having thus ensured that the corporate strategic issues are addressed, purchasing managers can then focus on both the subjective and the objective measures of the purchasing business.

The task here is to choose a lead KPI for each issue. Use the eight-point list above to identify the most effective measures that relate to these tactical supply chain operations.

In order to support these main KPIs the manager should select the transactional KPIs that feed upwards to the main KPIs.

The IT issue here is to select data and consolidate information that, wherever possible, already exists in the system. Special entries or searches are often valuable, but performance management measures that arise from regular process transactions and analysis are more robust and reasonably accessible on a long-term basis.

6

Learning activity 6.6

Develop a list of important purchasing and supply KPIs for your business.

Feedback on page 106

Now go on to tackle the final self-assessment question in this session.

Self-assessment question 6.6

Complete a purchasing and supply department questionnaire ready to be issued to a management meeting that will discuss and choose the KPIs for the next 12 months.

Feedback on page 106

Revision question

Now try the revision question for this session on page 332.

Summary

This session has focused on two main issues:

- the use of IT/IS systems in purchasing and supply chain management as applicable to all business and service sectors
- how purchasing managers use information covered in this subject area in relation to:
  - the purchasing function
  - supplier performance
  - buyer performance.

The session reviewed the IT links with corporate systems, and considered how these systems evolve within organisations large and small. It then reviewed the nature of data and information available to purchasing managers in order to undertake the process of measuring each of the above aspects of performance.

The final section considered the business case performance indicators for a purchasing manager, namely cost reduction and service improvement. These performance indicators are equally valid in private or public sector organisations.

These issues are all developed as session titles in the course book and students need to keep this IT information session in mind throughout their studies of each of the respective topics to follow.

Feedback on learning activities and self-assessment questions

Feedback on learning activity 6.1

A corporate IT/IS system will integrate data from all management and operational areas of action, including finance, marketing, production, HR, supply chain, R&D, administration/services and other special interests.

A totally integrated system will be based on the principles of an enterprise resource planning (ERP) system, and will interface with both inbound suppliers and outbound customers. A corporate IT system integrates with the movement of goods and information flows, as illustrated in figure 6.3.

Figure 6.3: Controlling and tracking the flow of information and materials

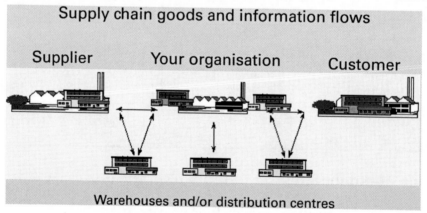

Within a supply chain process and system there will be interfaces with various other subsystems, such as the purchasing system, the materials requirements planning (MRP) system, stores and stock systems, distribution planning systems (DRP), HR systems, and finance systems.

Feedback on self-assessment question 6.1

Answers

1   B
2   C
3   D

Feedback on learning activity 6.2

Figure 6.4 is a generic diagram of IT relationships. It shows the supply chain IT system at the centre, surrounded by the possible departmental interfaces.

Figure 6.4: Supply chain IT relationships

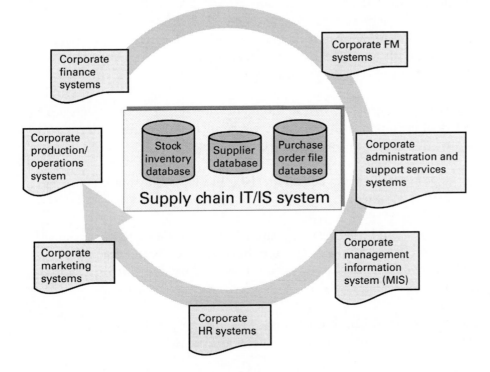

Feedback on self-assessment question 6.2

There is a wide cross-section of possible areas, including:

- purchase order details: supplier, volume and value
- back orders awaiting delivery
- details of contracts for call-off of goods and services
- cost per order raised
- spend per buyer
- spend per category
- saving or added value reports
- cost of purchasing: corporate turnover and/or corporate HR cost
- links to suppliers' prices, catalogues, discount structures
- supplier database details
- EDI, e-commerce links
- delivery schedules, planned and actual
- expediting progress data
- goods received records
- basic quality records: goods rejected/returned to suppliers
- vendor rating database
- invoice links to finance (linked to payment-days reports).

Feedback on learning activity 6.3

Your ranking will depend on the business sector you operate in, and on the nature of the goods or services you are involved with.

103

You could apply the reports you have listed to reviewing and reporting on the efficiency and effectiveness of the purchasing function. Such reports will lead to:

- an analysis of the volume and value of goods and services purchased
- an analysis of the number of transactions
- an 80:20 analysis of purchasing spend
- an analysis of the cost of the purchasing function, as a proportion of business turnover in the last full financial year
- an analysis of the cost savings targets achieved.

This is a broad, general list. You should develop this activity by considering an area of operation with which you are familiar and grouping your priority list into objective measures or subjective measures.

Consider how you would collect the data, and how you would report the information to others.

Reporting would be delivered upward to senior managers for operational, tactical and longer-term strategic use. Reporting across and down the hierarchy would be used to track workflows and productivity on a shorter-term basis.

This methodology can thus be applied to any aspect of supply chain management performance measurement, as required.

Feedback on self-assessment question 6.3

1 FALSE. The summation of a category spend is an objective measurable value.
2 TRUE. Savings made on direct/indirect costs will have a direct positive impact on gross profit.
3 TRUE. The TCA includes the actual cost of procuring goods and services.
4 TRUE. In many manufacturing and retail sectors purchasing departments operate as profit centres.

Feedback on learning activity 6.4

This activity leads to some basic information on the spend analysis of your active supplier base.

You can collect the data from the purchase ledger database, and start by listing the spend by supplier for a selected period in descending order, from highest to lowest values. From this data you can identify the total spend for the time period, and then calculate the percentage spend with each supplier. From this you will be able to undertake sub-analysis. The most useful first step is to identify your top 20% of suppliers by value.

The general principle of the 80:20 rule is that around 80% of the money you spend is typically with the top 20% of suppliers. From this basic data analysis you are in a position to identify your top 20% suppliers and thereby apply your skills to this group.

There are many other, more detailed techniques and analysis methods for the supplier base. However, the principle here is to illustrate how purchasing/business IT systems can facilitate data analysis.

Feedback on self-assessment question 6.4

This question takes you to the next step of using information. In learning activity 6.4 you gathered information and produced a basic 80:20 supplier base analysis. You now need to use this information to manage and/or report to others.

A management report would include the results of the supplier base analysis and the actions that a purchasing manager could take, including some or all of the following points:

- actions planned to use the information for purchasing leverage
- actions planned to undertake negotiations with suppliers
- actions planned to realign the supplier base
- actions planned to manage the supplier base more closely.

Feedback on learning activity 6.5

There are many examples. They include:

- web pages with interactive catalogues
- web supplier/product search facilities
- e-commerce applications
- e-government applications
- e-bidding/tendering facilities
- intranet developments
- supplier registration packages
- specialist professional trade body links
- interactive subscription services, such as the British Standards Institution (BSI)
- certain remaining or specialist electronic data interchange (EDI) applications
- conferencing and communications packages.

Feedback on self-assessment question 6.5

Your answer to this question will vary depending on the nature of your business or organisation and the evolutionary stage it is at.

Most organisations have benefited from basic web searches for products, suppliers and technical information.

You may also have considered some of the competences and competence development issues in working with these processes and systems.

Your answer should develop a response of a specific example.

Feedback on learning activity 6.6

Your list should include cost reduction and service improvement KPIs at each level:

- Strategic/corporate KPIs: linked to the longer-term mission and values of the organisation.
- Tactical/middle management KPIs: linked to delivering the current annual business plan.
- Operational/transactional KPIs: linked to managing the shorter-term transactions and operational processes.

Feedback on self-assessment question 6.6

Memo to Heads of:

Finance, IT, Production, Marketing, Human Resources, R&D, Administration

Management Team meeting with the CEO

Each management team has submitted its annual departmental business plan to the Board. Each manager is requested to enter the most important KPI with respect to the service that purchasing/supply management provides and interfaces with their respective department. From the responses to this questionnaire the purchasing manager will report back on the set of KPIs most relevant to the organisational aims and departmental customer needs.

Selection of key performance indicators	Customer requests	Issue/target to be measured
Strategic/corporate KPIs		
Tactical/middle management KPIs		
Operational/transactional KPIs		
Special KPIs		

Why measure suppliers?

Introduction

They may not be friends, but your key suppliers can be respected and developed, and they can provide support in bad times. It is estimated that the average business spends about 50–60% of its total operating costs on bought-in goods, works and services, although this percentage is often lower in public services such as healthcare and local government. It is clear that the performance of these external suppliers will have a significant effect on both the real and the perceived performance of the business or organisation. This therefore presents the purchasing department with a real challenge.

> 'What matters is working with a few close friends, people you respect, knowing that if times turn bad these people would hold together.'
> **Richard Branson**

7

Session learning objectives

After completing this session you should be able to:

7.1 Explain the link between supplier performance and business success.
7.2 Summarise the measurement of suppliers within the procurement function.
7.3 Define the contribution of measurement in 'quality management'.
7.4 Argue that the measurement process contributes to the building of relationships.
7.5 Distinguish between the measurement processes of supplier selection and supplier evaluation.
7.6 Describe a situation where both business stakeholders cooperate in performance measures for mutual advantage.

Unit content coverage

This study session covers the following topics from the official CIPS unit content document:

Statement of practice

- Explain how measuring performance in supply chain activities fits into the overall management process of an organisation.

Learning objective

2.2 Explain the importance of measuring a supplier's performance and distinguish from supplier appraisal.
- Supplier appraisal: assessment of supplier capability to control quality, quantity and price
- Supplier performance: comparison against a standard, performance on previous orders and against other suppliers' performances

Prior knowledge

A general understanding of the concept of the supply chain and the benefit to a business of good key suppliers.

Resources

No specific resources are required, but it will be useful to be or to have been involved in the measurement or monitoring of suppliers. If you have not, you may find it useful to discuss this issue with other students or colleagues, or a manager.

Timing

You should set aside about 4.75 hours to read and complete this session, including learning activities, self-assessment questions, the suggested further reading (if any) and the revision question.

7.1　Supplier performance and business success

The purchasing challenge is to secure the best suppliers, in terms of value for money, to supply goods and services to the organisation. This can only really be achieved if:

- The supplier's abilities and performance are measured.
- The measurement uses sensible and appropriate **tools** (a generic term for management techniques, ideas and ways of working for undertaking a particular task).
- The measurement takes place over time to show trends.
- The results are compared with past performance, and other benchmarks if available, such as your competitors, or published indices.

The impact of success on the organisation may be considered in terms of the traditional five rights of purchasing (see table 7.1).

Table 7.1 Impact of supplier performance

The right *price*	Reductions in price by purchasing impact directly on the **bottom line** of the organisation (management-speak for the profitability of a business: the profit is usually the bottom line of a profit and loss account).
	Typically savings by purchasing can equate to increased sales of between 5% and 10%, often hard to achieve in many markets.
	This is why there is increased focus on purchasing in many organisations.
The right *quality*	Quality improvements help with branding and satisfy consumer demand for reliability and service.
	Quality can save money when designed in from the start: hence the importance of **early purchasing involvement** (ensuring that purchasing are involved early in a deal, and not brought in at the last minute) and good specifications.

(continued on next page)

Table 7.1 *(continued)*

	Reduced product failure helps with warranty claims and consumer perceptions.
	Fixing quality problems is more expensive than preventing them.
The right *quantity*	It is a key objective of many organisations to reduce **inventory** (also known as stock), and this has direct benefits in efficiency and cost reduction.
	In manufacturing and retail the move to JIT and lean manufacturing is dependent on suppliers' abilities to deliver the needed quantities as and when required.
The right *place*	Failure to deliver to the correct location becomes critical as inventory reduces.
The right *time*	Failure to deliver at the right time becomes critical as inventory reduces and JIT-type systems are introduced. Late delivery can cause severe production or service problems.

Clearly, if all the above are effective then the impact on the business is significant.

Learning activity 7.1

Identify a supplier who you consider has performed successfully for your business. In a table like the one below, write down between three and five positive success features that you attribute to this supplier, and which you have been able to measure. Then rank them in order of importance to your business, showing what you have gained from each feature, and how it was measured.

Table 7.2

Success feature	Description	How measured
1		
2		
3		
4		
5		

Feedback on page 121

'Good' suppliers allow an organisation to perform efficiently and effectively, and to focus on its core activities. The organisation does not need to worry about supplier performance and quality, which are – as far as possible – 'right first time'. As we have seen, this leads to lower costs of operation. Conversely, if suppliers perform badly, then service to customers suffers, along with product or service image. Also, management time and resources are required to improve the situation.

Although it is purchasing's overall responsibility to acquire good suppliers, the actual result will depend on the performance of the suppliers they choose. Also, and depending on the importance to the organisation of the type of purchase involved, purchasing may be interested not only in the **primary supplier** – the one responsible for supplying to them – but also in their supplier's supplier(s) (the second-level suppliers). Increasingly this is leading to purchasing being involved in the whole supply chain, rather than merely focusing on the primary suppliers.

Whatever the industry, supplier performance is increasingly being seen as critical, and there is increased pressure on purchasing to select suppliers who can perform to these standards, and to monitor delivery to ensure that they do!

Self-assessment question 7.1

Give True or False responses to the following statements.

1   Measuring supplier performance is only effective if done over a period of time. TRUE/FALSE
2   It is cheaper to fix quality problems as they occur. TRUE/FALSE
3   Purchasing staff are increasingly measuring the performance of suppliers further up the supply chain. TRUE/FALSE
4   Our product image may suffer if our suppliers have problems. TRUE/FALSE

Feedback on page 121

7.2   Supplier performance measures within the procurement function

We can see from the above that purchasing management is increasingly expected to measure the performance of suppliers, and in study session 8 we shall look in more depth at how this is done. The amount of direct effort that the buying organisation will need to put into the scope of the measurement system will depend on the importance of the purchase to the organisation in terms of:

* the criticality of the order(s) to the buying organisation
* the value of orders likely to be placed
* the time and resources available to continually review and update the measurements
* whether the purchase is a one-off or an ongoing requirement
* factors outside the supplier's control.

Learning activity 7.2

Identify a 'key supplier' in your business and write down four points that illustrate which aspect of the supplier's performance contributes most to your organisation's success, brand image or reputation.

Feedback on page 121

7

Any issue can be measured, but realistically most issues relate to cost and performance. Table 7.3 shows typical areas for analysis using supplier performance measurement ratings.

Table 7.3 Supplier performance: basic measures

Delivery	Often measured as percentage received, in a stipulated acceptable condition, at the agreed time. Sometimes more complex to calculate on service contracts
Quality	On manufactured items failure or reject rates are often used, while service contracts measure the recorded fails in service.
	Increasingly performance is related to quality standards such as ISO 9000 or management systems such as total quality management (TQM)
Service	Often more subjective, but tries to measure acceptable performance in areas such as after-sales service, response to problems, dealing with emergencies, and so on.
Pricing and costing	How do they price, and where are they in the market? Will they provide information on costs breakdowns?

For even the most basic system to be effective, measurement must be ongoing, not just a snapshot at one time. The aim is to measure real performance over time, and to improve it through dialogue, communication and development.

In addition to these basic areas of performance we may also wish to consider those in table 7.4.

Table 7.4 Supplier performance: advanced measures

Overall ability	This is a holistic view of the supplier's performance as a business. Have they the ability to deliver the required service or product over the period of the working relationship? This may include opportunities to benchmark against other suppliers. (See also study session 13.)
Financial stability	What is the supplier's stability for the period in question, and do they meet the necessary financial tests? (See also study session 12.)
Ability to contribute	Does the supplier see the need for and have the ability to make a positive contribution to our business, perhaps through design or innovation ideas or by contributing to cost reduction programmes?

Because both supplier status and market conditions change, these factors need to be reviewed regularly.

Self-assessment question 7.2

Read the following mini case study, and then rank the factors in what you feel is the appropriate order, giving your reasons for doing so. Put the most important first.

(continued on next page)

Self-assessment question 7.2 *(continued)*

ABC Trading plc supplies rear-light clusters to several car and caravan manufacturers. The smallest and cheapest components used are threaded steel bolts, moulded into the assembly and used to lock the unit in place. ABC uses one supplier, but there are many for this item. ABC is running at full capacity and is doing well in sales and profit terms, but is in a JIT delivery environment with most of its customers. What does ABC most need from its bolt supplier, and why?

1   Good prices
2   Good delivery
3   Innovative input
4   Financial strength
5   Good quality

Feedback on page 122

7.3   Performance measurement and 'quality management'

Although all the performance areas in table 7.3 and table 7.4 are significant, quality is becoming increasingly important in supplier performance measurement. This is because the issue of quality has moved on from the basic 'does it work' principle, and now embraces many aspects of a supplier's business performance.

In addition, quality control and management have been 'pushed' up the supply chain as companies, trying to improve their own quality, pass their philosophy to suppliers in their supply chain. Figure 7.1 shows how the view of quality has changed.

Figure 7.1: The changing view of quality

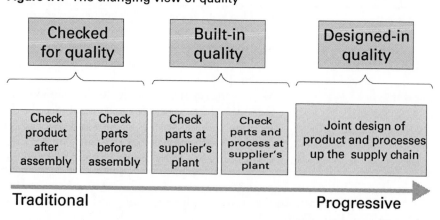

This change has required different and better relationships to be successful, but the intention is that every stage in the business process is inherently high quality, even on products and services that are of quite low value. In addition, a different philosophy now applies: it is less the quality of the product that matters, and more the overall quality of design, and the business process that produces it.

Learning activity 7.3

Consider one of your important suppliers. Give two examples of business activities you would like to measure for this supplier, and give reasons why you feel this is important to your organisation. You may wish to discuss this with your line manager, or quality manager.

Feedback on page 122

7

This change process now requires purchasing to find and hold on to suppliers that are capable of meeting these increasingly challenging requirements. Measurement plays a key part in this process, and purchasing will now consider measuring quality aspects in areas they would not have looked at previously. These might include:

- supplier's testing capability and facilities
- supplier's workforce training and skills
- supplier's equipment and machinery
- supplier's investment in technology
- supplier's production or process management methods
- supplier's organisation and management of quality systems, such as TQM or specialised mechanisms such as 'six sigma'
- supplier's quality certifications, such as ISO 9000
- supplier's general management structures and overall quality 'feel'.

It will be obvious from this that the move away from simple product or service checks has made the process of supplier performance measurement much more difficult, and has set purchasing departments a real challenge.

Self-assessment question 7.3

Answer the following multiple-choice questions.

1   Which of the following is an aspect of a supplier's business you would *not* measure for quality purposes?
    A supplier's workforce training and skills
    B supplier's sales force training and skills
    C supplier's equipment and machinery
    D supplier's investment in technology.
2   In quality thinking we are now focusing on:
    A checking quality more rigorously

(continued on next page)

Self-assessment question 7.3 *(continued)*

B assuming quality is right
C designing in quality
D building in quality.

3 Quality issues have been pushed up the supply chain because:
A it is the responsibility of suppliers in the supply chain
B it is cheaper to let suppliers do the checking at source
C it is required by modern production processes
D companies push their quality philosophy up the supply chain.

4 Moving to designed-in quality has created a need for:
A better training
B better relationships
C better facilities
D better quality checks.

Feedback on page 122

7

7.4 Supplier measurement and the building of relationships

For effective measurement to happen, purchasing must be successfully managing a triangle of complex relationships with both suppliers and internal customers. A large part of the service provision will depend upon the relationships between those involved, and these relationships need to be established early (during the procurement process), and then constantly reviewed and actively managed.

We have seen that the more progressive approach to quality has required relationships that are less adversarial. Relationships can be flexible and open, while maintaining proper businesslike and professional conduct. Good procedures help to establish this balance, and encourage mutual trust and open measurement between the parties.

There are two policies or strategic approaches to developing the necessary relationships: the traditional approach and the partnership approach. The players are the same, but the discussion and communication varies, as we shall see: the intention is to create a more focused approach.

Learning activity 7.4

Consider a major supplier to your organisation. Draw a diagram to illustrate the measurement processes involved in managing this supplier and the three-way relationships that are needed.

Feedback on page 122

In general, adversarial relationships are less likely to be productive, and very often we find that customers and suppliers are working together, while purchasing is under pressure and failing to drive the relationship, as figure 7.3 shows.

Figure 7.3: Traditional sourcing

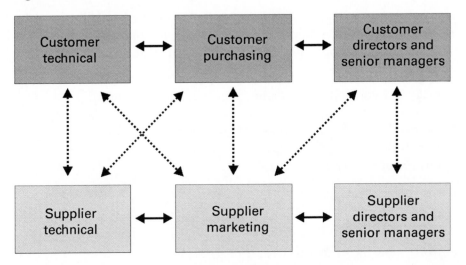

Figure 7.4 shows how the need to develop a more coordinated approach to suppliers has led to a team-based strategy, which aims to deliver much more focus in the developing of relationships. Often this will be led by purchasing, and measurement is a key component in the success of this type of relationship.

Figure 7.4: Partnership sourcing

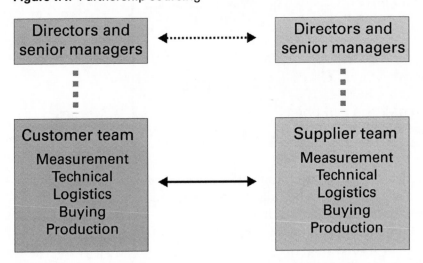

Although true partnerships are still rare, the principles are now well established between buyer and supplier. Partnership sourcing is a commitment by purchasing, customers and suppliers to a long-term relationship based on agreed objectives. Typically there are three key objectives:

- To minimise the total value cost chain, not just unit cost, and improve quality, through **partner development** (working to develop a partnered supplier to jointly improve cost, quality etc) and joint problem-solving.
- To ensure continuous improvement, through equal sharing of technical and cost information.

- To ensure information exchange and efficiency through long-term commitment, inter-organisational exchanges and frequent communication.

Such relationships will generally be longer-term, and can sometimes be more difficult to create in the tender-led public service environment. Figure 7.5 shows how these relationships develop and how the management of the relationship becomes increasingly important.

Figure 7.5: Development of the partnership sourcing relationship

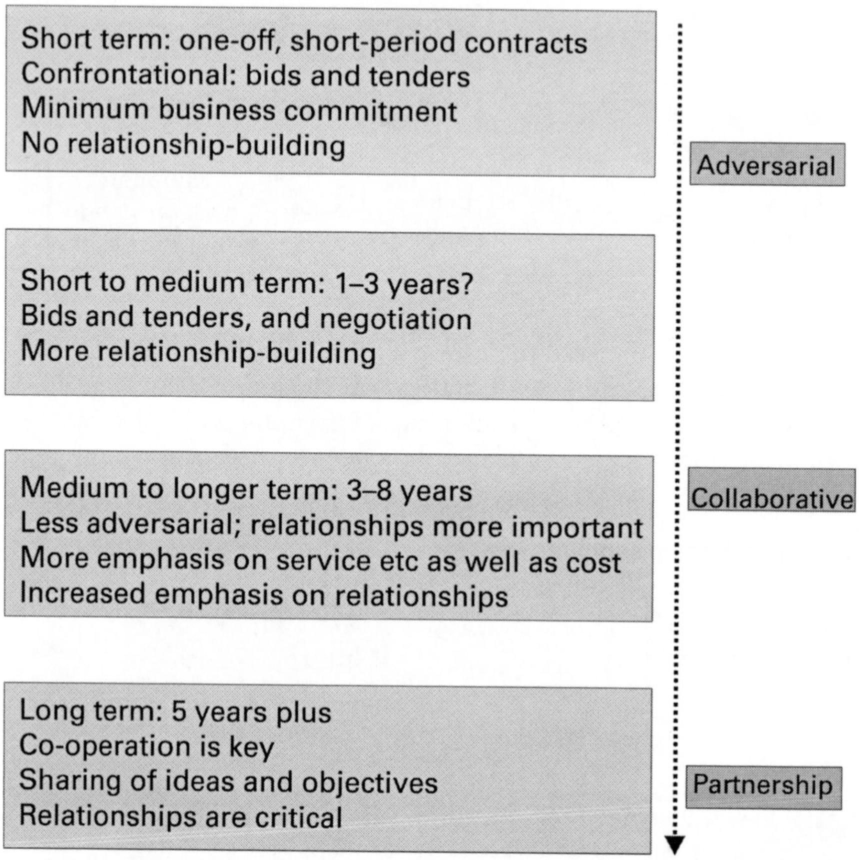

Short term: one-off, short-period contracts
Confrontational: bids and tenders
Minimum business commitment
No relationship-building

Adversarial

Short to medium term: 1–3 years?
Bids and tenders, and negotiation
More relationship-building

Medium to longer term: 3–8 years
Less adversarial; relationships more important
More emphasis on service etc as well as cost
Increased emphasis on relationships

Collaborative

Long term: 5 years plus
Co-operation is key
Sharing of ideas and objectives
Relationships are critical

Partnership

Note also that the use of large numbers of key performance indicators (KPIs) in a relationship can be a sign of insecurity, and it decreases as business strategies are aligned. It is possible that in very long-term partnerships measurement becomes less important, and performance is 'built in' to the relationship.

Self-assessment question 7.4

Complete the following statements:

1 True partnerships between buyers and suppliers are still _____.
2 Supplier and buyer relationships are often considered as a _____ that also includes _____ _____.
3 Today many organisations are seeking a less _____ style of supplier measurement.

(continued on next page)

4 Measurement is easier in a partnership style of relationship because there is more _____ between the parties.
5 In long-term partnerships performance may require less measurement and is _____ _____ to the relationship.

Feedback on page 123

7.5 Measurement in supplier selection and supplier evaluation

So far in this session we have considered various issues in regard to *why* we should measure supplier's performance. However, it is equally important to consider *when* we measure performance. In practice, supplier measurement takes place at two points in a typical purchasing process, as shown in figure 7.6. As you can see from the figure, different terms are sometimes used.

Figure 7.6: Stages in the purchasing process

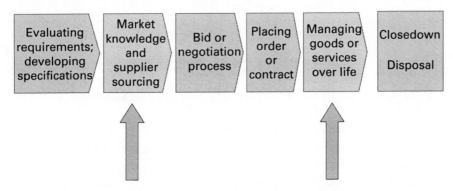

Learning activity 7.5

Based on your level of study so far write down a definition of each main measurement stage:

1 pre-award
2 post-award.

Which (if any) is the most important, and why? Give examples of each type as used in your organisation.

Feedback on page 123

At the sourcing stage we need to assess or appraise suppliers to see which ones are able to perform to the standards required, and we may also wish to certify or categorise suppliers based on the outcomes of this measurement.

When we have awarded a contract to a supplier (who has already been appraised), we then need to evaluate (measure) their actual performance. This is often called vendor rating, and it requires the cooperation of both the supplier and the internal customer if it is to be done effectively.

Self-assessment question 7.5

Write a report on your own experiences of pre- and post-award measurement, bringing out:

- the good and bad points
- any specific difficulties or problems
- how the suppliers and customers contributed.

Aim for around 1 page of A4.

Feedback on page 123

7.6   Performance measurement for mutual advantage

So far in this study session we have seen that it is in the interest of both the organisation and the purchasing and supply function that suppliers perform well. This also has major benefits in terms of improved quality and relationships. However, an important question is whether this feeling is shared by the supplier(s) involved. Is this a mutually beneficial approach?

Learning activity 7.6

Consider one of your major suppliers, and identify three measures that characterise the relationship you have with them. Given these, how would you think that the *supplier* sees the business relationship?

Feedback on page 124

To some extent, whether or not the relationship is mutually beneficial will depend on how the supplier views the buyer's company. Buyers often assume that their order, especially if high value, means the supplier automatically sees them as important.

This is not necessarily so. The four-box matrix in figure 7.7 shows that a supplier may see business relationships in various ways, as explained in table 7.5.

Figure 7.7: Supplier motivation

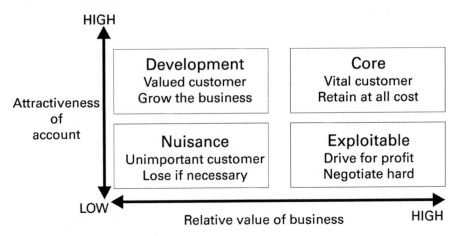

Table 7.5 How a supplier views relationships

Core	I see the buyer as my core business.
	Developing a relationship is highly desirable, and I see development and measurement as essential to the process.
	I may take the lead in proposing this.
Development	I wish to grow the business. The order is valuable, and so is the relationship.
	I am likely to want to work on developing the relationship, and will react well to development and measurement proposals.
Exploitable	I do not see a relationship as other than a way to get business.
	Attempts by the buyer to develop and monitor my performance are likely to be met with resistance or little real effort.
Nuisance	Frankly, the business is not of great interest, and you get transaction service at best.

Buyers who wish to implement performance management with suppliers must try to understand the nature of the relationship, or their effort may be wasted. Also, it is worth noting that this is not a question of the size of the order, but is a complex mix of factors, including:

- the volume of business
- the proportion of the supplier's business the buyer represents
- the supplier's business circumstances at the time, eg full order book, capacity problems etc
- any business history
- the supplier's view of the purchasing organisation
- the supplier's longer-term strategies and tactics.

When the relationship is in the core or development boxes in figure 7.7 the supplier may well be interested in developing the relationship, and be comfortable with enhanced performance measurement. There are several

7

benefits for suppliers that move this to being a mutually advantageous process. These include:

- The opportunity to prove how good their performance is in an 'open' environment.
- The opportunity to discuss problems they are experiencing with the buying organisation.
- The opportunity to submit ideas on design, cost reduction, inventory controls, new technologies and other issues of mutual benefit.
- The creation of an environment in which the concept that the supplier is in business to make a profit can be discussed.

Self-assessment question 7.6

The loner

Mrs Jones is Chair of Goody Foods plc, and has to lead a board-level discussion on developing supplier relationships over the next ten years. She is aware of the trend for a partnership style of relationship with suppliers, but prefers a more aggressive approach, and is a firm believer that quality must be measured on the production line to maintain Goody's product quality. Her purchasing director disagrees, and is proposing that for four of their 20 key suppliers they attempt to enter into longer-term agreements with a different style of relationship. He is a believer in measuring service, but believes that this should be undertaken further up the supply chain, and is less necessary if the relationship is better.

Also, there are major supply market problems that affect products supplied by two of the companies, which he believes this new approach could alleviate.

Provide five comments on this mini case study.

Feedback on page 124

Revision question

Now try the revision question for this session on page 333.

Summary

In this session we have tried to see the benefits of measuring performance for the organisation, and look at some of the broad areas that may be measured. We have also considered the major contribution made by measurement in the changing field of quality management and relationship-building, and have understood the difference between pre-award assessment and post-award measurement and vendor rating.

In the next three study sessions we shall consider some of these points in more detail.

Suggested further reading

For study sessions 7 to 14 students will find that chapter 9 of Neely et al (2002) provides a useful view of supplier, alliance and partner relationship measures, though without specific reference to procurement. Students should also look at Lysons and Farrington (2006), chapters 7, 11, and 17 which are also relevant to these eight sessions.

A useful website to support references for this session in particular is that of the official International Standards Organisation (ISO) http://www.iso.org.

Students who wish to read further on the quality management concept 'six sigma' should check Lysons and Farrington (2006), chapter 9, page 288.

Feedback on learning activities and self-assessment questions

Feedback on learning activity 7.1

You should have a table that shows the success features you have chosen. Your chosen features should have some fit with the five basic rights in the study session, but you must have derived this information through a measurement process.

Feedback on self-assessment question 7.1

1   TRUE. A 'one-off' exercise provides no information on trends or real-time performance.
2   FALSE. Fixing quality problems is usually more expensive than preventing them.
3   TRUE. The focus is no longer just on the primary supplier.
4   TRUE. Quality or delivery failures can have adverse and long-lasting effects on the image of a product.

Feedback on learning activity 7.2

There is no one right answer, but you may have identified some of the following criteria in your list:

* delivery performance
* quality performance
* service performance
* pricing performance
* overall capabilities

- financial performance
- innovation performance.

Feedback on self-assessment question 7.2

There is no absolutely correct answer, but your ranking could look like this:

2   Any delivery problems will put production at risk. Stock can be held, but even on low-priced items this should be avoided.

5   Even on a small component, failure can result in assembly rejection or warranty claims.

1   This is not a high priority, but costs will add up, because large numbers of components are used.

3   There is no real need for innovation in this area.

4   There are plenty of other suppliers if the current one fails.

Feedback on learning activity 7.3

There is no one correct answer, because what should be measured depends on the nature of the businesses involved. The areas you may have considered could include:

- testing capability and facilities
- workforce training and skills
- equipment and machinery
- production or process management
- quality systems such as TQM and 'six sigma'
- quality certifications (eg ISO 9000)
- management structures and overall quality 'feel'.

TQM is total quality management – a philosophy of quality management in which quality is seen as everyone's responsibility, and one that affects all aspects of business.

'Six sigma' is a high-level quality system used in industries where absolute quality is essential; it aims at a failure rate as low as 3–4 parts per million.

Feedback on self-assessment question 7.3

Answers

1   B
2   C
3   D
4   B.

Feedback on learning activity 7.4

There is no one correct answer. Your diagram might look something like figure 7.2 to show the role of the supplier and the customer.

Figure 7.2

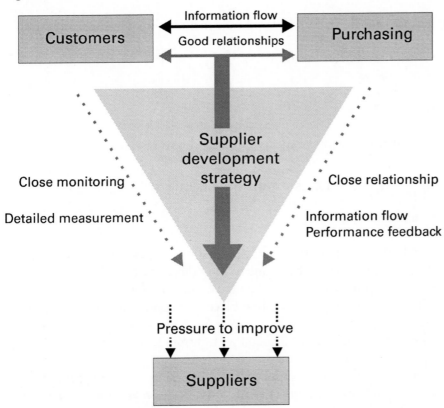

Feedback on self-assessment question 7.4

1 rare
2 triangle – internal customers
3 adversarial
4 trust
5 built in

Feedback on learning activity 7.5

There is no one right answer.

1 Pre-award (supplier assessment) is concerned with the process of choosing the right supplier, and measurements are aimed at ensuring that the supplier can perform well.
2 Post-award (vendor rating) is concerned with making sure the supplier is performing, and with helping to develop that performance.

Both are equally important activities; however, pre-award measurement can help to eliminate many problems, whereas even the best vendor rating system can struggle to improve a bad supplier.

Feedback on self-assessment question 7.5

There is no specific feedback, but your report must cover each of the three points of discussion.

Feedback on learning activity 7.6

There is no specific answer, but you may include such measures as:

- value or volume of business
- relationships
- dependence
- trading history.

Do not forget to see this from the supplier's point of view.

Feedback on self-assessment question 7.6

Your comments could include:

1 Mrs Jones may be right about the benefit of aggressive relationships: theory tends to swing from one to the other. The good buyer sees the relationship style as a tool to be used as appropriate.
2 Mrs Jones is wrong over the best place to measure quality; the current view is to prevent rather than correct.
3 The purchasing director is therefore right over quality: going further up the supply chain is often more cost-effective too!
4 In going for four of 20 suppliers the purchasing director is being sensible, at least in the short term; partnerships take a lot of time and resources to develop.
5 The purchasing director is right: if there are supply market problems, then a partner should give you better service if the relationship is working well.

Steps in the supplier measurement process

Introduction

As with many good management practices, supplier performance works best when it is the outcome of a process that has been well planned and organised, and has been implemented at the appropriate stages in the purchasing process.

Sometimes you can make things up as you go along; try this in performance management and you will not get the results you want.

Session learning objectives

After completing this session you should be able to:

8.1 Define the key stages in the buying process.
8.2 Describe the key steps in a pre-award assessment process.
8.3 Describe the key steps in a pre assessment process – supplier evaluation.
8.4 Analyse the importance of internal and external supplier feedback and corrective action.
8.5 Formulate a process to undertake a continuous review of the supplier measurement process.

Unit content coverage

This study session covers the following topics from the official CIPS unit content document:

Statement of practice

- Evaluate the benefits of implementing a well-structured approach to measuring organisational, functional and individual performance.

Learning objective

2.1 Analyse key areas associated with supplier selection.
  - The key stages in the buying process
  - The variables considered when making the purchasing decision

Prior knowledge

You should have a general understanding of the concept of the supply chain and the benefit to a business of good key suppliers. You should have read study session 7.

Resources

No specific resources are required, but it will be useful to be or to have been involved in the measurement or monitoring of suppliers. If you have not, you may find it useful to discuss this topic with other students or colleagues, or a manager.

Timing

You should set aside about 5.75 hours to read and complete this session, including learning activities, self-assessment questions, the suggested further reading (if any) and the revision question.

8.1 The key stages in the buying process

As we have seen in study session 7 there is a flow process to much purchasing activity, especially when we move away from basic transactional activity. Figure 8.1 shows this in a more detailed form as it might apply in public sector contracting. A similar process will apply in the private sector, but usually with less emphasis on tendering.

Figure 8.1: The flow of purchasing activity in public sector contracting

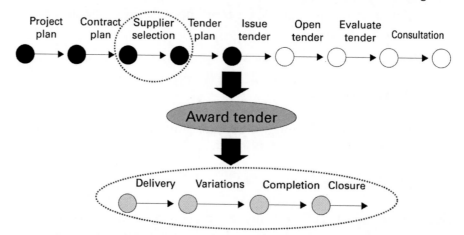

Basically, supplier measurement happens either as part of supplier selection or after a contract has been awarded. This is shown in figure 8.1 by the black circles. Of course, we may measure suppliers at other times if there is a specific requirement. For example, if a public sector organisation is particularly concerned with poor responses to bids or tenders, it may measure the quality of suppliers' responses in this activity.

Learning activity 8.1

Match figure 8.1 to the process typically followed in your organisation, and cross-reference the action points in table 8.1 with comments where appropriate.

(continued on next page)

Learning activity 8.1 *(continued)*

Highlight where you find the most supplier performance measurement.

Table 8.1

Stage	Common to my organisation	Comment
Project planning		
Contract planning		
Supplier selection		
Tender planning Negotiation planning		
Tender planning Negotiation process		
Award		
Delivery		
Variations		
Completion		
Closure		

Feedback on page 138

8

Although we can see two principal stages where performance measurement occurs, we should also recognise that the 'tools' can be applied at different degrees or levels of complexity, depending on what we want to achieve. This is shown in table 8.2.

Table 8.2 Levels of supplier measurement

Level	Purpose
Pre-award measurement	
Basic supplier selection	In order to narrow down a field of prospective suppliers, we undertake a series of limited measurements aimed at ensuring a basic level of supplier acceptability.
	• Applies to lower-value, less complex purchases and one-off arrangements.
	• Likely to require little resource input, and be desk based.
	• Likely to be based on basic quality and delivery functions.
Supplier categorisation	Many organisations have developed the above process and have divided suppliers into various categories. For example:
	Approved supplier: a supplier who has passed certain basic technical and quality requirements.
	Preferred supplier: an approved supplier who offers some additional value or who has some track record of performance.
	• Allows other users to buy from these suppliers without checking.
	• Allows suppliers to see where they stand, and move up the 'list'.
	• Allows for special measurements and process controls to be put in place.
	• Helps to distinguish between suppliers.

(continued on next page)

Table 8.2 *(continued)*

Advanced supplier selection	For key suppliers, or for high-value or high-risk purchases, a more advanced measurement process may be introduced.

- Will extend beyond the basic into areas of business competence (see also table 7.3).
- Will require sophisticated measurement tools and resources.
- Could include third-party involvement.
- Could require international accreditation, such as ISO 9000 series.

Post-award measurement

Basic vendor rating	Simple service monitoring to ensure compliance with the five rights.

- Mostly reactive.
- Some customer inputs.
- Little feedback or review.
- Only limited information.

Advanced vendor rating	A much more sophisticated approach, planned in advance and with supplier and customer active participation.

- Proactive.
- Can lead to better relationships.
- More information led.
- Much more review and feedback.

Supplier development	Can spin out of the above as good suppliers are identified and the buyer wishes to work more closely with the supplier to take the relationships towards the 'partnership' style.

- Supplier will have demonstrated acceptance of measurement and have contributed to business improvement.
- Measurement is still important but is moving from basic transactions towards processes, design and management issues.

Partner suppliers	- Suppliers have a different status. - Measurement of performance will continue, but is now less important.

Vendor rating is a systematic process of measuring supplier performance; it applies to suppliers with whom you are doing business. It is a particularly useful technique. It is often employed when dealing with suppliers that exist in a competitive market with many sources of supply. It is perhaps not such a useful tool if the supplier is a monopoly, and may have little interest in improvement. As with all purchasing tools, buyers must ensure they use vendor rating only to the degree necessary to achieve results for their organisation.

Supplier development is the process of identifying and working with a supplier to 'develop' the supplier's performance for the benefit of your organisation.

Self-assessment question 8.1

Give True or False responses to the following statements.

1   Vendor rating is extremely useful, and should be used with all our suppliers. TRUE/FALSE
2   In the private sector there is less emphasis on bids and tenders, so supplier performance measurement is less important. TRUE/FALSE
3   Performance measurement and vendor rating are capable of being introduced with different levels of complexity. TRUE/FALSE
4   Advanced vendor rating techniques can identify potential 'partner' suppliers for our business. TRUE/FALSE
5   Assessing suppliers' potential must be done by in-house staff. TRUE/FALSE

Feedback on page 138

8

8.2   Steps in a pre-award assessment

The requirement to select suppliers is a key function of purchasing. Sometimes the selection of suppliers is guided by an organisation's financial or procurement policies, and also to some extent by location and market conditions. The policy may be in the organisation's strategic documentation, and will then be governed by many factors, including legislation, business practice in a country or region, the management board, financial accountability and audit, best practice and organisational culture.

In some cases buyers and contract managers have limited choice as to supplier selection – for example on spares from an original equipment manufacturer (OEM). In many other cases the buyer, usually in cooperation with the customer, can influence supplier selection to good effect. In the public sector, tendering requirements and EU legislation are designed to encourage suppliers to bid for business; measurement of supplier ability is still very important.

Learning activity 8.2

You are the buyer for an engineering manufacturer. You have been asked to develop a new supplier assessment process, and have to prepare a checklist of the steps needed to undertake such work. Provide this checklist.

Feedback on page 139

In most cases, purchasing managers will need to establish a process for assessing new suppliers. Figure 8.2 shows some key steps to be followed, and these are described in more detail below.

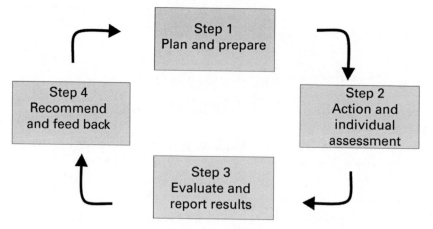

Figure 8.2: Steps in a pre-award assessment

Step 1: Plan and prepare

As in most aspects of business, good planning will help to achieve good results, and adequate time should be allowed in the procurement process for the necessary measurement activity. Planning can include:

- checking rules and policies
- checking feedback from existing vendor-rating schemes
- choosing a field- or desk-based approach
- certified or informal requirement
- the degree and coverage of the assessments
- communications strategy
- briefing and administration.

Step 2: Action and individual assessment

It is important that the assessments are carried out efficiently and effectively. Remember that at this stage the supplier is cooperating in the hope of gaining business; do not forget this process is also costing the supplier time and money.

- Undertake the assessments (see also study session 7).

Step 3: Evaluate and report results

After the assessments are completed, it is important that time is made available to study the results, undertake calculations, and analyse all collected data.

- Arrange review meetings if required.
- Appoint a 'secretary' to record details.
- Match assessments with other data, such as existing performance information or market research.
- Prepare a report if required and recommendations on supplier's status and areas of concern.

Step 4: Recommend and feed back

It is important that clear recommendations are produced from what will have been a complex process. In addition, the supplier should be

8

properly debriefed on both their strengths and weaknesses. This is especially important if the supplier's performance is not acceptable, because:

- It is good practice.
- The supplier should be allowed to respond.
- The supplier may be able to correct faults, and can be reviewed again in future.

Self-assessment question 8.2

This self-assessment question has been combined with self-assessment question 8.3 below, and you should complete it when you have read learning section 8.3.

Feedback on page 139

8.3 Steps in a post-award evaluation

Post-award supplier performance measurement is commonly known as vendor rating. It is intended to be a positive process that:

- Evaluates the supplier's performance against set performance criteria (sometimes known as key performance indicators or KPIs) that are built into the agreement between the parties.
- Collects performance data from reports and/or IT systems for use by the organisation in the future.
- Uses the information in positive discussion with the supplier to assist in improving performance.
- Allows the buyer to determine whether to develop the relationship or abandon it completely.

As we shall see in later study sessions, vendor rating can be a very complex and sophisticated tool. It has several special characteristics:

- the need to blend **quantitative** data (based more on measurements and figures) and **qualitative** data (based more on perception and opinion)
- the need for good data collection systems
- the need for good internal and external relationships
- the need to understand statistical tools.

Also, it may take place off the buyer's site.

Learning activity 8.3

You are the buyer for a public service organisation. You have been asked to develop a new supplier vendor rating process, and have to prepare a checklist of the steps needed to undertake such work. Provide this checklist.

Feedback on page 139

The nature of vendor rating will vary from supplier to supplier, depending on the value of the purchase and the degree of purchasing risk involved. Generally, however, the planning stages are similar to those for pre-award assessment.

Step 1: Planning

- Needs to be early in the development of the deal, and planned into the process, so that all parties are aware of the system and their own input.
- What style of vendor rating is to be used, and which vendor rating 'tools' will be applied?
- Who will be involved, and what is the definition of their role? This may need internal consultation and negotiation to resolve, as it may require the commitment of resources.
- What will be the required information flows, and do the systems (IT and manual) exist to collect and process the data?
- How will feedback and development take place?

Step 2: Introduction

- There may be a need to formally launch the proposed system.
- Introduce on a pilot basis if required.
- Implement the full system (amended as a result of the introduction and pilot if required).

Step 3: Action, monitoring and feedback

This is the working stage, and may last for a long period.

- Monitor information supplied by the system.
- Feedback to suppliers and users on a regular basis, with review meetings as required.
- Make minor changes and improvements to reflect information received.
- Identify scope for major changes and developments.

Step 4: Re-engineering

- Use output from step 3 to propose major changes (re-engineering) to the system.
- Review and agree these changes with the parties.
- Introduce amended system.

(The term **re-engineering** is management-speak for the act of looking at a business system or process and making changes and improvements to it.)

Step 5: Action, monitoring and feedback

This repeats step 3 using the re-engineered process and performance requirement. This cycle of review and improvement can continue, and may run several times.

Step 6: Closedown

At the end of the relationship the system is closed down. In a positive relationship both parties will wish to review what has been achieved, and for the buyer it is important that feedback goes as an input into the creation of new schemes. In this way the process constantly improves. Figure 8.3 shows this in diagram form.

Figure 8.3: Closedown

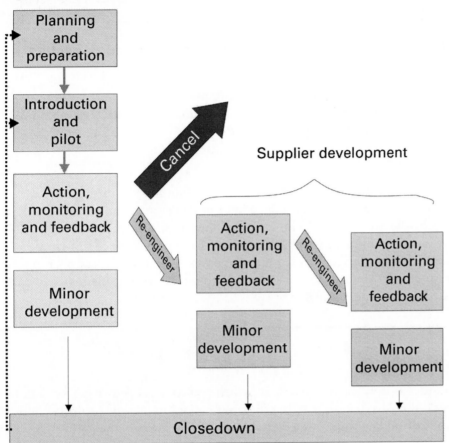

Self-assessment question 8.3

Complete the missing words in the following paragraphs relating to sections 8.2 and 8.3.

Miss M is senior buyer for Toytown plc, a major toy company. She has been asked to implement a supplier _____ programme as her company is about to begin _____ product from Thailand and China. Miss M is not constrained by her company's financial or procurement _____, but has never done this before. She understands how this differs from the _____ _____ used to measure the existing supplier base, and wonders whether the process steps are similar. Given her inexperience she feels a _____ approach might be useful, and has wondered whether there is scope for _____ _____ to be involved.

So far she can see four possible stages: planning, action, _____ and _____.

Toytown's current suppliers are subject to rigorous _____ measurement using a range of _____, and the process has been _____ several times as part of the company's attempts practice continuous _____. The company also places great emphasis on good _____ to suppliers. As a result, several

(continued on next page)

8.4 Internal and external supplier feedback and corrective action

We have already seen that, as part of both pre-award assessment and post-award vendor rating, we need to build in feedback and corrective action. But what do we really mean by these terms?

What is feedback?

In an acoustic sense feedback occurs when a sound passes through a microphone, is amplified through a loudspeaker system and is picked up again by the microphone. This creates a howl or whistle that you may have heard at concerts. Feedback in a management process of this type occurs when information is fed into the process, (in this case supplier measurement) and the outputs are analysed by the responsible manager and passed back to the originator.

Figure 8.4 shows a typical feedback arrangement.

Figure 8.4: A typical feedback arrangement

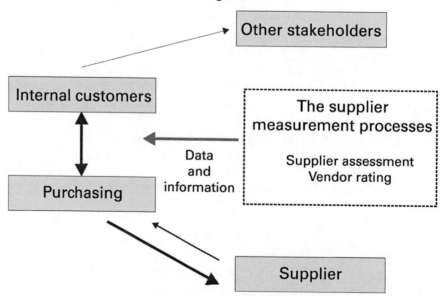

The principle of feedback is as follows:

1. Data flows out from the process to the performance measurement manager (often purchasing).
2. Processed data, conclusions and recommendations flow between purchasing and their internal customers.
3. Data, recommendations and suggestions are fed back to the supplier to allow for change and improvement.

There will also be some minor feedback, as internal customers (and purchasing) may share information and opinions with other stakeholders (including senior management) on the effectiveness of the process. Also, suppliers develop perceptions as to how the process is working, which they feed back to the relevant manager.

But why is this process really necessary? Unlike acoustic feedback this type of management feedback is desirable because:

- The supplier needs to know what the problems are if he is to correct them. This may sound obvious, but not all companies do in fact do this. (Lysons and Farrington (2006) refer to surprise by Jaguar suppliers when this was introduced in the 1980s.)
- A more formal process involves people in the supplier's organisation who may be more concerned with problem-solving than the sales and customer services staff who are the usual point of contact.
- The intention of performance measurement is usually to jointly improve, *not* to penalise and complain. This is hard to do without good feedback. Corrective action is easier with accurate feedback and good data.
- The feedback process helps to build team and personal relationships.
- Internal feedback helps to show the purchasing function as proactive in performance improvement.
- The feedback and corrective action process is likely to involve most of the departments involved in the measurement process itself, because the two elements are interconnected. It is essential at the planning stage to ensure that provision is made for such feedback to take place, and that systems exist for handling the data.

However, in terms of the actual communication of feedback it will often be found best to establish more formal channels, and this is discussed in section 8.5.

Self-assessment question 8.4

You have been asked to draft a new page for the purchasing procedures manual, providing advice on performance measurement feedback. Produce the first draft of this document, using the ideas in this section plus thoughts of your own. Write no more than one page of A4.

Feedback on page 139

8.5 Continuous review and the supplier measurement process

Given the emphasis placed on the importance of feedback, it is also important to note that neither vendor rating nor the feedback process can normally be a one-off exercise. Supplier measurement can be really effective only if the initiative is sustained, and in this section we shall consider some of the issues around a regular review process.

A review may take place in various ways, which can be adapted to the particular circumstances of the deal. Some of these different ways may also form steps in an escalating process on long-term contracts. This could be as shown in table 8.3, although few organisations will use every stage. The timescales are only examples, and in practice will be designed to suit the particular business environment.

Table 8.3 Schedule for performance review

Level 1 (say daily or weekly)	• Low-level contact and routine comment • Regular data exchange • Electronic or paper-based, with telephone or email support • Exceptions noted and flagged to next level with comment • Could be a short, low-level meeting, especially if suppliers have an on-site representative
Level 2 (say monthly)	• Summary data from Level 1 • Exceptions are reviewed to look for patterns • Recommendations for change/improvement (and termination of bad suppliers) are passed forward • Previous changes are reviewed • Meetings with key managers and staff • Notes are kept
Level 3 (say quarterly)	• Recommendations for change are made • Previous changes are reviewed and accepted/rejected • Key decisions on supplier terminations are made • Meetings with key managers and staff • Notes and minutes are kept
Level 4 (say yearly)	• High-level review • Key managers plus senior management • Formal meeting • Conformation of business position and future relationships
Special issues/ emergencies	• An ad hoc session will be held if necessary • Attendees as required

Learning activity 8.5

Develop a second page for the procedural manual you wrote in self-assessment question 8.4 above. This time add a section that recommends how to ensure that there is a proper review mechanism in place for all performance measurement arrangements.

Feedback on page 140

8

Attendance at review meetings will vary, and it will be useful to plan this in at the beginning, because the time commitment can be significant – especially if there are several suppliers being measured. There is no set list of who should be involved, but it is likely that the following departments will be asked for an input:

- Purchasing – who may well be leading the initiative.
- The internal customer(s) – note that when the supplier services many internal customers it may not be practical to involve them all!
- IT or data support – to provide and interpret information.
- Finance – a management accountant can often provide useful support.
- Specialist support – as required.
- The supplier's staff.

This process is intended to be constructive, and most meetings should be informal and positive. An aggressive approach is inappropriate, especially if the supplier is in a minority. The optimum location of meetings will depend on the nature of the contract, but buyers should be aware that there are benefits from visiting suppliers' premises from time to time; they should not assume all meetings are on their own premises.

This type of review process can be aided on large contracts by one of the parties placing a representative on the other party's site. This is common in the car industry on JIT contracts, and can help to share responsibility and improve communication and relationships.

Self-assessment question 8.5

Answer the following multiple-choice questions.

1   Review in post-award supplier performance management is never:
    A quarterly
    B yearly
    C infrequent
    D one-off.
2   Because all purchases and organisations are different, the review process tends to:
    A escalate
    B be the same
    C be adaptable to circumstances
    D be different every time.
3   On large or complex contracts what type of review process may be used?
    A escalating
    B manual
    C IT-based
    D third party.
4   Senior management is likely to attend:
    A every meeting
    B occasional meetings
    C high-level reviews
    D never on performance management.

(continued on next page)

Self-assessment question 8.5 *(continued)*

5　Performance review meetings should always be held:

A on the buyer's premises

B on the supplier's premises

C on neutral premises

D where the best results can be obtained.

Feedback on page 140

Revision question

Now try the revision question for this session on page 333.

Summary

Supplier performance measurement can be a complex process, which needs to be fitted into the right place in the procurement process. For best results it is essential that it is implemented well and that good feedback and review processes are in place, creating an environment in which results become the main objective.

We shall now move on to consider in more detail some of the tools that may be used.

Suggested further reading

Students will find the reference to the surprise of the Jaguar workers in Lysons and Farrington (2006).

Feedback on learning activities and self-assessment questions

Feedback on learning activity 8.1

There is no specific feedback for this activity, but your response should show where your organisation differs from this model, and where most supplier measurement takes place.

Typically, most supplier measurement will occur either as part of supplier selection or after the award stage.

Feedback on self-assessment question 8.1

1　FALSE. Buyers must ensure they only use it to the degree necessary to achieve results for their organisation.

2　FALSE. Supplier performance measurement is equally important in the public and private sectors.

3　TRUE. The complexity can be tailored to the purchase and to the available organisational resources.

4　TRUE. This can spin out of the above as good suppliers are identified and the buyer wishes to work more closely with the supplier.

5　FALSE. Although this is often true, third-party consultants may make a contribution if in-house skills or resources are not available.

Feedback on learning activity 8.2

There is no one correct definition, but your checklist is likely to pick up on at least four main steps:

1   preparation
2   action and assessment
3   evaluation
4   recommendation and feedback.

Feedback on self-assessment question 8.2

See self-assessment question 8.3.

Feedback on learning activity 8.3

There is no one correct definition, but your checklist is likely to pick up on some of the following steps:

1   planning
2   introduction or pilot
3   action, monitoring and feedback
4   alteration or re-engineering
5   closedown.

You should also pick up on the fact that steps 3 and 4 tend to cycle as improvements are required: this may happen several times over the life of the process.

Feedback on self-assessment question 8.3

You should have words similar to:

assessment – sourcing – policies – vendor rating – team – third parties – evaluation – recommendation – performance – tools – re-engineered – improvement – feedback – partnership – cancelled.

Feedback on learning activity 8.4

There is no right answer or diagram here. Your model may look similar to that in figure 8.4, or it may be much more complicated.

Feedback on self-assessment question 8.4

There is no one correct answer. As with all tasks of this type you may find it useful to consider the five Ws: Who, What, When, Where, Why (and How!).

A good order might be:

1   What is feedback?
2   Why is feedback necessary?

3 How do we feed back?
4 Who does the feedback?
5 When and where do we feed back?

Feedback on learning activity 8.5

There is no one correct answer.

You may wish to use the same methodology as in self-assessment question 8.4, but don't forget to add your own views based on your experience.

You should now have a two-page policy draft on the feedback and review process.

Feedback on self-assessment question 8.5

1 D
2 C
3 A
4 C
5 D

About measurement tools

'A bad workman blames his tools.'

Proverb. If your supplier performance measurement system isn't working, you may have chosen the wrong tools for the job!

Introduction

So far we have discussed some issues surrounding the concept of supplier performance measurement, both pre- and post-award of business. However, in reality, performance measurement is more a series of 'tools' that can be used in different ways, and in this study session we shall look in more detail at the concept of the 'performance measurement toolbox'. In study session 10 we shall then examine some of these tools in more detail.

Session learning objectives

After completing this session you should be able to:

9.1 Demonstrate the different performance measurement 'tools' for various categories of supplier and activity.
9.2 Distinguish between qualitative and quantitative measurements.
9.3 Appraise the issues involved in designing measurement systems and ensuring data availability.
9.4 Propose the involvement of other stakeholders in the measurement process.
9.5 Compare the benefits of a desk-based and a visit-based approach.

9

Unit content coverage

This study session covers the following topics from the official CIPS unit content document:

Statements of practice

- Appraise measures that can be used to improve supplier performance.
- Employ accounting techniques and ratios to measure suppliers' efficiency.

Learning objective

2.4 Analyse and explain a range of measures which may be used to develop sustained improvement of supplier performance.

Prior knowledge

You should have a general understanding of the concept of management tools, the way in which they can be used, and some of the factors in their design.

You should have read study sessions 7 and 8.

Resources

No specific resources are required, but it will be useful to be, or to have been involved in, the design of a supplier measurement system. If you have not, you may find it useful to discuss this topic with other students or colleagues, or a manager.

Timing

You should set aside about 4.5 hours to read and complete this session, including learning activities, self-assessment questions, the suggested further reading (if any) and the revision question.

9.1 Using the right performance measurement 'tools'

In purchasing we can liken the various techniques we have available to the toolbox a mechanic may use to fix your car. Sometimes there is just one tool for the job (say an oil filter remover); sometimes there are several tools that could do the job (spanners, sockets etc), and the mechanic uses the one that seems most appropriate to the job in question. Sometimes the tools relate only to servicing a car, and sometimes they are common tools that can be used in many different applications.

The same principle applies in performance management. There are some dedicated tools for vendor rating, or for financial appraisal, and we have to decide how best to apply these. Equally, there are other more general management tools that can help us as well. This section does not provide detailed explanations of each tool or technique, but shows only how it might be useful in performance management.

Learning activity 9.1

Consider a supplier whose performance you are currently measuring or are about to measure. List the tools and techniques that you are using, or will use, and indicate some of the reasons why you have chosen them.

Feedback on page 154

Figure 9.1 shows our toolbox in graphic form.

Figure 9.1: Performance measurement toolbox

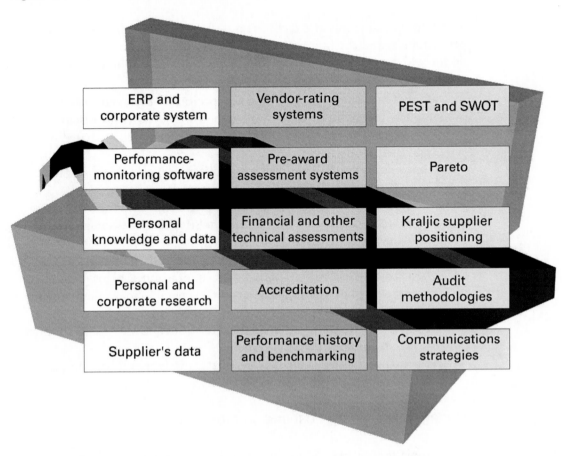

We can identify three main categories of tool (in this context tools may also be information and research):

- systems and information tools
- performance measurement and accreditation tools
- management, theoretical and support tools.

Systems and information tools

This includes a wide range of data and information tools that may be available to support performance measurement, and which may be particularly useful at the pre-award assessment stage. They may include:

- ERP, DRP and MRP systems and other corporate software tools. These can provide data to support performance management, and sometimes include a performance measurement software module.
- A dedicated supplier performance measurement software tool.
- Data from suppliers, either as part of a performance management agreement or from straightforward information-gathering. This may include financial, sales, general management and company information.
- Personal knowledge and data that you have acquired in your job.
- Personal or corporate research undertaken to assist supplier performance measurement projects.

9

Performance measurement and accreditation tools

These are specific tools and techniques designed to measure a supplier's performance, and the buyer needs to understand them well enough to decide which one is appropriate, and to what degree it should be applied.

- Supplier assessment tools. These are specifically designed to assess suppliers before business is awarded, and we have already discussed them in some detail. They may be internally designed, or based on established models.
- Vendor rating tools. There are many different models, and we shall discuss these in more detail in study session 10.
- Self-assessment tools, in which the suppliers check their own performance. The buyer may accept the supplier's measurements, or jointly devise the tools with the supplier.
- Technical assessments, which may take place particularly at the pre-award stage. This could include financial, personnel, plant, quality systems, customer service arrangements, general management and any other aspect of the supplier's business considered important.
- Quality or performance accreditation tools such as ISO 9000 (business process) or ISO 14000 (environment).
- Performance history. This may be a particularly useful benchmarking tool if the supplier has been used before.

Management, theoretical and support tools

These tools are not specific to performance management, but can be particularly helpful to buyers in helping to decide which suppliers to assess and how to manage data.

- There are a couple of 'quick' analytical tools that can help decision making and understanding. They are referred to by their acronyms, and you will probably have heard of SWOT (Strengths, Weaknesses, Opportunities and Threats) which is very useful in analysing relationships. PESTLE is a tool for analysing risk and relationships, and stands for Political, Economic, Social, Technological, Legal and Environmental. Lysons and Farrington (2006) give more details on these tools.
- Pareto analysis (also known as ABC analysis or the 80:20 rule) is a logistics technique often used in stock control, in which it is usually found that 80% of the value of stock is in 20% of the lines. It can equally be applied to the selection of suppliers, or to data supplied from performance management systems. Its main function is to help you concentrate on the important areas.
- Kraljic's 'four box' matrix is helpful in the classification of suppliers, and suggests that suppliers fall into four categories. (Lysons gives more details on this tool.)
  - Strategic items: high profit impact and supply risk to us. Performance measurement would be important in pointing to possible partner organisations.
  - Bottleneck items: little profit impact, but failure could be disruptive. Performance measurement would be important.

9

144

- Leverage items: high profit impact but little supply risk. The buyer has the upper hand here. Performance data is less important as supplier substitution is easier.
  - Non-critical: less need for performance measurement.
- Audit methodologies will help to ensure that performance measurement stays on track, and that there is no scope for fraud (see study session 10).
- **Communications strategies** will help to ensure smooth operations and effective problem-solving. (There are many types of communication, but the process works best when a plan or 'strategy' is developed.)

Self-assessment question 9.1

Read this mini case study and then provide answers, with comments, to the questions below.

Jacob's ladders

Jacob is the buyer responsible for a range of aluminium ladders produced by his company, Easy Ladders plc. There are shortages and supply difficulties in the world aluminium market, and Jacob has decided to introduce vendor rating on his two key suppliers of castings. Easy Ladders has an ERP system in place with an (unused) supplier performance measurement module, but there are extensive archived performance records sheets on quality and delivery.

Easy Ladders is a small company, with a tight management structure and budget. Historically, relationships with the two suppliers have been poor, and each party has repeatedly blamed the other for problems. Jacob believes he has improved this recently.

1 Is Jacob right to introduce vendor rating to deal with the shortage and supply difficulties?
2 Would there be any reason to involve external support in developing the scheme?
3 Should Jacob rely on the currently unused module in the ERP system?
4 Would the historical archive be a useful tool for Jacob?

Feedback on page 154

9.2 Qualitative and quantitative measures of performance

The criteria and factors listed above are capable of being measured either subjectively or objectively, and this difference will be a recurring theme in all aspects of performance management and measurement.

Table 9.1 shows some of the key characteristics of both types of measure.

Table 9.1 Quantitative and qualitative measures

Quantitative (objective) measures	Qualitative (subjective) measures
Based more around numbers and values	Based more around quality or service issues
More measurable and comparable over time	Less easy to measure
More easily turned into targets	More complex to turn into targets
Often more task-oriented	Designed more to measure processes and service than efficiency at tasks
Focus on efficiency and improvement (in the numbers) over time	Focus on improved perception, effectiveness and contribution over time
Particularly suitable for:	Particularly suitable for:
• leverage and non-critical items • transactional arrangements • post-award vendor rating systems • product-based purchasing	• pre-award assessment • where purchasing is seen as a key or strategic contributor • service contracts and purchases • gaining a 'feel' for a supplier • perception issues such as attitude, contribution
Examples	**Examples**
• Component quality • Delivery performance • Prices • Response times to call-outs • Financial performance • Equipment used	• Business contribution • Attitude to technology • Management strengths • Staffing issues • Market conditions • Overall financial strength

9

Learning activity 9.2

Draw up a table similar to table 9.2.

Table 9.2

Quantitative	Qualitative

From your experience and knowledge to date, set down some advantages and disadvantages of each type of measurement.

Feedback on page 154

Quantitative measures tend to be easier to define and to track, because they relate to actual performance, and 'real' data will exist. They also help to eliminate any bias in the reporting. Disadvantages can include:

- the cost of setting up recording systems and actually analysing all the data
- difficulty in interpreting the data
- ensuring all participants are working to the same guidelines.

Qualitative measures are more difficult, because they rely on the expertise of the individual(s) making value judgements on the supplier's performance. Care should be taken to ensure that bias is not allowed to enter the decision-making process when using qualitative measures. Often qualitative measures are turned into a 'numbers approach', as we shall see in study session 10. Disadvantages can include:

- ensuring a common basis for judgements
- holding too much data in the heads of individuals (who may then leave)
- too much emphasis on one success or failure (no matter how problematic).

In practice, many buyers will try to ensure that, when serious performance measurement is being introduced, a mix of different measures is used. Care should also be taken to ensure that issues are within the scope of the supplier to resolve.

9

Self-assessment question 9.2

Answer these multiple-choice questions.

1 Biased opinion can be a problem when dealing with:
A qualitative measurements
B vendor rating
C quantitative measurements
D customer service performance.
2 Which of the following would be best suited to qualitative measurement?
A leverage and non-critical items
B perception issues
C transactional arrangements
D post-award vendor rating systems.
3 Quantitative measurements rely on:
A the buyer's systems
B actual performance and 'real' data
C the supplier's systems
D ERP systems.
4 Which of the following is *least* likely to be a quantitative measurement?
A component quality
B delivery performance
C prices
D management strengths.

Feedback on page 155

9.3 Planning measurement systems and ensuring data availability

We have seen that there is a range of tools and techniques that we may wish to use to measure a supplier. We may be able to tap straight into an existing system or methodology, but often this is not the case, and the buyer will need to consider shaping a 'new' approach. In this section we shall look at some of the issues to be considered when choosing which tools to use.

Learning activity 9.3

Choose a supplier whose performance you would like to measure, and prepare a list of key issues you need to consider in planning the measurement system to be used. Why are these particularly important for you?

You may wish to discuss this with your line manager.

Feedback on page 155

We have already discussed the importance of planning when developing performance measurement, and table 9.4 provides a basic checklist of points to consider when undertaking this planning. (In this table, the term **IT capability** is usually applied to a group or organisation: it encompasses an audit of all aspects of IT, including hardware, software and user skills.)

Table 9.4 Performance measurement planning checklist

Key issue	Questions
What do we have already?	• Is there a system in existence? • What history and data do we have? • Do we have expertise in the organisation?
Who will be using the tools?	• Have they done this before? • Do they have the necessary skills? • Will they need training? • What are our relationships like at present? • Can the system be automatic?
What is the nature of the application?	• What is the detail of the job in question? • Do we know the key areas we need to measure? • Do we know the measurements we need in these areas? • Are we sure having these measurements will be helpful?
What is the optimum amount of data needed?	• We should measure only what is really necessary to obtain a result – but what is this optimum?
What are our available resources?	• Can we do this in-house? • Have we the overall skills and data-handling capability? • Do we need external guidance? • Do we need a third party to undertake the work?

(continued on next page)

Table 9.4 *(continued)*

Key issue	Questions
	• Do we have a budget constraint?
	• What are the supplier's resources?
Do we have to follow procedures or organisational policies?	• What are they? • Do they help or hinder the process?
What is our IT capability?	• Does the plan envisage a large IT requirement? • Do we have the IT capability? • Do existing systems have performance measurement modules or tools that could help? • Do we have the IT staff resource? • Do our people need training or re-skilling in this area?
How long will the process run for?	• If short-term, is it really necessary, or can it be kept simple? • If long-term, is it worth a real resource investment to get right? • Do we need to develop a project plan or management proposal?
What is the audit, review and feedback required?	• How will we check that it is operating effectively? • What will the meeting time commitment be? • What degree of administration will be needed? • Who will be involved?

9

Self-assessment question 9.3

Fill in the gaps in this paragraph of text:

Brian is planning a vendor rating system for a supplier. He is concerned over the size of the project, and realises the need to obtain the _____ amount of data, thus putting the least strain on _____ _____. He also feels that some staff lack the necessary _____, and that some _____ input might be beneficial.

This is the first time the company has done this, and there is no _____ information available as a starting point. However, the deal runs for 5 years, so some _____ of time and resources can be justified. However, if this happens it will be necessary to have proper _____ and _____ mechanisms built into the system to monitor results.

Feedback on page 155

9.4 Involving others in the measurement process

Sometimes performance measurement will be led by, and carried out by, the purchasing and supply function alone. This is not a problem, but there are stakeholders and others who may be able to make a contribution to the measurement process once they are involved. (**Stakeholders** are those people or bodies with an interest or 'stake' in the issue of buyer or supplier performance.)

Why involve others?

- To share responsibility on major projects.
- To widen the range of skills available, particularly in pre-award assessments.
- To spread the burden of providing time and/or financial resources across the organisation.
- To provide access to skills or resources that the buyer's organisation does not possess.
- To help build a team and break down communication barriers.
- To allow faster assessment or vendor rating implementation.
- There is an organisational requirement to do so.

Learning activity 9.4

Draw a diagram with purchasing at the centre, and name the main links to others who could be involved in the performance measurement process (see figure 9.2). Do not just think of internal departments.

Figure 9.2

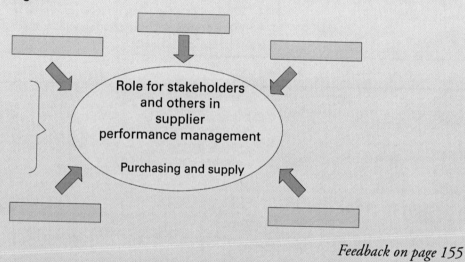

Feedback on page 155

Given that there are almost always some benefits from involving others in the process, figure 9.3 shows some of those most commonly involved, and table 9.3 provides more detail.

Figure 9.3: Involving others in the measurement process

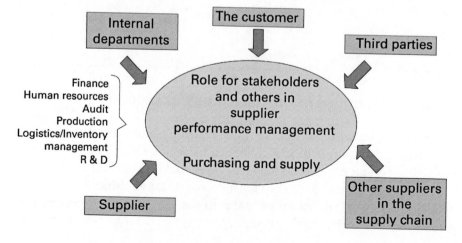

Table 9.5 Role for stakeholders and others in supplier performance management

Department or function	Role
Purchasing and supply	• Leadership and management • Coordination and implementation • Review and feedback • Overall responsibility
The internal customer	• Supplier monitoring • Determining quality and service requirements • Technical input
Other organisational functions	• Finance – assist in financial appraisal and budget issues • Human resources – assist with people and structural issues • Quality management – assist with quality issues • Audit – help devise review processes • Production – help assess supplier's capability to perform • Logistics/inventory management – assist with delivery and service capability • Research and development – advise on supplier's innovative abilities
The supplier	• Provides data and access • May undertake self-assessment or have existing internal measurements that can be utilised • Provides ideas for improvement • Provides feedback on the performance of the buyer's organisation • Provides data on other suppliers
Other suppliers in the supply chain	• There may be occasional benefits from involving others in the supply chain if there are areas of common interest or concern, eg rising oil prices, or shortage of steel
Third parties	• External consultants can provide advice and guidance, and draw up schemes if required • External testing houses can act for the buyer's organisation

(See also study session 10)

Self-assessment question 9.4

Draft a short management report commenting on the possible benefits to your organisation of involving some other stakeholders in supplier measurement.

Feedback on page 155

9.5 A desk-based or visit-based approach?

It will be clear from all of the above that effective performance measurement requires a significant amount of work. Some of this work can be undertaken from the buyer's desk, some of it will require meetings, discussion and consultation, and some may require visits to suppliers' premises.

Learning activity 9.5

Draft out three checklists showing some key benefits of:

- desk-based activity
- meetings, discussions and consultations
- supplier visits.

Feedback on page 156

Let us look at these in more detail.

At the desk

Desk-based work has several benefits for the buyer, not the least of which is that it is cheaper and maximises the use of time, which is not wasted in travel. Desk-based activity underpins the whole process, and should include:

- the detailed planning and administration
- reading or internet-based research (company information, annual reports etc)
- using internal data such as performance history
- studying and analysing data collected once a performance measurement scheme is operational
- recommendations and report writing.

Meetings, discussion and consultation

Inevitably there will be a need for consultation and meetings, often on a regular basis. Much of this may be internal, but there is a cost and time factor attached, as well as the usual diary-scheduling difficulties. Meetings and consultations do help to build up the team, and are a good communications opportunity. They may include:

- initial planning meetings
- implementation or project team meetings
- one-to-one sessions with key or difficult players
- regular review and feedback meetings
- pre-visit planning meetings.

Visits

Visits can be complex and hard to arrange, especially with overseas suppliers, but are essential for developing more qualitative measures about a supplier and the way the supplier operates. Of course the supplier will normally make a special effort during these visits – what you see may not be actual practice all of the time!

- Although supplier visits incur expenditure they are well worth doing because they help build knowledge and develop relationships.
- Visits by individuals are generally far less useful than those by a team from different functions: however those taking part must have a useful role to play and not be on a 'day out'.
- Visits should only take place when something useful can be gained. Visiting to an agreed programme can be less effective as it allows for preparation by the supplier. Remember that the timing of your visit is especially important if the supplier has any kind of cyclical aspect to their business.
- Visits should not just be to see the 'sales team' but should look at all aspects of the supplier's business. Remember to try and look at less obvious issues such as management capability, employee relationships and so on, and consider the general feel and appearance as well (often known as the 'housekeeping').
- A standard approach is alright as a starting point but suppliers should be visited as individual companies, and untried suppliers will need a different approach to existing suppliers.

9

Self-assessment question 9.5

Give True or False responses to the following statements.

1   Supplier visits can be expensive, but are essential for developing more qualitative measures. TRUE/FALSE
2   Regular review and feedback meetings help build a 'team'. TRUE/FALSE
3   It is best for the buyer to visit a supplier on his/her own to ensure that all aspects are covered. TRUE/FALSE
4   Desk-based work is little use once a system begins to operate. TRUE/FALSE
5   It is important to visit suppliers at regular intervals. TRUE/FALSE

Feedback on page 156

Revision question

Now try the revision question for this session on page 334.

Summary

In this study session we have looked at various aspects of supplier measurement tools:

- using the right tools
- quantitative and qualitative measures
- planning the use of measurement tools

- involving other stakeholders
- desk-based and visit-based activity.

In study session 10 we shall examine some specific tools in detail.

Suggested further reading

More details of SWOT analysis, PESTLE analysis and Kraljic's 'four box' matrix can be found in Lysons and Farrington (2006), chapter 2, pages 49–64. Pareto analysis (also know as ABC analysis or the 80:20 rule) is also used extensively in inventory management and details can be found in Lysons and Farrington (2006), chapter 10, page 319.

Students will find Neely et al (2002) especially relevant for this session as it particularly emphasises the role and input which stakeholders can make.

Feedback on learning activities and self-assessment questions

Feedback on learning activity 9.1

There is no one correct answer. You should have identified a list of tools and techniques, and should be able to match them to some of those identified in this section. At the least you should have identified:

- systems and information tools
- performance measurement and accreditation tools
- management, theoretical and support tools.

Feedback on self-assessment question 9.1

Your answer could read like this:

1   Jacob is right to introduce a rating system on these two suppliers, because they are key to business success. However, rating the suppliers will not in itself cure problems in the world market, although it may help develop partnership relationships, which should help him achieve better service.
2   External consultants might provide Easy Ladders with some good ideas on how to take the concept forward. They might also provide manpower resources that Easy cannot, which could help speed up the development process.
3   He should consider using this module. However, many such modules have limitations because they are generic in design, and he must also consider whether the company has the necessary IT resources to use the module effectively.
4   Yes, it would. History can show useful trends on performance, which can form the basis for discussions with suppliers. It will, however, be less useful in predicting what happens in the future.

Feedback on learning activity 9.2

Your table could include the answers shown in table 9.3.

Table 9.3

Quantitative	Qualitative
Expensive to set up and operate	Ensure a common basis for judgements
Difficult to interpret the data	Data is in people's heads
Standardising guidelines	Too much emphasis on one success or failure
Uses real data	Possible bias
Easy to track and trace	

Feedback on self-assessment question 9.2

1 A. Qualitative measurements can be affected by biased opinions.
2 B. Perceptions are best measured with qualitative measures.
3 B.
4 D. Management strengths would be a qualitative measurement.

Feedback on learning activity 9.3

There is no one right answer, but your list could include:

- current position
- who will be involved
- the detail of the application
- the minimum data needed
- available resources
- IT capability
- timescale
- audit and review required.

Feedback on self-assessment question 9.3

You should have some or all of the following:

optimum – available resources – skills – external – historical – investment – audit – review

Feedback on learning activity 9.4

Your diagram could have included:

- the internal customer
- other organisational functions
- the supplier
- other suppliers in the supply chain
- third parties.

Feedback on self-assessment question 9.4

You should feed back in report form on the benefits you feel are important, which should include some of those mentioned above. Your criticism should be balanced to show good and bad points, with suggestions for improvement and for widening stakeholder involvement if – on balance – you feel this would be useful.

Feedback on learning activity 9.5

There is no one right answer, but you should have identified at least some points from the text that follows.

Feedback on self-assessment question 9.5

1   TRUE. Visits are an essential part of much supplier measurement.
2   TRUE. Review and feedback help to develop the team.
3   FALSE. Team approach will provide a better mix of skills and trained observation.
4   FALSE. Desk-based work underpins the success of a measurement project.
5   FALSE. Suppliers should be visited when necessary, not to a timetable.

9

Performance measurement

'It ain't what you do it's the way that you do it – that's what gets results.'
Bananarama song lyric

Introduction

To get good results from performance measurement you need to understand the basic principles. In this study session we shall look in more depth at how performance measurement can be undertaken, using some simple examples. Generally, the measurement of a supplier's performance may be compared with:

- an agreed standard
- performance on a previous order
- another supplier's performance
- other criteria appropriate to your organisation.

Session learning objectives

After completing this session you should be able to:

10.1 Summarise some generic methodologies for performance measurement.
10.2 Explain and give examples of the basic process of vendor rating.
10.3 Explain and give examples of the category approach to supplier performance measurement.
10.4 Summarise the benefits of using weighted measurements.
10.5 Explain the advantages of third-party involvement and testing procedures.
10.6 Plan audit processes to avoid financial or performance fraud.

10

Unit content coverage

This study session covers the following topics from the official CIPS unit content document:

Statements of practice

- Categorise types of performance measures that are available to supply chain managers.
- Evaluate targets as a means of improving the performance of the purchasing function and individual buyers.

Learning objectives

2.4 Analyse and explain a range of measures which may be used to develop sustained improvement of supplier performance.

- Carter's model of supplier appraisal, the balanced scorecard (Kaplan and Norton 1996), plan–do–check–act (PDCA) cycle (Shewhart 1939, Deming 1986)
- Vendor rating calculations

2.9 Describe ways of measuring supplier achievement of service levels.
- Cost of initial purchasing measure
- Ongoing levels of performance in carrying out the service: quality, after-sales service, price, consistency of performance

Prior knowledge

You should have a general understanding of the concept of vendor rating and supplier measurement. There is some basic maths in this session.

You should have read study sessions 7, 8 and 9.

Resources

No specific resources are required, but it will be useful to be, or to have been involved in, the design of a suppler measurement system. If you have not, you may find it useful to discuss this topic with other students or colleagues, or a manager.

You may find a calculator useful, and access to the internet will allow you to check on testing houses and vendor rating in general.

Timing

You should set aside about 5.5 hours to read and complete this session, including learning activities, self-assessment questions, the suggested further reading (if any) and the revision question.

10.1 Generic methodologies for post-award performance measurement

Measurement will identify weaknesses on the part of the supplier. It will allow the supplier the opportunity to improve their performance (assuming of course that the cause of the weakness lies with the supplier). It will also allow the buying organisation to seek concessions and/or compensation for poor performance.

Feedback obtained during the measurement process may also be used to develop staff and organisational measurement skills, helping to ensure continuous improvement in overall supplier performance.

Learning activity 10.1

Draft a checklist of ways you could choose to assess one of your key suppliers.

Feedback on page 172

In table 10.1 we can see that there are several different methods we can use to measure suppliers. Variations in *italic* are discussed later in this study session. Some of the terms in the table merit a fuller explanation:

- **Cost ratio rating** is a measurement system for supplier performance, which applies a cost to a performance failure: for example, 'a late delivery costs us £125 per occasion'. These costs are then totalled for each supplier.
- **Categorical rating** is a measurement system for supplier performance that identifies a series of measurement categories and then rates suppliers against them using subjective criteria.
- **Standard** is a commonly used term that usually means an agreed company, national or international standard such as ISO 9000.

Table 10.1 Generic methods of measuring supplier performance

Type	Description	Variations
Statistics-based	Relies heavily on the availability of statistics, and is therefore orientated to measurable or transactional activities. There can be different levels of complexity in terms of content and statistical analysis.	• *Simple rating – a few selected categories are measured.* • Complex rating – a wide range of categories are measured. • *Weighted rating – a weighting is applied to the selected categories.* • Cost ratio rating – attempts to convert the performance failures into an actual cash cost to the organisation.
Perception-based	Is concerned with perceptions and opinions. Can be an easy way to undertake a simple review of a supplier's performance. In a more complex form it is used when a more 'rounded' view of the supplier is required. Opinions are often converted to figures for positioning purposes.	• *Simple rating – opinion is sought on a few selected categories.* • Categorical rating – a more complex approach with a wide range of categories and functions involved. • *The 10 Cs – a set of statements that can be used to assess suppliers.*
Research-based	Checking out a supplier's performance through research.	• Financial analysis • References

(continued on next page)

10

Table 10.1 *(continued)*

Type	Description	Variations
		• Historical performance • Reputation
Standards and accreditations	Using supplier's accreditations as a basis for performance. ISO standards are recognised worldwide, but there may be company or national schemes that could be used.	• ISO 9000 (series) • ISO 14000 • Supplier's total quality management systems • Others by discussion
Self-assessment	Using supplier's existing or proposed self-assessment of performance to avoid introducing a new performance measurement system in the buyer's organisation.	Supplier's existing systems of measurement are utilised. A new system of self-measurement is agreed with the supplier for this job.

Self-assessment question 10.1

Consider a supplier you believe is performing badly. Write a short report indicating the nature of the problems experienced, and recommending a method or model best suited to correct the situation.

Feedback on page 172

10.2 Simple vendor rating

Vendor rating is the process of measuring the performance of a vendor (supplier): it usually implies the use of a process or system. It is a tool that will act as a control on performance. Problems will be highlighted, allowing corrective action to be taken by either or both parties as appropriate.

At a simplistic level, supplier performance is typically measured by:

• Quality – could be the number of acceptable deliveries in relation to the total number of deliveries received. 'Acceptable' in this case is often defined as 'complete'.
• Delivery – could be the number of deliveries delivered on time in relation to the total number of deliveries received.
• After-sales service – could be the time taken in hours or days for queries to be resolved, measured against a target.
• Price – could be measured as the delivered price quoted by the supplier against the lowest delivered price for the same article by any one supplier.

However, other calculations can be used. This information would be received in purchasing, and simple calculations undertaken. Figure 10.1 shows an example in which:

• Quality is good: 15 out of 15 deliveries are acceptable.
• Delivery is less good: only 13 of the 15 deliveries were on time.
• Service: was poor, averaging 20 days to resolve a query instead of the target of 10.
• Price: is close to the lowest at £300 instead of £290.

Figure 10.1: Simple vendor rating

Factor	Score	Target	Score
Quality (by delivery)	15	15	1.00
Delivery timing (by delivery)	13	15	0.87
After-sales service (by days)	20	10	0.50
Price (by £s)	£300	£290	0.97
Total			3.33
	Target		4.00
	Actual		3.33
	Overall assessment		83%

The calculations

1. Express each factor as a proportion of 1. (For example, after-sales service is half of the desired performance, so it rates only 0.5)

2. Add up the scores (in this case 3.33).

3. Calculate the target (the maximum achievable – in this case 4).

4. Compare the actual with the target and express as a percentage – in this case 3.33 as a percentage of 4.

Note that in this type of rating system we do not normally 'add' anything for better performance. For example, if the after-sales service provided was 8 days against our target of 10, the answer would still be 1.

From this we can say that that this supplier's performance over the measured period of time was 83% of that required. Clearly, this information, supported by the raw data, can form the basis for serious discussion with the supplier on service improvements.

Learning activity 10.2

Examine this given data from a simple vendor rating system.

- Quality – 70 out of 75 deliveries are correct.
- Delivery – 13 of the 75 deliveries were late.
- Service – 4 days actual against 5 days target.
- Price – actual £250; best £250.

Create a matrix similar to figure 10.1 and calculate the supplier's overall rating.

Feedback on page 172

There is no separate self-assessment question for this section. These topics are covered in self-assessment question 10.2 below.

10.3 Perception-based rating

A more comprehensive approach will need to be taken to vendor rating when a supplier is more critical to the ongoing success of the organisation, or when more complex factors and factors that require subjective opinions need to be assessed.

An alternative to basic vendor rating is the category model, in which (often through a team exercise) the buyer can assess the supplier in some depth. Very often this will be centred around a checklist, which might look similar to that shown in table 10.3.

Table 10.3 Category rating form

Supplier:		Date:	
Performance category – typical examples		**Rating**	
	Good	**Acceptable**	**Poor**
Delivery performance (correct quantities)			
Delivery performance (on time)			
Price (performance over time)			
Quality and compliance to specification			
Invoicing and financial performance			
Service from representative and after-sales team			
Good accurate documentation			
Problem solving when difficulties occur			
Emergency backup if needed			

Plus other categories as appropriate to the supplier goods or service being evaluated

In this example a *good – acceptable – poor* rating has been used. Another common method is to allocate a numerical position: for example, '1 equals poor – 5 equals excellent'. This then allows some basic calculations to be made, which makes it easier to compare suppliers. Note that a standard form will be less useful than one devised for each evaluation.

Learning activity 10.3

Examine all supplier assessment you are aware of in your organisation, and look for an example of a simple form used in the measurement process.

List the categories of rating that the form covers. Is this a good list, in your view, and what if anything would you add, based on your reading so far? How does this compare with the example in table 10.3?

(continued on next page)

Learning activity 10.3 *(continued)*

You may wish to discuss this with your line manager or supervisor.

Feedback on page 172

A more sophisticated approach uses the '10 Cs' shown in table 10.4 (this is based on Carter's 1995 7 Cs model). This approach is equally useful in pre- and post-award assessment situations. A checklist is used to identify all the key categories in which the supplier is expected to perform. This is very useful when beginning the measurement planning, but the buyer must then determine in detail what mix of measurement tools and techniques will be used in each category.

Table 10.4 The 10 Cs of supplier performance measurement

Category	Description
Competency	The ability of the relevant key personnel within the supplier's organisation: for example, management, technical, administrative and professional staff.
Capacity	The ability of the supplier, in terms of physical, intellectual and financial resources, to meet the buyer's total requirements. For example, has the supplier the production and financial capacity to meet the requirement?
Commitment	Evidence available to the organisation in the form of statistical data on such items as process control, failures, or quality. Quality control records are a good example of this.
Control	Evidence available to the organisation of the existence of effective management controls and information systems. Quality management systems such as ISO 9000 are a good example.
Cash	The supplier's cash resources and financial stability over the previous five years or so. More details of this aspect are given later in this unit.
Cost	A measure of the total cost of acquisition rather than just the price.
Consistency	The ability of the supplier to demonstrate a high standard of delivery reliability and quality, preferably with evidence of improvement over time.
Culture	Compatible with similar values.
Clean	Environmentally sound, conforming with legislative requirements.
Communications	The supplier is fully integrated with information and communication technology.

The balanced scorecard

The concept of the balanced scorecard, used to measure performance in organisations, was introduced by Kaplan and Norton (1996). It provides managers with a holistic and balanced view of an organisation's performance, rather than simply focusing on financial measures of performance. The concept recognises that decisions should be made using qualitative as well as quantitative data.

The balanced scorecard considers an organisation's performance from four perspectives:

1 Financial perspective, which takes into account measures such as profitability, cost and dividends.
2 Customer perspective, which considers measures such as customer retention and customer satisfaction on the quality of the product or service delivered by the organisation.

10

3   Internal business perspective, which looks at issues such as inventory management, costs, the production cycle and technological capabilities.
4   Learning and growth perspective, which relates to organisational development and how the organisation has changed over a period of time. Employee retention and feedback on employee satisfaction are important measures of this.

For example, an organisation might have decided to reduce operating costs to increase overall profitability. From a financial perspective and an internal business perspective, this would indicate improved performance. However, from a customer perspective, this decision might have led to a lower quality product or service, which would indicate a reduced level of performance. Similarly, employee motivation might have been affected, leading to a higher level of staff turnover and reduced employee satisfaction.

The conclusion is that an organisation can only be developing if performance in all four perspectives is improving.

Plan–do–check–act (PDCA) cycle

Another technique that can be used to achieve continuous improvement in supplier performance is the plan–do–check–act (PDCA) cycle. This technique was introduced by W Edwards Deming, who is regarded as the 'father' of the total quality management (TQM) movement. The PDCA cycle is a sequence of activities, undertaken on a cyclical basis, to achieve improvement. It is a systematic approach to problem solving, particularly in relation to quality, and relies heavily on the use of data.

The cycle starts at the planning stage, which involves an examination of the methods currently being used, or the problem. Data about this are collected and analysed and a plan of action to improve performance is formulated. At the planning stage, objectives will be set and these will be used later to establish whether the plan has been successful. The next step is the implementation or 'do' stage, where the plan is put into operation. Next is the 'check' stage, where the implemented plan is evaluated to find out if improvement has been achieved and objectives met. If there has been no improvement, any lessons learned are noted and the cycle starts again. If the desired improvement has been achieved, there is the 'act' stage, where the change is consolidated into the organisation's operations.

An example of how this PDCA cycle might be used could be a supplier who is delivering a high percentage of faulty components. At the planning stage data about the problem would be collected and analysed. From this objectives would be set and could include the achievement of a 100% quality level. The supplier would be expected to formulate a plan on how to achieve this objective. The check stage would involve monitoring deliveries over a given time period to see if the desired improvements had been achieved. If there were no improvements, new objectives and plans would have to be formulated. However, if the improvements had been achieved, the changes would now be consolidated into the supplier's operations.

Self-assessment question 10.2

Study this mini case study.

(continued on next page)

Self-assessment question 10.2 *(continued)*

Benjamin's Blocks

Benjamin's Blocks plc are involved in producing block paving for local councils, and feel they need to introduce a more sophisticated supplier performance measurement system for one of their key suppliers. They hope this will create a better relationship with the supplier. They already have lots of performance 'numbers' and a basic numerical vendor rating system, but feel that this does not give a true 'feel' for the relationship.

The lead buyer at Benjamin's has been shown the 10 Cs by a CIPS-qualified member of staff, and feels they provide all that is needed to begin the process. At the first planning meeting he meets objections from his deputy, who believes they should look for a simpler approach. This should continue to utilise the basic rating system, but bring in references to the more subjective issues needed for a wider perspective.

Identify four points that you feel can be drawn from this scenario.

Feedback on page 172

10.4 The benefits of using weighted measurements

The rating systems that we have discussed so far can be either simple or complex, but they have the characteristic of treating each category or rating factor as equal. However, in practice this is not usually the case, and we therefore need to weight factors in relation to their perceived importance to the organisation.

Weighting simply means giving a higher priority (or weight) to one characteristic over another, but its effect on a rating system can be quite significant.

Figure 10.2 shows the same vendor rating calculation we used earlier. However, in this example we have made a judgement to emphasise quality and delivery and de-emphasise after-sales service. The weighting column shows how this is done. Note that, when using weighting, the total of the weight is always 1 or 100%

Figure 10.2: Weighted vendor rating

Factor	Score	Target	Score	Weighting	Weighted score
Quality (by delivery)	15	15	1.00	30%	0.300
Delivery timing (by delivery)	13	15	0.87	35%	0.303
After-sales service (by days)	20	10	0.50	10%	0.050
Price (by £s)	£300	£290	0.97	25%	0.242
Total				100%(1)	0.895
	Target				1.000
	Actual				0.895
	Overall assessment				90%

The calculations

1. Work out the score as before.

2. Apply the weighting (for example, delivery timing = 0.87 × 35% = 0.30).

3. Add up the weighted scores.

4. Compare the actual with the target score (1 or 100%).

So we can see that using the weighted score the same supplier providing the same service scores 90% as against 83% from simple rating – an increase of 7 points. In real terms this may mean a substantial change in our view of the supplier, and weighted systems, though more complex, are generally more useful.

There are, however, several factors that can distort this type of calculation. The most common ones are:

- Data is either inaccurate or taken from an inappropriate source.
- Weighting is inappropriate and data is therefore 'biased' towards an inappropriate performance measure.
- Qualitative data based on opinion can be either biased or inaccurate compared to quantitative data.
- Over time new systems and personnel can provide different data resulting in an apparent change of performance. Also over time systems often degrade unless regular management audits are carried out on their effectiveness.

Learning activity 10.4

Take the vendor rating matrix you prepared in learning activity 10.2 above. Weight it as follows:

- Quality: 30%
- Delivery: 35%
- Service: 10%
- Price: 25%

Create a matrix similar to figure 10.2 and calculate the supplier's overall rating.

Feedback on page 173

Now go on to tackle the following self-assessment question.

Self-assessment question 10.3

These questions also cover section 10.2.

Give True or False responses to the following statements.

1 In basic vendor rating there are only four factors that can be used. TRUE/FALSE
2 In basic vendor rating the maximum a supplier can score on any given factor is 1 or 100%. TRUE/FALSE
3 Quality will always be the number of acceptable deliveries in relation to the total number of deliveries received. TRUE/FALSE
4 The reason for weighting is that suppliers cannot be expected to perform equally well in all areas. TRUE/FALSE

(continued on next page)

Self-assessment question 10.3 *(continued)*
5   In weighted vendor rating the weighting applied must always add up to 1 (or 100%). TRUE/FALSE
6   The weighting factors applied should come from the user. TRUE/FALSE

Feedback on page 173

10.5 Third party involvement and testing procedures

In study session 9 we touched briefly on the potential role for **third parties** in the supplier measurement process. This involves the inclusion of another party in what is usually a two-party relationship: for example, in third party quality testing the work is undertaken by someone who is *not* the buyer or seller

But why would we wish to use a third party at all?

Learning activity 10.5

Investigate whether your organisation is using any third parties or testing bodies in any current supplier measurement activities. Why was this role given to the third party?

What are the advantages and disadvantages of third party input?

You may need to discuss this with your colleagues or line manager.

Feedback on page 173

Ultimately, the success of any measurement system depends on the skills of the people who operate and use it. Purchasing personnel should be familiar with the various applications discussed, but they may well lack experience in using them, especially if the systems are being introduced for the first time. Additional support and training may be needed, which may be available from either internal or external sources. Purchasing and supply management must decide this, based on their estimate of in-house capabilities and resources. This will include an assessment of:

- available finance
- available time
- staffing levels and staffing skills
- organisational policy and procedures
- quality of internal relationships
- size and technical content of the project or purchase.

Following this assessment, a decision can be made on the potential for involving third-party organisations. Typical areas of involvement include the following:

- The provision of skilled labour or a project manager for a period of time.

- Specialist consultants can provide advice and guidance on how to implement a supplier measurement project.
- The provision of related IT services.
- Market and supplier research.
- Specialist financial assessments.
- External testing houses can test specific components, assess a supplier's total capability, or assess for compliance with international standards such as ISO 9000. Some of these houses are members of the Association of British Certification Bodies (ABCB), and a well-known name internationally is the Norwegian firm DNV (Det Norske Veritas).
- On building projects a whole range of performance measurement can be carried out via architects and surveyors.
- For some service contracts, third-party suppliers will provide 'mystery shoppers', who will test service performance.

The principal disadvantages of using third parties include:

- Cost, especially over long periods.
- Regular changes of the contractor's personnel which often make continuity different.
- Loss of interest by the contractor. Consultants often offer high-level personnel at the beginning, but gradually change this over the life of the contract.
- The need to monitor the contractor's services.

Self-assessment question 10.4

Answer the following multiple-choice questions.

1 Which of the following is *not* a reason for using third parties?
   A availability of time
   B lack of skills
   C poor-quality internal relationships
   D the supplier requests it.
2 External testing houses can test:
   I products and components.
   II compliance with international standards.
   Which of the above statements is true?
   A I
   B I and II
   C II
   D Neither
3 Responsibility for involving third parties will lie with:
   A senior management.
   B purchasing and supply management.
   C quality management.
   D the internal customer.
4 A big disadvantage of third-party involvement is:
   A the time to award the contract.
   B cost over time.
   C lack of suitable contractors.

(continued on next page)

10

Self-assessment question 10.4 *(continued)*

    D difficulty in specifying what is needed.
5   Third-party contractors:
    I sometimes substitute lower grade personnel.
    II often fail to follow the required specifications.
    Which of the above statements is true?
    A I
    B I and II
    C II
    D Neither

Feedback on page 174

10.6 Audit and the planning of an audit trail

When considering the planning and implementation of a supplier measurement process, it is important that sufficient thought is given to the role of audit and the need for a good **audit trail** (documents or records that allow a process or action to be tracked back to its origin – a trail that an auditor can follow).

Learning activity 10.6

Draft a checklist to your head of audit that suggest issues or points of action that can give the audit team a useful role or roles in your supplier performance measurement activities.

You may wish to discuss this with your audit team manager.

Feedback on page 174

10

Although many occurrences of supplier measurement will be relatively simple and basic, a few will relate to large or complex projects that involve many people and last for significant periods of time. For these projects good audit practice is essential.

The terms can be defined as follows:

- Traditional financial audit, to ensure that all systems are compliant with good practice and organisational regulations.
- Process audit, to ensure that the systems and process are working properly and that the desired information is being provided.
- Value for money audit, to check whether the organisation is gaining more from the measurement than it is costing to undertake it.
- Audit trail: is there a sufficiently clear specification, supported by records, notes minutes etc, to allow audit to do their job?

Traditional audit

If the supplier measurement process involves the significant commitment of staff or financial resources it may be part of the normal organisational audit process, either of itself, or as part of the purchasing and supply audit. It may therefore take place through either internal or external auditors, and will typically focus on the following issues:

- Have all organisational policies and procedures been complied with?
- Are all expenditures being made in accordance with financial procedures?
- Are supplier visits being administered properly, for example fares and expenses?
- Is required documentation up to date?

This aspect of audit is often a necessary part of organisational life, but it is more a 'policing' function, and makes little positive contribution. However, some of the auditor's skills may be very useful in the other types of audit.

Process audit

On any measurement process that runs for a long time it is useful to check that the systems are working as intended. Typically this might be done once, as the system becomes live, and at regular intervals thereafter during its life. This type of audit would typically focus on compliance:

- Are all the required data flows working as intended?
- Are systems (IT and paper) working as intended?
- Are review meetings taking place as agreed?
- Are recommendations and actions being taken, once agreed?
- Is the supplier complying with its obligations (particularly in self-assessment)?
- Is the buying organisation complying with its obligations?

This type of audit should provide feedback, which can help correct mistakes that are being made, and ideas for improvement.

Value for money audit

Both of the above audits set out to check that the processes are working as intended, and that the organisation does not lose money through process or compliance failure. Value for money (VFM) audit sets out to establish whether the organisation is gaining value from the processes, and would typically focus on benefits:

- Can we show what we have saved relative to what we have spent?
- Are there cash savings?
- If there are no cash savings, have we gained in other areas, such as better quality of product or service?
- Can we put a value to intangible issues such as better relationships?

Audit trail

The audit trail is an important part of any management process of this kind. Much of it will be documentation, but the key principle should be transparency and openness.

- It should start with a well-documented 'project plan' that sets out what is to be achieved and how it is to be carried out. This is helpful, because it allows better planning, facilitates audit, and acts as a benchmark for assessing progress.

- It will include all necessary documents, files, records, data and minutes generated by activity as the process is running. This is particularly important, because the intention is to continuously improve, and this cannot be measured without data.
- It will include records of all significant decisions, such as the upgrading or downgrading of a supplier, and will be helpful should there be enquiries or protests.
- It will include regular reports to senior management as required.
- It will act as a valuable training 'library' for other projects, and for inducting new team members.

Self-assessment question 10.5

Provide the missing words in the following paragraph of text.

Simon has been reviewing the role of audit in one of his larger supplier performance measurement schemes. He is fairly satisfied that the _____ _____ is well documented, and that the various documents, records and notes provide a good _____ _____ for others to follow, but is concerned that other audit input has been more _____, focusing on procedures.

In discussions with the head of audit he has identified a need for a _____ _____ _____ audit to ensure that his company is really _____ from the measurement process. In addition, because the scheme has been running for a long period, he feels that a _____ audit would help to ensure _____ with the requirements of the scheme.

Feedback on page 174

Revision question

Now try the revision question for this session on page 334.

Summary

In this study session you have looked at generic methodologies for assessing suppliers and have undertaken some basic calculations as well as looking at how to incorporate more perception-based activities.

In addition we have looked at the roles for third parties and for audit, both of whom can make useful contributions.

In study session 11 we shall look at some issues relating to communications.

Suggested further reading

Students can find more detail on the 10 Cs in Lysons and Farrington (2006), chapter 11, page 389.

Useful websites to support references in this session are those of the Association of British Certification Bodies (ABCB) http://www.abcb.demon.co.uk and Det Norske Veritas (DNV) http://www.dnv.com/.

Feedback on learning activities and self-assessment questions

Feedback on learning activity 10.1

There is no one correct answer. Your checklist should include some of the variations covered in table 10.1, and you may also have been able to identify some of the main types of measurement.

Feedback on self-assessment question 10.1

There is no one correct answer, but your report will probably cover:

- Introduction
- The supplier, and the problem you believe exists
- Your recommended model
- Why this would be appropriate in your organisation.

Feedback on learning activity 10.2

Your matrix should look like table 10.2.

Table 10.2

Factor	Score	Target	Score
Quality (by delivery)	70	75	0.93
Delivery timing (by delivery)	62	75	0.83
After-sales service (by days)	4	5	0.80
Price (by £)	£250	£250	1.00
Total			3.56
		Target	4.00
		Actual	3.56
		Overall assessment	89%

Feedback on learning activity 10.3

You should have a sample form or checklist that you can compare with table 10.3. How many matches do you have?

You should have commented on your own form, and have a list of any suggested additional measures.

Feedback on self-assessment question 10.2

1 Benjamin's are right to hope that better relationships can come from introducing a more sophisticated measurement system, but only if this is done well and with the supplier's cooperation.

2   They are also right in their view that basic numerical rating systems show performance measurements well, but give no indications of thinking, strategy, attitude or commitment issues, which are important in long-term relationships.
3   The lead buyer is wrong: the 10 Cs are a comprehensive high-level checklist for aspects of a supplier's business approach and activity. They then need considerable time, effort and planning to work into specific actions.
4   The buyer and his deputy need to resolve this. The correct action depends on the pressures they are under. However, because the 10 Cs route would take time to implement, one solution would be to add a category-based assessment process to the current vendor rating, and use this with the aim of moving to a more comprehensive approach in the future.

Feedback on learning activity 10.4

Your matrix should look like table 10.5. Note that the supplier's performance is now lower as a result of his poor delivery, which you weighted at 35%.

Table 10.5

Factor	Score	Target	Score	Weighting	Weighted score
Quality (by delivery)	70	75	0.93	30%	0.280
Delivery timing (by delivery)	62	75	0.83	35%	0.289
After-sales service (by days)	4	5	1.00	10%	0.100
Price (by £)	£250	£250	1.00	25%	0.250
Total				100%	0.919
				Target	1.000
				Actual	0.919
				Overall assessment	92%

Feedback on self-assessment question 10.3

1   FALSE. You may use as many as you can handle; the principle remains the same.
2   TRUE. The maximum a supplier can score on any given factor is 1 or 100%, and the overall maximum is (1 × the number of factors).
3   FALSE. This is one basic measure, but there could be others.
4   FALSE. Weighting allows the buyer to bias the scoring in favour of those things that are important to his or her organisation.
5   TRUE. The weighting applied must always add up to 1.
6   FALSE. The weighting factors applied must accurately reflect the values of the organisation; usually some consensus will be needed.

Feedback on learning activity 10.5

There is no one right answer. Your response should match with some of the issues raised in this section.

Feedback on self-assessment question 10.4

1 D
2 B
3 B
4 B
5 A

Feedback on learning activity 10.6

There is no one correct answer. The quality of input from audit teams will vary according to how they see their brief, and according to the experience of the team. However, you should find some input opportunities under the following headings, which are developed in this section.

- Financial audit – good practice and organisational regulations.
- Process audit – of systems and processes.
- Value for money audit – checks the organisation is gaining from the measurement.
- Audit trail – ensuring there is one.

Feedback on self-assessment question 10.5

project plan – audit trail – traditional – value for money – benefiting – process – compliance

Communication

Introduction

Most organisations have a high awareness of the need to communicate, and have some sophisticated systems for doing so. Yet all too often people at all levels lack the real basic data they need to participate and do a job well. This applies just as much when measuring purchasing performance as it does to management in general.

'I've not got a first in philosophy without being able to muddy things pretty satisfactorily.'
John Banham, ex Director General CBI

Session learning objectives

After completing this session you should be able to:

11.1 Determine how different types of communication can support business relationships at all levels: strategic, tactical and operational.
11.2 Explain the link between communication, performance measurement and relationship-building.
11.3 Analyse the importance of good communication mechanisms within performance measurement systems.
11.4 Argue the importance of good communications in resolving disputes and managing conflict.
11.5 Describe some of the different types of communication mechanism available.

11

Unit content coverage

This study session covers the following topics from the official CIPS unit content document:

Statement of practice

- Evaluate the benefits of implementing a well-structured approach to measuring organisational, functional and individual performance.

Learning objective

2.5 Evaluate the importance of close and frequent buyer–supplier communication and its importance for supplier performance.
   - Demand–supply chain relationships
   - Inter-organisational partnering and long-term commitment
   - Benefits relating to working together: cost reduction, joint product and service development, joint performance measurement and appraisal

Prior knowledge

You should have a general understanding of the concept of communications in business and some of the methods used.

You should have read from study sessions 7 to 10.

Resources

No specific resources are required, but it will be useful to be, or to have been involved in, some aspects of communication with a supplier over performance measurement. If you have not, you may find it useful to discuss this topic with other students or colleagues, or a manager.

Timing

You should set aside about 4 hours to read and complete this session, including learning activities, self-assessment questions, the suggested further reading (if any) and the revision question.

11.1 Communication and business relationships at strategic, tactical and operational levels

In previous study sessions we have seen that introducing supplier performance measures will alter the nature of the relationships between the parties. When this is done well, the relationship will improve, and may eventually move from an adversarial to a partnership style of relationship.

Learning activity 11.1

Take a supplier with whom you are familiar. Use the template below to review who is involved in communication at present, and how you would ideally like to see this in the future.

Table 11.1

Function involved	Current involvement	Ideal involvement

Feedback on page 189

A large part of this change in relationship will be due to the improved communications that performance measurement should bring about.

Figure 11.1 shows some of the communications links and relationships that can be established.

Figure 11.1: Communication links and relationships

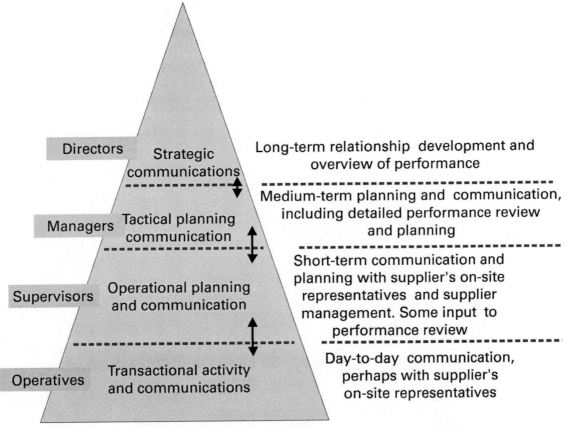

Source: Adapted from a diagram in Christopher (1985)

Director level

- Directors will not generally be meeting frequently, and when they do these may be quite formal sessions, usually with an agenda and notes or minutes. There will be an overview of performance to date, concentrating on the main issues that have emerged from the detailed reviews undertaken at other levels.
- Directors will concentrate on the health of the relationship, and the direction it will take in the future, but they are likely to be working on advice from the managerial level.
- A report may go into company newsletters or annual reports.
- This could be a level for **dispute resolution** (the solving of disputes through a process, or by having a policy, rather than just hoping things will sort themselves out).

Management level

- More frequent meetings, some of which may be informal, and some of which are likely to be formal performance review sessions. There is also likely to be one-to-one dialogue on issues. Managers will take a much more detailed look at performance management issues, because they will be making recommendations to their directors.
- Visits may take place.

- Outputs may go into company newsletters or general circulation and notice boards.
- Could be a level for dispute resolution.

Supervisor level

- There will be fewer formal meetings and much more informal contact, also via telephone and email etc. At this level investigative and corrective action is important, and much of the statistical data will be analysed at this level. Unless the supplier has an on-site presence there is likely to be less supplier contact.
- Outputs may go to management, general circulation and notice boards.
- Disputes are likely to be flagged at this level.

Operative level

- Day-to-day activity regarding performance management but especially important in identifying areas of poor performance. This is often the level responsible for generating many statistics. Little supplier contact
- Problems are flagged at this level.
- An area where perceptions can easily be generated, for example 'very unfriendly to deal with on the phone'.

The key point is that, when measuring suppliers' performance effectively, each part of the organisation has a part to play, and can contribute to the impression one organisation has of the other. It is important that, when planning a supplier performance measurement system, this aspect of communication and relationship-building is taken into account early in the planning stages. Ideally, a communications plan should be part of the system design: relationships and communications need to be managed, and this is not always easy to do.

Self-assessment question 11.1

Take the ideal situation you identified in learning activity 11.1 above and create a communication model diagram that graphically explains what you would like to see happening.

Feedback on page 189

11.2 Communication, performance measurement and relationship-building

Perhaps one of the most significant benefits that performance measurement provides is that it should allow each party to gain a better understanding of the constraints, deadlines and problems that affect the relationship. This higher level of understanding should provide significant opportunities for improvement within both organisations, and therefore opportunities to strengthen the relationship.

Learning activity 11.2

Involvement with suppliers can often lead to a better understanding of supply market conditions or a supplier's problems. Consider a supplier who, through discussion, visit or research, you have come to understand better.

Write a short report (300 words) explaining what you learned, the awareness this gave you, and how it helped in the job.

Feedback on page 190

Essentially, performance measurement should create a business relationship that has much more mutual dialogue and problem-solving than an ordinary business relationship. This in turn leads to altered levels of awareness, as table 11.3 shows.

Table 11.3 Altered awareness in performance management

Party	Awareness
The buyer	• Gains better awareness of the supplier's business. • Gains better understanding of the market and the supplier's supply chains. • Gains awareness of what effects his/her actions have on the ability of the supplier to manufacture or produce a product. • Gains awareness of problems within his/her organisation as seen by the supplier.
The supplier	• Begins to understand the customer's business problems • Begins to see how he/she can help the customer better • Begins to understand the buyer's downstream supply issues and his/her involvement in them. • Understands the buyer's use of the product, which may create opportunities to suggest ways in which it could be improved. • Begins to see problems in his/her organisation as seen by the buyer.
Both parties	• Begin to see opportunities for joint business improvement. • Begin to take a wider view of the supply chain. • Begin to recognise common problems elsewhere in each other's upstream and downstream supply chains. • Begin to see opportunities to cooperate outside the immediate business area.

If used correctly, performance measurement will provide an objectivity that would not otherwise be possible. Problems in both organisations will be highlighted, but in a positive way, where they are capable of being analysed and corrected. In many cases emotive issues such as the personal relationships between buyer and seller will become less important, to the benefit of both parties.

Interestingly, there can be a significant spin-off from a relationship of this kind as other parties see what is happening and feel it would be a better way to work:

• Other suppliers may wish to see a similar relationship established.

11

- Other internal customers see the benefits the new relationship is providing, and wish to participate.

This can often enhance the position of purchasing and supply within its own organisation.

Self-assessment question 11.2

Complete the following multiple-choice questions

1 Performance measurement should help a supplier gain awareness of all the following except:
A the customer's business
B the buyer's downstream supply issues
C problems in the buying organisation
D problems in his/her own organisation.

2 Performance measurement will always help to:
A create more dialogue
B design a better product
C improve quality
D reduce prices.

3 Performance measurement should be:
I subjective
II positive
Which of the above statements is true?
A I
B I and II
C Neither
D II

4 Other suppliers may become involved in performance measurement because:
I they observe the benefits.
II they are part of the joint supply chains.
Which of the above statements is true?
A I
B I and II
C Neither
D II

5 An unexpected benefit of performance measurement can be that:
A purchasing procedures can be simplified
B less board-level reporting is required
C purchasing position is enhanced
D risk management is simplified.

Feedback on page 190

11.3 The importance of good communication mechanisms within performance measurement systems

Performance measurement is an important tool in the contract management process, as we have seen earlier, but of course it is just one of several tools that may be used, and there are many activities within good contract

management that provide opportunities for communications and
relationship-building between the supplier and the buying organisation.

Learning activity 11.3

Consider a contract or buying agreement with which you are familiar.
Using the checklist in table 11.4, comment critically on each aspect of your
selected contract.

Table 11.4

Checklist	Comment
Description of contract	
Relationships need to be established early	
Relationships need to be actively managed	
Relationships are flexible and open	
Procedures are good	
Style (adversarial to partnership)	
Level of resource commitment needed	
Supplier's view of contract	

Feedback on page 190

Figure 11.3 summarises some of the most important activities of contract
management in graphic form, and table 11.6 provides further clarification
of the relationships involved. In the table, the term **risk management**
is used to denote a formalised process – increasingly common in many
organisations – of analysing all aspects of 'risk' to the success of the business,
and seeking solutions in advance.

11

Figure 11.3: Contract management activities

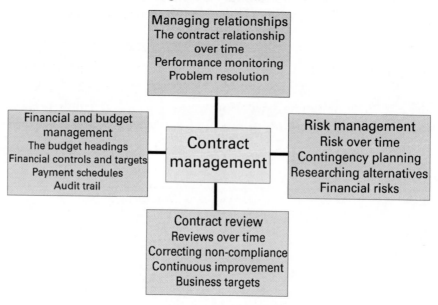

Table 11.6 Contract management relationships

Activity	Description	Key players
Contract review	The basic day-to-day process of making the contract work, changing amending and improving as appropriate	• Contract management • Users • Supplier's representatives
Financial and budget management	The basic process of ensuring that the financial aspects of the contract work, that payments take place as required, and that a financial audit trail is in place	• Accounts/finance • Audit • Contract management • Supplier's accounts
Risk management	A more sophisticated process, looking at 'what if?' in terms of the contract and possible failures	• Contract management • Finance (or risk management team) • Supplier (on occasion)
Managing relationships	A key role, making sure that all the complex relationships needed are working and, by definition, solving problems, networking and dealing with relationship difficulties	• Contract management • General management • Supplier's management

No matter how good the contract and the definition of the roles, effective performance measurement will depend upon the relationships between those involved. So what are some of the key requirements for good relationships?

- Relationships need to be established as early as possible, constantly reviewed, and actively managed.
- Relationships can be flexible and open, while maintaining proper businesslike and professional conduct.
- Good procedures help to establish a balance and encourage mutual trust between the parties.

11

- Adversarial relationships are less likely to be productive.
- Relationships will be based on the respective roles agreed between the parties, and care should be taken to avoid the generation of a performance measurement 'industry' whose costs exceed its benefits.
- Strategic contracts will place a greater emphasis on these relationships.
- The supplier must see the contract as important (see study session 7).

One difficulty on large contracts with many users is: who should be involved in the measurement process? Does one user act as a representative, or is a team of users put together? Communication plans and mechanisms must be considered, as for example must the extent to which local user/supplier communication is encouraged or permitted on measurement issues.

Self-assessment question 11.3

Consider the example of the agency staffing contract provided in the feedback from learning activity 11.3 above (reproduced here).

1   This contract arrangement is for the supply of agency staff. Our organisation needs to use these staff quite regularly and at short notice.
2   We let this contract by electronic tender, and there was little attempt to establish relationships at the beginning. This caused problems at first, as it was not clear who was really responsible for handling communications. It is now agreed that the contract manager leads on business issues and the lead customer on operational issues.
3   Relationships are still guarded, but improving. Procedures are good, and agreed by both parties.
4   We wish this to be adversarial at first, while the contract beds down, but our strategy is to move to a partnership style if the measurement system indicates good results. Resource commitment has been significant; it has reduced, but still takes too much time.
5   We have had some difficulty getting the supplier's view of the contract. We want to be a 'development' customer but at present we may be 'exploitable'.

Make at least five significant comments (good and bad) on what was said.

Feedback on page 191

11.4 Good communications and the resolution of disputes and management of conflict

As we have seen, good communications will help to build relationships, and performance measurement is a valuable communication tool. However, as we have also seen, measurement will on occasions raise issues that may be contentious or which may become the focus of disagreement between the parties. This is to be expected, and should not of itself be seen as a problem, because both the buyer and supplier organisations are trying to derive benefit from the measurement exercise.

Learning activity 11.4

Draft a procedure note for your purchasing manual on the correct process and procedure to be adopted in the event of dispute or conflict occurring

(continued on next page)

Learning activity 11.4 *(continued)*

in a performance measurement system for which you are responsible. Use a diagram if you feel it helps. (Maximum 1 page A4.)

Use the style of your own manuals or policy documents.

Feedback on page 191

A performance measurement system will raise issues that may cause disputes, but it should also create an environment in which these issues can be positively resolved. Disputes and conflict are different, and table 11.7 provides some simple definitions of the two terms.

Table 11.7 Definitions of disputes and conflict

Disputes	A dispute occurs when the parties fail to agree over something, but there is not necessarily any bad feeling. Very often this will be a technical or contractual issue.	For example, the performance measurement system calls for delivery information to be submitted monthly. The supplier has interpreted this as the calendar month, and has changed software to do this, but the buyer wanted it to be every four weeks. The supplier does not now want to change back, and a dispute exists. If this cannot be resolved at the operational level it will have to be escalated in some way until a decision can be reached.
Conflict	Conflict occurs when there is a clash between one person or organisation and the other. It is often due to different personalities or cultures. Disputes can become conflicts if they fail to be resolved. Conflict is often down to human relationships, and can be hard to resolve.	For example, the end customer and the supplier's production manager fail to get on, and are always arguing about quality issues, even though the data suggests there is not a problem. This must be resolved, but cannot really be escalated in the same way as a dispute can, because there is often an absence of 'willingness' to reach a result.

In order to manage disputes and conflict several points need to be considered:

- Disputes between businesses are rarely the result of deliberate actions but usually occur because of poor communications, changing circumstances, third party actions or unforeseen circumstances. This should be remembered when trying to solve them.
- Minor items should be dealt with directly at the lowest possible level, but more fundamental issues need to involve the contract manager or performance manager.
- It is more beneficial to solve problems jointly rather than have one party impose a solution on the other, and the continuous dialogue should help to identify problems early.
- A performance measurement system agreement may specify the system of arbitration or arbiter to be used in case of unresolved disputes.

- The purchasing manager has a responsibility to both parties and sometimes has to take the supplier's side as well as his or her own.
- When using overseas suppliers watch for disputes arising through differences in language, understanding or common practice.
- Where conflict is personality-based then changing the personalities may be the only solution.
- Conflicts can be resolved through the courts, but it is usually expensive and often the contract has already failed by this stage.

Although a good performance measurement system should allow the resolution of most problems, it is important at the planning stage to ensure that mechanisms exist to resolve disputes if they cannot be resolved in the normal course of business. Table 11.8 shows some alternatives for dispute and conflict resolution. In the table, both mediation and arbitration denote stages in a disputes procedure. **Mediation** is less formal, and simply involves a third party to try to help; **arbitration** is more formal, and the results are usually binding.

Table 11.8 Resolving disputes and conflicts

Method	Description
Normal course of business	• By far the best and easiest way. • Disputes and conflicts are settled by the parties in the course of performance measurement activities.
Internal escalation	• An escalation process is written into the performance measurement process. • May be to senior manager or director level. • May draw attention to failure at operational level.
Mediation	• The parties enlist the aid of a mediator (internal or external), who will listen to and question each side in an attempt to lead them to settlement. • Not usually binding.
Arbitration	• The parties present their cases to one or more arbitrators, who decide how the case should be settled. • Usually binding, and enforceable through the courts. • Has a cost and a visibility, and suggests a failure in the organisations.
Renegotiation	• The parties agree to renegotiate the contract, or at least the performance management aspects.
Litigation	• If unable to resolve the matter through the means listed above, the matter can be decided in the courts.

11.5 Types of communication mechanism

There are many types of communication mechanism that can be applied to performance measurement at both the pre- and post-award stages, and in this section we shall take a brief overview of some of these.

However, it will also be useful to consider what is meant by communication, because many organisations are almost obsessive about it (or about the lack of it!).

Learning activity 11.5

Consider the following situation.

Your vendor rating systems have thrown up quality blemishes in the skins of uPVC doors you are buying. This has been traced to airborne dust and debris at the moulding stage, and can be eliminated if the operators make a slight change to the way they work.

Comment on each of the following as an effective way for the supplier to advise employees of the required changes.

- Company newsletter.
- Internal memo.
- Memo on noticeboard.
- Issue new procedure notice.
- Change IT-based procedural manual.
- Email to all operators.
- Staff meetings.
- Phone calls to operators.
- Management walkabout.
- Quality meetings.

Feedback on page 191

In general terms, communication is an implied willingness to pass on or exchange information or data from one group to another. For this to work effectively there are three important criteria, and these are shown in figure 11.4.

Figure 11.4: Criteria for communication to work

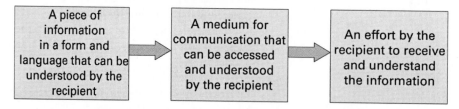

The third point (the right-hand box) is especially important: much communication is wasted because the intended recipients do not attempt to receive it.

Communication channels are formal or informal routes that are *regularly* used for communication, and which can be identified and used. Once communication channels have been established, they need to be kept open and used regularly. Occasional submission of data in a performance measurement system is unlikely to meet requirements, but is also going to be very easy to miss. In terms of performance measurement there are several types of information that may be shared, and different ways of doing it. Table 11.9 shows some of the main types of communication, and table 11.10 the most common methods of communicating, in relation to performance measurement.

Table 11.9 Types of communication

High-level plans	As a relationship moves towards partnership status there needs to be communication on longer-term matters and strategic issues.	• Strategic plans • Business plans • Procurement plans
Operational plans	Ensures that each of the parties is aware of how the others business is performing.	• Market prospects • Customer requirements • Procurement targets • New initiatives, eg e-business
Business performance statistics	The basic data that drives the performance measurement system. Especially important for ongoing vendor rating and other types of evaluation.	Examples would include: • delivery • quality • service price • responsiveness • initiatives
Change control proposals	As performance management develops, there will be a regular process of change, based on the review and feedback from the data.	Will potentially cover any aspect of the product or service that can be highlighted from the data acquired and from the improved relationships created.

11

Table 11.10 Methods of communication

Library and internet research	All manner of information can be accessed or supplied to help build up a profile of a supplier.	Particularly useful pre-award
Published documents	• Sales information • Company documents (eg environmental policies) • Annual reports Useful but obviously written with a positive spin by the supplier.	Particularly useful pre-award
Exhibitions, conferences and open days	Useful for research and for understanding of markets and supplier-based issues.	Particularly useful pre-award
Correspondence	Essential for major issues, and often helps to provide part of the audit trail on decision making, provided proper records are kept.	Useful at all times
Telephone and email	Essential for day-to-day operations. Essential that records are kept if major decisions are made via these mechanisms.	Useful at all times

(continued on next page)

Table 11.10 *(continued)*

Meetings	Useful for building relationships.	Useful at all times
	Good for reviewing progress and developing new ideas and recommendations.	
Notes and minutes	Essential for record keeping and audit trails.	Useful at all times
	May also function as action planning tools.	
Visits	Particularly useful for • assessing suppliers pre-award • evaluating new ideas or processes post-award • building relationships.	Useful at all times
Electronic data exchange	Essential where vendor rating systems require regular and detailed transfers of information between the parties.	Particularly useful post-award
Trade and professional publications	Useful for providing data and statistics that can be used to monitor markets and innovations (such as CIPS guide to market prices).	Particularly useful post-award
Newsletters	Company newsletters provide a high-level overview of what is happening inside the buyer's and the supplier's organisations.	Particularly useful post-award
Supplier awards	Award schemes are designed to give a high profile to suppliers who achieve targets for service or innovation.	Particularly useful post-award
	They help to build goodwill and cooperation between the parties.	

Having completed this, now try the following self-assessment question.

Self-assessment question 11.4

Give True or False responses to the following statements.

1   Proposals for change and improvement will be very important communications during pre-award assessment. TRUE/FALSE
2   Internal escalation is by far the best and easiest way of solving disputes. TRUE/FALSE
3   If used irregularly, communication channels may not be effective. TRUE/FALSE

(continued on next page)

Self-assessment question 11.4 *(continued)*

4   Serious performance measurement disputes are best resolved through the courts. TRUE/FALSE
5   Supplier award schemes are an important part of an audit trail. TRUE/FALSE
6   Communication planning is best undertaken early in the planning stage of performance measurement. TRUE/FALSE
7   An essential element of good communications is choosing the appropriate medium to use. TRUE/FALSE
8   In a good performance measurement system the system manager should be seen as fair by both parties. TRUE/FALSE

Feedback on page 192

Revision question

Now try the revision question for this session on page 334.

Summary

In this study session we have looked at various aspects of communication and its effect on performance measurement systems and relationships. We have also looked at some media that can be used, and have considered what might happen in the event that we are in dispute with our supplier.

We now move on in study session 12 to consider another particularly useful tool to use when measuring purchasing performance – financial appraisal.

Feedback on learning activities and self-assessment questions

Feedback on learning activity 11.1

There is no one right answer. An example might be as shown in table 11.2.

Table 11.2

Function involved	Current involvement	Ideal involvement
Procurement	Deals with sales and finance queries.	Coordinate contacts, and leads on communications strategy.
Customer	Deals direct with sales and production.	Deals with supplier via communication routes agreed with purchasing.
Quality	Deal with sales.	Deal with supplier's production and quality.
Senior management	Our MD knows their MD and plays golf occasionally.	Ideally only on a formal basis within the communications plan.
Receipts	Deal with delivery and despatch.	Deal with delivery and despatch.
Finance		Deal with finance queries.

Feedback on self-assessment question 11.1

Your model could look something like figure 11.2.

Figure 11.2: A communication model diagram

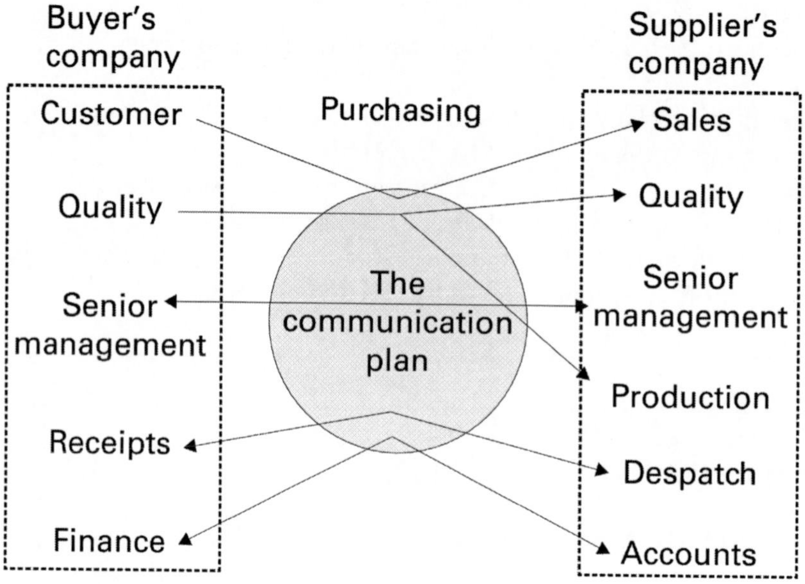

Feedback on learning activity 11.2

There is no specific feedback.

Feedback on self-assessment question 11.2

1 C
2 A
3 D
4 B
5 C

Feedback on learning activity 11.3

There is no one correct answer. An example would be as shown in table 11.5.

Table 11.5

Checklist	Comment
Description of contract	
This contract arrangement is for the supply of agency staff. Our organisation needs to use these staff quite regularly and at short notice.	
Relationships need to be established early	*We let this contract by electronic tender, and there was little attempt to establish relationships at the beginning. This caused problems at first.*
Relationships need to be actively managed	*This caused problems at first, as it was not clear who was really responsible for handling communications. It is now agreed that the contract manager leads on business issues and the lead customer on operational issues.*
Relationships are flexible and open	*Relationships are still guarded, but improving.*

(continued on next page)

Table 11.5 *(continued)*

Procedures are good	*Procedures are good, and agreed by both parties.*
Style (adversarial to partnership)	*We wish this to be adversarial at first, while the contract beds down, but our strategy is to move to a partnership style if the measurement system indicates good results.*
Level of resource commitment needed	*Has been significant; has reduced, but still takes too much time.*
Supplier's view of contract	*We have had some difficulty getting this view, as the supplier does not seem to think like this. We want to be a 'development' customer but at present we may be 'exploitable'.*

Feedback on self-assessment question 11.3

Your comments could include the following:

- Organisations required to use formal tendering can easily miss the communication opportunity to build up relationships by assessing suppliers thoroughly at the pre-award stage, and need to take positive action to correct this.
- Electronic tendering and communication can, in general, reduce administrative and printing costs, but does not help to build relationships.
- There was clearly little attempt to consider relationships and communications in the planning stages for this contract: hence the confusion with the lead user.
- There are clear indications in paragraphs 4 and 5 that planning and strategy discussions have taken place.
- 'Good procedures are in place' seems to conflict with other statements. Perhaps this refers to basic procedures for contract administration, payment etc. This might suggest an over-emphasis on this aspect at the planning stage.
- It is easy to underestimate the resources a project such as this can require, and contract managers must be very selective in applying measurement and monitoring systems where resources are insufficient.
- There is good awareness of the different views that suppliers may have.

Feedback on learning activity 11.4

There is no one correct answer. Your escalation path is likely to cover the following points:

- Resolve at operational level.
- Refer to relevant manager.
- Refer to senior management (or human resources if personality based).
- Refer to mediation or arbitration (internal or external).
- Refer to law.

Feedback on learning activity 11.5

- Company newsletter: not suitable for operational changes, but can be used post-event to highlight improvements

- Internal memo: limited effectiveness on its own; may not be read.
- Memo on noticeboard: may not be read, but useful if there is a known system of posting such details.
- Issue new procedure notice: good if necessary, and if procedures need updating. Effective if addressed to employees.
- Change IT-based procedural manual: necessary, but only as backup to another approach. Do operatives have regular IT access?
- Email to all operators: do operatives have regular IT access?
- Staff meetings: good, and a good place to confirm by memo or procedure note.
- Phone calls to operators: not likely to be effective.
- Management walkabout: helps to make a point, but needs follow-up action to sustain.
- Quality meetings: good if held, but staff meetings would do.

Feedback on self-assessment question 11.4

1. FALSE. they will be more important post-award.
2. FALSE. Disputes are best settled during the normal course of business.
3. TRUE. If not used regularly, communications may be missed.
4. FALSE. Recourse to law is a last resort, and is very expensive.
5. FALSE. Supplier award schemes are of little importance in an audit trail.
6. TRUE. Leaving communication planning until after an award is a poor way of working.
7. TRUE. The choice of media must be from those accessed by the recipient.
8. TRUE. Good performance measurement is not penalty based, so the manager should act for both sides.

11

Financial appraisal

'You know, we accountants are a much misunderstood lot.'
Sir Kenneth Cork

Introduction

In many organisations there has in the past been rivalry or conflict between finance and procurement, and in many structures the purchasing and supply function has been part of the corporate finance function. The 'bean counters' are not seen as having a creative input to make to the purchasing process in general.

In this session we shall look in some detail at the role for the finance department in measuring supplier performance, and how they can make a very positive input.

Session learning objectives

After completing this session you should be able to:

12.1 Describe the role and input for the finance department in performance management.
12.2 Explain the benefit of undertaking corporate financial appraisal on appropriate suppliers.
12.3 Demonstrate the advantages of specialist third-party versus internal appraisal.
12.4 List specific financial assessment measurement tools, and understand some specific application examples.
12.5 Explain how to carry out a cashflow analysis.

12

Unit content coverage

This study session covers the following topics from the official CIPS unit content document:

Statement of practice

• Employ accounting techniques and ratios to measure suppliers' efficiency.

Learning objective

2.6 Employ appropriate financial and accounting tools to assess organisational efficiency.
  • Cashflow analysis
  • Use of appropriate ratios – activity ratio, liquidity ratio, working capital – to assess organisational efficiency
  • Identification of supplier fraud

Prior knowledge

You should have a general understanding of the concept that finance and accounting staff can bring benefit to the measurement of supplier's performance.

You should have read from study sessions 7 to 11.

Resources

You will find a calculator useful.

It will be helpful to be, or to have been, involved in some aspects of financial appraisal of a supplier. If you have not, you may find it useful to discuss this topic with other students or colleagues, or with someone from your finance team.

Timing

You should set aside about 4.25 hours to read and complete this session, including learning activities, self-assessment questions, the suggested further reading (if any) and the revision question.

12.1 The role and input for the finance department

A comprehensive review of a supplier's financial data provides the purchasing manager with good information on where the supplier's organisation has been, and where it is going, in financial and business performance terms. In table 12.1 we can see various aspects of financial and business performance that are of concern in both pre- and post-award performance assessments.

Table 12.1 Role and inputs for finance department

Role	Description	Comment
Accounting measures, including ratio, income statement and balance sheet analysis	From balance sheets and income statements and other sources accountants can calculate: • return on capital employed • margin • asset turnover • liquidity, and many others. (We look at these measures later in this session.) A balance sheet analysis also provides a financial 'snapshot' of assets and liabilities.	Often they can be compared to those of other organisations in the same industry, providing useful performance benchmarks. Particularly useful pre and post award to check the financial strength and profitability of suppliers. Allow an on-going watch on the finances of key suppliers if checked regularly.

(continued on next page)

Table 12.1 (continued)

Role	Description	Comment
	These all provide a picture of the supplier's current financial condition.	
Audit and fraud prevention	We have already seen in study session 10 the contribution that can be made by audit including: • traditional financial procedures audit • process audit • value for money audit • audit trail.	A helpful range of services from the audit team which is typically a function of the finance department.
Cost control analysis	Has the supplier a history of attempting to reduce costs, and can they demonstrate this on a positive basis?	Particularly useful during pre award assessment to assess prices. It may be hard to obtain this type of data.
Credit rating checks	What is the supplier's credit history and, if poor, is this likely to affect the performance of the contract?	Useful at both pre and post award stages to help indicate the overall ability of the supplier to perform. Can provide an early view of future problems.
General financial support	An accountant can often provide useful support to all aspects of performance management especially when a team approach is involved. Typically they are good data analysts and provide a useful third party view on difficult decisions	Purchasing managers should use their financial support team skills whenever possible.
Review of annual report	Annual reports are produced by all publicly held companies at the end of the financial year. They hold data on many of the above aspects of financial performance	Especially useful at the pre award stage, and contain useful non financial information as well.
Third party financial report	Fee based services from third party suppliers such as Dun & Bradstreet. Their reports provide financial information about the supplier, including credit ratings, turnover, and so on.	A very useful and easily accessed service which finance staff can help interpret.

12

Learning activity 12.1

Consider supplier performance assessment and management in your own purchasing and supply organisation. Write a report (around 1.5 pages of A4) on the input (if any) from finance, accountancy or audit staff to this process

(continued on next page)

Learning activity 12.1 *(continued)*

at present, and how you feel this could be developed. You may wish to talk to a finance manager about this topic.

Feedback on page 208

Although a purchasing manager may be expected to understand these basic financial principles, he will usually call on colleagues for support as and when needed.

Annual reports and accounts should always be thoroughly reviewed. In addition to the core financial statements (profit and loss, cashflow and balance sheet), the explanatory notes should also be scrutinised. They may include a detailed breakdown of turnover by specific activity, changes in management staff, contingent liabilities, financial commitments and post balance sheet events. An analysis of turnover may identify or confirm a supplier's core business, and whether it is over-dependent on a particular customer.

Self-assessment question 12.1

Read this mini case study and provide answers, with comments, to the questions below.

Alan's appraisals

Alan is the procurement manager for a large local authority, reporting to the director of finance. He feels that, like many local authorities, they have paid insufficient attention to measuring the performance of their suppliers, and he would particularly like to improve their assessment of suppliers for a large service outsourcing contract on which he is about to start the planning.

He feels it would be especially useful to develop some financial and analytical skills, but is concerned that the staff in finance will not have the particular skill sets needed to appraise suppliers properly. He has, however, been impressed with the way the audit team have worked in the past, but feels this kind of traditional procedural audit has a very limited part to play in his plans.

In the past he has used D&B reports, and is familiar with annual reports that companies often present to the team, but he is unsure of the contribution they can make. He is a bit reluctant to raise this with the finance director (his boss) in case it exposes his ignorance.

1   Is Alan right that many local authorities are weak on supplier performance measurement?
2   Do service outsourcing contracts require more measurement than product-related contracts?
3   Why would he feel the finance staff may not have the skill sets needed?
4   Is he right to feel the audit role is limited?
5   Is he right to feel wary of revealing too much ignorance in front of his manager?

Feedback on page 208

12

12.2 The benefits of undertaking corporate financial appraisal

Today's business world is a complex place, both nationally and internationally. Although very few suppliers go into a contract knowingly promising things they cannot deliver, the purchasing and supply manager has a responsibility to his organisation to ensure:

- that before awarding a contract he is satisfied that the supplier has the financial resources and stability to perform acceptably for the period of the contract.
- that during the term of a contract he can check that the supplier's financial resources and stability are not affected by the supplier's own actions or other market situations.
- that in the event of the contract being heavily amended the supplier has the financial strength to cope.

Learning activity 12.2

Consider the suppliers with whom you deal regularly. Draw up a list of points that you need to consider when appraising a supplier's financial strength during the term of the contract. You may find it useful to discuss this activity with a member of the finance department.

Feedback on page 208

Corporate financial analysis (or appraisal) is an important tool for ensuring that the three criteria listed above are met, and although the purchasing manager should always retain overall responsibility, the finance department will often take a leading role in carrying out this appraisal.

Issues such as financial standing may have an impact up to the final award of contract, and ultimately even lead to cancellation. The credibility and stability of suppliers can change from month to month as their commitments vary, and, if possible, data and credit ratings from specialist online database providers (see table 12.1) should not be used as a substitute for detailed and ongoing examination of the audited accounts by the contracting team.

This examination should cover the prime bidder, subcontractors (if known), and, if applicable, the ultimate parent company/ies. (In a bid process the **prime bidder** leads the bid, and manages any other involved parties who are essentially subcontractors for the bid.) It should include an analysis of the latest available audited and interim accounts, and any other published information that may have a bearing on the company's financial position or ownership (eg credit facilities, debt rating, current takeover activity, restructuring, new capital investment). The analysis should draw attention to any significant items, including trading results and their trend, cash movements, and balance sheet strengths and weaknesses.

Undertaking such activity is time-consuming, and – as with all procurement tools – it should be applied only where the cost can be justified by the value or importance of the contract or purchase. Care should be taken if

12

doubts exist about a supplier's financial standing, particularly when a large-value, long-duration contract is being let. This can lead to interesting and rewarding discussions with the supplier, who will naturally try to put a positive spin on the published figures.

In the end the purchasing manager must be as confident of a supplier's financial ability to fulfil the contract as he is with other aspects of the supplier's performance.

Warning signals

Good, regular financial appraisal will help to indicate what may happen to a supplier in the future, and can often predict:

- falling profitability
- increasing debtor-days
- increasing debts and creditor-days
- increasing stocks, slower stock turnover
- deteriorating liquidity
- over-reliance on short-term debt
- high gearing
- late production of accounts
- qualified accounts
- changing auditor's and/or banker's name
- cash draining from the business
- major reductions in staffing.

Although poor performance in any of these areas may have a positive explanation, a buyer who has this information is well placed to ask probing questions at the next relevant meeting.

Self-assessment question 12.2

Give True or False responses to the following statements.

1 The responsibility for identifying a need for and carrying out financial appraisal usually lies with the finance team. TRUE/FALSE
2 Dun & Bradstreet type analysis can replace a more detailed and time-consuming appraisal. TRUE/FALSE
3 Because much information is public, it will not be difficult to get suppliers to reveal the real financial position. TRUE/FALSE
4 Financial measurements are good indicators of financial problems. TRUE/FALSE
5 Appraisal needs to go beyond the supplier, up as far as parent companies if possible. TRUE/FALSE

Feedback on page 209

12.3 Specialist third-party versus internally led financial appraisal

Although almost all organisations likely to undertake supplier performance measurement will have access to a finance department, there are often good reasons why it is appropriate to use external third-party support for a financial appraisal rather than to do it in-house.

Learning activity 12.3

Consider your organisation's procurement activity. Have you or your colleagues ever used external third parties to undertake financial appraisals or other performance-related activity?

If yes, please describe what it was, and your view of its overall effectiveness.

If no, why is this, and what scope would you see for doing so?

You may find it useful to discuss this activity with your manager or a member of the finance department.

Feedback on page 209

Most of the reasons for using third-party finance support in performance measurement are typical of the reasons why third-party contractors are used in any aspect of management. In a sense this is a typical 'make or buy' decision. Table 12.2 summarises the position. (In the table, the **Private Finance Initiative** refers to a politically driven process that tries to bring private sector skills and capital into the public sector. It is often said to be aimed at increasing efficiency, but critics of the scheme would argue over its long-term financial benefits.)

12

Table 12.2 Third-party versus internally based financial appraisal

Issue	Comment
Cost	Generally the use of third-party specialists is likely to prove expensive, particularly so in the case of banks or large accounting firms.
	Internal services will be cheaper, or not charged at all, depending on organisational policy.
	The costs of financial appraisal will have to be included in any value for money audit of the overall success of the performance measurement process.
Skills	In smaller companies, or some public sector functions, the internal teams may not have the necessary skills. In any organisation this will be true if financial appraisal has not been undertaken before, or is not undertaken on a regular basis
	On the other hand, if external contractors are used, the internal team will never acquire the skills, and this must be considered at the planning stage, especially if the skills will continue to be needed in the future.
	External firms sometimes change the staff provided from time to time, occasionally reducing the level of skills in the process!

(continued on next page)

Table 12.2 *(continued)*

Issue	Comment
Training	Following from the above, third-party support can be used to increase the competence of the internal resource. For example, initial appraisals could be undertaken by third parties supported by internal staff, who would gradually take over as the contract progressed.
Time	Such appraisal can be complex and time-consuming, especially on large contracts. Internal teams may need external support to be able to provide the desired level of support.
Political or procedural	There may be internal or governmental political or procedural constraints that lead to the choice of external third parties. Very often this would be for the provision of all financial services on a contract rather than just for the performance measurement aspects
Size	The size or complexity of the contract or purchase may mean that external third-party support is the only practical way of providing the resources.
Innovation and new methods	For example, the Private Finance Initiative (PFI) schemes in the public sector have introduced some unfamiliar concepts. Such arrangements tend to be intricate, particularly for large projects, and sometimes involve the formation of a separate company, a special-purpose vehicle, as the entity to deliver the required service.
	Usually the contracting authority will need specialist financial expertise to vet the PFI financing structure proposed by the bidders, and to undertake the necessary financial, sensitivity and risk analyses.
	It is advisable, at the start of the proposal process, to appoint financial advisers who have experience in the quantitative evaluation of complex contract pricing and funding structures.
Impartiality	Third parties may be used if the in-house operation is felt to be unable to be impartial in its evaluation. For example, if a major service is being outsourced or moved overseas the financial team might be biased in favour of the internal 'supplier'.
Conflict of interest	The reverse of the above happens when the contracting manager needs to ensure that there is no conflict of interest between the provider of advice to the buying organisation and the provider of advice or funding to the supplier.
	In this case an in-house operation may have the advantage of total independence.
Geography or location	Internal finance teams can appraise overseas or distant suppliers, but using a third party in the supplier's location will help to ensure local knowledge is applied and will minimise travel and logistical issues.

Clearly there is no right or wrong answer to the question of whether financial appraisal should be undertaken in-house or placed with a third party.

However, it can reasonably be assumed that third-party providers will be more expensive, and it should also be noted that not all third-party contractors will be capable of providing the required quality of advice. The

12

problem is knowing which contractor can, and this type of sourcing may require a performance management system of its own.

Self-assessment question 12.3

Answer the following multiple-choice questions:

1   Generally speaking a third-party contractor will be:
    A more competent
    B more expensive
    C more acceptable to the supplier
    D more focused on results.
2   A conflict of interest can happen because:
    A the in-house finance team favours the buyer's organisation
    B an external third party is working for another buyer in the same market
    C the in-house finance team favours the supplier
    D an external third party is working both for the buyer and for the supplier.
3   Innovative purchasing causes problems because:
    A an in-house team may not have the skills
    B a third-party team may not have the skills
    C the type of analysis needed is new
    D there are no procedures to cover it.
4   Are the following statements true or false?
    I Third-party contractors cannot train internal finance staff.
    II Internal finance staff cannot deal with overseas suppliers.
    A I and II
    B II
    C I
    D Neither

Feedback on page 209

12

12.4 Financial appraisal measurement tools

There are many useful financial tools, but ratio analysis is probably the single most important technique of financial analysis. However, a ratio is unlikely to provide any useful information about a company in isolation; it must be used as a means of comparison. This can be done by comparing the trend of a ratio for a particular company over time or with the corresponding figure for other companies, particularly those in the same sector.

Ratios can be considered in two groups when appraising a supplier's ability to perform:

- Performance ratios. These give an indication of how well the business is being run.

- Financial status ratios. These indicate the financial position of the company; of them, liquidity ratios measure the ability of the company to meet its short-term liabilities.

Note also that not all organisations use exactly the same methodology for financial calculations (though the principles are the same). Check with your finance team if you have any doubts.

Performance ratios

Figure 12.1 shows three of the most important measures. Each of the following example calculations uses the following figures: sales of £300m, an operating profit of £60m, and capital employed of £80m.

Figure 12.1: Performance ratios

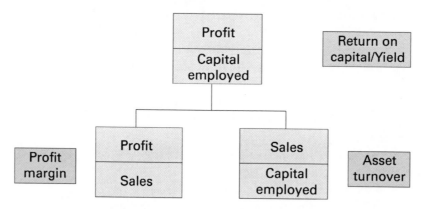

Return on capital employed

Return on capital employed (ROCE) is expressed as a percentage (figure 12.2). Capital employed is best defined as fixed assets plus stocks and trade debtors less trade creditors, ie the net operating assets in the business. This enables the ratio to measure the operating performance of the management.

Figure 12.2: Return on capital employed (ROCE)

Profit margin on sales

Profit margin on sales (margin) is expressed as a percentage (figure 12.3). This gives the profit that is earned as a proportion of sales. Thus, if the margin is 10%, 10 pence of each £1 of sales represents profit. The margin will vary from sector to sector. A manufacturing company might have a margin of 10%, whereas a food retailer's margin would be more like 5–8%. Service sector companies' margins may be higher.

The margin can be improved either by putting up selling prices or by reducing costs.

Figure 12.3: Profit margin on sales

Asset turnover

This ratio shows the level of sales that a company can generate from a given level of capital employed (figure 12.4). Capital-intensive industries (eg heavy engineering) will tend to have low figures for asset turnover. The asset turnover can be improved either by generating a higher level of sales from a given asset base or by disposing of assets that are not productive.

Figure 12.4: Asset turnover

Financial status ratios

Figure 12.5 shows two of the most important measures. Each of the following example calculations uses the following figures: current assets £8m, stock £4m and current liabilities at £4m.

Figure 12.5: Financial status ratios

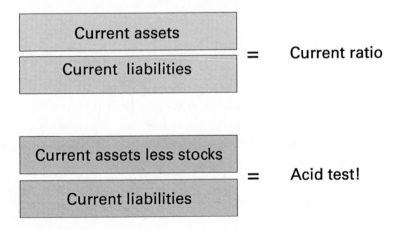

Current ratio

This ratio (figure 12.6) indicates the extent to which short-term assets are adequate to settle short-term liabilities. However, a current ratio of less than 1.0 does not necessarily mean that a company has liquidity problems, nor does a current ratio of more than 1.0 mean that a company does not. This is because liquidity is essentially concerned with future cashflows, whereas the current ratio considers the position at a given moment in time.

Figure 12.6: Current ratio

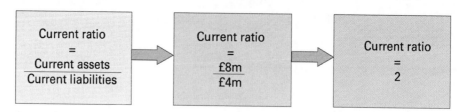

However, despite this limitation, the current ratio can still be a useful indicator, particularly when there is a sharp deterioration in the liquidity position.

It should be noted that whereas too low a current ratio may be worrying on the grounds of liquidity, too high a current ratio may be worrying on the grounds of profitability. Funds invested in working capital could be earning a return if invested elsewhere.

Acid test (or quick) ratio

The idea behind this ratio (figure 12.7) is similar to the current ratio. However, in this case the stock figure is excluded from the funds available to meet current liabilities, on the grounds that stock may take several months to turn into cash.

Figure 12.7: Acid test (or quick) ratio

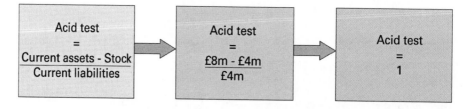

It is important to remember that these ratios represent the picture only at a moment in time. They need to be explored in more detail to find out what is behind them, and finance department staff should be able to help with this. It will also be helpful to record them over time, because a trend is often more informative than a snapshot.

Learning activity 12.4

Study the sample balance sheet and profit and loss statement in figure 12.8.

(continued on next page)

Learning activity 12.4 *(continued)*

Figure 12.8

Balance sheet of ABC Ltd	Year 2007 (£000's)	Year 2008 (£000's)
Fixed assets		
Buildings	1,200	1,400
Machinery	800	850
Vehicles	220	240
Total fixed assets	2,200	2,490
Current assets		
Stock	530	580
Debtors	410	460
Cash	120	160
Total current assets	1,060	1,200
Current liabilities		
Creditors	380	420
Bank overdraft	500	500
Total current liabilities	880	920
Net current assets (current assets – current liabilities)	180	280
Total assets (total fixed assets + net current assets)	2,380	2,770
Long-term loan	750	750
Net total assets (total assets – long term loan)	1,630	2,020
Financed by		
Issued share capital (1,000,000 £1 ordinary shares)	1,000	1,000
Profit and loss account	630	1,020
Total amount of finance	1,630	2,020
Profit and loss statement		
Sales turnover	8,230	9,150
Cost of sales	5,890	6,340
Gross profit (sales turnover – cost of sales)	2,340	2,810
Selling, distribution and administration expenses	1,450	1,640
Operating profit (before interest and taxation)	890	1,170
Interest payable	60	60
Taxation payable	250	330
Operating profit after interest and taxation	580	780
Dividend payable	190	200
Retained profit to profit and loss account	390	580

Calculate the following for each of the two years:

1   current ratio
2   acid test or quick ratio
3   gross profit percentage

(continued on next page)

Learning activity 12.4 *(continued)*

4 operating profit percentage (before interest and taxation)
5 return on capital employed
6 asset turnover ratio.

Feedback on page 209

Now go on to tackle the following self-assessment question.

Self-assessment question 12.4

Using the information from learning activity 12.4 above, answer the following questions.

1 What is the significance of the change in the two liquidity ratios: the current ratio and the acid test or quick ratio?
2 What is the significance of the change in the operating profit before interest and taxation and the return on capital employed percentages?
3 What is the significance of the change in the asset turnover ratio?

Feedback on page 210

12.5 Cashflow analysis

Learning activity 12.5

Go to the following website, www.bized.co.uk: http://www.bized.co.uk/.

Follow the links to Accounting, then Management Accounting, then the Cash Flow Learning Trail.

Find out the nature of a cashflow forecast and why companies prepare a cashflow forecast.

Feedback on page 210

Profit and loss accounts and balance sheets are prepared from information covering the previous financial year. Cashflow forecasts, however, are estimates about what is expected to happen over the coming financial year. They are an attempt to forecast when cash will be received from customers and other sources and when cash will have to be paid out to employees, suppliers and the government for taxes due. A cashflow forecast is an important planning tool because if a business runs out of cash, it is likely that it will cease trading.

If a cashflow forecast predicts that a business will not have enough cash to pay its bills, then the business must arrange to obtain the amount of money required from another source. The most common source is a bank overdraft, but companies could also raise the money from shareholders or through factoring their invoices.

The usual method of preparing a cashflow forecast is to start with the opening bank balance at the start of the month. Then, all expected cash received from customers is added to the opening balance and all expected payments to suppliers and employees are deducted. This will leave a closing balance and if this is positive, or within an agreed overdraft limit, no further action is needed. If the closing balance is negative, or an agreed overdraft balance has been exceeded, alternative finance will have to be arranged.

The significance of this in the supplier appraisal process is that when suppliers are bidding for a new contract, one of the first things they should do is to prepare a cashflow forecast. This will reveal whether they have the cash resources to fulfil the contract or whether they will have to find alternative sources of finance. The buyer in the customer organisation will want to be assured that this process has been carried out and may want to see evidence of it. If there is no evidence, this will count against the supplier in the appraisal process.

Self-assessment question 12.5

A small supplier has an opening balance at the beginning of February of £17,500. The supplier expects customers to pay invoices issued in January with a total value of £56,400.

The supplier knows that a tax bill of £15,700 is due to be paid to the government, £36,800 must be paid in wages to employees and £14,400 must be paid to suppliers.

1   What will be the supplier's closing balance at the end of February?
2   What would be the situation if half of the customers, by value, didn't pay their invoices as expected?

Feedback on page 210

12

Revision question

Now try the revision question for this session on page 334.

Summary

In this session we have looked at the important role that financial appraisal plays within the overall supplier measurement framework, and we have considered the advantages and disadvantages of outsourcing this activity. We have then worked on some practical examples to show how financial appraisal can help us see problems arising for our suppliers.

In study session 13 we shall look at some other aspects of supplier performance measurement.

Suggested further reading

Students seeking more information on external financial inputs can check out Dun and Bradstreet report analysis in Lysons and Farrington (2006), chapter 11, page 376 or visit their website at http://www.dnb.com.

A wide range of other useful information on financial services can be obtained by searching for 'financial services' through your web browser.

Feedback on learning activities and self-assessment questions

Feedback on learning activity 12.1

There is no specific feedback. Your report should have picked up some of the points covered in the main text, and you should ensure you comment on the appropriateness of the level of input you identified.

Feedback on self-assessment question 12.1

1   Yes, this is generally true: much local government procurement (and other public procurement) has tended to be short- to medium-term and tender-driven. However, this weakness is increasingly being recognised.
2   Not necessarily; it is the overall balance of risk and benefit to the organisation that matters most. However, most large outsourced service contracts will generally benefit from good pre- and post-award supplier measurement, which is not always true for product-based contracts.
3   Local authority finance staff have many skills, but are likely to have spent less time on this type of activity than many private sector colleagues (see also question 1).
4   No. Audit does not need to be limited to procedural matters, and Alan may gain from open discussion with the audit team on possible roles and inputs.
5   No. In general terms an open admission of weakness accompanied by a proactive proposal for remedying this will not seem a show of weakness, given a normal management relationship. Also, it is better to acknowledge this now, rather than once planning is under way.

Feedback on learning activity 12.2

There is no specific answer, but you may have some of the following:

- Poor financial standing may lead to cancellation.
- Financial standing can change from month to month.
- Dunn & Bradstreet type analysis is not a substitute for detailed checks.
- Appraisal should cover the prime bidder, subcontractors and parent company/ies.
- Appraisal should always include the latest available audited information.
- Appraisal activity is time-consuming.
- Care should be taken if doubts exist about a supplier's financial standing.
- Financial ability is as important as any other aspect of performance.
- Early warning signals can be spotted.
- Poor performance may have a positive explanation.
- Appraisal keeps a buyer well informed and in charge.

12

Feedback on self-assessment question 12.2

1   FALSE. The purchasing manager should always retain overall responsibility.
2   FALSE. This type of analysis is useful for a 'quick picture', but cannot replace a more detailed appraisal.
3   FALSE. Suppliers are likely to be reluctant to confirm poor financial performance: hence the need for the team to have an accountant with a real skill in interpreting financial data.
4   FALSE. They are pointers to possible problems, and there may always be good explanations for the figures.
5   TRUE. This should happen unless there is insufficient time or risk involved.

Feedback on learning activity 12.3

There is no specific answer. Whether your response is yes or no, some of the issues that may have been considered could include:

• the cost of external support
• lack of internal skills or training
• lack of time
• political requirements
• size, scale or complexity of the transaction
• the wish to gain impartiality
• the need to avoid conflict of interest.

Feedback on self-assessment question 12.3

1   B
2   D
3   C
4   D

Feedback on learning activity 12.4

Based on the information in this study session, your answers should look like figure 12.9.

Figure 12.9: Answer to learning activity 12.4

	Year 2007	Year 2008
1 Current ratio	1.20	1.30
2 Acid test or quick ratio	0.60	0.67
3 Gross profit percentage	28.43%	30.71%
4 Operating profit percentage (before interest and taxation)	10.81%	12.79%
5 Return on capital employed	37.40%	42.24%
6 Asset turnover	3.46	3.30

Feedback on self-assessment question 12.4

1   The current ratio has improved from 1.20 to 1.30, while the acid test ratio has improved from 0.60 to 0.67. This means that ABC will be in a better position to settle its current liabilities.
2   All three profitability percentages have improved. The operating profit percentage has increased from 10.81% to 12.79%, while the gross profit percentage has also increased from 28.43% to 30.71%. The return on capital employed has increased from 37.40% to 42.24%. This means that ABC is performing better and is using its capital more efficiently.
3   ABC's asset turnover has decreased from 3.46 to 3.30. One explanation for this could be that assets have increased by a greater proportion than sales turnover.

Feedback on learning activity 12.5

Your research should have revealed that a cashflow forecast is an estimate of how much cash will be available in a business at any given time. It is prepared by estimating how much cash will be received from customers and other sources and how much cash will be paid out to suppliers, employees and the government.

A cashflow forecast is important because it will reveal whether a company has enough cash to meet its obligations. If it reveals that there is insufficient cash to meet such obligations, then alternative sources of cash must be found, for example by arranging a bank overdraft.

Feedback on self-assessment question 12.5

1   The closing balance at the end of February will be £7,000 (£17,500 + £56,400 - £15,700 - £36,800 - £14,400).
2   If half of the customers by value did not settle their invoices, the amount of cash received by the company will be £28,200 less than anticipated. The closing balance would now be (£21,200), a negative figure.

12

Other performance measures

Introduction

So far we have concentrated on the main activities of supplier measurement, and the important role for financial appraisal. If you really want to do a better job then you will need to consider the wider picture. In this session we shall look at some other aspects of performance management, the benefits of joint performance measurement, and benchmarking.

If you do things well, do them better – be daring, be first, be different, be just!
Anita Roddick – Body Shop International

Session learning objectives

After completing this session you should be able to:

13.1 Describe the internal and external commercial relationships found in most organisations.
13.2 Propose other areas for measurement activity.
13.3 Describe the potential for joint performance measurement initiatives.
13.4 Explain supplier surveys and benchmarking.

Unit content coverage

This study session covers the following topics from the official CIPS unit content document:

Statement of practice

• Categorise types of performance measures that are available to supply chain managers.

Learning objective

2.8 Analyse qualitative supplier performance measures.
   • Research and development activity
   • Conformance to international industry standards and benchmarks
   • Cultural adaptation

Prior knowledge

You should have read study sessions 7 to 11.

Resources

It will be helpful to be, or to have been involved in, some aspects of benchmarking and other performance measurement activities.

13

Timing

You should set aside about 4.25 hours to read and complete this session, including learning activities, self-assessment questions, the suggested further reading (if any) and the revision question.

13.1 Internal and external commercial relationships

In study session 7 we looked at relationships, and at the development of partnerships between buying and supplying organisations. Before anything resembling a partnership can exist, good relationships must be developed both inside the buying organisation and between the buying organisation and the supplier.

Learning activity 13.1

In terms of your own purchasing department, can you identify any examples of relationships in which the supplier and the end user are closer than (from a procurement point of view) you might wish?

Write a short report (1 side of A4) explaining the problem, stating why it is affecting relationships and how this might be resolved.

Feedback on page 222

Often, at least at start-up, these good relationships do not exist. In fact it is surprising how often relationships, especially internal relationships, are a problem. Figure 13.1 shows how this might look in many organisations.

Figure 13.1: Typical commercial relationships

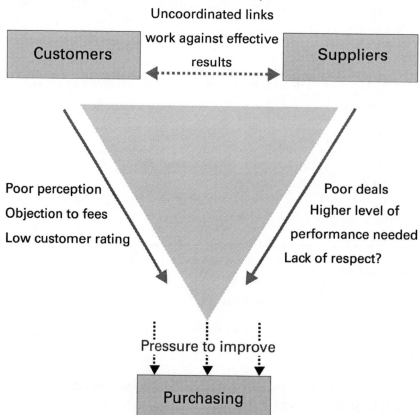

In this model the customers and the suppliers are in regular contact, which may include commercial issues, and there is little control exercised. Suppliers offer poor deals because purchasing has little effectiveness, and customers also have a low opinion of the service offered to them. The pressure is on purchasing and not on the supplier, and this is a problem in many organisations.

An example of this can be found in the NHS, where traditionally medical suppliers keep very close to medical staff, making it difficult for buyers to negotiate good deals.

Figure 13.2 shows how the relationships need to work if the buying organisation is to get the best from the relationship.

Figure 13.2: Relationships for effective buying

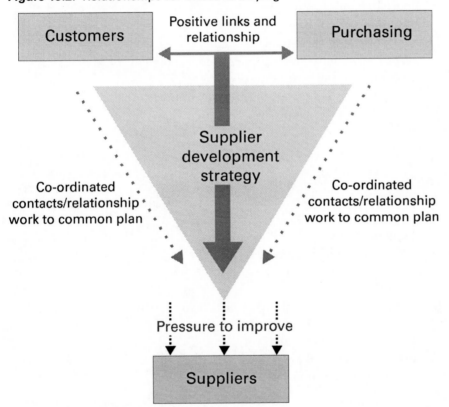

The customers and the purchasing team have managed to form a positive relationship, and develop a coordinated approach to dealing with the supplier. There is a development strategy for managing the relationship with the supplier, and the pressure is on the supplier to perform.

It will not always be easy to achieve this, but this type of relationship is essential if effective performance measurement is to work.

Note also that, although a relationship will often be focused on the purchasing team and the end user, other departments will be involved from time to time, and need to be integrated into the relationship management strategy:

- Senior management: contact through occasional meetings, trade associations, exhibitions and functions.
- Research and development: contact if joint development is taking place.

- Finance: contact through invoicing and payment plus financial appraisal.
- Health and safety: contact through any specific problems that may arise.
- Marketing: contact through any joint product or service development.
- Production: contact through any production problems or development sessions.

Self-assessment question 13.1

Answer the following multiple-choice questions:

1. In many organisations the closest relationships exist between:
   A purchasing and the supplier
   B purchasing and the end user
   C the supplier and the end user
   D the supplier and the payments section.
2. In regard to contact with a supplier, purchasing will try to:
   I keep contact to the minimum.
   II develop a coordinated approach to dealing with the supplier.
   Which of the above statements is true?
   A I and II
   B II
   C I
   D Neither
3. Generally speaking, the senior management role in relationship-building will be:
   A solving problems
   B promotion and development
   C mediation or arbitration
   D taking meetings.
4. Suppliers often like to deal direct with customers because:
   A purchasing has set the deal up that way
   B it saves time for sales staff
   C customers' technical knowledge is better
   D purchasing is not involved.

Feedback on page 222

13.2 Other areas of measurement activity

There are several aspects of a supplier's business that can be evaluated, especially if the contract to be awarded is large, complex or high risk for the buyer.

Learning activity 13.2

Draw up a checklist of the main aspects of a supplier's business that you feel you might need to measure at some stage in a comprehensive contract award and management process. Give a brief description of each header.

Feedback on page 223

Much of the focus in this section so far has been on the measurement of the basic services or products provided, and on the financial strength and stability of the supplier. However, the following are also important aspects of the supplier's business that are worth measuring on higher-risk projects.

The supplier's organisation and management

- General information: Who are they and what do you know about the company and its managers? The annual report can be helpful here, as can Dun & Bradstreet. How long has the management been in post? Supplier account management techniques (see study session 14) can be useful here.
- History: What do you know about the company and its trading record with you and other customers? Is it known for any bad practice or unethical activities, or do other customers or suppliers constantly rate it badly?
- Future plans: Where are they going as a business, and how does this fit in with your expectations and business plans?
- What level of investment has been made in plant and equipment and is it in good condition?
- The level of training and academic background of individuals. Are they signed up to schemes such as 'Investors in People' (see study session 15)?
- Many companies these days contract out services and sub-assemblies. Is the product or service you require supplied by a subcontractor, and if so do you need to know more about how this process works and might affect your contract?
- Where does the company stand on public issues such as environmental policies, support to the community, health and safety, and so on?
- The commitment of the supplier to research and development, as this will measure the extent to which the supplier will contribute to product or service improvement. Typical measures might be financial and include the percentage of total revenue or profits spent on research and development. Alternatively, they might be non-financial and include staff research achievements or links with academic institutions. An important aspect of this measure is to look at trends over a period of time to identify whether the commitment is increasing, reducing or remaining constant.
- The extent to which the supplier has adapted to the customer's culture. An organisation's culture is an amalgam of shared values, behaviour patterns, symbols, attitudes and ways of conducting business. It is important that the supplier adapts to the type of culture that exists in its customer's organisation if the relationship is to be effective and long lasting. If the supplier can't adapt, it is likely that problems in the relationship will develop and the relationship will be short.

The supplier's employees

- Skills and training provided: Many jobs now need higher-level skills and the supplier may well be able to show training plans and targets. Look also for evidence such as 'Investors in People' or the existence of a training needs analysis. (See study session 18.)
- Trade unions: Are employees represented by a union, or do they address their concerns directly to management? What is the public state of

management and employee relationships, and is there a history of strikes?

- Employee turnover: What is the turnover rate among management and employees? High turnovers may indicate skill shortages or bad industrial relationships.
- Is there evidence of good morale? Look for evidence of pride and support for the company and try to talk to some employees. What is the state of 'housekeeping' on the site?

The purchasing and supply team may be supported by management, human resources and production staff when measuring some of these activities.

It is also important to note that some aspects, such as employee welfare and ethics, can require a different emphasis if dealing with overseas or multinational suppliers, or if your own organisation requires certain standards to be met, eg achieving certain environmental standards, or avoiding 'sweatshop' labour.

Self-assessment question 13.2

Give True or False responses to the following statements.

1　The use of subcontractors by a supplier is not the concern of the buyer. TRUE/FALSE
2　High levels of management stability, and length of employment with the organisation, indicate a supplier who will do the job well. TRUE/FALSE
3　In the UK, strikes are now not so much of a problem as turnover and skills shortages. TRUE/FALSE
4　There can be a significant difference in the behaviour of multinational companies in different countries. TRUE/FALSE
5　A small team from purchasing and supply will be able to appraise all these factors as well as is necessary. TRUE/FALSE

Feedback on page 223

13.3 Joint performance measurement initiatives

We have seen from study session 7 that there is scope for joint benefit from performance measurement when the supplier considers that the buyer's organisation is important to its future plans. This can lead to the development of joint performance measurement.

Learning activity 13.3

Describe some 'win–win' opportunities for the buyer and the seller that can arise from the effective use of performance measurement indicators. Have you any examples of these occurring in practice?

(continued on next page)

13

216

Learning activity 13.3 *(continued)*
You may wish to discuss this with your line manager.

Feedback on page 223

Table 13.1 Benefits of joint performance measurement

Buyer and supplier

Improved solutions to operational difficulties:

- delivery schedules
- lead times
- invoicing and payments
- expediting
- basic customer service
- better operational communications

Buyer	Supplier
Elimination of 'waste' at the interface between the buyer and supplier	Market advantage, and reduced selling effort
Improved quality with positive supplier input	Improved technological capability and product development
Unnecessary cost can be 'designed' out of products	Can be more innovative in what it offers
Improved security of supply	Improved and secured payment arrangements
An increase in purchasing contribution to the profitability of the organisation on a continuous basis	Improved financial stability and security
Cycle time reduction in product development	Opportunities to improve and refocus management capability
Ability to concentrate on supplier management, not sourcing and award	Ability to plan resources over the longer period

Joint performance initiatives are expensive to both parties because of the commitment and resources that are necessary to make them work, and continuous improvement should be seen as the basis of the relationship. This is not possible without a review process for assessing performance.

Until recently, such processes have been restricted to the assessment of the supplier's performance but there is an increasing move to '360 degree' assessment in which the two parties assess each other. In this way obstructions that were caused by either party to the performance of the relationship can be identified and mutually resolved.

Generally, a shared measurement approach is a type of partnership, and is based on:

- shared mutual objectives and compatible benefits for both parties

13

- agreed problem-solving methods
- shared risks according to who can best manage them
- an active search for continuous measurable improvements
- a way of managing the relationship proactively.

Joint performance measurement impinges on design, manufacturing, logistics and other functions as well as on the commercial aspects traditionally of interest to the buyer. However, cross-functional teams are usually needed to inject specialist expertise into the process, and at the start of the relationship both the buyer and supplier organisations will form teams. As the relationship develops it is possible that the two teams may merge, creating 'cross-functional, cross-organisational' teams, as shown in figure 13.3.

Figure 13.3: Cross-functional, cross-organisational teams

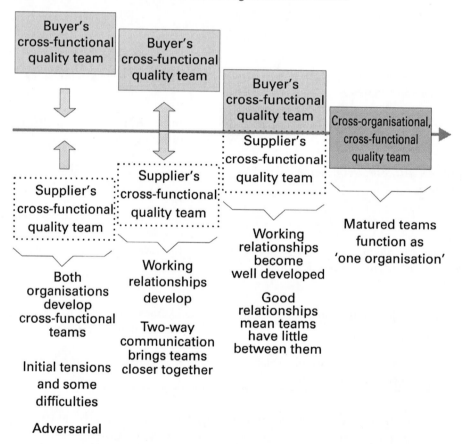

These teams have the task of analysing performance data, identifying the causes and effect of problems, and implementing solutions.

For example, the performance measurement data may show that the supplier is not meeting delivery targets. The cross-functional team examines the data, and finds that the late delivery is the effect of poor planning and scheduling by a buyer (the root cause of the problem). In traditional supplier measurement the 'blame' would lie inside the buyer's organisation. However, with cross-organisational cooperation one potential solution may be for the supplier to cross-transfer one of his production schedulers on either a temporary or permanent basis to help 'coach' the buying organisation until the problem is removed.

Self-assessment question 13.3

Read the following mini case study.

Flora's Flowers

Flora's nurseries supply flowers to a large florist chain, whose lead buyer has proposed the creation of a joint performance measurement action team, as part of a new five-year deal. The buyers already operate a vendor rating system, which has been running for some years, and internally Flora's have set up a cross-functional team that has effectively dealt with some of the problems weeded out by this system, working quite closely with the buyer.

Flora's sales director John and his team have come to recognise that being measured has sharpened up their business in several ways, and John feels they have gained from the process (he thinks that the buyers probably suspect this is his view). He also feels there will be significant benefits from the joint approach, especially in reduced sales effort, financial stability and long-term planning.

His new MD Shirley is less sure, however, and thinks the joint team will struggle to stay equal with the buyers, who will use this as an opportunity to simply pressure Flora's for better service and prices.

Based on what you have read in this session please provide at least four single-paragraph comments on the above scenario.

Feedback on page 223

13.4 Benchmarking and supplier surveys

Benchmarking

Although measurement of our supplier's performance is always useful, we have already said that the data then needs to be put in a context before we can start to make effective judgements. At the most basic level we test the result against the standard or target we require, and the result will indicate whether or not we have compliance. This is a good start, but it leaves two important questions unresolved:

- What is happening to the measured performance? Is it improving, or getting worse over time?
- How good is our standard? Are we aiming too high or too low?

The process by which we try to establish the answers to these questions is called 'benchmarking'.

Learning activity 13.4

Study your organisation in its entirety. Can you identify three areas of activity in which benchmarking regularly occurs? What are they, why are they chosen, and how effective is the process, in your view?

(continued on next page)

13

Learning activity 13.4 *(continued)*
For this activity, only one of the above should be procurement related.

You may wish to discuss this with your line manager.

Feedback on page 224

A benchmark is a measurement which can be used as a point of reference when comparing an aspect of business or personal performance. Typically the comparison is either with competitors or the 'best in class' (or relevant field of business) and the results highlight opportunities for improvement by showing where the purchaser is and where he or she could be in the future.

Virtually all aspects of an organisation's performance can be benchmarked, such as financial management, manpower statistics, operational performance, use of technology and so on. The technique is equally useful in the public and the private sector, though in the public sector it is sometimes used as a 'blunt' tool for such issues as council tax levels or hospital bed occupancy.

In this session we are concerned only with supplier performance management, and we would look to benchmark aspects of the supplier's performance, which might typically include:

- price and especially cost breakdown
- quality and quality control processes
- day to day performance and service delivery
- administration and overheads
- supply chain management
- employee performance standards.

As many of these are aspects of the supplier's business that we wish to assess as part of our performance management, it will be obvious that the ability to compare the results with the performance of other suppliers is essential if good decisions are to be made.

It is also important to note that the key issue with benchmarking is not obtaining the information, but understanding why the different performances are occurring.

For example, you have established that (on a like-for-like basis) a major competitor awards a contract at an average period of 12 weeks from notification of requirement to contract award. Your average is 16 weeks. However, this data is of little use. What you must find out is how this is achieved, and it is the investigation that will identify actions you may be able to take.

There are, however, some problems with benchmarking that you should be aware of, and table 13.2 provides a summary.

Table 13.2 Problems with benchmarking

Problem	Description
One snapshot compared with another	Unless the benchmarking is done well, comparisons are just snapshots and are less useful: your company may be doing badly and they may be doing well at the time of the exercise.

(continued on next page)

Table 13.2 (continued)

Problem	Description
Resource heavy	Benchmarking is time-consuming if done properly, and should not be started without adequate resources. This includes the obtaining and processing of the information.
Be careful when benchmarking prices	There are many factors, such as volume and marketing, that can distort price differences unrealistically.
'Apples for apples'	Comparisons are undertaken for products or services that are not to the same specification: eg our printer paper is 100gsm, theirs is 80gsm.
Choose the benchmark with care	'Best in class' may not be the best benchmark to aim for: • The differences may be too fundamental. • The pursuit may be too expensive. • The process may be too demoralising.
Getting the information	It may be necessary to benchmark to organisations with whom data can be shared, or about whom data is easily acquired.

Supplier surveys

We have talked above about joint performance measurement initiatives and the benefits they offer to both parties. One benefit that some companies offer to their suppliers is the opportunity to participate in occasional supplier surveys.

There is no particular form for these and the content will depend on what is to be achieved. Typically the issues covered relate to the ease of doing business with the company, how the buyers are seen to be performing, and whether payment processes are working effectively.

The buying organisation must however be prepared to accept criticism and suggestion for change. If it is not then the survey will have no effect, and future surveys will not be supported by the suppliers.

Surveys can be made anonymous, to avoid any suggestion of trying to please the customer, and they can also be undertaken through a third party if total impartiality is required. They can take many forms, ranging from telephone polls to formal visits and interviews, with questionnaires being a common approach.

Many organisations have been initially surprised by the negative feedback received from suppliers: some do not really care. However, it is worth bearing in mind that an organisation needs to be a world-class customer in order to obtain world-class suppliers.

13

Self-assessment question 13.4

Write a paragraph (3–5 lines) of critical comment on each of the following statements:

1   Benchmarking is not really relevant in my business.
2   Now the data tells us what can be achieved, we are halfway there.
3   We are pleased, because our supplier's performance has improved steadily from when we took the benchmark.

(continued on next page)

Self-assessment question 13.4 *(continued)*

4   You have to be very careful to compare the right things to get meaningful benchmark data, especially on complex issues.
5   The problem with supplier surveys is that they always say what they think we want to hear.

Feedback on page 224

Revision question

Now try the revision question for this session on page 335.

Summary

In this session we have looked in detail at the quality of relationships, some other important areas for measurement of supplier performance, the scope for joint performance measurement, and the details of benchmarking.

Each of these can be helpful in taking the quality of our purchasing performance measurement to another level, and in study session 14 we shall have a brief look at the more sophisticated concepts of supplier development and supplier account management.

Feedback on learning activities and self-assessment questions

Feedback on learning activity 13.1

There is no one right answer. Depending on the organisation, such problems develop because:

- Procurement doesn't have a good reputation.
- Customer and supplier share technical knowledge.
- Procurement are 'just following the rules'.
- Suppliers are trying to 'divide and conquer'.

Depending on the organisation, solutions include:

- improving buyers' skills
- improving technical knowledge among buyers
- promoting procurement as an added value process
- pushing the rules and procedures
- managing and understanding relationships better.

Feedback on self-assessment question 13.1

1   C
2   B
3   B
4   D

Feedback on learning activity 13.2

Your list might include:

- Ability to perform: suppliers who appear to be good candidates on paper may actually have old facilities in disrepair, outdated technology, or an overall inability to meet a purchaser's needs.
- Financial status: a comprehensive review of the supplier's financial data provides the purchasing manager with good information on where the organisation has been, and where it is going.
- Cost systems: measurement systems designed to track an organisation's costs.
- Quality assurance, quality control, and related systems: close examination is critical, because purchasing is responsible for ensuring the quality of supplies and services.
- Organisation and management: close examination of top management commitment and involvement, stability, training and certification.
- Workforce: close examination of labour relations, morale skills and unionisation.
- Housekeeping: housekeeping is an indicator of discipline and pride in the workplace.
- Process/material flow: efficient process and material flow are required to keep a supplier competitive.

Feedback on self-assessment question 13.2

- FALSE. The buyer needs to ensure that audits of subcontractors are made by the supplier to ensure that standards are met.
- FALSE. Management stability and length of employment are factors to be looked at in the supplier's management structure, but do not in themselves offer a guarantee of performance.
- TRUE. High turnover and skills shortages are major problems for some companies, and need careful appraisal by buyers.
- TRUE. Consistent standards are not always applied by multinational companies, and are often driven by in-country legislation as much as by ethical concerns.
- FALSE. Done properly, such appraisal will need support from across other functions.

Feedback on learning activity 13.3

Table 13.1 shows some of the most common benefits, but your list may well contain others.

Don't forget to provide examples if possible.

Feedback on self-assessment question 13.3

Your comments could include the following:

- The buyer's scheme appears to be working well, and the sales team can see progress and don't appear to feel threatened. This could be a good

13

basis for going ahead, provided there is no obvious change of attitude coming from the buyers.

- The setting up of the internal team has also worked well, and the fact that it already has positive links with the buyers argues for a joint set-up.
- The benefits that John can see are all possible advantages of a joint approach, which is in effect a partnership style of doing business.
- The MD's view is probably affected by being new in post. There is a natural suspicion inherent in buyer–seller relationships, which is often overcome only by involvement. Shirley needs to be prepared to discuss the issue with the team, and to look at the results to date.
- Where Shirley does have a point is in terms of the ownership of the joint team, and it would be reasonable to discuss the protocols around this team, such as how it works, where it meets, and who is in the chair before finally agreeing.

Feedback on learning activity 13.4

There is no specific feedback. Your non-procurement examples should be significant to the organisation. Your procurement example is likely to include one of the following:

- quality
- operational performance
- value
- costs
- service
- processes
- labour and training
- technological innovation.

Feedback on self-assessment question 13.4

Your comment could look like this:

1   I think you're wrong. Benchmarking is widely used in many industries and across most sectors of business and management activity. As it basically consists of comparing your performance with a known better performer, it is unlikely that it is not relevant to any business. Even a known good performer will wish to check they are not slipping backwards!

2   Getting your data right is an important first step, but it is really only a beginning. The main task is to critically analyse why the results are different and what actions can be taken. If there is a halfway point it might be after the action plan is developed but before implementation starts!

3   You are right to be pleased, because this is clearly a step in the right direction. However, the problem is that benchmarking should provide both start-point position and a target position so you know how far you have come *and* how far you have to go.

4   You are right. It is essential to ensure that like-for-like comparisons are made. Even on simple exercises such as price comparisons slight variations in specification can distort the results. On complex issues

such as buyer productivity many factors need to be carefully checked before results can be used.

5   This can happen if the buying organisation has not planned the survey properly. It is unlikely that this will happen where purchasing really own the project and genuinely wish to improve.

13

Supplier development and supplier account management

Introduction

In study sessions 7 to 13 we have discussed the benefits of supplier performance measurement, and have demonstrated that, properly managed, it can be a very powerful tool for purchasing and supply management. We have also seen how it can help facilitate partnerships, or at least move relationships towards more of a 'partnership' style. However, not all relationships suit this style, and not all organisations wish to have partnership-type relationships.

Session learning objectives

After completing this session you should be able to:

14.1 Develop and control suppliers in a more positive way.
14.2 Demonstrate the value of being able to identify key suppliers.
14.3 Define supplier development.
14.4 Define and understand supplier account management.

Unit content coverage

This study session covers the following topics from the official CIPS unit content document:

Statements of practice

- Categorise types of performance measures that are available to supply chain managers.
- Evaluate the benefits of implementing a well-structured approach to measuring organisational, functional and individual performance.

Learning objectives

2.5 Evaluate the importance of close and frequent buyer–supplier communication and its importance for supplier performance.
  - Demand–supply chain relationships
  - Inter-organisational partnering and long-term commitment
2.7 Analyse the use of performance measurement as a tool for supplier relationship development.
  - Measurement as a motivating factor for both parties
  - Mutual opportunities to create understanding to improve performance
  - Positive approach to relationship building and continuous improvement
  - Identification of weaknesses and problems

14

Prior knowledge

You should have read and have a good comprehension of the preceding study sessions and general management principles.

Resources

It will be helpful to be, or to have been involved in, some aspects of supplier development, and in more positive ways of managing suppliers. You may wish to talk to other colleagues on the issues in this study session.

Timing

You should set aside about 5.25 hours to read and complete this session, including learning activities, self-assessment questions, the suggested further reading (if any) and the revision question.

14.1 Developing and controlling suppliers in a more positive way

'To partner, or not to partner; that is the question.'

Learning activity 14.1

Complete a Pareto analysis of your suppliers by spend value and identify the top five. In each case consider the nature of your relationship with the supplier, and the main customer, using table 14.1.

Rate the supplier relationship from 1 = well managed to 10 = badly managed.

Rate the customer relationship from 1 = well managed to 10 = badly managed.

Table 14.1

Supplier	Value of business	Supplier relationship type	Customer relationship quality
1			
2			
3			
4			
5			
Total			

What is your judgement on the result?

Feedback on page 238

While it is generally the case that there will be benefits from measuring the performance of suppliers, it does not follow that a partnership or cooperative approach will necessarily be the desired relationship in all cases. There are a number of reasons for this:

- Either the buying or the selling organisation may prefer a more adversarial style as part of its organisational culture.
- Either the individual buyer or the seller may favour a different approach. This is not uncommon, and many buyers and sellers see themselves in a 'game', where they are on opposite sides.
- Relationship styles (as with many aspects of business management) go through phases when they are in or out of fashion.
- Organisational policies work against true long-term partnerships. For example, public sector tendering requirements are often seen like this as contracts are renewed to timescales, and good performance is no guarantee of repeat business. (This does not mean that a partnership *style* cannot be achieved.)
- Geographical and market issues may influence the way the relationship develops.
- The size of the organisations may work against a partnership approach. For example, a large company may need to source a critical part from a small or medium-sized enterprise (SME), or vice versa.
- The nature of the relationship may be a problem. There may be some 'rogue' buyers or sellers who just cannot work together, even in a supportive environment.

Each organisation will develop its own approach, which may be summed up as shown in figure 14.1.

Figure 14.1: Relationship styles

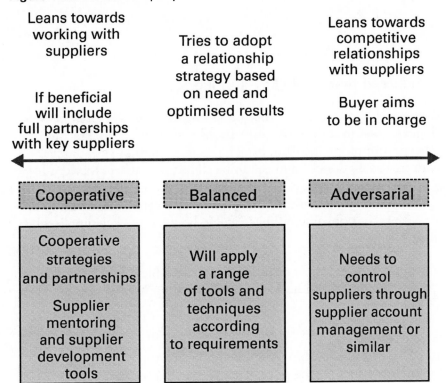

No matter what the chosen style of relationship, most buying organisations will wish to handle supplier relationships in a more positive way, and depending on the approach chosen there are other tools that can be used, including supplier mentoring, supplier development and supplier account management. These will be discussed later in this session. (The term **supplier relationships** refers to the range of relationships with suppliers, but with the implication of a more structured and organised approach.)

Whichever style or approach is chosen, good performance measurement needs to be part of the process, and the tools referred to are intended to complement not replace good performance measurement techniques.

Sometimes formal supplier measurement, appraisal or rating systems cannot be implemented. Buyers must recognise that it is still essential to have a method of monitoring progress and establishing targets and timescales. For each supplier there should be an agreed series of milestones, and progress against these milestones can then be reviewed on a regular basis and, if necessary, revised targets agreed. In this way, both parties have the reward of progress over time.

To provide an added incentive for the supplier, award schemes may be used or extra business may be offered. However, care must be taken to ensure that this is done in an open and transparent way.

Self-assessment question 14.1

Based on your analysis in learning activity 14.1 above, prepare a draft report (300–400 words) to explain why you wish to manage your top five suppliers more closely.

Feedback on page 239

14.2 The need to identify key suppliers

We have seen that cooperation is not necessarily the best approach in every situation, and that in some buying situations a more adversarial relationship might be more appropriate. Also, from a practical point of view purchasing resources are usually scarce and need to be allocated to where they can have the most benefit, and developing partnerships takes time. In this more balanced approach, how can the buyer decide what type of relationship to aim for with each supplier and, in particular, how can the key suppliers be identified?

In many organisations simple techniques will often identify the key, strategic or important suppliers, and no further sophistication may be needed. These may include:

- value of spend
- problems in a relationship (continued poor service)
- commodity issues (eg the price of a raw material such as copper)
- buyers' professional and business knowledge
- political or organisational sensitivity (eg potential environmental hazards)
- clear business exposure to risk from supply failure.

In other organisations buyers may wish to augment such knowledge with a more systematic approach, and in study session 9 we looked briefly at this concept using a 'four box' matrix (P. Kraljic). It will now be helpful to revisit this idea in more depth, because it provides a very useful model for breaking down the supplier base. Figure 14.2 shows the traditional model.

Figure 14.2: Traditional four-box matrix

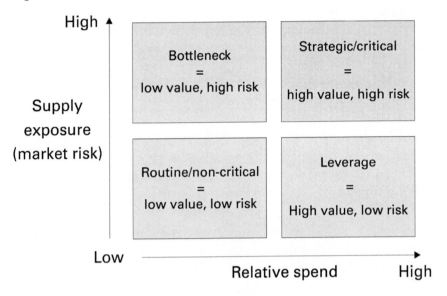

In purchasing, the term **product portfolio** denotes the range of goods or services purchased by the buyer; by implication it leans towards a commodity base rather than a customer base approach. The concept of the four-box matrix has been in circulation for around 30 years. You use it to classify your product portfolio within the four boxes, according to a balance of spend and risk:

- Critical/strategic items: high cost and therefore profit impact and supply risk to your business if supply fails. Any suppliers supplying these products must be highly competent, and purchasing resources can be concentrated here.
- Bottleneck items: little cost and profit impact, but failure could be disruptive. For example, cheap parts for a conveyor system could stop production. This high criticality or risk justifies some investment of time in supplier measurement and proactive management.
- Leverage items: you spend a lot on these but there is little supply risk, and so as a buyer you have the upper hand. Performance data is less important because supplier substitution is easier, and you can be much more adversarial if you choose.
- Routine/non-critical items: buy as you like, with little need for effort. Often these items can be delegated to users to acquire.

14

Learning activity 14.2

Take the top five suppliers identified in learning activity 14.1 above. Using the four box matrix (figure 14.2), categorise each of the five suppliers,

(continued on next page)

Learning activity 14.2 *(continued)*

and comment on the result, bearing in mind the report you wrote in self-assessment question 14.1 above.

Feedback on page 239

When using this model you are starting with the intrinsic qualities of the products you buy, not the suppliers you buy them from. The model acts as a basis for further consideration of the supply base available to you, and it is quite possible that a supplier may fall into two boxes. For example, the supplier could be supplying a critical production component and a routine spare. The buyer then makes a further choice:

- Determine the supplier as 'critical', dealing with all products supplied by the company.
- Continue with the product as 'critical', concentrating only on this item from this supplier.

As with all models of this kind you can design variations to suit your specific requirements: it is the principle of classifying the products (and hence the suppliers) in a consistent and structured way that is particularly useful.

Self-assessment question 14.2

Give True or False responses to the following statements.

1 In Kraljic's model critical/strategic items are those that have little supply risk but which are critical to keeping your business going. TRUE/FALSE
2 In many purchasing organisations shortage of resources means difficult decisions need to be taken when considering relationship development. TRUE/FALSE
3 You don't need complex models to know which are the key suppliers. TRUE/FALSE
4 Kraljic's model is based on product analysis. TRUE/FALSE
5 This type of model works only if you apply it exactly as written. TRUE/FALSE

Feedback on page 239

14

14.3 About supplier development

Imagine that you are dealing with a supplier and your performance measurement system indicates that the supplier is not performing well. If your general style for handling suppliers is adversarial, and if the market allows, you may move towards termination of the supplier.

If, on the other hand, your style is more cooperative (or if there are few suppliers), you may decide that it would be worth putting effort into helping the supplier to improve. More rarely it may be the case that you have a limited number of suppliers in a certain market and would like to encourage some new suppliers.

This is often known as supplier development or sometimes supplier mentoring.

Learning activity 14.3

Consider your suppliers and identify five suppliers who are not performing well. Using the template below, indicate whether you feel that your company could help these suppliers to perform better, and what support would be needed.

Supplier	Problem	How we could help
1		
2		
3		
4		
5		

Feedback on page 240

Supplier development means the provision of help to a supplier. There are no limits on what this might be, but it typically includes:

- Advice – on any issue that might help the relationship, such as quality or customer service.
- Finance – to help with capital purchases or even on occasions in time of hardship.
- Technology – large companies may provide access to their technology to help smaller or less competent suppliers.
- Personnel – key personnel may be loaned to the supplier for assistance, for example loaning engineers to give technical assistance with a manufacturing problem.
- Procurement – large buyers may help add 'muscle' to smaller companies' purchasing power.
- Supply chain benefits – allowing the supplier to access your supply chain for a particular purpose.

This is generally to enable the supplier to offer a product or service that better meets the buyer's needs, or to interface with the buying organisation in a mutually appropriate way. Suppliers are often selected for development as a result of supplier assessment or vendor rating. The use of supplier development is determined by supplier strategy, and will generally be targeted at those suppliers categorised as being of strategic importance.

14

233

Where several suppliers are strategically important to an organisation, supplier development programmes may be used.

Supplier development is a practical series of steps, based on developing more effective relationships, designed to get the best out of a supplier. You should note that:

- Supplier development is normally undertaken with existing suppliers who can be (and agree to being) improved. This agreement is important, and is a key characteristic of supplier development schemes.
- Supplier development depends on good communication. Suppliers will tend to view any client initiatives as just another means of exploitation – driving down the buyer's costs at the expense of the seller's profits. The key starting point, therefore, is to have a clear set of objectives, which are agreed internally. This should then form the basis of explaining and selling the concept to the supplier. The supplier needs to participate as a 'willing partner'.
- Supplier development is a good way in which larger companies can bring on SMEs that they feel have future potential, and this can help create competition and stimulate innovation.
- Before the programme starts, the supplier's performance must be measured against the agreed criteria in order to 'benchmark' the scope for development. This also allows the monitoring and measurement of improvement over time.
- Supplier development teams will generally be multifunctional, so that they can look at all aspects of any particular process or initiative. The aim is to identify areas where improvements can be made on a joint basis.
- Supplier development is not impossible in the public sector, but is often limited to advice or personnel rather than financial support, except on rare occasions.
- Even in a supplier development programme it is essential that the development should be bespoke to each supplier, and targeted at their particular needs.
- Supplier development in this context should not be confused with diversity and other such programmes, which aim to help small and ethnically owned businesses, by ensuring a more level playing field for business, and which may have grant support attached.

14

Self-assessment question 14.3

Write a paragraph (3–5 lines) of critical comment on each of the following statements.

1 We have a supplier development programme that supplies loan equipment and technical training to all suppliers on the programme.
2 I don't believe in helping suppliers – we have enough problems already!
3 Most of our problems with suppliers seem to be with administrative issues such as specifications, orders and invoicing problems. Supplier development won't help here.

(continued on next page)

Self-assessment question 14.3 (*continued*)

4   I have a feeling that a team approach would be useful here!
5   Supplier X is a real problem and I think needs developing!

Feedback on page 240

14.4 About supplier account management

You will have seen that supplier development works in a cooperative type of business relationship. Supplier account management, on the other hand, recognises and prospers in a more adversarial type of relationship.

Many procurement departments are at a disadvantage relative to suppliers' sales departments in terms of the amount of resource available, and the level of training received. As a result the supplier often 'manages' the relationship better, and often has undue influence on the user (see internal and external commercial relationships in study session 13).

Supplier account management is a sophisticated technique that aims to reverse this relationship, placing the buyer much more firmly in charge of the relationship. As with all such techniques it should be applied only where the time and effort required are likely to have a positive result, and is likely to be applied only to carefully selected suppliers.

A complicating factor is that some suppliers provide a range of products through various buyers to different end users. How this is to be handled will require some internal discussion, perhaps with one buyer taking the lead and a number of users being in the team.

As with supplier development, before the programme starts the supplier's performance must be measured against the agreed criteria in order to 'benchmark' the scope for development and allow the monitoring and measurement of improvement over time. However, unlike supplier development, cooperation is not essential, and indeed there may be some supplier resistance.

For the rest of this session we shall discuss a simple model of account management that most organisations could apply. Simplistically there are three stages:

1   Fully understand the supplier, your own business requirements of the supplier and the current state of business and relationships. This may sound simple but can be quite difficult to achieve, especially in large, complex businesses.
2   Develop a strategy for dealing with the supplier and building the internal relationships to implement this strategy. This will usually require a team approach, but can be very difficult to achieve, especially where internal relationships are poor. The internal relationship-building is needed to answer the question 'What do we want from this supplier and how do we get there?'

14

3 Design an action plan and implement the strategy, measuring progress over time, and having regular reviews within the internal team to take the necessary corrective action.

Once the strategy is working well the buying side may, if they wish, try to build the supplier into the arrangement, thus moving away from the adversarial approach to some extent.

Supplier account management requires significant time and resources to carry through well, though this will reduce as the principles become part of your organisation's standard way of working. It will often take a long time to get a result, and patience and some continuity of personnel will be useful.

Supplier account management requires data, and table 14.4 shows some minimum requirements. You can see that many of the techniques and tools mentioned in these study sessions form part of this schedule.

Table 14.4 Supplier account management

The current relationship

Activity	Description
Supplier background	• Basic supplier information: name, contacts, etc • Annual reports and other documents • Details on supplier's management (study session 13) • Overview of products/services supplied • Supplier's other major customers • Recent major news items of note • Main customer units served
Financial and commercial status	Current financial performance indicators *with your analysis* (study session 12) Current and forecast value of business transacted Value of your business to the supplier
Contract information	• Details of current contracts with supplier, including number, dates, type and products/services covered • Any special contractual commitments • Details of any non-contract supply (leakage, out of scope, etc) • Details of actual spend against contracts • Trend data relating to spend
Performance information (study session 10)	• The supplier's current performance • Benchmark information • Price/cost information • Have you any information on customer satisfaction in regard to this supplier? • If you have customer satisfaction data, what is the trend?
Account analysis	• SWOT and PESTLE on the supplier and the relationship (study sessions 9 and 11) • Supplier classification (this study session) • Reverse positioning – how the supplier sees the business (study session 7) • Details of supplier's account/sales management style

(continued on next page)

Table 14.4 *(continued)*

The future relationship

Activity	Description
Future relationship objectives	• What benefits are sought • Target relationships internal and external • New performance targets including specific price/cost targets • Any changes required to the supply chain. • Supplier conditioning – our special ways of working we need the supplier to comply with • SWOT analysis of the attractiveness to supplier of your business *after* you have implemented your proposed changes • Details of roles and responsibilities within the 'virtual team' managing the relationship with the supplier
Management points	Administrative details of all scheduled meetings, reviews, etc Communication plan that details of all scheduled communications, reports, contact points, news flows Escalation plan for disputes (study session 11)
Action plan	1 2 3 4 5 6 7 8 9 10

Management executive summary

Analysis summary, conclusions and recommendations with regard to supplier management approach based on above information

Learning activity 14.4

Note: This activity utilises table 14.4. It will take some time to complete.

Take a supplier with whom you would like to prepare a draft account plan and on whom you feel you already have a fair amount of knowledge. Study the draft checklist in table 14.4 and amend it to cover anything you feel is missing.

(continued on next page)

Learning activity 14.4 *(continued)*

Work through the checklist, acquiring the data you require, and taking a view on each header. You can do this individually, but may find working with a colleague useful. You may wish to open a file for this information.

Go as far as completing the action plan.

Feedback on page 240

Now go on to tackle the following self-assessment question.

Self-assessment question 14.4

Using the work you did in learning activity 14.4 above write the management executive summary and recommendations for the chosen supplier (300–400 words).

Feedback on page 241

Revision question

Now try the revision question for this session on page 335.

Summary

In this session we have looked mainly at how data used to measure purchasing performance can also be used in more unusual forms of supplier management, and in building up an extensive picture of a supplier to allow for supplier account management techniques to be developed.

This ends our work on measuring the performance of the supplier. We shall now begin to consider measuring the performance of another key player – you, the buyer!

Suggested further reading

Details of Pareto analysis (also known as ABC analysis or the 80:20 rule) can be found in Lysons and Farrington (2006), chapter 10, page 319.

Details of Kraljic's 'four box' matrix can be found in Lysons and Farrington (2006), chapter 2, page 64.

Feedback on learning activities and self-assessment questions

Feedback on learning activity 14.1

Your chart could look like the example in table 14.2.

Table 14.2

Supplier	Value of business	Supplier relationship type	Customer relationship quality
1	£3m	7	6
2	£2.7m	4	2
3	£2.1m	5	5
4	£1.6m	10	5
5	£1.2m	8	7
Total	£10.6m	34/50	25/50

For our top five suppliers I judge that we are generally operating with badly managed relationships, and that of supplier 4 is particularly poor. Our customer relationships are slightly better managed than those with our suppliers. I feel that for our organisation some repositioning of supplier relationships towards better managed would be beneficial.

Feedback on self-assessment question 14.1

There is no specific answer. Your report may include issues such as

- better relationships with customers
- better service, quality and prices
- earlier supplier involvement
- less interference by supplier's sales force
- placing the buyer in charge.

Feedback on learning activity 14.2

Your response may look like this example (as these are your top five by value, they will be either critical/strategic or leverage items):

- Supplier 1: Critical
- Supplier 2: Leverage
- Supplier 3: Leverage
- Supplier 4: Critical
- Supplier 5: Leverage.

Having done this analysis I feel we should not worry about suppliers 2, 3 and 5 but concentrate on suppliers 1 and 4, both of which scored as badly managed on both supplier and customer relationships.

Feedback on self-assessment question 14.2

1 FALSE. This describes 'bottleneck' items.
2 TRUE. We must concentrate resources to get maximum benefits.
3 TRUE. Many buyers will know this easily. However, in some organisations portfolios are large and harder to manage. Also, new buyers may find this technique useful.
4 TRUE. This model starts by looking at the product and then considers the supplier.
5 FALSE. You can modify the model to suit; the main thing is to apply it consistently.

14

Feedback on learning activity 14.3

Your chart could look like the examples in table 14.3.

Table 14.3

Supplier	Problem	How we could help
Supplier example 1	Performs well, but never understands our need for on-time deliveries.	Provide training on how we work – exchange personnel for short periods.
Supplier example 2	Is a very willing performer, but struggles to hit quality because of outdated equipment it cannot afford to replace.	Consider financing equipment, or purchasing and loaning/ hiring. Loan surplus plant from own operations
3	Etc	Etc
4	Etc	Etc
5	Etc	Etc

Feedback on self-assessment question 14.3

Your responses could be as follows:

1 Be careful, as your programme may be too prescriptive. Each supplier may have different needs, and the programme needs to respond with what is needed, not just determine a requirement for loan equipment and technical training.
2 Fair enough – but helping the supplier could be the easiest way of solving *your* problem, because supplier development is not done for the supplier's benefit but because it helps the supplier to offer a product or service that better meets the buyer's needs.
3 You may not appreciate it, but much supplier development is about helping to get administrative systems working better. This often includes exchange of personnel and 'training' schemes to improve contacts.
4 You are absolutely right. A cross-functional team approach (see study session 13) is most likely to be the way forward, unless the supplier's problems can clearly be related to one aspect of business performance.
5 Simply being a 'problem' is not a development issue; there has to be an identified underlying problem. Also, the supplier has to agree to be 'developed', and this may not happen if relationships are not right.

Feedback on learning activity 14.4

You should end up with a file of information on the supplier, and a series of judgements such as the SWOT analyses.

- Are any gaps in the data critical pieces of information you really should know about the supplier?

14

- Compare your future objectives with the current position. Are you being realistic?
- Look at your action plan – is it achievable?

Remember: this is only an exercise, but the information can be very useful in a real situation.

Feedback on self-assessment question 14.4

Your summary should explain how you propose to improve the management of this supplier. Your report could include:

- background and overview
- summary of current position
- outline of desired changes
- proposed actions to achieve this.

14

Why measure buyers' performance?

Introduction

This may seem a trite question, but if we do not perform, why are we here at all? We therefore need to **manage and measure the performance** of the purchasing and supply department. The importance that is attached to this will often reflect the profile that purchasing has within the organisation.

Performance management of purchasing and supply staff is *not* just about staff appraisal, although this may be a part of it. Performance management looks at all aspects of the purchasing and supply function.

Performance management should:

- include any measurement processes
- be continuous rather than scheduled
- focus on the business objectives and the 'bottom-line' performance
- be owned by everyone, rather than an end in itself
- not be driven by process or paperwork
- include inputs from **stakeholders** other than the manager and employee – all those people or bodies with an interest or 'stake' in the issue of buyer or supplier performance
- be something that employees want to be part of.

> 'In business, words are words; explanations are explanations, promises are promises, but only performance is reality.'
> **Harold S Geneen**

Session learning objectives

After completing this session you should be able to:

15.1 Describe the benefits to the buyer of good performance management.
15.2 Summarise the aims of measuring buyer performance for the organisation.
15.3 Distinguish between periodic, ongoing and annual measurement options.
15.4 Explain the links to reward and advancement.
15.5 Summarise problems with poorly managed measurement schemes.
15.6 Explain the wider national view and structured approaches such as Investors in People.

Unit content coverage

This study session covers the following topics from the official CIPS unit content document:

Statement of practice

- Evaluate the benefits of implementing a well-structured approach to measuring organisational, functional and individual performance.

Learning objective

3.1 Define and explain the benefits of a well-managed and structured approach to measuring an individual's performance.
- Investors in People (IIP) guidelines and structure
- Performance against target assessments
- Planning for improvements
- Using personality profiling to ensure that purchasing staff are appropriate to their role

3.4 Analyse and explain how an individual's knowledge, expertise and skills can be developed to the benefit of both that individual and the organisation.
- Individual benefits: level of responsibility, job satisfaction, career progression, skills development
- Organisational benefits: better-trained workforce
- Improved productivity and profitability
- Competitive advantages

Prior knowledge

No specific knowledge is required for this session. However, if you are already subject to a personal measurement system you may find some aspects of this session easier.

Resources

No specific resources are required. However, there is much general research information available on the internet, which you can use to support the recommended textbooks and learning materials.

Timing

You should set aside about 5.5 hours to read and complete this session, including learning activities, self-assessment questions, the suggested further reading (if any) and the revision question.

15.1 Performance management and the buyer

Organisations should be continuously helping to develop their employees' skills and knowledge. Clearly, this benefits both the individual employees and the organisation as a whole, but it requires a structured and well-managed approach that ensures that individuals:

- Have the skills and knowledge that they need to do the job, and to develop their full potential.
- Can improve their contribution to the organisation.
- Can participate more fully in the organisation, and understand the overall aims and business strategies better.
- Are motivated, and that their morale is high.

Learning activity 15.1

Reflect on any personal experience of performance measurement that you have had. How effective do you feel it has been? What benefits has it provided for you and for your organisation?

Feedback on page 255

Let's look at these four areas in more detail.

Improved skills and knowledge

A prime objective of the performance management process is to help employees improve their performance, particularly by developing useful skills and gaining relevant and up-to-date knowledge. This can be a continuous process, if say a manager interacts regularly with the employee, acting as a coach and mentor; or it may come from employee requests, or as output from a formal **appraisal** system. Appraisal is a systematic approach to checking aspects of performance, usually used for suppliers and employees. The term is often interchangeable with 'evaluation'.

A **training needs analysis** (TNA) can be of benefit here by providing a better view of the employee's learning needs. This is a systematic analysis undertaken to establish the training needs of staff in relation to the needs of the organisation. (See study session 18.)

The skills and knowledge acquired will benefit the employee in all future employments, but they must bring benefit to the organisation as well.

Making a better contribution

Well-skilled and developed employees can make a better contribution to the activities of the organisation activity, and they should therefore find their work more involving and enjoyable. Remember also that the employer is investing time and money in performance management, and will require a return on this investment. This may be measured in various ways (see below).

Having a better view of overall aims and business strategy

In many organisations employees complain that 'they never tell us what is going on', and that communication is poor. A good performance management system requires regular dialogue between staff and managers. It normally includes objectives and targets, which should be derived ('cascaded') from company business plans and objectives. We describe this cascade process more fully in study session 16.

Improved motivation and morale

Low morale among buyers is likely to lead to poor day-to-day performance, lack of interest in the job, and higher staff turnover. This in turn will mean that procurement targets are not achieved, expertise is lost, and recruitment costs increase.

15

There are many reasons for poor morale in an organisation, but a regular, well-managed performance and appraisal system should provide a positive improvement in morale.

Of course, some buyers might take a narrower view, and consider the main benefit of performance measurement to be merely the rewards that may be linked to it. This is understandable, but buyers who see this as the only benefit have failed to understand the wider aims and objectives of such measurement.

Self-assessment question 15.1

Give True or False responses to the following statements on the benefits of performance management for the buyer:

1   Bonus payments or rewards may be considered as a wider benefit of performance management for buyers. TRUE/FALSE
2   Internal communications should be directly improved as a result of a well-managed employee measurement system. TRUE/FALSE
3   Almost any training and development that an employee wants will help to benefit the organisation. TRUE/FALSE
4   The employing organisation will be looking for a measurable return on its investment in measuring and appraising employees. TRUE/FALSE
5   Individual departments should set their own targets and objectives derived from departmental plans. TRUE/FALSE

Feedback on page 255

15.2 Performance management and the organisation

An organisation will invest time and resources in a good performance management and measurement system. It will have various aims in introducing such a system.

Learning activity 15.2

Reflect on your organisation's aims for buyer performance management. You may need input from your line manager or HR department. What does the organisation see as the benefits?

Feedback on page 255

Improving employee performance

A performance management and appraisal system is designed to increase employees' performance in the long term. It does this by measuring performance against objectives and targets, and by providing the skills and training that employees need to support any areas of weakness.

For buyers this should eventually result in better prices, deals or contracts for the organisation, improved quality and service, and a bottom-line improvement. This is often difficult to measure directly, and improvements in the perception and profile of the purchasing and supply function within the organisation will be equally important.

Better communication and feedback

Most organisations recognise that there can be benefits from improving communication, especially around the business-planning process. Also, good 'honest' appraisals can provide valuable feedback to management on how the organisation is felt to be performing.

With good processes for setting objectives, regular appraisals and good feedback, an organisation can receive excellent input from staff on improvements to the systems and processes with which they are involved. This input can be taken into account when corporate and departmental plans are reviewed.

Gaining information

The system produces information about the employee, the manager, and the organisation. This can help in developing the employee, the team, and the recruitment process.

For example, appraisal might reveal a weakness in negotiation skills. This would lead to successful training across the team, spin off into other parts of the business, and become a key part of the job profile for future recruitment.

Procedural or legal requirements

An effective performance management system must be professionally sound, and should enable managers to ensure the organisation complies with all relevant legislation and organisational policies.

For example, a good appraisal system might help identify issues such as harassment or prejudice, so that appropriate action can be taken.

A structured approach ensures that personnel-related decisions (such as promotion or termination) can be supported if they are subsequently subject to legal challenge.

15

Self-assessment question 15.2

From the above material, arrange a list of benefits in the best order for your organisation, and explain why you have chosen this order.

Feedback on page 255

15.3 3 Periodic, ongoing and annual measurement

In any performance management system, the frequency of measurement and review is important.

A good process requires effective communication between employee and manager all year round, and it will suffer if this is not the case. The employee and the manager must both feel comfortable with the system. If they have little regular contact, the process will be less effective.

The manager's key appraisal tasks are to observe and identify performance that has occurred, and communicate those observations to the employee. The manager should also look for feedback and make suggestions for improvement.

The employee's key appraisal tasks are to accept assessments that are fair, and defend himself or herself against assessments that are not. He or she should also provide sensible feedback, and consider the suggestions made. There can be a degree of negotiation in such reviews, especially if financial rewards are involved.

Learning activity 15.3

Consider any appraisal or measurement systems that apply to your own job. What frequency is used? Is this effective? If not, what frequency would be best?

Feedback on page 255

Typically, we find three different frequencies:

- Ongoing. In an ongoing process there is regular contact on performance and appraisal matters throughout the year. Often this contact is informal. There may be milestone meetings as well, especially if quantitative data has to be produced and considered. This approach may be particularly useful in fast-moving businesses, or in smaller organisations where contact is easy to arrange.
- Periodic. This usually involves a series of scheduled appraisal interviews, typically either quarterly or half-yearly, for which both manager and employee prepare. This is helpful if external sources need to prepare data or statistics as it provides a series of target dates. Quarterly meetings are better if manager/employee contact is less frequent.
- Annual. Managers who view the process as only a once-a-year activity lose significant opportunities for performance improvement. Annual interviews, even with a manager with whom the employee has regular contact, can be uncomfortable and hard to handle. Also, it is harder to change objectives and apply corrective actions if you only meet once every 12 months.

Self-assessment question 15.3

List the advantages and disadvantages of each of the approaches described above.

Feedback on page 256

15.4 The links with reward and advancement

In many organisations, performance and appraisal information helps to determine career paths for individuals and identify talent. Often it is also linked to salary or bonus payments.

Learning activity 15.4

Reflect on your organisation's policy or process in relation to linking appraisal to reward and advancement. Does it bring benefit to the business, and increase employee motivation? If not, why not? (Your HR department or line manager may be able to help you.)

Feedback on page 256

Developing talent

Appraisal can allow employees (especially those comfortable in such situations) to 'advertise' themselves within the organisation. They can be monitored, given special training or extra objectives, or even **fast tracked** according to organisational policy. (Fast tracking is scheduling a supplier or employee for advancement or development faster than the norm.)

Their performance in a more demanding role can also be monitored closely, and in a formal system the results can be seen by managers elsewhere in the organisation (if this is allowed by confidentiality rules).

Care should be taken to ensure that the talent is genuine; the ability to perform well in an appraisal is not the only test for a good buyer.

Improved motivation

When good rewards follow from a fair and respected system there should be increased morale, greater effort, and more ideas and innovation.

Financial reward

Financial rewards significantly sharpen employees' perception of the measurement and appraisal process. There are different types of reward. They can be:

- Manager's discretion. The manager has full authority to reward as he or she sees fit. This is a powerful role for the manager, and it can easily be abused unless there is some type of rigorous checking system.
- Next increment. Performance to a certain level automatically moves the person to a new salary point.
- Organised bonus schemes (performance-related pay or similar). These are schemes devised by the organisation and based around the performance measurement process. There are usually limits on the size of the payments, and there may be opt-out clauses for staff who do not wish to participate, especially in the public sector.

15

The danger is that employees may see financial rewards as the key reason for a performance appraisal. Managers should ensure that this aspect does not predominate, or the other benefits of performance measurement will be lost.

Self-assessment question 15.4

Give True or False responses to the following statements:

1   Although many staff might disagree, reward or promotion are not the key reasons for performance appraisal. TRUE/FALSE
2   The performance appraisal process provides good opportunities for employees to be identified for promotion or development. TRUE/FALSE
3   Next increment reward schemes are no longer common because organisations do not wish to pay financial rewards. TRUE/FALSE
4   The power that a manager has in a system where rewards are at the manager's discretion is not a problem. TRUE/FALSE
5   Appraisal interviews give all staff an equal opportunity to present themselves for consideration for reward or advancement. TRUE/FALSE

Feedback on page 256

15.5 Problems with poorly managed measurement schemes

Measurement and appraisal requires the interaction of several different individuals and systems to work effectively. As you might expect, there are plenty of opportunities for problems to occur.

Learning activity 15.5

Reflect on performance management in your organisation. Can you see any problems with the way it is managed? How do these affect the credibility of the system?

Feedback on page 257

Some of the most common difficulties are as follows:

*   'We have an appraisal system because we feel ought to.' To work effectively, measurement and appraisal must be owned by the management and given real priority within the organisation. Without this they fall into disrepute. For example, if a manager is called to a meeting when he has an appraisal organised, the appraisal must be given priority.
*   There is too much pressure and slippage. Managers and employees have full diaries, and it is easy for four meetings a year to slip. If an appraisal has to be cancelled, it should be immediately be rescheduled. Failure to hold meetings is always a sign that the system isn't being taken seriously.
*   There are changing targets and priorities. Fast-moving organisations often need to change targets and objectives. This must be allowed for,

but it can make results hard to judge. It is important not to arrive at a yearly interview to discuss performance and targets against objectives that are no longer high priority.

- There is a lack of confidentiality. Information is often quickly available to all; staff often tell each other how they 'got on'. Management must assume that information will leak out; fairness and equality are essential.
- 'You're not listening.' Managers don't listen to feedback from review sessions. This is self-defeating, and employees gradually lose confidence in the system and provide less input as time goes on.
- There is a lack of good information. This can be a problem for both management and employees, and if the appraisal process requires data that is unavailable there may be disagreement over what has actually been achieved.
- There is a failure to review and update. The measurement and appraisal process has been operational for a long time, but has not itself been 'reappraised'. Employees easily spot this, and the process becomes discredited.
- There is a lack of training and practice. Often, training takes place when a scheme is introduced, but is not then continued to cover new staff and managers. Personal measurement can be difficult, and many people are uncomfortable in such situations. Training can help. So too can regular participation and attendance, which acts as practice, and significantly improves contributions.

Self-assessment question 15.5

Mini case study with questions: Jack's dilemma

Jack works for the purchasing department in a large local authority. The authority has operated a performance measurement system for several years, linked to some well-understood and fair performance targets. Good performance is recorded on an employee's record and used in interviews for promotions, but staff sometimes share these comments, which they often find interesting. The measurement system has always been quite strong on qualitative data, but the authority shows little sign of improving the level of quantitative input.

The authority wishes to introduce a financial reward for achieving savings targets. Jack has no problem with the principle of this, but he does have some concerns, because of what he sees as weaknesses in the current system.

1 From the information given, what might be Jack's main area for concern given the need to link rewards to savings made?
2 From the information given, what could be his second concern now that financial rewards are involved?
3 In this scenario, does it seem sensible for the authority to consider this type of target?
4 What might be done to ensure that the scheme continues to work well?

Feedback on page 257

15.6 The wider view, and Investors in People

Increasing the measurement of performance in the workplace is seen as part of the wider educational and development framework for the country at large; it is not just an organisational tool for improving in-house performance. It is argued that a well-measured and developed workforce will ultimately benefit everyone, and should be supported both by both individual organisations and by a national initiative.

In the UK, the basic components of a structured approach are set out in the national standard **Investors in People**, a national scheme that aims to provide a 'kitemark' of excellence in training.

Learning activity 15.6

Disappointment for Jill

Jill has just started working in a company that proudly displays an Investors in People plaque in the reception area. This was one of the things that drew her to this company, but she has found that her colleagues and managers are not concerned with training and development, and that few plans have been drawn up for training.

Identify some key issues that you would expect Jill to see in a company that has achieved this standard. (You may wish talk to your line manager or HR department, or look on the internet for companies with IIP policies.)

Feedback on page 257

The Investors in People standard is a benchmark of excellence in training, based loosely on the total quality management model. It comprises the following elements:

* Commitment from senior management to develop all employees to achieve business objectives. Organisations need written flexible plans that set out business objectives, how employees will help the business meet its objectives, and how their personal and development needs will be assessed and met.
* Regular senior management review of the training and development needs of all employees.
* Action to train and develop individuals, not only when they are recruited bur throughout their employment;
* Set out in the organisation's business plan a mechanism for continuous evaluation of the effectiveness of the investment in training, to assess and improve its future effect.

These are good management practices and disciplines in their own right, irrespective of whether the organisation goes on to achieve formal recognition in the form of the IIP standard or a similar standard of quality.

15

Personality profiling

Personality profiling is a self-awareness tool that provides individuals with a detailed analysis of their personal behavioural style. From this, practical guidance can be given on making appropriate modifications to behaviour, which will improve the performance of an individual purchasing officer.

Team profiling is where the personality profiles of all the members of a team are established. Where a team has a mixture of profiles, there is likely to be a positive and constructive environment, where the team performs well. If all members of a team have a similar profile, it is likely that such benefits will be lost.

One of the most widely used personality profiling systems is the Myers Briggs Type Indicator (MBTI), based on the work of Katherine Briggs and Isabel Myers in the 1940s. This provides information about four aspects of personality:

- How and where a person focuses and gets their energy.
- How a person prefers to take in information.
- How a person makes decisions.
- How a person relates to the world.

The MBTI can help individual employees understand why some behaviours are natural to them and why others require a lot of effort. It can provide an insight into areas such as managing stress, dealing with conflict, how people work best and career development.

In a team context, MBTI can give useful information about how a team might communicate and work together more effectively. It can also reveal how the team might need to develop to improve overall performance.

Another well-known system for assessing personality characteristics is DISC, which is based on the work of Dr William Marston. It is based on the concept that all personalities are a combination of four core styles:

- Dominant, characterised by the individual being forceful, direct, decisive and pioneering.
- Influencing, characterised by the individual being optimistic, friendly, talkative and charismatic.
- Steady, characterised by individuals being patient, loyal and practical.
- Compliant, characterised by individuals being precise, sensitive, analytical and diplomatic.

The DISC system measures several variables:

- How a person solves problems and responds to challenges.
- How a person attempts to influence others.
- The pace at which a person responds to change.
- How a person responds to rules and regulations.

Personality profiling systems can be used to improve the performance of individual purchasing officers and purchasing teams. Once the behavioural style of an individual has been established, methods of changing this

15

through training and development can be determined. If, for example, it is discovered that an individual's predominant core style is steady and the team leader requires that individual to be more decisive, appropriate training can be provided.

Similarly, if it is discovered that the majority of the members of the team are compliant, the team leader can introduce appropriate training to change the behavioural style of some or all members of the team. A variety of behavioural styles in a team is preferred to improve its performance.

Self-assessment question 15.6

Write a short memorandum on the importance (or otherwise) of a national framework of performance management for the nation, the organisation and the individual.

Feedback on page 257

Summary

We have looked at the reasons why we should consider measuring buyers' performance, and we can now identify the following key issues:

- Measuring performance is part of the wider process of managing performance.
- Benefits should accrue both to the employee and to the employer.
- There can be differences in the frequencies with which measurement is undertaken, and these can have significant implications for effectiveness.
- Reward and advancement are common outcomes of performance measurement, but they need careful management to be effective
- Performance management can also be said to have a wider benefit to the economy as a whole, by steadily increasing the skills and competence of the workforce.

Suggested further reading

For study sessions 15 to 19 students will find that chapter 8 of Neely et al (2002) provides a useful view of performance measurement from the perspective of employees as stakeholders. Students should also look at Lysons and Farrington (2006), chapter 17 for brief information on employee-related issues especially:

17.2 Management by objectives

17.8 Miscellaneous approaches to measuring purchasing performance

17.11 Ethical codes and training.

For this session in particular students can find useful information on the Investors in People initiative at their website http://www.investorsinpeople.co.uk.

Feedback on learning activities and self-assessment questions

Feedback on learning activity 15.1

You should reflect any experiences you have had to date, asking yourself:

- What did you gain?
- What was learned or improved?
- Did you feel more or less motivated after the involvement?
- What did the organisation gain?
- Were there any benefits or failures in communication or participation?

Feedback on self-assessment question 15.1

1   FALSE. Rewards are a narrow way of considering the benefits of performance measurement.
2   TRUE. This is one of the key benefits of a well-managed scheme.
3   FALSE. The skills and knowledge must bring benefit to the organisation as well as to the employee.
4   TRUE. Ultimately, the organisation has to improve performance for all stakeholders, not just employees.
5   FALSE. Objectives and targets should be derived from company business plans and objectives.

Feedback on learning activity 15.2

You should be able to identify why your organisation operates a buyers' performance measurement system, and what its *main* reason is for doing so. The reasons might include:

- improved employee and business performance
- better communication and feedback
- better information
- compliance with procedural or legal requirements
- more employee benefits
- benefits specific to your organisation.

Feedback on self-assessment question 15.2

There is no one right answer. Your list should include most of the above points, plus others that you feel are relevant. In general, you should include improved business performance towards the top of your list.

Feedback on learning activity 15.3

You should examine the approach used for any appraisal or measurement that you are involved in. Does it:

- Happen all the time?
- Happen to a schedule?
- Happen only once a year?

15

Do you feel this is the best frequency? Explain why, or, if not, why a different frequency would be better.

Feedback on self-assessment question 15.3

Your answer might include some or all of the following:

Ongoing

- Advantages: regular contact, less formality, better relationships, fast and adaptable.
- Disadvantages: time input, lack of milestones, difficult in some organisations.

Periodic

> Advantages: allows coordinated inputs, more structured; formality may mean it is taken more seriously.
> Disadvantages: generally more difficult to manage; relationships are more difficult.

Annual

- Advantages: less time input.
- Disadvantages: formal, lack of relationship, hard to change or develop objectives.

Feedback on learning activity 15.4

You should be able to look at your own organisation and identify whether there is a direct link between measurement of buyers' performance and the rewards they receive. You could have identified:

Pros

- identifying talented staff
- positive motivation and rewards
- bottom-line performance improvements
- innovation and effort.

Cons

- focused too much on rewards
- perceived unfairness
- power of managers.

Feedback on self-assessment question 15.4

1   TRUE. This aspect can become too dominant. If it does, the other benefits of performance appraisal will suffer.
2   TRUE. Performance and appraisal information will help the organisation to determine career paths for individuals and spot and develop talented staff.

15

3   FALSE. Many organisations are happy to give financial rewards but
     dislike next increment systems.
4   FALSE. Rigorous checks are necessary to prevent abuse and favouritism.
5   FALSE. Staff may perform well in general, but feel uncomfortable in
     this particular situation.

Feedback on learning activity 15.5

By now you should have thought about your own organisation's
measurement process in some detail. Problems could include any or all of
the following:

- The scheme exists, but it has low priority in the business.
- There is pressure and slippage in the process.
- The scheme doesn't allow for change.
- There is a lack of confidentiality.
- Management ignores feedback.
- There is a lack of good information.
- There is a lack of training or practice.

Feedback on self-assessment question 15.5

1   Jack's main concern should be the lack of measurable data. To measure
     savings targets effectively, very clear numbers will be needed.
2   Jack's second concern could be the current lack of confidentiality,
     though this does not come from the organisation.
3   Probably not. A savings target is perfectly reasonable, but setting targets
     without ensuring the data is available for measurement is likely to lead
     to faults with the measurement scheme.
4   First, the authority needs to put effective data collection systems in
     place. The issue of confidentiality can perhaps be covered more easily by
     discussion with the staff involved. In any case, a major change such as
     this would be a good opportunity to review the way the scheme works.

Feedback on learning activity 15.6

Your list of issues might include the following:

- commitment from senior management
- written flexible plans for personal and development needs
- regular review of training and development needs of all employees
- action to train and develop individuals
- a mechanism for continuous evaluation.

Feedback on self-assessment question 15.6

Your memorandum should cover several of the points covered in this section
of the study session, including:

- commitment from senior management
- written flexible plans
- regular senior management reviews

15

- action to train and develop individuals
- action throughout an individual's employment
- mechanisms for continuous evaluation of training effectiveness
- accepted standard of standardisation
- goes beyond one organisation.

Cascading targets and objectives

'The odds of hitting
your target go up
dramatically when
you aim at it.'
Mal Pancoast

Introduction

It may seem an obvious statement, but the activities any group of staff need
to be 'aimed' via a series of targets and objectives. This is the concept of
management by (or through) objectives (MBO). In this study session we
shall look at how this concept works, and at how objectives cascade down
from the business-planning process. We shall consider some of the issues
and problems of objective-setting.

Session learning objectives

After completing this session you should be able to:

16.1 Define the concept and benefits of managing through objectives.
16.2 Summarise the way in which targets and objectives cascade down from
the business-planning process.
16.3 Design positive objectives that conform to the SMART approach to
objective-setting.
16.4 Demonstrate the possibilities of different timescales for objectives.
16.5 Analyse some of the problems that can arise during objective-setting.
16.6 Demonstrate the benefits of feedback, audit and review of the objective-
setting process.

Unit content coverage

This study session covers the following topics from the official CIPS unit
content document:

Statement of practice

* Explain how measuring performance in supply chain activities fits into
the overall management process of an organisation.

Learning objective

3.3 Analyse and explain how individual components of a purchasing role
link to the overall objectives of the organisation.
* Contribution of individuals to an organisation's profitability
* Management of basic workload
* Development of purchasing infrastructure

16

Prior knowledge

You should have read study session 15. Some familiarity with corporate or departmental planning processes would be useful, as would participation in an objective-setting process.

Resources

No specific resources are required. However, there is much general research information available on the internet, which can be used to support the recommended textbooks and learning materials. You may find discussion with your manager or HR department to be useful.

Timing

You should set aside about 5.75 hours to read and complete this session, including learning activities, self-assessment questions, the suggested further reading (if any) and the revision question.

16.1 Managing by objectives

Managing by objectives (MBO) requires that the aims and objectives for the business are cascaded down through the organisation, providing direction for departmental planning, staff and management targets, and eventually personal objectives.

MBO can be misused, and this can lead to an overemphasis on results, competition between staff, and workers being pushed to accept inappropriate targets. A balance needs to be struck between:

- a proactive set of objectives that provide employees with a clear indication of what the organisation expects and why and
- an over-demanding set of rigid objectives that override every other consideration.

Learning activity 16.1

Reflect on the term 'managing through objectives'. What do you think this means, and what would be the benefits for the employee and the organisation?

Feedback on page 271

If properly implemented, management through the use of objectives should:

- lead to focused, business-driven objectives at all levels in the business
- encourage individuals to become involved in setting and reviewing their own objectives

- help identify skill shortages and bespoke training opportunities for the participants.

The basic steps to establishing an individual employee's objectives are as follows:

1. Management should ensure that all employees clearly understand the corporate business direction and departmental objectives. (This may require some special briefing or communication.)
2. Manager and employee need to review the employee's job description and responsibilities, preferably by discussion and agreement. The objectives should not conflict with this, or the job description may need to be amended.
3. Jointly match the targets for the business and department with ideas from the employee. Usually this results in objectives for a defined period, for example one year ahead.
4. Discuss and agree the objectives. The employee should take ownership of them as far as is practical within the cascade process. Whenever possible the manager's role should be that of questioner and developer, rather than director.
5. Agree the evaluation criteria that will be used in evaluating progress towards achievement of the objectives. Typical examples might include project due dates, profit contributions, savings targets, quality targets, or contract coverage.
6. Agree the timetable for joint review of performance and comparison with the plan.
7. Agree the required outputs, because feedback from the subsequent review sessions may provide business challenges for the manager and highlight training and development needs for the employee.

Self-assessment question 16.1

Fill in the blanks in the following text:

If we have a good process for management through objectives, then employees will have more _____ and _____ objectives, which typically results in more _____ job performance and allows _____ training and development for each individual. Care should be taken that there is a high degree of employee _____ in the process, or else _____ may suffer.

_____ from the process is essential if management is to _____ the scheme over time.

Feedback on page 271

16

16.2 Targets and objectives, and the business-planning process

Many larger organisations will have a high-level corporate business-planning process. This should include a procurement plan, or at least a reference to procurement's role within the business. Smaller businesses may lack a formal structure for doing this, but they are often better at more informal communication of organisational strategies and plans.

The basic question is always 'What is the function and direction for procurement?'

Learning activity 16.2

Look at your department's objectives. Can you track them back up the organisation and into the planning process?

Feedback on page 271

High-level planning should cascade down through the business. This is summarised in figure 16.1: the thick black track highlights the individual employee's objective-setting process.

Figure 16.1: High-level planning should cascade down through the business

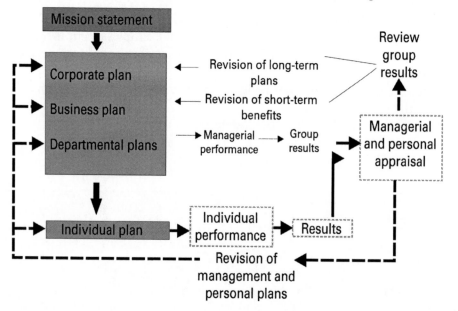

The various parts of this cascade are described below.

Mission (statement)

This is a broad statement of why the organisation exists, and what it hopes to achieve. This is often aspirational. For example, a car manufacturer's mission might be:

'To lead the market in the development of low-cost, environmentally safe transport'

From this we might assume that the company will emphasise low-cost, environmentally friendly manufacturing, and safety.

The mission statement gives focus and direction to the organisation. We should see the key issues of cost, safety and the environment echoed throughout the objective-setting process. These aspirations are turned into positive actions for the company in the corporate plan and the business plan.

Corporate plan

This is long-term and strategic, looking ahead perhaps 3–10 years. It focuses on the larger issues: for example, a decision to cease manufacturing in high-cost countries.

Business plan

This is medium-term, covering perhaps the next 1–3 years. It contains more detail on particular projects within the corporate plan: for example, the planned transfer of an engine-manufacturing facility from the UK to China.

Departmental plan

This is short-term, covering typically 12 months. It includes the department's contribution to the business and corporate plans. It provides the manager's objectives, and therefore influences those of his or her staff: for example, re-sourcing components in the project to move the UK engine-manufacturing facility.

Employee plan

This is usually short term, covering typically 12 months, and is derived from the departmental plan. Its content influenced by the job description and responsibilities: for example to re-source components X, Y and Z in line with the project to move the UK engine-manufacturing facility.

Outputs from departmental and individual plans are reviewed and fed back into the planning process; organisational demands can result in changes to individual targets.

This is an ideal model, but if individual employees cannot track their objectives back through the organisation they would have a reasonable case for asking 'Why am I doing this?'

Self-assessment question 16.2

Write a short essay analysing how this process of cascading objectives works in your organisation. (Maximum one side of A4)

Feedback on page 271

16

16.3 Designing positive and SMART objectives

As we have now seen, individual objectives should be derived from the main business-planning process, with of course the inclusion of some internal departmental and personal objectives.

How many objectives should there be? This is often a problem. There is no one correct answer to the question, but consider the following points when setting objectives:

- If there are too many objectives, this can be both unrealistic and demotivating.
- If there are too few, this is not sufficiently challenging.

Objectives are not tasks, but they do *contain* tasks. They should be broader than tasks, and should allow the employee some creativity.

The optimum is probably between eight and ten well-developed objectives.

An objective will typically have four elements. A simple example for a purchase order controller is shown in table 16.1.

Table 16.1 Elements of an objective

Objectives	Example
The key task (May be in several employees' objectives)	Improve the payment of invoices
The objective (A description of the objective for *this employee*)	To ensure that invoices received are checked for accuracy and paid in a timely manner
The performance measures (*How the performance or improvement will be measured*)	Average time (days) from receipt of invoice to payment date
	Monthly total of settlement discounts claimed (£s)
	% of inaccurate invoices received
The timescale (by when) (The objective milestones and review timetable)	By December 200? – review every month

It is not easy to write good objectives. To ensure good 'quality' objectives it is sound practice to follow the principles embodied in the acronym **SMART**:

- Specific: The objective should be clear and unambiguous. It should refer to a specific area of activity, and be clearly expressed.
- Measurable: It should be possible to measure the outcome. If not, employees or managers will not know whether it has been achieved. **Quantitative** measures (measurements that are based on figures and data) are popular, but they are sometimes difficult to obtain. For example: 'To undertake a survey of customer perceptions of the purchasing service'. The only measurable here might be whether or not the survey has been undertaken.
- Achievable: It is clearly undesirable to set objectives that are unachievable by the employee or unrealistic in their scope. For example, it might be unrealistic or not achievable to set the employee the objective 'To improve the perception of the purchasing service'.
- Realistic: As 'Achievable'.
- Timed: Objectives should have a timetable for achievement and review. Some objectives may need special reviews outside the normal object review process. For example, if our invoicing objective is a high priority,

16

it may need a special monthly review outside the regular quarterly review.

Learning activity 16.3

Compare any two real examples of objectives used in your organisation with the model described above. How do the real-life examples stand up?

Feedback on page 271

When we choose a measurement, we need to decide whether to make it **zero based** or continuous. Zero basing starts each period from zero: it effectively forgets previous performance, and looks afresh at what is achievable. Continuous improvement builds on data all the time, but this can be a problem, because improvement in a given area usually gets harder to achieve over time.

Self-assessment question 16.3

Read the following:

Mr X is a contract manager looking after a range of very good, well-priced hotel service contracts in an NHS hospital. He has 14 objectives this year, of which two are detailed below. He has a wide authority to take actions.

Comment on whether each of the two examples shown below meets the SMART criteria for objective-setting.

Do you have any other comments?

Table 16.2

Objective 1: To achieve savings of around 10% across all your contracts during the financial year subject to progress review at two-monthly intervals.	
	Comment
Specific	
Measurable	
Achievable	
Realistic	
Timed	

Table 16.3

Objective 2: To improve the service provided to the catering department in response to complaints received on quality and payment of invoices by the end of July	
	Comment
Specific	
Measurable	
Achievable	
Realistic	
Timed	

Feedback on page 271

16

16.4 Timescales for objectives

Learning activity 16.4

Reflect on how different objectives need different timescales to achieve. Use the table below to write a brief outline of the relevance of timescales to aspects of your job, your work environment (team or colleagues) or your department.

Table 16.6

Area of activity	Main timescales	Relevance
My job		
My immediate environment		
My department		

Feedback on page 272

Objectives have different timescales, which fit broadly into the level they occupy within the cascade process we described above. In general we can see five broad levels of timescale as we move down through this process. These time periods are just suggestions; the actual periods will vary from one organisation to another.

Very long-term (10 years plus)

The mission statement and the higher-level strategic aims and objectives fit here. They should be carefully chosen, because constant change at this level will cause more problems than it solves.

Long-term (3 to 10 years?)

The corporate plan fits here. Corporate plans are not rigid; they change over time as the organisation moves forward. They also have to reflect changes outside the organisation, such as developments in technology and new legislation. However, as for the mission statement, rapid changes at this level can have negative effects.

Medium-term (1 to 3 years?)

The business plan fits here. Some flexibility is desirable at this level, because of the shorter timescale and the need to incorporate issues such as design and marketing, which move on faster cycles. Here the organisation can respond to business pressures (or government policy in the case of public services).

Short-term (up to 1 year?)

The departmental and individual plans fit here. There is more scope for change and adaptability here, as activity is largely tactical, and fast moving.

Day-to-day

These are department and individual actions and plans, which vary and develop to suit immediate organisational needs. These are always fast moving, but can still have a major impact on business success. Too much day-to-day focus can easily distract management from the need for longer-term objectives.

Self-assessment question 16.4

Give True or False responses to the following statements on timescales for objectives:

1   Different timescales apply at different levels in the organisation because the nature of the objectives set is different. TRUE/FALSE
2   Operational buying staff have lots of long-term objectives. TRUE/FALSE
3   If possible, buyers should be set some longer-term objectives. TRUE/FALSE
4   It is the day-to-day activity that really drives a business forward. TRUE/FALSE
5   Dedicated planning teams and process can sometimes become 'divorced' from the rest of the business activity. TRUE/FALSE

Feedback on page 272

16.5 Problems with objective-setting

Learning activity 16.5

Sometimes objective-setting does not work well. Compare the list of reasons in table 16.7 with any real examples you have experienced or come across in your career.

Table 16.7

Reason	My experience
Failure to write SMART objectives	
Inadequate information for measuring success	
Constantly changing plans	
Failure to hold review sessions	
The organisation likes to dictate the objectives	
Lack of qualitative objectives (too much emphasis on numbers)	
Objectives are too easy	

Feedback on page 272

16

Clearly, there are many things that can go wrong with the objective-setting process. Some of the more common ones are listed below:

- *Changing plans and focus:* Probably the greatest cause of problems with objective-setting. The cascade process works badly, so objective-setting drifts from core business aims. Sometimes objectives are changed by instruction from further up the organisation. This causes frustration for both management and employees.
- *Failure to review adequately:* This leads to an assumption that the objectives do not matter. It is unreasonable to set regular reviews and then to fail to do this but still demand results at a yearly review. Failure to review also means that changes cannot be properly incorporated into the objective-setting process.
- *Failure to be SMART:.* This is a failure of both manager and employee. The objectives do not meet the SMART criteria, perhaps because of poor construction or lack of development time and thought
- *Inadequate information:* It is often difficult to obtain the information needed to measure the objectives. This means the objectives fail to be properly measured, or there is disagreement over the values used.
- *Too much organisational control:* Employees discover that there is less 'give' in the system when it comes to selecting objectives than they were led to believe. If they disagree with an objective, the manager forces it through. Participative goal-setting becomes top-down objective-setting, and the entire process loses credibility.
- *Lack of qualitative objectives* (those based more on perception and opinion, rather than on figures and data). Evaluation criteria need to be SMART. However, sometimes effective performance management requires the evaluation of behaviours and subjective issues, which are often avoided because they are harder to evaluate.
- *Setting easy objectives:* Performance theory suggests that best results are achieved when challenging objectives are set. However, employees who receive linked rewards may prefer easier objectives to ensure a good financial reward. Also, some managers may set easier objectives to avoid difficult issues with employees, or to give a false impression of departmental success.

Self-assessment question 16.5

Write a short report (around one sheet of A4) critically analysing a couple of sample objectives from your organisation, bearing in mind your responses to learning activity 16.5 above. You may include other problems in the analysis if you feel they are important

Feedback on page 272

16.6 Feedback, audit and review of the objective-setting process

Regular review will help to validate the objective-setting process and ensure that both manager and employee treat it seriously. It will also provide advance notice of any difficulties or problems that the employee is experiencing, and allow the manager or the employee to change the objective in the light of real world developments.

Learning activity 16.6

Identify the key points in regard to review and feedback on objectives from the following short scenario.

Oliver is a new buyer (9 months in post). He has inherited an objective to improve the lead time on some pumps kept in stock for ready-use spares. He was previously a stationery buyer. These pumps are critical items and during his investigations he discovers that the long lead time is caused partly by major problems with the single supplier used. During his first review in month 8 the topic is discussed, but he doesn't mention the cause, as he feels this will look as though he is trying to avoid coming up with good ideas and is just blaming the supplier.

Three months later (month 12) the supplier fails, and there is a temporary supply crisis with lost production for his company. His manager calls for a review in the next month, at which this will be discussed.

Feedback on page 273

Feedback should be a two-way process: the employee needs to know how the manager sees his or her performance, and the manager needs to know whether the employee is experiencing difficulties or problems.

Provided the atmosphere is right, there should be useful feedback during appraisal review sessions, and the manager should ensure that whenever possible this includes some positive elements as well as any negative ones.

Feedback should generally be:

- Precise: Both manager and employee should avoid speaking in general terms, as what they say could be interpreted in different ways. This will make it more difficult to achieve any correction or change.
- Timely: As soon as possible after the poor (or outstanding) performance or behaviour has taken place, or when there is a major issue around one of the objectives.
- Impersonal: Criticism of personal traits should be avoided unless essential: it can cause emotional reactions that are both undesirable and obscure the main issue
- Given often: Understanding of performance is enhanced when there is frequent review, and when feedback is received early enough to identify problems in achieving goals.

As well as the day-to-day feedback from appraisal meetings it is also necessary for the organisation to review and perhaps audit the operation of the entire measurement and appraisal process. This will help ensure that:

- The organisational and employee benefits are being obtained.

16

- No major problems are occurring.
- The scheme is up to date and relevant.
- The necessary outcomes are being dealt with effectively.

Organisations with the Investors in People award are under a requirement for senior management to undertake such checks and audits.

Self-assessment question 16.6

Arrange the following measurement process steps in a suggested correct sequence:

1   Appraisal meetings take place.
2   Senior management review and audit progress and outcomes.
3   Manager and employee agree/confirm job roles and responsibilities.
4   Manager and employee discuss/propose individual objectives.
5   Manager ensures employee understanding of corporate business direction and departmental objectives.
6   Manager and employee agree evaluation criteria and appraisal meeting outputs.
7   Manager and employee agree appraisal timetable and process.
8   Manager evaluates feedback from appraisal/measurement process.
9   Manager and employee agree and sign off objectives.

Feedback on page 273

Revision question

Now try the revision question for this session on page 335.

Summary

In this study session we have seen:

- How objective-setting should be part of an overall cascade of planning and performance measurement, beginning at the top of the organisation. Without this the objective-setting process will lack real focus.
- How to write well-structured objectives using the SMART criteria, and some of the problems that can arise when objective-setting does not happen properly.
- How failure to feed back and review can negatively affect the objective-setting process.
- Although sometimes managing through objectives may lack flexibility, or convey a 'command and control' image, it can be very useful when properly applied with these limitations in mind.
-

Feedback on learning activities and self-assessment questions

Feedback on learning activity 16.1

Benefits could include:

- a good information 'cascade'
- realistic and acceptable objectives
- involvement of employees
- feedback to management
- agreed measurement criteria.

Feedback on self-assessment question 16.1

You should have found words close to or equivalent to the following:

focused – business-driven – effective – bespoke – involvement – morale – feedback – improve

Feedback on learning activity 16.2

You should demonstrate that there is some link between your department's aims and objectives and those of the organisation. Preferably this should include reference to organisational documents such as annual reports, business plans and mission statements.

Your own objectives should also clearly 'fit' within this process.

Feedback on self-assessment question 16.2

Your essay should track the cascade process described above, as applied in your own organisation. You may decided that not all the stages described are applicable: if so, it would be equally interesting to know why they do not apply in your organisation.

Feedback on learning activity 16.3

You should have identified two example objectives from your organisation and have provided a short analysis of their effectiveness or otherwise, measured both against the main content of an objective and against the SMART criteria.

Feedback on self-assessment question 16.3

Table 16.4

Objective 1: To achieve savings of around 10% across all your contracts during the financial year subject to progress review at two- monthly intervals.	
	Comment
Specific	OK, but could perhaps define what type of saving
Measurable	Easy to measure provided data is available. Yes provided the data is available
Achievable	Yes – he owns the contracts and has a wide spread of authority

(continued on next page)

16

Table 16.4 *(continued)*

Objective 1: To achieve savings of around 10% across all your contracts during the financial year subject to progress review at two- monthly intervals.

	Comment
Realistic	Perhaps not - the contracts are already very well priced
Timed	Good – clearly states regularity of review

Table 16.5

Objective 2 – To improve the service provided to the catering department in response to complaints received on quality and payment of invoices by the end of July

	Comment
Specific	Reasonable in pointing at the broad objective
Measurable	Harder to measure, perhaps using reduced complaints. Poor overall
Achievable	Not clear. The contracts are his responsibility, but some of the issues, eg invoicing, may not be
Realistic	Not as written, though he could obviously make a contribution
Timed	Very precise

Other comments could include the following:

- Two-monthly review conveys priority on savings.
- 14 objectives may be an overload.
- Objectives may need more detail; they look rushed.

Feedback on learning activity 16.4

Your outlines should identify different timescales (or explain why they are all the same), and pick out which aspects of your job, environment and department have different timescales and why.

Feedback on self-assessment question 16.4

1   TRUE. It is the job of the objectives set at senior level to give direction to the business over longer timescales.
2   FALSE. Operational buyers generally work on day-to-day through to medium-term timescales.
3   TRUE. Although most objectives will be short-term, it may benefit the individual to have, say, one objective that runs over a longer period of time.
4   FALSE. Successful companies get the day-to-day right, but they are driven by good medium-term and long-term planning.
5   TRUE. Dedicated teams can be very effective, but sometimes they can make the planning an end in itself.

Feedback on learning activity 16.5

You should be able to identify at least two or three examples from your own experience.

Feedback on self-assessment question 16.5

You should evaluate by using the above list of problems and identifying new ones if relevant.

Feedback on learning activity 16.6

Key points should include the following:

- Did the buyer have the chance to feed back?
- Was the 8-month delay acceptable?
- Should the buyer have asked for a review?
- Should a critical item have been reviewed more often?
- Feedback was not given to the manager, who could have taken action.
- Is the final review too late?

Feedback on self-assessment question 16.6

The response should be broadly in the following order:

5 – 3 – 4 – 6 – 9 – 7 – 1 – 8 – 2

16

Appraisal and evaluation techniques

Introduction

Does this sound familiar? This session focuses on the appraisal process and interview – still very common in many organisations – which can be a stressful experience for many employees (and some managers).

Session learning objectives

After completing this session you should be able to:

17.1 Describe informal and formal appraisal and evaluation techniques.
17.2 Evaluate the benefits of a quantitative or qualitative approach.
17.3 Explain the main components and issues in an interview-based appraisal process.
17.4 Summarise the self-assessment approach to appraisal.
17.5 Propose the involvement of others in the appraisal process.
17.6 Define the issues that can arise if the appraisal process fails to work effectively.

Unit content coverage

This study session covers the following topics from the official CIPS unit content document:

Statement of practice

- Categorise types of performance measures that are available to supply chain managers.

Learning objective

3.2 Explain how appraisal and evaluation techniques can be employed to measure and improve performance.
   - Periodic reviews
   - Informal and formal appraisals

Prior knowledge

You should have read study sessions 15 and 16. Some personal experience will be beneficial, especially experience of appraisal interviews.

It's that time of year again, and your organisation has gone into performance measurement frenzy. There's panic to complete the appraisal process and sign off this year's objectives, and a hectic round of appraisal interviews for all concerned.

17

Resources

No specific resources are required, but you may find it useful to discuss this issue with other students or colleagues.

Timing

You should set aside about 5.75 hours to read and complete this session, including learning activities, self-assessment questions, the suggested further reading (if any) and the revision question.

17.1 Formal and informal appraisal and evaluation techniques

In many organisations, appraisal includes an interview, typically between the line manager and the employee. These interviews take different forms but in broad terms we can identify two extremes of formality in interview structure (see figure 17.1).

Figure 17.1: Two extremes of formality in interview structure

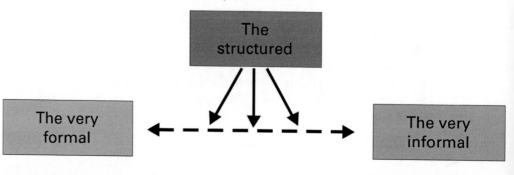

Learning activity 17.1

Look at your organisation, and make brief notes on the degree of formality in the appraisal or measurement process for buying staff. What strengths and weaknesses result from this choice?

Feedback on page 285

Formal

Formal interviews are often included in organisation-wide appraisal schemes, which typically have fairly tight rules and requirements, precise written objectives, set interview requirements and standards for measurement of achievement. Such schemes often include a requirement to keep records for administration purposes.

There may also be guidelines on the interview structure, and the minimum interview timetable is often dictated by the rules. For example, there may be a requirement for at least four interviews per year.

In the formal interview the buyer and his or her manager are more likely to attempt to use scoring mechanisms as part of the evaluation process, and this can be likened to the vendor rating used for suppliers. Good preparation is needed for this type of interview to work effectively.

Informal

This appraisal process will be far less structured and disciplined, and is often based on regular day-to-day discussion or shorter, more relaxed meetings. Undertaken well, this can still be very demanding, and is well suited to organisations where employees are able to demonstrate their progress without significant preparation. Equally, however, informal systems can simply hand control to the manager to praise and reward as he or she sees fit.

The paperwork content is likely to be minimal, or absent all together.

Structured

This represents a balance of the above two approaches, with a minimum of control and formality but designed to avoid the ad hoc nature of the informal system.

Self-assessment question 17.1

Fill in the blanks in the following text:

Mr Johnson is manager of a small printing company with two buyers. He favours a formal system of measuring their performance with precise _____ objectives, set _____ requirements and standards for _____ of achievement. He has also taken steps to produce _____ on interview _____ and technique.

He is aware that this can make the interviews quite _____, and therefore he tries to ensure that the atmosphere is as _____ as possible when he meets with the buyers.

Feedback on page 286

17.2 Quantitative and qualitative measurement approaches

As when we are evaluating supplier performance, the measures used to evaluate buyers' achievement of their targets and objectives may fall into two categories – quantitative and qualitative.

We need to understand the difference between these, and how this can affect the appraisal process.

17

Learning activity 17.2

Look at your objectives or those of a colleague, and make brief notes that assess the balance between quantitative and qualitative objectives.

(continued on next page)

Learning activity 17.2 *(continued)*

Does your organisation tend to favour one or the other, or is the balance about right?

Feedback on page 286

Table 17.1 shows some of the main characteristics of each approach.

Table 17.1 Quantitative and qualitative measures

Quantitative measures	Qualitative measures
Based around numbers and values	Based around quality or service issues
Objective and measurable	Subjective and less easy to measure
Easily turned into targets	Difficult to turn into targets
More task orientated	Designed to measure satisfaction and service rather than efficiency at tasks
Common where purchasing is seen as a process driven or clerical activity	More likely where purchasing is seen as a key contributor
Focus on efficiency and improvement (in numbers)	Focus on perception, effectiveness and contribution
Examples	Examples
1 To increase the number of orders processed from an average of 4 to 5 per hour	1 To strive for significant improvement in relationships with key internal customers
2 To increase business margin from 21% to 25% over 12 months through better procurement	2 To improve product quality over a range of goods

Most purchasing teams will be exposed to a mix of these measures, and indeed this is often desirable. If the appraisal process is very demanding, or is linked to rewards, employees may well prefer quantitative measures if they feel measurement will be easier or more accurate.

Self-assessment question 17.2

Give True or False responses to the following statements on timescales for objectives:

1 Quantitative measures are concerned with numbers and data; qualitative measures are concerned with facts and opinions. TRUE/FALSE
2 Qualitative measures are usually easier to turn into targets. TRUE/FALSE
3 Failure to obtain good data is more likely to cause problems in quantitative measurements. TRUE/FALSE
4 Task-related functions tend to be measured using qualitative measures. TRUE/FALSE
5 Quantitative measures may be preferred by employees when bonus payments are involved. TRUE/FALSE

Feedback on page 286

17.3 Interview-based appraisal

The interview is by far the most popular way of undertaking formal appraisal. This interview is an important part of the process, but it is one that both parties – employee and manager – can find difficult. Although the term 'interview' is most frequently used, the general aim should be to have a relaxed atmosphere, and a supportive approach from the manager.

Of course, managers undertake many sorts of interview, and it is important that the right style be used in appraisals in order to get the best results. Some of the different styles that could be used are listed below:

- Interrogative/forceful
  - Used in a disciplinary session, or when interviewing a difficult supplier.
  - The interviewer is an interrogator, and has total control, which may have to be exercised in a forceful way.
  - Very inappropriate as a style for appraisals.
- Planned/directive
  - Used in job interviews, and with suppliers and customers.
  - The interviewer has an agenda, but tries to guide the process positively, rather than exerting control directly – to steer the direction the interview takes, but not try to control the whole process.
  - Might be suitable in a very formal appraisal session. Not ideal.
- Loose/relaxed
  - Typical style for appraisals, counselling and personal issues.
  - The interviewer tries to create a sympathetic 'partnership' relationship with the employee, to reduce the possibility of friction or tension, and help ensure the individual feels able to contribute. There is a minimum of direct control, but a result is needed, and the employee must have a large input.
  - The style to aim for in appraisals.

Learning activity 17.3

Reflect on what you have now read about interview style. Prepare a short comparison between the theory and any practical examples or situations in which you have taken part.

Feedback on page 286

We can break an appraisal interview down into three main stages:

Before the interview

17

- Plan and prepare for the interview. Failure to do this is a common cause of difficulty in appraisals.
- Identify new objectives, remembering the links to the business planning process. You may have to do some 'negotiation' in the interview.
- Review existing objectives and form your view of progress. You may need to ask for data to be available.
- Review last year's interview notes, especially if you do not know the other person well.
- Book rooms and appointments.

The interview

- Must be in private, with as few interruptions and distractions as possible.
- The atmosphere should be informal, but performance improvement and problem solving should be the main item for discussion.
- Managers must give employees adequate time to speak, allowing them to describe their performance throughout the year.
- Data should be tabled and agreed.
- A set of objectives with performance targets should be produced, or drafted for completion at a later session.
- Changes and amendments to the objectives can be discussed and agreed.
- Notes should be kept as required.

After the interview

- Notes should be written up and agreed. Both parties will keep their own notes.
- Unagreed points can be confirmed.
- Actions can be set in place.

The outcomes from the interview should include:

- A clear view of the employee's performance over the period concerned.
- A recommendation for reward or for counselling/development.
- A review of the objectives and the job, with changes to both objectives and job descriptions as required.
- Feedback from both parties on the wider view of the business.
- Identification of skill and knowledge gaps that may need training or development.

This last point is important: one of the great benefits of a sound appraisal system is the input it provides to the development of training. (See study session 18.)

Self-assessment question 17.3

Fill in the blanks in the following text:

The HR department at Company X is very concerned about some aspects of the appraisal interview process. At least one manager has adopted the wrong _____ in interviews, being rather _____, which employees feel is inappropriate for these interviews.

Several other managers are failing to undertake the necessary pre-interview _____, and some have not held interviews in _____ owing to a failure to_____ _____.

_____ are not being taken, and the necessary _____ from both parties is often missing.

Feedback on page 286

17

17.4 Self-assessment

Self-assessment is the process by which an individual assesses his or her performance either as part of, or instead of, a wider evaluation process. Typically self-assessment will involve a form or questionnaire in order to ensure consistency for all participants. Usually the outcome will be evaluated by the line manager or an appointed group.

Self-assessment builds on the employee's undoubted knowledge of his or her own personal strengths and weaknesses and as such should create a more open and honest appraisal. However in practice employees usually find it difficult to be objective and often either under or over estimate their performance.

Learning activity 17.4

Reflect on whether you think self-assessment could work in your department or organisation, and prepare a short management report on your views. (If it is already in use, report on how successful you feel it is.)

Feedback on page 286

There are several points to consider in regard to self-assessment:

- It can feed a bigger process, where the self-assessment becomes part of the preparation work that the employee should be undertaking anyway.
- It can be rigid in application. If the self-assessment uses a rating or measuring system it can create a very mechanistic or 'tick box' approach to performance measurement.
- It can be useful for training and professional development. Self-assessment is particularly useful in helping to identify skill gaps and training and professional development opportunities.
- Filling in forms, especially if they are complex, is usually unpopular.
- It is hard to avoid personal bias, and if rewards are linked to the appraisal process then staff may have a vested interest in overstating their success.

When self-assessment replaces an interview this may remove a difficult stage from the process. However, it can also remove an opportunity for feedback and relationship-building as well.

The content of a self-appraisal form will vary, but typically it will be a mix of verbal responses, numbers and dates. It is also common for such forms to include simple rating of the '1 equals low, 6 equals high' type. There may be sections for each level of management who will sign the form.

Typical content of the form might include:

- the key objectives
- the progress made on each objective
- appropriate numbers for measuring progress
- perceived skill shortages or training needs

17

- personal initiatives outside the main objective process
- a signing-off section for all participants
- a rating section for the manager.

Self-assessment question 17.4

Fill in the blanks in the following text:

It is always difficult to assess the value of self-assessment in performance measurement. When it is _____ of a wider scheme it forms part of the employees' _____, and it is also extremely useful for assessing _____ gaps and _____ needs.

On the other hand it often means completing a _____, which can be unpopular, and _____ _____ can often make the results less satisfactory.

Simple forms often include a numerical _____ system, and different levels of _____ may need to sign off the forms. The whole process can create a '_____ _____' mentality towards performance management

Feedback on page 287

17.5 Involving others in the appraisal process

Most appraisal takes place down the line management structure. There is nothing wrong with this, but the wider performance management concept discussed in study session 15 envisages other inputs to this process. In particular, it envisages input from those who can be considered as 'stakeholders' of the purchasing department.

(Stakeholders can be defined as groups with similar characteristics who have a 'stake' in a particular issue, function or organisation. For example, passenger groups can be considered as a stakeholder for a transport company.)

Learning activity 17.5

Write a management report on how other stakeholders could be (or already are) involved in performance measurement of buyers in your organisation. You may wish to discuss this with your manager.

Feedback on page 287

Some potential stakeholders for purchasing and supply staff are listed below:

- Team and/or peer input
    - Used for many years in education and the military.
    - Peers often have unique first-hand knowledge, which supervisors do not.

- Must be handled carefully, as it can cause stress, bad relationships and undesirable competition.
- Internal customer input
  - Particularly useful when assessing staff or functions that provide a service, for example expeditors or stores staff.
  - The manager may obtain useful performance appraisal data, such as whether the internal customers' needs are being met promptly, courteously, and accurately.
- Suppliers
  - If the organisation is keen to improve relationships with suppliers, their input can provide a very different focus to the appraisal.
  - Many buyers have been surprised by what suppliers say about them and their organisation.
  - However, suppliers may tend to say 'nice things' to avoid upsetting their customers.
- Other stakeholders
  - Could include senior managers, board members, end customers, trade unions etc
  - The principle is that the stakeholder should be involved because their input provides a useful and different contribution to the appraisal process for purchasing staff.
- Junior staff
  - Unsurprisingly not especially common, but can be applicable in organisations that place a premium on good employee relationships, or where very close teamwork is common.
  - Would need very careful design and management to work effectively.

Self-assessment question 17.5

Give True or False responses to the following statements on stakeholders:

1 Stakeholders are generally people with shares in an organisation. TRUE/FALSE
2 Stakeholders have always been involved in the performance measurement of buyers. TRUE/FALSE
3 Involving junior staff as stakeholders is best suited to organisations with strong trade unions. TRUE/FALSE
4 Internal customers can provide a valuable insight into buyers' performance. TRUE/FALSE
5 Suppliers' input may tend to be distorted for fear of avoiding upsetting a buyer. TRUE/FALSE

Feedback on page 287

17

17.6 Problems with the appraisal process

If the appraisal process is not undertaken properly, there are two major consequences:

- The employee fails to be motivated, and begins to lose confidence in the whole process, perhaps seeing it as a management 'game'.

- The organisation fails to gain the benefits it seeks, which include employee participation and empowerment. Ultimately it also begins to see a fall-off in performance and a failure to achieve targets.

Learning activity 17.6

Arrange the following list of statements in order of priority in terms of the problems you feel they cause in an appraisal process. Show the biggest problem first.

Give a brief explanation of your reasoning for the order you have chosen.

The problems of poor appraisal can include the following:

1. The rewards in our systems are not worth the effort we put in.
2. We often lack the data we need for measuring performance.
3. Our interview techniques are poor, and need improving.
4. There is favouritism and unfairness in our appraisal process.
5. A failure of the 'cascade' of communication means we sometimes do not know how our objectives relate to the business objectives.
6. Failure to prepare is a major problem in our appraisal process.

Feedback on page 287

The problems of poor appraisal can include the following:

- Failure to prepare. The interview dates are adhered to, but very little preparation is undertaken. Significant harm is done if only one party has devoted a lot of time to preparation.
- Favouritism and unfairness. The good manager will make every attempt to avoid this, but appraisal is an emotive time, and managers must be prepared for such feelings even where they are not justified. It may be helpful to document the process.
- Poor interview techniques. Many managers do not like this type of interview, and consequently are not good at it.
- The process becomes mechanistic. The danger in regulated systems is that, over time, a comfortable process can develop, but there is little real achievement.
- Failure of the 'cascade' of communication. The best systems have a good relationship between appraisal and organisational targets, but this is frequently a weak link in many systems.
- Failure to follow up. Often interviews can reveal skill shortages and weakness, for example a need for some negotiation training, but there is no follow-up, and the training is not provided.
- Lack of data. Systems fail to provide the data necessary to allow the achievement of targets to be measured.
- Inappropriate rewards. Where appraisal is used as part of the reward system, managers must ensure that employees can receive large enough pay increases. Well-structured and managed appraisal processes that lead to very small rewards may be perceived as not worthwhile.
- Trading success. Employees frequently try to trade off success in some objectives against failure in others. Although this is understandable,

17

objectives are set against business needs, and cannot be substituted in this manner except when formalised as part of the review process.

Self-assessment question 17.6

Analyse the following short case study, and identify possible problems and any plus points.

Sam is attending his end of financial year appraisal interview on Tuesday 30 April, after having returned from two weeks' sick leave.

This interview has been postponed twice, (once in March, because the manager had to cancel at the last minute, and two weeks before, when Sam went off sick), and there is now some pressure to have the meeting.

Through no fault of his own, Sam has had a lot of sickness this year, and he is worried, as he has not achieved all his targets, and his manager doesn't always appear sympathetic. However, Sam has some very good data on all aspects of his performance, and he believes that he has exceeded a couple of targets. He feels that this may help him against those targets that he has not done so well in.

Feedback on page 287

Revision question

Now try the revision question for this session on page 336.

Summary

In this session we have considered various surrounding the appraisal and evaluation process, especially appraisal interviews, which are still a core component of many performance measurement schemes for buyers. We have also considered:

- self-assessment
- the inclusion of other stakeholders in the process
- the problems that can occur during appraisal.

Suggested further reading

Students may enjoy Goodworth (1989) which, though quite old, makes a number of good points in a humorous way.

Feedback on learning activities and self-assessment questions

Feedback on learning activity 17.1

Your notes should show:

- Whether your organisation leans to the formal or the informal.

17

- The strengths and weaknesses of this approach.
- Some examples to illustrate the process.

Feedback on self-assessment question 17.1

You should be able to identify the following words from the text:

written – interview – measurement – guidelines – structure – difficult – relaxed

Feedback on learning activity 17.2

Your notes should show some objectives, with your comments on whether they are quantitative or qualitative measures. You should also indicate how you see the balance, and why.

Feedback on self-assessment question 17.2

1   TRUE
2   FALSE. They work more on subjective judgements, and are therefore harder to turn into targets.
3   TRUE. Quantitative data is more dependent on numbers.
4   FALSE. Tasks are often more suited to quantitative measures.
5   TRUE. There should be less scope for disagreement with quantitative measures.

Feedback on learning activity 17.3

Your comparisons should bring out some of the issues around:

- The different interview styles, and whether they were wrongly applied.
- The structure of the process, and whether it was broadly followed.
- Whether there were good outcomes from the process.

Feedback on self-assessment question 17.3

You should have the following words:

style – interrogative – planning – private – book rooms – notes – feedback

Feedback on learning activity 17.4

You should provide a view as to why you feel self-assessment will or will not work in your organisation or department. This could include the following points:

- as part of a wider process
- rigidity or formality in application
- use in training and professional development
- problems of personal bias
- lack of interview – a good or bad thing.

17

Feedback on self-assessment question 17.4

You should have identified the following

part – preparation – skill – training – form – personal bias – rating – management – tick-box

Feedback on learning activity 17.5

There is no set response. You should identify some groups who could be involved, and show the contribution they could (or do) make.

Feedback on self-assessment question 17.5

1 FALSE. Stakeholders can generally be defined as groups with similar characteristics who have a 'stake' in a particular issue, function or organisation.
2 FALSE. Involving stakeholders is a relatively new idea in most organisations.
3 FALSE. It is best suited to organisations that place a premium on good employee relationships.
4 TRUE. Customers' perceptions are tremendously important but often overlooked.
5 TRUE. Supplier input is valuable, but care must be taken to check its validity

Feedback on learning activity 17.6

There is no one right answer, but a good order would be: 4 – 6 – 2 – 5 – 3 – 1.

Number (4) is first, because any perceived favouritism and unfairness will cause the whole scheme to be badly viewed by staff (and by some managers). Following this is number (6), because failure to prepare is always likely to be a major problem. Lack of data (2) causes many problems, as does (5), failure of the objective 'cascade' process. Poor interviewing (3) is relatively easy to improve with practice and training, and inadequate rewards (1) are rarely a 'showstopper' in practice.

Feedback on self-assessment question 17.6

Your responses could include the following:

- Cancellation by the manager at this stage in the year should have been avoided. Had the March session gone ahead, there would be far less pressure.
- Sam has had little chance to prepare for the Tuesday interview, which might have been better later in the week. (Of course, he should have prepared for the earlier sessions.)
- Lack of sympathy in a manager may be common, because sickness and absence cause operational problems. However, this does not mean that the manager is likely to be unfair in his treatment of Sam.

17

- Sam has done well to get good data. This will always be helpful in this type of interview, whether it reveals a good or a bad result.
- Exceeding expectations on a couple of objectives is good, but not if it is at the expense of the other objectives. Sam is being optimistic to hope for a trade here, as the organisation is not getting the results it requires.

17

Study session 18

Training and staff development

Introduction

Thirty years ago people worked for the company; now they work for themselves. Organisations need to recognise that different employees are motivated in different ways: some by their career aspirations, some by reward, and many others who just want to do a good job and contribute usefully to the organisation.

By continuously helping to develop their employees' skills and assisting them in achieving their aspirations, managers are also enabling the organisation to achieve its business objectives.

'If hard work were such a wonderful thing, surely the rich would have kept it all to themselves.'
Lane Kirkland

Session learning objectives

After completing this session you should be able to:

18.1 Describe the stages and benefits of developing a training needs analysis (TNA).
18.2 Distinguish between job profiles and job descriptions, and how they influence a TNA.
18.3 Argue the benefits of focused rather than non-focused approaches to training and staff development.
18.4 Summarise the different types of training available.
18.5 Explain the concept of continuous professional development.
18.6 Evaluate the success of training for the individual and for the business.

Unit content coverage

This study session covers the following topics from the official CIPS unit content document:

Statements of practice

- Explain how measuring performance in supply chain activities fits into the overall management process of an organisation.
- Evaluate the benefits of implementing a well-structured approach to measuring organisational, functional and individual performance.

Learning objective

3.5 Evaluate and explain the use of a range of techniques to analyse the training needs of individual buyers.
- Job profiles
- Key objectives

- Performance measures
- Appraisals

Prior knowledge

You should have read study sessions 15, 16 and 17. Some previous experience of participating in organised training courses will also be of benefit.

Resources

No specific resources are required, but you may find it useful to discuss this issue with other students or colleagues, and with your training department or responsible manager.

Timing

You should set aside about 6 hours to read and complete this session, including learning activities, self-assessment questions, the suggested further reading (if any) and the revision question.

18.1 Developing a training needs analysis

In many organisations training is a 'scattergun' process. When an organisation makes a positive attempt to structure training, based on what is needed to help the employees achieve the organisation's business goals, the result is a training needs analysis (TNA). The TNA process concentrates on matching the skills of the individual with the needs of the organisation. The result shows strengths, which can then be utilised, and weaknesses, which can be dealt with through training and development programmes.

Learning activity 18.1

Reflect on the approach that your organisation takes to analysing staff training and development needs, and prepare a short critical outline of the good and bad points. You may find it useful to talk to colleagues and your training department.

Feedback on page 302

18

Often an organisation's training needs are identified through the activities shown in figure 18.1. Of these, the data from the appraisal interview is the key, because it allows for a two-way comparison between what the organisation requires from the employee and whether the employee understands his or her roles and responsibilities.

Figure 18.1: Identifying training requirements

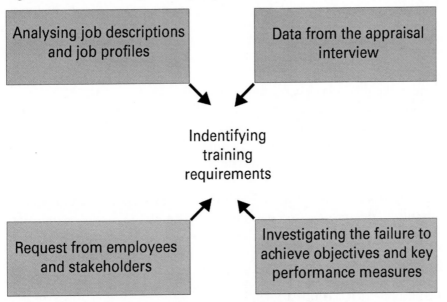

The information obtained can be analysed, and particular areas of weakness can be identified and remedied. This is specialist work, and it may require input from the human resources or training departments.

When the 'normal' processes shown in figure 18.1 are not working well, information on training needs will be poor. There may also be a need to establish a longer-term training plan, or to set a **benchmark**, perhaps after a restructuring or before a major change in direction. (A benchmark is a target that is established – benchmarked – and against which performance can be compared. It is often used in comparisons between organisations.)

In this case a special training needs analysis may be required, and this can be undertaken in various ways. Two common methods are by self-assessment and by interview, as follows:

- Self-assessment
  - Using a questionnaire to establish how employees see their own skill base and training needs, and to identify strengths and weaknesses.
  - Relatively easy to organise, but results can be subject to personal bias, and can easily form a 'wish list'.
- Interview based (internally or externally led)
  - Employees attend an interview similar to an appraisal interview, to discuss their strengths and weaknesses.
  - This is led by a manager or delegated member of staff. In order to encourage open discussion it is usually best if this is not the line manager.
  - Employee and interviewer discuss and agree the areas of strengths and weaknesses. Difficulties with this approach are the possible lack of open discussion, and the amount of management time required.
  - External interviewers, perhaps from a training or consultancy firm, can be used. This is more expensive, but can be faster, and it helps to ensure the open debate that is necessary.

18

In general, the steps in arranging a TNA are as follows:

1 Agree the method to be used (and recruit external interviewers if you need to).
2 Agree the group(s) of staff involved.
3 Agree and prioritise the areas of performance and the skills and competences that the organisation requires (that is, the desired benchmark).
4 Undertake the interviews or self-assessment.
5 Compare the results with the benchmark requirements, and identify any major problem areas (the skills gaps).
6 Devise and implement suitable training to remedy these skill gaps.
7 Review and feed back as appropriate.

A TNA can be a complex process, but if it is well managed, it can provide good results and a training and development programme that is capable of driving a business for several years.

Self-assessment question 18.1

Draft a management-type report on how training needs are (or could be) assessed within your organisation, with a shortlist or timetable of actions required.

Feedback on page 302

18.2 Job profiles, job descriptions and their influence on a TNA

A **job profile** defines the skills and abilities necessary for the successful performance of a job. A **job description** defines – both for the organisation and for the employees – all the essential functions of the job.

Job profiles and job descriptions can make a major contribution both to the appraisal process and to a training needs analysis. They do this by defining what the job is, what the expected outcomes are, and the key skills, knowledge and attributes that it is believed are necessary to do the job well.

Job descriptions and job profiles are both used extensively in recruiting staff, as well as in appraisal and performance management.

Learning activity 18.2

Compare your job description with the list of contents in table 18.1. Note any significant points of difference and any useful additions, and state whether you feel these have a positive or negative effect on your job. (If you

(continued on next page)

Learning activity 18.2 *(continued)*

do not have a job description, ask a colleague or friend to work with you – it does not need to be purchasing-related)

Table 18.1

Model	Included in my job description? Y/N	Comment
Job title		
Job outline and position in the organisation		
List of essential activities (prioritised if appropriate)		
Specific output measures (if appropriate)		
Reporting relationships		
Other working relationships		
Size of budget or impact of job		
Tools and technology to be used		
List specific behaviours that might be required		
Conditions of service, and pay issues		

Feedback on page 302

Job profile (sometimes called job specification)

This defines the skills and abilities that are needed to perform the job successfully. The following are typically included in a job profile:

- The knowledge, skills and abilities required to perform the task, together with some indication of the degree of ability required. These are often known as the key competences, and they are very important when developing a TNA.
- Any educational requirements, usually stated as 'a minimum of...' or 'must be studying for...'. This is useful if the TNA is to cover educational requirements and qualifications.
- The level of experience required, often including the markets and industries, and perhaps with stipulated time periods in each area of experience. May also refer to skills gained and tasks accomplished during these employments. Useful in the TNA because it can help highlight experience gaps.
- Any professional certificates or training required, often including evidence of continuous professional development. This is useful if the TNA is to include professional development requirements.

The job profile therefore provides a very useful checklist when preparing a TNA, as well as being used in short-listing and selection activities. Job profiles need to be updated over time – as do job descriptions.

Job description

This defines – both for the organisation and the employee – all the essential functions of a job, and also what makes it different from other jobs.

18

293

Job descriptions have sometimes had a bad press, accompanied by images of employees waving a piece of paper and stating, 'It's not in my job description.'

In reality this is more an issue of morale and industrial relations. However, managers must appreciate that, having gone into some detail to explain the content of a job description to an employee, it is necessary to take equal care when explaining the need for changes and developments.

Table 18.2 shows the contents of a typical job description.

Table 18.2 Job descriptions

Content	Contribution to TNA
Job title	A broad indication of the nature of the job
Job outline and position in the organisation	Helps outline the broad skills required and wider reporting relationships
List of essential activities (prioritised if appropriate)	Helps determine the core skills that will be needed
Specific output measures (if appropriate)	Helps determine some specific skills that will be needed
Reporting relationships	Contributes to communication skills needs
Other working relationships	Contributes to communication skills needs
Size of budget or impact of job	Indicates a need for financial skills
Tools and technology to be used	Indicates a need for technical skills
List specific behaviours that might be required	Picks up more specialist skills that may be needed
Conditions of service and pay issues	N/A

Job descriptions are extensively used in recruitment, but often they are not updated in line with organisational developments. As a result, it is not uncommon for different employees doing the same job to have different job descriptions.

Self-assessment question 18.2

Fill in the blanks in the following text:

In most businesses both job _____ and job _____ can provide good inputs for the development of a _____ _____ _____. They are also very useful documents in the _____ process: the job _____ is especially useful to the interviewers and the job _____ to the interviewee. In the past, job _____ have sometimes been misused, and it is essential that both documents are _____ regularly to keep pace with changes in the organisation.

Feedback on page 302

18.3 Focused versus non-focused training and development

We have seen that, if an organisation has the necessary activities in place, training needs flow out of a well-managed process, which is itself directly linked to the organisation's needs and objectives. We may consider this

18

to be a process in which the organisation – from the senior management down – has focused on training, and on the need to make it work for the organisation.

Learning activity 18.3

Consider the above statement, and then prepare a short report on whether you feel the process of determining training requirements in your organisation can be considered as 'focused'. You may wish to talk with your manager or training department.

Feedback on page 303

Focused training

The advantages of adopting a focused approach to training are as follows:

- Employees are trained only in skills or competences that relate directly to their jobs or their role in the organisation. For example, they may be trained in word-processing because it is a skill they need in their job, *not* because it is part of the IT training package.
- Employees are trained only in areas in which they have a skills or knowledge gap. This allowing training to be targeted at individuals, and not at a group or department.
- Training can be targeted to address real weaknesses, rather than being generic in nature, because all those taking part have similar knowledge gaps. For example, in the public sector negotiation training needs to concentrate on internal negotiation rather than supplier negotiation.
- The results from the analysis are very helpful in course development, which ensures that trainers deliver less generic training.
- Training budgets can be utilised better. Without this type of approach many people receive training that provides little benefit – a clear waste of money and time.
- Identifying staff or departments with skills gaps will also identify those with particular strengths in any given area of activity. This means that internal resources can often be used to supplement or replace external training.

Unfocused training

In many organisations training is unfocused, and as a result is less effective than it should be. When training *does* take place, it may arises from various sources:

- As a result of an employee's request: 'I have seen this supplier-sourcing seminar advertised, and would like to attend.'
- As a result of a manager's initiative: 'I have seen this excellent course on supplier sourcing, and think we should send some people on it.'
- As a result of senior management policy: 'We always send all our people on supplier-sourcing courses, and they really benefit from it.'

18

- As a result of a training company sales push: 'We are organising training sessions on supplier sourcing, and think your staff would benefit.'

Sometimes training is rushed to ensure that a budget is spent, and as there is no internal guidance the first available courses are chosen. Whatever the source of the initiative, this type of unfocused training is less likely to achieve the results or to be as cost-effective for the organisation.

It is also debatable whether it is better than no training at all!

Self-assessment question 18.3

Give True or False responses to the following statements on training:

1 Sometimes training is rushed through to spend a budget. TRUE/FALSE
2 Providing training as a result of an employee's request is not a good way of choosing training. TRUE/FALSE
3 Senior management play no part in establishing focused training needs. TRUE/FALSE
4 Focused training allows skilled employees to become involved in training others. TRUE/FALSE
5 External trainers can develop good courses without TNA outputs. TRUE/FALSE

Feedback on page 303

18.4 The different types of training available

Once the training need has been identified, there are several different ways in which training can be provided, and a number of different sources of the training.

Job-based training

This is training that takes place in the job situation, generally using existing staff and resources. It may include:

- Orientation or induction of new employees. Good induction is recognised as a factor in developing employee morale in the first few days.
- Learning by doing ('sitting with Annie'). An employee picks up a job by trial and error or sits with another employee for a period. Still common, though not especially effective and can easily allow the passing on of bad practices.
- **Buddying**. Employees are allocated a 'buddy' with whom they can work and learn, usually at a similar level to themselves. This can be effective, especially in the early days, but some skill is needed to select the right people to place together.
- **Mentoring**. Development or training is provided by a more senior employee, or by an equal with greater skills in a particular area. This

can work very well where a gap analysis has shown both strengths and weaknesses in a team, and can also help build up good staff/management relationships

- Rotational. Employees move around the organisation learning different jobs and gaining a wider view of the business. This is used more in supervisor or management training, and may be best not undertaken until the employee has had some time to settle in and learn the business
- Involvement and practice. Many skills, such as negotiation, presentational skills and taking meetings, benefit from involvement and practice. Whenever possible management should arrange this for those employees who need it.

Specific skills-based

This is training aimed at learning how to do something specific, such as operate a new machine or computer program, or understand a new staff appraisal process. It may be an external course, or it may take place in the workplace. It is often delivered by external trainers, or by representatives of the supplier or installer involved.

Generic

This is training aimed at broadening generic skills used in the job, and which form a 'toolbox' for the employee that grows over time. In procurement, examples of such skills might include negotiation, cost price analysis or sourcing overseas. Generic training is often delivered by external trainers, and may be open access (available to all) or bespoke (tailored to one company or market). This type of training is often difficult to apply immediately in a job, and its real benefit is in developing a knowledge base that can be used when required.

Professional or academic

This is training based around the addition of formal educational requirements, such as GCSEs, A-levels, degrees or masters degrees. Typically it will be focused on a few individuals, and will be taken though a college or e-learning route. This category also includes professional exams such as those offered by CIPS, the principle procurement qualifications body in the UK.

Many organisations require employees of a certain grade and above to have a professional qualification.

Learning activity 18.4

Examine training and training courses that you have been on (or have been offered) and match them to the categories in this section.

Feedback on page 303

18

Now go on to tackle the following self-assessment question.

Self-assessment question 18.4

Give True or False responses to the following statements on the different types of training:

1   Nowadays experience is most important, and it is rare for organisations to expect buyers to have professional qualifications. TRUE/FALSE
2   The problem with generic training is that it is often hard to apply in the job. TRUE/FALSE
3   'Buddying' is the term for development or training provided by a more senior employee or an equal with greater skills. TRUE/FALSE
4   Externally sourced training is always better than internal training, but it is usually more expensive. TRUE/FALSE
5   Orientation of employees early on is a very useful training technique. TRUE/FALSE

Feedback on page 303

18.5 Continuous professional development

A manager who expects to use employees effectively over a long period must recognise that training and skill development is not a one-off exercise. Equally, employees, especially those wishing to progress their careers, must recognise the need to keep updating their skills, training and experience if they are to be attractive to an employer.

Indeed, for some professionals (doctors for example) this is compulsory, and is built into their contract of employment.

Also, under risk management requirements many organisations see **continuous professional development** (CPD) – the process of keeping skills, training knowledge and experience up to date – as a way of demonstrating that employees are competent in their jobs.

Learning activity 18.5

Reflect on what you have read, and comment on whether the concept of CPD could (or does) apply in your current position, and what benefits it could (or does) offer you and your employer. How would it work? You may wish to discuss this with your manager or HR department.

Feedback on page 303

The concept of CPD is based on formalising the need to constantly review and update knowledge and skills. This can be personally driven, or it can be organisationally or professionally driven.

Personally driven CPD

The employee or the manager takes it upon themselves to ensure this happens, by actively reviewing and refreshing their skills, or those of their employees, from time to time.

Organisationally or professionally driven CPD

In this case employees are part of a formal process, usually run by the employer or a professional body. Often there is a requirement to record a specific amount of development per year, and training courses often carry contribution ratings to help the individuals achieve their CPD ranking.

Typically CPD can be achieved through a mix of the following:

- your own efforts, using any available resources and activities such as audio/DVD/video tapes, books/publications, computer-based training and internet research
- professional association meetings and involvement
- evening courses or 'distance learning'
- seminars and workshops sponsored by academic bodies, professional associations and suppliers
- management training courses
- formal training programmes and courses
- site visits
- job rotation both inside and outside your own department
- acquiring additional qualifications including professional certificates, formal education or advanced degrees.

Self-assessment question 18.5

Fill in the blanks in the following text:

Continuous professional development is based on the need to constantly _____ and update _____ and _____ For employees this helps to keep them _____ to an employer; for an organisation it ensures that _____ from poor employee skills is minimised.

Even when an employer does not require it, employees can develop _____ CPD for themselves to keep _____ _____ _____ with their training and experience. In some professions, however, CPD is a _____ requirement.

Feedback on page 303

18.6 Evaluating the success of training

An organisation that is prepared to make a high level of commitment to training must be equally clear on the need to review and evaluate the success (or otherwise) of the training provided.

Unfortunately, it is difficult to evaluate the success of training, because it is often hard to apply quantitative measurement to the process. Also, the

18

amount of time required can be significant and costly. For these reasons many organisations do not evaluate training properly, and because of this they lose confidence in training, sometimes even abandoning projects while they are still running.

The value of training becomes harder to measure as its complexity increases. For example, it will be relatively easy to place a value on training employees to work a new procurement software system, but less easy to assess the value of negotiation training.

Learning activity 18.6

Reflect on what you read, and comment on the degree to which evaluation of training takes place in your organisation. Do you feel money is being wasted in this area? You may wish to talk to your manager or training department.

Feedback on page 304

A good training evaluation should answer a couple of reasonable questions:

- Is there evidence of a link between the training and a performance improvement?
- What is the bottom-line value to the organisation of the training (has it saved us more than it cost?)

Evaluation is also important because it can help in the design and delivery of future courses by providing clear feedback into the training planning process on the quality of the training undertaken. This ensures that the content of training courses is also the subject of continuous improvement, and helps when designing requirements and briefing training suppliers.

We can evaluate training in various ways:

- By asking participants: verbal feedback, usually on an informal basis. This needs recording and analysing to be of real value.
- By questionnaire: commonly done at the end of the training session to get a quick reaction. Needs to be done quickly, and not left for weeks. Often 'knee jerk' reactions prevail, and the job is rushed so that the attendee can leave.
- By discussion with the trainers: In particular, when external or funded training is provided there should be a follow-up to review the results.
- By a review group: a complex process, justifiable only on large training projects. The review may be by questionnaire or by interviews, or by a combination of the two. The training providers could be present.
- Through the appraisal process: This has the benefit of providing distance, and allowing the attendee to put the knowledge into practice.

A widely used model for training evaluation was devised by Donald Kirkpatrick (1975). This is a complex model, which basically attempts to evaluate training across four levels: reactions, learning, behaviour and results (see figure 18.2).

Figure 18.2: Kirkpatrick's model of training evaluation

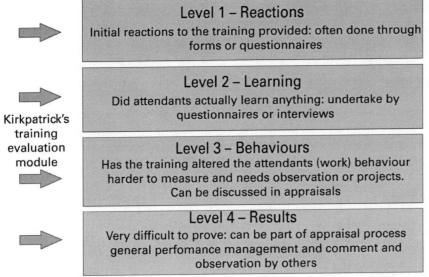

Source: Kirkpatrick (1975)

Obviously, training must deliver a return for the business, but there should be a benefit for the trainee as well. The benefits for the individual can be seen as:

- better, more enjoyable training
- responsibility and job satisfaction
- career opportunities and rewards
- skills and knowledge development.

Self-assessment question 18.6

Identify some potential issues and problems in the following statement, received confidentially from a purchasing manager:

'Our organisation has little time for the evaluation of training, which we feel is virtually impossible, except for easily measured skills such as using equipment or programs, or health and safety. We know external trainers sometimes ask for feedback, but we don't usually see this, and are not sure it would be helpful, as usually they simply want to show how well they have performed. Occasionally we do have complaints from delegates, and then we do not run the training again; however, we are always under pressure from HR to spend the training budget, so we often have to push a series of courses towards the end of the financial year.'

Feedback on page 304

18

Revision question

Now try the revision question for this session on page 336.

Summary

In this study session you have seen that training undertaken in an unfocused way is a waste of time and money, both for the organisation and for the employee. TNAs can provide this focus, and when they are combined with well-managed job profiles and job descriptions, and the encouragement of continuous professional development, there are great benefits to be gained for the organisation and the employee.

However, you have also seen that there is little point in doing all this without attempting to evaluate the success or otherwise of the training and development provided.

Suggested further reading

Students can find excellent references and checklists on training in Bailey (1997). A wide range of other useful information on training and staff development can be obtained by searching for 'training and staff development' through your web browser.

Students looking for more information on the subject of evaluation in general or on the Kirkpatrick training evaluation model should consider Kirkpatrick (1975) and Kirkpatrick and Kirkpatrick (2005).

Feedback on learning activities and self-assessment questions

Feedback on learning activity 18.1

You should show how training and development needs are assessed in your organisation, and whether or not this works well. Points to be brought out from this learning activity might include the following:

- Is there any type of formal or informal TNA process?
- If not, how is training developed in your organisation?
- What are the strengths and weaknesses?
- Any personal experience.

Feedback on self-assessment question 18.1

In learning activity 18.1 you identified how training is currently planned. This short report should turn this reflection into a management report that outlines some positive steps for improvement in your organisation.

Feedback on learning activity 18.2

Your responses should indicate which items are in your job description, with comments. You should also show useful additional items, and explain what you feel they add to the job description.

Feedback on self-assessment question 18.2

profiles – descriptions – training needs analysis – recruitment – profile – description – descriptions – updated –

Feedback on learning activity 18.3

Your response should bring out the nature of the training you (or your colleagues) have had to date, and whether you felt it fitted the definition of focused training or not.

Feedback on self-assessment question 18.3

1 TRUE. Many organisations cannot carry over training expenditure to a new financial year.
2 TRUE. Just because it is requested does not mean the employee or business will benefit.
3 FALSE. Senior management support is essential for the creation of a focused training environment.
4 TRUE. The process identifies such employees, who can then become involved.
5 FALSE. Without the TNA input the courses will be more generic and less useful to the organisation.

Feedback on learning activity 18.4

You should have provided a list of courses, showing which category you feel each one best fits into.

Feedback on self-assessment question 18.4

1 FALSE. Experience is important, but many organisations still require professional qualifications for the wider knowledge they can bring.
2 TRUE. Its real benefit is in developing a knowledge base that can be used when required.
3 FALSE. This is mentoring. In buddying, employees are allocated a 'buddy' with whom they can work and learn, usually at a similar level to themselves.
4 FALSE. Externally sourced training is usually more expensive than internal training, but it is not necessarily better.
5 TRUE. Good induction is recognised as a factor in developing employee morale in the first few days.

Feedback on learning activity 18.5

Your response should bring out whether you feel CPD could or does work for you, and the benefits to both parties. Under 'How would it work?' you may have picked up some of the points in the text:

- personal or business-driven
- a professional requirement
- many different sources and inputs.

Feedback on self-assessment question 18.5

review – knowledge – skills – attractive – risk – personal – up to date – compulsory

18

Feedback on learning activity 18.6

Your response should bring out whether you feel training is evaluated properly in your organisation, and whether or not value for money is being obtained. Some of the points in this section could appear, including:

- Why do you do the evaluation?
- How do you do it?
- Do you use a particular model or technique?

Feedback on self-assessment question 18.6

You should be able to identify the following inaccuracies:

- Evaluating training is not virtually impossible, but it does require some time and effort to do well, especially on more advanced material.
- There is no reason at all why the trainer's feedback cannot be shared with the organisation, and many external trainers will welcome the opportunity to do this.
- Of course trainers wish to see good results, but they are often genuinely anxious to identify any areas for improvement, especially if the training is likely to be repeated.
- Delegates' complaints should be investigated, and are a good source of feedback, but simply not doing the training again is not necessarily the right answer.
- End-of-year spending on training often places the training system under pressure and is likely to result in poor results. This is a bad reason for initiating training.

Information and individual performance management

Introduction

We saw in study sessions 15, 16, 17 and 18 the benefits to both the employee and the organisation of good performance management systems, positive appraisal processes, and a well-focused training and development programme. We can identify many things that are important if these systems are to work well, but one of the most important is the availability of good data.

The use of the wrong data, or data that is disputed by managers or employees, is highly likely to cause problems in a buyer performance measurement system, and can lead to the process (especially appraisal) falling into disrepute.

In this context 'data' means statements and views as well as figures, and it can therefore be both objective (based on facts) and subjective (based on opinion).

Session learning objectives

After completing this session you should be able to:

19.1 Describe the importance of data to the measurement process.
19.2 Explain the need for access to the corporate and departmental planning process, and effective systems design.
19.3 Summarise the types of data that may be used.
19.4 List the sources of data that may be used.

Unit content coverage

This study session covers the following topics from the official CIPS unit content document:

Statement of practice

- Evaluate targets as a means of improving the performance of the purchasing function and individual buyers.

Learning objective

3.6 Explain how to measure individual performance against pre-set targets.
- Cost reduction
- Profitability
- Productivity

Prior knowledge

You should have read study sessions 15, 16, 17 and 18, and also study session 6 (IT and data management). Knowledge of data acquisition issues and problems will also be useful

Resources

No specific resources are required, but you may find it useful to discuss this issue with your IT department or responsible manager.

Timing

You should set aside about 4 hours to read and complete this session, including learning activities, self-assessment questions, the suggested further reading (if any) and the revision question.

19.1 The importance of data in the measurement process

It may seem obvious that lack of suitable data will be a problem, and yet appraisal systems often fail because objectives are chosen that prove to be hard to measure. In addition we often find that insufficient thought has been put into ensuring that the necessary data will be available when required.

Of course objectives should not be chosen just to fit the information that *is* available. When an objective is necessary, and measurement information is not available, the employee and his or her manager need to carefully agree some terms of reference for assessing progress.

Learning activity 19.1

Reflect on any measurement data you are currently collecting that contributes to your appraisal or measurement process. Present a short report indicating whether the data is easily obtained, and whether you are happy with the quality of the data.

Feedback on page 315

Useful data needs to fit into the following categories:

Relevant

The data needs to be as closely relevant as possible to the issue or the objective that is being measured. There is little point in having information on a closely related subject just because the data needed for the main objective is not available.

For example, if we wish to reduce lead times on transactional purchasing we cannot measure this without data on all aspects of lead time (requisitioner to purchasing, inside purchasing, purchasing to supplier, and supplier to requisitioner). Without all the data, any individual pieces of data are less useful.

The same applies in more qualitative measurement. For example, when assessing presentation skills in business meetings it is not directly relevant that an individual plays a leading role in the organisation's amateur dramatic productions.

Properly targeted

An employee should be judged in relation to what is expected of them at their level or position. Avoid average measures wherever possible.

For example, it might be unfair to use a common measure of achieved savings for a group of buyers if they each have different commodities or groups of customers. In this case it would be unfair to have the same targets. Can the data be made to allow for these distinctions?

The same applies to a department. It would be unfair to set a department a savings target based on a given budget if the department cannot influence all of this budget.

Accurate

Is the data accurate, or from a trusted source? Very often, data is provided from corporate systems such as financial systems that were not set up to provide purchasing information, at least in a form suitable for accurate appraisal.

For example, we may have obtained a list of all suppliers from accounts and started a supplier rationalisation exercise, only to discover that the data does not include information for several key departments.

The need for accuracy is a particular problem when we are using subjective opinion, and in appraisals linked to rewards. Whenever possible, opinion-based data should be supported by multiple sources. For example, there is a big difference in emphasis between 'One of your customers says...' and 'Several of your customers have said...'.

Timely

Data should be as up to date as possible, and should be available at the requested time. This ensures that it reflects recent efforts and developments, but it can pose a strain on systems, and requires significant collection effort.

- Can the data sources keep up to date?
- Is the data available on request?
- Does the data require batch processing or special request?

Fair and impartial

All subjective data must be scrutinised to remove, as far as possible, any chance of unfairness or impartiality. This is both ethically desirable and essential for the good workings of the systems; it is also necessary by law.

19

Usable

Data collection on a large scale will be complex and can be expensive, especially if we are seeking personal opinions and views. Care should be taken that all data collected is used to avoid wasting time and effort. It is all too easy to have piles of data and printouts produced that are hardly used.

Self-assessment question 19.1

Give True or False responses to the following statements on the importance of data:

1 The more data you have available, the easier it will be to measure a result. TRUE/FALSE
2 If there is no data for measurement, you should not set the objective. TRUE/FALSE
3 It is best to set buyers individual targets, even if the department has an average overall target to achieve. TRUE/FALSE
4 Subjective opinions should always be sought from more than one source. TRUE/FALSE
5 Data from corporate systems is always directly usable in performance measurement. TRUE/FALSE

Feedback on page 315

19.2 Accessing corporate and departmental planning

We have seen that performance management systems should operate as part of the overall business-planning process. As with the organisational and supplier performance measures discussed in study sessions 1 to 14, much of the quantitative data needed for individual performance measurement *should* be available from corporate systems. However, we cannot assume that this means it *is* available, or that it is in the form we need. Much thought and planning may be needed to access this information as and when necessary.

Learning activity 19.2

Prepare a list of any areas of your own activity where data flows seem inadequate to allow good measurement of your performance. Can you say why this data is poor? Do you feel the provision of data has been well thought through?

You may wish to discuss this with your IT department or line manager.

Feedback on page 315

19

We can see two main categories of information requirements: ongoing, and specfic or bespoke.

Ongoing requirements

This is data that an employee (or a department) needs to access over the long term in order to perform properly. It does not follow that all of this data will be used for performance measurement at any given time, but elements of it will be used when required. Much of this will be operational or day-to-day performance data.

In procurement, this type of data might include measurements relating to:

1 transactional activity, such as orders placed, invoices cleared or customers visited
2 budgetary conformance, such as staffing budgets, non-pay expenditures or training budgets
3 operational performance, such as savings targets, supplier appraisal or vendor rating system management
4 strategic contributions, such as margin improvements, supplier rationalisation programmes or international sourcing initiatives.

Often this type of data will come from corporate systems such as ERP (enterprise resource planning) systems, financial systems, HR systems and indeed dedicated procurement or logistics systems. However, such systems do not always provide the data needed, and frequently do not provide it in the desired format. The procurement department may need to set up local PC-based systems to extract and manipulate data to its own requirements, especially for use in performance measurement. However, where there is a consistent shortfall between the data required and the data available, purchasing management need to make every attempt to have the corporate systems enhanced.

It will also be necessary to establish regular information flows with other departments and perhaps customers and suppliers, and this will also take time. These links cannot be established quickly, and need to be carefully designed, often with support from IT staff.

Much of this data is objective or quantitative, either transactional or process driven, and it is likely to be less easily available for categories 3 and 4 above, where we begin to have more bespoke data requirements (see below).

Specific or bespoke requirements

This is data that is needed so that a specific task or objective can be measured, and it could be required for any period from a few months to several years. So careful research is needed when writing and agreeing the objective, to ensure that adequate data is available to evaluate the performance achieved.

Examples of this sort of requirement might include information on:

- timescales and budgets for a specific purchasing project or capital scheme
- supplier or customer relationship initiatives
- special sourcing and market initiatives, for example overseas sourcing
- staffing or training and development initiatives
- quality of service surveys with suppliers or customers

19

- quality initiatives, value analysis or value engineering projects
- strategic initiatives.

Some of this data will be quantitative, but much of it will be qualitative, and therefore it will be dependent more on subjective opinion and less on figures. But, whether quantitative or qualitative, it is also less likely that the data will be easily available from existing systems.

Whether the requirement for information is ongoing or specific, the links to the business-planning process and the interaction with the organisation's business systems are critical, and need to be thought through during the process of cascading objectives. Equally, it is essential that the organisation has the skills and flexibility to create a new data flow when needed. In the case of more qualitative measures this may need some good **relationship management** as well as good systems design. Relationship management is the process of positively managing all the internal and external relationships with which the individual is involved. In procurement it is often linked to the internal customer and the supplier.

Self-assessment question 19.2

Give True or False responses to the following statements:

1   Qualitative data is often harder to get hold of and process accurately than quantitative data. TRUE/FALSE
2   Data for measuring strategic activity will be no harder to obtain than other data. TRUE/FALSE
3   The time to consider the data flow for an objective is during the business-planning process. TRUE/FALSE
4   When assessing buyers' performance we shall often need data from outside purchasing, including customers and perhaps suppliers. TRUE/FALSE
5   Sometimes data will need reprocessing in purchasing before it can be used for performance measurement. TRUE/FALSE

Feedback on page 316

19.3 Types of data used

The data and information used in performance management will vary according to the task or objective and the organisation. For a purchasing and supply organisation some typical measurement and target areas include those listed in table 19.1.

It is also important to recognise the nature of this information, which we can categorise as quantitative or qualitative, or a mix of both. This is important because, as we have seen earlier, there can be difficulties with the quality and availability of some information.

These lists are just typical examples, and you should be able to identify measures of your own that are not shown here.

Table 19.1 Measurement and target areas

Typical measurement	Category
Basic or transactional activity	
• Number of requisitions handled, orders placed etc	Quantitative
• Speed of turn round (purchasing lead time)	Quantitative
• Overall lead time (from request to receipt)	Quantitative
• Number of complaints	Mix
• Number of invoice queries	Quantitative
• Expediting activity	Quantitative
• Quality and effectiveness of service	Mix
• Internal and external customer satisfaction	Mix
Departmental or internal performance	
• Staffing costs and levels to budget or targeted reductions	Quantitative
• Non-pay cost to budget or targeted reductions	Quantitative
• Staff appraisal and development/training targets	Mix
• Activity ratios per employee	Quantitative
• Personnel and welfare issues	Qualitative
• Staff recruitment/retention targets	Mix
Operational performance	
• Savings or margin contribution	Quantitative
• Amount of delegated procurement activity	Quantitative
• Use of procurement cards	Mix
• Inventory reduction	Quantitative
• Quality or service improvements	Qualitative
• Environmental targets	Quantitative
• Impact on current business objectives	Mix
• Performance against corporate milestones	Mix
• Legislative and process compliance targets	Mix
• Project milestones	Mix
Strategic performance	
• New sourcing strategies	Mix
• Product and materials development	Mix
• Supplier relationships and development	Mix
• Contribution to company performance	Mix
• Make or buy strategies	Mix
• Value analysis and value engineering	Mix
• Globalisation targets	Mix

Learning activity 19.3

Complete table 19.2 to analyse the type of data needed to measure the key tasks in your job description. Is it shown in the list of typical measures in table 19.1? Comment on the quality of data used to measure you.

Table 19.2

My key objectives	Shown in list? Y/N	Comment
1		
2		
3		
4		

Feedback on page 316

19

Now go on to tackle the following self-assessment question.

Self-assessment question 19.3

Answer these multiple-choice questions.

1   Quantitative data is more concerned with:
    A opinions
    B views
    C facts
    D reviews.
2   Which of these statements does *not* apply to qualitative data:
    A It is harder to obtain.
    B It is harder to judge as right or wrong.
    C It is generated from IT systems.
    D It comes from many sources.
3   Generally. measures used for assessing strategic level performance will not be:
    A based on quantitative measurements
    B based on others' judgements
    C based on a wider view of business activity
    D based on qualitative measurements.
4   Many performance measurements will be based on:
    A a mix of different inputs
    B inputs from ERP systems
    C inputs from human resources
    D inputs from the employee.
5   Welfare targets for employees would generally be considered as:
    A strategic measures
    B departmental measures
    C transactional measures
    D operational measures.

Feedback on page 316

19.4 Sources of usable data

Clearly there will be a wide range of sources of data available, depending on the performance measure in use and the sophistication of the organisational systems. Those working in smaller organisations may have less access to corporate data systems (though this is not always a disadvantage), but note that volume of information is not the most important factor.

We should not assume that all data comes from IT systems. Although much data *is* available from IT systems, many organisations still have substantial paper records available, and much of the qualitative or subjective information will be written (or emailed) or verbal.

Learning activity 19.4

Investigate the sources of performance management data that your organisation uses, list them in table 19.3, and comment on how useful you

(continued on next page)

Learning activity 19.4 *(continued)*

feel each one is. Identify any other sources that you feel could be used, and state why.

You may wish to discuss this with you IT department or line manager.

Table 19.3

Data sources used	Comment
Other source	
Other source	
Other source	

Feedback on page 316

Sources of data for use in performance measurement might include organisational systems, personally managed systems, forms and pro formas, internal customers, suppliers, external organisations and research.

Organisational systems

These could include ERP, MRP and DRP systems, financial systems, HR systems, logistics systems and organisational procurement systems.

Departmental systems

In some organisations, systems are run only at departmental level. These can often be adapted more quickly than corporate systems, and may be more suitable for bespoke measurement data.

This is often the best level for gathering, storing and processing subjective data.

Personally managed systems

Most procurement staff will have access to a PC, and will have some sort of personal filing system of their own. This can often be used or modified to provide data for a performance management activity, though some validation of the data may be necessary from time to time. Personal systems are often kept as backups, or as duplicates when employees are not entirely happy with the main recording systems.

Forms and pro formas

Much long-term procurement can be monitored during delivery to ensure that performance of both the contractor and the procurement team is satisfactory. The completion of regular returns of this nature is common in service contract monitoring and vendor rating systems, and can provide a useful contribution to procurement performance measurement.

19

Input from internal customers

Many areas of performance can be measured with the help of input from internal customers who are the recipients of procurement services. This input will tend to be subjective, and will need to be used carefully to ensure accuracy. It can be especially useful in the measurement of purchasing service quality and when measuring supplier performance. Customer surveys and questionnaires can be useful, but it is worth bearing in mind that improvements over time cannot be measured unless these are undertaken regularly, which can be time-consuming.

Data from suppliers

Supplier data is commonly used (especially where e-business links are in place), to monitor such measures as service levels, lead times and delivery performance. Many organisations also still rely on supplier information to find out what product ranges and volumes they are using.

This is basically transactional activity, and some organisations go further and look to measure aspects of buyers' performance by asking for suppliers' views. This can either be direct or via supplier surveys, and the results can be revealing, to say the least.

External organisations

Sources such as trade organisations, professional bodies, government agencies and statistical organisations can provide good sources of up-to-date and independent data that can be used in performance management. For example, buyers may wish to use the RPI index of inflation or the CIPS market price indices when calculating price savings or analysing cost breakdowns. Such organisations would not usually have a direct input into a buyer's measurement or appraisal, but the data they provide can be very useful.

Research

Data suitable for use in performance measurement can also be gained from newspapers, magazines and the media, library research, and of course the internet. However, this 'raw' data will often need validation before it can become acceptable evidence.

Self-assessment question 19.4

Draft a short report critically examining what you have found as detailed in learning activity 19.4 above, and making recommendations for widening the sources used for performance measurement data in your organisation.

Feedback on page 316

19

Revision question

Now try the revision question for this session on page 336.

Summary

We have looked in some detail at the availability and need for good data if our performance measurement systems are to be effective and if they are to retain credibility with both the organisation and the employees who are being measured. Clearly, there are many aspects of good performance management schemes, but good data is always essential, and the absence of this data has created weaknesses in many systems.

We have also looked at several activities that are commonly measured, and have suggested the degree to which data needs to be quantitative or qualitative or a mix of both.

Finally we have looked at potential sources of performance data.

Feedback on learning activities and self-assessment questions

Feedback on learning activity 19.1

Your report might include some comments on the following aspects of the data in question:

- Is it relevant?
- Is it properly targeted?
- Is it accurate?
- Is it timely?
- Is it fair and impartial?
- Is it in usable format?

Feedback on self-assessment question 19.1

1   FALSE. Too much data is as bad as too little, and is unlikely to be used.
2   FALSE. If the objective is a necessary organisational requirement, it must be set.
3   TRUE. Setting the departmental average for each buyer does not allow for differences in buyer portfolios, training and ability, or market conditions.
4   TRUE. This helps to remove bias and provide a more realistic view of performance.
5   FALSE. Corporate data needs editing, as does all data, to fit the specific measurement criteria required.

Feedback on learning activity 19.2

You should have prepared a list highlighting inadequate data flows in relation to your job and organisation, with comments on the inadequacy of the data where possible. Issues could include:

- shortage of day-to-day data
- poor paper or IT systems
- no longer-term information
- no qualitative information
- bad interdepartmental communication.

19

Feedback on self-assessment question 19.2

1 TRUE. Quantitative data is often available from existing systems.
2 FALSE. Data for strategic or bespoke projects will be harder to obtain, and may need special data collection methods.
3 TRUE. At this stage a new data flow can be developed if needed.
4 TRUE. Customers and suppliers may provide quantitative and qualitative data.
5 TRUE. Procurement may need to set up local PC-based systems to extract and manipulate data to its own requirements.

Feedback on learning activity 19.3

There is no specific answer. You should be able to identify with some of the points listed in the text or, if not, identify your own objectives. You should also analyse how satisfied you feel with the quality of the data.

Feedback on self-assessment question 19.3

Answers

1 C. Quantitative data is concerned more with facts.
2 C. Qualitative data generally does not come from IT systems, though such data may be used in making qualitative judgements.
3 A. Strategic-level performance will generally be based less on just facts and figures.
4 A. Many measures, especially those above transactional level. require a mix of inputs.
5 B. Welfare issues would be departmental targets or objectives.

Feedback on learning activity 19.4

You should have completed the table and provided details of other sources that you believe could be used. You may have identified some of the following broad categories:

- systems in your organisation
- systems in your department
- systems of your own (or a colleague)
- existing or new forms and pro formas
- input from internal customers
- input from selected suppliers
- inputs from external organisations or stakeholders
- research data.

Feedback on self-assessment question 19.4

You should provide feedback in report form on the data sources used, which should include a number of those mentioned above. Your criticism should be balanced to show good and bad points, with suggestions for improvement and for widening of the sources of data used.

Buyer and supplier performance links

Introduction

Many organisations are increasingly recognising that purchasing departments have to be able to prove they are adding value to the procurement process or the supply chain. It is certainly not always acceptable that judgements on good performance should be left within procurement, and it is becoming more important to take a wider view of procurement success.

Often the problem with measuring buyers' performance is that it satisfies the purchasing and supply management team, but it rarely addresses the views of everyone else who comes into contact with the purchasing service.

In study session 17 we looked briefly at the role that other stakeholders could play, and perhaps the only real way to measure any department's performance is to ask those who have dealings with it for their views. In this session we shall develop this idea further.

> Involving suppliers in our performance measurement is like sleeping with the enemy – we may find it interesting in the short term, but what will the long-term implications be?

Session learning objectives

After completing this session you should be able to:

20.1 Evaluate the weaknesses of existing approaches to performance measurement.
20.2 Argue that there is a need and benefit from relating performance to wider issues.
20.3 Define potential performance measurement links to suppliers.
20.4 Define possible performance measurement links to other stakeholders.

Unit content coverage

This study session covers the following topics from the official CIPS content document:

Statement of practice

- Appraise measures that can be used to improve supplier performance.

Learning objective

3.7 Compare the relative performance measures of the buyer with those of his or her respective suppliers.
  - Key measures of supplier performance: competency, commitment, capacity, control

20

- Key measures of buyer performance: skill and knowledge, plus contribution to an organisation's goals and targets

Prior knowledge

You should have read sessions 15–19.

Resources

No specific resources are required, but you will find it useful to discuss this issue with fellow students, with other colleagues, and perhaps with line managers.

Timing

You should set aside about 4 hours to read and complete this session, including learning activities, self-assessment questions, the suggested further reading (if any) and the revision question.

20.1 The weaknesses of existing approaches to performance measurement

We have already seen that there can be difficulties in establishing a performance measurement system that works well, and that there are various processes and relationships that must work effectively over a long period of time for good schemes to make sustained progress. Inevitably, this fails to happen in many organisations. Indeed, even where the processes within performance and appraisal systems appear to be working well, the results may not provide the real benefits that the organisation deserves and requires.

Learning activity 20.1

Consider your organisation, and list any broad weaknesses of its approach to buyer performance measurement.

Feedback on page 327

Why may a performance measurement system not provide the benefits the organisation needs? There are several reasons for this.

The programme satisfies only the 'owners'

A measurement system has been developed that is believed to be working well at all levels within the purchasing department. Management and staff are broadly satisfied, and the results are good in terms of the numbers and the targets used. However, in reality the scheme has lost sight of the wider picture, and is measuring only what purchasing believe is important. It is 'inward-looking'. This can be the case if the measurement system no longer links to the wider business goals, or is not really being monitored from senior management level.

There is too much information

We have talked about the difficulties that may arise if data is not available to support measurement and appraisal. However, the rapid growth of data management systems in the last 15 years has often resulted in a situation where there is too much data or too many 'numbers', and this can effectively swamp appraisal systems. Indeed, the latest thinking in IT terms is that a decision management system should now sit above an ERP system in order to sift data and present only the absolutely key information. The same thinking needs to be applied to personal performance measurement. In particular, an overemphasis on measurables can reduce the qualitative content of the measurement process.

Setting unachievable targets

On occasions the targets and objectives set in even the best-managed systems are incapable of being achieved. This is not uncommon in the public sector, where political pressure can set targets for which the structure or resources of an organisation are inadequate or incapable. Closely linked to this is the issue of unrealistic timescales.

As an example, over the last 20 years the UK government has regularly changed the structure and ownership of the central purchasing function in the National Health Service, largely in order to improve procurement practice and achieve savings. At the same time it has also encouraged a great deal of procurement freedom and autonomy at hospital and clinic level. The two strategies may well be incompatible with the hoped-for savings gains, and lead to the setting of unachievable targets.

When this sort of thing happens consistently, performance measurement schemes begin to fail, or seek easier targets.

Unsuited to this department

Not all organisations and departments lend themselves to the kind of measurement systems that we have discussed in the study sessions so far. This is especially the case if the nature of their work does not fundamentally lend itself to measurement, or is almost entirely subjective. In purchasing this might be the case with strategic policy units or 'think tanks', IT or data analysts, commodity advisers, or quality control teams.

Nobody wants to drop it

Sometimes faults within the performance measurement system have caused it to become a mechanistic process, driven only by the fact that the organisation will not face up to (or is unaware of) the need to review

20

the arrangements. This is often the case in public sector schemes, and in organisations without good two-way communication. It is also a problem when the system is 'championed' by a director or senior manager.

Blame cultures

Good performance and appraisal process require open, two-way communication and regular, managed feedback up the organisation. They also need performance management to take place in a 'no blame' environment, where those involved do not fear making mistakes or occasional failures. If this is not the case communication becomes limited, and the measurement system becomes unwieldy and penal.

However, although the above factors are important, many of those involved in performance measurement are now arguing that failure to adequately take into account the views and wishes of stakeholders is the greatest weakness of all.

Self-assessment question 20.1

Fill in the blanks in the following text:

The HR department of Big Factory plc believes it has identified weaknesses in the purchasing performance measurement system. It has become _____ as the process has taken over, and seems to have lost sight of the _____ _____. There are several processes and _____ that must work _____, and this sometimes fails to happen, and some targets are _____, causing employees concern. However, the biggest problem is that some _____ feel the department fails to take their views into account.

If purchasing was less _____ _____ it could consider involving its _____ or _____ in the process, with positive results.

Feedback on page 327

20.2 The wider involvement of stakeholders

The argument used for the positive inclusion of stakeholders is that, in today's global economy, the perceived performance of many organisations is about more than just the balance sheet.

For example, at a corporate level several oil companies have experienced bad publicity around environmental issues, and car manufacturers are occasionally shown to be disregarding safety issues. When this happens the stakeholders are the general public (and investors), and their confidence in these organisations can be significantly undermined by such problems.

Figure 20.1 shows some of the common stakeholder groups for any department.

Figure 20.1: Common stakeholder groups

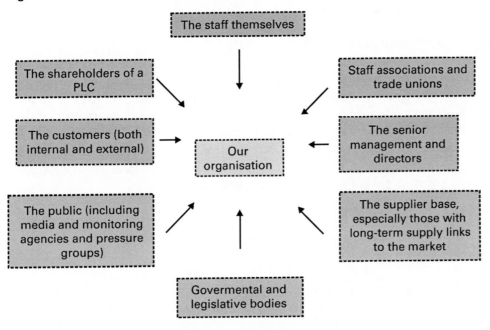

In addition, the involvement of stakeholders helps to ensure that performance management does not become too 'cosy' as discussed above.

Learning activity 20.2

Reflect on what you have read and write a short analysis of the scope for involving other stakeholders in the measurement of purchasing performance in your organisation. You may wish to discuss this with your line manager.

Feedback on page 327

In purchasing departments there are generally three major stakeholders to be considered: the corporate management team, the internal customers, and the suppliers.

The corporate management team

The corporate management team will have two main concerns:

- In a narrow sense, they will wish to see purchasing perform well to the performance targets set through the type of cascade process we have considered already.
- In the wider sense, the corporate team will have views on how these targets are achieved. and on the wider implications for the business.

For example, the buyers in a food manufacturing business will be expected to maintain or improve quality while improving margins and reducing costs. However, if in the process of doing this they fall out with farmers, who then start lobbying Parliament and the media, this may be seen as a

20

321

failure at corporate level. The procurement objective is met, but the business consequences can be unforeseen.

The internal customers

As we have seen elsewhere in this course, there is often tension between the traditional role of the purchasing function and the wishes of the end users or customers, who see purchasing as a mechanistic organisation that interferes with their getting the products and services they want. This can in part be resolved by better communication and stronger links between the functions, and involvement in the purchasing performance measurement process can be a very useful contribution to this process.

If the purchasing function is not perceived to be providing its customers with the service they require, then arguably it is failing to satisfy a major stakeholder.

For example, a hospital wishes to buy Brand A physiotherapy equipment because it sees it offering improved facilities, but purchasing buys Brand B, which is more cost-effective and compatible with existing equipment. The procurement objective is met, but the customers perceive purchasing to be ignoring their views as users and experts.

If we are an internal customer (and stakeholder) we shall expect two levels of performance from our purchasing colleagues. At one level we expect them to provide us with the operational service we require, and this can be summed up in ensuring that the 'five rights' apply: 'the right products, of the right quality, at the right prices, at the right timing and delivery, and in the right quantities'.

However, we also expect a reasonable level of service and professionalism, and increasingly we expect what might be considered as added value services: services that place purchasing high on the list of departments helping to drive the business forward. These include strategic contributions such as sourcing strategies, supplier and product development, and cost reduction programmes. They might also include softer contributions such as expanding product knowledge, training and development of non-purchasing staff, and developing better customer relations.

The suppliers

It has often been argued that a purchasing department is only as good as its suppliers. This view has been around for many years, but is especially true from the perspective of other stakeholders in the organisation who use the suppliers that purchasing has chosen.

Of course, there is often a problem even in well-structured organisations, because the demands of stakeholders conflict. This is quite normal, and in this situation purchasing and supply management will have to prioritise its stakeholder input – not always an easy thing to do.

In the next section we shall discuss this link between buyers and suppliers in more depth.

Self-assessment question 20.2

Give True or False responses to the following statements:

1 In a well-managed organisation there is little conflict between stakeholders' aims and objectives. TRUE/FALSE
2 The general public are unlikely to be considered as stakeholders for a purchasing team. TRUE/FALSE
3 Shareholders are exercising their power more in many companies. TRUE/FALSE
4 In many organisations public perception can be affected by bad procurement decisions. TRUE/FALSE
5 Suppliers' performance really has the biggest impact on our internal customers. TRUE/FALSE

Feedback on page 328

20.3 Performance measurement links to suppliers

A supplier is a stakeholder for the period for which it holds a contract to supply a particular organisation with a given product or service. That is to say, it has an interest in how the organisation performs, not least because it wishes to do business under the contract.

However, some suppliers are also stakeholders in the industry or service in question and therefore have a stake in the success of the industry as a whole, even though they do business with only parts of it at one time.

For example, a UK-based supplier of oil drilling pumping equipment has a contract with two large oil companies. This supplier has a direct stake not only in these companies performance but also in the performance of the whole industry.

Learning activity 20.3

Consider to what extent (if at all) suppliers influence procurement performance measurement in your organisation.

Feedback on page 328

When suppliers fail to perform well there are often problems in the relationship that are the fault of the buying organisation. Suppliers may therefore feel entitled to a view as to how business is conducted, an opportunity to add value to the process, and perhaps even an opportunity

20

to measure the effectiveness of the purchasing department. The organisation may also support this view!

The attitude and contribution of suppliers can have a major impact both on a business and on how the purchasing team with whom they deal is perceived, so it should be in the interests of the purchasing team to involve willing suppliers in this way.

Suppliers' contributions to measuring purchasing performance can be broadly divided into two elements.

How is purchasing's operational performance?

This is where the supplier passes judgement on the day-to-day performance of purchasing. We can see several potential issues here:

- Is the purchasing organisation dealing well with the transactional and basic operational process involved in servicing the buying arrangement?
- Does the supplier find purchasing easy to deal with and accessible?
- Is day-to-day communication good?
- Are queries dealt with promptly?
- Are payments processed quickly?
- Are tenders and bids (where used) handled in a supplier-friendly manner?

What value does purchasing add?

This is where the supplier passes judgement on the added value that purchasing contributes to the relationships the supplier has with the buying organisation:

- Is purchasing trying to work with the supplier in a positive way to bring additional benefits?
- Does purchasing respond to savings opportunities when offered?
- Will they let suppliers contribute to value analysis and value engineering studies?
- Is there a role for suppliers in the development of specifications?
- Will they allow suppliers to train and develop users and purchasing staff?
- Do they respond to ideas on manufacturing or process improvements, or on new technologies and materials?
- Will they accept ideas on ways to improve communications?

Suppliers who wish to work in this way should receive active support from the purchasing department, and together they can provide a better service to the customer. This type of supplier relationship will enhance the image of procurement within an organisation, so there should be mutual benefit. Including the supplier in the performance measurement process may help to create the right environment.

Purchasing (with the customer's help) remains responsible for measuring and monitoring that the service proved is satisfactory, but the customer (the stakeholder) will also express their view through an input to the measurement and appraisal process.

20

The process is shown diagrammatically in figure 20.2.

Figure 20.2: Input to the performance measurement process

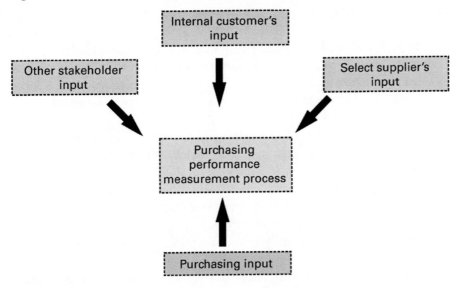

Attempting to introduce a measurement system with this kind of involvement can create a number of potential problems. These might include the following:

- Selling the idea in the business. Will other stakeholders and management accept the idea?
- Selling the idea to the staff involved. How will it be received by the staff dealing with this supplier?
- Choosing appropriate suppliers. Clearly not all suppliers will wish to work in this way, and only a few with a major stake in the business or the industry are likely to be suitable.
- Control and audit. How can we ensure the information is accurate?

Care should also be taken to ensure this is a bona fide wish on the part of the supplier, and not just an attempt to weaken or bypass procurement!

Self-assessment question 20.3

Following on from learning activity 20.3, write a short report on the potential benefits of introducing an approach involving suppliers in measuring purchasing performance. What difficulties would you envisage?

Feedback on page 328

20.4 Performance links with other stakeholders

We have seen that typically there can be three major stakeholders for a purchasing team, and we have considered in some detail the contribution that suppliers can make. The other stakeholders may also be able to provide a useful perspective on how purchasing is performing (apart from any views

20

as customers), which should also be included in the measurement and appraisal process.

These other stakeholders could include:

- Finance: Are all budget targets being met, and is there sufficient emphasis on real savings and margin improvements?
- Operational management: Is purchasing adding real value to the organisation, and are the contributions ensuring minimum adverse reactions or bad publicity?
- Human resources: Are staffing issues and problems being dealt with effectively, and are appraisal and development programmes operated well?
- Risk management: Are the products and services supplied contributing to, and in line with, risk management strategies?
- Specialist departments, eg health and safety: Do all products and services supplied comply fully with heath and safety policies and guidance?
- Staff associations: Does purchasing have good employee relations, and manage and develop staff well?
- The wider public: Is the organisation perceived to procure in a public-minded way, including environmental and ethical issues, eg exploiting child labour?

Learning activity 20.4

Consider to what extent – if any – other stakeholders already influence procurement performance measurement in your organisation. List some of those involved, and the contribution they make.

Feedback on page 328

Now go on to tackle the following self-assessment question.

Self-assessment question 20.4

Write a second report, following on from your views on involving suppliers, that looks at the potential benefits of introducing other stakeholders into the assessment process.

Feedback on page 329

Summary

In study sessions 15 to 19 we have considered the benefits of performance management for the organisation and the employees, and have looked at how this links to training and development, including continuous professional development. We have also considered the issues that can arise if the information flow necessary for good performance management does not work effectively.

In all these study sessions we have been looking at what might be considered as the conventional model of performance management and appraisal, based on cascaded objectives and a departmental or organisational appraisal system.

In this session we have tried to move away from the conventional model by involving those who have a stake in an effective purchasing and supply department in the performance measurement process. If this is done well, the final outcome should be a much fairer measure of the true contribution that purchasing is making.

Suggested further reading

Students will find Neely et al (2002) especially relevant for an overview of approaches that may be of use in considering the subject of this session.

Feedback on learning activities and self-assessment questions

Feedback on learning activity 20.1

You should identify those that are the biggest issues in your organisation. These could include the following:

- The programme is too inward-looking.
- There is too much information'
- Unachievable targets are set.
- The process is not suitable for this department.
- Nobody wants to drop it!
- There is a blame culture.

Did you identify the need to involve external stakeholders?

Feedback on self-assessment question 20.1

mechanistic – wider picture – relationships – effectively – unachievable – stakeholders – inward looking – suppliers – customers

Feedback on learning activity 20.2

Your analysis should nominate some stakeholders who could participate in the measurement process, and indicate the contribution they could make.

Table 20.1

Stakeholder	Potential Contribution

20

Feedback on self-assessment question 20.2

1   FALSE. Conflicting stakeholder ambitions are not a function of poor management but of the different roles each stakeholder has.
2   FALSE. Decisions made by purchasing teams (especially in the public sector) can sometimes impact directly on the public, eg disposal of waste in a service contract.
3   TRUE. Shareholders have increasing expectations of company performance.
4   TRUE. Bad procurement can lead to visible rows, overspends or bad news stories.
5   TRUE. In some organisations the real measure of a successful supplier is one who keeps the customer happy.

Feedback on learning activity 20.3

You should comment on whether or not any suppliers are involved in measuring purchasing performance and, if so, what impact and issues it has created.

Feedback on self-assessment question 20.3

There is no specific right answer; you should look for issues of real benefit to your organisation. Try to bring out some of the points highlighted in this section, if they are relevant.

Show who the suppliers could be, the degree of contribution they could make, and what the contribution could be.

Feedback on learning activity 20.4

Your list of stakeholders might include:

*   operational/production management
*   finance
*   HR
*   risk management
*   specialist, eg health and safety
*   staff associations or trade unions
*   the public.

Table 20.2

Stakeholder	Involved in your organisation Y/N	Comment on contribution
Stakeholder		
Operational/production management		
Finance		
HR		
Risk management		
Specialist, eg health and safety		
Staff associations or trade unions		
The public		

20

Feedback on self-assessment question 20.4

There is no specific right answer; you should look for issues of real benefit to your organisation. Try to bring out some of the points or stakeholders highlighted in this section if they are relevant, but consider others that are applicable in your business.

Show who the stakeholder could be, the degree of contribution, and what the contribution could be.

Revision questions

Revision question for study session 1

You have been recently appointed as the supply chain manager to a medium-sized manufacturing company producing engineering components and employing a workforce of some 1,500.

Your remit is to source all goods and services for the business, and manage the supply chain for your business.

You have line responsibility for three managers: the purchasing and contracts manager, the stores and stock control manager, and the transport and distribution manager.

You are preparing a report to be submitted to the Board to recommend new targets for, and reporting of, key performance indicators (KPIs) for your department.

Draft the outline of this report. The report should have a clear introduction of the issues, and should detail the performance indicators for each manager in your team. The report should state the methodology you would use to identify the KPIs, and should conclude with some management recommendations linked to your business.

Feedback on page 339

Revision question for study session 2

Your company has a programme of cross-functional training sessions planned to ensure a good understanding of departmental principles and processes.

As the purchasing manager, you have been asked to deliver a one-hour presentation to a group of internal operational managers and user departments on the subject of 'total cost of acquisition', and how this relates to costs and performance.

The presentation timescale is:

Introduction – 10 minutes
Subject presentation – 35 minutes
Questions – 15 minutes.

You have decided to prepare six PowerPoint slides for the subject presentation, and you now have to draft the bullet points for each slide, together with brief trainer's notes, which will be given out with the slides as handouts.

Describe the content and points that you will include in your presentation.

Feedback on page 339

Revision question for study session 3

The management of a business operates at various levels: strategic management, tactical/operational management, and transactional management.

Write an essay discussing how a purchasing manager would select key performance indicators (KPIs) for each level of management under his or her control, and how these KPIs interface with corporate plans.

Feedback on page 340

Revision question for study session 4

As purchasing manager for your organisation you have identified your top 20% of products by spend value.

You have decided that in future your requests for quotation (RFQs) will request detailed cost information from your suppliers rather than just unit selling prices.

You need to give the suppliers a brief guidance note on what you want and how you need the information.

Taking an example of a manufactured engineering component, what information will you ask a supplier to detail in future offers?

Set out how you will present this guidance note to suppliers bidding for future supply contracts.

Feedback on page 340

Revision question for study session 5

You are the stores and stock control manager for your organisation. Your managing director is concerned about the level of stock held and the cost of holding stock.

The stores is being set up as a cost centre, and you are to identify all costs of holding stock in order to set a stores on-cost percentage.

Describe how you will calculate the real cost of stockholding and, having set this, how you will manage the stores and stock control performance indicators for the future.

Feedback on page 341

Revision question for study session 6

Your organisation is reviewing its IT systems, and discussions are under way with two suppliers who offer corporate integrated IT management systems.

As purchasing manager you have been asked what are the most important elements for you to operate the purchasing system within the proposed corporate IT process.

Prepare a set of headers and brief notes on each point as part of your response to the IT manager.

Feedback on page 341

Revision question for study session 7

You are the purchasing and supply manager for a medium-sized manufacturing company that has a few problems with supplier deliveries and pricing, but some major concerns over quality are your biggest worry. Currently your supplier measurement systems are poor to non-existent.

Write a report for your board to:

- demonstrate how introducing systems for measuring supplier performance might impact on different aspects of the five basic 'rights' of purchasing
- analyse the particular impact it might have on solving your quality problems
- make some brief recommendations for consideration by the board.

Feedback on page 342

Revision question for study session 8

You are the deputy supplies manager for a large trust hospital. About 60% of procurement comes through your department, and you have some good supplier measurement systems in place. Your manager has asked you to make a presentation to the estates, pharmacy and TSSU departments who manage the rest of the spend, clarifying in particular:

- where supplier performance measurement fits into a typical procurement process
- the differences between pre-award assessments and post-award evaluation
- the basic steps to be taken to implement each.

Your final presentation will be in PowerPoint form, but your manager wants to see your rough draft of the text and diagrams first. You should prepare this in writing in the following format:

- Slide 1: Title; points or paragraph to be presented, with diagram if required
- Slide 2: Title; points or paragraph to be presented

and so on to the end of your presentation.

Feedback on page 343

Revision question for study session 9

You are probably familiar with the concept of the buyer's 'toolkit', and also with the idea that not all performance management activity can be desk based.

Write an essay discussing the merits of the different kinds of tool that are available for supplier performance management, and clarify the base through which they could be applied.

Feedback on page 343

Revision question for study session 10

You work in the purchasing department of a large university, which is just outsourcing its office cleaning services.

Your manager has asked you to prepare a management report for him outlining the generic post-award performance measurement systems that could be used to monitor the supplier, with some simple examples. He also wants you to make a recommendation in the report as to which system might be most appropriate, and give your reasons why.

Feedback on page 344

Revision question for study session 11

You are the senior buyer in a medium-sized food processing company that is currently experiencing disputes and conflicts with its supplier base. To provide some background for a meeting of departmental managers your managing director has asked you to prepare a short paper that:

- classifies the communications links and relationships that *can* be established across the different levels in the business
- appraises the nature of disputes and conflicts
- selects some appropriate ways for helping to resolve these disputes and conflicts.

Feedback on page 345

Revision question for study session 12

Kieran is head of the purchasing department of a large local authority. The authority has recently undergone a large reorganisation, and has moved much of the transactional activity (order placing, expediting etc) to the users, leaving the central team free to concentrate on higher-value, longer-term contracts.

As part of this restructuring the head of finance (Kieran's boss) wishes to outplace one of his staff to provide full-time support to Kieran, as he believes there is a valuable role to fill. Kieran is less sure, believing this is the start of financial interference in procurement.

Discuss this scenario in an essay, and demonstrate the benefits you think will come from such a placement.

Feedback on page 345

Revision question for study session 13

Your organisation has recently announced plans to implement joint performance measurement initiatives with a number of key suppliers, starting with the setting up of some cross-functional teams. After this was announced, several questions were raised at your team meeting, and you have agreed to write an explanatory paragraph on each question for the next purchasing newsletter. The questions raised were:

1 Why do we need joint initiatives? Isn't our existing measurement system enough?
2 Isn't this going to be very expensive to implement?
3 If we have a team and they have a team, aren't we just going to end up arguing?
4 Why would the suppliers want to participate in this process?

Your response should have a short introduction clarifying (for other readers) what joint performance measurement is, plus four specific answers to the questions (do not restate the question).

Feedback on page 346

Revision question for study session 14

You are buying in a difficult market, and have identified a supplier who is not performing well. You are surprised by this, as the supplier seems keen, and showed promise during the initial pre-award assessments.

Write an essay discussing the options you have for dealing with this supplier, and demonstrate why developing the supplier might be beneficial for your business.

Feedback on page 346

Revision question for study session 15

You are working in defence procurement, and your HR department has decided to extend the departmental performance review scheme to procurement staff, linking it to performance-related pay and advancement opportunities.

Using a report style, prepare an information bulletin for issue to staff that highlights the positive benefits that both they and the department will gain from having such a performance review scheme in place.

Feedback on page 347

Revision question for study session 16

It is essential to write good, clear objectives if performance measurement for buyers is to work effectively.

(a) Describe four common elements found in typical simple objectives.
(b) Classify the five key principles used when writing objectives.

(c) Demonstrate the application of the elements and principles you have identified in (a) and (b) by writing one objective for each of the following activities:
  (i) achieving purchasing savings
  (ii) improving the quality of a product
  (iii) writing objectives for members of your team
  (iv) producing a departmental newsletter.

Feedback on page 348

Revision question for study session 17

Consider the process of staff appraisal/evaluation, which is often at the heart of performance management for purchasing and supply staff. Organisations can have very different views on how this is done, and on who should be involved in the process.

Write an essay that:

- discusses the advantages and disadvantages of the different levels of formality and administration
- demonstrates the practicality of involving other parties than the line manager.

Feedback on page 349

Revision question for study session 18

Your organisation is planning to identify a targeted training programme for purchasing and supply staff, and intends to undertake a training needs analysis (TNA) to help establish exactly what training is required.

Planning is still in the early stages, but to help keep staff informed you have been asked to write an internal memo/email that:

- introduces the TNA concept
- demonstrates to staff the reasoning behind the decision to use a TNA, and tells more about the steps involved
- classifies a selection of potential training solutions that might be used once the outputs of the TNA are available.

Feedback on page 349

Revision question for study session 19

In procurement there is often an ongoing requirement for information and data to allow effective buyer performance measurement, and this information and data will be both qualitative and quantitative in nature.

(a) There are four main categories of performance. State what these categories are, and demonstrate the different characteristics of each. (33% of marks)

(b) Using the categories you have identified, select at least four example measures for each category, providing a brief description of the measure and whether it is qualitative or quantitative in nature. (66% of marks)

There is no set requirement for a style of response, but you may find a table-type format useful.

Feedback on page 350

Revision question for study session 20

'A supplier is a major stakeholder in the performance of the buying team it deals with.'

Discuss this concept in an essay, demonstrating how the buying team performance may be viewed by the supplier, and evaluating the issues that might occur if suppliers are brought into the measurement process for buyers.

Feedback on page 351

Feedback on revision questions

Feedback on revision question for study session 1

Your report could have the following structure. The writing times are for guidance only.

(a) *Introduction*
Explain the principles and importance of setting KPIs for the supply chain. This should be only a summary for the benefit of Board members who may not be familiar with the value of KPIs (say 15% of writing time).

(b) *Identify the role of each element in the supply chain*
There are three elements in the flow of goods through the supply chain:
- inbound contracts and purchasing
- intra-site stores and stock control
- outbound transport and distribution.
(This will need about 25% of writing time.)

(c) *Methodology*
Explain how the three department managers work together and with other operational managers on the flow of goods into, through and out from the business.
State a model or methodology of how you will review, coordinate, identify, set and report on KPI targets.
This is the largest section of your report (say 35% of writing time).

(d) *Recommendations*
State how you will report the results, and how you will interface with other operational managers and systems. For example, in this business you may well be working on an MRP system with production management. Ensure that the issue of continuous improvement is covered in the recommendations
Around three recommendations will do (say 25% of writing time).

Note: This question is focused on the following sections in study session 1:

- 1.1 The importance of performance management in business
- 1.6 The importance of measuring purchasing and supply chain performance in public and private sector organisations

Feedback on revision question for study session 2

The main headers would need to cover the following six points:

(a) Setting the scene; definition of total cost of acquisition (TCA).
(b) Why all managers need to understand this concept.

(c) How user departments and purchasing can work together to add value to TCA solutions.

(d) How you would measure TCA performance over time.

(e) How you would learn from decisions and operations to ensure continuous improvement for the organisation.

(f) How this best practice process benefits the organisation as a whole.

Note: This question is focused on the following sections in study session 2:

- 2.1 Added value performance management in corporate business operations: general principles
- 2.5 Added value opportunities of negotiating improved procurement and contract terms with suppliers

Feedback on revision question for study session 3

Your essay could contain:

(a) *Introduction*
A brief explanation of the key issues for a purchasing manager at each level and the relationship to the wider corporate plans (say 20% of writing time).

(b) *The main issues*
The purchasing issues as developed from a model similar to table 3.3. An explanation that the KPIs need to pass the SMART criteria set out in the course book, with purchasing examples.
How each management level interfaces with the departmental plan. How the departmental plan is a part of the wider company plan.
(This part of the essay would take some 60% of writing time.)

(c) *Conclusion*
Confirming what you have said, emphasising the business benefits and closing the essay (say 20% of writing time).

Note: This question is focused on the following sections in study session 3:

- 3.1 How do purchasing and supply managers contribute to the KPI targets set by corporate management?
- 3.2 How do purchasing and supply managers select and set KPIs for their core business operation?

Feedback on revision question for study session 4

(a) *Introduction*
It would be useful to explain why more detailed cost analysis data is of use to a purchasing manager (say 20% of writing time).

(b) *The main body*
Your main areas are likely to be as follows:
- Give suppliers a brief definition of the cost categories: fixed, variable, other costs
- The main elements of cost for which you require a breakdown: see section 4.2.
- How the base costs are set for labour and materials.

- Create a pricing table for the suppliers to complete. This will set the standard for comparison against your definitions outlined in the introduction.
- Identify the main basis of indexing on price elements: labour/material indexes.
- Set out how you will manage price reviews over time on longer contracts.

Some 80% of your writing will be in this main body section.

Note: this question is focused on the following sections in study session 4:

- 4.2 How are costs allocated and accounted for in a commercial organisation?
- 4.3 Introduction to cost price analysis: how are variable costs managed?
- 4.4 Using cost analysis and measuring your purchasing performance

Feedback on revision question for study session 5

Your report could have the following structure. The writing times are for guidance only.

(a) *Introduction*
An explanation of the main costs involved in holding stock, based on the model illustrated in section 5.2 (say 25% of writing time).

(b) *The cost elements*
- financial opportunity costs
- physical opportunity costs
- calculation of a stores on-cost based on annual turnover.
(This will need about 35% of writing time.)

(c) *KPIs*
Identify a set of KPIs for stores, stock control and management (say 20% of writing time).

(d) *Recommendations*
State how you will report the results, and how you will interface with other operational managers and systems.
Around three recommendations will do (say 20% of writing time).

Note: this question is focused on the following sections in study session 5:

- 5.2 The cost of holding stock
- 5.3 Building up the stockholding cost base and identifying links to performance management
- 5.4 Stores and inventory key performance indicators

Feedback on revision question for study session 6

Your report could have the fllowing structure. The writing times are for guidance only.

(a) *Introduction*
An outline of the links with the organisation, both upstream and downstream A summary of the data needed for purchasing decisions (see figure 6.2) (say 15% of writing time).

(b) *Identify some details in purchasing management reports you wish to generate*
 • inbound contracts and purchasing management
 • intra site stores and stock control operations
 • outbound transport and distribution operations.
(This will need about 25% of writing time.)

(c) *State how purchasing information links to the corporate system*
Identify the interdepartmental links (see learning activity 6.2) (say 35% of writing time).

(d) *Recommendations*
State how you would need the system to be set up for transactions, contract records and strategic data analysis.
Around three recommendations will do (say 25% of writing time).

Note: this question is focused on the following sections in study session 6:

 • 6.1 Information systems in business, and the links with supply chain systems used to measure performance
 • 6.2 The key elements of a purchasing IT system
 • 6.6 Best practice: which KPIs will help supply chain managers reduce cost and improve service?

Feedback on revision question for study session 7

Your report could have the following structure. The writing times are for guidance only.

(a) *Introduction*
Explain the background and problems you face. This is a report, so it needs an introduction, but this has mostly been given to you, so keep it relatively short (say 10% of writing time).

(b) *Impact on the five 'rights'*
The five 'rights' are price, quality, quantity, place and time. You should not spend time here commenting on quality, as you will pick this up later; a brief reference will show you are aware of it. You should then give a brief explanation of the impact that performance measurement could have on each of the remaining four 'rights' (say 30% of writing time).

(c) *Contribution to improving quality*
Here you could use two or three themes to emphasise the importance of this element. For example:
 • an introductory theme on basic quality measurement issues
 • a comment on how this can move quality further up the supply chain, and the benefits this brings
 • some of the wider issues to be measured, such as workforce training or investment in technology.

This is the largest 'section' of your report (say 40% of writing time)

(d) *Some recommendations*
These will be very much down to you, but should provide the board with some good ideas. There are no clues in the question, so use your knowledge of supplier performance management. Around three recommendations will do (say 20% of writing time)

Note: this question is focused on the following sections in study session 7:

- 7.1 Supplier performance and business success
- 7.3 Performance measurement and 'quality management'

Feedback on revision question for study session 8

Your PowerPoints might read as follows:

- Slide 1: Introduction and purpose of presentation.
- Slide 2: Brief description of supplier performance management.
- Slides 3–4: Explain a typical public sector procurement process, showing all the stages from project planning to closure. Emphasise the points at which performance management has particular relevance. You might use diagrams here as well.
- Slides 5–7: Explain in a little more depth the difference between pre-award and post-award measurements. For example, post-award measurements are often sustained over time with the chosen supplier, whereas pre-award measurement is concerned with helping to select suitable suppliers.
- Slides 7–9: Pick up the stages in the process, emphasising particularly that post-award assessment is a 'live' process and one that can change and develop through review and feedback.

Note: this question is focused on the following sections in study session 8:

- 8.1 The key stages in the buying process
- 8.2 Steps in a pre-award assessment
- 8.3 Steps in a post-award evaluation

Feedback on revision question for study session 9

Your essay could contain:

(a) *Introduction*
   Showing you know what the question is about, and outlining how you intend to cover it (say 15% of writing time).
(b) *Section on performance management tools*
   A description of the available toolkit, which should pick up the three main categories of tool, with a description and at least one example (say 40% of writing time):
- systems and information tools: a wide range of data and information tools that may be available to support performance measurement and which may be particularly useful at the pre-award assessment stage, eg corporate IT systems
- performance measurement and accreditation tools
- management, theoretical and support tools:
(c) *A section on 'base'*
   This should highlight the three main types of activity:
   1   desk based: activity best undertaken in the office, eg Internet research
   2   meeting based: activities best undertaken by meetings, eg planning and communication session

3   visit based: activities best undertaken through visits, eg supplier's process and material flows.

Be sure to have cross-linkage to the tools. The use of different examples would be a bonus. (Say 30% of writing time.)

(d) *Conclusion*

Confirm what you have said, and close the essay (say 15% of writing time). Try to make a telling point at the end. For example:

'We can see that in determining which tools and techniques to use we are also to some extent deciding the degree to which our activities will be focused outside the office.'

Note: this question is focused on the following sections in study session 9:

- 9.1 Using the right performance measurement 'tools'
- 9.5 A desk-based or visit-based approach?

Feedback on revision question for study session 10

Your report will need to cover those methodologies detailed in the course material but selecting only those suitable for use post-award. In the section on recommendations there is no right answer: you may choose whichever method you feel is appropriate, as long as you can justify this sensibly and in line with the course content, or a university scenario.

Your report might contain:

(a) *Introduction*

Explain the background, and the problems you face. This is a report, so it needs an introduction, but this has mostly been given to you, so keep it relatively short (say 10% of writing time).

(b) *The main body*

Your main areas are likely to be
- statistics based, eg simple rating, complex rating, weighted rating
- perception based, eg categorical rating, the 7Cs
- self-assessment.

You will need some detail of each example, and should show a simple calculation or form design if you think it necessary, as the manager has asked for examples. Keep any maths simple. (Say 60% of writing time.)

(c) *Recommendations*

As indicated, you cannot be wrong, but your answer should reflect the given situation. A weighted complex rating system, heavily dependent on external support to deliver, would probably be too expensive for this type of project.

Therefore you might recommend a simple six-point category-based approach using a small team, undertaken on a monthly basis. This would be practical, not too expensive, easy to establish, and not too time-consuming.

Note: this question is focused on the following sections in study session 10:

- 10.1 Generic methodologies for post-award performance measurement
- 10.2 Simple vendor rating

- 10.3 Perception based rating
- 10.4 The benefits of using weighted measurements

Feedback on revision question for study session 11

Your paper will have three main sections, but may benefit from a short introduction.

(a) *Introduction*
The question is suggesting a link between conflict and disputes and communications, and you should pick this up, as well as the loss of time and effort that conflict can cause (say 10% of writing time).

(b) *Classifying communications*
Relationships can develop at all levels in a business, but a four-part breakdown into director, management, supervisory and operative levels will be sufficient. Show the nature of the relationship at each level, perhaps linking it to disputes and conflicts (say 35% of writing time).

(c) *Nature of disputes and conflicts*
Explain the difference between disputes and conflict, and show how disputes can lead to conflict (say 20% of writing time).

(d) *Resolution of disputes and conflicts*
Solutions can range from normal course of business up to litigation, and you should provide an indication of a preferred route, with explanations (say 35% of writing time).

Note: this question is focused on the following sections in study session 11:

- 11.1 Communication and business relationships at strategic, tactical and operational levels.
- 11.4 Good communications and the resolution of disputes and management of conflict

Feedback on revision question for study session 12

Your essay should support the placement, because there several benefits from close collaboration, especially on longer-term, higher-value purchasing. Your essay could include:

(a) *Introduction*
Showing you know what the question is about, and outlining how you intend to cover it (say 10% of writing time).

(b) *Some of the roles and inputs*
A description of the available tools, such as balance sheet analysis, annual report analysis, and cost control analysis (say 25% of writing time).

(c) *The benefits of corporate financial appraisal*
(Say 25% of writing time.)

(d) *Some specific financial appraisal tools*
For example, return on capital employed (ROCE), profit margin on sales (margin) (say 25% of writing time).

(e) *Conclusion*
Confirm what you have said, and close the essay (say 15% of writing time). Try to make a firm conclusion. For example:

We can see that Kieran will gain substantially from this new appointment, which will....

Note: this question is focused on the following sections in study session 12:

- 12.1 The role and input for the finance department
- 12.2 The benefits of undertaking corporate financial appraisal
- 12.4 Financial appraisal measurement tools

Feedback on revision question for study session 13

(a) *Introduction*
Will emphasise the positive benefits of working with the suppliers rather having than one-sided measurement (say 12% of writing time).

(b) *Question 1*
Could include comment on improving relationships, creating a partnership style, getting early supplier involvement, going a step beyond the existing system (say 22% of writing time).

(c) *Question 2*
Could include comment on cost versus expected benefits, application only where business justifies it, the need to take a longer-term view, the cost being shared between the parties (say 22% of writing time).

(d) *Question 3*
Could say this is possible at first, but there is a likelihood that the teams will start to work together as time goes on. Emphasise the need for good management of the process and real empowerment of the teams (say 22% of writing time).

(e) *Question 4*

Could include:

- market advantage and reduced selling effort
- improved technological capability and product development
- enhanced innovativity in what the organisation offers
- improved and secured payment arrangements
- improved financial stability and security
- opportunities to improve and refocus management capability
- ability to plan resources over the longer period.

(Say 22% of writing time.)

Note: this question is focused on the following section in study session 13:

- 13.3 Joint performance measurement initiatives

Feedback on revision question for study session 14

Your essay could contain:

(a) *Introduction*
Showing you understand the question, and that you have identified the two themes that you need to consider in detail (say 15% of writing time).

(b) *A section discussing the options you have*

There is no correct answer, but you may develop the following options (say 35% of writing time):

- terminate – but this is a difficult market
- 'discipline' and penalise the supplier in some way – but this may not help if the supplier is trying hard
- take no action at all, and hope for improvement – not very proactive in a difficult market
- take some simple steps to see what the supplier's problems are – worth considering, and has no major resource implications
- look at introducing a 'supplier development' approach.

This leads you into:

(c) *A section on supplier development*

The question is leading you into arguing in favour, but you should not ignore some of the potential negatives. You could cover:

- what supplier development means.
- what it might include: eg advice, technology and even finance
- some key requirements: eg good communications, establishing benchmarks, multi-functional approach, could be part of a programme
- some disadvantages: eg needs good management, costly in time and resources, must be reviewed regularly, can be applied only to a limited number of suppliers.

(Say 35% of writing time.)

(d) *Conclusion*

Confirm what you have said, and close the essay (say 15% of writing time). Try to make a telling point at the end. For example:

'Supplier development should not be undertaken lightly, but in the right situation it can bring positive benefits both to the buyer and to the supplier.'

Note: this question is focused on the following section in study session 14:

- 14.3 About supplier development

Feedback on revision question for study session 15

Your bulletin could contain the following:

(a) *Introduction*

Explain the purpose of the bulletin, and how it is intended that both parties will benefit – it should be 'win–win' (say 10% of writing time).

(b) *The employees*

Could include comment on:

- improved skills and knowledge
- training opportunities
- career prospects
- making a better contribution
- having a better view of overall aims and business strategy
- improved motivation and morale.

(Say 25% of writing time.)

(c) *The department*

Could include comment on:
- improved departmental performance
- improved prices, deals or contracts, improved quality and service, and a 'bottom-line' improvement
- improved perception and profile of the procurement function
- better communication and feedback with staff
- meeting procedural or legal requirements.

(Say 25% of writing time.)

(d) *Links to rewards and advancement*

Could comment on:
- developing talent
- improved motivation and innovation
- financial reward
- organised bonus schemes
- need for careful management.

(Say 25% of writing time.)

(e) *Conclusion and summary*

This will wrap up the bulletin, and needs a positive 'spin' to inspire the target audience and give them confidence (say 15% of writing time).

Note: this question is focused on the following sections in study session 15:

- 15.1 Performance management and the buyer
- 15.2 Performance management and the organisation
- 15.4 The links with reward and advancement

Feedback on revision question for study session 16

There is no set style for this question, and each part should be treated as roughly equal in terms of writing time.

(a) Common elements (with description):
- the overall task or area of activity
- the objective
- the performance measures
- the timescale, by when, milestones and review timetable:

(b) Key principles (with description):

S = Specific

M = Measurable

A = Achievable

R = Realistic

T = Timed.

(c) Examples

As an example you might have:

(iii) Writing objectives for members of your team

Performance management – to write at least five good quality objectives for each member of the team, in line with the departmental strategies and objectives: to be agreed and in place by 1 April with a schedule of three review meetings in the following 12 months.

Note: this question is focused on the following section in study session 16:

- 16.3 Designing positive and SMART objectives

Feedback on revision question for study session 17

Your essay could contain:

(a) *Introduction*
Showing you understand the question, and that you have identified the two themes that you need to consider in detail (say 15% of writing time).

(b) *A section discussing levels of formality*
You should develop the following options (say 35% of writing time). Some topics are suggested below, but you will need to decide whether they are advantages or disadvantages.
- *Formal.* Include comments on: organisational, rules and requirements, written objectives, set interview requirements, standards for measurement of achievement, timetables, scoring mechanisms, preparation. Suitable for which type of organisation?
- *Informal.* Include comments on: less structured and disciplined, based on regular day-to-day discussion, shorter, more relaxed meetings, less paperwork, can still be demanding. Suited to which type of organisation?
- *Structured*: a mix of the two.

(c) *A section demonstrating the potential for involving others*
The question is leading you into arguing in support of involving others, but you should not ignore some of the potential negatives (say 35% of writing time). You could cover:
- why involve others?
- who might be involved (team and/or peers, internal customers, suppliers, etc)?

(d) *Conclusion*
Confirm what you have said, and close the essay (say 15% of writing time). Try to make a telling point at the end. For example:
'I believe that in general the very formal style of appraisal should be avoided, and that, wherever possible, appraisal should include input from outside the procurement team'

Note: this question is focused on the following sections in study session 17:

- 17.1 Formal and informal appraisal and evaluation techniques
- 17.5 Involving others in the appraisal process

Feedback on revision question for study session 18

Your memo/email should contain:

(a) *The introduction section*
The key word here from the question is 'targeted', and you can outline why a TNA can provide a more accurate appreciation of staff training needs than some other ways of selecting training (say 30% of writing time).

(b) *A section on the TNA and a typical process*

Remember nothing is yet agreed, so you are concerned only with a typical TNA. The steps can include:

(i)   Agree the method to be used (and recruit external interviewers if needed).

(ii) Agree the group(s) of staff involved.

(iii) Agree and prioritise the areas of performance, skills and competences required.

(iv) Undertake the interviews or assessment.

(v)   Compare the results with the benchmark requirements and identify any major problem areas (the skills gaps).

(vi) Devise and implement suitable training to remedy those skill gaps.

(vii) Review and feed back as appropriate.

(Say 35% of writing time.)

(c) *A section on potential training solutions*

You are asked for a selection. Choose which ones you like, but your reasoning must be sound and logical. Some options are:

- job based: orientation or induction, learning by doing, buddying, mentoring, rotational
- specific skills based: training aimed at learning how to do something specific, such as operate a new machine or computer program
- generic: training aimed at broadening generic skills used in the job and which form a 'toolbox' for the employee that grows over time
- professional or academic.

(Say 35% of writing time.)

Note: this question is focused on the following sections in study session 18:

- 18.1 Developing a training needs analysis
- 18.4 The different types of training available

Feedback on revision question for study session 19

The marking schedule has indicated how you should allocate your writing time, and there is no need for an introduction or conclusion if you use a list- or table-type format.

(a) The four categories are:

- Transactional activity: data relating to basic, day-to-day activity such as orders placed, invoices cleared.
- Budgetary conformance: data relating to adherence to departmental or project budget activities, often at management level and including pay and staffing levels etc
- Operational performance: data relating to more advanced 'tasks' of procurement, including the real added value issues such as savings targets, supplier appraisal.
- Strategic contributions: data relating to strategic and organisational contributions that help drive the business, such as margin improvements, supplier rationalisation programmes.

Examples are not asked for here but will add value to your answer if they do not overlap with part (b).

(b) Examples would be:

Table 21.1

Basic or transactional activity	
Number of requisitions handled, orders placed etc	Quantitative
Speed of turn-round (purchasing lead time)	Quantitative
Overall lead time (request to receipt)	Quantitative
Number of complaints	Mix
Number of invoice queries	Quantitative
Expediting activity	Quantitative
Quality and effectiveness of the service	Mix
Internal and external customer satisfaction	Mix

Table 21.2

Departmental or internal performance	
Staffing costs and levels to budget or targeted reductions	Quantitative
Non-pay cost to budget or targeted reductions	Quantitative
Staff appraisal and development/training targets	Mix
Activity ratios per employee	Quantitative
Personnel and welfare issues	Qualitative
Staff recruitment/retention targets	Mix

Table 21.3

Operational performance	
Savings or margin contribution	Quantitative
Amount of delegated procurement activity	Quantitative
Use of procurement cards	Mix
Inventory reduction	Quantitative
Quality or service improvements	Qualitative
Environmental targets	Quantitative
Impact on current business objectives	Mix
Performance against corporate milestones	Mix
Legislative and process compliance targets	Mix
Project milestones	

Table 21.4

Strategic performance	
New sourcing strategies	Mix
Product and materials development	Mix
Supplier relationships and development	Mix
Contribution to company performance	Mix
Make or buy strategies	Mix
Value analysis and value engineering	Mix
Globalisation targets	Mix

Note: this question is focused the following section in study session 19:

- 19.3 Types of data used

Feedback on revision question for study session 20

Your essay could contain:

(a) *Introduction*

showing you understand the question, and that you have identified the three themes you need to cover (say 10% of writing time):

- Discuss the concept.
- Demonstrate the supplier's view.
- Evaluate the issues.

(b) *The concept*

Argue whether the supplier is a stakeholder showing ('discuss') you can see two sides (say 25% of writing time).

- *For* the argument you could cite the service received, the need for good specifications, involvement in the whole industry etc
- *Against* you might suggest the supplier simply wants a sale, is not a real stakeholder, might like procurement out of the way etc

(c) *The supplier's view*

A section showing how the supplier sees procurement. You could cover:

- operational performance – its impact on making business work smoothly and payments happen on schedule.
- value added performance – is the relationship being developed? is there early supplier involvement? etc

(Say 25% of writing time.)

(d) *The issues*

Relationship with the customer, vested interests, staff reactions, choosing the suppliers etc (say 25% of writing time).

(e) *Conclusion*

Confirm what you have said, and close the essay (say 15% of writing time). Try to make a telling point at the end. For example: 'Involving suppliers in a buyer's performance measurement system is likely to be controversial, but there may be some real benefits to be gained for both the buyers and the buying organisation.'

Note: this question is focused the following section in study session 20:

- 20.3 Performance measurement links to suppliers

References and bibliography

This section contains a complete A-Z listing of all publications, materials or websites referred to in this course book. Books, articles and research are listed under the first author's (or in some cases the editor's) surname. Where no author name has been given, the publication is listed under the name of the organisation that published it. Websites are listed under the name of the organisation providing the website.

Association of British Certification Bodies (ABCB) http://www.abcb.demon.co.uk/.

Bailey, D (Associates) (2001) *The Training Handbook,* London: Gee Publishing.

British Electro-technical and Allied Manufacturers Association (BEAMA) http://www.beama.org.uk/.

Christopher, M (1985) *The Strategy of Distribution Management.* Aldershot: Gower.

Deming, WE (1982) *Quality, Productivity and Competitive Position.* MIT Press.

Det Norske Veritas (DNV) http://www.dnv.com/.

Drucker, P (2003) *The Essential Drucker,* 2004 edition, Harper Collins.

Dun and Bradstreet http://www.dnb.com/.

Goodworth, C (1989) *The Secrets of Successful Staff Appraisal and Counselling,* 1st edition, UK: Butterworth /Heinemann.

Institute of Civil Engineers (ICE) http://www.ice.org.uk/.

International Standards Organisation (ISO) http://www.iso.org/.

Investors in People http://www.investorsinpeople.co.uk/.

Ishikawa, K (1985) *What is total quality control? The Japanese Way.* Prentice Hall.

Kaplan, RS, and DP Norton (1996) *Balanced Scorecard: Translating Strategy into Action* Harvard Business School Press

Kirkpatrick, D (1975) *Techniques for Evaluating Training Programmes,* Alexandria, VA: American Society of Training Directors (originally published in the *Journal of the American Society of Training Directors*, 1958/59).

Kirkpatrick, DL, and JD Kirkpatrick (2005) *Evaluating Training Programmes – the four levels,* 3rd edition. USA: Berrett-Koehler.

Little, N (2004) *Price, Cost, Value, Benefit, Gain, Worth … which way do I turn.* Eli Broad Graduate School, Michigan State University, USA.

Lysons, K (2000) *Purchasing and Supply Chain Management,* 5th edition, London: Pearson/Prentice Hall.

Lysons, K, and B Farrington (2006) *Purchasing and Supply Chain Management,* 7th edition, London: Pearson/Prentice Hall.

Neely, A, C Adams and M Kennerley (2002) *The Performance Prism*, 1st edition Pearson/Prentice Hall.

Poister, T (2003) *Measuring performance in public and non-profit organisations* 1st edition. San Francisco: Wiley.

Porter, ME (1985) *Competitive Advantage.* Free Press.

Taguchi, G (1986) *Introduction to Quality Engineering.* Asian Productivity Association.

Index

Nurse Practitioners

Clinical Skills and Professional Issues

Edited by

Mike Walsh PhD BA(Hons) RGN PGCE DipN(London)

Reader in Nursing, St Martin's College, Carlisle, UK

SECOND EDITION

BUTTERWORTH
HEINEMANN

ELSEVIER

EDINBURGH   LONDON   NEW YORK   OXFORD   PHILADELPHIA   ST LOUIS   SYDNEY   TORONTO   2006

BUTTERWORTH
HEINEMANN
ELSEVIER

First edition 1999
  Reprinted 1999, 2001, 2002
Second edition 2006
  Reprinted 2008

ISBN 978 0 7506 8801 7

British Library Cataloguing in Publication Data
A catalogue record for this book is available from the British Library

Library of Congress Cataloging in Publication Data
A catalog record for this book is available from the Library of Congress

Notice
Knowledge and best practice in this field are constantly changing. As new research and experience broaden our knowledge, changes in practice, treatment and drug therapy may become necessary or appropriate. Readers are advised to check the most current information provided (i) on procedures featured or (ii) by the manufacturer of each product to be administered, to verify the recommended dose or formula, the method and duration of administration, and contraindications. It is the responsibility of the practitioner, relying on their own experience and knowledge of the patient, to make diagnoses, to determine dosages and the best treatment for each individual patient, and to take all appropriate safety precautions. To the fullest extent of the law, neither the publisher nor the editor assumes any liability for any injury and/or damage.

The Publisher

 ELSEVIER your source for books, journals and multimedia in the health sciences
www.elsevierhealth.com

Printed and bound in the United Kingdom
Transferred to Digital Print 2009

Working together to grow
libraries in developing countries

www.elsevier.com | www.bookaid.org | www.sabre.org

ELSEVIER   BOOK AID International   Sabre Foundation

The
publisher's
policy is to use
**paper manufactured
from sustainable forests**

Contents

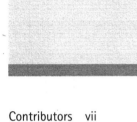

Contributors

Claire Callaghan BA(Hons) MSc RGN
Lecturer, St Martin's College, Lancaster, UK

Alison Crumbie MSN BSc RGN DipNP Dip App ScN
Nurse Practitioner, Windermere Health Centre,
Windermere, Cumbria, UK

Wendy Fairhurst-Winstanley BA (Hons) PGCE RGN MSc
Nurse Partner, Honorary Lecturer (University of
Manchester), Marus Bridge Practice,
Wigan, UK

Kay Holt MA MSc Dip BSc(Hons)
Nurse Practitioner, Cleveley Health Centre,
Cleveleys, UK

Lesley Kyle DN NP BA(Hons) MSc RGN RM
Nurse Practitioner/Partner, Canonbie Medical Practice,
Canonbie, UK

Sally Panter-Brick BSc(Hons) NP RGN RSCN
Paediatric Nurse Practitioner, Children's Ward,
Cumberland Royal Infirmary, Carlisle, UK

Anita Powell RGN
Heart Failure Nurse, Community Offices,
Lancaster, UK

Fiona Smart PhD MA BEd(Hons) RGN RSCN DipN RNT
Director of Studies: Advanced Clinical Practice,
St Martin's College, Carlisle, UK

Mike Walsh PhD BA(Hons) RGN PGCE DipN(London)
Reader in Nursing, St Martin's College, Carlisle, UK

Preface

*No man has a right to fix the boundary of the march
of a nation; no man has a right to say to his country
– thus far shalt thou go and no further*

(Charles Stewart Parnell 1885)

These ringing words from Parnell were used to introduce the first edition of this book published in 1999. We make no apologies for repeating them in this edition as while we have made huge strides in advancing the cause of nurse practitioners (NPs) and making people realise the tremendous contribution they can make to health care, there are those who still say 'thus far and no further' to nurse practitioners.

There are many examples of areas where nurse practitioners are making a huge difference to health care but there is one in particular we would like to highlight and that is the area of child health whether it be through the specialist paediatric nurse practitioner or the more general primary care NP. The year 2004 saw the launch of the National Service Framework for Children and Young People's health services with the critical message that children are not just little adults and have to have dedicated care provision that rests firmly on this principle. We look forward to seeing NPs play a major role in the provision of holistic, family centred care in both hospital and primary care settings over the next few years.

Inter-professional collaboration underpins quality health care and we can think of numerous examples of successful NP collaboration with medical colleagues which illustrate this point. Further collaboration with other health care professionals such as paramedics is taking shape and promises much for the future. Perhaps our biggest collaborators however are patients themselves. This underpins one of the unique aspects of NP led health care, the ability to take the patient with you as a partner, exploring the holistic family and social related aspects of health and illness in addition to the biomedical science.

The NP concept has spread beyond the boundaries of the USA where it originated, to encompass Canada, Australia, New Zealand and increasingly European countries. There is no doubting the contribution NPs can make to the health of the Third World given the resources and political stability needed to provide effective health care. This is particularly true of the area around the Indian Ocean devastated by the Tsunami of December 26 2004. Our own academic travels since the last edition have taken us to the USA, Canada and Australia where we have spoken to many NPs and if it is any consolation to readers, they share the problems and aggravations that are experienced in the UK. They also share the personal triumphs of a good job well done as a patient's health is turned around by skilled NP care. Whichever part of the world you go to, NPs are moving health care forward and Parnell's words are as equally true in Oswaldtwistle as they are in Ontario.

As this book goes to press the NMC are consulting on nurse practitioner registration in the UK. When you buy this book we will know the outcome. It is 14 years since the first RCN course was set up for NPs, and since then we have been campaigning for recognition. Let us hope that now our time has come.

Mike Walsh, 2006

PART 1

Clinical practice

Chapter 1

Problem–solving

Alison Crumbie

INTRODUCTION

Nurse practitioners consult with patients who have undifferentiated, undiagnosed conditions. Patients are assessed, receive a diagnosis and are offered education, treatment, referral or discharge. This type of activity exemplifies the autonomous practice which characterizes the work of a nurse practitioner. Indeed, Offredy (1998) found that important factors relating to decision-making in nurse practitioner consultations include: the ability to recognize patterns in clinical situations, the ability to concentrate simultaneously on both obvious and masked patient cues and an appreciation of the consequences of inappropriate action. This points to the complexity of the activity carried out during consultations. In order to remain within the Nursing and Midwifery Council's Code of Professional Conduct (Nursing and Midwifery Council 2002), the nurse practitioner should accept responsibility for autonomous decision-making. It is therefore essential that the nurse develops an effective and secure clinical reasoning strategy to guide the problem-solving process.

Problem-solving is not unique to nursing. Indeed, most professionals face problems in their area of practice. A detective is an obvious example of a person presented with a problem who works through a certain process in order to arrive at a solution to a crime. Engineers are faced with problems of constructing bridges across increasingly large stretches of water; a builder faced with the problem of a leaking roof has to employ a problem-solving strategy to discover the leak and repair it. There is an enormous amount of literature relating to theories of problem-solving and clearly different approaches are valuable in different settings. The problem-solving process which is most appropriate for nurse practitioners may not be the same as for nurses working in other areas of practice.

Hurst et al (1991) carried out a series of interviews with nurses to gain insight into their understanding of the problem-solving process. They found that nurses gave a high degree of attention to the implementation stage of problem-solving but attached little importance to evaluation. Hurst et al suggest that this may be because nurses concentrate on the 'doing' aspects of nursing, at the expense of the analytical processes of problem-solving. Nurse practitioners, however, are making autonomous decisions and therefore have to address the analytical processes of problem-solving rather than adopting the traditional approach of 'doing things, for the patient'. The nurse practitioner will take a history from the patient, carry out appropriate physical examination techniques and make decisions about further tests, referral or treatment regimes. This process may involve doing things with and for the patient but the expertise lies in the analysis of problems and the ability to arrive at accurate diagnoses in an efficient and effective manner. A problem-solving strategy which underpins the nurse's clinical decision-making will contribute to accurate diagnoses and the implementation of more effective treatment regimes. Through reflective practice, the nurse will learn from the process, building up a level of expertise for future encounters with clients. A secure clinical reasoning strategy enables the nurse to progress as far as his or her level of knowledge will allow.

There are two major theories of problem-solving – the information-processing system theory (Newell & Simon 1972) and the stages model theory. The information-processing system is based on the theory that problem-solving is a product of two processes – understanding and solving. Understanding is based on your immediate thought processes when you meet a problem and your knowledge and experience of similar situations. The solving process is a search for the solution using your experience of similar situations, identifying, analysing and synthesizing knowledge gathered during the understanding process (Hurst et al 1991). Hurst et al state that there is little research to support the application of the information-processing system to real-life problems such as those found in dealing with patients. The information-processing system theory is most often associated with well-defined problems; frequently, the problems faced by nurse practitioners are complex and ill-defined.

Hurst (1993) points out that a review of the literature relating to stages model theory over the last 50 years elicited 55 different representations of stages models. The stages theory of problem-solving is a stepwise process involving different stages and different numbers of steps depending on the model used. According to Hurst (1993), the stages model encourages systematic thinking which can be applied to each new problem. It is flexible: when problem-solving is unsuccessful, it is possible to isolate the weak link in the process and therefore its use can facilitate learning.

There are, however, several criticisms of the stages model. It is suggested that the stages represent a rigid process of discrete steps and that this does not adequately reflect what really happens in practice (Hurst 1993). In clinical practice the stages become blurred and there is a dynamic process which does not necessarily follow a logical stepwise approach. Barrows & Pickell (1991) developed a model of clinical problem-solving which is presented as a stages approach to the clinical decision-making process. The model is built up in a series of steps; however, the authors suggest that it is a dynamic process including ongoing feedback and development of the initial impressions of the patient. The clinician may work through the steps in a matter of seconds, and then work through the steps again as more information becomes available through the patient inquiry.

The Barrows & Pickell model was primarily written for medical students. It incorporates issues of patient education, compliance, physical examination, diagnosis and viewing the problem from the patient's perspective and therefore has relevance to the work of nurse practitioners. Barrows & Pickell point out that there are two components of clinical problem-solving which are inexorably linked. One component is content, which is the knowledge base of the practitioner. The second component is process, which is the method of manipulation used by the practitioner to apply knowledge to the patient's problem. A well-developed problem-solving process enables the practitioner to utilize knowledge and experience to provide the most effective care for patients. Barrows & Pickell suggest that effective, efficient and fast clinical reasoning skills are the skills behind intuition. Intuition is not a magical phenomenon representing the art of clinical practice – it can be developed and taught. According to Barrows & Pickell, the more a practitioner focuses on the skills of problem-solving, the more intuitive his or her practice will become. The skills of the problem-solving process within Barrows & Pickell's model of clinical reasoning will now be applied to the problems faced by nurse practitioners in the clinical setting.

FORMING THE INITIAL CONCEPT

It is essential that each part of the encounter with a patient is an active process on the part of the nurse practitioner. The first impressions of the patient provide the nurse with an enormous amount of information which should be noted and which will form part of the initial concept. All significant factors should be considered, including quality of the patient's voice, smell, appearance, how they enter the consulting room and the people accompanying the patient. This information is gathered in seconds and provides the basis for the practitioner's initial perceptions. The practitioner analyses these perceptions and develops the initial concept (Barrows & Pickell 1991, p. 34):

Patient information available at the outset
↓
Perceptions
↓
Analysis
↓
Initial concept

The patient's appearance, age, sex and opening comments add to the initial concept developing in the mind of the practitioner. A patient who walks into the consulting room and sits down before complaining of hip pain will provide a different picture to the patient who limps in with the help of a relative and gingerly lowers himself down on to the chair with an outstretched leg and then complains of hip pain. A patient who comments on feeling tired and low and is judged to be approximately 55 years of age, female and slightly overweight will create a different initial concept to a patient who complains of feeling tired and low, is judged to be approximately 25 years of age, female and very thin.

The initial concept is gradually developed from deliberately sought observations. For example, in the case of the female patient who is 55 years of age, slightly obese, tired and low, the nurse may particularly concentrate on observing her hair for quality and quantity, looking at her skin for hydration and listening to the quality of her voice. All of this information can be added to the initial concept. In the case of the 25-year-old female who is tired and low and very thin, the nurse may in particular observe her facial expressions, general appearance and manner of approach to the consulting room and add this information to the initial concept of the patient. In each of these cases the practitioner is gathering information which is relevant to the presenting complaint and, whilst avoiding the dangers of jumping to conclusions too quickly, a focused exploration for the signs of hypothyroidism in the first case and for depression in the second expedites the problem-solving process.

It is also important to note the demeanour of those who have accompanied the patient. Observations of body language and listening carefully to the speech of the carer or relative will provide further information about the patient's problem. Patients quite frequently attend the surgery because they have been asked to do so by friends or relatives. It is important to ascertain this fact as it provides information about the patient's perception of the problem.

There are a number of threats to the accuracy of the formation of an initial concept; one such threat is prejudice and bias. The practitioner's own beliefs and assumptions will weaken the effectiveness of the assessment. It is clearly important to become self-aware and to recognize any prejudice which may cloud judgement in the clinical setting. This differs from the need to be aware of culturally specific disease processes. For example, if a 50-year-old Asian person complained of feeling tired and low it would be quite reasonable to entertain an initial hypothesis of diabetes mellitus. The analysis of the patient's problem must remain objective in order to preserve accuracy and therefore other assumptions about culture, gender, sexual orientation and class should be deliberately checked for elements of personal bias which could contaminate the problem-solving process.

A further threat to the process of developing an initial concept is the possibility of making a translation error. This occurs when a patient uses a term which the practitioner immediately translates into something which does not accurately represent the patient's experience. For example, a patient may complain of being sick and the practitioner notes nausea and vomiting. The patient could mean feeling ill, feeling nauseous, feeling guilty or depressed or feeling feverish – therefore it is essential for the practitioner to check the meaning of the patient's words with him or her before making assumptions.

It is important at this stage to keep tentative hypotheses separate from the initial concept. The initial concept includes information gathered from the patient's appearance, observations of people accompanying the patient, awareness of a hidden agenda, the patient's perception of the problem and any evidence which may support initial hypotheses.

For example, in the case of the woman who complains of feeling tired and low, the nurse practitioner can collect information and develop a summarized version of observed facts:

> *A 55-year-old Caucasian woman, who states she is feeling tired and low, appears to be slightly overweight, has coarse thin hair, has dry skin and a hoarse voice, is not accompanied by a relative, walked into the consulting room with no restrictions and states she doesn't know what is wrong.*

It would be a mistake at this stage to note 'a 55-year-old woman with hypothyroidism'. Hypothyroidism is simply one of several potential hypotheses. Similarly, with the 25-year-old woman who is complaining of feeling tired and low, it would be a mistake to note 'a 25-year-old depressed woman'. It is more accurate to note: 'a 25-year-old woman who states she is tired and low, appears to have a low body mass index, has slow speech and movement, with a depressed appearance'. Depression is a potential diagnosis for this woman and is one of several hypotheses until further evidence can be added to the initial concept.

GENERATING HYPOTHESES

A hypothesis is a provisional explanation for the occurrence of the patient's problem. It provides a label for the information which has been collected and allows the practitioner to focus a line of enquiry in a certain direction (Chase 2004). Once the initial concept has been formulated, several different hypotheses may spring to mind. This can happen in a matter of seconds and the number and type of hypotheses will vary according to the clarity of the patient's complaint. The generation of hypotheses

will also depend upon the experience and clinical knowledge of the practitioner. A nurse who has little experience of women's health and the menopause, for example, may come up with differential diagnoses of anxiety disorder or depression for a woman who complains of sleeplessness and feelings of distress during meetings at work. A nurse with experience in caring for women experiencing the symptoms of the menopause may generate hypotheses of menopause, anxiety disorder or depression and the subsequent enquiry will have a broader perspective covering different issues.

Nurse practitioners are frequently presented with vague complaints from patients such as 'I feel tired all the time', 'I have been experiencing headaches' or 'I have been feeling dizzy'. For each of these vague complaints there are many potential hypotheses and once the initial concept has been developed, the hypotheses have to be narrowed down to provide a focus for the consultation. For the complaint of 'dizzy', for example, the nurse has to ask initial questions to help focus the enquiry. 'When does it occur?' 'What makes it better and what makes it worse?' 'Are there any other symptoms associated with the dizziness?' 'Can you describe the feeling?' The questions at this stage are broad and should not bias the responses of the patient. For example, asking the question 'Are there any other symptoms associated with the dizziness?' is different to asking 'Do you feel nauseous when you are dizzy?' Questions which are too focused at this stage can contaminate the patient's story and lead the patient into providing information which does not necessarily represent the reality of his or her experience but rather tells the practitioner what he or she wants to hear.

It is possible to generate broad hypotheses which can be focused after gathering further information from the patient. For example, if a patient complains of pain in the hand and the forearm, the practitioner may generate a hypothesis of 'painful forearm'. Further information may lead the practitioner to generate several more focused hypotheses. If the patient states that he doesn't remember sustaining an injury but the pain has been present for many months and is now stopping him in his work, the hypotheses of 'nervous injury to the median nerve, radial nerve or ulnar nerve' could all be generated. These hypotheses then provide the basis for further enquiry and the practitioner needs to generate a strategy to provide evidence which may support or refute the hypotheses generated so far.

FORMULATING AN ENQUIRY STRATEGY

The initial concept and the hypotheses must remain flexible and open to change in the light of new information. As the nurse becomes aware of new information, this must constantly be checked against the initial concept and the hypotheses. Hypotheses may be ruled out or substantiated by further enquiry and it is here that the nurse practitioner must utilize physical examination skills and focused history-taking to elicit the information required to generate a working hypothesis which will underpin the subsequent management plan. The aspects of physical examination to be carried out, the tests which may need to be performed and the sequence of questions to be asked form the enquiry strategy.

The enquiry strategy is a process of analysis and synthesis of information. For example, in a patient who complains of headache, the initial concept may be: 'Woman who appears to be 30 years old states she has been experiencing headaches with increasing frequency over the last 12 months but does not have one today'. On asking broad questions the woman states that she feels nauseous with the headache, paracetamol has helped slightly, the headache is made worse by noise and she tends to go to bed if she has one, the headaches seem to come on in the evenings and she has never experienced anything like this before. At this stage the hypotheses could be focused to 'migraine', 'tension headache', 'cluster headache', 'eye strain', 'sinusitis', 'side-effects of medications' or, less likely, 'brain tumour' or 'severe hypertension'. The differential diagnosis of 'meningeal irritation' has already been ruled out as meningitis presents with a sudden severe, generalized headache which would have been present during the consultation.

The nurse practitioner's knowledge of anatomy and physiology, pathophysiology and previous experience will then guide the history-taking process to ask some more focused questions, such as: 'Please show me where you feel the pain.' 'Do you notice any other symptoms with the headache?' 'When did you last have an eye examination?' 'What type of work do you do?' 'Are you on any other medications?' 'Do you have any neck pain?' 'How long do the headaches last for?' 'What do you think your headaches are related to?' 'Do any of your family members have problems with headaches?' 'Is there any link between the headaches and your menstrual cycle?'

Several of these questions will allow the practitioner to rule out some of the potential generated hypotheses. For example, if there is a negative reply to 'Are you on any other medications?', side-effects of medications can be ruled out. A positive response to the question relating to neck pain enhances the possibility of tension headache. The associated symptom of nausea may heighten the possibility of migraine, while the location of the headache bilaterally around the occipital region may support tension headache. If the woman reports that the headaches last for 4–6 hours and there is no history of family migraine or similar headaches, tension headache may again be considered. In response to the menstrual cycle question, the patient answers that she would not know as she has not had a period for a few months. This information clearly changes the initial concept and generates further hypotheses for analysis and synthesis with the original concept, for example, in this particular case, relating to potential pregnancy.

The enquiry strategy is a deductive process. The information obtained will allow the practitioner to reject some hypotheses, support others or generate new ones in the light of fresh information. Some questions will effectively rule out certain hypotheses. Patients who attend the clinic with headaches are often concerned that they may have hypertension. Practitioners are aware that hypertension is an unlikely cause of headache, however, it takes only a few moments to check a patient's blood pressure and this will quickly reassure the patient on being told that the reading is normal. Similarly, some patients fear a brain tumour with unexplained headaches, so it is worthwhile addressing this and enquiring about the type of headache (deep, steady and dull); what makes it worse (coughing or straining); when it is worse (worse on waking and often improves with upright position), and then letting the patient know that a headache which has been intermittent over 12 months and worse in the evenings is unlikely to be associated with a brain tumour. By doing this, however, you may have addressed the patient's fears – this in itself can be therapeutic.

The methods described in the enquiry strategy are described by Barrows & Pickell (1991) as a searching process. Searching is focused on the particular presenting problem. Scanning is another process used by practitioners to scan the horizon for further clues. This includes the review of systems, review of past medical history, family history, demographics and social situation. This may produce useful information which may generate new hypotheses or support the present hypotheses. The scanning process also provides the nurse with information which is incredibly valuable when considering treatment options. If in the scanning process the nurse finds that the patient left home when she was 16 and now lives in shared accommodation with four other women, is employed at present but only on the minimum wage and has no savings, this will have serious implications for suggestions regarding treatment options.

After searching and scanning, the practitioner may need to redesign the enquiry strategy. Clearly, in the case of the woman with the headache, the new hypotheses may include 'pregnant' and experiencing 'tension headaches'. This would have to be checked with further history-taking, now focused on sexual activity, the nature of the nausea, weight loss or weight gain and the possibility of being pregnant. The process remains dynamic and flexible and the practitioner must be open to change and regeneration of new hypotheses throughout the process.

APPLYING APPROPRIATE CLINICAL SKILLS

Clinical skills include the ability to carry out an appropriate physical examination and to focus the history to dissect and elaborate on the patient's complaint. Most of a diagnosis is made on the history alone and much of the physical examination is conducted to support or refute hypotheses generated during the enquiry and history-taking process. History-taking skill involves the ability to adapt to the particular patient's communication style. The use of broad questions followed by more focused questions helps to elicit as much information as possible in the patient's own words. Barrows & Pickell (1991) suggest that direct questions help to dissect the specifics of the patient's problem. Direct questions should cover reasons for the encounter, onset of the problem, quality and intensity of the symptoms, associated symptoms, sequence and localization of symptoms, physical or emotional stress preceding the problem and relieving or palliation factors. The history-taking process is covered in greater detail in Chapter 2.

In taking the patient's history, questions should generally be open, as closed questions tend to bias the patient's responses. Open questions allow patients to elaborate on their symptoms and to tell their story. There are some occasions, however, when closed questioning is appropriate. In an emergency situation such as an acute asthmatic episode a closed question, 'Have you already taken your blue inhaler?' will help the practitioner to understand the severity of the attack. In a consultation with a patient who does not easily elaborate on the story of the problem, closed questions may be necessary to elicit responses to specific questions.

The history-taking process in a person with headaches might start with an open question such as 'How do your headaches affect you?' This may be followed by a series of more focused questions, including: 'When do they occur?' 'Where do you feel the pain?' 'How long have you been experiencing them for?' 'Do you experience any other symptoms?' Depending on the responses to the more focused questions, the practitioner might want to go on to ask a series of closed questions to confirm or rule out certain hypotheses, for example 'Do you find the light makes it worse?' or 'Does your neck feel painful?' It is important not to channel the patient down a specific line to support the hypotheses that were generated in the first few seconds. Open questioning avoids this problem and allows the practitioner to build a broad picture of the patient's problem. This will reduce the likelihood of missing a vital clue.

The physical examination is guided by the generated hypotheses. Physical examination is a further searching process and is most often carried out simply to confirm or refute the hypotheses. Physical examination can be carried out after the history-taking process or the two processes can be carried out at the same time. If a patient complains of abdominal pain but is unable to describe the exact location of the pain, is in his mid-40s, tells you that the pain sometimes keeps him awake at night and sometimes makes him vomit, the hypotheses of pancreatitis, peptic ulcer, intestinal obstruction, gastroenteritis, reflux oesophagitis, irritable colon and ureterolithiasis are all possible. For efficient use of time it is worthwhile examining the patient's abdomen whilst carrying out further questioning. The physical examination helps to provide more precise information about the location of the pain. When the patient places his hand over the epigastric area of his abdomen and does not complain of any tenderness in the costovertebral angles or in the lower abdomen, several of the hypotheses can be rejected and the practitioner can focus the history-taking and further physical examination on the remaining hypotheses.

This very brief initial examination can assist the history-taking process and, whilst it is important to carry out a thorough abdominal examination and urinalysis and it is important to take a thorough history including systems review, allowing the patient to point to the area of discomfort on his exposed abdomen will help focus the searching techniques during the consultation. When the patient points to the epigastric area, the initial concept of the patient is developed further, the practitioner employs the enquiry strategy to collect more information, analyses the information, utilizes further searching techniques of physical examination and history-taking and adds all the information to the initial concept. Eventually enough data will have been gathered to analyse and accurately identify the patient's problem. At this point the practitioner can develop a problem synthesis.

DEVELOPING THE PROBLEM SYNTHESIS

Once the initial concept has been developed and refined and the information has been checked for accuracy with the patient, the enhanced initial concept develops into the problem synthesis. This is a representation of the patient's problem. Once a problem synthesis has been developed the practitioner should be able to represent the patient's problem with accuracy and clarity. This does not necessarily mean that the practitioner has confirmed a diagnosis. In some cases it is not possible to do so because further tests are needed or because the patient has a rare condition with which the practitioner is unfamiliar. The patient may require referral for a specialist opinion and therefore it is important that the practitioner is able to represent the problem synthesis without necessarily offering a diagnosis.

The problem synthesis is developed from the data-gathering process – the enquiry strategy. The following is an example of the developing problem synthesis. A male patient in his 60s walks into the consulting room complaining of a cough which will not go away. The practitioner develops an immediate initial concept of 'a male patient with a recurrent cough who is in his 60s'. It is possible to

develop several hypotheses from this initial information. The patient may have developed chronic bronchitis, chronic obstructive airways disease, congestive heart failure, gastroesophageal reflux, asthma, postnasal drip, a viral upper respiratory tract infection, pneumonia or bronchitis. The patient has a problem associated with the respiratory system and an experienced practitioner will immediately focus observation on the patient's fingers to look for evidence of nicotine staining, looking at his face, hair and mouth for evidence of the yellow hue of many years of smoking, noting any smell of smoke, observing the lips for signs of pursed-lip breathing and noting the mucous membranes for signs of cyanosis and respiratory distress. The practitioner may also glance at the patient's ankles to see if there is any evidence of peripheral oedema which may provide a clue that the patient has a cardiac condition. This all happens in seconds and immediately the practitioner has developed the initial concept and has gathered vital clues to support or refute the generated hypotheses.

This patient has no signs of smoking and it is not possible to see his ankles underneath his trousers. The practitioner commences with an open questioning style to try and understand more about the nature of the cough. 'Tell me a bit more about your cough'. The patient explains that he has had it for months and it is bothering him at night. He has fits of coughing and it is keeping his wife awake. The practitioner has gathered vital information here. If the patient has had the cough for months, it is more likely to be a chronic condition and not an acute one. It is therefore possible to focus on the conditions which are more likely to be chronic such as chronic bronchitis, chronic obstructive airways disease, congestive heart failure, gastroesophageal reflux, asthma or postnasal drip and the hypotheses of the acute respiratory conditions, including a viral upper respiratory tract infection, pneumonia or bronchitis are less likely. The initial concept has already changed to 'a man in his 60s who has no signs of smoking, with a cough which he has had for months; the cough is troublesome at night'.

The practitioner must then develop an enquiry strategy which includes history-taking and physical examination. The history will include more focused questions about the cough. Questions about the timing, whether it is productive, whether there are any other associated symptoms, what makes it worse and what makes it better will help to build upon the initial concept. When the patient states that the cough is productive, the practitioner asks an open question to discover exactly what sort of sputum is being produced. When the patient answers that it is 'gooey', that doesn't help the practitioner much. 'What colour is the sputum?', which is different from asking 'Is the sputum green?' will result in the patient describing the sputum as white, green, yellow, black or red – all of these responses would be significant. If the question had been: 'Is the sputum green?' the patient could answer 'yes' or 'no'. As the patient was not provided with any options the reply may not be an accurate reflection of the nature of his sputum. If he answers 'no' then further questioning is required; if he answers 'yes', it is possible that the practitioner is leading the patient down a particular path towards a diagnosis and may inadvertently miss a vital clue.

When the patient states that the sputum is white, it is worse at night, nothing seems to help once he has started a coughing fit, sometimes he feels sick and dizzy with the effort of coughing and he often feels short of breath during an attack, he does not smoke and his wife is very worried about him, the initial concept has changed again, and the hypotheses can be reviewed. A cough which is aggravated on recumbency can be due to postnasal drip, congestive heart failure or gastroesophageal reflux. There is a possibility that the diagnosis could be asthma, where the cough is triggered by the presence of dust mites in a poorly ventilated bedroom. The presence of white sputum could support the hypothesis of asthma; however, further examination and enquiry are required before eliminating other possible causes of the cough. The initial concept has now developed to 'a man in his 60s who does not smoke has had a cough for months which produces white sputum; the cough is worse at night, nothing relieves it, he feels sick and dizzy during an attack, his wife is worried about his health'. .

The enquiry strategy must now go a stage further to ask more searching questions and to carry out the appropriate physical examinations. A practitioner might choose to continue to take the history, including present social situation, past medical history, current medications and relevant family history and follow this with a physical examination. In the history-taking process the nurse finds that the patient has recently retired and moved house, is currently decorating, had a history of 'bronchitis' as a child, has been very fit and well and rarely consults with health care professionals

and is not taking any medications. To reject or support hypotheses which now seem to be less likely than at the beginning of the encounter, the practitioner might now specifically ask closed or focused questions about heart or gastric symptoms. 'Do you notice any heartburn?' 'Do you notice a strange taste in your mouth when you lie down?' 'Have you noticed any swelling in your ankles?' 'Do you get breathless when you exercise?' These questions would help rule out with greater certainty gastric reflux and congestive heart disease.

The physical examination component of the enquiry strategy would be focused on the respiratory system and include examination of the cardiovascular system and the sinuses for postnasal drip. It is clear from the history that the practitioner might be working on a preferred hypothesis of asthma and the data-gathering physical examination would be focused on auscultation for bilateral wheezing. Examination of the posterior pharynx for secretions and the mucosa of the nose for cobblestone appearance, followed by palpation of the sinuses for tenderness would help support or rule out the hypothesis of postnasal drip. Examination of the extremities for pitting oedema, assessment of the heart rate for tachycardia and auscultation of the lungs for crackles or wheezes and the heart for extra heart sounds would address the cardiovascular possibilities and add to the developing problem synthesis.

Eventually the data-gathering system comes together. Several hypotheses have been rejected and the practitioner can then form a problem synthesis. The problem synthesis represents the patient's problem and therefore in the example of the man in his 60s with a recurrent cough, the practitioner would develop a problem synthesis as follows:

A man in his 60s who does not smoke has had a cough for months which produces white sputum, the cough is worse at night, nothing relieves it, he feels sick and dizzy during an attack, his wife is worried about his health. He has no breathlessness on exercise and does not complain of heartburn. He had a history of bronchitis as a child and no other past medical history. He does not take any medications and is usually well. He has recently retired and moved house. He is currently decorating his present house. There is no evidence of cyanosis in the mucous membranes and no evidence of pursed-lip breathing. Mucous membranes of the oropharynx and nose are pink and moist and there is no evidence of mucoid secretions in the posterior pharynx. He

*has a pulse rate of 82 and normal heart sounds. He
has wheezes throughout both lungs.*

Once a problem synthesis has been developed
the practitioner can compare the problem synthesis
with the generated hypotheses. A judgement is
made as to which (if any) of the hypotheses fits the
problem synthesis. Drawing on clinical knowledge
and experience the practitioner is able to apply the
pathophysiological processes to the patient's
problem and make a judgement about the possible
diagnosis. It may be necessary to utilize a variety of
tests or to initiate a trial of treatment to be sure that
the diagnosis is correct.

It is essential that throughout the problem-
solving process the practitioner is checking the
accuracy of the findings with the patient's perception of the problem. Communicating with the
patient throughout the process helps him or her to
understand the diagnostic process and therefore to
understand the treatment plan. It is essential to get
to know the patient to help direct subsequent decisions about treatment and tests. If these decisions
are made without the patient's contribution, the
chances of compliance with the treatment plan are
reduced and therefore the success of the intervention will be threatened.

LABORATORY AND DIAGNOSTIC FINDINGS

It is clearly important in some patient encounters to
support or reject the generated hypotheses with
tests. For example, in the previous case of the
female patient who was 55 years of age, slightly
obese, tired and low, the practitioner might want to
follow the history-taking process and physical
examination with thyroid function tests to support
or reject a hypothesis of hypothyroidism. In the
example of the man in his 60s with recurrent cough,
the nurse may wish to do a reversibility test with
pre- and post-salbutamol peak flow readings
followed by a week's diary recording of peak flow
readings and a follow-up appointment.

When deciding which tests to utilize it is important to consider the inconvenience to the patient,
the harm caused to him or her, the cost of the test
and what information the test is going to provide.
Sometimes tests are used as part of the scanning
procedure in an attempt to search for other clues,
for example, the battery of tests that many clinicians carry out for the complaint of tired all the time
(full blood count, urea and electrolytes, liver function tests, blood glucose, thyroid function tests,
monospot (or Paul Burnell for glandular fever), erythrocyte sedimentation rate and urinalysis) may
help provide a clue where the history-taking and
physical examination process have not produced a
significant result. It is essential to consider the role
of the tests in the enquiry strategy and the relevance of positive or negative results to solving the
patient's problem.

The sensitivity, specificity and relevance of the
test for the hypothesis must be considered to determine if it is worthwhile proceeding with that test.
Sensitivity is measured by the number of false-
negatives it might produce. If a test detects most
cases of a disease in a tested group of people with
few false negative results, then it is sensitive for
that disease. If the test is specific for the disease
then it will only show a positive result in people
who have the disease. If a test shows a positive
result in people who do not have the disease then it
is not specific. The relevance of a test is the effect it
will have on the diagnosis and management of the
patient. The reasons for carrying out laboratory
testing according to Barrows & Pickell (1991) are to
reassure the patient, to provide the practitioner
with further evidence to support a hypothesis and
to assess the severity of the disease. The results of
testing when considered with the rest of the
enquiry strategy may support your diagnosis.

DIAGNOSTIC DECISION-MAKING

Eventually the practitioner is faced with the need to
make a diagnostic decision. It may not be possible
to make an immediate decision about a patient's
problem and in some cases it is necessary to live
with uncertainty until test results are available or
until further evidence comes to light. If the diagnosis is uncertain the clinician has to decide how to
progress. It may be that after the enquiry strategy is
complete a patient's problem may still have two
hypotheses. For example, chronic obstructive airways
disease and asthma may be difficult to differentiate
in some patients. It may therefore be necessary to
implement a course of treatment, monitor the result
and then make a diagnostic decision based upon
the results of the therapy. If a decision can be made
the practitioner then has a further decision-making
process to address – how to treat the patient.

THERAPEUTIC DECISION-MAKING

Evidence which has been collected throughout the patient encounter will have helped the practitioner understand the patient's perception of the problem and learn about the patient's values and beliefs. This is essential when making a decision about treatment with the patient. If a patient has concerns about the overuse of steroids in the treatment of asthma, for example, this issue may have to be addressed and alternatives may have to be explored. Similarly, if the patient expects to receive antibiotics for a cough but the practitioner makes a therapeutic decision to offer no treatment because it is a viral cough of short duration, this decision will have to be considered in the light of the patient's expectations and time will have to be devoted to explaining this decision to the patient.

It is also important to consider the cost of the treatment – both to the patient and to the health service. More expensive treatments are sometimes worthwhile when there is proof that they are more effective. It is essential to consider the patient's perspective and needs here, as a rapid response to an initial treatment may enhance compliance with treatments later in a chronic disease process. The patient must be fully informed of what to expect so that he or she realizes that there is some partnership in the decision-making process. The practitioner must also consider the risks of the treatment and whether the risks outweigh the benefits. This is not always easy, and, like diagnostic decision-making, it is a dynamic cyclical process which alters according to information gathered from the patient and the knowledge and experience of the practitioner (Fig. 1.1).

REFLECTION IN AND ON PRACTICE

The Barrows & Pickell stages model of clinical problem-solving allows the practitioner to reflect upon an encounter with a patient and to consider the stages which went well and stages which did not go well. The model provides a framework for learning from each client encounter and allows the practitioner to identify skills which need to be developed. It is possible to use this framework to carry out reflection in action, as described by Schon (1987). The practitioner can carry out scanning techniques whilst reflecting upon past experiences and synthesizing that knowledge with the information gathered in the present encounter.

The problem-solving process is a dynamic cyclical process which allows the initial concept of the patient to evolve and develop. The whole process

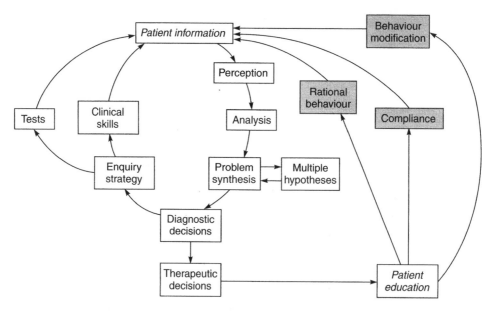

Figure 1.1 Diagnostic decision-making process (Figure 14, from *Developing Clinical Problem-solving Skills* by Howard S. Barrows and Garfield C. Pickell. Copyright © 1991 by W. W. Norton & Company, Inc. Used by permission of W. W. Norton & Company, Inc).

may happen in minutes or it may take months, depending upon the need for test results or diagnostic interventions. A structured approach to problem-solving enables the nurse practitioner to utilize the skills of history-taking and physical examination to generate hypotheses and to minimize the possibility of missing a vital clue. A thorough approach will finally enable the nurse practitioner to make diagnostic and therapeutic decisions with a confidence that enhances the success of the consultation process.

References

Barrows H S, Pickell G C 1991 Developing clinical problem solving skills: a guide to more effective diagnosis and treatment. Norton Medical Books, New York

Chase S 2004 Clinical judgement and communication in nurse practitioner practice. F A Davis, Philadelphia

Hurst K 1993 Problem solving in nursing practice. Scutari Press, London

Hurst K, Dean A, Trickey S 1991 The recognition and non-recognition of problem solving stages in nursing practice. Journal of Advanced Nursing 16:1444–1455

Newell A, Simon H A 1972 Human problem solving. Prentice-Hall, New Jersey

Nursing and Midwifery Council 2002 Code of Professional Conduct. NMC, London

Offredy M 1998 The application of decision making concepts by the nurse practitioners in general practice. Journal of Advanced Nursing 28(5):988–1000

Schon D 1987 Educating the reflective practitioner. Jossey Bass, San Francisco

Chapter 2

Taking a history

Alison Crumbie

INTRODUCTION

In order to operate in advanced clinical roles, nurse practitioners must be skilled in taking an accurate history. All nurses are used to assessing patients and asking questions but the nurse practitioner expands this skill to include an assessment of the medical history. The history-taking interview must be of a high quality so that the patient's symptoms are accurately and precisely recorded. The importance of taking a history cannot be over estimated – Epstein et al (2003) estimate that 80% of diagnoses are based on the history-taking process alone.

Listening to the patient's story is not just an opportunity for data collection but also for establishing a therapeutic relationship. The encounter may also be an opportunity for a healing or teaching moment. Health care does not have solutions for all the problems that people present with and often all that can be done is to listen and validate the patient's experience.

This chapter will focus on the history-taking aspects of nurse practitioner consultations. The skills of physical examination, health education and the management of many common conditions will be presented in later chapters.

As mentioned in the previous chapter, history-taking is a problem-solving process, it involves, searching for clues, collecting information without bias yet staying on track to solve the puzzle. As the data comes from a human being and is received by another human being, it is subject to error. Patients forget symptoms or get the sequence of events out of order or withhold embarrassing details. Often people may tell their story in a way they think you want to hear it or they may try to please you. They may describe their actions in a way that they think a normal sensible person would behave rather than how events occurred. Clinicians may misunderstand, overlook relevant information, fail to ask key questions or jump to premature diagnostic conclusions. The assessment is a continuing process and finding out the patient's story is sometimes ongoing rather than being limited to one encounter. Effective communication is clearly the key to success as the history is usually the single most important part of the whole assessment process.

Nurse practitioners consult with patients in a variety of settings. They may see patients in emergency situations in the accident and emergency department or in acute situations in a walk-in centre. In general practice, nurse practitioners may consult with a patient on a single occasion or may have several encounters with the person, spreading over many years. In the case of chronic disease management, for example, the nurse practitioner will be meeting the patient at regular intervals over a lengthy period. It may therefore be necessary to be selective and to prioritize in any particular consultation, as it may not be necessary to address the whole range of the patient's needs in one session. The nurse practitioner and patient therefore have to work as a partnership.

The nursing focus of the interview is on the person and his or her experience. It is important to 'stay in the moment' and appreciate the significance of that moment to the patient. Being there and witnessing the person may be therapeutic in itself when there is no treatment to offer. Simply acknowledging suffering, pain or the wide range of human emotions and social conditions can have a therapeutic effect.

The history should be seen as only one component of assessment and diagnosis; it is the initial stage in data collection. In some instances, such as a chronic disease, the history would be an extensive and important guide to diagnostic tests, whereas a minor skin condition may be diagnosed mainly by visual inspection and only a few questions are needed to reach a conclusion.

The nurse practitioner should start with a fresh mind, collecting information, and try to refrain from jumping to conclusions too quickly. Although history-taking may appear to be a daunting task at first, experience and practice will allow the practitioner to focus on the likely cause of the patient's problems with increasing confidence and rapidity.

FACTORS AFFECTING THE INTERVIEW

SELF-AWARENESS

Before starting an interview it is important to have taken some time to consider your own feelings, beliefs, values, strengths and weaknesses. Ask yourself what you bring to the relationship both culturally and emotionally, and cultivate inter-personal factors such as liking and respect for others, empathy and the ability to listen. Burnard (1992) presents a model of the outer and inner aspects of self. Outer aspects include facial expressions, gestures, touch, movement and dress; inner aspects include thinking, feeling, sensing, intuition and experience of the body. Through learning about the outer and inner aspects of oneself a sense of self-awareness can be developed.

Taking a complete history can be an intimate experience as you are asking the patient to share personal experiences. It is a privilege to listen and it often demands maturity to deal with the information and listen in a nonjudgemental way. In a busy clinical situation it is easy to bring charged emotions from a previous encounter with you. Taking a break or a quick refocusing meditation can help bring you back to centre for the next encounter.

ENVIRONMENTAL FACTORS

Provide privacy and try to ensure that there are no interruptions from the busy culture of our health care system, such as telephone calls, beepers, mobile phones or colleagues entering the room. Try and discourage interruptions except in cases of emergency. An interruption can disturb concentration and destroy the feeling of a safe environment that takes time to build up and, once lost, may not be fully restored. The room should be a comfortable temperature, with minimal noise. Remove distracting equipment or clutter from view. Arrange the furniture to enable the person to sit comfortably at the same eye level and at an angle which allows eye contact but also allows you to look away easily if desired.

PERSONAL SPACE

It is worth considering your proximity to the patient. The physical distance between yourself and the patient can send a powerful message and can generate feelings of anxiety or discomfort in some clients. The physical examination takes place in an intimate zone and it is important to remember when moving to this part of the consultation process that you should warn the patient that you are going to move in closer. If a patient feels uncomfortable with the distance from the clinician it may interfere with the development of trust in the relationship.

PERSONAL APPEARANCE

Nurse practitioners should think carefully about clothing. Most patients seem to prefer clothing appropriate to the setting, which tends towards conservative, conventional and professional. It is important not to impede or distract patients from being comfortable in telling their story, which may be the case if you are inappropriately dressed.

OTHER NONVERBAL COMMUNICATIONS

Body language can encourage or discourage the flow of conversation. Eye movements, facial expressions, body gestures and posture are all important (Table 2.1). Videotaping consultations can give you useful feedback, especially concerning mannerisms that may discourage patients from talking.

Table 2.1 Non-verbal behaviours of the interviewer

Positive	Negative
Professional appearance	Inappropriate dress
Equal status seating	Standing over or behind desk
Comfortable close proximity	Too close or too far away
Relaxed open posture	Tense
Leaning slightly forward	Slouched away
Occasional facilitating gestures	Critical or distracting
Facial animation or interest	Yawning, pointing, finger tapping
	Looking at watch
Appropriate smiling	Frowning
Maintaining eye contact	Avoiding eye contact
	Focusing on notes/computer
Moderate tone of voice	Strident or high pitch
Moderate rate of speech	Too slow or too fast
Appropriate touch	Too frequent or inappropriate touch

THE INTERVIEW

Medical history-taking has developed into a fairly set format and the nurse practitioner must be sure to include questions pertinent to a medical diagnosis, as this will assist communication with medical practitioners. When appropriate, you should also expand into psychosocial areas of questioning which include more about the person and his or her experiences. The skilled nurse practitioner therefore includes sufficient data for a baseline medical assessment but also obtains information that will provide a picture of the patient's experience of the condition.

At the beginning of the interview it is important to consider why the patient is there and what his or her expectations are. The patient also needs to know who you are, why you are there and what your intentions and expectations are. He or she may never have been interviewed in such depth before by a nurse or even heard of a nurse practitioner. The purpose of the interview is to establish a rapport with the patient to gather background information about any problems, current health, past medical history and social history. Patients want someone who is competent to address their concerns. Some may expect to be seen by a doctor and therefore withhold information, thinking a nursing interview is just a preliminary screen. Others may misunderstand time limitations or the expertise of the nurse. It may be helpful to introduce yourself with a simple brief explanation of your role so that patients understand the aim of the interview and its relevance to their care.

Patients must feel comfortable in telling their story and therefore need to know that the interview is confidential. Neighbour (1987) points out that patients have most control over the first part of the interview. Often they modify their first words depending on the environment and their initial remarks give valuable clues to their main concerns. It is helpful to leave as much space as possible for the patient to talk at the beginning of the interview. Blackwood & Hatton (2003) suggest that after asking the first question you should normally allow the patient to talk uninterrupted for at least two minutes. Simpson et al (1991), in their review of communication, mention one study where patients were interrupted by the clinician on average within 18 seconds of starting to describe their problem and, not surprisingly, failed to go on to disclose significant concerns.

Pendleton et al (1987) identified seven tasks of the consultation:

1. To define the reasons for the patient's attendance
2. To consider other problems
3. To choose with the patient an appropriate action for each problem
4. To achieve a shared understanding with the patient of the problems
5. To involve the patient in the management and encourage him or her to accept responsibility
6. To use time and resources appropriately
7. To establish or maintain a relationship with the patient which helps to achieve the other tasks.

Pendleton's seven tasks can be encapsulated by dividing the interview into three phases – introduction, working phase and termination phase. In the introduction phase it is important to take steps to ensure comfort and privacy. The patient should be welcomed and this may involve you introducing yourself and shaking hands with the patient. Social chat is acceptable and is useful when walking from the waiting area to the consulting room. It is particularly important to know and use the patient's name.

During the working phase it is necessary to elicit the patient's story by gathering information. The patient's past medical history, family history, psychosocial history, current problem and current health status should be explored and a review of systems carried out. Start with open questions, and then become more focused. It is common for patients to have a multitude of problems and it is often impossible to pursue all the problems in one consultation. Therefore it is necessary to prioritize and pursue the most urgent problem. Sometimes a summary of the problems stated so far is helpful to prioritize with the patient. Other problems should be identified and, if they cannot be addressed in this interview, it is important to let the patient know that they will be addressed at a later date.

The termination phase involves a further summary of the important points. The consultation then moves on to physical examination if necessary, a discussion of treatment options and the plan for follow-up if required.

INTERVIEW TECHNIQUES

It is possible to develop interviewing techniques which can assist with the flow of the history-taking

---

Box 2.1 Helpful interview techniques (Morton 1993)

- Offer general leads
- Restating to clarify
- Reflecting
- Verbalizing the implied meaning
- Focusing the discussion
- Placing symptoms or problems in sequence
- Encourage participation and evaluation
- Making observations that could encourage the patient to discuss symptoms
- Using silence
- Summarizing

Box 2.2 Interview techniques to avoid

- Asking 'why' or 'how' questions
- Using probing, persistent questions
- Using inappropriate or technical language
- Giving advice
- Giving false assurance
- Changing the subject or interrupting
- Using stereotyped responses
- Giving excessive approval or agreement
- Jumping to conclusions
- Using defensive responses
- Asking leading questions, suggesting 'right answers'
- Social chat: the person is expecting professional expertise

---

process. Helpful techniques are summarized in Box 2.1 and unhelpful techniques in Box 2.2. The nurse practitioner should use reflective practice to analyse the techniques used in each interview and should be able to build on the experience to develop an effective history-taking strategy.

FRAMEWORK OF QUESTIONS

When interviewing patients it is easy to be sidetracked or omit important questions. Developing a framework of questions can help to gather information in an orderly way. There are many different approaches to history-taking. The traditional medical

> **Box 2.3 Key elements of a medical history**
>
> - Identifying data
> - Chief complaint
> - Present illness
> - Past medical history
> - Current health and medications
> - Family history
> - Psychosocial history
> - Review of systems

history is structured so that the clinician can focus easily on the presenting problem and the interviewer can easily record all data in well-organized sections. Patients tell their stories in different ways and usually not in a structured way. It is up to the clinician to gather the data in a logical sequence. The history obtained should be made up of the components summarized in Box 2.3.

Identifying data

Date, time, age, date of birth and sex are usually included, with a brief description of the patient's appearance to help in identification.

Chief complaint

Patients should be encouraged to state the problem in their own words. This statement should be recorded.

Present illness

This expands upon the chief complaint, describing it more fully and explaining the chronological development of symptoms. It should include what the patient thinks and feels about the illness and what concerns led to the decision to seek help. The patient's perception of the problem is crucial. Ask patients what they think caused the symptoms and why they have come today for treatment. How the symptoms have affected the person's life should also be checked. Symptoms may become meaningful in a broader sense and may be linked to relationships or significant events in a person's life. It is therefore important to understand the meaning of the symptoms or illness to that person especially, as this may be very different from your perspective as a professional. Remember to allow the patient to speak uninterrupted.

SYMPTOM ANALYSIS

In order to encourage patients to describe their symptoms in the most expansive manner, several frameworks have been developed, one of which is PQRST (Morton 1993). This mnemonic is most useful in describing pain but can be used for other symptoms:

P: provocative/palliative
Q: quality
R: region/radiation
S: severity
T: temporal/timing.

Provocative/palliative

The nurse practitioner should explore what provokes the symptom or the pain and what relieves it. The patient should be asked if movement, lying down, breathing, over-the-counter medications, heat, cold or any other factors exacerbate or alleviate the symptom.

Quality

The quality of the symptom is a description of how it appears to the patient. Patients use a variety of words to describe their symptoms and this is particularly useful in arriving at a diagnosis. The complaint of crushing chest pain, for example, is almost diagnostic of myocardial infarction. Such is the subjective nature of pain that the patient may use a wide range of words to describe it. McCaffery et al (1994) suggest that if patients are having difficulty in describing the pain, a questionnaire can be used to provide a few words which may help them explain the sensations they are experiencing. For example, throbbing, shooting, stabbing, sharp, cramping, gnawing, hot, burning, aching, heavy, tender, splitting, tiring, exhausting, sickening, fearful, punishing and cruel are all words which can be used to describe discomfort.

Region/radiation

It is important to discover where the pain or symptom is being experienced. Ask the patient if it travels anywhere. This is particularly useful in exploring the pain of shingles or gathering information about skin disorders. A patient may only complain of the acne which appears on his or her face when in fact it has spread to the patient's back. Without asking the relevant questions to explore radiation, the nurse practitioner may never discover the true extent of the problem.

Severity

A rating scale can be used in the assessment of pain. It is important to ensure that all members of the health care team are using the same scale. A scale of 0–10 is most commonly used. It is also useful to ask the patient to compare it with other common experiences, such as toothache, menstrual cramp, earache or headache. A rating scale is also a useful tool for the assessment of skin disorders such as psoriasis or eczema and can be applied to any condition which tends to fluctuate over time.

Timing

The timing of the symptom is an important factor in several disease processes. Exploring with the patient when the symptom started, how long it lasted or lasts for, the timing in the day, week or year, the pattern of the symptom, its consistency or if it is intermittent, is useful in generating a clear picture of the problem. This can be particularly helpful when exploring symptoms such as a runny nose in allergic rhinitis or cough in asthma, as it can help with the diagnosis and subsequent treatment.

The information comes from the patient but the nurse practitioner must organize the data, clarifying symptoms and quantifying how severe and how frequent they are before finally placing them in order.

CURRENT HEALTH

This may be reviewed briefly or expanded to detailed questions depending on the time available. Important topics to review are listed in Box 2.4. It is useful to explore the patient's smoking history in some detail. This can be a sensitive issue as people who smoke feel that they are being judged by health care professionals. However, smoking status and history are an important part of the history. You need to ask what is smoked (cigarettes, cigars, etc.), how many and for how long. If the person does not smoke, you need to find out if he or she ever did, for how long and when he or she gave up. It is also worth checking current interest in wanting to stop, enquiring what it would take to make the person stop, possible support and difficulties. Passive smoking should also be explored. It is useful to be

> **Box 2.4 Issue to be covered when examining current health**
>
> - Current medications
> - Allergies
> - Tobacco consumption
> - Alcohol consumption
> - Use of other nonprescribed drugs
> - Exercise pattern
> - Dietary habits
> - Sleep pattern
> - Engagement in screening such as smear tests
> - Immunization history

able to calculate the patient's pack year history. If a patient has smoked 20 cigarettes for 1 year this is calculated as one pack year. If they have smoked 40 cigarettes for one year this is calculated as two pack years. Carry out the following calculation:

(cigarettes smoked per day)/20 × number of years of smoking = pack years

A pack year history of greater than 15 increases the patient's risk of long-term lung disease and could be a valuable clue in the history-taking process.

Another important area of the current health history is the patient's current medications. It is important to ask about both prescribed and over-the-counter medications and to ask how long the patient has been taking each of these drugs. It is important to explore the potential side effects of the medications being taken. For example, many patients think that nonsteroidal anti-inflammatory drugs are harmless as they are so readily available from chemists; they can however, cause serious and potentially fatal health problems such as gastrointestinal bleeding.

PAST MEDICAL HISTORY

This is needed to put the present illness into context. Here the clinician asks about childhood illnesses, hospitalizations, surgery, blood transfusions and any specialist consultations. Any relevant previous medical history should be explored with the patient. It is also important to ask about recent history of foreign travel, including immunizations taken before travelling and any obvious exposure to potential health hazards during the journey.

FAMILY HISTORY

You should ask if the patient's parents are alive and if they have any illness. Establish ethnicity and health of blood-related family members. If there is a hereditary disease, enquire about all family members affected for at least two generations. Particularly important diseases to consider include cardiovascular and respiratory disease (including asthma and any cases of sudden death), cancer (particularly bowel, ovarian and breast), hypertension, diabetes, osteoporosis, renal disease, allergies and any mental health disorder.

For diseases which have a genetic component a genogram may be useful: this is a quick visual guide which gives a snapshot of the person's place in the family (Fig. 2.1). Genograms are used in family systems theory where the family is viewed as influencing current illness. The family tree can reveal patterns of illness, genetic traits and social and cultural factors. They can be relatively simple with names, dates of birth, death and marriage, or more complex, to include repetitive family themes, genetic traits, alcoholism and marital dysfunction. At least three generations should be studied and presented in the diagram.

PSYCHOSOCIAL HISTORY

This section is focused on collecting information to build a picture of how this person functions in society and who is around for social support. There is overwhelming evidence to show that lower social class and poverty are associated with poorer health. Those who are socially connected to others and feel part of a community have better health outcomes. Clinicians are often unaware of the issues people face in their everyday lives and make assumptions that deter them from revealing intimate problems. This may lead to selective awareness in clinicians. For the nurse practitioner it is important to establish a level of trust that allows patients to reveal problems that may influence their health. From a nursing perspective it is important to build a picture of patients in their social setting so that their experience of health and life is properly understood. Examples of questions that could be used to elicit useful social information can be found in Box 2.5.

To follow on from the information gathered by enquiring about the patient's social history, it might be useful to ask about work environment, recent job

---

Box 2.5 Questions to elicit a social history
• Tell me about your living situation
• Who lives with you at home?
• What is your occupation?
• Tell me about your hobbies and leisure interests
• How far did you go with education?
• Do you have any financial worries?
• Who would you call if you needed support or in an emergency?
• How stressful has life been recently?
• How do you feel about the future?

changes, work conditions, hours, shifts, chemical hazards, protective clothing required and availability of an occupational health service. Throughout the history-taking process it is important to keep an open mind and not to rush into a diagnosis before all the information is gathered.

REVIEW OF SYSTEMS

A history is not complete without a review of systems. To the beginner it often seems an onerous task to continue with yet more questions, but the idea is to search for hidden clues and double-check that significant information has not been left out in the symptom analysis of presenting illness. It may prompt patients to recall further details about their health, help construct a picture of health and spot areas that might be important to target for health promotion. The review is customarily taken in a logical 'head-to-toe' order. As you focus the history and move your line of questioning, it is important to lead into each new section so that the patient has some understanding of the framework and topic to be discussed. This technique may help minimize uneasiness or feeling that the question is not relevant to the original concern.

General

Questions here are focused on general state of health apart from the new symptoms of the presenting illness. Useful questions include:

- Generally, how have you been feeling?
- How is your appetite?
- Is your weight stable?

- Do you have any fatigue?
- Any fever, chills or night sweats?
- Are you sleeping well?

Head/nervous system

Ask the patient if he or she has experienced any headaches, dizziness, faintness or head injury. Has the patient noticed any numbness, tingling, tremors, weakness, difficulty coordinating movement or other unusual sensations? It may also be important to explore whether the patient has noticed any change in his or her ability to remember things. Sometimes it is useful to seek the advice of other family members if the patient is unable to clearly answer questions around memory.

Eyes

Any change in vision including diplopia and blurred vision, or any changes with the eye such as redness or irritation, watering or discharge should be explored. The nurse practitioner should check if the patient wears glasses and when the last vision test or glaucoma test was carried out.

Respiratory (including ENT)

Breathing problems such as wheezing, feeling short of breath, pain, cough, production of sputum or coughing up blood should be explored. Ask the patient if there has been any earache, sore throat or hearing problems. Check the date of the last chest x-ray, TB skin test, pneumococcal or flu vaccination.

Cardiac

Enquire about any heart problems, dyspnoea or palpitations. Check for ankle swelling and ask the patient if he or she experiences ankle swelling that builds up throughout the day. Check for high blood pressure, anaemia, recent ECGs or heart stress test.

Gastrointestinal

Check for any difficulties in eating certain types of food, heartburn or indigestion, use of antacids, nausea or vomiting, flatulence, wind or excessive burping and level of appetite. Enquire about any change in bowel movements, constipation or diarrhoea, use of laxatives, rectal problems, haemorrhoids or fissures. It is important to note any changes in weight and to enquire whether these changes were related to a weight-reducing diet.

Genitourinary

Recent changes in pattern of micturition should be discussed. Check for symptoms such as frequency, urgency, nocturia, change in colour or smell of urine or pain. It is valuable to check for urinary incontinence. The patient may not volunteer this information unless asked. For men it is worthwhile asking if there are any problems in the genital area, any rashes or lumps on the penis, scrotum or testes. Check if the patient carries out regular testicular examination. For women the last menstrual period and the pattern and duration of her cycle should be recorded. Problems with periods, amenorrhoea, mennorhagia, inter-menstrual spotting, vaginal discharge, itching, foul smell, pelvic pain, menopause symptoms, use of contraception and date of last cervical smear should all be explored.

Sexual health

It is worth pointing out that you are concerned about all aspects of health and that many people have questions about sexual health. This paves the way for asking whether the patient has any concerns in this area.

Musculoskeletal

Ask the patient about pain, stiffness or swelling of the joints and any muscular pain, cramp or loss of strength.

Endocrine

It is likely that clues to an endocrine disorder will have been identified during the history-taking process, however, it is important to consider this system as one of the additional areas to cover in general review to ensure a full and complete history is gained. Ask the patient if he might have any of the symptoms of diabetes mellitus such as polydipsia, weight loss or polyuria. It is also worthwhile considering the symptoms of hypothyroid disease such as the insidious onset of constipation, weight gain, altered skin texture and changes in cold tolerance. Hyperthyroidism results in heat intolerance, weight loss, irritability, increased appetite and palpitations.

Psychological

Start by asking the patient to describe his or her mood. Check how patients generally feel about themselves, what bothers them most about their present condition, how they cope with it and where they look for hope or strength.

The review of the systems concludes the history-taking process. The nurse practitioner should now be in a position to focus more clearly on the physical examination or may feel the need to return to earlier questions to confirm the results with the patient.

SENSITIVE AREAS

History-taking may well take you into some sensitive areas but if you are to obtain a holistic picture of the patient's health status, you need to obtain truthful information in such a way that a therapeutic relationship can be established and maintained. The following discussion explores some of these areas, including cultural competence, alcohol and drug use, sexual problems and domestic violence.

CULTURAL COMPETENCE

Most nurses would like to think of themselves as sensitive to different cultures. Many nurse scholars have suggested that sensitivity is not enough but that culturally competent care is essential to meet the needs of patients. Increasingly diverse societies with greater immigration to developed countries, inter-cultural marriages and changing borders lead to a greater need to be culturally aware. Culturally competent care has been defined (Meleis 1996) as:

'Care that takes into account issues related to diversity, marginalization and vulnerability due to culture, race, gender and sexual orientation.'

Campinha-Bacote (1994) proposes a culturally competent model of care which involves cultural awareness, cultural knowledge, cultural skill and cultural encounter. Cultural awareness is the process of becoming sensitive to interactions with other cultures. The nurse practitioner must be aware of bias and prejudice and must refrain from imposing his or her own beliefs on others. Cultural knowledge relates to the educational foundation that the nurse acquires. Cultural skill allows the nurse to assess a person's beliefs and practices without relying on written information or stereotyping about cultures. The cultural encounter is a further process whereby

the nurse directly engages in cross-cultural interactions with clients of varied cultural backgrounds.

Two assessment tools that might be useful in providing a culturally sensitive structure for history-taking are the framework of Kleinman et al (1978) and Leininger's (1978) transcultural framework.

Kleinman et al (1978) developed a framework for cultural assessment and suggested that the following series of open-ended questions would be useful during the history-taking process:

- What do you think has caused your problem?
- Why do you think it started when it did?
- What do you think your sickness does to you?
- How severe is your sickness?
- What kind of treatment do you think you should receive?
- What are the most important results you hope to achieve from these treatments?
- What are the chief problems your sickness has caused?
- What do you fear most about your sickness?

Leininger (1978) developed a theory of transcultural care: one of her main underlying assumptions was that clients who show signs of cultural conflict, noncompliance, stresses and ethical or moral concerns need nursing care that is culturally based (Reynolds & Leininger 1993). The theory identifies nine domains to consider during cultural assessment:

1. Patterns of lifestyle
2. Specific cultural values and norms
3. Cultural taboos and myths
4. World view and ethnocentric tendencies
5. General features that the person thinks are different or similar to other cultures
6. Health and life care rituals and rites of passage to maintain health
7. Degree of cultural change
8. Caring behaviours
9. Folk and professional health-illness systems used.

People of varying cultures are not only of varying ethnicity but also have differing sexual preferences, live in different parts of the country, are of varying gender type or are of different ages. Cultural sensitivity is essential in history-taking with all people. In the last 20 years there has been a cultural shift to more openness about lifestyles. Gay, lesbian, bisexual and transgender groups have become more outspoken, pointing out the heterosexual bias of society and health care professionals. Morrisey (1996) points out that stereotyping or stigmatizing may interfere with care and, if nurses are to provide quality care, they must examine any homophobic feelings they may harbour.

It is important to demonstrate respect for people as unique individuals – culture is only one component that makes them who they are. Recognizing that there is diversity, being open to learn about different cultures and taking an open attitude without stereotyping is a beginning towards cultural competency. Nursing research has also turned to anthropology to explore culture. By studying culture we have to explain it in relation to ourselves and therefore gain insight into human life. Caring acts and rituals are found in all cultures and by appreciating culture we understand and appreciate ourselves better.

ALCOHOL AND OTHER RECREATIONAL DRUG USE

Alcoholism is a stigmatizing illness (Hennessey 1992) which causes a multitude of health problems for both men and women. An association exists between alcoholism and several obstetric and gynaecological problems such as infertility, sexual dysfunction, miscarriage and breast cancer and therefore women are particularly at risk of the detrimental effects of alcohol. Alcohol is part of the British culture – the 'pub' is a central place in many communities. Often people understate the amount they drink because they may feel judged as deviant or are embarrassed to admit to their full alcohol consumption. The person who has an alcohol problem often denies the amount consumed or may try to rationalize consumption by stating that last week was an exception. Despite these difficulties it is important to establish an average alcohol intake without judging or offending the patient. If alcohol-related questions are included in the main body of the history-taking process it can appear to be part of the routine interviewing and data collection that contribute to the whole health assessment, and therefore reduces the stigma associated with the question. General screening questions include:

- Do you drink alcohol?
- How much do you drink?
- When was your last drink?
- What do you like to drink?

If necessary it might be important to explore the patient's use of alcohol in more depth. Mayfield et al (1974) developed the CAGE framework as a tool to identify patients who have a problem with alcohol. If the person answers yes to any of these questions it indicates that there is a problem:

- Cut down: ever felt the need to cut down?
- Annoyed: ever felt annoyed by criticism of your drinking?
- Guilty: ever had guilty feelings about drinking?
- Eye-opener: ever felt the need for a morning drink (eye-opener)?

The diagnostic accuracy of the CAGE framework has not been fully established (Taner & Antony 2004), however, it is considered to be a valuable indicator that there might be a problem and that further exploration with the patient might be necessary.

Following on from screening questions about alcohol it may be necessary to ask about the use of other recreational drugs or the possible misuse of prescription drugs. It is useful to integrate the questions into the routine history after a rapport has been established. Most experts recommend a nonjudgemental approach, which means not apologizing for asking such questions, as an apology may imply that stigma or embarrassment is attached.

An example of an introductory question might be: 'I have asked you about smoking and drinking alcohol, now I would like to ask you if you use any recreational drugs'. If the person says 'no', it is worth following up by asking if he or she has ever used drugs in the past. Depending on the response, other questions may include:

- What is your drug of choice and how often do you use it?
- Have you had any bad reactions?
- Have you ever got into trouble or had family problems because of your use?
- Ever tried to quit?

More detailed history for alcohol or substance abuse

1. Normal use or pattern
2. Date and time of last drink (or drug use)
3. Substances used (type of alcohol or drug)
4. Quantity
5. Past history of blackouts, tremors, hallucinations

6. Past history of abstinence
7. Normal pattern of eating
8. Legal problems
9. Family problems
10. Occupational problems
11. Family history of alcoholism
12. Other drugs/medications used.

SEXUAL PROBLEMS

A sexual history provides the nurse with information about the person's lifestyle and may highlight areas of need for risk assessment. We live surrounded by sexual messages in our music, literature, films and television. Nudity and titillating articles appear daily in the tabloid press and yet many nurses find it difficult to ask questions about sexual issues. Although part of a holistic assessment, it is usually an area which is left to another time – which never comes.

There are many barriers to taking a sexual history. The nurse practitioner can feel that the patient does not want to talk about it or that you may be protecting the patient in some way by not addressing the subject. These are often excuses, however, which only serve to cover up personal discomfort with this subject. It is important to recognize whether it is your own discomfort rather than the patient's that is preventing you from asking questions. Looking at your own feelings, attitudes and values about sexuality may help to identify any personal defences that stand in the way of making a thorough assessment.

Some practitioners use a questionnaire to help break the ice on this subject (Tomlinson 1998), however, this may not always be possible within the time constraints of a normal consultation. When taking a sexual history it is useful to start with a general question that sets up a safe, comfortable environment for the patient. Your choice of question depends on your personal style and the context of the situation, but the following are a selection that might be useful:

- Many of the people who come to this clinic have concerns about sexual health. Is there anything you would like to ask?
- People with your symptoms (illness) often experience other problems, sometimes in the area of sexual functioning. How has this affected your life?

- Many people around this time have questions about sexual activity. Do you have any concerns?
- The medications you are taking can sometimes cause sexual problems as a side effect, have you noticed any of these side effects?

If the patient has concerns you may want to use more focused questions. If your attitude is matter of fact, the patient is likely to relax and become matter of fact too (Tomlinson 1998). Often people talk about the genitalia or sexual issues using euphemisms which are intentionally vague to avoid embarrassment. It is important for the interviewer to gain an accurate understanding and therefore it is useful to ask specific questions to clarify the situation. More specific questions could focus on how long the problem has been occurring, loss of sex drive, any pain felt by either partner during intercourse, any stress factors or problems with the relationship and whether the problem is related to a specific time, place or partner. Gaining answers to these questions may take considerable time and patience and the use of silence in these consultations may be extremely helpful while the patient searches for appropriate words and terms to describe the problem.

Many people are eager to ask questions once the subject of sexual health has been introduced. By introducing the subject in a nonjudgemental way you let the patient know it is permissible to discuss this subject with you. This may also enable the patient to return to the issue at a later time.

DOMESTIC VIOLENCE

Health professionals are not very good at asking questions about this topic. Domestic violence is so prevalent, however, that it is now being viewed as a public health issue. A strategy to deal with the problem effectively should include health professionals and should be a multidisciplinary approach. The nurse practitioner needs to be familiar with community resources in order that she or he may refer appropriately.

Often health professionals have difficulties dealing with patients who suffer domestic violence and either ignore symptoms or label the person 'difficult'. When a woman continues to stay in a violent situation, health professionals may get frustrated and feel that intervention is futile. The patient may be caught in an emotional double-bind with little control over her life. Choosing to leave the environment with which she is familiar but which may contain the only support she knows is a difficult decision. Empowering a woman to make such major changes can take a long time. It is still worth trying to get the real story and obtain any information that may help an intervention rather than ignoring the issue. A useful way in might be: 'Many patients have told me they have been hurt or abused at home. How is it at home for you?' Domestic violence includes child abuse. You may therefore include a question such as: 'Most parents get upset when their baby cries a lot. What do you do when your baby won't stop crying?' Or, more directly, 'Are you afraid you might hurt your child?'

The history-taking process might highlight a number of red flags or risk factors for domestic violence and the nurse practitioner needs to be alert to these clues. If a patient describes excessive alcohol consumption, use of recreational drugs or a history of domestic violence it is worthwhile considering their current situation and potential threats to other family members. This is particularly important when children are involved and nurse practitioners must ensure that they are intimately familiar with local guidelines on the referral procedures for families and children who might be at risk.

RECORD-KEEPING

The problem-oriented record is one of the commonest ways of recording medical information. The initial collection of data should be made as significant and complete as possible. The only limitations should be the discomfort to the patient. The reason for discussing this in a history-taking chapter is that the processes of obtaining and recording data are intrinsically linked and often force us to gather our information in a problem-oriented way. For the nurse practitioner it is important to create a format that allows a health-oriented approach. One frequently used format for recording notes in the medical record is SOAPIER (Eggland & Heinemann 1994). The acronym SOAPIER stands for subjective data, objective data, assessment, planning, intervention, evaluation and review. This has been shortened to SOAP, SOAPIE or even PIE (problem, intervention and evaluation). The method chosen will depend on the norms of the nurse practitioner's area of practice. It is essential that the notes allow health care professionals to communicate effectively with each other.

CLOSURE OF HISTORY-TAKING AND TRANSITION TO PHYSICAL EXAMINATION

During the history-taking process, it helps the patient if you can give him or her a sense of structure by summarizing at the end of each section or using a simple phrase to indicate you are moving to another section. For example, 'I've asked you about your past history, now I'd like to ask about your family history.' At the end of the interview you should offer a simple summary of the main points to make absolutely sure that the patient is in agreement with your perception of the story. Always conclude by asking: 'Is there anything more that you would like to add?' You are now ready to move to the examination.

In practice, clinicians will often ask questions as they perform an examination. However, once the physical examination starts, the clinician is in a more directing position and the patient may feel vulnerable and therefore wary about answering sensitive questions fully. This has obvious implications for the type of questions asked. For the beginner it is also essential to separate history-taking from physical examination as it is easy for the inexperienced to get muddled and lose a sense of order.

History-taking is an important skill and is often the key to diagnosis. Keeping a logical order can help the nurse practitioner cover a lot of ground and discover extensive information. The art is to be thorough without being too interrogative and to listen to patients' responses and encourage them with verbal and nonverbal signals to tell their story.

Nurse practitioners struggling to master the art of asking difficult questions can take heed from studies in doctor–patient communication. Simpson et al (1991) reviewed the literature and found communication problems were common; most patient complaints could be linked with poor communication. The skills needed in an interview were identified as data-gathering, forming and maintaining relationships, and being able to deal with difficult issues such as sexual history-taking or breaking bad news. These are skills that can be learned but need continual development. Reflection on practice, peer review and continuing education are important to develop the art of questioning so that history-taking is appropriate and relevant to culture and context.

References

Blackwood R, Hatton C 2003 Clinical skills, 4th edn. Blackwell Science, London

Burnard P 1992 Know yourself! Self awareness activities for nurses. Scutari Press, London

Campinha-Bacote J 1994 Cultural competence in psychiatric mental health nursing: a conceptual model. Nursing Clinics of North America 29(1):1–9

Eggland E T, Heinemann D S 1994 Nursing documentation: charting recording and reporting. J B Lippincott, Philadelphia

Epstein O, Perkin G, Cookson J, de Bono D 2003 Clinical examination, 3rd edn. Mosby, Edinburgh

Hennessey M B 1992 Identifying the woman with alcohol problems. Nursing Clinics of North America 27(4):917–924

Kleinman A, Eisenburg L, Good B 1978 Culture illness and care. Annals of Internal Medicine 88:251.

Leininger M 1978 Transcultural nursing: concepts, theories and practices. John Wiley, New York

Mayfield D, McLeod G, Hall P 1974 The CAGE questionnaire. American Journal of Psychiatry 131:1121

McCaffery M, Beebe A, Latham J (eds) 1994 Pain clinical manual for nursing practice. Mosby, London

Meleis A 1996 Culturally competent scholarship: substance and rigor. Advances in Nursing Science 19(2):1–16

Morrisey M 1996 Attitudes of practitioners to lesbian, gay and bisexual clients. British Journal of Nursing 5(16):980–982

Morton P G 1993 Health assessment in nursing, 2nd edn. F A Davis, Philadelphia

Neighbour R 1987 The inner consultation. MTP Press, Lancaster

Pendleton P, Schofield T, Tate P, Havelock P 1987 The consultation: an approach to learning and teaching. Medical Publications, Oxford

Reynolds C, Leininger M 1993 Madeleine Leininger: cultural care, diversity and universality theory. Sage, London

Simpson M, Buckman R, Stewart M et al 1991 Doctor patient communication: the Toronto consensus statement. British Medical Journal 303(6814):1385–1387

Taner M T, Antony J 2004 Reassessment of the CAGE questionnaire by ROC/Taguchi methods. International Journal of Technology Assessment Health Care 20(2):242–246

Tomlinson J 1998 ABC of sexual health. Taking a sexual history. British Medical Journal 317:1573–1576

Chapter 3

Disorders of the skin

Mike Walsh

INTRODUCTION

Dermatological conditions account for a substantial proportion of the nurse practitioner's work; many systemic diseases also produce significant alterations in the skin and its appearance. In addition, nurse practitioners (NPs) in many settings have to deal with a wide range of wounds. The external nature of the skin means that any lesion or disorder is more readily apparent to the individual than a problem affecting many of the internal organs. The effect on the patient's perception of his or her appearance may also be profound. The NP is therefore likely to see many patients whose presenting condition will involve a skin disorder of one sort or another. This chapter will cover the more common presenting conditions but the NP wishing to know more should consult a dermatology textbook.

PATHOPHYSIOLOGY

DEFINITIONS OF FREQUENTLY USED TERMS

The following terms are frequently used in describing skin disorders:

- macule: a small, flat, clearly delineated area of altered colour such as a freckle or spot
- papule: a small elevated and therefore palpable solid mass up to 5 mm across
- nodule: as for a papule but greater than 5 mm across
- vesicle: a superficial, fluid-filled elevation of the skin; the cavity is filled with serous fluid but

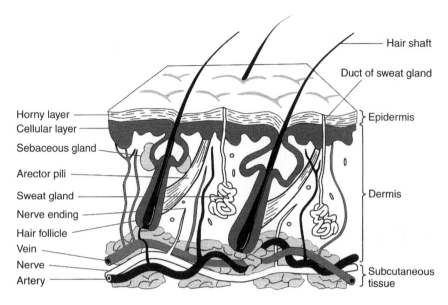

Figure 3.1 A cross-section of dermis and epidermis.

Hair shaft

Duct of sweat gland

Epidermis

Horny layer

Cellular layer

Sebaceous gland

Arector pili

Sweat gland

Nerve ending

Hair follicle

Vein

Nerve

Artery

Dermis

Subcutaneous tissue

less than 5 mm across, e.g. lesions of herpes simplex

- bulla: a vesicle but greater than 5 mm across, e.g. a burn blister
- pustule: similar to a vesicle but filled with pus, e.g. acne.

Figure 3.1 shows a cross-section through normal skin.

COMMON CONDITIONS PRIMARILY AFFECTING THE SKIN

Inflammatory disorders

Eczema refers to a pattern of inflammatory skin reaction which may be caused by outside (exogenous) or internal (endogenous) agents. Technically therefore it is not a disease, rather it is a pattern of inflammatory reaction which can have many causes and present in many clinical forms (Underwood 2000). In some individuals both factors may be present, producing a mixed picture. The term dermatitis is synonymous with eczema (Penzer 2002). Although there are different forms of eczema, all involve both the dermis and epidermis and feature the formation of vesicles; the patient experiences dry, itchy, scaling skin. Eczema may be either acute or chronic and may spread from the site of the initial appearance.

Outside agents may have a chronic irritant effect upon the skin and eczema develops as a result of an accumulation of exposure (e.g. a trainee hairdresser exposed to large quantities of shampoo) or as a result of exposure to a substance leading to an irritant reaction which may be immediate or develop within 24 hours. This latter situation is called contact dermatitis as the rash occurs at the point of contact and is frequently caused by occupational exposure to an irritant substance. Gould (2003) cites evidence indicating some 84 000 people each year in the UK develop an occupational contact dermatitis; commonly affected groups are beauty therapists, hairdressers, bakers, metal workers and those employed in the chemical industry.

Atopic eczema is a common example of endogenous eczema and predominantly affects children. There is a genetic predisposition towards developing eczema but other environmental and emotional influences are involved. The disorder often appears before the age of 2 and, while initially it may be generalized, subsequently tends most frequently to affect skin around joints such as the wrists, elbows and knees. Itching leads to the child scratching, which exacerbates the formation of skin lesions (erythema, vesicles and crusts) and therefore leads to more itching. The problem may continue into adult life but some 90% of childhood sufferers have outgrown the condition by adulthood (Penzer

2002). Other forms of eczema are known but poorly understood, such as stasis eczema associated with varicose veins and seborrhoeic eczema which may affect the scalp and face of infants in the first few months of life or the scalp, face and upper torso of adults.

Gardening may cause a range of skin disorders associated with the irritant effects of chemicals contained within certain plants such as the *Euphorbia* species, cow parsley, hogweed and rue, in addition to allergic reactions which may occur. The tulip bulb ('tulip finger' is a contact dermatitis) and the pot plant *Primula obconia* are two common plants that produce allergic problems (Northall 2003).

Psoriasis is one of the commonest inflammatory skin disorders and usually presents as patches of red scaly plaque which, if removed, may expose bleeding tissue. The scalp, knees and elbows are common sites but anywhere on the body may be affected. The condition is not usually itchy. The cause is unknown but a genetic predisposition is suspected in many cases. Trigger factors include trauma and infection.

Acne is a common and distressing problem, particularly amongst adolescents. Although in most people the problem resolves over a 2–3-year period, it may persist into adult life in a small number of cases. The number of spots varies over time but is often worse at stressful periods. Although the face, neck and upper trunk are most affected, other parts of the body may be involved. The person first becomes aware that the skin and scalp have become more greasy (due to increased secretion of sebum) before spots erupt. The nurse practitioner will usually notice that the spots are at different stages of development. The so-called blackhead is a blocked hair follicle and these lesions are characteristic of acne. Other lesions are found, such as papules and pustules, and scarring may also be present. The psychological distress caused by acne to adolescents when they are at such a vulnerable stage in their development cannot be overemphasized.

Acne is sometimes confused with rosacea, which is a chronic, inflammatory, cutaneous vascular disorder of unknown origin. Although men may be affected, this condition most commonly affects women, typically around the menopause, and produces a picture of facial flushing, erythema, oedema, telangiectasia (fine irregular red lines due to capillary dilatation), papules and pustules. The central part of the face is most affected, from the chin up to the forehead. In men, the nose is affected and

becomes large, bulbous and puffy with connective tissue hypertrophy. This is known as rhinophyma and Chalmers (1997) points out that the familiar face of the great early Hollywood star, W. C. Fields, was a classic example of this condition!

Drug reactions account for many presentations in primary care, often taking the form of a generalized erythema – although some fixed reactions recur in a localized area. The distribution may be confined to exposed areas of skin, indicating a photosensitive reaction with light has occurred. The term urticaria indicates intense local itching and swelling in addition to erythema.

Skin cancer

Although malignant lesions of the skin are much less common than nonmalignant ones, they are potentially serious and are best classified as melanoma and nonmelanoma skin cancer. The key difference is that melanoma is much more aggressive (case fatality approximately 20%) and more likely to metastasize rapidly if not treated promptly, although it occurs far less frequently than other forms of skin cancer. Nonmelanoma skin cancers are the most common form of malignancy in Caucasian populations but carry a low mortality as they are readily managed (Haslett et al 2003). The ultraviolet component of sunlight is implicated as the major causative factor in skin cancer and people of Celtic origin with skin that burns easily are most at risk.

Melanoma tends to affect younger adults and is commonly found on the legs in women and trunk in men, particularly in those whose skin type predisposes them to burn rather than tan in the sun, such as red-haired individuals or those of Celtic descent. The common presentation is the appearance of a new mole or an existing mole that has recently changed in appearance. Moles (melanocytic naevi) are benign, localized proliferations of melanocytes whose cause is unknown. The challenge is to distinguish between a melanocytic naevi or other relatively benign lesion and a melanoma soon enough to make a difference to the outcome, A melanoma usually appears as a superficial, pigmented and spreading lesion more than 7 mm across. The prognosis is good if detected promptly and if the lesion is excised while less than 1.5 mm thick, but poor if detected late.

The principal nonmelanoma skin cancers are basal cell carcinoma (rodent ulcer) and squamous cell carcinoma (epithelioma). Rodent ulcers are by far the most common of the skin cancers and, although they do not usually metastasize, they can be very invasive. They occur most commonly in older people on those parts of the head and neck most exposed to the sun. They may be nodular or pigmented in appearance. Squamous cell carcinoma also affects mostly older people and involves sun-damaged skin. Unlike a rodent ulcer, it may metastasize and may also arise from an existing diseased area of skin. The initial appearance may be a nodule or plaque but it usually progresses to a nonhealing, irregular ulcer.

There are some other skin lesions which may be described as premalignant. Bowen's disease will progress to epithelioma and others, such as solar keratoses (red scaly patches which come and go over time), also have the potential to become malignant. Prolonged exposure to the sun in fair-skinned people of advanced years is a common feature of solar keratoses.

Infectious diseases

The varicella-zoster virus causes both chickenpox and herpes zoster (shingles). Shingles occurs most frequently in those over 50 and is thought to be due to the virus being reactivated after lying dormant for many years after an earlier attack of chickenpox. Pain or a burning sensation may precede the appearance of any lesions by 3–5 days and is localized to a single dermatome. Tissue is erythematous – a group of vesicles marks the affected area. The skin lesions clear after approximately 2 weeks but may leave some scarring. Pain may persist after the attack has resolved.

Herpes simplex type II (genital herpes) is considered in more detail in Chapter 10. Type I virus produces itchy, uncomfortable cold sores commonly affecting the lips. This may be a recurrent phenomenon as groups of vesicles coalesce, burst and resolve in 2 weeks or so. Attacks may be brought on by fever or exposure to strong sunlight.

Warts are benign lesions which are viral in origin. The human papillomavirus (HPV) group is usually the culprit; different strains produce different types of wart. The term verruca refers to a wart on the sole of the foot. Warts are not usually painful; this distinguishes them from a whitlow, which is a painful lesion on the finger produced by the herpes simplex virus. Although warts are usually self-limiting with no long-term consequences for health, genital warts have been linked to cervical cancer and perianal warts in children may indicate sexual abuse (Springhouse 2002).

Individuals working in agriculture are prone to contract *orf*, a viral disease which normally affects sheep and goats but which can be transmitted to humans, usually producing a single lesion on a finger. This develops into a domed haemorrhagic pustule which may rupture, leaving a nodular ulcer which will usually resolve within 2 months.

Infection of the skin with *Streptococcus pyogenes*, usually after a small wound, can lead to *cellulitis*. This is most common in the lower limb, especially in oedematous tissue, and the elderly are most at risk. This is often associated with leg ulcers. The tissue is red, feels hot and appears swollen. Tissue necrosis may occur along with systemic effects such as pyrexia, malaise and even a confusional state in older patients.

Localized staphylococcal infections give rise to *furunculosis* or boils. Usually a hair follicle becomes infected. The boil matures and then discharges its central contents. A group of adjacent hair follicles may become infected, giving rise to a rounded lesion, typically on the neck, known as a carbuncle. This ruptures and discharges pus after a few days, similar to a single boil.

Fungal infections of the skin, such as *Tinea pedis* (athlete's foot), are common. Itchiness gives way to soreness as skin in the toe webs becomes scaly and broken. Athlete's foot is usually contracted as a result of cross-infection in areas such as swimming pools and sports changing rooms. *Tinea pedis* is one example of a type of fungus known as a dermatophyte which inhabits the stratum corneum and the dead keratin of hair and nails. *Tinea corporis* infects areas of skin and gives rise to the term ringworm – so called because an outer inflamed area surrounds a paler healing zone (Epstein et al 2003).

Candidiasis (thrush) is caused by infection of the skin and mucous membranes by *Candida albicans*. This yeast fungus normally occurs in the gastrointestinal tract and vagina without causing disease. If there is a change in the local environment, however, such as reduced resistance in immunocompromised individuals (for example, those with diabetes), it can become invasive and cause disease. Other trigger factors include antibiotic therapy and endocrine disorders such as diabetes. Common sites for disease include the mouth, vagina, beneath the breasts and in the groin, while balanitis may develop in the uncircumcised male. Persistent oral infections may be the first sign of AIDS. Intertrigo describes the occurrence of macerated skin, possibly colonized by *Candida*, where two skin surfaces meet, such as under the breasts.

The skin is also vulnerable to attack from parasitic organisms. The mite *Sarcoptes scabiei* gives rise to *scabies*, which is passed from one person to another through close physical contact. Children and young adults are most at risk, as the female mite burrows into the skin to lay her eggs, giving rise to itchiness and small linear skin lesions. Itchiness is also associated with head lice, which are frequently a problem in schools as the wingless insects can only be transmitted by direct hair-to-hair contact. Head lice feed on blood in the scalp and lay their eggs at the base of the hairs. Nits are the empty egg cases and are most frequently found in the occipital region of the scalp and above the ears. Body lice are usually associated with a person wearing the same clothes for prolonged periods of time as they only move on to the body to feed. They are most likely to be found on vagrants and rough sleepers who live in one set of clothes. Pubic lice are transmitted by direct physical contact and may live in hair other than the pubic region, such as the axilla or beard. Itchiness is usually the symptom that makes the infected person aware of the problem and the lice are clearly visible to the naked eye on inspection.

SYSTEMIC DISEASE AND THE SKIN

Systemic diseases may produce significant changes in the skin. It is therefore worth briefly summarizing some of the main diseases producing signs affecting the patient's skin.

Infectious diseases of childhood

Measles has an incubation period of 7–14 days, followed by a prodromal period of 2–4 days when the patient is most infectious. This is accompanied by the appearance of symptoms such as a cough, runny nose, loss of appetite and pyrexia. Measles is accompanied by a characteristic rash consisting of pink macules which first appear behind the ears, before spreading over the face to the trunk and limbs. The rash consists of irregular spots which may join together to form larger, dark red areas on the trunk and limbs. The classical picture of

measles is completed by the finding of Koplik's spots, which are very small bluish-white spots on the buccal mucosa towards the end of the prodrome period.

Rubella produces a characteristic rash consisting of separate pink macules which appear on the face and trunk, lasting for only 1–3 days. Adults tend to have been unwell for several days before the rash appears, whereas children are much less affected.

Chickenpox occurs most often in winter and usually affects children under the age of 10. Unlike measles, the rash may be the first sign that something is wrong, as prodromal symptoms often do not occur in children, although adults are usually unwell for 2–3 days before the characteristic rash appears. The rash usually starts on the scalp and as it spreads tends to be more concentrated on the trunk; spots appear in waves over several days. The rash consists initially of small superficial macules which progress through a papular phase before becoming vesicopustular. The itchy nature of the rash leads to scratching, the formation of scabs and subsequently scars as the scabs drop off.

Parents of young children with a rash may be concerned about the risk of *meningitis*. Young children who develop acute meningococcal meningitis due to infection with *Neisseria meningitidis* may become seriously ill in a matter of hours with septicaemia, septic shock and disseminated intravascular coagulation, in addition to the other signs of meningitis. The condition is associated with the rapid appearance of a petechial or purpuric rash due to disorder of the normal clotting mechanism.

Endocrine disorders

The increased risk of *Candida* infections in patients with diabetes has already been referred to. Amongst other effects are the formation of neuropathic ulcers on the soles of the feet and the development of fat hypertrophy at frequently used injection sites.

Hypothyroidism produces characteristic changes in the skin – it becomes thickened, dry and may take on a yellowish tinge due to the deposition of carotenes. Swelling may develop around the eyes while the hair becomes thinner and more brittle. Excess thyroid activity leads to warm moist skin and redness of the palms as well as rare conditions such as thyroid acropachy – a form of finger clubbing.

Other diseases affecting the skin include Cushing's syndrome (thinning of the skin, purple striae on the trunk, hair loss and easy bruising) and Addison's disease (hyperpigmentation).

TRAUMA

Wounds

Although various wound classification systems have been developed, the most practical approach is probably to classify wounds according to the characteristics that relate directly to their treatment. The following points are therefore important:

- The age of the wound – this determines the method of closure and the risk of infection as wounds over 6 hours old are much more likely to become infected (Cole 2003).
- Whether there has been any tissue loss, as this also affects wound closure.
- Presence of contamination and/or devitalized tissue – this increases the risk of infection and can delay healing. Infection with *Clostridium tetani* is particularly of concern. This anaerobic organism, whose activity is encouraged by the presence of devitalized tissue in the wound, can have a devastating impact. The neurotoxin it produces – tetanospasmin – blocks the sympathetic nervous system and the normal inhibition of motor reflexes, leading to severe muscle spasm and disruption of the autonomic nervous system. The results are potentially fatal, despite all the resources of modern intensive care.
- The risk of damage to other structures, ranging from superficial nerves and tendons to internal organs such as the spleen or bowel in deep penetrating wounds.

Burns

Damage to the respiratory system and the possible toxic effects of the inhalation of smoke and fumes represent the most immediate threat to life in victims of a fire. Oedema and swelling may obstruct the airway, while most household furnishings are capable of releasing a lethal cocktail of toxic fumes when burnt. Carbon monoxide poisoning and the development of pulmonary oedema are other possible and rapidly fatal outcomes.

Burn injuries lead to 130 000 patients needing treatment in UK A&E departments each year. Whatever the cause, the normal protective outer layer of skin is lost, exposing the individual to risk of infection. The depth of the burn injury is extremely important as this determines the possibility of regrowth of normal dermis and epidermis (Fig. 3.2). A superficial burn involves only the surface epithelium (e.g. sunburn). Blisters are rare and the tissue is erythematous. If deeper layers of the epidermis are involved, this is known as a superficial partial-thickness burn. Localized fluid loss from damaged capillaries and the consequent formation of blisters occur in partial thickness burns. Healing occurs by regeneration of new epidermis from surviving tissue. A deeper partial-thickness (deep dermal) burn which has destroyed the epidermis and part of the dermis, leaving only islands of epidermis deep within hair follicles and glands, will take considerably longer to heal (3–4 weeks) as new epidermis has to be generated from these surviving fragments. The quality of the new skin will be much poorer than the original. All these types of burn injury are extremely painful and often accompanied by a great deal of psychological distress, as the person fears being scarred for life.

A full-thickness burn reaching down to the underlying fat and muscle will only heal very slowly after the formation of much granulation tissue and consequent scarring. Blistering and oedema are common but the burn is characterized by leathery devitalized tissue which may be slate-grey or black in colour. This tough, leathery eschar tissue formed at the time of the injury is inelastic and may create a tourniquet around the limb (or even chest) in the case of circumferential burns, leading to gangrene of the limb or respiratory impairment in the case of a chest/back burn. A full-thickness burn also destroys nerve endings and, although the most severe form of burn, may be less painful than a more partial-thickness or superficial burn, where the nerve endings survive. The picture is usually complicated as the patient often presents with a mixture of full- and partial-thickness burns. Surgical intervention and grafting is the only solution for such a deep burn.

The fluid loss from damaged tissue can rapidly cause hypovolaemic shock, which is exacerbated by the effects of pain and toxin release in burns of larger areas. The composition of the burn fluid closely resembles that of plasma. Shock is likely in 10% surface area burns in children and 15% in adults (Bosworth 1997). In calculating burn area it is important to exclude superficial erythema as tissue fluid loss is negligible from these areas.

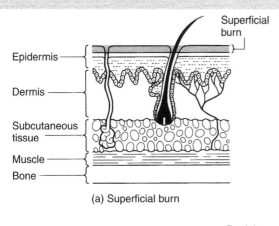

(a) Superficial burn

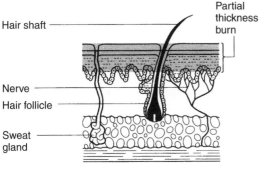

(b) Partial thickness burn

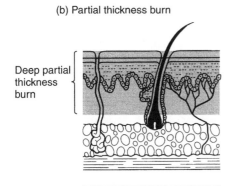

(c) Deep partial thickness burn

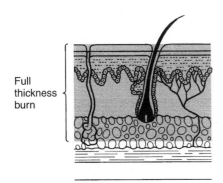

(d) Full thickness burn

Figure 3.2 The depth of burn injuries from (a) superficial to (d) full-thickness.

TAKING A FOCUSED HISTORY

Skin disorders and wounds have a striking visual appearance which invites immediate examination. The principle of obtaining a history before examination still applies however. The normal pattern of starting with the patient's own version of the problem should be followed. The PQRST symptom analysis is then useful as a basis for questions:

- Provocation/palliation: key questions relate to the possible cause of the skin problem, such as exposure to chemical agents or close contact with others. Any medication, whether prescription or over-the-counter, should be noted. Contact with new materials may explain contact dermatitis, while extensive sun exposure over a period of years suggests the risk of skin cancer. Check if any systemic symptoms have preceded the rash such as fever, sore throat, or vaginal discharge. The NP should also ask if anything improves the condition.
- Quality: the patient should be asked to describe the appearance of the skin or lesions. An accurate description of the sensations associated with the rash or lesion is essential, particularly whether it is itchy, painful, irritable or causes discomfort. Any history of bleeding, discharge or odour should also be noted.
- Region: it is important that the patient describes all affected regions of the body, not just the obvious currently visible areas.
- Severity: the impact of the disorder on the patient's everyday life should be ascertained, as this may be profound. An adolescent with acne may be distressed at his/her physical appearance, whilst an adult who presents with a new or changed mole (naevi) may be seriously worried about skin cancer.
- Time: the time interval between the onset of the condition and presentation should be determined, together with any variation in appearance and sensation that has occurred over time.

The past medical history should then be checked. Key areas include previous skin disorders, known allergies, tolerance of sunlight and the presence of any systemic disorders such as diabetes or cardiovascular disease. Enquire whether the patient is on any medication or is using over-the-counter or recreational drugs. Any other general symptoms which may be relevant should be enquired about, such as stress or general malaise.

Relevant family history should be explored, especially focusing on similar conditions and any known family history of allergy. There is some evidence of a genetic link in melanomas such that Haslett et al (2003) recommend any person with a suspicious mole and a history of melanoma in a first degree relative should be referred for a specialist opinion. The personal and social history is equally important; occupational or recreational exposure may provide clues to the possible disorder. It is important to know if the person has been abroad recently or bitten by any insects. The person's skin care habits should also be explored tactfully so as not to give offence. It may be important to know how frequently the person washes or shampoos, what cleansing agents and cosmetics are used and how much exposure there has been to sunlight or artificial tanning.

A detailed history is also essential if the patient presents with a wound. The exact mechanism of injury needs to be ascertained, as well as the time since the accident. The importance of this is illustrated by the example of a patient presenting with small puncture wounds around the metacarpophalangeal joints. They could be teeth marks caused by hitting another person in the mouth. The significance of this is that the human bite is extremely infective and such a wound could rapidly develop serious sepsis. The history of the wound is therefore crucial.

The patient's tetanus immunization status should be determined in all cases of wounding, including burns. Tetanus immunization only became universal in the UK in 1961 so although cases are rare, averaging about 14 per year in England and Wales (Cole 2003), the potentially fatal outcome means that this is an essential question in the history, especially amongst older patients.

Relevant medical information such as known allergies (e.g. penicillin, elastoplast) and general health (e.g. diabetes, cardiovascular disorder) should be ascertained as this will affect treatment and healing. Social factors should be explored to determine whether the patient can continue work or how well he or she will cope at home after discharge. This is particularly important when dealing with wounds affecting the hand where an occlusive dressing may need to be kept in situ, clean and dry, for several days.

In cases of burn injury it is essential to find out what caused the injury. Electrical burns may cause severe deep injuries which are not immediately apparent. Burns are sometimes associated with child abuse and neglect. The history of children who present with burns should therefore be carefully checked against the injuries for consistency. The first-aid steps taken at the time should be determined as these may be helpful or harmful. Application of cold water in moderation relieves pain and limits the extent of the injury but over-enthusiastic use of cold water can lead to hypothermia, especially in children. The risk of inhalation injury should be checked.

PHYSICAL EXAMINATION

A warm, well-lit but private environment is necessary for a good examination. The patient should be undressed as appropriate and any cosmetics removed. A hand lens may be helpful for detailed examination of lesions. Findings may be best recorded using predrawn blank outlines of the body, although a Polaroid camera may be used to record details of an extensive lesion or wound.

The distribution of a skin disorder over the body is a crucial element in its correct diagnosis, so a general inspection should precede detailed examination of individual lesions. Be systematic and thorough, starting at the head and working downwards including both hands. Examine the eyes carefully as jaundice readily shows as yellowing of the sclerae when skin discolouration may not be so obvious. Always include the nails when examining the hands noting particularly asymmetrical splinter like lesions, logically called splinter haemorrhages, which indicate subacute bacterial endocarditis. Pitting of the nail is commonly seen in psoriasis. Redness, swelling and tenderness of the skin where it joins the nail is called a paronychea and indicates infection.

If a disorder is related to sunlight, its distribution on exposed parts of the body will be apparent, while lesions distributed along a specific dermatome make the diagnosis of herpes zoster straightforward. An eruption confined to the flexor surfaces of joints such as the wrist, elbow and knee is characteristic of atopic eczema (p. 28). A generalized or symmetrical distribution usually indicates a systemic or constitutional disorder, whereas fungal, bacterial or viral infections normally have a focus from which spreading may have occurred. The arrangement of lesions within a rash should also be noted. As skin disorders change and evolve over time, it may be necessary to re-examine the patient at a later date to help confirm the diagnosis and assess the impact on the patient.

A careful examination of individual lesions should follow the general overview. The terms used on p. 27 should be used when describing findings. It is also essential to note the colour, size and shape of lesions together with the nature of their margins. A useful prompt to help record the details of a lesion is to think of ABCDE: A, asymmetry; B, border; C, colour; D, diameter; E, elevation (profile). A melanoma typically is **A**symmetrical, has an irregular **B**order and **C**olour distribution, a **D**iameter greater than 5 mm and an irregular **E**levation (Haslett et al 2003).

If the patient presents with a pronounced swelling it is essential to document its position, shape and size exactly. This should be measured with a ruler as changes need to be recorded accurately. The colour and warmth of the lesion are important pointers; if it is inflammatory in origin then increased warmth and redness are to be expected, as well as pain and tenderness. Whether the lesion is mobile or fixed to underlying struc-

tures should be determined. This latter finding suggests a tumour, especially when seen in association with the familiar peau d'orange skin of breast cancer. The swelling should be palpated to see how hard it is or whether it is fluctuant, which would indicate a fluid-filled cyst or abscess. Palpation will also reveal whether any pulse is present within the swelling.

The patient's history may indicate that the swelling is located over a lymph gland. It is therefore necessary to examine the lymph glands by palpation to check for lymphadenopathy (Fig. 3.3). Lymphadenopathy can be either generalized or localized and the cause is most likely to be infective or due to malignant disease. It may be necessary to examine the abdomen to assess the size of the liver and spleen (p. 154) while observing carefully for any evidence of clotting disorders. Examination of the glands should be assessing consistency (in Hodgkin's disease they are said to feel rubbery), tenderness (acute bacterial infection usually produces tenderness) and mobility (fixation is associated with malignant disease).

Lymph glands should always be compared immediately with the same glands on the opposite side of the body. The cervical and axillary glands should be checked with the patient sitting (Figs 3.4

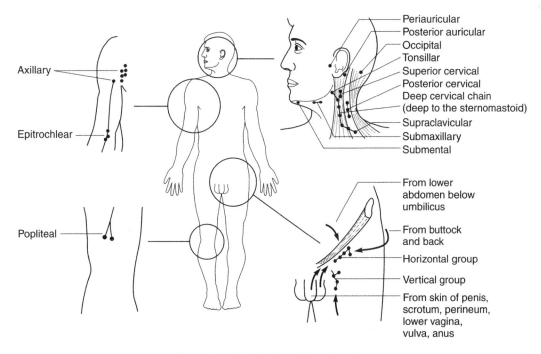

Figure 3.3 Distribution of lymph nodes.

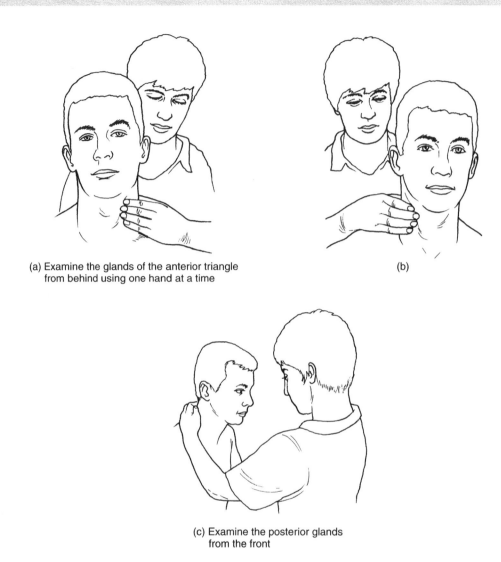

(a) Examine the glands of the anterior triangle from behind using one hand at a time

(b)

(c) Examine the posterior glands from the front

Figure 3.4 Techniques for palpation of lymph nodes.

and 3.5). The NP should face the patient while examining the occipital, posterior cervical and axillary nodes but be behind the patient to examine the other cervical nodes. The abdominal, inguinal and popliteal glands should be examined with the patient lying down.

Examination of a wound should focus on the key points mentioned on p. 32 – the first point must be to check whether bleeding has actually stopped. It is necessary to clean the wound carefully before examination so that all relevant structures are visible. Universal precautions should be observed at all times due to the risk of contracting a blood-borne disease. The possibility of skin closure should be assessed in light of any tissue loss, wound site, general condition of the patient's skin and the time since injury. This is particularly true in elderly patients. Evidence of contamination and devitalized tissue should be noted together with any signs of other structures such as tendons being involved. The exact site, size and shape of the wound should be recorded, using a predrawn chart if possible.

It is important not to focus only on the obvious wound, as there may be other injuries, such as a fracture, which require examination. A small puncture wound caused by a section of bone may be the only external evidence of an open fracture. A thorough examination is especially needed for

Burn victims should be immediately assessed to ensure there is no evidence of airway involvement, as oedema affecting the airway can lead to rapid death, whilst the effects of inhaled hot gases and toxic fumes can be equally lethal. External burns should be fully assessed to determine the area and depth of burn and the amount of pain the patient is experiencing. Predrawn charts of the body are invaluable for sketching the extent of the burn, although erythema should be excluded. For a rapid assessment of area, Wallace's rule of 9 may be used for an adult (Fig. 3.6), to which may be added the fact that the patient's own hand is approximately 0.75% of his or her own surface area (Wyatt et al 1999). The difference in relative size of parts of the body means that for children the Lund & Browder charts should be used. For example, an adult's head is 9% of body area whilst in an infant the figure is 17% (Fig. 3.6). Vital sign monitoring is essential if the burn is over 10%, because of the risk of shock. Depth of burn should be estimated using the criteria mentioned on p. 32, remembering that a full-thickness burn is characterized by a loss of sensation caused by destruction of the nerve endings. Circumferential full-thickness burns are particularly

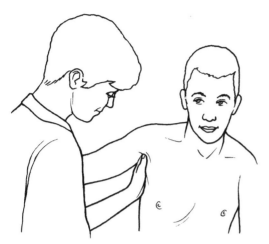

(a) Examine the glands on the right side

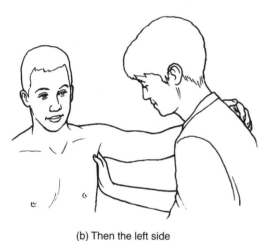

(b) Then the left side

Figure 3.5 Palpation of the axillary glands.

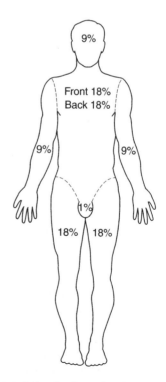

9%

Front 18%
Back 18%

9%   9%

1%

18%   18%

Figure 3.6 Rule of 9 for estimating area of burn.

assault and more seriously injured victims, as well as individuals who are drunk. In cases where the patient is brought in lying down a potentially serious error is to fail to examine the patient's back, which may show evidence of a serious penetrating wound or severe blunt trauma such as tyre marks. The amount of internal damage done by a stabbing or gunshot may bear no resemblance to the size of the wound, which may be very small. The energy and track of the penetrating object are the key determinants. The victim's clothing is potential forensic evidence in such cases and should be stored safely after removal. In serious wounding cases the patient's vital signs should be recorded as a baseline measure and repeated as necessary.

significant – gangrene may develop rapidly because of the tourniquet effect of devitalized tissue. Pain levels should be continuously monitored, not only to assess the initial level but also to check the effectiveness of whatever pain relief is given.

The management of burns and other wounds requires careful documentation and a structured approach. When examining a wound, always check the history given by the patient to check whether the findings match the story. This is particularly true in the case of children because of the risk of abuse. Bruises from accidental falls are common in small children but tend to occur on exposed sites such as the shins. Bruises on less exposed areas such as the back or buttocks therefore are particularly suspicious (Epstein et al 2003). Careful documentation is crucial at all times, and is even more so when dealing with victims of violence where the NP may be required to give evidence in court.

INVESTIGATIONS

Swabs from a wound or lesion suspected of being infected are frequently taken to try and identify the causative organism. All wounds will contain some bacteria; it is the presence of pathogenic organisms that is significant. The aim of taking a swab is to identify the causative organism and to determine its sensitivity to antibiotics. This requires using a sterile swab and avoiding contamination with ordinary skin flora. The swab should be carefully labelled and sent to the laboratory within 24 hours, using a transport medium where appropriate.

Dermatological clinics use a range of other techniques, such as microscopic examination of scrapings from the skin or of nails and hairs, and skin biopsy is an important investigation. These lie outside the scope of the nurse practitioner.

TREATMENT OF COMMON CONDITIONS

ECZEMA

Where contact dermatitis seems a likely diagnosis the patient should be advised to avoid all contact with the suspected material. Emollient creams have been found to be very effective, especially when the person is wearing gloves (Gould 2003). Topical steroids are a major part of the treatment of eczema, although they should never be used for an infective condition and should always be used sparingly due to their side effects. The more severe the disorder, the stronger the steroid that may be used, ranging from mild preparations such as 1% hydrocortisone through moderately potent agents such as flurandrenolone, potent agents such as betamethasone valerate (Betnovate) or clobetasol propionate (Dermovate). No improvement in outcome is achieved by combining steroids with topical antimicrobial agents (Haslett et al 2003).

Topical steroids produce local side effects in proportion to the strength of the preparation used. Thinning of the skin (atrophy) is a potential problem whilst inappropriate use on the face for acne leads to periorbital dermatitis. The area around the mouth and chin becomes erythematous and erupts in papules and pustules. Application of potent steroids should be stopped and replaced with a mild topical steroid and oxytetracycline should be prescribed – initially 500 mg twice daily, reducing over a period of several weeks.

Children with atopic eczema benefit from the use of emollients to reduce the problem of dry skin. If itching is a problem a systemic antihistamine is needed, which will also help with sleep (Candy et al 2001). A topical steroid will also be helpful and may be applied at bath-time. If there is a secondary infection it should be treated with systemic antibiotics such as flucloxacillin.

Seborrhoeic eczema (cradle cap) in infants is best managed by the application of an emollient such as olive oil or white petroleum which will soak and soften the crust, allowing later removal with shampoo. Gill (2003) recommends that for more severe cases the moisturizer should be left for several hours before shampooing and removing any scale left behind with an adult comb, Careful education of the parents is essential to help them manage the condition. In adults, troublesome seborrhoeic eczema should be treated with a mild topical steroid and/or a topical antifungal agent such as ketoconazole cream, due to the risk of pityrosporum infection.

PSORIASIS

There is a wide range of topical agents available for the treatment of psoriasis, although their use and appearance are usually unpleasant. Mild cases may only require an emollient but more severe eruptions are treated with vitamin D analogues such as calcipotriol, coal-tar preparations, the retinoid tazarotene or dithranol. Care must be taken when using dithranol near sensitive areas such as the face as it is liable to cause severe skin irritation. It should only be used on chronic plaques on extensor surfaces. Initial treatment should be with 0.1% concentration increasing gradually as tolerated; usually the application is washed off after an hour (BNF 2003). Ultraviolet light is another well-established effective treatment for psoriasis, especially when combined with other agents such as dithranol and tar. Systemic treatments for severe cases include methotrexate or oral retinoids such as acetretin.

ACNE

The psychological impact of acne on immature adolescents is such that empathy and understanding are important parts of the management, together with some basic health education. A range of commonly held beliefs about the condition can be dismissed as myths. Acne is not related to fatty foods and sweets, lack of skin hygiene, hormonal problems or sexual activity. Topical preparations of benzoyl peroxide are most likely to be effective as this peels the skin and suppresses the bacterium which colonizes sebaceous glands, *Propionobacterium acnes* (Candy et al 2001). More severe cases require the addition of an oral antibiotic such as tetracycline or erythromycin (500 mg twice daily) to the regime if the child is aged over 12. Treatment may continue for several months before there is significant improvement. Topical steroids should not be used.

Rosacea may be treated by topical metronidazole 0.75% gel (Metrogel) which should be applied twice daily after cleaning with a nonirritating agent. The skin should be washed gently with lukewarm water and patted dry before applying the metronidazole preparation. Skin care products which contain irritants such as alcohol or witch hazel should be avoided. Oxytetracycline is recommended for the treatment of pustules (BNF 2003). Other advice includes keeping a diary to try and identify any triggers which cause flare-ups so that they can be avoided, e.g. exposure to strong winds, alcohol or spicy foods.

SKIN CANCER

There are numerous benign skin lesions, many of which are associated with exposure to sunlight, which may bring a patient to the health centre anxious about the risk of skin cancer. This anxiety should be recognized in the consultation. Any lesion suspected of being malignant should be referred for an immediate medical opinion.

Health education about the harmful effects of sunlight should be offered at every opportunity, particularly with patients travelling abroad to hot climates or in general during the summer months. Individuals should be advised to avoid the strongest sunlight for 2 hours either side of noon during the summer, whilst parents should be advised of the importance of shade, T-shirts and sun hats for young children. Penzer (2002) cites evidence indicating that some 80% of sun damage to skin occurs during childhood.

The ultraviolet radiation within sunlight is most harmful to skin, especially in the medium wavelength where it causes a range of conditions, including sunburn, premature ageing and skin cancer. This form of ultraviolet is known as UVB, as opposed to longer-wavelength ultraviolet (UVA), which, while not causing sunburn, contributes to long-term skin damage and cancer, as well as problems of short-term photosensitivity. Many sunscreens are only effective against UVB; the sun protection factor (SPF) on the packaging indicates how many times more protection it gives compared to unprotected skin. Patients should therefore be advised to check the label on sunscreen products carefully and only buy a product that offers protection against both UVA and UVB. Protection against UVA is rated by a star system: a four-star preparation indicates that it gives the same protection against UVB as it does UVA, while lower ratings mean the protection against UVA is progressively less than against UVB. This system is controversial however (BNF 2003). The danger exists that people may counteract the benefits of using sunscreens by simply staying in the sun longer. Clothing offers more protection than sunscreen on bare skin. Tanned skin should not be praised and the health risks of sun exposure should be raised whenever possible, particularly with young men, who often use no sunscreen at all.

INFECTIOUS CONDITIONS

The use of antibiotics is under constant review due to the emergence of resistant strains. To be effective, conditions such as cellulitis require a systemic course of antibiotics if enough antibiotic is to reach the site of the infection via the blood stream. Local policies should always be followed concerning antibiotic therapy, especially the principle that swabs for culture and sensitivity should be taken before any course is started. Topical antibiotics should therefore be generally avoided, especially for leg ulcers, as in many cases they are not necessary or will be ineffective. Mupirocin is however an effective topical antibacterial which is recommended for treating impetigo, whilst silver sulfadiazine is an effective agent in the prophylaxis and treatment of infected burns.

Antibiotics have no part to play in the management of viral infections. Common warts are self-limiting and eventually disappear spontaneously; they may be treated by the use of salicylic acid, which need to be applied for up to 3 months to be effective. Cryotherapy is the painful alternative, involving application to the lesion of a bud of cotton wool frozen in liquid nitrogen. To be fully effective it should be held against the wart until it – and at least 1 mm of surrounding skin – has turned white (Reifsnider 1997). This may need repeating at 2–3-week intervals until the lesion is fully removed.

Herpes simplex infections affecting the genitals are very painful and best treated with analgesics and a 5-day oral course of acyclovir, famciclovir and valaciclovir whilst the lesions are still developing. Subsequent eruptions may be treated with saline bathing but may be severe enough to warrant a repeat of such a drug regime (Haslett et al 2003). Hospital admission may be needed in severe infections. Clotrimazole is effective against a wide range of fungal infections, including ringworm, and is commonly available as Canesten; nystatin is a familiar treatment for *Candida* infection but is not effective against the Tinea group of fungi. The patient should be advised to keep the area clean and dry to promote healing in both candidiasis and Tinea infections. If infections recur, a capillary blood glucose test should be performed to test for diabetes and the possibility of HIV infection should be considered. As transmission via sexual contact is possible in candidiasis, both partners should be treated together when a genital infection occurs.

Scabies is best treated with malathion or permethrin preparations. The *whole* body should be treated with the lotion twice, one week apart. Every member of the family should be treated. Lotions of malathion or carbaryl are better than shampoos for the treatment of head lice and pubic lice as shampoos are often not in contact with the lice long enough to kill them.

WOUNDS

Nurses have a great deal of expertise in the management of chronic wounds. This section will therefore only consider trauma and will concentrate on the initial presentation. The following key principles are well known and have been summarized by Cole (2003):

- For healing to occur there must be adequate blood supply. Patients whose peripheral blood supply is compromised are likely to experience delays in wound healing and this must be taken into account in their management by arranging follow-up and review if needed. Pretibial flap lacerations in elderly patients are notoriously difficult to heal and should be treated by steristrip closure and a firm dressing. If the flap is distally based (Fig. 3.7), this will have an even poorer blood supply and need close follow-up. The nurse practitioner should always check that there is adequate circulation distal to any serious injury because of the risk of compromise of the arterial blood supply to the rest of the limb.
- Necrotic or devitalized tissue should always be removed before wound closure. This reduces the risk of infection and contamination by foreign bodies (e.g. grit or soil). It also improves the person's defences against infection, as these are impaired by any foreign bodies in the wound. This may be done by sharp debridement with a scalpel but great care is

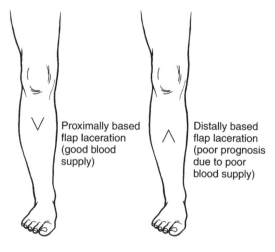

Proximally based flap laceration (good blood supply)

Distally based flap laceration (poor prognosis due to poor blood supply)

Figure 3.7 Pretibial flap lacerations.

necessary to ensure all suspect tissue has been removed while healthy tissue is not damaged. If there is any doubt about the viability of tissue, a medical opinion should be obtained prior to closure.

- Irrigation of the wound is essential to remove contaminants and reduce the infection risk. Sterile normal saline is commonly used but a systematic review by Fernandez et al (2003) shows ordinary tap water of drinking quality produces no adverse effect upon infection or healing rates when compared with sterile normal saline or any other specialist solution. In dirty wounds, soap and water may be necessary and even a scrubbing brush may be required. Analgesia such as Entonox should be made available to the patient if such measures are necessary.
- Before closure is considered, careful exploration of the wound is necessary to ensure that no underlying structures are involved and that all contamination and necrotic tissue has been removed.
- Prophylactic antibiotics are no substitute for thorough cleaning and debridement. Tetanus status must be determined and a booster given if needed.
- Wound closure should only take place if the wound is clean, tidy and less than 12 hours old. Suture technique cannot be learnt from a book alone; the basic principles should be to close the wound in such a way that the skin edges are opposed (with no dead space) but not under tension (Fig. 3.8). The smallest size suture should always be used. Typically, 5/0 and 6/0 are best for the face, 4/0 and 5/0 for the upper limbs and 3/0 for the lower limbs, trunk and scalp. In many cases wounds can be closed using steristrips or glue, although sites such as joints and the scalp require suture, as do deep wounds.

Wound closure should not be attempted if:

- Tissue of dubious viability is present or if contamination cannot be fully removed.
- Tissue loss has occurred.
- The wound is a bite. Human bites are particularly infective. A common presentation is a puncture wound to the hand caused by a tooth during a fight. Such apparently trivial wounds are potentially serious and should be admitted for formal surgical debridement in theatre, due to the risk of soft tissue infection

and osteomyelitis. Diseases such as hepatitis B, hepatitis C and HIV can all be transmitted by human bites. Dog bites account for some 200 000 A&E attendances per year in the UK and carry infection rates of up to 30% (Higgins et al 1997). In addition, for correct wound management, the nurse practitioner also needs to think about a health education approach to reduce the risk of future bites. Prophylactic antibiotic therapy appears to be effective in reducing infection from human bites but not from common animal bites such as cat or dog (Cole 2003). In certain circumstances, such as a child bitten on the face, the cosmetic benefits of suture may outweigh the risk of infection and the wound therefore is sutured under antibiotic cover.

- A foreign body is present in the wound. This should be removed in theatre.
- There is any risk of involvement of other structures such as nerves and tendons.
- The wound is ragged and may need specialist surgical closure to achieve a good cosmetic result.
- Tissue oedema is present, making closure very difficult.
- The wound is 24 hours old or more.

In any of the above circumstances, a medical opinion should be obtained promptly.

Wound dressing is a complex area and the nurse practitioner can easily be confused by the plethora of products now on the market. It is best therefore to stick to basic principles. If a wound has been thoroughly cleaned and closed, a dressing should be applied which protects the wound, is nonadherent, thermally insulating, capable of absorbing any exudate, nonallergenic and comfortable for the patient. The dressing should also be secured in such a way as to remain in place. It should only be removed prematurely if there are localized/systemic signs of infection, or it has become soaked through by exudate or externally contaminated.

Clean wounds with little exudate such as minor abrasions or wounds closed by suture/steristrip should be dressed with low-adherence dressings such as N-A Dressing or Melolin. They allow exudate to pass through and may require the addition of some extra sterile gauze backing to ensure they remain effective.

Wound beds with superficial infection benefit from the application of medicated dressings such as

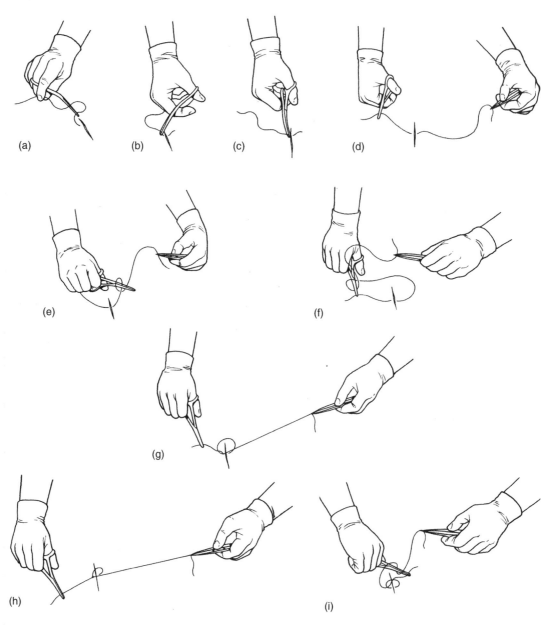

Figure 3.8 Suturing technique. (a) The point of the needle is perpendicular to the skin at the point of entry, which should be 3–4 mm from the wound. (b) The needle should be brought through and out of the wound. (c) Re-enter the needle on the opposite edge of the wound, by rotating the wrist, to bring the needle out 3–4 mm from the opposite side of the wound. (d) Pull the suture through the wound, ready to tie the knot. (e) Start tying the knot by making a loop with the needle holders. (f) Grasp the end of the suture. (g) Pull the end of the suture through the loop. (h) Pull the suture firmly but not too tightly and lay the knot to one side of the wound. (i) Repeat this method twice, looping in the opposite direction on each occasion.

Inadine or Iodoflex (good for *Pseudomonas*), while Actisorb is effective against a broader range of pathogens. These dressings may need changing daily at first if the antibacterial agent is to be effective.

If the wound is exuding heavily, the alginates such as Sorbsan or Tegage should be used. They form a hydrophilic gel as they absorb the exudate, and can be used as ropes to pack deeper wounds as well as sheets for more superficial wounds. Foams such as Allevyn or Lyofoam can be used for cavities. All these dressings can stay in place for several days but should be changed once saturated.

Wounds requiring autolytic debridement are best treated with the hydrogels (Smith 2003) but this requires daily dressing changes. Hydrocolloid dressings (Granuflex, Comfeel, Tegasorb) will also facilitate autolysis of devitalized tissue from the wound bed and are good for exuding wounds as they can absorb substantial amounts of exudate. They should be changed when saturated, typically every 4 days or so. An alternative is enzymatic debridement using Varidase, which should be applied directly to the wound bed. This breaks down fibrin, denatured collagen and elastin.

Superficial wounds that require observation may be dressed with a semipermeable film such as Opsite or Tegaderm. These are self-adherent and can stay in place for several days but should be changed if leakage of exudate looks imminent or has occurred.

BURNS

The treatment of serious burns revolves around the basic principles of airway and respiratory management, opioid analgesia, intravenous resuscitation, simple occlusive dressings and transfer to an A&E department or regional burns unit. These injuries lie outside the scope of this book; we will concentrate on minor burns in the rest of this section. It should be pointed out that such a burn may not seem minor to the patient.

Local protocols will normally determine which patients will be managed by the NP and which should be referred for a medical opinion. The following useful principles will help in drawing up such protocols or in managing patients in the absence of local guidelines. Patients must see a doctor if:

- the burn is full- or deep partial-thickness
- opioid analgesia is needed for pain control
- there is a risk of smoke or fume inhalation

- there is airway involvement
- special areas such as the face, hand, perineum and ears are involved
- surface area of burn exceeds 1%,
- nonaccidental injury is suspected
- infection is already established in an old burn.

Minor burns with none of the above characteristics are suitable for primary management by the nurse practitioner as they should heal with little or no scarring, providing they are correctly dressed. The basic principles of wound management apply to burns as they do to any other wound, particularly the need for a scrupulous aseptic technique. Irrigation is essential to clean and expose the wound for careful examination. Blisters should initially be left intact but devitalized tissue, especially the roof of a blister which has subsequently ruptured under a dressing, should be removed with sterile forceps and scissors to minimize the risk of infection. A fresh burn wound will exude considerable amounts of fluid for at least 24 hours. As a consequence, several layers of paraffin gauze, preferably with a low-adherence dressing, should be used in contact with the burn and it should have a thick backing layer of sterile gauze to ensure that the dressing remains patent. The dressing should be reviewed after 48 hours. Hydrocolloid dressings may be used for the long-term management of partial-thickness, epithelializing wounds after the initial exudate has subsided. Before discharge, an adequate course of analgesia should also be administered, together with advice about wound elevation to control oedema.

Silver sulphadiazine cream (Flamazine) has a broad-spectrum antibacterial effect and is useful in treating burns. Pankhurst (1997) recommends its use prophylactically in burns affecting the perineum or the ear. Serious deformity of the ear could ensue if the cartilaginous pinna is allowed to dry out, therefore after it has been applied a paraffin gauze dressing held in place with a head bandage should be used. Silver sulphadiazine is also very useful in treating burns to the hand or foot. The need to retain joint mobility precludes bulky dressings; after cleaning and debridement, silver sulphadiazine cream should be applied to the hand or foot and then it should be encased in a Gortex bag. It may also be used to treat infected burns or in the conservative management of fingertip injuries. Contraindications to the use of silver sulphadiazine are pregnancy, breast-feeding and known sensitivity to sulphonamides (BNF 2003).

The psychosocial impact of burns should also be considered as an integral part of long-term management. Patients may be anxious about scarring. The only honest answer the NP can give is to say that it is too early to predict the outcome. If the patient is a child, parents may be feeling guilty and blaming themselves. Sensitivity is necessary in handling the parent who may be upset by their child's distress. In particular, injuries to the hand may prevent someone from working, caring for a child or an elderly relative or from carrying out normal activities of living. These aspects should be checked before discharge to see if any help can be arranged.

There is a great potential for health education work in the field of wounds and burns, ranging from first aid to prevention. All patients (and other family members) attending with a wound or burn are potential recipients of health education (leaflets, posters) assuming they are well enough. Prevention strategies can be explored by asking how the accident occurred. This may identify unsafe working practices, such as not wearing protective clothing.

First-aid advice for burns involves copious irrigation with cold water to remove any residual heat and therefore limit burn damage. This also gives considerable pain relief; however, excessive irrigation, especially in small children, can lead to hypothermia. Patients should be advised to leave any blisters intact and not apply any lotions or creams to the burn. Tight constrictions such as rings should be removed because of the risk of swelling. If the burn can be covered with a clean dressing this should be done; cling film is especially suitable for this purpose. Before discharge, explain the need to keep the wound dressing clean and dry; point out signs that may indicate infection or that the dressing needs changing. Reinforce this information with printed leaflets or cards the patient is given to take away and which should also include details of any follow-up appointment. Tetanus prophylaxis should also be discussed and a written record of any booster injection given to the patient in the form of a card.

Summary

Skin disorders can vary from the acute and painful to the long-term and chronic. Whatever the presentation, it is important to retain the holistic nursing perspective and consider the unique psychological impact of such a highly visible condition as a skin disorder. The implications for work, recreation and family life must also be talked through with the patient. Every opportunity should be taken to be an active health educator, whether by displaying material in the waiting room, working with individual patients during a consultation, or engaging in community activity such as liaising with schools and sports centres. The NP should therefore combine a broader psychosocial approach with the specific medically-focussed treatment of the skin disorder to offer the patient holistic health care.

References

Bosworth C 1997 Burns trauma. Baillière Tindall, London

BNF 2003 British National Formulary 45: March 2003. British Medical Association/Royal Pharmaceutical Society of Great Britain, London

Candy D, Davies G, Ross E 2001 Clinical paediatrics and child health. W B Saunders, Edinburgh

Chalmers D 1997 Rosacea: recognition and management for the primary care provider. Nurse Practitioner 22(10):18–30

Cole E 2003 Wound management in the A&E department. Nursing Standard 17:45–52

Epstein O, Perkin D, Cookson J, de Bono D 2003 Clinical examination, 3rd edn. Mosby, Edinburgh

Fernandez R, Griffiths R, Ussia C 2003 Review; wound cleansing with water does not differ from no cleansing or cleansing with other solutions for rates of wound infection or healing. Evidence Based Nursing 6(3):81

Gill S 2003 Infantile seborrhoeic dermatitis (ISD) or infantile eczema (including cradle cap). In: Barnes K (ed) Paediatrics: a clinical guide for nurse practitioners. Butterworth-Heinemann, Oxford

Gould D 2003 Occupational irritant contact dermatitis. Nursing Standard 17(31):53–60

Haslett C, Chivers E, Boon N, Colledge N 2003 Davidson's principles and practice of medicine, 19th edn. Churchill Livingstone, Edinburgh

Higgins M, Evans R C, Evans R J 1997 Managing animal bite wounds. Journal of Wound Care 6(8):377–380

Northall F 2003 Vegetation, vegetables, vesicles: plants and skin. Emergency Nurse 11(3):18–23

Penzer R 2002 Nursing care of the skin. Butterworth-Heinemann, Oxford

Reifsneider E 1997 Common adult infectious skin conditions. Nurse Practitioner 22(11):17–33

Smith J 2003 Review: debridement using hydrogel appears to be more effective than standard wound care for healing diabetic foot ulcers. Evidence Based Nursing 6(3):83

Underwood J 2000 General and systematic pathology. Churchill Livingstone, Edinburgh

Wyatt J, Illingworth R, Clancy M, Munro P, Robertson C 1999 Oxford handbook of accident and emergency medicine. Oxford University Press, Oxford

Chapter 4

The head and neck

Alison Crumbie

CHAPTER CONTENTS

INTRODUCTION

The head and neck area involves many overlapping systems, including alimentary, respiratory, neurological, cardiovascular, musculoskeletal, ear, nose and throat (ENT). This chapter focuses on those conditions associated with the nose, ear, mouth, neck and throat, which represent the most common reasons for patients seeking help from nurse practitioners. It is therefore important that the nurse practitioner can carry out an appropriate assessment of the patient and has an understanding of the pathophysiology relating to the head and neck.

PATHOPHYSIOLOGY AND CLINICAL PRESENTATIONS

A thorough examination of the head and neck includes the nose and sinuses, the ears, the mouth, the face, the neck and throat. The eyes are also included in the head and neck; however, ophthalmic examination will be covered in Chapter 6. It is reasonable to break the examination down into discrete sections as the nurse practitioner will choose to focus upon a particular area depending upon the patient's presenting symptoms.

THE NOSE AND SINUSES

Symptoms of nasal disease include nasal obstruction, discharge and deformities. Nasal obstruction is associated with nasal or sinus disease and may be due to a number of causes, including anatomical abnormality of the nose, mucous membranes or of the autonomic control of the mucosa. An anatomical abnormality may be due to a deviated nasal septum or congenital atresia of the conchae. Abnormalities of the mucosa include polyps, hypertrophy of the mucous membranes and excessive abnormal secretions. Abnormalities of the autonomic control of the mucosa include allergic disorders, including swelling of the mucous membranes and excessive production of secretions.

Nasal discharge is a common symptom of nasal and sinus disease. The discharge may be watery or thick. Watery discharge occurs with the onset of a common cold and may also be due to exposure to allergens or irritants. A thick discharge may be produced in a chronic condition of the nose or sinuses such as perennial allergic rhinitis.

Allergic rhinitis is a condition in which both nasal discharge and obstruction are present. Allergic rhinitis may be seasonal (hayfever) or perennial; both are due to the protective mechanisms of the nasal mucosa being triggered by harmless particles such as pollens. Particles trapped in the nose of people allergic to the specific allergen result in the release of mediator molecules such as histamine from the cells near the epithelial surface of the mucous membranes. Histamine directly stimulates receptors causing vasodilation, oedema and exudation of plasma. Sneezing and hypersecretion are the result of reflex activation and account for the unpleasant symptoms associated with rhinitis (Cross 1998).

If nasal discharge is excessively sticky, the normal ciliary action of the nasal lining may become impeded and mucus collection can accumulate. If infection is superimposed, the secretions may become purulent or mucopurulent. Persistent discharge of yellowy secretions or pus is indicative of sinus disease. Thick blood-stained discharge may be indicative of a tumour in the nose or sinuses. A unilateral discharge in a child may suggest a foreign body in the nose.

Pain is a symptom often associated with sinus trouble; however, facial pain may have other causes. It is worthwhile checking over the area of distribution of the trigeminal nerve to check for trigeminal neuralgia. Alternatively, dental or ear problems may lead to referred pain being experienced in the facial area.

A direct blow to the nose can result in trauma to the cartilage or bones. Injury to the nose may result in cartilaginous destruction, resulting in a flattened bridge and an alteration in shape. Diseases such as

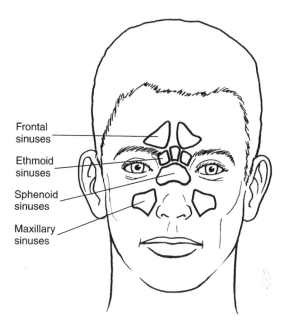

Figure 4.1 The sinuses.

cancer, tuberculosis or syphilis may result in severe nasal deformities, requiring the specialist care of an ENT consultant.

The nasal sinuses are air spaces in the bones of the skull which communicate with the nasal cavity. There are two groups of sinuses: the anterior group is made up of the frontal air sinus, maxillary air sinus and ethmoidal air cells; the posterior group comprises the posterior ethmoidal cells and the sphenoidal sinus (Fig. 4.1).

Sinusitis is an inflammatory condition of the mucous membrane lining of the sinuses and often progresses to pus formation. Any condition which tends to obstruct the drainage of the sinuses will predispose the patient to sinusitis. Deflection of the septum, nasal allergy, foreign bodies and tumours all predispose to sinusitis. The mucous membranes of the sinuses pass through the usual stages of infection, including increased secretions, oedema of the membranes, and increased ciliary activity, followed by a decrease in ciliary activity. The infection may be in one sinus or it may spread to all of the sinuses, this condition is known as pansinusitis.

Differential diagnosis in disorders of the nose and sinus

When a patient complains of the vague symptoms of the common cold or a stuffy nose it is important to consider the differential diagnoses of these symptoms so that the patient can be reassured and appropriate self-management advice provided. It is important to differentiate between allergic rhinitis, sinusitis and the common cold by taking a thorough history and carrying out an examination of the head, neck and respiratory tract. A patient with a fever of greater than 39°C is unlikely to be suffering from a simple upper respiratory tract infection and should be assessed for pharyngitis, otitis media, sinusitis, meningitis or bacterial pneumonia. A patient who complains of malaise, chills and shivering may be suffering from flu and patients who complain of pain over the sinuses which is exacerbated by coughing are likely to have sinusitis.

THE EARS

Common conditions associated with the ears include earache, discharge, deafness, tinnitus and vertigo or dizziness. It is useful to consider clinical conditions of the ears in three categories – the external ear, the middle ear and the inner ear. Figure 4.2 is a diagrammatic representation of the ear.

The external ear

In children it may be possible to detect congenital abnormalities of the external ear, including bilateral protruding pinnae ('bat ears') or atresia of the pinna. These may be associated with congenital abnormalities of the middle and inner ear. The pinnae of any patient can become inflamed due to acute dermatitis, perichondritis or infections such as herpes-zoster oticus (Ramsay Hunt syndrome). Acute dermatitis may occur due to an extension of otitis externa or to sensitivity to topical treatment; this in turn may develop into perichondritis. This is inflammation of the covering of the cartilage and may be caused by ear piercing, trauma to the ear or extending otitis externa, as described above. This condition may be extremely destructive, causing the patient great pain and discomfort. On inspection the pinna appears red and shiny. Herpes-zoster oticus may involve the seventh and eighth cranial nerves. Symptoms may include facial paralysis, giddiness, nystagmus and hearing loss in addition to the herpes-zoster lesions and herpetic pain.

The pinna of the ear is frequently omitted when people apply sunscreen to protect themselves against the damaging effects of the sun. For this reason it is not uncommon to observe squamous cell and basal cell carcinomas on the edge of the pinna. On close inspection of the pinna it is possible to discover areas of hyperkeratosis and small lesions which may be early carcinomas. Biopsy is necessary to determine the histology of the lesion.

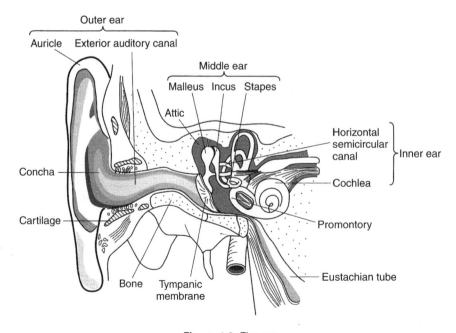

Figure 4.2 The ear.

Diseases of the external meatus include infections and blockages. Infections may include furunculosis, which is a very painful infection of a hair follicle caused usually by *Staphylococcus aureus*, and otitis externa, which is a generalized infection of the whole skin of the external canal. Otitis externa can be fungal or bacterial; and the irritation of the meatus is accompanied by desquamation and scanty discharge. Conditions predisposing to otitis externa include hot humid climates, swimming baths, dusty environments and traumatized skin following scratching of the ears or the presence of eczema. Many organisms have been linked to otitis externa, including *Staphylococcus pyogenes*, *Pseudomonas pyocyanea*, *Escherichia coli*. Otitis externa is most commonly bilateral; unilateral otitis externa is so uncommon that an underlying middle-ear infection should be considered as a possible cause of the problem. Furunculosis and otitis externa can both lead to an impairment in hearing, indeed, anything which causes an obstruction in the external auditory meatus can cause deafness.

One of the commonest causes of impaired hearing is the presence of wax in the ear. Wax or cerumen is a completely normal finding in examination of the ear. Impacted wax may cause irritation and can occasionally cause tinnitus if the wax presses on the eardrum. Pieces of Lego, beads, insects and cotton buds are all possible finds in the external auditory canal of small children. In adults, foreign bodies tend to be those associated with cleaning the ears, such as matchsticks and cotton buds.

A further fairly common abnormal finding on examination of the external auditory meatus is exostosis or osteomata. An exostosis is a bony outgrowth from the wall of the external auditory meatus and is associated with people who have engaged in a lot of swimming in cold water, although the cause is unknown. Patients are often unaware of the presence of the exostosis, which only becomes apparent when the meatus is finally closed due to the collection of wax or the presence of other inflammatory conditions.

Middle ear

The tympanic membrane can be damaged by trauma or by the infection of otitis media or other problems with the ear. Trauma to the ear can be direct, e.g. from attempts to clean the ears with cotton buds, or indirect, such as a slap to the ear or a blast from an explosion. The patient will complain of acute pain at the time of the rupture, may report hearing loss

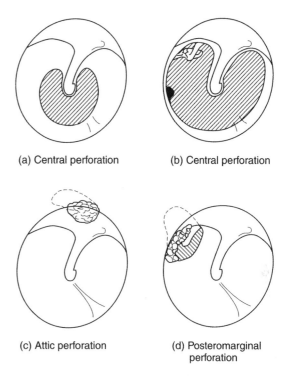

(a) Central perforation   (b) Central perforation

(c) Attic perforation   (d) Posteromarginal perforation

Figure 4.3 The main types of perforation.

and may occasionally complain of tinnitus and vertigo. There may be bleeding from the ear and a visible tear in the eardrum. The message in the management of traumatic perforation is to leave the ear alone. In virtually all cases the membrane will repair rapidly and all that is required is a protective dressing and prophylactic antibiotics.

Perforations of the eardrum may also be caused by infection. In general, if an ear discharges and there are no signs of external otitis, there must be a perforation. There are three main types of perforation – central, marginal and attic, depending on location (Fig. 4.3). Marginal and attic perforations are characteristic of progressive disease and are associated with bone destruction. This is a potentially dangerous situation which requires referral to prevent further hearing loss.

Otitis media

Otitis media may be acute or chronic. Acute otitis media is an inflammation of the lining of the middle ear; if this fails to resolve a mixed infection may persist which can lead to further damage to the middle-ear structures and greater potential for conductive deafness.

Acute otitis media

Acute otitis media is common in infants and young children with 66% of all cases occurring before the age of 3 (Candy et al 2001). It often follows an acute upper respiratory tract infection. Without a culture of discharge from the ear it is impossible to differentiate between viral and bacterial causes of the condition. Organisms invade the mucous membrane of the middle ear via the eustachian tube or occasionally via the external auditory meatus, causing inflammation, oedema, exudate and, later, pus. The swelling causes closure of the eustachian tube, preventing aeration and drainage. Pressure from the pus rises, causing the tympanic membrane to bulge; necrosis of the tympanic membrane results in perforation and the ear drains until the infection resolves. The patient may complain of earache (which may be slight or severe) and often there will be a history of resolution of the pain if the tympanic membrane perforates. Deafness always accompanies acute otitis media and may be the presenting complaint in adults. There may be pyrexia and a child can appear quite flushed and ill. Pain, impaired hearing and discharge are the cardinal signs of acute otitis media.

Chronic otitis media

Chronic otitis media may be caused by late or inadequate treatment of acute otitis media, upper airway infection, immunosuppression and particularly virulent diseases such as measles. There are two major types – mucosal disease and bony disease. In mucosal infection the ear often discharges copious amounts of mucoid fluid. The ear may improve from time to time and the perforation may heal spontaneously. In bony disease there may be scanty discharge with aural polyps (which may fill the meatus), granulations and cholesteatoma. Cholesteatoma is formed by squamous epithelium and results in the accumulation of keratotic debris which may be visible through the perforation and may be smelly. This can lead to intracranial complications if left untreated and requires referral to assess the extent of the disease and possible surgical intervention.

Glue ear

Mucous otitis is otherwise known as glue ear. This is a common condition in childhood and involves the accumulation of fluid in the middle ear in the absence of acute inflammation. The fluid may be thin and serous or even partially solid. The condition is most often bilateral and the child's hearing will be impaired. The cause of glue ear is debated, although it is probably linked to poor eustachian tube function and low-grade infection. Bull (1996) states that other causes include parental smoking, allergic rhinitis, untreated acute otitis media and barotrauma, such as descent in an aircraft when suffering from a cold. The eardrum will appear dull, may have visible vessels and a yellow/orange or a blue-grey tinge and will be retracted. In long-standing cases the eardrum may become atrophic and even collapse. The eardrum will be immobile on testing for mobility. As impaired hearing and the presence of fluid in the ear may cause permanent conductive hearing loss and impaired development, it is essential that children who have mucous otitis are treated appropriately. Referral to an ENT specialist should be considered if the problem does not resolve.

Complications of otitis media include acute mastoiditis, meningitis, extradural abscess, brain abscess, subdural abscess, labyrinthitis, lateral sinus thrombosis, facial nerve paralysis and, rarely, petrositis affecting the sixth cranial nerve, resulting in diplopia and trigeminal pain. These are serious and in some cases life-threatening illnesses – this emphasizes the importance of making an accurate diagnosis and correctly treating diseases of the ear.

The inner ear

The inner ear includes the cochlea, vestibule and the semicircular canals and is often termed the labyrinth. Labyrinthitis is a complication of acute or chronic otitis media and may be the precursor to meningitis. The usual symptoms of middle-ear disease – loss of balance, giddiness, vomiting, hearing loss and nystagmus – are seen. If the disease progresses, all hearing ability will be lost and the labyrinth may fill with bone.

Differential diagnoses of ear disorders

The major symptoms associated with ear disease include earache, hearing loss, tinnitus, dizziness and vertigo. The following section will consider each of these complaints and possible differential diagnoses.

Earache

Seller (1993) states that most earaches are caused by acute infections of the middle ear or external

Table 4.1 Differential diagnoses of earache

Otitis media	Tends to occur in children with unilateral severe pain
Serous otitis media	Occurs in children and some adults; unilateral; less painful
Otitis externa	Tends to be bilateral and occurs in people who are diabetic, swimmers and people who have eczema
Trauma	History of a traumatic event
Mastoiditis	Presents as pain in and behind the ear
Foreign body/wax	Tends to cause vague discomfort and may impair hearing
Referred pain	Such as dental abscess or temporomandibular joint dysfunction; in adults, tumours occur more frequently with advancing age

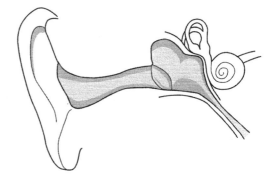

Figure 4.4 Conductive deafness is caused by an abnormality of the external auditory canal in the outer or middle ear.

Table 4.2 Causes of hearing loss

Conductive	Sensorineural
Cerumen, foreign body	Presbycusis (deafness of old age)
Acute or chronic otitis media	Noise-induced (occupation)
Otitis media with effusion (glue ear)	Congenital
Trauma to the tympanic membrane	Ménière's disease
Otitis externa	Drug-induced
	Infections

auditory meatus. If examination does not reveal the cause, then referred pain should be considered. The possibilities are listed in Table 4.1. Bull (1996) points out that malignant disease of the posterior tongue, vallecula, tonsils, larynx or pharynx will produce earache. This earache tends to be intractable. The cervical lymph nodes should be examined and any history of dysphagia checked. Malignancy should be considered until proven otherwise.

At least half of the cases of otitis media are viral in origin rather than bacterial and it is not possible to reliably distinguish clinically between them (Valman 2000). During the history-taking process the nurse practitioner might find that otitis media is secondary to a recent upper respiratory tract infection, which suggests a viral cause. Alternatively there may be a history of tonsillitis with marked pyrexia, suggesting a bacterial cause. A history of purulent and bloody discharge from a spontaneous perforation associated with pain relief also suggests bacterial otitis media. However there is no *reliable* way to differentiate between the two possible causes of the infection.

Hearing loss

It is important to understand that there are three classifications of deafness: conductive deafness,

sensorineural, and mixed conductive and sensorineural deafness. Conductive deafness results from the mechanical obstruction of the sound waves in the outer or middle ear, preventing the stimulation from reaching the cochlear fluid of the inner ear. Figure 4.4 shows the area of the ear which, if blocked for some reason, may result in conductive hearing loss.

Sensorineural deafness results from the defective functioning of the cochlea or auditory nerve and this prevents neural impulses from travelling to the auditory cortex of the brain. Mixed deafness is a combination of conductive and sensorineural deficits. Table 4.2 lists the most common causes of hearing loss. Hearing loss has a variety of causes and a thorough history and examination are necessary to determine an accurate diagnosis.

Tinnitus

Tinnitus is a common condition which can cause a great deal of suffering for patients. It is the constant

Table 4.3 Causes of tinnitus

Damage to the ear	Other general cause
Blockage in the ear	Fever
Presbycusis	Cardiovascular disease
Ménière's disease	Anaemia
Impacted wisdom teeth	Multiple sclerosis
Otosclerosis	Alcohol abuse
Ototoxic medications	Tiredness and anxiety
Tumour (glomus jugulare/	Head injury
acoustic neuroma)	
Aneurysm (intracranial)	

Table 4.4 Vertigo associated with ear problems

Episodic	Constant
Ménière's disease	Ototoxicity
Acoustic neuroma	Chronic otitis media with labyrinthine fistula
Solitary attack	
Vestibular neuronitis	
Labyrinthine fistula	

or intermittent perception of noises in the ears and has been described as a swarm of bees, whistling, a diesel lorry ticking over or a cistern filling with water (Fisher 1998). Tinnitus is a symptom which is often a feature of general ill health and it has several causes (Table 4.3).

When the history and physical examination reveal normal findings for the ear, the other general causes of tinnitus should be considered. The management of tinnitus will be discussed later in this chapter and, regardless of the cause of the problem, patients must be taken seriously and referred to self-help groups for support and information.

Dizziness and vertigo

The history-taking process is particularly important to differentiate between true vertigo and dizziness. Vertigo is the illusion of rotation either of the surroundings or the self. Nystagmus is the objective sign of vertigo. Dizziness is a much looser term associated with feeling faint or light-headed associated with, for example, postural hypotension, hypoglycaemia, hyperventilation or a cardiac dysrrhythmia. The accompanying symptoms of the dizziness or vertigo help to differentiate between diagnoses and clearly the origin or cause of the problem depends on the underlying pathology. It is important to determine the timing and persistency of the episodes, aural and neurological symptoms. The peripheral causes of vertigo, associated with ear problems, are summarized in Table 4.4. Central vertigo refers to vertigo caused by disruption of the central connections of the vestibular nerve associated with cerebrovascular disease or multiple sclerosis.

THE MOUTH

Patients may present with concerns about oral infection, lesions, loss of taste, bleeding around the gums or discomfort of the tongue. A few of the commoner conditions will be considered here.

Ulceration

This is the most common disease to affect the oral mucosa. There are several different forms of ulcers and diverse aetiological factors have been implicated in the pathogenesis. Nutrition, hormones, psychological causes, infection and trauma are all potential causes of ulcers. In the case of persistent ulceration it is important to consider the possibility of HIV infection, which is commonly linked to disorders of the mouth. Ulcers can occur in isolation or in crops which may disappear for weeks and then return. In the case of herpes-zoster there may be hundreds of tiny ulcers which cause the patient considerable discomfort and suffering. Herpes simplex can cause painful oral ulcers in small children and can be one cause of a toddler crying, unwell and off feeds.

Leucoplakia

Leucoplakia is associated with people who have AIDS. It appears as whitish patches of irregular size, often in several sites in the mouth and it is considered to be premalignant – careful observation and biopsy are necessary to monitor the condition. Smoking, drinking spirits, syphilis and sharp teeth are other predisposing factors.

Moniliasis

Moniliasis (thrush) most commonly occurs in the mouths of immunosuppressed patients, people on antibiotic therapy or chemotherapy in malignant disease, debilitated elderly patients and sick children.

The lesions appear as creamy-white curdy patches over the soft palate and may extend to the tongue. Monilia has even been noted on dentures and an essential part of the patient's treatment is a thorough cleaning of false teeth.

Raw red tongue

A raw red tongue suggests possible deficiency syndromes such as iron-deficiency anaemia, malabsorption and pellagra. Further investigation and examination of the patient are required to determine the cause.

Gingivitis

The state of the gums and the teeth gives a good indication of the patient's general health and wellbeing. Swelling and redness of the margins of the gums are often the result of irritative calculus formation. This may progress to peridontitis – an inflammation of the deeper tissues around the teeth and a common cause of the loss of teeth in adults. Gross hypertrophy of the gums with infection, bleeding and necrosis may be a sign of acute leukaemia.

Salivary disorders

The parotid, submandibular and minor salivary glands can be affected by acute or chronic inflammation, cysts, calculi and tumours. Mumps is the most common acute inflammatory condition of the salivary glands which causes swelling in the parotid glands, resulting in great pain and discomfort for the patient. Chronic inflammation is usually due to sialectasis (duct dilatation leading to stasis and infection). The gland becomes thickened and the patient complains of pain. Salivary retention cysts occur most often in the floor of the mouth and can become very large, expanding to involve the loose tissues. The saliva produced from the submandibular gland is mucoid and this results in the development of calculi in some patients.

As salivary glands contain lymph nodes within their structure, they may become the site of metastases from a primary site or from blood dyscrasias such as leukaemia. A solid parotid tumour in a child under the age of 16 is more likely than not to be malignant (Bull 1996).

Cancer

Cancer can occur anywhere in the mucosa of the lips, mouth, tongue and palate. Smoking, chewing tobacco, drinking spirits and poor oral hygiene may all play a role. The most common presentation is on the edge of the tongue as an ulcer. The ulcer will bleed easily and has a typical rolled edge. Occasionally a tumour may present as a lump beneath the surface of the tongue or as a fissure. Urgent biopsy is required in all of these cases.

Carcinoma of the lip

A localized chronic ulceration of the lips may be due to a carcinoma. The lower lip is the commonest site. Predisposing factors include pipe smoking and exposure to sunlight.

Loss of taste

Loss of taste is a problem which may not necessarily be linked to the function of the tongue. The ability to taste relies upon tactile, gustatory, thermal and olfactory sensations. If there are blockages in the nose due to polyps, a head cold or the inflammatory responses due to sinusitis, the patient will not be able to taste properly. If there is no abnormality to be found in the nose, the problem may be caused by viral infection, head injury or concussion.

Tonsillitis

Tonsillitis is common in children but can occur at any age. Under 3 years of age it most often presents as a child who is feverish and refusing to eat while older children may complain of a sore throat. Enlarged and possibly painful cervical lymph nodes may also be found (Valman 2000). Children and adults commonly present with fever and enlarged tonsils which are red and may exude pus; the pharyngeal mucosa will be inflamed and cervical lymph nodes may be enlarged. The cause may be bacterial or viral. Tonsillitis may develop into acute otitis media or, rarely, peritonsillar abscess (quinsy) in which case an urgent medical opinion is needed due to the risk to the airway.

Pharyngitis

Pharyngitis is common and may be caused by simple irritants such as exposure to cold, fumes, certain fruits or viral infection. Infective pharyngitis is most often caused by streptococcal infection. In simple acute pharyngitis the patient will be dysphagic and the mucosa of the pharynx will be hyperaemic. Infective pharyngitis leads to more severe dysphagia, pain and malaise.

Table 4.5 Differential diagnoses of pharyngitis

Without pharyngeal ulcers	With pharyngeal ulcers
Viral	Herpangina
Infectious mononucleosis	Candidiasis
Streptococcal pharyngitis	Herpes simplex
Gonococcal pharyngitis	
Allergic pharyngitis	

If the soreness of the throat is persistent, the patient may have developed chronic pharyngitis. Predisposing factors include smoking, drinking spirits, mouth-breathing, chronic sinusitis, chronic periodontal disease, use of antiseptic throat lozenges and repeated exposure to industrial fumes.

Differential diagnoses of sore throat

Seller (1993) differentiates between pharyngitis with ulcers and pharyngitis without ulcers when considering the differential diagnoses of sore throat. Most commonly the causes will be bacterial or viral pharyngitis; other causes are considered in Table 4.5.

THE FACE

A general review of the face can provide vital information. The face will reflect a variety of systemic diseases, including Cushing's syndrome, acromegaly, myxoedema, Parkinson's disease and Down's syndrome. In more localized conditions it may be possible to detect the swelling of the parotid glands in salivary gland disorders or the slightly gaping mouth of a patient who is unable to breathe effectively through the nose, for example in perennial allergic rhinitis. More specifically associated with the structure of the face is facial nerve paralysis.

Facial nerve paralysis

The causes of facial nerve paralysis are numerous and are listed in Table 4.6. The patient will present

Table 4.6 Causes of facial nerve paralysis

Cerebral vascular lesions	Suppuration (otitis media)
Poliomyelitis	Multiple sclerosis
Cerebral tumours	Guillain-Barré syndrome
Bell's palsy	Sarcoidosis
Trauma	Herpes-zoster oticus
Tumours	

with weakness of the facial muscles, causing an asymmetry which is accentuated on smiling or attempting to close the eyes. It is essential to be aware of the innervation of cranial nerve VII and the different findings you might expect for each of the differential diagnoses. In supranuclear lesions such as cerebral vascular lesions or cerebral tumours, for example, movements of the upper part of the face are likely to be unaffected as the forehead muscles have bilateral cortical representation.

Bell's palsy

The aetiology of Bell's palsy is unknown. However, the symptoms result from an acute inflammatory response which causes swelling in the facial nerve. Swelling within the myelin sheath of the nerve results in ischaemia in the axon. It usually has an acute onset and slowly progresses over 7–10 days. Patients often complain of pain behind the ear and may also complain of tinnitus, fever or a mild hearing deficit. Voluntary and involuntary movements of the face will be affected in varying degrees.

Bell's palsy is a diagnosis of exclusion and a high degree of suspicion of tumour must be maintained in the presence of associated tics or spasms, slow onset of paralysis and paralysis of isolated branches of the facial nerve. A thorough physical examination is essential to determine the exact location of the neural deficit.

THE NECK

The neck contains a vast number of structures, any number of which can be the source of ill health in a patient. This section will focus on the commonest complaints associated with the neck. For neck pain associated with the cervical vertebrae, see Chapter 12.

Neck swellings

Swellings in the neck may result from thyroid swelling, an acute abscess, cysts or metastatic nodes due to malignant involvement of a lymph node. A thyroid swelling may be a solitary nodule or a diffuse goitre which moves on swallowing.

Laryngitis

Laryngitis is commonest in the winter months and is usually caused by the common cold or influenza. The patient will present with hoarseness (dysphonia) or loss of voice (aphonia) and the larynx will appear red and dry with stringy mucus between the cords. Laryngitis is commonest in the winter months and is usually caused by the common cold or influenza. Predisposing factors include shouting, smoking and the consumption of spirits. Acute laryngitis in children can lead to airway obstruction. The child will be unwell, have a harsh cough, hoarseness or aphonia.

Acute epiglottitis is an emergency in children usually affecting those over 2 years of age. Infection of the epiglottis by *Haemophilus influenzae* causes severe swelling which obstructs the laryngeal inlet and potentially can cause complete airway obstruction. The child will have stridor, dysphagia, prefer to sit up, leaning forward slightly whilst drooling as s/he is unable to swallow. Acute epiglottitis is a pediatric emergency and the child should be referred to hospital immediately.

HISTORY-TAKING

As with all history-taking, it is essential to be thorough and include the past medical history, family history, social history, a systems review and a full analysis of the presenting symptoms. The following are examples of history-taking for the various components of the head and neck, with a specific focus on the main problems associated with each area. In exploring the history of a problem within the head or neck it is important to consider not only the presenting problem but also the surrounding structures.

NOSE AND SINUSES

The blocked nose

Nasal obstruction may or may not be associated with nasal discharge. This history and initial assessment are particularly important when the patient complains of a blocked nose because they provide clues as to whether the problem is due to a functional abnormality or a mechanical obstruction. Nasal obstruction in children is most likely to be caused by a foreign body rather than a polyp, which is rare in a child. In adults the opposite is true and therefore the patient's age is an important factor in the assessment process for a blocked nose.

Rhinorrhoea

In nasal discharge it is important to assess the chronology of the illness. Is it seasonal, intermittent or continuous? Does the patient feel that the nose is blocked or irritable? Is it unilateral or bilateral? Unilateral rhinorrhoea requires careful consideration as the cause may be a deviated nasal septum, foreign body or tumour. Is it associated with any other symptoms, such as sneezing, watery eyes, facial pain, headache, fever or sore throat? It is important to enquire about medications as certain drugs, such as oral contraceptives, are related to a stuffy nose.

Rhinitis

A careful history charting the chronological history of rhinitis is essential to discover potential allergens and triggers of the condition. The history should check clues relating to seasonal or diurnal variations or obvious exacerbating factors such as the work place. Personal and family history are also important when the patient presents with this problem, as a history of atopy makes the diagnosis of rhinitis more likely.

THE EARS

If the patient complains of ear pain, local causes are most likely in children. In adults it has been estimated that half of all ear pain is due to secondary causes (La Rosa 1998). Disorders of a wide range of structures such as the sinuses, teeth, jaw, salivary glands and laryngopharynx may cause pain to be referred to the ear. A thorough history is therefore important to explore all possible causes of the problem.

The external ear

The history relating to otitis externa should focus on hearing loss, location of pain, facial twitching, paralysis, dizziness and trauma. It is also important to explore occupation, swimming habits, methods of cleaning the ears and any problems with the mouth, sinuses, nose or throat. Recent ear-piercing is an important clue in perichondritis and a history of atopy is useful in determining whether the patient may have eczematous ear canals.

Ask the patient to describe the drainage from the ear. A milky or bloody drainage may be linked with otitis externa but, more specifically, a cheesy green-blue/grey discharge may result from *Pseudomonas* infection, and clear drainage suggests eczematous weeping (La Rosa 1998).

The middle ear

It is important to explore drainage from the infection of the middle ear. Timing of drainage linked to the patient's report of pain will assist in determining whether there may be a perforation of the tympanic membrane and will therefore help guide the physical examination.

The inner ear

It is important to encourage the patient to describe the sensations associated with dizziness or vertigo. It is possible to differentiate between true vertigo and dizziness (p. 52). If the patient states that tinnitus is present in association with vertigo, Ménière's disease is most likely, as tinnitus will be absent in benign postural vertigo. Nausea and vomiting may be present in all cases of dizziness or vertigo; unilateral weakness, diplopia, numbness or tingling may be due to brainstem disease. The duration and timing of the symptoms are important, as in positional vertigo the symptoms last from minutes to hours, in Ménière's disease from hours to days and in brainstem disease from days to weeks. In all conditions of the ear it is useful to know the patient's occupation to determine exposure to irritants such as dust and any recent trauma to the ear such as a gunshot, barotrauma or air travel.

THE MOUTH

Many of the disorders associated with the mouth have a systemic component and it is important to ask the patient about general health and other illnesses. There is a close link between lesions of the mouth and HIV infection and therefore issues of HIV status should be explored with the patient. Treatments in malignant disease such as radiotherapy and chemotherapy will predispose the patient to candida of the mouth; information on current illnesses and medications should be elicited.

As there is a close link between smoking and carcinomas of the lips and mucosa of the mouth, the patient's smoking history should be explored. The type of tobacco used is important, as pipe smoking is a predisposing factor to carcinomas of the lip and chewing tobacco is a predisposing factor for cancers of the mouth. Alcohol consumption is also important here, with particular reference to the quantity of spirits consumed.

THE FACE

Important questions in the focused history of a patient with unilateral facial palsy include determining whether the weakness is unilateral, if postauricular pain is present and if there is ipsilateral (same sided) lacrimation. These three signs are strong indicators of Bell's palsy (Biullue 1997). Other important questions include whether the onset was acute or slow, duration of symptoms, history of chronic disease, drooling, altered taste, skin lesions, asymmetrical facial expressions, history of a tick bite and pregnancy. Differential diagnoses to be considered with Bell's palsy include Herpes simplex, HIV, tumours, infectious processes, diabetes mellitus, hypothyroidism and demyelinating disease.

THE NECK

A swelling in the neck may be due to a variety of causes and can be related to systemic diseases as well as local causes. Focusing on the patient's general health to explore level of energy and family history to consider thyroid disorders will assist in the subsequent physical examination and further investigations.

PHYSICAL EXAMINATION

As with all examinations, physical examination of the patient who presents with a problem in the region of the head or neck should commence with observation. The examination will be focused on the problem area, however, it is important to look beyond the presenting symptom and consider these surrounding structures and potential links between these structures. Palpation of the affected area follows observation. Percussion and auscultation are generally not required in an examination of the head and neck.

THE NOSE AND SINUSES

A general inspection of the external nose is necessary to note any deformity, swelling or erythema. Observe for signs of the allergic crease, which is a small wrinkle that develops just above the tip of the nose and is due to the constant rubbing associated with allergic rhinitis. This is known as the allergic salute. The inspection is continued by placing gentle pressure on the tip of the nose to widen the nostrils. A penlight or otoscope is necessary to provide a view of the nasal vestibule. The nasal septum can be observed for signs of deviation, which is not uncommon and rarely obstructs airflow.

The inside of the nose can be inspected using a nasal speculum with a good light source. The speculum must be inserted gently and with care to avoid pressure on the very sensitive nasal septum. Seidal et al (2003) recommend holding the speculum in the palm of the hand, using the index finger to stabilize the speculum whilst controlling the patient's head position with the other hand. The nasal mucosa is sensitive and the patient will automatically withdraw and tilt the head away from the examiner. It is important to view the nasal septum, inferior and middle turbinates in a systematic way, focusing on the mucosa for signs of swelling, bleeding or exudate and the septum for deviation, perforation or inflammation. Observe for any abnormalities such as ulcers, polyps or a foreign body.

Palpation of the sinuses should be carried out with care and consideration: the patient may be experiencing discomfort and pain from infection and inflammation of the mucous membranes. Palpate for areas of local tenderness by pressing up on the maxillary sinuses (just below the cheekbones) and over the frontal sinuses (just below the eyebrows).

THE EARS

Observation of the ears commences with an inspection of each auricle and the surrounding tissues, noting any lumps, skin lesions, deformities, discharge from the ear and areas of erythema. Otoscopic examination of the ear canal should be carried out with the largest ear speculum that the canal will accommodate. The ear that is causing the problem should be inspected second, the normal ear providing a reference point for comparison. It may be necessary to straighten the ear canal by grasping the auricle and pulling it upwards, backwards and slightly away from the head. This movement may be painful for the patient and may be a sign of acute otitis externa. It is essential to ensure that the otoscope is held in a firm and secure manner by anchoring the instrument with the examiner's hand placed firmly against the patient's head (Fig. 4.5). This prevents any injury should the patient move and is particularly valuable in the examination of a child.

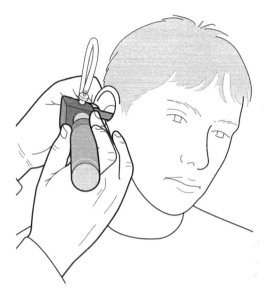

Figure 4.5 Examination of the ear: correct position for holding the auroscope (adapted from Epstein et al 2003).

The ear canal should be observed for cerumen, foreign bodies or any discharge or oedema; the skin of the ear canal should be inspected for signs of inflammation.

The eardrum should be shiny with a clear cone of light and the handle and short process of the malleus should be visible. Abnormalities of the eardrum may be present, including perforations, red bulging drums, the amber colour of a serous effusion or chalky white patches of tympanosclerosis. It may not always be easy to achieve a full view of the eardrum and the examiner will have to move the otoscope around gently to gain as full a view as possible.

If the patient has complained of poor hearing or the examiner suspects that the hearing has been impaired, a gross hearing test can be carried out during the examination. Auditory acuity is tested by standing 30–60 cm away, exhaling and then whispering softly towards one ear while the second ear is occluded. This process should be repeated for the second ear and the results of the two sides compared.

Two important hearing tests which should be carried out together are Weber's test and the Rinne test. The latter helps confirm the findings of the former. Weber's test for lateralization can be utilized to assess for unilateral conductive hearing loss. A 512 or 1024 Hz tuning fork is gently struck to set it vibrating and then placed midline on the patient's head. The patient states whether the sound can be heard equally on both sides or if it can be heard more clearly on one side. In unilateral conductive hearing loss the sound is preferentially heard in the impaired ear. In unilateral sensorineural hearing loss the sound is heard in the good ear.

Air and bone conduction can be compared by carrying out the Rinne test. The tuning fork is struck and then placed on the mastoid bone behind the ear and level with the ear canal. Normally, sound conducted by air is louder than sound conducted by bone. Therefore if the patient is asked to compare the loudness of the sound in this position with that produced by holding the vibrating ends of the fork by the ear, an abnormal result would be to say that the sound heard with the fork on the mastoid process is louder. Further information can be obtained after placing the fork on the mastoid and asking the patient to state when the vibrations can no longer be heard. The tuning fork is then quickly moved to be placed just at the entrance of the ear canal and the patient asked if they can still hear the sound. If they can, this is a positive Rinne test and indicates that air conduction is better than bone conduction in that ear, the normal state of affairs (Epstein et al 2003). This is recorded in the

patient's notes as AC > BC (positive Rinne). If the tuning fork is heard more clearly when in contact with the mastoid, bone conduction is better than air conduction (negative Rinne test, AC < BC) indicating a conductive hearing loss due to a foreign body or cerumen in the ear canal, for example. Table 4.7 provides a summary of the interpretation of Rinne and Weber tests.

The diagnostic decision is based on the rest of the patient's history and physical examination.

THE MOUTH

Examination of the mouth should begin with the lips to observe for colour, ulcers, cracking or discoloration. The corners of the mouth should particularly be checked for cracking as this may be a sign of iron deficiency. It is useful to wear gloves and to use a tongue depressor to examine the oral mucosa. With a good light the roof of the mouth, the gums and teeth and the underside of the tongue should be inspected carefully for lesions and signs of infection.

Ask the patient to put out his or her tongue. An assessment of cranial nerve XII can be made depending on whether the protruding tongue is symmetrical or asymmetrical. The condition of the tongue, its hydration and the turgor of the skin reflect the degree of hydration. The tongue should have a smooth even appearance with no evidence of ulceration or other lesion. Asking the patient to touch the palate with the tongue allows inspection of the floor of the mouth and the under (ventral) surface of the tongue for any abnormalities.

With the patient's mouth open and the tongue not protruded the pharynx and tonsils can be inspected by asking the patient to say 'aaah'. This also checks the movement of the soft palate and pharynx and includes an assessment of cranial nerve X. In Xth nerve paralysis the soft palate fails to rise and the uvula deviates to one side. The soft palate, pharynx, uvula and tonsils can be inspected for swelling, erythema, exudate or white spots.

THE FACE

A general inspection of the face provides an overall idea of systemic illness, for example, enlargement of the bones in acromegaly or a fixed expression of Parkinson's disease. The face should be symmetrical – asymmetry is therefore an indication of

Table 4.7 Interpretation of Rinne and Weber tests*

Right ear	Left ear	Interpretation
Rinne positive	Rinne positive	Normal or mild/moderate or severe bilateral sensorineural loss
(AC > BC) Weber central	(AC > BC)	
Rinne positive	Rinne negative	Left conductive or mixed hearing loss
(AC > BC) Weber → left	(AC < BC)	
Rinne negative	Rinne negative	Bilateral mixed or conductive loss
(AC < BC) Weber central	(AC < BC)	

*Adapted from Toghill (1995).

abnormality. Facial pain or paralysis requires a more detailed examination of the facial cranial nerve (cranial nerve VII). All branches of the facial cranial nerve must be assessed, as involvement of just one branch may indicate a tumour. Ask the patient to puff out the cheeks, grimace, clamp the eyes together and wrinkle the brow. Test taste sensation on the anterior two-thirds of the tongue. Further detail on the cranial nerves can be found on p. 70. A careful examination of the skin includes checking for herpes-zoster and the ear canal should also be checked for the vesicular lesions of herpes.

THE NECK

The neck should be inspected for symmetry, signs of swelling and any visible lymph nodes. The patient must be relaxed for palpation of the lymph nodes and the examiner should follow a structured pattern to cover all 10 areas. Lymph nodes should be noted for size, shape, mobility and tenderness and it should be possible to roll a node in two directions. An enlarged supraclavicular node is highly suggestive of metastatic disease, any hard or fixed nodes suggest malignancy and tender nodes suggest inflammation. Table 4.8 provides an overview of the lymph nodes and a systematic method of

examination; see Figure 4.6 for a diagrammatic representation of the lymph nodes.

Continuing on the external surface of the neck, the trachea and thyroid gland should be inspected for symmetry and any signs of swelling. It should be possible to place your finger between the trachea and the sternomastoid and the space should be equal on both sides. By asking the patient to swallow, the thyroid cartilage, thyroid gland and cricoid cartilage will all rise and it should be possible to note the symmetry of the movement. The same assessment is carried out during palpation. The patient is examined from behind and the examiner places the

Table 4.8 Examination of the lymph nodes

1.	Periauricular
2.	Posterior auricular
3.	Occipital
4.	Tonsillar
5.	Submandibular
6.	Submental
7.	Superficial cervical
8.	Posterior cervical
9.	Deep cervical chain
10.	Supraclavicular

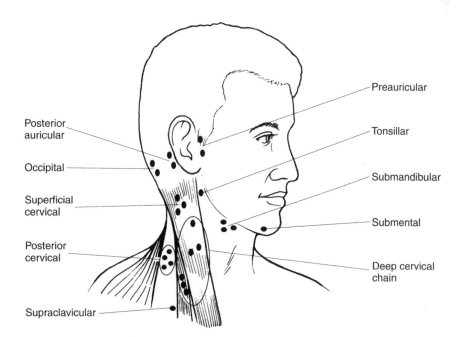

Figure 4.6 Lymph nodes of the head and neck.

fingers of both hands on the patient's neck so that the index fingers are just below the cricoid. By asking the patient to swallow, it may be possible to palpate the glandular tissue as it rises and then falls back to the resting position. Benign and malignant nodules may be palpated and the patient may report tenderness in thyroiditis. If the thyroid gland is enlarged, listen over the lateral lobes with a stethoscope for bruits. A bruit over the thyroid may suggest hyperthyroidism.

Indirect laryngoscopy can be carried out to visualize the vocal cords, epiglottis and larynx. This requires considerable practice and requires the use of a laryngeal mirror. Specialized examination techniques available on referral include the use of a flexible nasendoscope, fibreoptic laryngoscopy or direct laryngoscopy under general anaesthesia.

MANAGEMENT AND PATIENT EDUCATION

Some of the most frequently seen conditions are summarized below.

ACUTE OTITIS MEDIA

Treatment is initially symptomatic with a simple analgesic such as paracetamol. If perforation of the eardrum occurs, it will normally heal spontaneously and, apart from cleaning and swabbing out the ear, no further intervention may be needed apart from a subsequent review (Cross & Rimmer 2002). Culture and sensitivity of the discharge should be carried out if antibacterial therapy is to be offered, however. Generally, antibacterial agents for acute otitis media are of limited value as the cause is frequently viral but if they are to be used they should be administered systemically according to local protocols. Otitis media with an effusion ('glue ear') does not require antibacterial therapy but if it persists for over a month or so, specialist referral to an ENT surgeon is indicated (BNF 2003) as this may lead to deafness and significantly interfere with the child's development.

OTITIS EXTERNA

Prevention is ideal and patients should be encouraged not to clean their ears with hairgrips or cotton tips and should also be advised to wear ear plugs when swimming. If patients develop otitis externa they should be advised not to swim for 7–10 days. Petroleum jelly (Vaseline) can be used to provide a simple yet effective barrier to water when showering and the patient should be encouraged to dry both ears thoroughly if they do get wet.

If the patient presents with otitis externa, careful aural toilet and/or gentle syringing may be sufficient to deal with the problem. A more persistent condition may be treated with a ribbon gauze dressing soaked in corticosteroid eardrops but if infection is present, a topical anti-infective agent such as neomycin or clioquinol may be indicated combined with corticosteroid in an ear drop preparation. The tympanic membrane must be intact for the safe use of such agents.

Instillation of ear drops

The patient should be instructed to lie down on the side that is not infected (if there is bilateral involvement, the patient has to do one ear at a time with adequate rest in between). The drops are then dropped into the ear one at a time. The patient may need to move the pinna gently to help the drops move down into the canal. The patient must remain lying in the same position for 2–3 minutes. Before returning to the upright position it is useful to place a piece of cotton wool which has been soaked in a few of the drops in the outer part of the ear. The cotton wool prevents the drops from running out of the ear and can be removed after an hour or so (La Rosa 1998).

SORE THROAT AND UPPER RESPIRATORY TRACT INFECTIONS

Most sore throats are viral in origin, therefore antibacterial medication is frequently of no value. Patients have to be educated about inappropriate use of antibiotics and may initially be unhappy that they are not offered 'a course of antibiotics'. The same comment applies to most common colds that present, especially in winter. Local protocols should therefore be developed and adhered to in order that only those patients who will be likely to benefit, are prescribed antibacterial therapy such as someone with a demonstrated beta-haemolytic streptococcal pharyngitis.

General health advice about drinking plenty of fluids, eating a healthy diet, keeping warm, resting and taking simple analgesia should be offered, not courses of antibacterial drugs.

Instillation of nasal drops

Nasal congestion associated with the common cold or rhinitis can be relieved with the use of decongestant drops or spray which contain sympathomimetic drugs causing vasoconstriction of mucosal blood vessels. Xylometazoline is commonly used for adults and children. There is a danger, however, of a rebound effect when the patient stops taking the drops. This is caused by a temporary vasodilation leading to increased congestion and so the patient may be tempted to take more drops, setting up a vicious circle (BNF 2003). Patients require instruction on the use of nasal drops as they frequently administer them in an upright position and most of the medication runs down into the oesophagus or runs straight back down the nose and into a handkerchief. The head-back or Mecca position (Fig. 4.7) is the most effective and the patient should hold the position for a few minutes after administration of the drops.

(a) The patient lies prone on the bed with head hanging over the side

(b) The Mecca position

Figure 4.7 Recommended positions for using nasal drops.

TINNITUS

Often little can be done to relieve the suffering of tinnitus. Patients may become depressed, fearful and anxious and will search for a cure. Bull (1996) suggests that there are several points which are helpful in the management of tinnitus:

- Take the patient seriously
- Treat any abnormalities of the ear
- When appropriate, reassure the patient that the condition is benign
- Examine the patient thoroughly
- Be honest with the patient
- Sedatives and tranquillizers may help in some situations
- Treat depression thoroughly and expertly
- A hearing aid may help if the patient also has hearing loss
- Tinnitus maskers are available to produce white noise
- Playing a radio at night may help the patient to sleep
- Relaxation techniques may help some patients
- Refer to self-help groups and other sources of information.

RHINITIS

Some helpful tips for people who suffer from seasonal allergic rhinitis have been suggested by Scadding (1997). These tips can form the basis of a self-management plan and are specifically aimed at reducing the risk of exposure to allergens:

- Listen to the pollen forecast and plan your day accordingly
- Wear wrap-around sunglasses
- Rub petroleum jelly (Vaseline) into the inside of your nose
- Avoid irritants such as paint or cigarette smoke
- Bring in the washing and close bedroom windows before the evening as pollen grains descend as the air cools
- Keep car windows closed and consider buying a car filter
- Avoid walking through or cutting grass
- Avoid picnics and camping
- If you go out in the countryside, shower and wash your hair when you return
- Take an intranasal spray regularly if prescribed.

References

Biullue J S 1997 Bell's palsy: an update on idiopathic facial paralysis. Nurse Practitioner 22(8):88–105

BNF 2003 British National Formulary 45, March 2003. British Medical Association and the Royal Pharmaceutical Society of Great Britain, London

Bull P D 1996 Diseases of the ear, nose and throat, 8th edn. Blackwell Science, Oxford

Candy D, Davies G, Ross E 2001 Clinical paediatrics and child health. W B Saunders, Edinburgh

Cross S 1998 Perennial allergic rhinitis. Practice Nursing 9(11):34–38

Cross S, Rimmer M 2002 Nurse practitioner manual of clinical skills. Bailliére Tindall, London

Epstein O, Perkin D, Cookson J, de Bono D 2003 Clinical examination, 3rd edn. Mosby, Edinburgh

Fisher P 1998 Tinnitus. Practice Nursing 9(3):33–36

La Rosa S 1998 Primary care management of otitis externa. Nurse Practitioner 23(6):125–133

Scadding G K 1997 Rhinitis explained. Asthma Journal 2(1):11–17

Seidal H, Ball J, Dains J, Benedict W 2003 Mosby's guide to physical examination, 5th edn. Mosby, St Louis

Seller R 1993 Differential diagnosis of common complaints, 2nd edn. W B Saunders, Philadelphia

Toghill P 1995 Examining patients: an introduction to clinical medicine, 2nd edn. Edward Arnold, London

Valman B 2000 ABC of One to Seven. BMJ Publishing, London

Chapter 5

The nervous system

Mike Walsh

INTRODUCTION

The importance of the nervous system, and in particular the central nervous system (CNS), cannot be overestimated, as it is this system which makes us essentially human. The higher cerebral functions distinguish us from the rest of the animal kingdom and give us the power to think and reason. Without such an advanced CNS and the special sense of vision, you would not be able to read this book, neither would we have been able to write it.

Patients with migraines and headaches, minor head injuries, faints, fits, dizziness and collapses will be encountered frequently in primary health care and minor injury settings. The nurse practitioner (NP) may also see patients with early signs of more serious disorders such as Alzheimer's disease, Parkinsonism or a cerebral tumour, whilst peripheral nerve problems such as carpal tunnel syndrome may also present. It is important therefore to be able to recognize signs and symptoms suggestive of more serious disease which require medical management and differentiate these patients from others with less serious conditions that the NP can manage.

PATHOPHYSIOLOGY

HEADACHE

A headache is a symptom of an underlying disorder rather than a disease in itself. The underlying problem is usually minor, although the headache itself may be causing considerable distress; in a small number of cases there may be serious pathology such as meningitis.

The two most common presentations are tension headache and migraine. The exact process involved in a tension headache is unclear but it typically presents as a generalized aching sensation which may become localized to the rear of the head or around the temporal region. It may be brought on by any activity requiring sustained concentration, such as driving, and is often associated with anxiety and high stress levels. The patient usually complains of recurrent headaches over a substantial period of time which can be relieved by mild analgesics such as paracetamol.

Migraines are more serious and debilitating. They are caused by arterial dilatation inside or outside the skull. The pain is usually localized to one or more specific areas; it is severe and persistent and may be associated with nausea and vomiting. The onset may be associated with visual disturbances and may be provoked by certain foods. Mild analgesics alone often do not relieve the pain, which may last for hours or even days in severe cases.

Other causes of headache include visual problems in a patient who needs glasses. S/he may be unaware of this fact and has been attempting to compensate for loss of vision by prolonged contraction of the extraocular muscles. The pain is a steady dull ache localized around the eyes and a visual acuity test will quickly reveal the cause of the problem. Sinusitis may also lead the patient to attend, complaining of frontal headaches across the forehead and cheeks. Trigeminal neuralgia, another potential cause of presentation, causes severe, stabbing facial pains, typically of only a few seconds duration but recurring frequently. Patients are frequently middle aged or older. The pain follows the path of the second and/or third divisions of the trigeminal nerve. Unusual loops of the cerebellar arteries are thought to press on the trigeminal nerve rootlets where they enter the brain stem, causing the pain. A similar pain is sometimes experienced by patients with multiple sclerosis. Specific triggers for the pain such as shaving or touch may be identified by the patient.

Meningitis, subarachnoid haemorrhage and brain tumours are the commonest serious disorders producing severe headaches. Each has its own pattern of associated signs and symptoms. The pain is typically constant and severe and is not relieved by over-the-counter analgesics. Onset is usually rapid with meningitis and subarachnoid haemorrhage, and associated with neck stiffness and photophobia as a result of meningeal irritation. Pain associated with a tumour has a more gradual onset and neurological symptoms vary depending on the site of the tumour.

TRAUMA

Head injuries are one of the most common causes of presentation at A&E/MIU although it is injury to the actual brain that is the potentially serious problem, consequently facial injuries should always be considered as producing potential brain injuries as well. Most 'head' injuries are minor, but still account for 320 900 bed days in England alone (Hall 2003). However only 1–3% of those admitted require active medical intervention, so there is great scope for more effective management to prevent unnecessary admission.

Most patients are simply dazed but do not lose consciousness. Where loss of consciousness does occur it involves simple concussion where the brain impacts against the internal surface of the skull, leading to a brief interruption of the reticular activating system and consequent loss of consciousness (less than 5 minutes) and a short period of amnesia. These may be thought of as primary brain injuries which are diffuse in nature. Injuries involving higher energy levels may produce a primary focal injury localized to the point of impact (or directly opposite), such as contusion of the brain which leads to a more prolonged period of unconsciousness. Skull fracture may occur whilst severe injuries involve ruptured blood vessels and haematoma formation. There may also be widespread primary diffuse brain tissue damage. Delayed secondary brain damage may occur in severe head injuries due to cerebral hypoxia, ischaemia or brainstem herniation due to raised intracranial pressure. Occasionally patients present with a lucid interval when they have regained consciousness, but then as intracranial pressure rises (usually due to haematoma formation), the level of consciousness deteriorates into coma.

CONVULSIONS AND COLLAPSES

It is important to differentiate between convulsions or seizures, simple faints and other causes of loss of consciousness such as transient ischaemic attacks. Epilepsy still carries a social stigma and the word is often avoided for that reason but is best understood as *recurring* seizure episodes which frequently do not have an obvious physical cause (idiopathic). Baddeley & Ellis (2002) estimate that the average general practice in the UK has 10–15 patients with active epilepsy and will diagnose a further 1–2 patients each year.

Convulsions or seizures are classified by Springhouse (2000) into those that commence with focal manifestations (partial seizures) and generalized seizures that affect the whole body, producing bilateral convulsions and/or loss of consciousness. Partial seizures are usually caused by a localized lesion within the cerebral cortex such as a tumour or an area of scarring. Partial seizures may be of the Jacksonian type, where motor activity dominates, leading to localized tonic-clonic movements, although consciousness is retained throughout.

Generalized seizures may cause a temporary decrease in consciousness (absence seizure or 'petit mal') or produce a full tonic-clonic seizure with loss of consciousness ('grand mal'). They have a bilateral cortical cause which is frequently idiopathic in origin and manifestations usually appear in childhood. However, if the onset is in later life the cause may be a cerebral lesion such as a tumour, scarring from an old head injury or withdrawal from alcohol or sedative drugs when there is dependence. The seizure may be metabolic in origin and disorders such as uraemia, hypoglycaemia or hyperglycaemia are possible. The effects of flashing lights cannot be ruled out in inducing generalized seizures.

During a tonic-clonic seizure there is an initial collapse and loss of consciousness, the person passes through a tonic phase of muscle rigidity and cyanosis, followed by the clonic phase of generalized convulsions during which significant head injury may occur. A period of unconsciousness follows associated with profound muscle relaxation, which may lead to incontinence before the patient passes through a confused, drowsy period. This postictal phase may be characterized by an elevated temperature associated with the clonic muscular activity. A positive Babinski response is commonly found (p. 74) postictally and the patient will have no recollection of events surrounding the seizure.

Collapse due to a sudden reduction in blood reaching the brain is known as syncope. Simple fainting (vasovagal syncope) is due to a sudden fall in blood pressure caused by peripheral vasodilatation with no compensatory rise in cardiac output. A syncope attack is often associated with some form of generalized motor activity such as twitching, hence it is often confused with a fit. The cause is usually a major emotional disturbance such as fear or pain and predisposing factors include hunger, tiredness and a hot stuffy atmosphere. If someone stands up suddenly he or she may faint as a result of postural hypotension if there is an insufficient reflex response to increase cardiac output and blood pressure. This may be caused by antihypertensive medication or a disorder of the autonomic nervous system. As soon as the person reaches the horizontal position, the brain receives adequate blood flow and consciousness is regained, although there may be a short period of confusion immediately afterwards.

Cardiac arrhythmias may also cause a sudden collapse as they may lead to inadequate cardiac output (p. 109). This may be associated with tachycardia or bradycardia. More seriously, ventricular fibrillation may have occurred, in which case there is no effective cardiac output and immediate resuscitation is required. In an elderly patient, it is always worth checking whether s/he is on a pacemaker as a failure in the pacemaker can lead to profound bradycardia.

The collapse may have been caused by a hypoglycaemic state. In this case the classic picture of increasing confusion, sweating and tremor before collapse, in a known diabetic, coupled with a low capillary blood sugar reading, makes the diagnosis simple. Some individuals with disordered personality may also collapse. This is usually hysterical behaviour and is accompanied by normal vital signs and no obviously abnormal signs. Hysterical overbreathing will produce signs of tetany (carpopedal spasm) due to imbalance in blood gases as carbon dioxide levels fall, inducing respiratory alkalosis. Drug misuse should always be considered in cases of collapse.

The possibility of a transient ischaemic attack (TIA) due to temporary cerebral ischaemia should also be borne in mind. Problems may be associated with emboli in the internal carotid artery which often present with a mild or transient hemiparesis and/or transient blindness, whilst vertebrobasilar ischaemia can produce a sensation of vertigo leading to unsteadiness, nausea and vomiting. Vertigo means the person perceives the surroundings as being in motion ('spinning') and this error of perception can either be due to disorder of the vestibular organs in the inner ear or a brain stem lesion.

A presentation which may lead patients to worry that they have had a stroke is the unilateral facial paralysis of Bell's palsy which is often associated with sensory changes in the affected area. This is thought to be due to reactivation of latent herpes simplex 1 virus leading to inflammation and compression of the facial nerve and hence muscle paralysis. Symptoms usually develop over a few hours (Haslett et al 2002). Recovery begins after 2 weeks and for 80% of patients is complete within 3 months. Older patients may, however, be left with a permanent facial deformity.

Sometimes it is not possible to distinguish clearly between a collapse and a fall. Elderly patients in particular may present with a vague history of falling and it is important to try and establish whether the person did fall accidentally as a result of tripping or loss of balance, or whether s/he collapsed as a result of a medical reason such as syncope or TIA. Eye-witness accounts are crucial in deciding between these two possibilities. How much the person can recall of the event is also a valuable guide – if s/he cannot recall hitting the ground, this suggests s/he lost consciousness first and then fell, which makes an accidental fall unlikely.

DEGENERATIVE BRAIN DISEASE (ALZHEIMER'S DISEASE)

In the process of a consultation the NP may easily miss the early signs and symptoms of Alzheimer's disease. Behaviour which may be dismissed as inattentiveness or carelessness may be the first warning signs before the disease progresses to more advanced stages where there is recent and long-term memory loss, personality changes, apathy, loss of initiative, neglect of personal hygiene and appearance, disorientation followed by motor aphasia (inability to recall words even though the person wishes to say them) and speech-slurring.

In the later stages there is complete disintegration of the person with total loss of recognition of family and friends, disorientation, inability to perform simple cognitive tasks such as writing their own name and loss of motor function, including the ability to walk. Finally the person loses all language skills, becoming doubly incontinent and immobile. Although at present there is no cure, early detection could lead to better management of the disorder, whilst there is hope that in the future treatments may become available to slow down the progress of the disease and may be one day lead to a cure.

OTHER NEUROLOGICAL DISORDERS

Many disorders of the CNS have signs and symptoms of problems with balance, walking and coordination. It is possible that a consultation with the nurse practitioner may be the first point of contact with the NHS for a patient in the early stages of such a disorder. It is therefore essential to recognize abnormal signs or suggestive features in a history so that the patient may be speedily referred on to a medical practitioner. It is beyond the scope of this book to go into a detailed account of such neurological disorders; however, we will briefly mention some of the more common neurological diseases.

Many patients who present with problems associated with balance or gait are suffering from disease of the CNS. Parkinson's disease (paralytic agitans) is one such disease which affects one person in every 100 in the 60–70-year age group. The disease is a complex clinical syndrome which stems from a lack of dopamine, which usually exerts an inhibitory effect on movement by opposing or inhibiting the effects of the neurotransmitter acetylcholine. Lack of dopamine induces tremor, rigidity, difficulty in voluntary movement and slowness, but the person's higher mental faculties may escape damage for many years. This produces the classical shuffling gait of Parkinson's disease where the person appears to be about to fall forwards, the loss of facial expression and also the characteristic tremor of the upper limb which is maximal at rest and produces a pill-rolling movement as the thumb moves back and forth across the fingertips. It is possible to encounter the patient in the early stages of the disease before such a classical picture has developed and the NP has to be alert for early signs of stiffness and slight tremor.

Multiple sclerosis commonly presents in young adults: 60% of patients have their first attack aged between 20 and 40. The disease affects 80 people per 100 000 in the UK, the male to female ratio is 1:1.5 and a person in the UK has a 1 in 800 lifetime risk of developing MS (Haslett et al 2002). This chronic, progressive disease leads to patchy demyelination of the brain and spinal cord and its early signs and symptoms can be variable, depending on the exact location of the damage. Symptoms such as bladder or bowel dysfunction, fatigue, muscle weakness, visual disturbance, transient tingling sensations or numbness (paraesthesia) are all associated with multiple sclerosis. Unlike parkinsonism, tremor is pronounced when the person is trying to do something (intention tremor) rather than at rest. Relatives may report personality changes and increased emotional lability.

Head injury or a brain tumour can lead to the signs of raised intracranial pressure. These may develop in minutes (head injury) or over a period of weeks and months in the case of a brain tumour. Rising intracranial pressure leads to a reduction in perfusion of cerebral tissue and cerebral hypoxia. A key early sign in response to a cerebral tumour is papilloedema (p. 92), while later signs of rising intracranial pressure include decreasing level of consciousness, unreactive dilated pupils (only one pupil may be affected if the lesion is localized), raised blood pressure and bradycardia. The history may reveal complaints of headaches and nausea. Neurological deficits may also be observed depending on the area of the brain affected, whilst convulsions and changes in mental capacity may also occur.

The term peripheral neuropathy describes a disorder of the peripheral nerves which may be generalized or localized, usually involving sensory and motor tracts. The disease process involves either demyelination or damage to the axon itself. The patient tends to complain of altered sensation and weakness in varying degrees depending on which sort of nerve tracts are attacked. The longest nerves are affected first, hence symptoms tend to start at the feet and work upwards, affecting the hands later. There is a wide range of causes such as Guillain-Barré syndrome, vitamin B12 deficiency, diabetes, chronic renal failure and alcohol abuse. Peripheral nerve problems associated with trauma and compression are discussed in chapter 12, with particular reference to the upper limb and the lumbar spine.

The CNS may be attacked by pathogens – acute bacterial meningitis is a particularly feared disease. Viral meningitis is, however, more common and much less serious. Various organisms may cause this infection, giving rise to meningeal inflammation, raised intracranial pressure, disturbance of cerebrospinal fluid circulation and cerebral ischaemia. This pathology manifests as pyrexia, headache, photophobia, neck stiffness, vomiting and reduced level of consciousness. The most serious form of the illness involves *Neisseria meningitidis*, possibly leading to septicaemia, a petechial or purpuric rash, disseminated intravascular coagulation, septic shock and death within a few hours. A rapid diagnosis and initiation of therapy improves the prognosis; however, mortality remains high.

TAKING A FOCUSED HISTORY

Neurological disorders may produce no obvious signs at the time of the examination therefore diagnosis depends heavily on taking a good history. The picture is complicated by the fact that neurological symptoms may be induced by stress alone.

HEADACHES

The PQRST mnemonic may be used to explore the main symptoms. If the main complaint is headaches, start by asking what brings them on (provocation); possible causes include sleeping, posture, reading or other activities involving concentration. What relieves the headaches (palliation)? Ask the patient to describe the pain in his or her own words (quality); it may be a dull ache, tight, boring, burning, pressing. It is important to describe where the pain is and whether it radiates (region), together with how intense it is (severity) using a five-point scale and a description of how the pain affects the person (e.g. 'I have to go and lie down'). Finally, duration of episodes needs to be discovered together with any particular time of day or month (time). A good description of headaches obtained in this structured way greatly facilitates diagnosis.

IMPAIRED FUNCTION AND ABNORMAL SENSATION

The same approach can be applied to other presenting complaints. Problems with gait, coordination, weakness or unusual sensations can be explored, attempting to discover what brings the problem on and whether rest relieves the problem (P). Patients' own descriptions of their feelings and perceptions together with an account of how the problem affects them should be explored (Q). The areas of the body affected should be ascertained (R). It is important to know how severe and disabling the symptoms are (S). Speed of onset and variation of symptoms with time should be checked (T). Problems such as numbness and paraesthesia (tingling or other abnormal sensation) affecting the sensory nervous system should be assessed in the same way.

LEVEL OF CONSCIOUSNESS AND ORIENTATION

In dealing with a head injury, collapse or convulsion, it is important to discover how much the patient can remember. If there is a gap in memory this indicates that the patient was probably unconscious. Eye witness reports are invaluable and should be checked against the classic stages in a grand mal convulsion to see if the story matches. Alternatively the person may have fallen and recovered consciousness quickly with no evidence of tonic-clonic phases, indicating that a syncope (simple faint) is the most likely explanation. The presence of any odd feelings or sensations immediately before the collapse should be checked, such as dizziness, palpitations or an epileptic aura. It is important to know if this has happened before and, if so, whether the person is taking antiepileptic medication or whether there is a pattern to these episodes.

Orientation in time and space should be ascertained to ensure the person has fully recovered and for their own safety. (Where are you? What time is it?) The first sign of deterioration in a head-injured patient will be a decreasing level of consciousness, related to rising intracranial pressure. If the patient presents in a confused condition, it is important to ascertain from relatives or friends the normal level of mental functioning and whether this has changed significantly recently, as well as any change in personality. For non-trauma patients, it is possible to check orientation and memory tactfully in the guise of confirming information held in their notes, but not by asking closed questions that have a yes/no answer, where the patient can guess the correct answer. Questions such as 'When did you last see us?' 'What is your address?' 'Who do you live with?' 'What day is it today?' can easily be asked in a manner which will not cause offence to the fully alert, oriented person.

If the patient has had a generalized seizure (grand mal) s/he will remain sleepy, confused and disoriented (postictal) for up to several hours afterwards, whereas in a simple syncope attack the person will be oriented and able to answer questions within a few minutes. This is a useful aid to making a differential diagnosis between these two possibilities.

OTHER SYMPTOMS

In addition to the three main features discussed above, patients should be asked whether they have noticed any other unusual symptoms recently. This open-ended question may reveal important information. Visual disturbances should be noted, together with any complaints of dizziness. The term vertigo should only be used if the patient describes rotational movement; dizziness in the absence of rotation suggests postural hypotension or some other cause of imbalance. Nausea and vomiting are key indicators of raised intracranial pressure and should be included in the history.

PREVIOUS MEDICAL HISTORY

It is important to ask about previous medical history. Key questions include whether the person suffers from diabetes, epilepsy or Ménière's disease, is under treatment for hypertension or cardiac arrhythmias, or has a history of transient ischaemic attacks. In some cases of neurological disorder the causative event may have happened many years previously; a careful medical history should include questions about childhood and early adult life. Significant aspects of the previous medical history include recent infections, head or spinal injury, congenital abnormalities, birth trauma, meningitis or any previous cerebrovascular accident. Any previous mental health problems which may be relevant should also be explored.

MEDICATION

It is important to enquire about medication as this will give important clues about relevant factors in the medical history, such as cardiovascular disease, diabetes or epilepsy. It is also necessary to ask about recreational drugs as they all act upon the CNS. Assumptions about illegal drug use should not be made. This is now a widespread phenomenon across all sections of society, particularly with the young, and it is not restricted to deprived urban areas. In dealing with persons who collapse, questions about drug use should always be asked, especially with younger individuals.

FAMILY HISTORY

The history should also bring in family history, as many neurological disorders involve a genetic predisposition such as multiple sclerosis and migraine. Other rarer diseases such as muscular dystrophy and Huntington's chorea are known to be genetic disorders.

PERSONAL AND SOCIAL HISTORY

The personal and social history is important as stress or occupation could be contributing to the disorder. Symptoms such as headaches and migraines can be brought on by stressors such as divorce, bereavement, other domestic problems, moving house or changing jobs; these factors may also be associated with exacerbations of multiple sclerosis or epilepsy. Occupational factors include prolonged concentration on VDUs leading to headaches, exposure to dangerous chemicals such as organophosphates in farming and recurrent overuse of certain joints such as the wrist which may lead to carpal tunnel syndrome. Drug use is a key area of social history. Alcohol intake is particularly important as it may be contributing to the problems of diabetes or epilepsy.

The history should also explore whether there have been any recent changes in memory or behaviour, particularly focusing on the ability to care for self (dressing, hygiene, toileting) as consistent deterioration in self-care and memory are early signs of dementia. Intermittent lapses in memory are probably less significant, being related to mood changes and other psychological factors. Sleeping patterns should be explored together with factors which may have increased stress recently, such as financial worries. The patient's general educational level and understanding may be usefully ascertained whilst taking a history.

The possibility of having acquired HIV infection should be explored as a large number of patients with AIDS develop neurological disorders, ranging from vascular myopathy (which leads to degeneration of the spinal cord, ataxia, loss of sensation in the feet and paraplegia) through to full-blown AIDS encephalopathy and dementia. Anxiety and depression in AIDS patients are frequently seen, related to the likely outcome of the disease and the implications of living with AIDS.

History-taking which focuses on mental health problems such as anxiety or depression is dealt with in Chapter 20.

PHYSICAL EXAMINATION

The physical exam follows a logical structure, starting with observing how patients walk into the room and sit down, looking at their general appearance, personal hygiene and demeanour before focusing on the cranial nerves, motor and sensory nervous systems and finishing with an assessment of higher cerebral functioning.

GAIT AND GENERAL MOBILITY

Close observation of how patients walk across the consulting room and sit down by your desk, how mobile they are and how easily they can undress will yield important information. Check the patient's gait and look for any abnormality such as an obvious hemiparesis. Parkinsonism produces a characteristic gait involving difficulty in starting, small steps which become more rapid and inability to swing the arms in the normal way when walking. Alternatively, the patient may show signs of foot drop, including pronounced hip flexion on the affected side while walking and the foot being noisily stamped on the ground. Ataxia is demonstrated by walking with the feet an abnormally wide distance apart and difficulty in remaining upright, grabbing at objects for support. This usually indicates disorder of the cerebellum. A range of other abnormal walks is possible and the nurse practitioner should be able to describe the gait accurately using the correct medical terminology, in his/her notes, for possible discussion with a medical practitioner later. Note factors such as whether there is adduction or abduction, length and rate of stride, balance, width of gait and whether feet are picked up cleanly.

Normally a person maintains balance through several mechanisms, some of which do not involve vision. The semicircular canals in the inner ear play a key role in maintaining balance via the vestibular nerve fibres, various structures in the brainstem, the cerebellum and ultimately nerves which innervate skeletal muscle. With the eyes closed and no visual input to the brain, balance depends on the vestibular system together with proprioceptors. The effectiveness of this system may be assessed by Romberg's test: the patient stands with feet together and closes his/her eyes for 20 seconds. Observe how well the patient maintains balance. Stand immediately behind the patient to steady him/her if s/he loses balance. Instruct the patient to open the eyes immediately if s/he, loses balance – this is a positive Romberg's test and indicates failure of the vestibular system. In cerebellar ataxia the person has difficulty standing with feet together even with eyes open.

The neck and spine should be examined before moving on to the nervous system, as degenerative changes are commonly associated with neurological complaints in older persons. Check passive movements of the neck (rotation from side to side and flexion-extension) to ensure there is no restriction or pain on movement. Observe how readily the patient can undress and take off a shirt or blouse.

If the meninges become inflamed due to bleeding (subarachnoid haemorrhage) or infection (meningitis), this produces a reflex muscle spasm and consequent neck stiffness (nuchal rigidity) so that it is impossible to touch the chin to the chest even with a passive movement. This test should be carried out gently, with the patient lying on the back (supine) and the occipital region of the head supported by both hands. Kernig's sign is another related sign – this is caused by meningeal irritation in the lumbar region. The resultant spasm means that passive flexion of the hip and knee in the same leg followed by passive extension of the knee with the hip still flexed produces pain and resistance. This procedure is carried out with the patient lying supine –a positive result indicates meningeal irritation.

Auscultation for cranial and cervical bruits should be carried out as vascular disease is a common cause of brain dysfunction in the late middle-aged and elderly.

CRANIAL NERVES

This section will focus on testing the cranial nerves during a basic physical examination. Abnormal findings usually indicate local nerve damage or could be associated with disorders affecting the cerebrum. Students should refresh their knowledge of the anatomy and physiology of the 12 cranial nerves so that examination technique is underpinned by the necessary knowledge to make an accurate differential diagnosis.

Olfactory nerve (I)

The absence of a sense of smell is known as anosmia and is most frequently due to obstruction of the nasal passages, although it may be caused by an old head injury damaging the olfactory nerve. Vials of various substances can be used to test the sense of smell and should be administered with the patient's eyes closed via one nostril at a time, while the patient occludes the other by pressing with a finger.

Optic nerve (II)

Detailed examination of the optic nerve is covered on p. 91.

Oculomotor, trochlear and abducens nerves (III, IV and VI)

These nerves are considered on p. 86; their functions are closely interrelated, controlling pupil size and eye movement.

Trigeminal nerve (V)

This has both motor and sensory components. The motor fibres innervate the muscles responsible for chewing, movements of the jaw and swallowing. Muscle wasting may be observed best as hollowing above the zygomatic arch. The patient should be asked to open and close the mouth against resistance (hold the jaw) to test muscle tone. Muscular wasting or weakness may be found in myasthenia gravis or various myopathies while the jaw deviates to the weakened side if a unilateral trigeminal lesion is present.

The sensory fibres transmit sensation from the face and frontal part of the scalp. The three sensory divisions of the trigeminal nerve are the ophthalmic, maxillary and mandibular branches; the names broadly indicate the areas of the face served by these fibres. Examination of pinprick and light touch sensation should be carried out with the patient's eyes closed and working in an unpredictable pattern over all areas of the face. The sensations reported on the left side of the face should be compared with the right; normally they will be the same. The end of a needle and cotton wool may be used to test for sensation and moist cotton wool should also be used to test the corneal reflex (ophthalmic branch). A light touch on the cornea should produce an immediate bilateral blink reflex.

Unilateral impaired function is a serious finding and commonly indicates a tumour affecting the fifth cranial nerve or higher sensory pathways, although a patchy deficit may be due to trauma damaging some peripheral branches of the nerve.

Facial nerve (VII)

Many facial movements are innervated by the motor branch of the facial nerve whilst it provides sensation to the frontal portion of the tongue. It is also involved in the corneal blink reflex and the production of tears and saliva. The motor branch can be tested by first checking for any obvious asymmetry in the patient's facial appearance and then asking him/her to perform the following manoeuvres and examining for asymmetry or weakness:

- Raise both eyebrows
- Frown and then smile
- Close both eyes and keep them closed while you try to open them
- Show both upper and lower sets of teeth
- Blow out both cheeks.

Upper motor neuron lesions tend to have a minimal effect on the upper part of the face (e.g. the eye can still be closed) but cause significant paresis in the lower facial muscles, with drooping of the corner of the mouth and dribbling of saliva. Lower facial asymmetry is usually obvious. Tumours and vascular lesions occurring in the brainstem may cause abnormal seventh nerve signs, whilst this nerve is the most commonly affected cranial nerve in Guillain-Barré syndrome.

If the lower motor neuron is involved this causes a unilateral weakness of all the facial muscles. An acute onset is commonly seen in Bell's palsy, though the exact cause is unknown. There may also be a loss of taste over the frontal two-thirds of the tongue in Bell's palsy, indicating sensory involvement. The eye should be thoroughly examined if Bell's palsy is suspected as the corneal reflex is diminished and blindness may develop. Abnormal lacrimation may also be noted.

Vestibulocochlear nerve (VIII)

The eighth nerve has two branches: the vestibular, which is concerned with balance and posture and the cochlear, which is concerned with hearing. Assessing the patient's hearing is dealt with in Chapter 4, whilst testing the vestibular branch is normally the preserve of hospital medical specialists.

Glossopharyngeal and vagus nerves (IX and X)

These nerves are usually considered together because of their close anatomical relationship. Hoarseness may indicate vocal cord paralysis whilst a nasal tone may be produced if the palate is functioning abnormally. Observing the patient saying 'Aah' will reveal any abnormality in movement of the uvula or palate. Deviation of the uvula indicates a tenth nerve lesion (such as a meningioma or fractured base of skull) on the opposite side and will usually be seen with asymmetrical elevation of the soft palate. The gag reflex may be tested (after warning the patient first) by touching either the tonsil or pharynx on each side. If the reflex is absent on one side this indicates a lesion affecting either the ninth or tenth cranial nerve.

Accessory nerve (XI)

This important motor nerve innervates the intrinsic muscles of the larynx, the sternomastoid muscles and part of the trapezius. The patient is best examined from behind to check for any paralysis of the trapezius, shown by drooping of the shoulder and downward lateral displacement of the scapula. S/he should then be asked to shrug the shoulders and maintain that position against downward pressure to check for any weakness which would be indicative of a peripheral nerve disorder.

The sternomastoid muscles should be inspected and palpated for any signs of atrophy. Test their strength by asking the patient to rotate his/her head against resistance with firm pressure to the opposite side of the face. The contraction of the sternomastoid should also be noted during this procedure. If there is bilateral wasting of the sternomastoids, the patient will have difficulty raising the head from the pillow while lying in the supine position. Isolated lesions of this nerve are rare, but findings indicative of a myopathy may be noted.

Hypoglossal nerve (XII)

The XIIth nerve is the motor nerve responsible for innervating the muscles of the tongue. When the patient's tongue is protruded it should lie symmetrically in the midline with no fasciculations or atrophy. If there is a unilateral lesion the protruded tongue deviates towards the affected, weaker side. The patient should be able to move the tongue equally well to either side of the mouth and in the vertical plane as if to lick the chin or the tip of the nose.

Unilateral abnormalities are often due to cranial tumours or vascular lesions, although they may also be traumatic in origin. Diseases such as myasthenia gravis result in abnormal findings such as dysarthria and dysphagia whilst a cerebrovascular accident may cause deviation of the protruded tongue in the acute phase.

MOTOR SYSTEM

This section should be read in conjunction with Chapter 12. Examination of the motor system begins as the patient walks into the room and sits down as problems of gait and balance together with evidence of muscle wasting may be immediately obvious. Fasciculations should be noted. This term describes repeated spontaneous contractions of muscle fibres in the same motor unit and can vary from a delicate flicker through to an obvious twitch.

The examiner needs to be competent in testing for normal coordination, deep tendon reflexes and plantar responses, together with assessment of muscular tone and power. Abnormalities can indicate whether the problem is an upper or lower motor neuron disorder or whether it involves the muscles. The exam can only be carried out properly with the patient undressed to underwear, therefore a warm and private environment is essential.

Coordination and balance

Proprioception and cerebellar function are essential for coordination and balance. In a simple test the patient carries out rapid alternating movements such as touching each finger of the right hand with the right thumb in sequence and then reversing the sequence before repeating the movements with the other hand. Alternatively, ask the patient to hold out the right hand palm upwards and repeatedly touch the upwards-facing fingertips with the front and back of the fingers of the left hand, rapidly rotating the left hand to accomplish the manoeuvre. Repeat with the other hand. The patient should be able to carry out these movements smoothly and rhythmically; jerky, slow or irregular movements are abnormal.

Accuracy of movement may be tested using the finger-to-finger test. The NP should hold his/her index finger about 45 cm in front of the patient and ask the person to touch his or her nose tip and the nurse practitioner's finger alternating between the two. The patient should have the eyes open and the finger should be held in several different positions during this test. Both hands should be tested. The patient should be able to perform this test smoothly and accurately but if the finger repeatedly goes past the NP's finger this may indicate cerebellar disease. In a variation of this test the patient closes the eyes and repeatedly touches the tip of his/her own nose with the index finger of

each hand. A further test for accuracy involves asking the patient to lie down and then to run the heel up and down the shin of the opposite leg in a straight line.

Abnormalities in these tests indicate disorder of the cerebellum. Cerebrovascular disease, multiple sclerosis, alcoholism and degenerative disease are the most likely competing explanations.

Romberg's test for balance has already been described (p. 69); in a further test the person stands on one foot for 5 seconds with the eyes closed and then hops on to the other foot, holding that position for a further 5 seconds.

Deep tendon reflexes

The effect of a reflex arc is to produce an involuntary response when the appropriate stimulus is provided. The involuntary nature of the response provides the examiner with objective information about the nerve pathways involved, if only the appropriate tendon is stimulated by the tendon hammer.

When testing reflexes it is important that the patient should be relaxed and comfortable. The hammer should be held between the thumb and index finger: a flick of the wrist provides a sharp tap on the tendon. The major tendon reflexes should be tested systematically, comparing responses on opposite sides of the body. Results may be recorded on a stick figure using the following standard notation:

- +++   Exaggerated response
- ++   Normal
- +   Just present
- ±   Present only with reinforcement
- 0   Absent

Considerable experience is needed before such a scoring system can be used confidently.

- Biceps jerk (reflex arc involves spinal segment C5 and C6): the patient's elbow is flexed at 45° the elbow is held with the fingers over the biceps muscle and the thumb on the biceps tendon (Fig. 5.1) and the thumb (not the tendon) is struck. The reflex jerk should produce visible or palpable flexion of the elbow as the biceps contracts.
- Supinator jerk (reflex arc involves spinal segment C5 and C6): the patient's arm rests on the NP's arm with the elbow flexed at 45° and the arm slightly pronated (Fig. 5.2). The aim is to strike the patient's brachioradial tendon

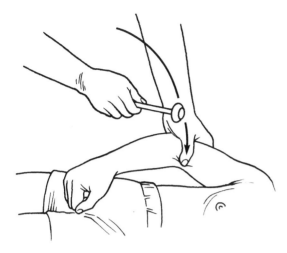

Figure 5.1 Testing biceps jerk.

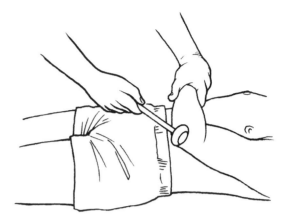

Figure 5.3 Testing triceps jerk.

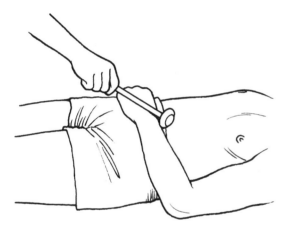

Figure 5.2 Testing supinator jerk.

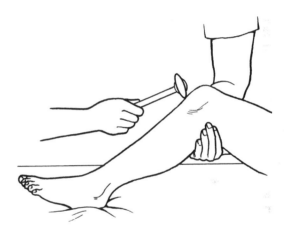

Figure 5.4 Testing for knee jerk.

some 5 cm above the wrist – this should produce pronation of the forearm and flexion of the elbow.

- Triceps jerk (reflex arc involving spinal segments C6 and C7): the individual's elbow is flexed to 90° with the arm resting against the side of the body (Fig. 5.3). The aiming point is the triceps tendon just above the elbow. This should produce contraction of the triceps muscle, which will cause visible or palpable contraction of the elbow.
- Knee jerk (reflex arc involving spinal segments L3 and L4): the patient sits with the lower limb hanging loosely and the knee flexed at 90°. The upper leg should be supported (Fig. 5.4) and the patella tendon is struck just below the

patella. The lower leg should extend in response to contraction of the quadriceps muscle.

- Ankle jerk (reflex arc involving spinal segment S1): this is most readily tested with the patient kneeling on a chair, toes pointing towards the floor, although it may be tested with the patient lying recumbent (Fig. 5.5). The Achilles tendon is struck at the level of the malleoli. This should produce contraction of the gastrocnemius muscle and therefore plantar flexion of the foot.

If reflexes are difficult to elicit or absent, use reinforcement to make them easier to observe. For the lower limb the patient interlocks the flexed fingers and attempts to pull them apart just as the tendon

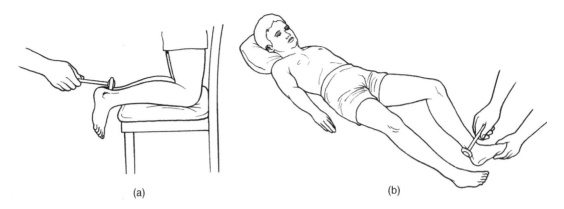

(a)   (b)

Figure 5.5 Testing for ankle jerk of (a) kneeling patient and (b) recumbent patient.

is about to be struck, while for the upper limb, the patient squeezes the knees together immediately before testing. If reinforcement has been used to elicit a reflex, it is recorded as ±.

Exaggerated reflexes usually indicate upper motor neuron disease. Muscles may show some loss of strength but little evidence of atrophy in upper motor neuron disease. If reflexes appear to be brisk or hyperactive it is worth testing for clonus, which is a series of rapid muscle contractions in response to a stimulus. This suggests a disorder of the pyramidal tract. The knee should be supported in a partly flexed position and the foot briskly dorsiflexed; if rhythmical tremors in the foot are felt, clonus is present. If there is a symmetrical loss of reflex this may indicate generalized peripheral neuropathy, whereas a single lost reflex suggests a localized problem. Absent or diminished reflexes are found in lower motor neuron disorders which are usually associated with loss of muscle tone and muscle wasting. A delayed reflex suggests hypothyroidism.

Stimulation of the lateral border of the sole of the foot leads to plantar flexion (toes curl downwards). Dorsiflexion of the big toe (Babinski response) indicates an upper motor neuron lesion or may be found after an epileptic seizure.

THE SENSORY SYSTEM

The patient may present with a history of reduced sensation (hypoaesthesia) or altered sensation (paraesthesia). It is important to test sensitivity to light touch, pressure and temperature with the patient's eyes closed and to map the results carefully in order to build up an accurate picture of sensory disturbance over the affected area. The correct interpretation of areas of altered sensation requires knowledge of the distribution of the major peripheral nerves and dermatomes (Fig. 5.6). Normally, sensation should be distributed symmetrically about the body and the person should be able to describe correctly the stimulus (sharp/dull) and differentiate between sites (proximal/distal) in successive stimuli.

Superficial touch can be tested with light strokes of a piece of cotton wool. Superficial pain can be tested with a pin. Hypodermic needles should be avoided because they are too sharp and may accidentally puncture the patient's skin. A disposable pin should be used to avoid any risk of transmitting a blood-borne disease. The patient can be asked to differentiate between sharp and dull sensation (use the side of the needle). Only if superficial pain sensation is abnormal should temperature be tested, using sample bottles of warm and cold water, which can be pressed against the skin. Great care should be taken to ensure that the water is not too hot. Deep sensation can be tested by squeezing muscle between finger and thumb.

Vibration can be tested with the aid of a tuning fork held against various bony prominences (e.g. sternum, shoulder, wrist) whilst joint position is tested by holding a distal phalanx laterally and moving it up or down and asking patients (still with their eyes closed) which direction the movement takes in a short series of random movements. If the patient is unable to identify correctly the direction of movement, continue to work proximally along the limb, repeating the test.

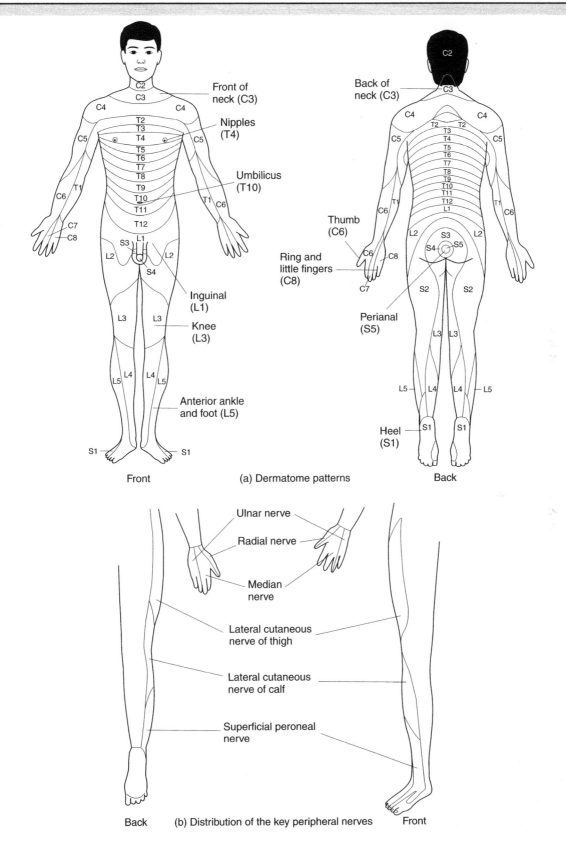

Figure 5.6 The distribution of (a) dermatomes and (b) key peripheral nerves.

Two-point discrimination can be tested with an unfolded paper clip. Either one or both ends are applied to the skin at random on the pulp of both index fingers and thumbs. The distance between the two ends can be varied to ascertain the minimum separation that the patient can identify. Again the patient must have the eyes closed. A normal person can distinguish between two points 3–5 mm apart on the pulp of the index finger.

Disorders affecting specific single peripheral nerves (mononeuropathy) normally give rise to reduction in all sensations and/or a feeling of numbness in nerve distribution. Common examples include carpal tunnel syndrome (median nerve, usually affecting the dominant hand first) and damage to the sciatic nerve producing foot drop, absent Achilles tendon reflex and anaesthesia over the foot. The radial and ulnar nerves may suffer from compression or direct trauma in arm injuries. Peripheral neuropathies and spinal injuries are associated with disorders of touch, pain and temperature perception together with joint position and two-point discrimination. If the pattern of sensory loss is symmetrical, this suggests a polyneuropathy. Such disorders affect the peripheries of the longest nerves first and progress proximally. The feet are therefore commonly affected first. Patchy sensory disorder suggests a spinal cord problem rather than a polyneuropathy, which tends to be uniform in its distribution. Complex patterns of sensory disturbance may present with various cerebral lesions, which are often vascular.

Cortical function and the sensory system

A lesion in the posterior (ascending) columns of the spinal cord or in the sensory cortex may be demonstrated by testing the patient's ability to interpret and discriminate between sensory inputs. The following simple tests may be performed, all with the patient's eyes closed:

- Stereognosis: can the patient identify by touch alone common objects such as a coin?
- Extinction: touch both hands simultaneously with a pin and ask whether the patient is being touched on the left, right or both hands.
- Graphesthaesia: draw a number on the patient's palm and ask what it is.
- Point location: touch the patient's skin and ask him/her to point to the area touched.

A failure in one or more of these tests suggests a lesion in the sensory cortex or the posterior columns

of the spinal cord (Seidal et al 2003). It is important in these tests to check that the patient's touch and position sense are normal, or only slightly impaired, as these parts of the sensory nervous system must be functioning to carry out valid tests on the sensory cortex. If touch and position sense are normal but the patient has an abnormal two-point touch test result (see above) of > 5 mm when the finger pad is tested, this indicates probable disease of the posterior columns in the spinal cord.

THE UNCONSCIOUS PATIENT

The primary assessment must follow the well-known ABCD format, checking for patent airway (A), effective breathing (B), cardiac output (C) and evidence of disability (D) associated with a spinal injury. It is crucial that a history be obtained from anybody who witnessed the incident to find out whether the patient has suffered a head injury, fit or collapse, is likely to have taken drugs or alcohol or whether there is no known history. Check for signs of intravenous drug misuse and the smell of alcohol on the breath.

It is necessary to have an objective measure of the patient's level of consciousness and this is provided by the well-known Glasgow Coma Scale (GCS; Fig. 5.7), which should be recorded initially and at regular intervals thereafter (15 minutes while unconscious, more frequently if the level of consciousness is fluctuating). The patient is in coma if s/he does not open the eyes in response to painful stimulus (nail bed pressure), utters no sounds and fails to respond to any command (GCS = 3).

Vital signs should be monitored at 15-minute intervals. If the intracranial pressure is seriously elevated after head injury, this produces a reflex slowing of the pulse as blood pressure rises in an attempt to increase brain perfusion. On the other hand, unsuspected internal injuries may lead to the rapid development of hypovolaemic shock.

Pupil size and reaction should also be closely monitored. Pressure on the third cranial nerve will lead to a sluggish pupil response and to a fixed dilated pupil on the affected side. This may be due to an expanding haematoma in head injury. Bilateral fixed dilated pupils in head-injured patients indicate major brain swelling and hence damage as both branches of the third cranial nerve are affected. Early observations are essential as developing periorbital haematoma may soon make it impossible to open a patient's eyes sufficiently

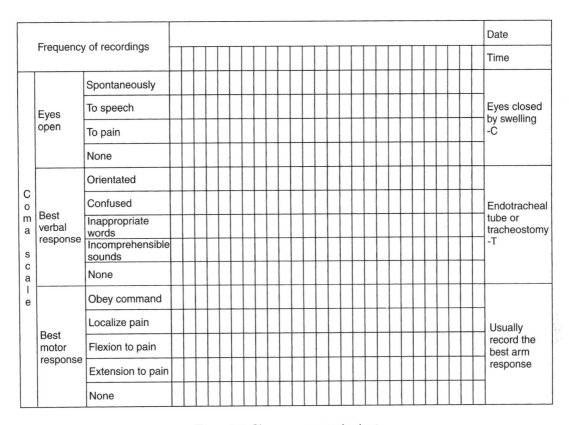

Frequency of recordings																									Date
																									Time
C o m a s c a l e	Eyes open	Spontaneously																							
		To speech																							Eyes closed by swelling -C
		To pain																							
		None																							
	Best verbal response	Orientated																							
		Confused																							Endotracheal tube or tracheostomy -T
		Inappropriate words																							
		Incomprehensible sounds																							
		None																							
	Best motor response	Obey command																							
		Localize pain																							Usually record the best arm response
		Flexion to pain																							
		Extension to pain																							
		None																							

Figure 5.7 Glasgow coma scale chart.

to observe the pupils. Overdose of tricyclic antidepressants may also produce bilateral dilated pupils due to their anticholinergic effect. Pinpoint pupils suggest opioid drug use as the most likely cause of coma. In the absence of head injury, a capillary blood glucose reading should be taken to eliminate hypoglycaemic coma.

Motor function should be checked bilaterally as part of the GCS together with reflexes. This may provide crucial information about spinal cord involvement.

Head-injured patients should also be examined for cerebrospinal fluid leakage or bleeding from within the ear, indicating a basal skull fracture. Bruising over the mastoid process is known as Battle's sign and indicates a fracture through the middle fossa. The scalp should be carefully examined for lacerations; as well as exacerbating the risk of hypovolaemic shock due to other injuries, scalp wounds may indicate the possibility of an open and/or depressed skull fracture with the risk of meningitis from contamination of the meninges.

If the nurse practitioner has to assess and manage an unconscious patient without access to immediate medical assistance it is important that s/he remembers that maintenance of a patent airway and effective breathing at all times is essential for the patient's survival. In undressing and examining the patient, the nurse practitioner should also assume there is spinal injury until proven otherwise.

DIFFERENTIAL DIAGNOSIS

The patient's history is the single most important factor in arriving at a differential diagnosis. It also guides the physical examination. The following common presenting complaints are analysed to illustrate the steps to follow in arriving at a differential diagnosis of the patient's health problem.

Headache

It is important to differentiate between a potentially sinister cause such as meningitis or cerebral tumour, migraine and other less serious causes such as tension headaches, sinusitis and eyestrain. The PQRST mnemonic will assist in making this differential. Key diagnostic features of migraine include a pain that has high impact upon the patient's daily activity, is moderate to severe, throbbing in nature and unilateral. The pain lasts for between 4 and 72 hours although attacks are relatively infrequent and the patient is symptom free between attacks. Nausea, vomiting and photophobia are frequently associated with the pain as well as sensory disturbance producing an aura. Patients are in the young to middle age groups and females are more common than males (MIPCA 2003). Tension headaches are bilateral and have a low impact upon daily living activity; they are not associated with nausea and vomiting. They can affect all ages and genders equally. Sinusitis or eye strain are other possible causes of a generalized headache; facial pain distribution and a story of rapid stabbing and severe pains suggest trigeminal neuralgia.

More serious pathology, such as meningitis or subarachnoid haemorrhage, is suggested by cerebral irritation and impaired consciousness. A patient complaining of headaches should always have a blood pressure check to eliminate hypertension. Other signs of a more sinister aetiology include the presence of a rash, fever, neurological deficit which remains after the pain has gone or behavioural changes.

Collapse

Recovery rate is a key guide to the possible cause. If the person has had a stroke there will be little improvement in their condition over the short term (unless it is a transient ischaemic attack). If the person has had a generalized seizure s/he will be in a confused and disoriented (postictal) state for possibly several hours afterwards, unlike syncope where orientation is quickly regained. If a convulsion is ruled out, it is necessary to eliminate the possibility of a cardiac arrhythmia (perform ECG, check history) or in the case of an elderly person a simple fall (check history). A capillary blood glucose test will eliminate the possibility of a hypoglycaemic attack. An eyewitness account helps to differentiate between causes such as a simple vasovagal syncope or a convulsion. If the patient is found in a collapsed state, the smell of alcohol or evidence of other drug use (e.g. intravenous needle marks, respiratory depression) point towards alcohol

or drug abuse as a likely cause; nevertheless, the nurse practitioner should also carry out a careful exam to eliminate the possibility of a coexisting head injury. Abnormal neurological findings indicate the possibility of a stroke.

Other neurological problems

There are many circumstances where the nurse practitioner might observe a significant neurological sign and it is essential therefore that s/he is able to develop an early line of clinical thinking with a differential diagnosis, record findings accurately and

Table 5.1 Attribution of signs to probable lesions in the nervous system*

Sign	Region of nervous system
Weakness or paralysis of movement	Upper motor neuron
Increased tendon reflexes	
Extensor plantar response	
Wasting, weakness or paralysis of muscles	Lower motor neuron
Diminished tendon reflexes	
Reduction in tone	
Ataxia of gait	Cerebellar lesions
Disordered coordination and fine movements	
Intention tremor	
Reduced superficial sensation in peripheries	Generalized neuropathies
Wasting and weakness of distal musculature	
Early loss of tendon reflexes	
Impaired position sense (positive Romberg test)	Sensory tracts, dorsal columns
Decreased appreciation of vibration	
Ataxia of gait	
Muscle wasting and weakness, usually proximal	Muscles
Reduced reflexes with marked muscle wasting	
Amnesia and cognitive disorders	Cerebral cortex dysfunction
Dysphasia	
Right/left disorientation	
Hemiparesis	
Apraxia	
Visual field defects	

*Adapted from Munro & Edwards (1995).

consult or refer appropriately. A useful approach is to ask what is disturbed, where and why? This requires an accurate record of the observed abnormality, its location and a suggestion as to its cause. The following simplified table (Table 5.1) indicates specific signs which can be attributed to lesions in the nervous system.

MANAGEMENT AND PATIENT EDUCATION

This final section of the chapter will focus on the management of common neurological conditions.

HEADACHES

Migraine

The patient with a history of migraines may be distressed because of the debilitating nature of the attacks and the disruption they cause to everyday life. This may lead to time off work, disruption of study for a student or serious problems for a mother bringing up a young family, particularly if she is a lone parent. The person may also be anxious, interpreting the migraines as a symptom of a more serious disorder such as a brain tumour.

A key step in managing migraine is to try and identify any precipitating factors which the patient may be able to avoid. The patient may find it useful to keep a diary over a period of time recording the frequency of attacks and associated symptoms, the presence of an aura, and what s/he was doing immediately before the attack. This may lead to the discovery that attacks coincide with the menstrual cycle. Clinical trials have failed to provide evidence that it is possible to reduce the frequency of migraines by hypnosis, using a TENS machine or avoiding certain foodstuffs such as cheese, chocolate, red wine or caffeine. However, there is evidence that relaxation therapy, biofeedback techniques and avoiding known triggers do reduce the frequency, as does exercise and massage linked to stress reduction (Campbell et al 2000). The contraceptive pill aggravates migraine and if an increase in frequency of attacks coincides with a woman starting oral contraception, she should be advised to use alternative methods.

The nurse practitioner may therefore explore stress reduction strategies with the patient as a means of lessening the incidence of migraines. If the patient is caring for young children, s/he may

need to work through some coping strategies with the nurse practitioner, which may include identifying helpful relatives or friends who can look after the children while s/he recovers.

Evidence (Matchar et al 2000) indicates that paracetamol, paracetamol/codeine combinations (e.g. Migraleve) or antiemetics alone are of no value in treating migraine. Efficacy has been demonstrated however for the use of aspirin and the NSAIDs (Clotam Rapid) or aspirin/paracetamol combinations with metaclopramide such as Migramax or Paramax.

The most effective drugs are the 5-hydroxytryptamine agonists known collectively as the triptans. Sumatriptan (50 mg orally) is the most effective and has the quickest onset when given subcutaneously (dose 6 mg). Autoinjectors are available for this route. The nasal spray form (20 mg in one dose) is quicker to act than any of the oral triptans. The drug has potential side effects and should not be taken by patients with a history of coronary artery disease or combined with any other drug to treat migraine because of the risk of interactions (BNF 2003).

If migraine is seriously affecting the patient, betablockers are effective in preventing attacks. The side effects of these medications are such that their use for more than 6 months is not recommended. Addressing lifestyle issues may successfully reduce the frequency of attacks. There is also some evidence that alternative therapies such as feverfew, vitamin B2 or magnesium preparations, or acupuncture, can reduce the frequency of attacks (Downson & Cody 2002). The long-term management of migraine is most effective if a team approach is taken involving both the patient and health care providers such as GP, NP, other nursing staff, the local pharmacist and possibly hospital specialist in severe cases.

Tension headache

A good place to start is to explore the causes of stress and anxiety before looking at what measures can be taken to reduce these factors. A diary may be helpful to identify particular situations which lead to headaches so that they can be avoided. This can be reviewed at a follow-up appointment, together with progress on stress reduction strategies. Positive reinforcement is important for the patient.

The consultation is a good opportunity to educate the patient about the dangers of paracetamol which may be consumed in significant quantities as the patient tries to deal with the symptom (headaches) rather than the cause of the problem (stress). Many people do not realize that paracetamol may cause serious liver damage and is therefore contraindicated in those with liver disease, including those with a history of alcohol abuse. Between 20–30 paracetamol tablets (10–15 g) taken over a 24-hour period can cause severe liver damage or renal tubular necrosis (BNF 2003). Symptoms may not become apparent however until 4 or 5 days later. It is important to stress that if the patient is taking paracetamol to relieve headache the maximum daily dose is 4 g or eight tablets. Tactful enquiry should also be made about alcohol intake.

Other causes of headache

If a Snellen test has revealed eyesight problems, the patient should be referred to an optician. If sinusitis is the cause of the patient's pain, a course of amoxicillin, doxycycline or erythromycin is the recommended antibiotic therapy (BNF 2003).

If the nurse practitioner suspects trigeminal neuralgia the patient should be referred to the GP. Carbamazepine is effective at reducing the severity and frequency of attacks, although side effects include rashes, dizziness, nausea and vomiting. The usual approach is to start the patient on 300 mg/day in divided doses and gradually increase the dose until it is effective without problems from side effects. Patient education about side effects is essential. As a last resort it is possible to destroy the trigeminal nerve to relieve pain, but this leaves the patient without any sensation on the side of the face and at risk of corneal ulceration.

The nurse practitioner may receive a phone call from an anxious individual worried that their child or relative may have meningitis. In children the peak incidence is between age 6 and 12 months and early signs include drowsiness, irritability and refusal of feeds (Valman et al 2000). Rapid development of a nonblanching purpuric rash is a serious sign indicating meningococcal septicaemia in infants and toddlers (Epstein et al 2003). In older patients the rapid onset of severe headache worse than anything experienced before, photophobia, neck stiffness, fever, confusion, drowsiness in addition to the classic rash are all signs indicating immediate admission and treatment to a critical care facility. Antimicrobial therapy with parenteral benzylpenicillin (preferably IV) should be commenced immediately, if possible, whilst waiting for an ambulance. The BNF (2003) recommends children over 10 and adults should receive an initial dose of 1200 mg, 1–9-year-olds 500 mg and children under 1 year 300 mg.

COLLAPSE

Generalized seizure (grand mal)

Do not interfere with the patient during the tonic and clonic stages of the seizure. Any hard objects which may cause injury should be removed from the immediate vicinity and if it is possible to place a blanket or something similar under the patient's head as a means of protection, this should be done. Once the clonic stage is over, the individual will remain deeply unconscious and may occasionally have a further fit. S/he should therefore be placed in the recovery position to protect the airway and, if suction is available, this should be used to remove secretions from the oral cavity. The profound muscle relaxation which accompanies this stage may lead to urinary incontinence if the individual's bladder contained significant amounts of urine. This should be checked and if possible wet clothing removed to prevent embarrassment when consciousness is recovered. Recovery proceeds through the postictal stage, during which time the patient slowly regains consciousness but may be confused and disoriented; s/he should be kept under observation until fully oriented.

It is possible that the fit happened elsewhere and the patient has been brought to the nurse practitioner (e.g. in a minor injuries unit). The nurse practitioner should try and obtain a reliable eye witness account in order to assess the probability of a generalized seizure. By the time the patient arrives at the unit s/he will usually be in the postictal phase if this is the case.

After checking the ABCD, the NP should then carry out a careful neurological examination (including checking for evidence of head injury) and obtain a history of the event. In the immediate postictal period, observation and regular assessment of level of consciousness are essential and it is important to ascertain whether the individual has a history of epilepsy. If this is positive, local protocols may allow the patient home with a responsible adult and notification of the GP. If the patient has no history of epilepsy, s/he should be carefully followed up by a medical practitioner – epilepsy is not a disease in itself, rather it is a sign of some possibly serious underlying pathology.

If the person has a history of epilepsy, the nurse practitioner may make a follow-up appointment to discuss medication and lifestyle. Good control is essential if chronic accumulative brain damage from repeated fits is to be prevented. Patients should be advised about the need to take medication regularly to maintain effective plasma concentrations. Adherence to medication is often poor because there are no obvious effects if a single dose is missed. If the person suddenly ceases medication altogether, this can produce rebound seizures. Many antiepileptic drugs can interact with other drugs. A particular problem occurs with drugs that reduce hepatic enzyme activity, as this leads to a considerable reduction in the efficacy of combined and progestogen-only oral contraceptives (BNF 2003). Examples include phenytoin, carbamazepine and phenobarbitone.

Patients will be particularly concerned if they drive as epilepsy will lead to the loss of their driving licence and therefore possibly their job. Even after a single seizure a person in the UK is required to cease driving and has to be seizure free for 1 year to regain their licence. The regulations concerning heavy goods vehicle and public service vehicle licences are much stricter as the person has to be seizure free and off medication for 10 years to regain a licence.

Syncope

Laying the person flat allows sufficient blood to reach the brain for him/her to regain consciousness rapidly. It is important to have made a differential diagnosis that rules out possibilities such as hypoglycaemia, transient ischaemic attack or cardiac arrhythmia. The examination should also have ruled out any possibility of head injury incurred secondary to collapse. Under these circumstances, the patient should be allowed to leave when well enough, preferably in the company of a responsible adult.

Alcohol or other drugs

Individuals may present in a comatose or drowsy state as a result of alcohol and/or other drug misuse. It is essential to carry out a thorough examination so that head trauma or other injury is not missed. Assuming that there are no other injuries, the intoxicated individual is best placed in the recovery position to safeguard the airway, and allowed to sleep it off under observation. The floor is the safest place to lay such individuals as they have a habit of falling off trolleys, even if cot sides are in place.

If opioid drug use is suspected, careful observation must be maintained, watching out for respiratory depression and possible respiratory arrest. Oxygen saturation should be continually monitored with a pulse oximeter. The specific antidote, naloxone, should be readily available if the person is comatose or there is doubt concerning respiratory function. It is given intravenously in small amounts (1–2 mg at 2-minute intervals) up to a maximum of 10 mg and is quick-acting in reversing the effects of opioids. Naloxone has a short half-life and its effects soon wear off. This latter point is important as on regaining consciousness, many individuals wish to leave quickly. The risk of lapsing into coma shortly afterwards should be explained and if possible the person kept for observation to ensure this does not happen. If such a patient insists on leaving, someone else known to the individual who could keep him or her under observation should be made aware of the risks. Universal precautions should be observed at all times as a protection against HIV and other blood-borne infections.

The use of Ecstasy is not confined to large city centres; young adults collapsing after taking this drug or other related amphetamines may be brought to a minor injuries unit anywhere. Ecstasy is therefore a possible cause of collapse in a previously fit young adult brought from a party or nightclub. The presenting picture is one of dilated pupils, tachycardia and hyperpyrexia. The person may become comatose, hypertensive and develop cardiac arrhythmias. The history will include collapse and possibly convulsions. This is a serious medical emergency as death from the rapid subsequent onset of respiratory failure, cardiovascular collapse and disseminated intravascular coagulation may follow (Haslett et al 2003). Urgent transfer to medical care and an intensive treatment unit is essential. Steps to cool the patient in order to reduce the risk of hyperpyrexia should be taken whilst waiting for an ambulance.

Cocaine is a stimulant producing euphoria in mild to moderate doses coupled with excited and aggressive behaviour. Severe intoxication, however, leads to convulsions, coma, hypertension and hyperpyrexia, and can induce a stroke or myocardial infarction with a rapidly fatal outcome.

Other causes of collapse

If examination reveals neurological deficits suggestive of a stroke or other CNS pathology or if there are signs consistent with syncope due to a cardiac problem, the patient should be referred for an immediate consultation with a medical practitioner, in accordance with local protocols.

HEAD INJURY

The traditional approach to head injury management has always been very cautious with high numbers of patients admitted for observation, of whom only a very small proportion have any significant pathology. As a result a new set of guidelines have been developed by NICE (2003) which emphasize the need for CT scanning as the investigation of choice. Conventional skull radiography is now to be regarded as a second choice when CT scans are not available. Implementing these guidelines will be challenging (Hall 2003). The NICE guidelines also list the following types of patients (Box 5.1) who present in any non-A&E setting as being those who should be referred to A&E.

The same criteria apply to anyone telephoning for advice. While a patient is awaiting transfer to A&E it is important to be re-assessing their GCS at least half-hourly as a deterioration in their GCS is the usual first sign of developing intracranial pathology. If the patient is being discharged from your care home, it is important to educate the patient about the risk of dizziness, poor memory and loss of concentration which may last for days after a minor head injury.

As we have seen in the history-taking and physical examinations sections, the nurse practitioner may elicit evidence suggestive of a range of more serious neurological disorders than those covered in this section. Such disorders clearly fall within the remit of the GP and hospital consultant and it is essential that there are well-defined nurse practitioner referral mechanisms to ensure prompt medical attention.

Box 5.1 Conditions for referral of head injured patients to A&E

- Glasgow Coma Score < 15
- Any loss of consciousness due to injury
- Focal neurological deficit since injury
- Suspicion of skull fracture or penetrating head wound
- Amnesia before or after injury
- Persistent headache and/or vomiting since injury
- Seizure after injury
- Previous cranial surgery
- High energy injury e.g. road traffic accident
- History of bleeding/clotting disorder or current use of anticoagulant medication
- Currently intoxicated with alcohol or other drug
- Age 65 or over
- Suspicion of non-accidental injury
- Continuing concern about diagnosis

In addition the patient should be referred if there is irritability or observed behavioural changes, especially in the case of infants and children. Social circumstances should also be taken into account in deciding whether to refer, even if none of the above criteria are met.

Source: NICE 2003.

Summary

Neurological disorders may be encountered in a wide range of clinical settings. Often nothing is found on physical examination and the nurse practitioner will have to be guided by the history provided by the patient or witnesses. Many patients with headaches, minor head injuries or who have momentarily collapsed due to a faint can be successfully managed by the nurse practitioner. The first signs of more serious disorder which need medical management may be noticed by an observant nurse practitioner. It is possible that the nurse practitioner in primary health care may be involved in the long-term management of these individuals as part of the multidisciplinary team.

In conclusion, although the nurse practitioner may at first be intimidated by the complexity of the nervous system, it is essential that s/he can take a thorough focused history and perform a systematic baseline neurological examination if s/he is to refer appropriately and collaborate in the management of patients.

References

Baddeley L, Ellis S 2002 Epilepsy; a team approach to management. Butterworth-Heinemann, Oxford

BNF 2003 British National Formulary. British Medical Association/Royal Pharmaceutical Society of Great Britain, London

Campbell J, Penzien D, Wall E 2000 Evidence based guidelines for migraine headache; behavioural and physical treatment. Neurology 54. Available: www.aan.com

Downson A, Cady R 2002 Rapid reference to migraine. Mosby, London

Epstein O, Perkin D, Cookson J, de Bono D 2003 Clinical examination, 3rd edn. Churchill Livingstone, Edinburgh

Hall G 2003 Tackling injury head on. Emergency Nurse 11(4):18–21

Haslett C, Chilvers E, Boon N, Colledge N 2003 Davidson's principles and practice of medicine, 19th edn. Churchill Livingstone, Edinburgh

Matchar D, Young W, Rosenburg J et al 2000 Multispeciality consensus on diagnosis and treatment of headache; pharmacological management of acute attacks. Neurology 54. Available: www.aan.com

MIPCA 2003 Migraine. In: Primary Care Advisers Guidelines. Available: www.mipca.org.uk/guidelineword

Munro J, Edwards C 1995 Mcleod's clinical examination, 9th edn. Churchill Livingstone, Edinburgh

NICE 2003 Head injury: triage, assessment, investigation and early management of head injury in infants, children and adults. Online. Available: www.nice.org.uk

Seidal H, Ball J, Dains J, Benedict G 2003 Mosby's guide to physical examination. Mosby, St Louis

Springhouse 2000 Handbook of pathophysiology. Springhouse Corpn, Springhouse, Pennsylvania

Valman B 2000 ABC of one to seven. BMJ Books, London

Chapter 6

Vision and the eye

Mike Walsh

INTRODUCTION

Patients complaining of 'something in my eye' or 'my eye is all red and sore' are seen regularly in practice. Alternatively, the patient may present with a story of visual disturbance. All patients require careful assessment in order to distinguish between minor problems and those with a more significant problem that needs referral to a medical practitioner or optician. A full physical examination involves an assessment of vision and examination of the eye, with an ophthalmoscope. The nurse practitioner should be alert for signs of serious visual problems, such as glaucoma; other systemic disorders such as hypertension and diabetes also produce telltale signs which may be detected with an ophthalmoscope. Taking a focused history and carrying out a careful assessment of vision is an essential part of practice in all clinical areas.

PATHOPHYSIOLOGY

A logical approach is to start at the outside and work inwards. The basic structure of the eye is shown in Figure 6.1. The optic nerve, extraocular muscles and nerve supply will therefore be considered first. Complaints of visual impairment or diplopia (double vision) are the most likely clinical presentation, indicating that there may be a problem in this area. The eye itself will then be considered, again working inwards from the exterior.

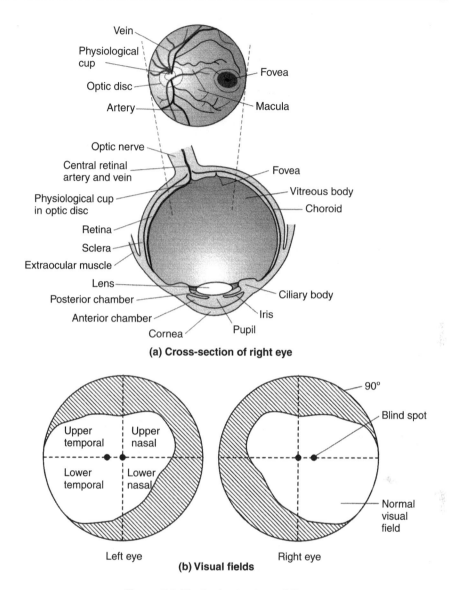

(a) Cross-section of right eye

(b) Visual fields

Figure 6.1 The basic structure of the eye.

CRANIAL NERVES AND THE EYE
(see p. 70)

Optic nerve (II)

Lesions affecting the optic nerve, such as neoplasms, usually lead to loss of vision. Figure 6.2 shows the complicated nature of the visual fields as the nerves from the eyes join at the optic chiasma before proceeding separately to the primary visual cortex. A lesion at (a) will cause total blindness in the affected eye whereas a lesion affecting the optic chiasma (such as a pituitary tumour) at (b) causes bitemporal hemianopia. The term hemianopia means defective vision or blindness in half of the visual field. If the lesion occurs at point (c), this causes a homonymous hemianopia involving nerve tracts arising from the same side of each eye, therefore the visual defect will occur on either the left or right of both eyes. Compare this with the bitemporal hemianopia shown in (b).

The pupillary reflex depends on nerve impulses being conducted along the optic nerve from the eye that has light shone into it. The reflex response is

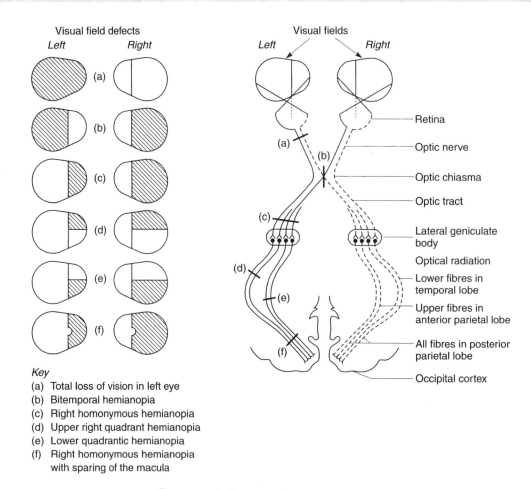

Visual field defects
Left   Right

(a)
(b)
(c)
(d)
(e)
(f)

Visual fields
Left   Right

(a)
(b)
(c)
(d)
(e)
(f)

Retina
Optic nerve
Optic chiasma
Optic tract
Lateral geniculate body
Optical radiation
Lower fibres in temporal lobe
Upper fibres in anterior parietal lobe
All fibres in posterior parietal lobe
Occipital cortex

Key
(a) Total loss of vision in left eye
(b) Bitemporal hemianopia
(c) Right homonymous hemianopia
(d) Upper right quadrant hemianopia
(e) Lower quadrantic hemianopia
(f) Right homonymous hemianopia
    with sparing of the macula

Figure 6.2 Lesions affecting the optic nerve.

controlled by the oculomotor nerve (III) and results in both pupils being constricted. A response of the eye that has not had light shone into it is known as the consensual reflex. If light is shone into an eye and there is no direct reflex, but there is a consensual reflex when light is shone into the other eye, this logically indicates that there is a defect in the retina or optic nerve leading from the nonresponsive eye. However, if the pupil is fixed and dilated and does not respond to light, but there is a consensual reflex in the other eye, this indicates that the lesion is affecting the oculomotor nerve supplying the unreactive eye. The ocular nerve is functioning or there would not be a consensual reflex.

Oculomotor, trochlear and abducens nerves (III, IV and VI)

The close relationship between these three cranial nerves is such that they are normally considered together. The oculomotor nerve is responsible for innervation of the iris and the pupillary reflex. It also innervates key muscles involved in eye movements, as do the trochlear and abducent nerves. These are shown in Table 6.1 working clockwise around the right eye.

The effects on the oculomotor nerve of a swelling intracranial lesion after head injury are discussed in Chapter 5. A tumour may have a similar effect, producing a third cranial nerve palsy which involves ptosis (drooping of the upper eyelid) as well as a dilated and nonresponsive pupil. The nerve may be compressed bilaterally by a large tumour or the problem may be due to an aneurysm compressing the nerve trunk. Lesions distorting the brainstem may affect the abducent nerve (VI) due to their anatomical closeness at the tentorium. The abducent nerve (VI) is rarely the subject of an isolated lesion; where this does occur, diabetic mononeuropathy and head injury are the main causes.

Table 6.1 Innervation of muscles involved in movement of the eye

Muscle	Movement of globe	Nerve
Superior rectus	Upwards	Oculomotor (III)
Inferior oblique	Upwards	Oculomotor (III)
Medial rectus	Medially (towards the midline)	Oculomotor (III)
Superior oblique	Downwards when eyes adducted	Trochlear (IV)
Inferior rectus	Downwards	Oculomotor (III)
Lateral rectus	Laterally (away from midline)	Abducens (VI)
Levator palpebrae superioris	Opens upper eyelid (no effect on globe)	Oculomotor (III)

Nerve palsy produced by pressure from a tumour or aneurysm leads to diplopia or double vision. The normal eye is able to move to keep the image of the object on the macula but the affected eye, as a result of the nerve palsy, cannot track the object in the same way. The image therefore falls on the retina some way off the macula. The brain interprets the picture as a double image: the largest discrepancy between the images is in the direction in which the muscle is not functioning correctly would act. If the patient states that double vision is worse on looking sideways, then this indicates that it is a third and/or sixth cranial nerve problem (Table 6.1); if looking up and down makes the problem worse, then it is likely to be a third and/or fourth cranial nerve problem (Table 6.1). The false image from the affected eye is always the outermost one, consequently, in a sixth cranial nerve lesion, as the person gazes towards the affected side the diplopia is always worse, since the lateral rectus muscle is not functioning properly on that side.

In children, strabismus (squint) is the main ophthalmic problem that the nurse practitioner is likely to encounter. Intermittent strabismus is brought on by looking in a particular direction or concentrating on a specific distance. Strabismus can also be permanent where there has been an abnormal development of the synapses in the visual cortex. In either case, one or another of the eyes will have a visual axis not directed towards the object being looked at. The term amblyopia refers to a loss of visual form in one or both eyes. This occurs only in childhood and happens when the brain cannot cope with two images, one from each eye, and as a result suppresses one of the images (Barnes 2003).

EXTRAOCULAR PROBLEMS

Infection of the hair follicle of one of the eyelashes produces a painful, tender, inflamed-looking pimple, known as a stye, which is located on the lid margin. It is not to be confused with a chalazion which is an inflamed meibomian gland. This too forms a tender, inflamed-looking pimple but is usually located inside the lid rather than on the margin as in the case of a stye. In either case the eyelid may become inflamed. Other lumps include a marginal cyst developing from a sweat-secreting gland or a basal cell carcinoma (rodent ulcer), usually affecting the lower lid.

Inflammation of the eyelids is known as blepharitis and is most pronounced at the margins. It may be associated with eczema or psoriasis. Herpes simplex or herpes-zoster ophthalmicus infections present with a characteristic vesicular rash in addition to inflammation of the eyelid and may lead to herpetic ocular disease affecting various structures within the eye.

The elderly are prone to problems associated with a lid margin. It may be turned inwards (entropion), in which case the lashes irritate the conjunctiva, or the lower lid may be turned outwards (ectropion), interfering with normal drainage and leading to continual tears in the eye. Graves' disease (hyperthyroidism) frequently leads to exophthalmos (protruding eyeballs) and other secondary ophthalmic problems associated with excess exposure of the cornea. Involvement of the ophthalmic muscles may lead to diplopia.

Trauma to structures around the eye may produce swelling and bruising which can quickly close the eye, making later inspection impossible. Lacerations which go through both surfaces of the lid or which involve structures such as the lacrimal duct may lead to complications and should therefore be referred to a medical specialist.

Perhaps the commonest cause of presentation is a foreign body in the eye – most commonly dust, grit, a splinter of wood or metal. The foreign body will be found lodged on the cornea or the undersurface of the eyelid (subtarsal foreign body). Corneal foreign bodies can cause severe irritation, infection and, in the case of metallic objects, staining of the cornea with rust. High-energy particles can penetrate the eye with much more serious consequences and chemicals splashed in the eye can have devastating effects. Alkalis containing lime (such as wet cement) can rapidly penetrate the cornea, damaging the iris, ciliary body and lens.

It may be that no evidence of the foreign body can be found, despite the discomfort felt by the patient. This suggests that the object has led to a corneal abrasion. This painful condition is often caused by a glancing blow from something as innocent as the edge of a piece of paper.

The other common presentation is the patient complaining of a sore, red eye. The person with conjunctivitis presents with discomfort and redness of the conjunctiva. The cause is usually infective (bacterial or viral) but it may also be due to an allergic reaction. A subconjunctival haemorrhage may occur as a result of trauma or a sudden increase in venous pressure caused by coughing. It presents as a well-defined red area that fades to yellow as the red blood cells deteriorate over the next few days and finally the haemorrhage disappears. Trauma to the cornea has already been mentioned. The cornea may also become inflamed (keratitis) as a result of extension of a pre-existing conjunctivitis, the herpes simplex virus which causes dendritic ulcer formation on the cornea, exposure to ultraviolet light (careless use of sun lamps or arc welding without proper eye protection) or corneal exposure.

INTRAOCULAR PROBLEMS

The cause of an inflamed red eye may lie within the eye itself. Obstruction of the outflow of aqueous humour leads to increased intraocular pressure causing visual impairment, pain and dilated blood vessels, giving the eye a reddish appearance. This is the serious condition of glaucoma, which may occur as an acute emergency or as a more gradual disease process. It causes damage to the optic disc and loss of vision. Glaucoma can be primary or secondary to some other disease process such as a tumour within the eye, inflammation or infection. Painful inflammation of the iris (iritis) for example may lead to glaucoma. Inflammation of the choroid, iris or ciliary body is known as uveitis and may be due to infection or associated with collagen disorders such as rheumatoid arthritis.

Bleeding within the inner eye (vitreous haemorrhage) from retinal or ciliary vessels is a serious problem which threatens vision. It may be associated with trauma, retinal detachment, hypertension or diabetic retinopathy in which microaneurysms and atheromatous plaques develop in retinal blood vessels. Retinal detachment is a serious disorder which can cause severe visual impairment. It is

usually due to degenerative changes associated with ageing or trauma such as penetrating eye injury or head injury. Needless to say, any penetrating injury to the eye can have serious consequences for vision in that eye. It may also lead to the development of sympathetic ophthalmia, a poorly understood inflammatory condition that affects the uninjured eye and that may lead to loss of vision in that eye unless promptly treated.

Opacification of the lens produces a cataract. The commonest cause by far is ageing; the person's vision in the affected eye steadily deteriorates as the cataract develops either in the centre of the lens or on the margin. Congenital cataracts are associated with children whose mother had a viral infection such as German measles in the first trimester of pregnancy or who have inherited a genetic defect leading to an inborn error of metabolism.

TAKING A FOCUSED HISTORY

Patient anxiety is to be expected in any consultation, but particularly so when patients come to see the nurse practitioner concerning a problem with their eyes. Fear of blindness is an understandable cause of high levels of anxiety and the nurse practitioner should be tactful and understanding when taking a history. The following section focuses on the key areas in history-taking but the nurse practitioner should always remember the broader holistic perspective as well.

PRESENTING COMPLAINT

The most likely symptoms that the patient will relate are pain or soreness, foreign body, redness of the eye or visual disturbance. In assessing pain the PQRST mnemonic is most useful, thus it is important to ascertain what brings on the pain and what relieves it (P). It may be an activity involving continual concentration such as driving, reading or working on a VDU screen, which suggests eye strain and an eyesight test is required as spectacles may be needed. Pain may also be associated with a tension headache (p. 64). If questions about the quality (Q) and severity (S) of the pain reveal that it is severe and associated with nausea and vomiting whilst questions about the region (R) indicate that it is within and around the eye (rather than the head, which would suggest migraine), this strongly suggests an intraocular inflammatory problem or glaucoma. This history may also be due to shingles affecting the trigeminal nerve (herpes zoster ophthalmicus). The time (T) of onset of pain should also be ascertained. This key fact should be established whatever the presenting complaint, including those mentioned below.

If a foreign body is the cause of the problem, the patient will usually be able to give an accurate account of the accident. It is important to try and ascertain what material is involved, when the accident occurred and whether it was a high velocity particle (e.g. from chiselling, grinding or windscreen glass in a road accident) which may have penetrated the cornea. If it is a chemical it is again important to find out what, especially whether it is alkaline, such as wet cement or mortar, given the potentially catastrophic damage that lime can inflict on the eye. First-aid measures taken at the time of the accident should also be ascertained.

The patient may complain of a sensation like having something in the eye, but cannot recall a particular incident. This sensation of grittiness and discomfort, accompanied by redness and tears, suggests damage to the cornea. Ask about pain, whether photophobia is present, whether there is any discharge from the eye and redness, checking particularly the duration of symptoms. Ask whether the person wears contact lenses, whether there has been even a trivial glancing blow to the upper face or the possibility of exposure to ultraviolet light (p. 87). The patient may be distressed and agitated, therefore a calm reassuring manner is particularly important.

If the patient is complaining of a disturbance of vision, try and ascertain which of the following applies:

- Blurred vision: usually caused by an ocular problem interfering with the transmission of light through the eye, e.g. cataract formation or refractive errors in the lens.
- Loss of vision: check carefully whether this has occurred in one eye or both as this indicates whether the problem is anterior or posterior to the optic chiasma respectively (see Fig. 6.2). Sudden loss of vision suggests that the cause of the problem is vascular. Fixed blind spots within the field of vision are known as scotomas and should be distinguished from floaters (see below). The presence of a scotoma suggests damage to the retina or within the visual pathway.

- Double vision: it is important to check that the patient does not interpret blurred as double vision.
- Haloes and flashes of light: haloes are caused by water drops diffracting light rays as they pass through the eye and are therefore associated with corneal oedema or cataract. Flashes of light (photopsia) are caused by the vitreous tugging on the retina.
- Floaters: everybody notices floating objects within their vision from time to time and this is not abnormal: however, a sudden increase in the number of floaters is abnormal and is likely to be due to a vitreous haemorrhage.

PAST MEDICAL HISTORY

It is essential to find out if the person has had vision problems in the past, including whether they wear contact lenses or spectacles and if they have had any history of trauma affecting the eye or the region immediately around the eye. Ask whether the patient has had any previous problems with the herpes simplex or herpes-zoster virus. Date of the last eye test should be noted. If the person wears contact lenses, it is essential to check that s/he is following recommended good practice for care of the lenses and eyes. Previous eye surgery should be ascertained. Chronic diseases which have serious implications for vision by causing retinopathy include diabetes and hypertension, and these should be checked out with the patient.

FAMILY HISTORY

Any family history of visual problems and disorders affecting the eye should be checked.

PERSONAL AND SOCIAL HISTORY

The person's work should be discussed as this may contribute to eye strain, be responsible for allergic reactions or, in the case of a welder, directly cause inflammation of the cornea as a result of not taking proper precautions against ultraviolet light (arc eye). Exposure at work to VDU screens, high-speed machinery or hazardous sporting activity such as squash or boxing should be explored as health education may be necessary to prevent a recurrence of the problem. The precautions the person is currently taking should be discussed. Ask about any recent problems with reading or changes which suggest problems with distant vision.

PHYSICAL EXAMINATION

This section will also follow the principle of working from the outside inwards, starting with assessment of the orbit, eyelids and outer eye before moving on to look at the inner eye and finally vision.

EXTERNAL EXAMINATION

The examination starts as soon as the patient walks into the room. Eye contact is an essential part of greeting any new patient and affords an excellent opportunity for the nurse practitioner to assess for any obvious signs such as exophthalmos or strabismus.

Swelling around the orbit of the eye is an abnormal finding; it may be due to allergy or in a young person such oedema could suggest renal disease. Fading bruising is evidence of a periorbital haematoma caused by a blow to the eye region. Particular attention should be paid if abuse is suspected in the case of a child or woman. A vague explanation such as 'I walked into a door, or 'I can't remember' should be treated with caution, whilst the presence of a haematoma around the left eye is particularly suspicious as most punches are thrown with the right hand, making contact on the left side of the face. The human fist fits within the orbit whereas a vertical object such as a door does not, making periorbital bruising unlikely, especially when the person states that s/he walked into the object. At such low speeds there is unlikely to be sufficient energy in the collision to cause extensive bruising. Suspicion should not be taken too far, however, as one of the authors well remembers the consultant in charge of an A&E department appearing one Monday with spectacular bilateral periorbital haematomas as a result of an accident with the boom of his sailing dinghy that weekend!

The presence of orbital cellulitis is a serious sign; usually it is a result of spread of infection from the sinuses. The patient usually has orbital swelling around one eye, no history of trauma or evidence of bruising, restricted eye movements, tenderness over the sinuses and a history of feeling unwell. It is particularly serious in children, where blindness is possible in a matter of hours (Barnes 2003).

The eyelids should be checked for normal symmetrical appearance and the ability to open and close the eyes. A drooping eyelid (ptosis) suggests problems with the oculomotor nerve. It is also essential to check whether there is any inversion or eversion of the eyelashes and for the presence of any lumps or abscesses in the eyelid or at its margin (stye or chalazion). The patient should be asked to close the eyes in order to check that the lids completely cover the globe; corneal ulceration will result if this is not the case. Intraocular pressure may only be measured accurately with the use of specialist equipment. The eye may, however, be gently palpated and it should be possible to push the eye back into the orbit slightly without causing any discomfort. If there is resistance and the eye feels hard, this suggests glaucoma, hyperthyroidism or possibly a tumour (Seidal et al 2003).

OUTER EYE

The conjunctiva should be examined by pulling the lower lid downwards. Any signs of redness or sticky discharge should be noted as they are usually found in the presence of conjunctivitis. The upper tarsal conjunctiva should always be examined if the patient complains of a foreign body, as this is frequently where it will be found. To do this it is necessary to evert the upper eyelid: ask the patient to look down while you gently pull the lid downwards and away from the globe of the eye. It is then possible to bend the lid backwards over a cotton wool applicator to expose the conjunctiva on the undersurface of the lid. Any foreign body can be removed, before gently replacing the lid by reversing the manoeuvre. The steps involved in this procedure should be carefully explained to the patient before commencing, as some may find this rather alarming.

The cornea can then be examined by shining a light across it tangentially. It should be perfectly clear, as the cornea is avascular except for the area of the limbus where it joins the conjunctiva. A general loss of transparency is therefore abnormal and indicates oedema of the cornea or extensive epithelial damage, as occurs for example in chemical injury or prolonged dryness of the cornea. Yellow fluorescein eye drops may be instilled in the eye in order to show up a localized area of epithelial damage such as that found in ulceration, abrasion or with a foreign body. The corneal reflex depends upon sensory nerve fibres in the trigeminal nerve (V) and motor nerve fibres in the facial nerve (VII). It may be tested by gently touching the cornea with a wisp of cotton wool; the result should be an immediate blinking of the eye. Loss of this protective reflex is serious as the eye is highly susceptible to trauma or infection.

PUPILS

The pupils should be equal in size, regular in shape and react briskly to light both directly and consensually. However, in some people the pupils are naturally unequal in size. The medical term for unequal pupils is anisocoria and this may be more pronounced in bright light as the larger pupil cannot constrict properly. In this case it does indicate disorder – usually glaucoma or oculomotor nerve paralysis. In the latter case, it is usually accompanied by ptosis and lateral deviation of the eye as the nerve damage means the lateral rectus muscle is not functioning properly. The effects of head injury and opioid drug use on pupil reaction have been discussed on p. 76. A nonresponsive pupil may also be due to a realistic prosthesis!

The response of the pupils to accommodation should be examined. Ask the patient to focus on a distant object. Hold a finger 10 cm from the end of the nose; the pupils should be seen to constrict. A normal set of pupil responses may therefore be summarized as pupils equal and reacting to light and accommodation (acronym: PERLA).

If a squint has been observed, it should be remembered that in a young child it is likely to be a nonparalytic strabismus as the fault is a congenital problem in the central nervous system controlling the coordinated movement of the eyes to focus together on an object. The patient can focus with either eye separately, but not together. A paralytic strabismus presents in later life and is caused by a nerve palsy affecting the extraocular muscles. If the eye is turned medially this is known as a convergent strabismus (esotropia) while a lateral deviation is known as a divergent strabismus (exotropia). An intermittent convergent strabismus commonly occurs in the first 6 months of life but disappears beyond that age with maturation (Engel 2002). The person may or may not be complaining of diplopia, depending on whether the central nervous system adapts to viewing two separate images. A simple test involves asking the patient to look into the distance and then cover one eye. If the uncovered eye then moves to fix on the object, this is the eye with the squint.

OPHTHALMOSCOPY

This represents a significant new area of practice for nurses. It can provide vital information about the optic disc and retina and is therefore a skill well worth mastering. The ophthalmoscope produces an upright image magnified to the power 15 and the viewer can rotate different lenses into place to compensate for long- or short-sightedness in both the patient and the nurse practitioner. A well-dilated pupil is essential to obtain a good view and therefore the procedure is best carried out in a darkened room.

The bright light may be tiresome for the patient so the nurse practitioner should allow short breaks in carrying out the exam and not prolong the proceedings unnecessarily. Hold the ophthalmoscope in the right hand if you are looking through the instrument with the right eye. Use the other hand to stabilize the patient by holding his or her shoulder. Your face will be close to the patient's face (10 cm) for some time during this procedure, so think about what your breath smells of, particularly if you smoke.

Begin with the ophthalmoscope set to zero. Examine the right eye using your right eye and the left eye with your left eye. Ask the patient to look at a distant object and examine the eye from a distance of 30 cm. At this distance the red disc of the retina should be visible (the familiar red-eye effect produced by amateur photographers taking flash photographs). Absence of a red reflex usually indicates that the ophthalmoscope is in the wrong position, although it is also absent if there is total opacity of the pupil as a result of a cataract. Any localized opacities will be visible as dark patches against the background red glow.

Slowly approach the patient until a good view of the retina or fundus is obtained. It will not be possible to view the whole retina at once; you will only see a portion at any one time. At a distance of 3–5 cm the first blood vessels should be seen and, as these always branch away from the optic disc, this should allow visualization of this landmark. The index finger can be used to adjust the lens wheel until a sharp image is seen. Arterioles are usually slightly larger and of a brighter red than venules. It is important to distinguish between them as their crossing points may reveal important information. The optic disc should have a well-defined margin, although occasionally myelinated nerve fibres are visible, creating a soft white, ill-defined edge to the disc. This is an essentially benign condition. The macula or fovea centralis may be found two optic disc diameters temporal to the optic disc but is difficult to see in an undilated pupil as the pupil reflex may obscure the view. It helps to ask the patient to look directly at the light; the macula should appear as a yellow dot surrounded by a deep pink periphery.

Description of the view is carried out systematically in a clockwise direction, viewing the retina as a clockface with the optic disc at the centre. The unit of measurement of distance is the diameter of the optic disc. Any abnormal features can be described as so many optic disc diameters from the optic disc at whatever hour it would be on a clockface.

It is important to become confident of your technique when carrying out fundoscopy, and to be familiar with the normal appearance of the fundus. Only frequent practice will bring this about and this is necessary if abnormalities are to be recognized. We will briefly mention some of the more common abnormal findings; those interested in this area may wish to consult a more advanced medical text for further information.

- Papilloedema: this is usually produced by increased intracranial pressure or cerebral oedema and results in swelling of the optic disc so that its normal cup shape is lost, veins are dilated and the margins become blurred. Venous haemorrhages may also be seen. Vision is not affected initially.
- Glaucoma: the increased intraocular pressure disrupts the normal vascular supply to the optic nerve, resulting in blood vessels seemingly disappearing under the optic disc, which in turn shows cupping as it is depressed backwards. The disc also appears much paler than normal due to its diminished blood supply.
- Haemorrhages: they can vary in size, shape and location depending upon their cause. Bleeding into the anterior chamber is known as a hyphaema and may initially appear as nothing more than a clouding of the chamber on ophthalmoscopy, although later a distinct fluid level will be seen. Glaucoma tends to lead to

haemorrhages at the margin of the disc, while hypertension can lead to flame haemorrhages, which are superficial flame-shaped areas. A dark red blot indicates a deep haemorrhage, although a microaneurysm usually cannot be distinguished from a deep haemorrhage. Both are seen in cases of diabetic retinopathy. In a vitreous haemorrhage the fundus view is usually lost altogether as blood has oozed throughout the vitreous humour.

- Hypertensive retinopathy: hypertension is associated with disease of the arterial walls and this leads to the characteristic finding of arterioles causing venules to appear pinched where they cross. This is because the thickened arteriole wall is compressing the venule. Flame haemorrhages may be observed (see above) and papilloedema may also be present.
- Diabetic retinopathy: haemorrhage has already been mentioned and is the early sign of diabetic retinopathy. Retinal ischaemia may become apparent later, as shown by venous dilation, creamy-coloured lesions known as hard exudates because of their well-defined borders (they consist of lipoproteins leaking from damaged blood vessels) and similar-looking but fuzzy-edged lesions, known as cotton wool spots, which represent infarcted nerve fibres. In advanced disease (proliferative diabetic retinopathy) new blood vessels may be seen developing; they are narrow and tortuous and may give rise to bleeds, causing loss of vision.

VISUAL FUNCTION

Visual acuity should be tested first using the standard Snellen chart at a distance of 6 metres. It is useful to have a permanent mark, measured at 6 metres from a wall, ready to carry out this test if required. When asking the patient to read down the chart, the nurse practitioner is assessing which is the last line that can be read and noting the number of that line. The numbers (6, 9, 12, 18, 24, 36 and 60) represent the distance at which the normal eye can read each line of print. Visual acuity is then expressed as the distance in metres from the chart (usually 6) over the number of the last line read. A rating of 6/6 is therefore normal eyesight whereas a score of 6/9 means that at 6 metres the person can only read what a normal eye could read at 9 metres. The legal limit for driving is 6/12 and 3/60 is classified as legal blindness.

The test should be carried out on each eye in turn with the other eye obscured. In testing the second eye it helps to ask the person to read from right to left as this minimizes the memory effect. You should always check whether the person is wearing contact lenses before carrying out the test. If vision is less than 3/60, you should ask the person to count how many fingers they can see when you hold your hand up 1 metre away. It is also important to test whether they can detect movement or see light.

VISUAL FIELDS

Peripheral vision can be tested simply with the confrontation test. Sit opposite the patient at a distance of 1 metre and ask him or her to cover the left eye. Cover your right eye, extend your left arm out wide horizontally and start to bring it inwards, asking the patient to tell you when he or she first sees your fingers. Compare your first perception of your fingers with the patient's to see if they are about the same or whether the patient is seeing your fingers significantly after you do, indicating a loss of peripheral vision. This should be repeated in the vertical plane, testing both above and below the patient's line of vision and also in the horizontal plane, but using the right hand to test peripheral vision from the midline (the nasal field will be less than the others because the nose limits this field of vision). The other eye may then be tested by reversing this procedure. It is important to be confident that you do not have any impairment of your own field of vision if the patient's responses are to be interpreted correctly.

Record any visual field defect and refer the patient on for more accurate determination of its extent (see p. 86 for possible causes). In addition to defects in the periphery, the patient may report having an area of blindness surrounded by an area of vision – a scotoma. If attempting to fix the gaze on an object with one eye leads to the loss of vision of the object, this is a central scotoma and indicates disease of the macula, whereas if the scotoma occurs in the same area in each eye, this suggests an intracranial lesion affecting the visual pathway.

Summary

In carrying out a physical examination the following areas should be covered:

- external inspection of the area around the eye and the eyelids
- the vision in each eye acuity and field of vision
- peripheral vision by confrontation testing
- ocular movements
- pupil size and reaction
- inspection of the cornea and testing the corneal reflex
- fundoscopy to examine the optic discs and retina.

LABORATORY STUDIES AND OTHER INVESTIGATIONS

A swab should be taken for culture and sensitivity if the patient presents with evidence of infection (inflammation and discharge leading to a 'sticky eye'). This is often the case with conjunctivitis, although the infective organism may be viral rather than bacterial.

Other more specialist equipment includes the applanometer, slit-lamp and a perimeter. The applanometer is an electronic measuring instrument measuring intraocular pressure (normal 16–21 mmHg). If you detect signs suggestive of glaucoma, intraocular pressure measurements are needed as a matter of urgency. The slit-lamp microscope permits detailed viewing of the eye and is particularly useful in dealing with foreign bodies, corneal abrasions and ulceration. A slit-lamp microscope is therefore extremely useful in A&E work. Fluorescein eye drops are used in conjunction with the slit-lamp to visualize corneal lesions. The perimeter is a semicircular instrument which permits accurate measurement in degrees of the patient's field of vision. If confrontation testing shows a defect, the patient should be referred for perimetry.

Detailed testing of visual acuity for a prescription for spectacles or contact lenses is, of course, the work of the optician. The nurse practitioner may be the first health professional who diagnoses the need for such specialist intervention.

Other highly specialized tests may be carried out in ophthalmology units, including gonioscopy to measure the angle of the anterior chamber, echo-ophthalmography using ultrasound to examine the interior of the eye when cataract prevents direct visualization or to check for retinal detachment, and fluorescein angiography, which assesses vascular structures within the eye and the condition of the retina.

DIFFERENTIAL DIAGNOSIS

SORE RED EYE

This can be due to:

- Foreign body: check history, examine for object; evert the upper lid in case it is a subtarsal body and use fluorescein eye drops.
- Stye or chalazion: examine eye lids carefully.
- Allergic reaction: check history, examine periorbital area for signs of oedema.
- Conjunctivitis: characteristic pattern of inflammation, complaint of mild discomfort rather than severe pain.
- Corneal abrasion or ulceration: painful; check history, including exposure to ultraviolet light; corneal damage is usually visible on examination with fluorescein eye drops; corneal discharge is present.
- Acute glaucoma: painful, fixed dilated pupil; ophthalmoscopy shows raised intraocular pressure.
- Iritis: small pupil, painful, redness restricted to immediate area of iris.

VISUAL DISTURBANCE

It is important to obtain a clear history as the diagnosis is based upon essentially subjective information given by the patient. The main causes are likely to be:

- Refractive errors: history of eye strain; test visual acuity.
- Double vision: check history, especially for any trauma. Observe movement of eyes; ascertain in which direction of gaze the diplopia is most pronounced to test whether this is an acquired paralytic condition caused by neuropathy affecting the oculomotor muscles.
- Haloes, floaters and flashing lights: usually associated with a loss of vision (discussed

below). Check whether migraine can be eliminated. Note that an occasional floater is not abnormal.

LOSS OF VISION

A sudden loss of vision suggests a vascular cause rather than the progressive loss of vision associated with a space-occupying lesion, such as a pituitary tumour affecting the optic nerve or problems such as cataract formation. The following are the main causes of loss of vision:

- A lesion affecting the macula, or the optic nerve, anterior to the chiasma may produce total loss of vision in one eye only (assuming the lesion is on one side only).
- If the optic chiasma is affected by a lesion such as a pituitary tumour, visual loss will occur in both eyes but on opposite sides of the visual fields (bitemporal hemianopia).
- A lesion proximal to the optic chiasma produces loss of vision in both eyes but on the same side (homonymous hemianopia).
- Cataract leads to a history of gradual loss of visual acuity in one or both eyes and is readily visible on ophthalmoscopy as the lens appears opaque when viewed through the pupil.
- Chronic glaucoma is associated with a history of progressively reduced peripheral vision, persistent haloes around bright lights and pain as a late symptom. Ophthalmoscopy and intraocular pressure measurement will confirm the diagnosis. Acute glaucoma is an ocular emergency caused by blockage of the drainage of aqueous humour. The dramatic rise in intraocular pressure leads to compression of the retinal blood vessels and destruction of the optic nerve cells. The patient will complain of rapid onset of severe pain, nausea and vomiting, blurred vision and haloes around bright lights. Characteristic changes include cupping of the optic disc and a much paler appearance than normal and these are visible on ophthalmoscopy.
- Retinal detachment leads to sudden onset of floaters and loss of vision in the affected eye. Vitreous haemorrhage may be visible on ophthalmoscopy.
- Diabetic retinopathy may lead to sudden loss of vision associated with sudden vitreous

haemorrhage. There will normally be a significant history of diabetes and diabetic retinopathy.

TREATMENT AND MANAGEMENT

This section will focus on those conditions that the nurse practitioner can manage alone. Other conditions that need referral to an optician or a medical practitioner who is possibly a specialist in ophthalmology will be briefly mentioned. You must appreciate that some disorders need urgent referral and be aware of any immediate first-aid steps. It is greatly to the patient's advantage if there are agreed referral pathways as this is no time for interprofessional political wrangles.

It is important in caring for patients presenting with an eye injury always to remember that the patient may be very anxious about possible blindness. You must consider the patient's psychological welfare and adopt a calm reassuring manner throughout. Social factors also need to be considered, such as how the patient will get home afterwards, whether s/he is safe to drive and how s/he will cope at home; this is particularly important in elderly individuals. As a general principle you should also be thinking about health education advice to prevent future problems.

TRAUMA

Simple lacerations around the eye may be closed in the normal way, preferably with steristrips or tissue adhesive to minimize scarring. If the laceration involves the eyelid or margin it is best to refer to a medical specialist. A history suggesting that a wound to the orbit may be penetrating should also alert the nurse practitioner to the need for medical referral as foreign material may be retained deep within the wound and intraocular structures may have been damaged. Radiography will reveal any metallic or stone fragments.

Blunt trauma involving an object the size of a squash ball can have serious consequences as the object fits within the orbit and may impact fully against the eye. The result may be haemorrhage into either the anterior chamber which will be visible as a collection of blood with a clear fluid level (a hyphaema) or into the vitreous, with the added risk of retinal detachment. Immediate referral to a medical specialist is indicated.

FOREIGN BODY

A subtarsal foreign body can be removed after everting of the lid. Local anaesthetic will usually be required (amethocaine 0.5% eye drops), after which a cotton wool bud moistened with normal saline can be used to remove the object gently. A good light source and a confident but gentle manner are essential.

If the object is located on the cornea it may be removed by irrigation using saline and either an eye undine or intravenous giving set. Jones (1998) recommends trickling the saline into the inner part of the eye and letting it run outwards, do not let it drop directly on to the cornea as this is painful. Alternatively a moist cotton wool bud may be used. Amethocaine 0.5% eyedrops should be instilled first. They are rapid-acting (within a minute) but wear off after 20–30 minutes. Local anaesthetic eye drops should never be used in the management of symptoms (BNF 2003). If the eye remains sore after removal of the foreign body, local anaesthetic drops should not be given to the patient to take home as an anaesthetized eye is prone to further injury and may also have its healing impeded. Prophylactic antibiotic cover is recommended with chloramphenicol 1% ointment or 0.5% drops due to the risk of a corneal abrasion. The eye should also be padded for protection for 24 hours (Cross & Rimmer 2002).

If the object is not readily removed from the cornea, the patient should be referred to a medical specialist because of the risk of corneal damage and infection. In the meantime, an eye pad should be fixed over the eye as protection and the patient advised not to rub it.

Penetrating foreign bodies may leave little or no trace of their passing and therefore may be easily missed. The history is vital – if the patient was engaged in the kind of activity that may have produced high-velocity particles such as using a hammer and chisel, a drill or garden machinery, the nurse practitioner should suspect the possibility of a penetrating foreign body and seek a medical opinion. In some cases signs such as a distorted pupil or a vitreous haemorrhage may be apparent, but such is the potential damage from an untreated intraocular foreign body, even if there are no obvious signs, that you should act on the history and refer.

If chemical damage has occurred, copious irrigation with water should take place and any obvious solid particles should be removed from the conjunctival sac (e.g. cement or mortar, both of which contain lime). Local anaesthetic drops should be used to facilitate this process and an immediate medical referral is essential.

Do not miss a potential health education opportunity in the case of eye injury. The use of protective eye equipment should be emphasized, whether for work or for playing squash.

DISORDERS INVOLVING THE EYELIDS

- Chalazion: some may be persistent, become infected and even lead to disturbance of vision by causing astigmatism. In these cases medical referral for surgical treatment is necessary. The large majority can be dealt with conservatively by advising warm compresses such as a face cloth soaked in warm water and the application of chloramphenicol ointment to deal with any infection. The patient should be asked to return if this regime fails to clear up the problem.
- Stye: this should be treated in the same way as a chalazion. The warm compresses will help draw the stye and lead to its eventual discharge while the chloramphenicol ointment will deal with the infective organism.
- Blepharitis: chloramphenicol ointment should be prescribed for application to the edge of the lid after it has been cleaned. This should be carried out three times daily. Artificial tears may also have to be prescribed. If little improvement occurs after follow-up, medical referral is necessary to treat the sebaceous gland dysfunction that probably lies at the root of the problem.
- Acute inflammation of the eyelid: the cause of the inflammation may be a stye or chalazion, in which case the treatment described above will be sufficient. However, in the presence of a vesicular rash, herpes simplex or herpes-zoster ophthalmicus is likely to be present, either of which could lead to serious herpetic ocular disease. This indicates the need for a rapid medical referral. If orbital cellulitis is suspected, urgent specialist referral is needed as this can lead to blindness in a matter of hours.
- Entropion: a first-aid solution involves taping down the lid and applying chloramphenicol ointment. Surgical correction is necessary for a long-term solution.

- Ectropion: this too requires surgical correction; chloramphenicol ointment will assist in the short term.
- Ptosis: as this may be a sign of serious systemic disease such as an aneurysm causing third cranial nerve palsy, prompt medical referral is necessary whatever the patient's age.

CORNEAL DAMAGE

Whether the problem is caused by ulceration, abrasion or exposure to ultraviolet light, the approach to treatment is the same, although such are the potentially serious consequences of corneal damage (loss of vision) that rapid referral to a medical specialist is recommended. Fluorescein eye drops should be used for examination of the cornea as ulceration or abrasions will be readily apparent. Treatment aims to protect the eye in the interim (whilst waiting to see a specialist) with a pad and prevent infection with the use of chloramphenicol 1% eye ointment. The discussion on treatment of corneal abrasions on p. 95 should be borne in mind if any significant delay is expected in seeing an ophthalmology specialist or in transfer to an A&E department. Systemic analgesia (such as paracetamol) should also be recommended to relieve the pain. Before any chloramphenicol is used, swabs should be taken to help identify any organisms present.

Chloramphenicol ointment lasts longer than eye drops as it is less likely to be diluted by tears. It should be administered three to four times daily and you should carefully explain that it is only administered to the affected eye and that a thin smear along the lower lid is all that is required. If both eyes are affected, as in ultraviolet light exposure, one tube should be used for the left and another for the right eye, both clearly labelled. This is to prevent the risk of cross-infection. The patient should be made aware of the dangers of exposure to ultraviolet light when using an artificial sunlamp or when skiing (reflected sunlight off the snow surface). If welding has been the cause of the problem the opportunity should be taken to check the individual's understanding of health and safety regulations at work as protective wear must be provided for those working with welding equipment. It is essential to check how the patient intends to get home after treatment for corneal damage as driving is not advised.

CONJUNCTIVITIS

The infective organism may be bacterial or viral and in the latter case it is often associated with an upper respiratory tract infection. Viral conjunctivitis may produce a clear discharge as opposed to the mucopurulent discharge seen in bacterial cases. The treatment is the same in either case – chloramphenicol eye ointment (1%) in two tubes clearly labelled left and right. If it is a bacterial infection, the chloramphenicol will deal with it; if it is a viral problem, it will stop the secondary bacterial infection which often occurs, making the situation worse. Viral conjunctivitis is fortunately a self-limiting condition. Conjunctivitis is contagious so great care must be taken with measures to avoid cross-infection of other patients, staff or the nurse practitioner. Patients should be informed about the risk of infecting other family members and advised to use only their own face cloth and towel. It is wise to ask the patient to return if the problem does not resolve within a few days.

Conjunctivitis in a young baby may have been acquired at birth and needs to be cultured to identify the causative organism (e.g. gonorrhoea or chlamydia). A 'sticky eye' in an infant less than 21 days old is a reportable disease (Barnes 2003).

If the conjunctivitis is allergic in nature, antihistamine eye drops such as antazoline (2–3 times daily) or levocabastine (twice daily) may be prescribed together with oral antihistamines. It is important to ascertain the likely cause of the reaction and what steps can be taken to remove the patient from exposure to the causative agent.

IRITIS AND UVEITIS

If either of these conditions is suspected on the grounds of a red eye and photophobia, you should refer the patient to a medical practitioner as there may be serious underlying pathology, either local (intraocular tumour, detached retina) or systemic, such as one of the arthropathies (ankylosing spondylitis, juvenile arthritis), sarcoidosis or infections such as syphilis, tuberculosis or herpes-zoster ophthalmicus. Sometimes the cause remains obscure, but as the possible effects on the eye are serious, a medical practitioner should be involved at an early stage.

OTHER OPHTHALMIC EMERGENCIES

Sudden visual disturbances, such as the appearance of:

- floaters due to possible detached retina or vitreous haemorrhage
- haloes due to the onset of acute open-angle glaucoma
- loss of vision in an eye due to arterial occlusion or disciform macular degeneration require prompt referral to an ophthalmic specialist, as would any case of penetrating eye trauma, chemical injury or severe pain in and around the eye which you are confident is not a migraine.

OTHER OPHTHALMIC CONDITIONS

There are many other conditions which may present to the nurse practitioner. These vary from disorders such as squints and diplopia through to conditions such as cataracts or chronic open-angle glaucoma. Medical referral is necessary as these are serious disorders which may lead to loss of vision or even, in the case of diplopia, be signs of underlying pathology affecting the cranial nerves which innervate the extraocular muscles. Refractive errors of vision are best referred to an optician together with individuals seeking advice about contact lenses. A contact lens lost in the eye may be difficult to find but will usually be in the lower fornix or under the subtarsal plate (Jones 1998).

References

Barnes K 2003 Paediatrics: a clinical guide for nurse practitioners. Butterworth-Heinemann, Oxford

BNF 2003 British National Formulary. British Medical Association, Royal Pharmaceutical Society of Great Britain, London

Cross S, Rimmer M 2002 Nurse practitioner manual of clinical skills. Bailliére Tindall, London

Engel J 2002 Pediatric assessment, 4th edn. Mosby, St Louis

Jones G 1998 Foreign bodies in the eye. Accident and Emergency Nursing 6:66–69

Seidal H, Ball J, Dains I, Benedict G 2003 Mosby's guide to physical examination, 5th edn. Mosby, St Louis

Chapter 7

The cardiovascular system

Anita Powell

INTRODUCTION

This chapter will concentrate on the more commonly encountered conditions and, by acquainting the nurse with some history-taking and physical examination skills that have traditionally belonged in the medical sphere, aims to show how nursing practice can be expanded to the patient's benefit. The cardiovascular system will be considered in terms of the heart itself, the arterial system and the venous system.

PATHOPHYSIOLOGY

THE HEART

Coronary heart disease (CHD) is a preventable disease that kills more than 110 000 people in England alone every year. It is the country's single biggest killer (National Service Framework for CHD 2004). The importance of this disease needs no emphasis, and in most cases the cause of CHD is atherosclerosis, although other less frequent causes include thrombus, embolism and coronary artery spasm. Atherosclerosis affects blood vessels elsewhere in the body, leading to peripheral vascular disease (p. 118). The main risk factors are well known – hypertension, smoking, obesity, lack of exercise, Type 2 diabetes and hypercholesterolaemia.

Blood lipids are divided into high-density lipoproteins (HDL) and low-density lipoproteins (LDL). High levels of LDL associated with low levels of HDL are associated with increased risk of

CHD. There is growing evidence for the treatment and reduction of blood lipids in combination with the assessment of cardiovascular risk of patients.

Atherosclerosis causes narrowing of the artery lumen. When this exceeds 75% of the lumen and starts to compromise blood flow, symptoms of angina pectoris usually start to appear, especially when there is increased demand for oxygen by the myocardium. An abrupt reduction or complete loss of blood flow in the coronary artery may occur when an atheromatous plaque suddenly fissures and develops an associated thrombosis. This manifests itself as a myocardial infarction (Nowak & Handford 2004). Tissue beyond the obstruction loses its blood supply and rapidly dies before any collateral circulation can be established. One or more layers of the heart may be involved and the infarcted zone may be a volume of 1–2 cm across. Fibrous scar tissue eventually replaces the dead area of myocardium.

Heart failure is a complex syndrome that can result from any structural or functional cardiac disorder that impairs the ability of the heart to function as a pump to support a physiological circulation (NICE 2003). The effect of this failure is that body tissue does not receive sufficient oxygen, an effect which becomes more pronounced on exertion. McMurray & Stewart (2003) state that the most common causes of chronic heart failure are coronary heart disease and/or hypertension. The cardiomyopathies, valvular dysfunction, cardiac arrhythmias, pericardial disease and infection are the other main causes.

Although reference is commonly made to left- or right-sided heart failure, the close relationship between the two sides of the heart means that, in practice, whichever side starts to fail first the other will soon follow. The pattern of presenting signs and symptoms reflects this close association.

In left-sided failure (left ventricular systolic dysfunction – LVSD), the problem is the heart's inability to pump blood efficiently into the systemic circulation, leading to congestion of the pulmonary vessels (backward heart failure) and accumulation of fluid in the alveoli (pulmonary oedema). This causes symptoms of acute and chronic respiratory distress such as dyspnoea and coughing. The reduced cardiac output that follows from left-sided failure (forward failure) results in reduced renal perfusion. The body consequently retains sodium and water due to activation of the renin-angiotensin system and aldosterone production. Failure of the right

side, which may be secondary to left failure, causes congestion of the venous system with congestion and oedema of peripheral tissues and organs.

Cardiac arrhythmias may produce no symptoms and may only be discovered when a routine ECG is performed. Some arrhythmias are persistent but others are short-lived, their effects may be transient and patients may present with a normal ECG, even though they have a history of 'funny turns', or 'palpitations'. More persistent arrhythmias may have significant haemodynamic effects, reducing cardiac output and leading to heart failure (e.g. atrial fibrillation or bradycardia associated with heart block) or may predispose to thrombus formation. Most serious of all, some ventricular arrhythmias can be life threatening (ventricular tachycardia) and can result in complete collapse with cessation of cardiac output (ventricular fibrillation). Arrhythmias and ECG interpretation will be dealt with in more detail later in this chapter (p. 109).

Hypertension is associated with a substantial rise in mortality rates. It is either due to increased peripheral resistance in the arterioles (essential hypertension) or secondary to some other disorder such as renal disease, which usually involves the renin-angiotensin mechanism. Grade 3 (severe hypertension) is defined as blood pressure (BP) in excess of 180/110 mmHg, whilst Grade 2 (moderate hypertension) is defined as a BP in the range 160/100 to 179/109 mmHg. In Grade 1 (mild hypertension) the BP lies in the range 140/90 to 159/99 mmHg (Williams et al 2004). There is evidence that Afro-Caribbean people are twice as susceptible to hypertension as Caucasians but this is accounted for by a greatly increased susceptibility only amongst women; Afro-Caribbean males have the same incidence as white British males (Gerrish 1996). In many cases the patient is asymptomatic and hypertension is diagnosed as a result of a routine BP reading. Concern remains that national surveys continue to show substantial under-diagnosis, under-treatment and poor rates of blood pressure control in the United Kingdom (Primatesta et al 2001). In severe fulminating hypertension, the patient presents as an acute medical emergency with severe headaches, vomiting, visual disturbances, papilloedema and retinal haemorrhages.

Disease of the valves within the heart may be either congenital or acquired, usually after rheumatic fever. Congenital problems usually cause stenosis of the pulmonary or aortic valves (a whole range of other congenital cardiac malformations are possible) whilst the mitral and aortic valves are most susceptible to the inflammatory response associated with rheumatic fever, which leads to scarring and thickening of the valve tissue.

Congenital pulmonary stenosis leads to a build-up of backpressure within the venous system and reduction in pulmonary blood flow, hence oxygenation. This leads to chronic fatigue, shortness of breath and sometimes cyanosis. Although this is a congenital problem, the child may be several years old before symptoms become serious enough for the parent to bring him or her for attention. Aortic stenosis leads to reduced cardiac output and a reduced arterial blood pressure.

Inflammatory disease of the valves can also produce stenosis, which in turn increases the work of the heart chamber behind the damaged valve as it strives to force blood through the narrowed opening. In some cases loss of tissue occurs; this prevents the valvular cusps from coming together and regurgitation or back-flow occurs (valvular incompetence). It is not uncommon for both conditions to co-exist, seriously impairing the heart's ability to function normally and leading to serious damage (dilatation and hypertrophy) to the chamber behind the incompetent valve. This is commonly seen in patients with aortic stenosis who may present with an enlarged left ventricle.

Other presenting conditions include pericarditis and infective endocarditis. The former is an inflammation of the pericardium, usually associated with a viral or bacterial infection, trauma or an autoimmune reaction. The inflammatory process can lead to the accumulation of fluid in the pericardium, which inhibits normal cardiac expansion (cardiac tamponade). Infective endocarditis may be associated with rheumatic fever, routine dental procedures, minor infections, parenteral drug use or valvular abnormalities. It may be acute with mortality rates of 60–80% (Nowak & Handford 2004) and be caused by virulent organisms such as *Staphylococcus aureus* or have a slower sub-acute presentation, which may develop secondary to other cardiac problems or heart surgery. Cardiac tamponade may occur in cases of trauma where an object penetrating the chest strikes the heart, leading to the accumulation of blood in the pericardium.

ARTERIAL DISORDERS

The same pathological processes that cause damage to the coronary arteries can affect arteries elsewhere in the body. Weakening of the wall of the aorta in the abdomen leads to the development of an aortic aneurysm, which may present as an acute emergency or as a chronic problem. Symptoms are often not what might be expected (e.g. back pain) and this can cause a delay in diagnosis. A leaking aortic aneurysm is potentially fatal, therefore caution is necessary if seeing a male over the age of 60 with abdominal pain as a leaking aneurysm is a potential cause of such pain (Epstein et al 2003).

Arterial disease may affect the main arteries of the legs in such a way as to produce a sudden blockage and loss of circulation (arterial embolism) or chronic deterioration in blood supply leading to intermittent claudication (pain on walking caused by a similar mechanism to angina pain) and peripheral gangrenous ulcers (Table 7.1). Eventually the limb may be lost as a result of gangrene and the patient's life may be endangered through toxaemia and other metabolic disturbances secondary to gangrene if medical assistance has not been sought soon enough.

A less severe arterial condition is Raynaud's disease. The cause is unknown but it most commonly affects young adults (females more than males). The patient experiences severe episodes of vasospasm affecting the hands and sometimes the feet, which go white before turning red as the circulation returns, often causing significant pain and discomfort. These features may occur as a consequence of some other disorder (secondary Raynaud's), such as working with vibrating machinery, but then they are more localized.

VENOUS DISORDERS

Deep venous thrombosis (DVT) is a well-known complication of prolonged immobility, usually affecting the iliac, femoral or calf veins. The associated risk of a pulmonary embolism due to a fragment of the clot dislodging is least if the thrombosis is only found within the calf veins. Other risk factors for DVT include heart disease, Type 2 diabetes, use of the contraceptive pill and malignant disease. Long-haul airline flights have recently been recognized as another risk factor where the above factors are complicated by potential dehydration and cabin pressures well below atmospheric.

Incompetence of the vein wall and/or valves is a common cause of varicose veins. Obstruction of venous return is also a contributory factor. The result is the development of distended and tortuous

Table 7.1 Differential diagnosis: causes of chest pain

	Angina	Gastrointestinal	Musculoskeletal	Respiratory
Provocation	Exercise Emotional upset	Related to food consumption	Related to trauma, physical effort	Increases with inspiration or trunk movement
Palliation	Rest GTN	Antacids	Mild analgesics, heat, rest	Little relief
Quality	Tightness	Burning, discomfort, wind	Ache	Sharp, grabbing (pleurisy, pneumothorax or pulmonary embolism) or dull, aching in pneumonia
	Stops patient activity	Patient carries on activity	Patient carries on activity	Lower chest, sometimes bilateral
Region	Retrosternal	Epigastric/retrosternal	Intercostal	Pneumothorax on entire side of chest
Radiation	Arm, wrist, hand, jaw	Unlikely, though possibly through to back	Backache	Pneumothorax radiates to back
Severity	Moderate	Variable	Moderate, though variable	Moderate to severe
Timing	Recent specific onset	Vague onset, though may waken patient from sleep	Shortly after physical effort	Sudden onset and then continual pain

veins in the lower leg, which, apart from being unsightly, cause the patient considerable pain. Consistently raised venous pressure around the ankles is associated with peripheral oedema and venous insufficiency. It leads to the breakdown of the skin on the medial and lateral aspects of the lower leg and the formation of chronic ulcers, which are notoriously difficult to heal, due to poor circulation, risk of infection and advancing age of the patient.

TAKING A FOCUSED HISTORY

CARDIAC DISORDER

Pain

The PQRST framework (p. 18) is valuable in evaluating the symptoms of pain associated with the cardiovascular system. Chest pain which is provoked (P) by exertion but palliated (P) by rest is characteristic of angina, whereas the pain of myocardial infarction (MI) is usually unrelieved by rest or taking GTN. Emotional upset, cold weather and exertion after a large meal may also provoke an angina attack. However, the patient frequently cannot point to anything that brings on the pain associated with MI.

This is the key difference that will appear in the history between the two conditions.

Other symptoms are similar, for example the patient usually describes the quality (Q) of the pain, whether due to angina or myocardial infarction, in terms of tightness, such as a crushing weight on the chest, although it may be described in terms of wind. The region (R) in both cases is retrosternal, located towards the base of the sternum, with radiation (R) occurring to the left arm, hand, jaw (the patient may present with toothache!) or even the ear. The pain may be severe (S), although some elderly patients may have an MI with little apparent pain (a silent MI). There is little association between the severity of chest pain and the seriousness of the illness (Hill & Geraci 1998). It is clearly important to know how long ago the pain began (time: T).

Chest pain is not uniquely caused by cardiac disorder. It is frequently musculoskeletal or associated with gastrointestinal problems. It may also be due to a respiratory disorder such as pneumothorax, pulmonary embolism, pneumonia or pleurisy. Table 7.1 is based on work by Hill & Geraci (1998) and should allow the NP to distinguish between the most likely causes of the patient's chest pain.

Dyspnoea

Difficulty in breathing or shortness of breath brought on by lower than normal levels of exertion is a second major symptom. This needs to be explored to ascertain exactly what the patient means by a phrase such as 'short of breath'. The PQRST framework guides the NP in checking what brings on the symptom. If it is exertion, it is important to find out how much, such as climbing the stairs at home or walking up hills. The cause may be nothing to do with exertion as the patient may wake up suddenly short of breath with signs of pulmonary oedema, coughing and expectorating frothy sputum. This person would probably be in acute left ventricular failure, and require immediate treatment. If the symptom is persistent even when resting during the day, this suggests chronic heart failure, assuming a respiratory cause can be eliminated. Pulmonary oedema will be associated with dyspnoea in acute left-sided heart failure.

Other symptoms

Other symptoms may include fatigue, depression, poor concentration and even confusion.

Impaired cardiac output leads to fatigue and difficulty in keeping up a normal level of exertion. The patient may perceive cardiac arrhythmias as palpitations or a sensation of feeling lightheaded. Momentary loss of consciousness or syncope attacks may occur with some arrhythmias such as heart block (p. 110). The patient may complain of swollen ankles; oedema has been referred to above and is frequently found in heart failure or venous stasis. Alternative causes of oedema such as hepatic disorder or nephrotic syndrome should be eliminated before confirming a diagnosis of heart failure.

Past medical history

Check whether the patient has a previous cardiac history of hypertension, angina or a previous MI. Also enquire about associated diseases such as Type 2 diabetes or rheumatic fever.

Family history

There is a strong genetic element associated with many cardiac diseases. Identify whether there is any family history of Type 2 diabetes, hypertension, hyperlipidaemia, congenital heart defects or other heart disease. Any unexplained sudden deaths in the family may also be significant evidence of cardiovascular disease.

Social history

Identify known risk factors such as whether the person smokes and how much. It is also useful to ask if the person has recently given up and when. Information regarding diet, exercise, occupation, how s/he deals with stress and alcohol consumption are essential when identifying risk factors.

TAKING A FOCUSED HISTORY FROM THE PATIENT WITH PERIPHERAL VASCULAR DISEASE

Arterial disease

The previous medical, family and social histories should be explored as above because the underlying disease process is likely to be the same as that causing angina pain, i.e. atherosclerosis. The main difference is that the site of pain is in the leg. It is usually brought on by exercise such as walking and is due to diminished blood flow being unable to meet the tissues' metabolic demands. This type of pain is known as claudication; in more advanced cases the pain may be severe and present at rest. It is important to ascertain how far the patient can walk before the pain (P) comes on, how long s/he has to rest before it is relieved and the nature of the pain, typically cramping (Q). Ask where the pain occurs (R) as this type of pain is usually in the calf; and enquire how severe it is (S). The effect on the person's lifestyle should also be noted as increasing difficulty in walking may be causing major problems. Time (T) since the patient first noted the problem is important; claudication usually has an insidious onset but an arterial embolus is a sudden event, which the patient can pinpoint.

Venous disease

Pain is again the most common symptom and should be explored carefully in a focused history. Pain and swelling in the calf are suggestive of DVT; however, a DVT may produce no pain at all. The patient's previous medical history is important as an indicator of risk factors for DVT formation. Check whether they have been on any recent long haul flights. The pain from varicose veins typically gets worse during the day as the patient is standing; lying down and elevating the legs relieve the pain.

The association between peripheral oedema and heart failure means that, although the patient may present with a complaint of swollen ankles, discolored skin and possibly a venous leg ulcer, you must take a full cardiac history.

PHYSICAL ASSESSMENT

GENERAL APPEARANCE

An initial decision must be made as to whether the patient is haemodynamically stable. If s/he is in a collapsed state with low blood pressure or absent pulse, then emergency cardiopulmonary resuscitation is necessary. However, if the patient has walked into the room then s/he may be assumed to be reasonably stable and a methodical assessment can be carried out, after obtaining the history.

The patient's general appearance holds several important clues. Dyspnoea on walking across the room clearly indicates a problem of cardiac or respiratory origin. Central cyanosis affecting the lips and mucous membranes of the mouth suggests impaired gas exchange in the lungs, raising the possibility of pulmonary oedema or respiratory disease. Congenital cardiac disorders may also cause central cyanosis. Peripheral cyanosis affecting the hands and feet, which look pale and feel cold with possibly weak or absent pulses suggests impaired cardiac output, peripheral vascular disease reducing blood flow to the extremities or vasoconstriction as found in Raynaud's disease. Inspection of the eye may reveal two significant signs of hypercholesterolaemia. Corneal arcus is the deposition of cholesterol at the edge of the cornea while xanthelasma is a yellowish deposit at the inner side of the eyelid of similar origin.

PULSE AND BP

Check pulse and BP. The BP reading should be done carefully, ensuring that the right-sized cuff is used, the sphygmomanometer is at the same level as the patient's arm, there is no tight clothing around the arm, the patient is suitably relaxed and the arm is extended horizontally but well-supported. If BP cannot be obtained at first, the end of the patient's finger should be compressed and the time taken for the colour to return to normal noted. If this is 2 seconds or greater, this indicates a shocked patient with a systolic BP of 60 mmHg or less.

JUGULAR VENOUS PRESSURE

Before moving on to examine the chest, the jugular venous pressure (JVP) should also be recorded. This is a measure of pressure in the right atrium – raised pressure indicates either right-sided heart failure or an increase in the pressure in the pericardial sac, which is restricting the return of blood to the right atrium (e.g. cardiac tamponade). JVP measurement is made relative to the sternal notch, which is always located 5 cm above the right atrium in the average adult, and is expressed as the vertical height above the sternal notch at which oscillations within the internal jugular vein can be seen. These oscillations are caused by pressure changes within the right atrium during the cardiac cycle.

In order to visualize these oscillations the patient should be reclining at 45° above the horizontal. If s/he is in a more upright position the oscillations become hidden by the clavicle and associated structures. If the jugular venous pressure is visible more than 4 cm vertically above the sternal angle, this is considered to be abnormally elevated (Fig. 7.1). The exact angle that the patient is reclining at will not affect the measurement.

CHEST EXAMINATION

Useful information can be obtained by simply examining the chest visually. Privacy and a warm consulting room are essential. Evidence of old scars should be noted and their cause established (surgery or trauma). The general shape of the chest should be observed for any abnormalities. An important observation is the location and extent of the apical beat, which should be visible in the mid-clavicular line in either the fifth or fourth intercostal space. It is best seen with a tangential light source and may also be felt by gentle palpation. It is unlikely to be visible in muscular or obese individuals. If the apical beat is visible in two intercostal spaces, this suggests an enlarged heart – obviously a key observation.

HEART SOUNDS AND AUSCULTATION

In order to carry out a full physical exam, you must be able to use a stethoscope to check whether heart sounds are normal or abnormal. You must therefore understand the physiology behind what you are listening to in order to make a correct decision about referral.

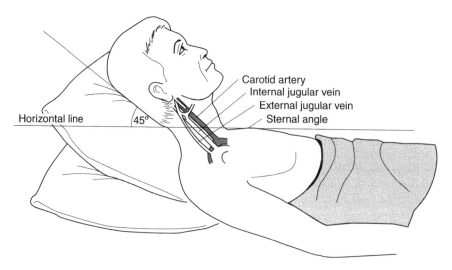

Figure 7.1 Measurement of jugular venous pressure (JVP); the JVP reading is the maximum height in centimetres above the sternal angle at which venous pulsations are visible.

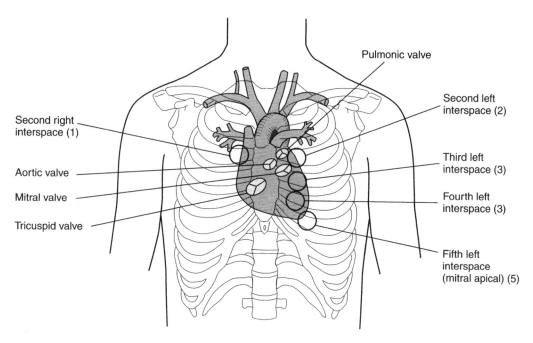

Figure 7.2 Sites for auscultation of heart sounds.

The main heart sounds are caused by the closure of valves; their opening should be a silent event. It is the closure of the tricuspid and bicuspid valves at the beginning of systole that causes the first heart sound (S1). The opening of the aortic and pulmonary valves should be silent; their closure at the end of systole, as the ventricles begin to fill with blood, produces the second heart sound (S2). This sound may be split, as the two valves often do not close at exactly the same time. A deep inhalation may also produce a splitting of S2. Neither situation is abnormal. The tricuspid and bicuspid valves open to allow ventricular filling at this time, but these are silent events. The sound of blood filling the ventricles under the effect of gravity is faint but may just be heard as a third sound (S3). The contraction of the atria, which expels the last fraction of blood into the ventricles at the end of diastole, may also produce a faint sound (S4). The soft, faint third and fourth heart sounds are best heard using the bell of the stethoscope placed over the apex, with the patient tilted on the left side at an angle of 45°.

Figure 7.2 shows the correct positions to place the stethoscope to carry out standard auscultation of the heart sounds. Positions 1 and 2 in the second intercostal space either side of the sternum will produce the clearest S2 sounds, while position 5 at the apex gives the best S1 sound (using the diaphragm). Work systematically through the five positions, slowly moving the stethoscope over the chest wall, following each sound as you proceed. Continual practice will produce a smooth and competent technique allowing you to confidently recognize normal heart sounds.

Abnormal heart sounds may be due to many causes and may not even indicate pathology. Always refer to a doctor if abnormalities are detected. Diseased valves produce murmurs, clicking or snapping sounds; yet the presence of abnormal sounds may be benign. The S3 and S4 sounds are normally very faint; if they become pronounced the result is a gallop rhythm, rather than the normal 'lub dub'. Likely causes include resistance to ventricular filling due to loss of compliance in the ventricular walls associated with hypertension and coronary artery disease or abnormally high stroke volumes associated with thyrotoxicosis, severe anaemia or pregnancy. Whenever an abnormal sound is detected, place it in the context of the patient's history and appearance, asking whether it can be linked to any obvious signs and symptoms, in order to assess its possible clinical significance. A medical opinion should always be obtained.

PERIPHERAL EXAMINATION

The patient's history and general appearance may indicate peripheral vascular disease. Cold, pale feet indicate a poor blood supply but the absence of both the dorsalis pedis and posterior tibial pulses (Fig. 7.3) indicates significantly reduced arterial blood flow. The popliteal and femoral pulses should be assessed in such cases (Fig. 7.4) and the results recorded as suggested in Figure 7.5. A popliteal or femoral aneurysm may be discovered in this way. It

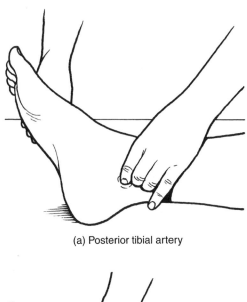

(a) Posterior tibial artery

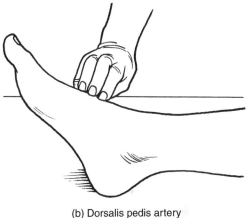

(b) Dorsalis pedis artery

Figure 7.3 Examining peripheral pulses in the foot: (a) the posterior tibial artery and (b) the dorsalis pedis artery.

will feel too obvious to be a normal pulse and is often described as expansile in that it pushes the examiner's fingers apart when gentle pressure is applied to both sides of the pulse.

If a Doppler probe is available, this can be used to assess the extent of peripheral ischaemia. A correctly sized BP cuff should be applied to the mid-calf region with the patient lying flat, and systolic BP estimated using the Doppler probe to detect arterial blood flow into the foot. This can then be divided by the systolic BP recorded in the arm to produce a ratio of ankle to brachial systolic BP. According to Black & Hawks (2004), the ratio should be at least 1.0, 0.8–0.5 is consistent with claudication, whilst severe ischaemia is present with a ratio < 0.4.

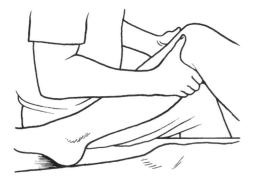

Figure 7.4 Examining the popliteal artery.

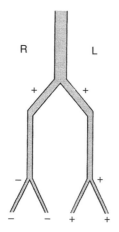

Figure 7.5 Recording peripheral pulses.

In severe ischaemia the foot may appear red but if it is elevated above the level of the heart it rapidly becomes pale, slowly turning red again if lowered below heart level due to capillary pooling. This is known as Buerger's test. Arterial ulcers may be seen on the toes or the sole of the foot and heel (dorsum). Gangrene and cellulitis may also be present.

Assess for peripheral venous disorder if the history is indicative of such problems. Both calves should be checked for size and tenderness (use a tape measure and ensure that circumference is measured at the same point on both legs with equal tension on the tape). The appearance, colour and warmth of the skin should be assessed for ulceration, oedema, varicose veins and engorgement.

Oedema in the lower limbs can be associated with oedematous changes elsewhere if the cause is heart failure. Localized oedema indicates restriction of blood flow in the veins of the leg; the most probable cause is DVT. A red painful area close to a superficial vein is likely to be thrombophlebitis (superficial venous thrombosis), which does not carry the same serious potential threat as DVT. Prolonged immobility will produce localized oedema as the patient has lost the pumping action of the calf muscles.

Chronic venous insufficiency produces swelling and discoloration and may be associated with venous ulcers around the shins. This picture is usually seen in elderly patients and there are often other pathological processes at work, including arterial disease (giving a mix of arterial/venous signs and symptoms), Type 2 diabetes and primary skin conditions.

INVESTIGATIONS

ELECTROCARDIOGRAPHY

The electrocardiograph (ECG) is a useful adjunct to the physical examination and focused history. However it is just that, an adjunct, and you should always be mindful of caring for the patient rather than the ECG!

The 12-lead ECG is a three-dimensional picture of the electrical activity of the heart, as opposed to cardiac monitoring, which is concerned with arrhythmia detection, normally using chest leads only, in a coronary care or ambulatory setting. A 12-lead ECG can reveal evidence of myocardial ischaemia, myocardial infarction or ventricular hypertrophy. A short rhythm strip is routinely recorded as part of a 12-lead ECG, which will help clarify any arrhythmia present, although continual monitoring is necessary if the arrhythmia is life threatening.

The ECG machine has electrodes attached to both wrists and ankles (only the left ankle is a recording lead as the right ankle serves as an earth) and has six separate chest (precordial) leads. The first six readings are designated I, II, III, aVR, aVL and aVF. The term bipolar or standard leads is used to describe I, II and III, while aVR, aVL and aVF are called unipolar leads. Each is the result of the machine making different combinations of the limb leads giving a three-dimensional picture of the heart's electrical activity, e.g. lead I is the voltage recorded in the left arm minus that recorded in the right. Figure 7.6 shows the views obtained.

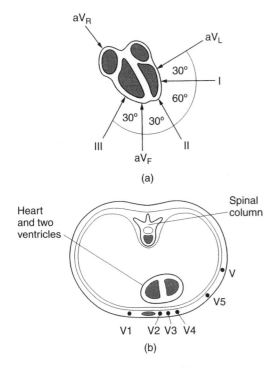

Figure 7.6 A 12-lead ECG showing (a) the views of heart obtained in the vertical plane by the limb leads and (b) views obtained by chest leads.

The chest leads must be attached in the correct positions (Fig. 7.7), which are as follows:

- V1: fourth intercostal space, immediately to the right of the sternum
- V2: fourth intercostal space, immediately to the left of the sternum
- V3: midway between V2 and V4
- V4: left fifth intercostal space, mid-clavicular line
- V5: left fifth intercostal space end of clavicle
- V6: left fifth intercostal space mid-axillary line.

This ability to build up a three-dimensional picture of cardiac activity is of diagnostic significance. The interpretation of the ECG assumes that all the leads have been placed in the *correct* positions.

In order to record an ECG successfully it is important to explain carefully what is going to happen to the patient in order to obtain cooperation. A simple explanation, such as 'This machine will give us an accurate tracing of how your heart is beating', is more meaningful than a cryptic statement such as 'I am just doing an ECG'. It is important to expose the chest fully; therefore privacy is required, especially for a female patient. Body hair seriously interferes with the trace so it must be shaved off as appropriate. Tremor will interfere with the recording so

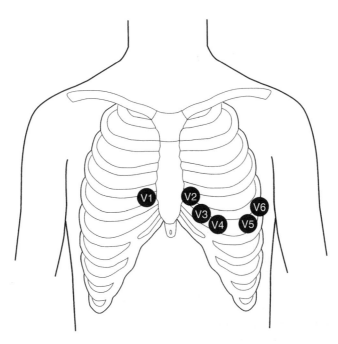

Figure 7.7 The correct positions of chest leads for a 12-lead ECG.

the patient must be still and relaxed. Calibration of the machine must be checked whenever it is used, along with paper speed. Interpretation assumes a vertical deflection of 1 cm corresponding to an electrical potential of 1 mV and that the paper speed is 25 mm/second. The most important piece of information on the ECG is the patient's name, the date and time of the recording. If the patient has presented with chest pain this information should also be documented on the ECG. Remember to write these on at the end. Many general practices are able to store the ECG recording on the computer so any additional comments should be added to the clinical notes on the system.

Key findings

There are many advanced texts on ECG interpretation. This section will concentrate on the more common significant findings. A normal ECG is shown in Figure 7.8 and the key stages are as follows:

- P wave: sinoatrial node (pacemaker of the heart) discharges an electrical impulse through the atria.
- PQ interval: time taken for impulse to travel from the atrioventricular node down the bundle of His and left and right bundle branches into the ventricles. Normally less than 0.2 seconds.
- Q wave: beginning of electrical discharge in ventricles; occurs in the right lower section of the intraventricular septum and spreads into the right ventricle. As this electrical activity is normally moving away from the electrode it produces a downward deflection as the machine is set to record in that way.
- RST complex: electrical discharge throughout the rest of the ventricles; normally obscures the Q wave almost completely as it follows so quickly.
- T wave: electrical activity associated with repolarization of cardiac muscle cells before next contraction.

One other key idea is the concept of the cardiac vector. A vector is any entity that has both magnitude and direction. An everyday example is the wind. The cardiac vector is the sum of all the electrical activity in the heart over one cycle. It has a magnitude, which can be measured in normal electrical units, and a direction, which is normally aligned in the general direction of lead II. This

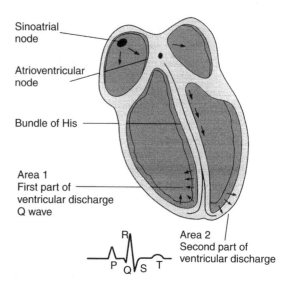

Figure 7.8 The spread of electrical activity via conducting mechanism.

explains why leads such as II normally produce the largest complexes whereas a lead such as aVL, which is at right angles to the normal cardiac vector, produces the smallest.

Armed with these basic facts about electrocardiography, it is possible to make some significant deductions from a 12-lead ECG. ECG machines are now able to analyze the recording and give a diagnosis. The person interpreting the ECG should not rely on this alone, the patient's clinical condition remains of overriding importance.

Myocardial infarction

Ischaemic heart disease produces three characteristic changes on the ECG, any or all of which may be visible, depending on the individual patient's condition (Fig. 7.9).

The Q wave may become more prominent than normal if the area of myocardium that normally obscures the Q wave is infarcted. As this myocardium now consists of dead tissue, there is no electrical activity taking place and therefore the full Q wave is now visible as if through an electrical window. A pathological Q wave of this nature is more than 4 mm in depth and will be found in those ECG leads which are looking at the infarcted tissue, enabling the MI to be localized within the heart. As this is a record of dead tissue it tends to be a permanent characteristic of an ECG and therefore this limits its value as a diagnostic observation. The

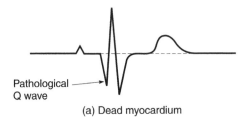

(a) Dead myocardium

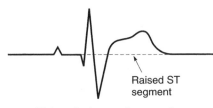

(b) Acutely damaged myocardium

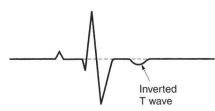

(c) Myocardial ischaemia
Note: There are a range of other causes for T wave inversion

Figure 7.9 Ischaemic ECG changes: (a) dead myocardium, (b) acutely damaged myocardium, (c) myocardial ischaemia; NB: there are a range of other causes for T wave inversion.

presence of an abnormally deep Q wave indicates that the patient has had an MI, but not when – it could have been last week or last year.

Of more use in diagnosing an acute infarct is the presence of an elevated ST segment on the ECG. This should normally be at the same baseline level as the rest of the trace. However, acutely damaged myocardial cells will leak potassium ions, each carrying a positive charge, with the result that after each myocardial contraction (QRS complex) there will be a surplus of positive charges with the result that the electrical baseline will be elevated above normal. This shows as an elevated ST segment of the ECG. This is an acute change that is visible on an ECG during an MI. This slowly resolves over a period of 1–2 weeks. It is possible that if the ECG is performed quickly after the patient complains of chest pain, the ST elevation will not have fully developed. This underlines the importance of lis-

tening carefully to the patient's history and looking at all the evidence prior to making a diagnosis.

Myocardial ischaemia

Inverted T waves may indicate cardiac ischaemia. There are other causes for this phenomenon (see below). If a patient is experiencing angina pain, the 12-lead may show ST depression. A patient with a history of angina who is experiencing no pain at present will probably have a normal ECG.

Ventricular hypertrophy

If one ventricle is abnormally enlarged, there will be an excess of electrical activity in that area of the heart compared to normal. This will pull the cardiac vector away from its normal alignment (towards the left in left ventricular hypertrophy and the right in right hypertrophy) and as a result this will produce changes in the size of various components of the ECG complex and possibly in the whole complex. Recognizing these changes and knowing which leads they occur in can give useful information about the presence of ventricular hypertrophy.

Knowing the normal is the key to recognizing the abnormal. In a normal ECG the largest upright complex should be in lead II and leads I and II should both show an R wave which exceeds the S wave. Count how many squares the R wave stands above the baseline and how many the S wave lies below the baseline. R should exceed S.

The following changes may be expected, though not all may be visible:
Right ventricular hypertrophy:

- Lead I, S wave > R
- V1, R wave > S
- V6 there is an obvious S wave
- V1 and V2 show T-wave inversion
Left ventricular hypertrophy:
- Lead II, S wave > R
- T-wave inversion in I, aVL, V5 and V6
- QRS complex is generally increased in height.

This last point shows the importance of ensuring the machine is correctly calibrated, as this could potentially result in the wrong interpretation.

Arrhythmias

This section will briefly review the most significant and frequently encountered arrhythmias. The key to rhythm interpretation is lead II – a lead II rhythm strip is automatically produced by most modern machines to allow arrhythmia detection. If your machine does not do this, then a 15-second lead II strip should be recorded after completing the 12-lead ECG.

Atrial fibrillation (Fig. 7.10)

The normal regular firing of the sinoatrial node is replaced by disorganized atrial activity. As a result the regular P waves disappear and the normally flat baseline becomes irregular. It is important to distinguish this from movement or electrical interference, both of which also produce irregularities in the tracing of QRS complex. As the atrioventricular node is not receiving strong, regular electrical impulses, the bundle of His conducts electrical impulses of varying strengths at rapid but irregular intervals to stimulate ventricular contraction. This causes QRS complexes to occur at irregular intervals, and this is reflected in an irregular pulse rate which when palpated is also of unequal strength. This situation will eventually lead to heart failure as the heart's pumping mechanism becomes increasingly inefficient. Occasionally the chaotic atrial activity may become organized producing a saw-tooth effect

along the baseline with a regular pattern of two or four small atrial waves to each QRS complex. This is known as atrial flutter (Fig. 7.11).

Paroxysmal supraventricular tachycardia (Fig. 7.12)

Despite this daunting name, PST is simply an arrhythmia caused by an atrial impulse being recycled between the atria and ventricles. The result is sudden bursts of tachycardia, which the patient experiences as palpitations or fluttering in the chest, it can also cause chest pain, sweating, and hypotension if symptoms persist for long periods. Alarming though this may be, it is not a life-threatening arrhythmia but may require hospitalization if sustained.

Heart block (Fig. 7.13)

This is a progressive condition which occurs as a result of ageing and degeneration of the conducting mechanism or as a result of acute damage to the bundle of His after an MI. First-degree block is shown on the ECG by lengthening of the PQ interval to 0.2 seconds or more as the electrical impulse is delayed in the conducting fibres. This

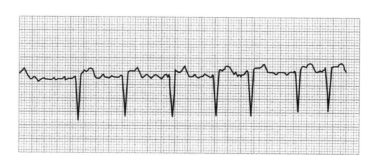

Figure 7.10 Atrial fibrillation: note the irregular rhythm and absence of normal P waves.

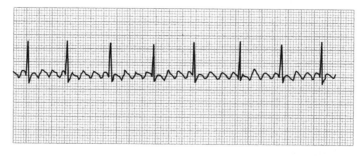

Figure 7.11 Atrial flutter: note regular rhythm (P waves) but ventricular rhythm depends on conduction pattern.

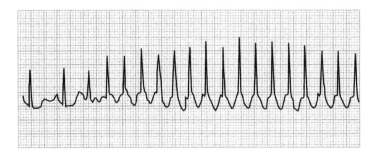

Figure 7.12 Paroxysmal supraventricular tachycardia: note development from normal sinus rhythm.

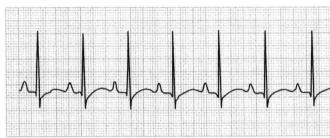

(a) First degree (note lengthened P–R interval)

Figure 7.13 Heart block: (a) first degree (note lengthened P–R interval), (b) second degree (occasional dropped beat), (c) second degree (2:1 conduction), (d) third degree (P wave and QRS complex not related).

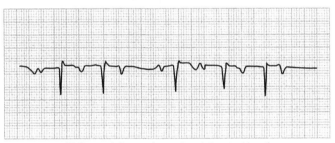

(b) Second degree (occasional dropped beat)

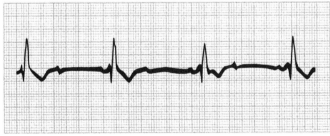

(c) Second degree (2:1 conduction)

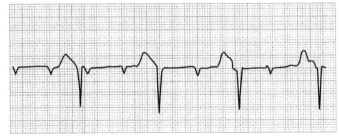

(d) Third degree (P wave and QRS complex not related)

in itself does not produce any clinical signs or symptoms. As the disease advances some electrical impulses fail to make it through the conducting mechanism and therefore do not produce a ventricular contraction. A P wave is present but no associated QRS complex occurs. This may occur at random (Mobitz type 2 block) or in an organized way where the PQ interval progressively lengthens over 3 or 4 beats and then there is a completely missed QRS complex (Mobitz type 1 or Wenckebach's phenomenon). A more progressive form of the disorder sees a consistent pattern of alternate electrical impulses failing to make it through the bundle of His. This is known as 2:1 block as only alternate P waves produce a QRS complex and may start to produce symptoms of heart failure if the effective ventricular rate is slow enough.

Complete or third-degree heart block is present when there is a complete breakdown of the conducting mechanism and, despite regular P waves appearing on the ECG, there are no associated QRS complexes. An alternative ventricular pacemaker takes over. This may be located within the bundle of His below the blockage or elsewhere within the Purkinje fibres in the ventricles. The former produces narrow QRS complexes as conduction is quicker but the latter situation leads to slower conduction and a much broader QRS shape. The patient is likely to develop heart failure as with a slow heart rate (bradycardia) any exertion leads to dyspnoea. Syncope attacks are possible if there is any delay in the alternative pacemaker's action as the pulse may be only 20–30 beats/minute.

Ventricular extrasystole (Fig. 7.14)

Extraventricular contractions (ventricular ectopics) are a result of stimulation by a group of cells outside the main conducting system. The occasional ventricular extrasystole does not produce any clinical effect; however, if they become more frequent or organized this is a matter of concern for two reasons. If an extrasystole were to coincide with the normal T wave (R on T), this could trigger ventricular fibrillation (cardiac arrest), as cardiac output falls to zero. Ventricular extrasystoles may increasingly occur in short consecutive runs (two VEs bigemony, three VEs trigemony; any more is termed runs of VT) that unchecked may become sustained ventricular tachycardia – a serious life-threatening

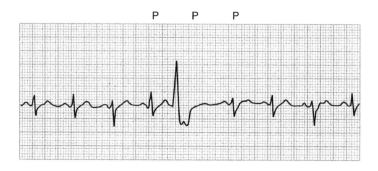

Figure 7.14 Ventricular ectopic with refractory period afterwards.

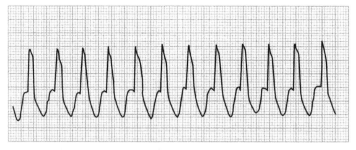

Rate: 100–170 beats/min, no P waves, broad QRS complexes

Figure 7.15 Ventricular tachycardia.

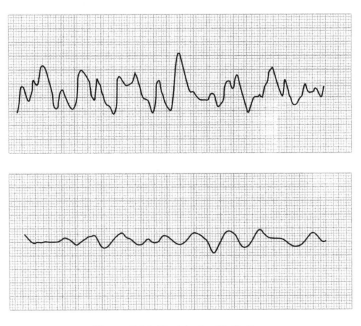

Figure 7.16 Ventricular fibrillation.

arrhythmia (Fig. 7.15). In this situation an ectopic focus in the ventricle has taken over the pacing of the heart and is firing rapidly (150–200 beats/min). The oxygen demand of the myocardium increases dramatically whilst the filling time between beats is reduced by a half or two-thirds of normal and cardiac output falls. This will rapidly lead to ventricular fibrillation (Fig. 7.16) unless it reverts to a normal sinus rhythm quickly. In ventricular fibrillation there is uncoordinated chaotic twitching of the ventricular muscle with no cardiac output. Cardiopulmonary resuscitation should be initiated.

OTHER INVESTIGATIONS

Troponins are integral protein compounds of striated muscle. There are three types: troponin C, troponin T and troponin I bound to each other and to tropomyosin. Troponin C has the same structure in both cardiac and skeletal muscle but the cardiac troponins, troponin T (cTnT) and troponin I (cTnI) are products of different genes and are specific to cardiac muscle tissue. The cardiac troponins have a specific feature; they are only released following cardiac damage and within 4–6 hours of that damage, they are present for a long time and they are very sensitive (Collinson 1998). Unlike the enzymes creatinine kinase (CK) and its cardiac specific iso-enzyme CK-MB (the previous cardiac diagnostic markers) these are detectable for longer periods following infarct. cTnT is present for 7–10 days and cTnI is present for up to 5 days. These two tests are now considered Gold Standard biochemical tests but you should ensure you are aware of the preferred investigation for your locality (British Heart Foundation 2003).

Hypercholesterolaemia is recognized as a risk factor in heart disease. The ratio of plasma total cholesterol LDL to HDL cholesterol may be used as an aid to risk calculations as the greater the ratio, the greater the risk. There is no threshold limit above which the person is suddenly at risk. The risk increases gradually as the cholesterol level increases.

DIFFERENTIAL DIAGNOSIS

The approach to history taking, the physical examination and investigations discussed above should enable you to make a differential diagnosis. The most likely scenario is the patient who presents with a history of chest pain – you must decide whether this is of cardiac origin rather than a gastrointestinal, respiratory or musculoskeletal pain. The history is usually sufficient to make this diagnosis. Having decided that the problem is cardiac, next you need to decide between the two most likely causes, angina or MI. Again the history is likely to point one way or the other; an ECG and a physical exam should quickly confirm the diagnosis in most cases.

An alternative presentation is the breathless patient who is generally unwell. It is important to be able to distinguish between a cardiac problem such as heart failure and other possible causes such as respiratory disease. Again a thorough history, clinical examination and ECG are required. NICE (2003) recommends referral for a chest x-ray to exclude respiratory disease. If the ECG and history are indicating the possibility of heart failure then the patient must be referred for an echocardiograph to confirm diagnosis. A simple blood test to detect naturatic peptides (BNP or NTproBNP) may soon be widely available to confirm a diagnosis of LVSD. (BNP is a hormone released by stretched cardiac muscle).

Peripheral circulatory problems need careful consideration to distinguish between venous and arterial disorders; in some cases there may be a mixed presentation. As the approaches to treatment are different – the wrong diagnosis could be potentially harmful – it is essential to combine careful physical examination with a good focused history.

If a patient is found to have raised BP, it is necessary to consider whether this is due to stress and/or exertion prior to the appointment, or a sign of hypertensive disease. In the former case it may be apparent that the patient is breathless after hurrying to keep an appointment or has just had a stressful experience. The diastolic pressure is relatively unaffected, even though the systolic may be above normal. When checked 15 minutes or so later, BP will have returned to normal. It is the sustained elevation of both diastolic and systolic BP with no apparent short-term cause that indicates hypertension.

TREATMENT

CARDIAC DISEASE

Acute disorders

Approximately 275 000 people in the UK suffer a heart attack each year. Between a third and two-thirds of heart attack deaths take place outside hospital, many within the first few minutes of the onset of symptoms (NSF for CHD 2004). The patient therefore needs to be admitted to a coronary

care unit as soon as possible. Immediate treatment involves intravenous opioid analgesia and an antiemetic, oxygen therapy and psychologically supportive care in a quiet restful environment before transfer to coronary care. An intravenous line should first be secured. Diamorphine 2.5–5.0 mg should be given as it combines analgesia with a strong sedative effect. The dose may be repeated if it is not effective in controlling pain. Prochlorperazine is the standard antiemetic given as a 12.5 mg intramuscular injection. Frequent observations of vital signs are necessary (15–30 minutes depending on the patient's condition) and, if an ECG monitor is available, the patient should be attached for rhythm monitoring. Ventricular fibrillation is the major danger in this initial period. A defibrillator should be readily available and you must know how to use it – the sooner the patient is defibrillated, the better the prognosis. Automated external defibrillators are now widely available in public places, for example, airports and sports centres.

In recent years the introduction of fibrinolytic drugs, which break up thrombi by degrading fibrin, has significantly improved the outlook for patients who have had an acute MI. The benefits of treatment decrease rapidly as time elapses since the MI; however, administration within the first 12 hours can produce substantial benefits. It is important to consider the risk of bleeding caused by fibrinolytic therapy in patients with a history of cerebrovascular disease, recent surgery, trauma or known clotting disorders, before deciding whether the benefits of their use outweigh the risks. Streptokinase, alteplase and anistreplase have all been shown to reduce mortality when administered intravenously (BNF 2004). Aspirin has an additive effect with streptokinase, and heparin should be given with alteplase to produce the best results. Local protocols will determine which drugs should be given and the nurse practitioner should be fully involved in this key therapeutic intervention. The Coronary Heart Disease NSF set a target of a 60 minutes call to needle time and a 30-minute door to needle time to encourage swift treatment with thrombolytic agents. The Myocardial Infarction National Audit Project (MINAP) was set up to enable clinicians to examine the management of acute MI within their hospitals (NSF for CHD 2004). Paramedic and pre-hospital services are now able to give patients thrombolysis prior to arriving at hospital, increasing the patients chances of survival and preventing sustained damage to cardiac muscle.

The other acute presentation commonly encountered is the patient in acute heart failure. This is most likely to be due to left ventricular failure secondary to an MI or some other cardiac event such as failure of the aortic or mitral valves leading to aortic or mitral regurgitation. The patient has marked pulmonary oedema and is underperfused due to the failing pumping action of the left ventricle. This results in hypotension, cold extremities, possible confusion and a reduced urine output. Immediate hospital treatment is required, but in the interim the patient should be cared for sitting upright to help lung expansion and oxygen administered to help correct the hypoxic state that has arisen due to hypoperfusion. The immediate medical management should consist of intravenous morphine, which will cause vasodilatation, respiratory suppression and relieve anxiety, all of which will relieve dyspnoea. Intravenous frusemide will also assist by producing a prompt diuresis. If there is likely to be a delay in admission to hospital, these measures should be instituted at once.

The nurse practitioner may receive a phone call from a member of the public about someone experiencing chest pain. Briggs (1997) suggests that the following indications should dictate whether the caller rings for an emergency ambulance – pain, tightness, pressure or discomfort in the chest, accompanied by any of the following:

- shortness of breath
- dizziness, weakness, nausea or vomiting
- cool moist skin
- pain affecting the neck, shoulders, jaw, back or arms
- heart palpitations
- pallor or blueness.

Other factors, which should alert you to advise immediate medical care, are:

- the chest pain is unrelieved by rest, antacids or nitroglycerine or if it has awoken the person
- chest pain is accompanied by pain, swelling, warmth or redness in a leg
- sudden onset of swollen ankles
- recent history of childbirth, surgery, immobilization or blood-clotting disorder
- fever, cough, shortness of breath
- age over 60
- medical or family history of heart disease, diabetes or blood-clotting disorder
- smoker.

Chronic disease management

The nurse practitioner has a major role to play in the long-term management of patients with conditions such as heart failure, hypertension and ischaemic heart disease. A great deal of information is available about lifestyle modification such as smoking cessation, increasing exercise and losing excess weight. Such health education initiatives must be targeted to produce beneficial effects.

There is ample international evidence that screening the general population for cholesterol levels and giving advice about diet to those with elevated levels has little effect (York Centre for Review and Dissemination 1998). Low-fat diets perform poorly in cholesterol reduction due to non-compliance; they also often leave the LDL/HDL ratio unaffected as they merely substitute carbohydrates for total fat in the diet. Williams et al (2004) recognize that lifestyle measures that reduce risk of cardiovascular disease include smoking cessation, reducing intake of total saturated fats, increasing the consumption of fish, engaging in aerobic physical exercise for 30 mins or more on at least 3 days a week, reducing salt intake to less than 100 mmols/day, aiming for a BMI of 20–25 kg/m^2 and, finally, limiting alcohol consumption to less than 3 units/day. They go on to suggest that effective implementation of these measures requires knowledge, enthusiasm, patience, and time spent with the patient. The NP plays a key role in securing adherence to drug therapy. An essential component of this work is fully explaining the benefits of drug therapy and the expected side effects so that patients are fully informed about and involved in their treatment. This is consistent with the approach needed to secure lifestyle changes.

The Heart Protection Study of 2002 recommended treating patients at high risk for vascular events with statins, regardless of the initial levels of serum lipids or age. Statins are recommended by National Cholesterol Education Program Adult Treatment Panel III as first-line therapy for high-risk patients with hypercholesterolaemia and as second-line therapy after diet for intermediate and low risk patients. The National Institute for Clinical Excellence is currently reviewing evidence to produce guidelines for the management of blood lipids in the United Kingdom.

When enlisting the patient as a partner in care it is useful to follow the health belief model (Rosenstock 1974), which suggests that people make decisions about their health based upon judgements about several variables. These may be summarized as the perceived susceptibility to an illness, the effect upon the individual of that illness and the costs and benefits of seeking treatment. It may help to use the Joint British Societies Coronary Risk Prediction Chart found in the BNF when talking these issues through.

To illustrate the model, consider a patient with hypertension being managed in primary care. Stress that the person already has high BP and point out the probabilities of a subsequent stroke or MI. This needs to be done in such a way as to make the patient perceive that s/he is highly susceptible but without causing undue anxiety and fear. The consequences of a stroke or MI to the patient and family should then be explored. Whilst there may be a fatal outcome, it is more likely that the person will be disabled. Who will look after the rest of the family? Who will look after the patient? These are the issues that need to be talked through sensitively without causing too much alarm, but in such a way as to motivate the patient to make a serious attempt to avert these possible future events.

This brings the discussion on to drug therapy and lifestyle modification. The perceived costs or disadvantages should be carefully explored. Some may be removed from the equation, as they may be mistaken beliefs or folk tales. Those that remain, such as the side effects of drugs, have to be acknowledged so that at least there are no unexpected unpleasant surprises for the patient who, in the process, is becoming a real partner in care. It then remains to show the potential benefits of adhering to drug therapy, weight reduction, exercise and smoking cessation. It may take several consultations to work through these issues but at the end, you may well find a motivated patient who fully grasps the risks concerned and who is able to make an informed decision about antihypertensive therapy. The outcome is more likely to be positive adherence to the therapeutic regime than if you simply lecture the patient on the evils of smoking, supply a prescription and send him or her away with a leaflet on blood pressure.

Despite intensive follow-up and discussion with the patient, risk is notoriously difficult to calculate, and even where it can be measured accurately, the same absolute risk will be perceived very differently by different people and in different contexts (World Health Organization 2003). There is much discussion about compliance and concordance. Lewis et al (2003) show that patients and health professionals find the concepts of risk and benefit difficult to understand, and in deciding whether to start preventative treatment doctors were more likely to accept smaller benefits than patients. Jackevicius et al (2002) demonstrated this by finding that two-thirds of older patients prescribed a statin for coronary heart disease will have given up within 2 years.

The health belief model approach can be used to manage a wide range of chronic diseases other than hypertension. It is important to be fully aware of the medications used and that their side effects need to be explored with patients. The patient's understanding of the medication must be assessed as some patients may be vague and have little idea about each type of drug, how much to take and when, let alone know the side-effects to look out for. Detailed information can be found in the British National Formulary; the following paragraphs summarize the most likely types of drugs used in treating cardiovascular disorders.

Calcium channel blockers

These drugs interfere with the displacement of calcium through active cell membranes, affecting cells in the myocardium, conducting mechanism and vascular smooth muscle. Myocardial contractility is reduced, leading to arteriolar dilation, thereby reducing blood pressure. Different calcium channel blockers have slightly different effects. Thus nifedipine acts mostly on blood vessels, whereas verapamil has a stronger effect on the myocardium and should not be given to patients in heart failure. Constipation is a side effect and verapamil may produce nausea, vomiting or dizziness.

Beta-blockers

By blocking the beta-adrenoreceptors in the sympathetic nervous system, these drugs reduce cardiac contractility and heart rate. They also reduce renin release from the kidney and hence angiotensin II synthesis. The net effect is to reduce blood pressure and beta-blockers are often combined with thiazide diuretics to enhance this effect. Side effects include bradycardia, conduction disorders, bronchospasm and peripheral vasoconstriction.

Nitrates

Both the above groups of drugs are used prophylactically to treat patients with angina. If an angina attack occurs, nitrates provide immediate short-term relief. Glyceryl trinitrate has been the standard drug for many years although its effects are short-lasting (20–30 minutes). It is usually administered sublingually or via an aerosol spray. It is also available as a transdermal patch for prophylaxis; each patch usually lasts 24 hours. Another commonly used nitrate is isosorbide mononitrate, which is used prophylactically in tablet form. Nitrates may produce severe headaches, postural hypotension, dizziness and flushing as side effects.

Angiotensin–converting enzyme inhibitors (e.g. Ramapril)

Drugs that prevent the conversion of angiotensin I to angiotensin II have proved very effective as an alternative to beta-blockade and thiazide diuretic therapy in managing hypertension, and also in treating heart failure, especially when combined with digoxin and diuretics. This group of drugs is best avoided in patients known or suspected to have renovascular disease, as they may stop glomerular filtration and lead to renal failure (BNF 2004).

Cardiac glycosides (e.g. digoxin)

By increasing the force of myocardial contraction and reducing conductivity within the heart this group of drugs has proven effective in the treatment of atrial fibrillation and heart failure. Side effects depend not only on plasma concentrations but also on the sensitivity of the myocardium or conducting mechanism to the drug, which varies considerably between patients. Bradycardia and other arrhythmias may occur in one patient but not in another, even though both are on the same dose. Simply monitoring plasma concentration is therefore not sufficient if toxicity is to be avoided. The nurse practitioner should follow up each patient on an individual basis, checking that the pulse remains in sinus rhythm with a rate above 60 beats/min, and that the patient has none of the other side effects of toxicity, such as nausea, vomiting and loss of appetite.

Diuretics

The thiazides, such as bendrofluazide, act by inhibiting reabsorption of sodium in the distal convoluted tubule. Loop diuretics such as frusemide inhibit reabsorption in the ascending loop of Henle in the renal tubule. Both types of diuretic produce an effect within 1–2 hours. This should be remembered when educating the patient, as the individual should

be advised to take the diuretic in the morning not the evening and not to miss doses. Although useful in the management of heart failure and hypertension, these drugs have an extensive range of possible side effects, including nausea, gastrointestinal disturbance and hypokalaemia. This latter problem has led to the development of drugs which are potassium sparing as an alternative to giving the patient potassium supplements; examples include spironolactone and amiloride.

Statins

This class of drugs is effective in lowering LDL cholesterol levels by inhibiting a key enzyme involved in cholesterol synthesis, especially in the liver. The Standing Medical Advisory Committee (1997), based on evidence from a large randomized controlled trial, has recommended that patients with angina who have a total cholesterol level 5.5 mmol/l or more (or LDL 3.7 mmol/l) should be considered for statin treatment.

Warfarin

The prophylactic anticoagulation effects of warfarin are well known. The number of patients for whom it is prescribed has increased substantially as it is now used to prevent embolization in patients with atrial fibrillation. Careful follow-up and monitoring of patients on long-term anticoagulation are essential and the NP should be aware of local policies relating to this.

An earlier systematic review of the management of stable angina by the York CRD concluded that there was no long-term difference in effectiveness between the major types of drugs such as beta-blockers, nitrates and calcium channel blockers (CRD1 1997). This review also found powerful evidence for the effectiveness of aspirin therapy in reducing the incidence of MI amongst those with stable angina. Discussions with patients concerning surgical options for the treatment of their angina will usually be carried out by the GP. Patients may wish to discuss the options with the nurse practitioner, so it is useful to know that the CRD1 review showed that, while in the short-term angioplasty is more effective than drug therapy in relieving symptoms, after 2–3 years the beneficial effect had disappeared, while overall angioplasty had no beneficial effect on survival rates. Coronary artery bypass improved quality of life and relieved angina more effectively than drug therapy over a much longer period (up to 10 years) but was associated with a significantly higher mortality rate in the initial period of treatment. There are therefore advantages and disadvantages and what might be best for one patient might not be the most appropriate option for another. Patients need to discuss the arguments and carefully consider which is the best option for them as individuals. Surgery is not a quick fix, which allows the patient to forget about drug therapy and lifestyle modification – a key point to be reinforced.

PERIPHERAL VASCULAR DISORDERS

Arterial problems

An acute arterial embolism or leaking aneurysm are major surgical emergencies and immediate transfer to a general hospital is essential after appropriate pain-relieving measures and once intravenous resuscitation has been started locally.

A patient may present with a history of intermittent claudication and signs of peripheral arterial disease affecting the foot, such as small gangrenous ulcers. If these ulcers become infected they may worsen rapidly as the poor blood supply means that the body's natural defence mechanisms are ineffective in dealing with the infective organisms. Cellulitis and possibly septicaemia may develop. The patient requires urgent referral to a vascular surgeon. Meanwhile, an honest dialogue using the health belief model approach is necessary. The aim should be to persuade the patient to stop smoking immediately and to take great care of the affected foot. If s/he is also diabetic, a thorough diabetic check (see Chapter 14) should be completed also examining the unaffected foot, and discussing diet and medication regimes (NICE 2004). Dressings are necessary for any ulcers and a referral should be made for a podiatrist to assess and treat any foot lesions. Patients should be dissuaded from home remedies but be advised on how to care for their feet.

Venous problems

If a DVT is suspected a medical opinion should be sought immediately in view of the potentially fatal outcome of a pulmonary embolism. Intravenous heparin should be commenced with oral warfarin for medium-term management.

Varicose veins are best managed by compression stockings and discussing the patient's daily routine. Periods of extensive standing should be identified and strategies explored to reduce these periods, especially at work. The importance of calf movements when standing to pump blood out of the affected veins should be emphasized together with the value of leg elevation when resting. It should be explained that to be effective this means elevating the legs above the level of the heart, not just sitting with the feet on a footstool. Referral to a doctor to consider the surgical option should always be offered.

Venous leg ulcers respond best to compression bandages that provide a pressure gradient within the lower part of the leg to reduce venous congestion. A significant number of patients may have arterial as well as venous disease and high compression bandaging would be contraindicated for such persons. It is important to measure ankle/brachial pressure index (ABPI, p. 105), as part of the assessment, noting that this is a more reliable indicator of peripheral arterial circulation than measuring whether peripheral pulses are present.

The patient should be encouraged to avoid sitting with the feet on the ground for long periods as this exacerbates venous congestion. A good dressing technique using one of the modern occlusive products, combined with the correct form of compression bandaging, has a major role to play in promoting healing of leg ulcers. Established ulcers can also be painful, therefore analgesia should be discussed with the patient and various analgesics may be tried until one is found that is effective for that patient. The elderly are increasingly susceptible to the side effects of nonsteroidal anti-inflammatory drugs (e.g. gastrointestinal disorders and hypersensitivity reactions); therefore other drugs such as paracetamol should be tried before these are used for pain control (BNF 2004).

Summary

The nurse practitioner has a major role to play in both the acute and long-term management of patients with cardiovascular disorder, in primary care or hospital settings. Whatever the situation, the NP is likely to be the *first* point of contact with the health care system and, in many cases, the *only* point of contact for some time. The principles of patient assessment and management outlined in this chapter, together with locally devised protocols and agreements, are therefore essential for care of the highest quality.

References

Black J, Hawks J 2004 Medical surgical nursing, 7th edn. Elsevier Saunders, St Louis

Briggs J 1997 Telephone triage protocols for nurses. Lippincott, Philadelphia

BNF 2004 British National Formulary. British Medical Association/Royal Pharmaceutical Society of Great Britain, London

British Heart Foundation 2003 Cardiac troponins. Factfiles: 8-2003

Collinson P 1998 Troponin T or troponin I or CK-MB? European Heart Journal 19:N16-N24

CRD1 1997 Management of stable angina. Effective Health Care 3(5). NHS Centre for Review and Dissemination, York

Epstein O, Perkin G, Cookson J, de Bono D 2003 Clinical examination, 3rd edn. Churchill Livingstone, Edinburgh

Gerrish K, Husband C, Buckingham J 1996 Nursing for a multi-ethnic society. Open University Press, Buckingham

Heart Protection Study 2002 Heart Protection Study Collaborative Group. MRC/BHF Heart protection study of cholesterol lowering with simvastatin in 20,536 high-risk individuals. A randomised placebo-controlled trial. Lancet 2002 360:7–22

Hill B, Geraci S 1998 A diagnostic approach to chest pain based on history and ancillary evaluation. Nurse Practitioner 23(4):20–45

Jackevicius C A, Mmdani M, Tu J V 2002 Adherence with statin therapy in elderly patients with and without acute coronary syndromes. JAMA 288:462–467

Lewis D K, Robinson J, Wilkinson E 2003 Factors involved in deciding to start preventative treatment: a qualitative study of clinicians' and lay people's attitudes. BMJ 2003; 327:841–845

McMurray J, Stewart S 2001 The increasing burden of chronic heart failure. Cited in: Stewart S, Blue L (eds) Improving outcomes in chronic heart failure: a practical guide to specialist nurse intervention. BMJ Books, London

National Service Framework for Coronary Heart Disease 2004 Winning the war on heart disease, progress report 2004. Department of Health Publications, London

NICE 2004 NICE guidance: type 2 diabetes – foot problems. Prevention and management of foot problems in people with type 2 diabetes. National Institute for Clinical Excellence, London

NICE 2003 NICE clinical guideline 5 – chronic heart failure. Management of chronic heart failure in primary and secondary care. National Institute for Clinical Excellence, London

Nowak T, Handford G 2004 Pathophysiology, 3rd edn. McGraw-Hill, Boston

Primatesta P, Brookes M, Poulter N R 2001 Improved hypertension management and control; results from the health survey for England 1998. Hypertension 38:827–832

Rosenstock I 1974 Historical origins of the health belief model. Health Education Monographs 2:328–335

Standing Medical Advisory Committee 1997 The use of statins. Department of Health, London

Williams B, Poulter N R, Brown M et al 2004 The BHS Guidelines working party, for the British Hypertension Society. British Medical Journal 328:634–640

World Health Organization 2003 Chapter 3. Perceiving risk. In: World Health Organization Report 2002. WHO, Geneva

York Centre for Review and Dissemination 1998 Cholesterol and coronary heart disease: screening and treatment. Effective Health Care Bulletin 4(1)

Chapter 8

The respiratory system

Kay Holt

INTRODUCTION

Respiratory problems are among the commonest causes of illness and can range from a minor cold to a life-threatening asthmatic attack or pneumonia. The challenge is to be able to differentiate between minor, largely self-limiting conditions and more serious pathology requiring urgent intervention and/or specialist consultation. The health promotion role of the nurse practitioner is to the fore in areas such as asthma management and smoking cessation. The holistic nurse practitioner approach can therefore make a major contribution to respiratory health.

PATHOPHYSIOLOGY

Some of the commoner or more serious conditions will be reviewed here before looking at the major symptoms of respiratory disease and how they relate to their underlying pathology.

THE COMMON COLD

The cold is caused by viral infection from numerous different groups, e.g. rhinoviruses, respiratory syncytial virus, adenoviruses, influenza viruses and parainfluenza viruses. Incubation is from 1 to 5 days with viral shedding up to 2 weeks. Rhinoviruses are the commonest but there are over 100 types with no immunity after infection and it is not uncommon to be immediately reinfected with another type. The viruses are transmitted through inhaled droplet infection and direct contact from hands to mucous membranes. Host response to the virus is an important factor in developing a cold. Inflammatory mediators, particularly proinflammatory cytokines, appear to be significant instigators of symptoms and research is targeted towards interfering with their production. Being cold or damp does not contribute towards the risk of infection.

ACUTE BRONCHITIS AND PNEUMONIA

Infections involving the lower respiratory tract can vary between those easily managed at home and life-threatening conditions. Three basic issues need to be considered:

- Is the condition confined to the bronchi or does it affect lung tissue, as in pneumonia?
- Is the patient at risk for cardiopulmonary problems (such as an elderly person)?
- Is the infection bacterial or viral?

The same organisms may be implicated in acute bronchitis and pneumonia (Table 8.1). Acute bronchitis refers to infection and inflammation of the bronchi usually involving a virus but lung tissue and sometimes the trachea and larynx may also be involved (Underwood 2000). In both acute bronchitis and pneumonia, the patient will usually present with a productive cough, fever and feeling unwell. Usually the person with pneumonia appears ill and has higher fevers, chills and hypoxia. Pneumonia involves infection of the distal airways and alveoli

Table 8.1 Comparison of physical findings in acute bronchitis and pneumonia*

Bronchitis	Pneumonia
Hacking cough with thick sputum	Increased respiratory rate
	May have guarding of affected side
	Expansion may be asymmetrical
	Decreased on affected side
Resonant to percussion over area	Dull to percussion
Normal breath sounds	
Voice sounds normal	Increased clarity of voice with egophony, whispered pectoriloquy
May have occasional wheeze	Bronchophony
	Crackles over area and sometimes low-pitched wheezes (rhonchi)

*Adapted from Jarvis (2000).

with the formation of inflammatory exudates. A patient is therefore likely to complain of breathlessness, pleuritic pain and, with bacterial infection, to have copious amounts of sputum. The presentation of pneumonia in the elderly may be very subtle with mental confusion being the only obvious symptom. The diagnosis is made on clinical examination and confirmed by chest x-ray.

It is beyond the scope of this book to review all the possible causes of acute lower respiratory tract infections but the commonest cause of pneumonia (acquired outside hospital) is the bacteria *Streptococcus pneumoniae*, which accounts for approximately 30% or more of cases. Other causes include *Chlamydia pneumoniae* (10%), *Mycoplasma pneumoniae* (9%), *Legionella pneumophila* (5%) and viruses, but in 40% of cases no microbiological diagnosis is ever established (Haslett et al 2003). Hospital-acquired pneumonia refers to a new case of pneumonia developing at least 48 hours after admission for whatever cause. Different organisms are usually involved, especially Gram-negative bacteria such as the *Klebsiella* species, *Pseudomonas aeruginosa* or *Escherichia coli*. *S. aureus* is the most likely Gram-positive bacteria involved.

TUBERCULOSIS

There has been a significant increase in cases in the UK during the last few years, which may be summarized as follows (Health Protection Agency 2004):

- In 2001 there were 6652 new cases in England, Wales and Northern Ireland
- This represents an increase of 42% since 1988
- 41% of all new cases were in London
- 63% of cases were amongst people born abroad, Black African and Pakistani ethnic groups having the highest incidence
- 6.7% were resistant to isoniazid and 0.8% exhibited multi-drug resistance.

Poverty, malnutrition, overcrowding and poor living conditions reduce the effectiveness of the person's immune system, making him or her more likely to contract TB if exposed to the organism. Those infected with HIV are at particular risk of TB. Reactivation of the disease amongst immigrants from the developing world areas seems to be the main driver behind this worrying increase.

TB is caused by *Mycobacterium tuberculosis*. It most commonly affects the lungs but can migrate to other places such as lymph nodes, kidneys, bones and skin or wounds. It is spread by droplet infection from someone who has active respiratory disease. Systemic symptoms are fever, night sweats, weight loss, fatigue and loss of appetite. Respiratory symptoms include dry cough, dyspnoea, haemoptysis and chest pain. Infection can lead to a chronic state in which the disease, although not active, retains the capability to be reactivated many years later (Black & Hawks 2004).

ASTHMA

Asthma is a disease characterized by chronic airway inflammation with increased airway responsiveness resulting in symptoms of wheeze, cough and breathlessness. Nowak & Handford (2004) consider that two key factors are involved:

- an immune hypersensitivity reaction involving antibody formation (IgE) to an airborne allergen (atopic asthma)
- a non-immune response involving disorder of the autonomic nervous system leading to abnormal bronchoconstriction and mucus production. Factors such as occupational pollutants, exercise and severe cold can trigger an attack.

In addition, asthma is known to be caused as a side effect of non-steroidal anti-inflammatory drugs. Airway obstruction is variable over short periods of time or reversible with treatment. It is estimated that in the UK the prevalence of asthma is 7% in adults and 15% in children (Russell 2001, LAIA 1999).

Childhood is the most common age of onset, with another peak in the 30s age group, however asthma can begin at any age. Classical symptoms include breathlessness, tightness in the chest, cough and wheezing. Pathological findings include inflammation, hypertrophy of smooth bronchial muscle, mucosal oedema, hypertrophy of mucous glands and thick mucus plugs which all lead to obstruction of the airways. Symptoms are variable but may be worsened by triggers such as allergens, infection or exercise.

Asthma can be either atopic or non-atopic but patients do not always easily fit into one category.

Features of *atopic* asthma are:

- childhood onset
- intermittent
- positive skin test
- clear trigger factors
- family history of allergy
- good prognosis
- association with hay fever and ezcema.

Features of *non-atopic* asthma are:

- adult onset
- persistent
- negative skin test
- trigger factors not clear
- possible family history of asthma
- fair prognosis.

With atopic asthma IgE antibodies are produced on first exposure to an allergen and attach to mast cells, which stay at the tissue level, and basophils, which circulate in the blood. On subsequent exposure the allergen binds to IgE antibodies on mast cells. The cell releases potent chemicals or mediators of the allergic response – histamine, prostaglandin D, leukotrienes and eosinophilic chemotactic factor have all been implicated. They constrict the bronchial airways, stimulate secretion of mucus in the airways and increase the permeability of small blood vessels, causing wheezing, swelling of tissue and congestion of airways. A second or late-stage reaction can occur 6–12 hours later (Phillips et al 2001). It is believed to be a continuation of the inflammatory response at this stage and does not respond well to bronchodilator drugs.

Common airborne allergens include house dust mite, pollen and pets and it can be extremely difficult to achieve successful allergen avoidance with any of these. For example it can take several months to remove allergens from a room after the last exposure to a cat or dog, as shown by the fact that 25% of homes without a resident cat or dog have detectable levels of allergen (Custovic et al 1998). Pet allergens are carried on small respirable particles which remain airborne for long periods (Custovic et al 1996). Sensitization to a pet is an important risk factor for asthma, however current evidence is not clear about whether pet ownership is a risk factor for sensitization or protection (Simpson & Custovic 2004). Advising families on this issue can be a dilemma for the nurse practitioner.

Occupational asthma is asthma caused by an antigen inhaled at work and is now the commonest industrial lung disease. A clear cause is almost always identifiable and if the patient is kept away from the substance their asthma can resolve completely, as long as the condition has been diagnosed at an early stage. An asthma history in adults should always include careful enquiry about symptoms in relation to time at work and away from work.

The diagnosis of asthma is relatively straightforward in most cases and starts with a good history. Due to the variable nature of the condition physical examination may be unremarkable or may reveal signs of airway narrowing such as wheeze. The reversible nature of the condition can be used to diagnose the disease; this can be done in several ways:

- Peak flow reversibility. A baseline peak flow is measured, then repeated 15 minutes after 200–400 mcg of a beta 2 agonist such as salbutamol or terbutaline. A rise in peak flow of 20% and at least 60 l/min will confirm the diagnosis of asthma (BTS/SIGN 2003).
- Spirometry reversibility. An improvement in FEV_1 by 15%, together with a 200 ml change is an alternative to peak flow reversibility. In patients where poor effort is suspected on peak flow, spirometry may be more reliable as poor effort can be easily detected.
- Serial peak flow diary. A diurnal variation (i.e. the difference between the lowest and highest of the daily readings) of more than 20% on 3 or more days indicates asthma (BTS/SIGN 2003).
- Exercise testing. This may be useful when a child or young person gives a history of asthma triggered by exercise but produces a normal peak flow in the clinic. Peak flow is measured pre and post 6 minutes exercise. It is measured every 10 minutes for 30 minutes post exercise and a decrease of 20% is a positive exercise test.
- Oral steroid trial. This may be necessary if previous diagnostic tests have been negative or inconclusive. In an adult 30 mg prednisolone is prescribed daily for 2 weeks. Peak flow or FEV_1 pre and post steroid trial can confirm the diagnosis.

An acute exacerbation of asthma can be as a result of exposure to a trigger or can present with gradually worsening symptoms over days or weeks, perhaps due to under use of inhaled corticosteroids. Patients may present reporting recent nocturnal symptoms and their inhalers becoming less effective. A thorough assessment of acute asthma should include peak flow, pulse, respirations, respiratory examination and pulse oximetry. Life-threatening features include a peak flow of 33% (or less) of normal, cyanosis, feeble respiratory effort, a silent chest on auscultation, bradycardia, hypotension, confusion or coma. If pulse oximetry shows saturation levels dropping below 92% or there is any evidence of a general deterioration in the patient's condition, arterial blood gases should be taken if possible as severe hypoxia ($O_2 < 8$ kPa, $CO_2 > 5$ kPa and a low pH) is likely (Cross 1997).

CHRONIC OBSTRUCTIVE PULMONARY DISEASE (COPD)

Chronic obstructive pulmonary disease (COPD) is characterized by airflow obstruction. The airflow obstruction is usually progressive, not fully reversible and does not change markedly over several months. The disease is predominantly caused by smoking (NICE 2004) and about 15–20% of smokers become COPD sufferers. There are other risk factors, e.g. family history and airway hyper-responsiveness, but it is not clearly predictable which smokers will develop the disease. Smoking cessation is the only effective intervention to slow the accelerated decline in lung function.

COPD involves a spectrum of disease processes including: chronic bronchitis, emphysema and long-standing asthma that is no longer fully reversible:

- Chronic bronchitis is a diagnosis based entirely on the patient's history; the production of sputum on most days for at least 3 months in at least 2 consecutive years.
- Emphysema is defined in structural and pathological terms describing the destructive process that goes on in the lungs, usually as a result of cigarette smoking. Snider et al (1985) define the condition as microscopic changes at the cellular level characterized by abnormal permanent enlargement of air spaces distal to terminal bronchioles with destruction of their walls and without obvious fibrosis.
- Chronic asthma is variable airway obstruction that is reversible spontaneously or with treatment.

COPD can incorporate features of any of the above but is a more objective diagnosis based on spirometric assessment. Spirometry measures airflow and lung volumes and with the correct equipment and training COPD diagnosis can be undertaken in primary care. Severity of COPD is based on the patient's forced expiratory volume in 1 second (FEV_1), which is the volume of air that can be exhaled in the first second of a forced expiratory manoeuvre. Unfortunately patients typically present when much lung volume is already lost, blaming their increasing respiratory symptoms on their increasing age and smoking. It is not unusual for a patient to be first diagnosed with an FEV_1 of less than 50% of predicted. A diagnosis of COPD should be considered in any patient who has symptoms of cough, sputum production or dyspnoea and/or a history of exposure to risk factors for the disease (GOLD COPD guidelines). The airflow obstruction in COPD is due to a combination of parenchymal damage. Mucociliary dysfunction and inflammation play important roles but the inflammation involves different cells to the inflammation in asthma.

COPD involves macrophages and basophils whereas the inflammation of asthma is mainly eosinophilic. The pathological changes in COPD include:

- Narrowing of the airways causing increased airflow resistance.
- Loss of elastin in the alveolar walls contributing to collapse of small airways.
- Hyperinflation causing flattening of the diaphragm and use of accessory muscles of respiration.
- Loss of alveolar/capillary interface causing disruption of gas exchange. The degree of blood gas disruption depends on the individual responsiveness of the respiratory drive.
- Cor pulmonale, which involves complex pathological changes leading to fluid retention and pulmonary hypertension caused by chronic hypoxia.

BRONCHIAL CARCINOMA

The strong association with tobacco smoking is well known, although factors such as exposure to asbestos dust, radiation and passive smoking are other important causes. The patient may present with a history of generally feeling tired, unwell and with loss of weight and appetite. More localized chest symptoms include chronic cough, shortness of breath and possibly haemoptysis. Complaints of chest pain indicate probable involvement of the pleura. The prognosis is poor.

INTERSTITIAL LUNG DISEASE

The term refers to a diverse range of diseases which affect the alveoli and septal interstitium of the lung and may progress to diffuse lung fibrosis. The effect is to reduce the lung's elasticity (Nowak & Handford 2004) and so increase the work of breathing whilst decreasing the effectiveness of ventilation. Patients often present with dyspnoea, dry cough and crackles on auscultation. Lung function tests usually show a restrictive defect. Impaired gas diffusion with reduced transfer factor are often found. Specific conditions include:

- cryptogenic fibrosing alveolitis
- connective tissue diseases such as rheumatoid disease
- extrinsic allergic alveolitis such as bird fancier's lung
- sarcoidosis.

OTHER CONDITIONS

Sudden onset of chest pain and respiratory distress may be due to a spontaneous pneumothorax or pulmonary embolism. Chest trauma should always be taken seriously as a pneumothorax (or haemopneumothorax if bleeding into the pleura has occurred) is potentially fatal, particularly if it is a tension pneumothorax. Fractured ribs are always painful and will interfere with good chest expansion and coughing, leading to the risk of bronchopneumonia. If ribs are fractured in two places, this segment of chest wall is known as a flail segment and, as it has become detached from the rest of the ribcage, will expand and contract out of step with the chest wall, giving rise to paradoxical respirations – the flail segment goes inwards on breathing in and outwards on expiration.

REVIEW OF COMMON RESPIRATORY SYMPTOMS

Dyspnoea can be caused by disease of the lung tissue, pleura or chest wall or may be due to extra-pulmonary conditions such as heart disease, particularly heart failure, shock, anaemia, hypermetabolic states, abdominal distension, obesity, anxiety and a low level of physical fitness. It is a sensation of breathlessness, often described by the patient as feeling short of breath. The current severity of the symptom can be gauged by asking the patient to rate the breathlessness on a scale of 1–10 during your examination, where 10 represents the worst it has been and 1 the easiest since the problem started. When assessing chronic dyspnoea it is helpful to use objective measurements such as the MRC dyspnoea scale (Fletcher 1960).

Paroxysmal nocturnal dyspnoea is a periodic attack of breathlessness that occurs at night or when lying down. This can occur in asthma and is usually triggered by a cough or wheezing episode.

Orthopnoea is discomfort in breathing, except when sitting or standing. It is often reported by people with left-sided heart failure and may also occur with asthma or COPD.

Coughing involves a forceful expulsion of air from lungs. The person may experience a single cough or episodes of repeated coughing. Everyone coughs from time to time during health to clear mucus from the pharynx or airways, but it is often a presenting symptom. It can be a voluntary or involuntary action, usually stimulated by secretions, irritation from a foreign body or inflammation.

Sensory nerve endings for the cough reflex are branches of the vagus in the larynx, trachea and bronchi. A cough may also be induced by stimulation in the external acoustic meatus, which is supplied by the auricular nerve (Arnold's nerve), a branch of the vagus. A foreign body or wax in the ear, hair touching the tympanic membrane or a subphrenic abscess (pus beneath the diaphragm) can stimulate a cough. A cough lasting more than 3 weeks is considered abnormal.

Chronic cough is often associated with smoking, asthma and chronic bronchitis. Other common causes are:

- COPD
- Postnasal drip due to chronic sinusitis, in which secretions flow from the postnasal area into the pharynx causing irritation and desire to cough
- Bronchiectasis; productive cough with copious amounts of purulent sputum
- Bronchial carcinoma
- Pulmonary tuberculosis
- Gastro-oesophageal reflux leading to aspiration at night
- Medication-related – angiotensin-converting enzyme inhibitors and beta-blockers produce a dry cough.

Sometimes a cough from an upper respiratory infection can persist for 6–8 weeks due to induced airway inflammation and increased sensitivity, often referred to as hyper-responsiveness. Less common causes of chronic cough are congestive heart failure, occupational inhalation of bronchial irritants and psychogenic factors.

Croup is a barking cough that occurs in infants and children. It usually begins at night after several days of a viral upper respiratory infection.

Haemoptysis is the term used for coughing up blood or blood-tinged sputum. Vigorous coughing may bring up a minimal amount of blood. Bright red, frothy blood is usually from the bronchial area and this may indicate bronchiectasis, carcinoma or TB. Frothy, pink sputum indicates pulmonary oedema whereas coughing up mostly blood with little mucus is usually associated with a pulmonary embolism. Haemoptysis is a serious symptom that should be investigated. The amount of blood, colour and whether mixed with sputum should be ascertained. It is important to find out if the blood is truly coming from the lung and not from the nose or pharynx.

OTHER ABNORMALITIES

A wheeze is a musical sound. Air is forced through narrowed airways which vibrate, producing a high-pitched sound as in asthma, or low-pitched sound as in bronchitis. A wheeze is most pronounced on expiration.

Stridor is a harsh, crowing sound caused by the turbulent flow of air through a narrowed upper airway. It is a musical sound of constant pitch which is most prominent on inspiration and can be heard at some distance from the patient. Stridor is usually produced in central airways and may be due to an obstruction, laryngeal spasm or oedema.

Chest pain related to the respiratory system usually arises from the pleura, chest wall or from the bronchial tree. Inflammation of the pleura (pleurisy) produces sharp, stabbing pain made worse by coughing, breathing or laughing. It usually makes the person try to stop and hold the breathing movement to avoid the pain. The parietal pleura has many sensory nerve fibres joining the intercostal nerve branches that also innervate the overlying skin. Pleural pain is caused by stretching the inflamed pleura or by separation of fibrous adhesions between the two pleural surfaces. The visceral pleura has no sensation. Rib fractures produce localized bony tenderness over the fracture site and pain is also produced by pressing on the same rib but away from the fracture. Costochondritis of the rib is common, starting with a dull pain which increases with respiratory motion. It is diagnosed by palpation and finding tenderness at the junction of the rib and cartilage.

Burning pain along the path of a dermatome on one side that does not cross the midline might suggest the beginning of herpes-zoster. Erythema on the skin is followed by clusters of tiny blisters which burst and scab over. The discomfort can vary from minimal to disabling pain and sometimes subside in a week, or may persist long after the skin has cleared, as in postherpetic neuralgia.

Diaphragmatic pain is sharp and may be localized along the costal margins, epigastric area and lumbar regions or radiate to the shoulder. The peripheral area of the diaphragm is supplied by the intercostal nerves but the central portion is served by the phrenic nerve that also supplies the neck. Mediastinal pain from organs behind the sternum is usually deep, poorly localized pain. Oesophagitis usually has a burning sensation and tumours or lymphadenopathy are associated with dull central pain.

When a patient complains of chest pain it is important to rule out angina. The diagnosis is made from the history.

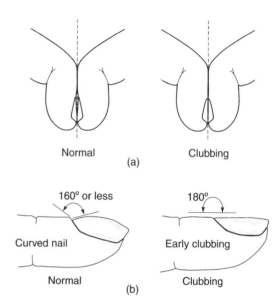

Figure 8.1 Clubbing.

REVIEW OF COMMON SIGNS OF RESPIRATORY DISEASE

Tachypnoea is rapid shallow breathing, usually greater than 18 breaths/min in an adult. Hyperventilation or overbreathing leads to an increase in air entering the alveoli, causing hypocapnia (arterial $PCO_2 < 5–6$ kPa).

Asymmetrical chest movement can be caused by scoliosis, chest wall injury or loss of lung volume on one side. Symmetrically reduced lung expansion can be a sign of emphysema or neuromuscular disease. Asymmetrical chest movement during inspiration can be a sign of airway obstruction on one side, pleural or pulmonary fibrosis, or splinting due to chest pain.

Cyanosis, a bluish discoloration of skin and mucous membranes, is caused by increased amounts of unsaturated haemoglobin in the blood. Central cyanosis occurs in respiratory failure; pulmonary oedema and congenital cardiac defects can best be seen in the tongue and mouth and are a late sign of serious respiratory failure with oxygen saturation

levels of around 80–85%. Peripheral cyanosis is more likely to be due to a circulatory problem.

Clubbing – bulbous swelling seen in the nail beds and fingertips – can indicate serious respiratory disease such as bronchial carcinoma, bronchiectasis, fibrosing alveolitis and empyema. It is also found with congenital heart defects, hepatic cirrhosis and inflammatory bowel diseases such as ulcerative colitis and Crohn's disease. It is said to exist when the anteroposterior thickness of the index finger at the base of the fingernail exceeds the thickness of the distal interphalangeal joint. There is also flattening of the angle between the nail plate and proximal skin fold. When healthy nails of the left and right hands are held together a diamond-shaped space appears between them, but in fingers with clubbing this disappears (Fig. 8.1). Patients rarely complain of clubbing so it is up to the nurse practitioner to observe this important sign and find out if this is a recent change in appearance.

TAKING A FOCUSED HISTORY

The main symptoms of concern in respiratory illness are cough, sputum production and changes in breathing pattern or sensations of feeling short of breath. Any report of chest pain must also be carefully checked to rule out a cardiac origin.

The PQRST approach to symptom analysis can be useful when exploring a patient's cough.

Enquire what brings the cough on and what relieves it (P). To help the patient describe the quality (Q) of the cough, ask if it is dry or whether it produces phlegm. The nature of the cough should also be checked (hacking, barking or bubbling) and whether it feels like it comes from a tickle in the back of the throat or deeper in the chest (R). Encourage the patient to rate the severity of the cough on a scale of 1–10 (S) and link this to the timing of the cough to check whether the severity varies with time of day (cough causing sleep disturbance is common in asthma but less so in COPD). You also need to check how long the symptom has been present (T).

If sputum is produced, a description should be obtained, including the quantity, consistency, colour (clear, white, creamy, yellow, green, brown) and presence of blood.

Breathlessness can also be checked using a PQRST approach. The key finding is how far the patient can walk without feeling out of breath, such as 10 paces on level ground or a flight of stairs. Ask whether the patient has noticed any hoarseness which might indicate laryngeal problems.

Previous medical history should check whether there has been any past respiratory disease, chest trauma or cardiac disease. Immunization status should be checked, specifically immunizations related to the respiratory system, e.g. BCG vaccination, pneumococcal and influenza vaccines. When asking about current health it is important to take a careful smoking history and also to note any allergies.

The current medication part of the history is particularly important as many drugs have pulmonary side effects. Angiotensin-converting enzyme (ACE) inhibitors can cause a dry cough. They are valuable in treating hypertension and heart failure; however, coughing occurs as a side-effect in 5–20% of patients – but this usually resolves when the drug is withdrawn. Beta-blockers can also stimulate a cough, which resolves when the medication is stopped. Aspirin, other non-steroidal anti-inflammatory drugs and beta-blockers can all trigger asthmatic episodes and should therefore only be used with great care by a person with asthma (BNF 2003). The respiratory-depressant effect of drugs such as alcohol and the opioids should always be borne in mind if called to deal with a collapsed, unresponsive individual where alcohol and drug abuse are suspected.

In the psychosocial history, occupation should be carefully checked. Ask about exposure to environmental hazards such as passive smoking, silica, asbestos or coal dust. Hobbies should be noted as pets such as pigeons, parrots and parakeets can spread disease to their owners, such as pigeon fancier's lung. Travel abroad to areas where there is a risk of exposure to specific respiratory pathogens should also be checked.

The family history should enquire whether there is any history of TB, allergic disorders or asthma. The review of systems should check overall health and for any general symptoms such as fevers, night sweats, fatigue or weight loss. You should ask about any nose and throat complaints, in particular sinus congestion, postnasal drip or allergic rhinitis, and any cardiac symptoms to rule out pulmonary problems linked to heart failure.

Table 8.2 summarizes how to take a focused history, incorporating the PQRST tool (see Chapter 2) for a typical patient with a respiratory complaint.

PHYSICAL EXAMINATION

The basic anatomical landmarks of the chest are shown in Figure 8.2. These will be useful in finding your way around and in documenting examination findings. You should familiarize yourself with the exact location of underlying structures such as the diaphragm and lungs in relation to the surface appearance of the chest.

A common mistake in examining the respiratory system is to rush in to listening to the breath sounds before systematically examining the person. It is important to have a good view of the chest and to take a moment to stand back and observe how the person holds himself or herself, the body shape and the movement of the chest wall on breathing.

Explain to the patient you are going to examine the chest and that it is necessary to remove clothing from the upper body. Offer a gown that can be slipped off easily at the appropriate time. The patient should sit comfortably on an examination table with the chest at your eye level so that you have a good view.

The order of examination for the chest is:

- inspection
- palpation
- percussion
- auscultation.

Always compare one side with the other, looking for symmetry. Each step in the examination builds

Table 8.2 Summary of focused history for respiratory system

1. *Identifying data*: Patient's name, etc.
2. *Chief complaint*: Cough going to my chest
3. *History of present illness*
   Cough: symptom analysis using PQRST tool:
   - Provocation/palliation: what brings the cough on? What relieves it?
   - Quality: patient's description, e.g. rattling. Is it productive? If so, what of?
   - Region: is it in the chest or does it feel more in the throat?
   - Severity: is it keeping you awake at night? Does it cause pain?
   - Time: how long have you had it? Is it worse at different times of the day?
   Type of sputum: colour, smell, consistency, blood?
   Shortness of breath: how far can you walk without getting out of breath?
   Hoarseness
   Pain: any associated chest pain
4. *History of previous illness*
   Hospitalizations/specialist consultations
   TB/pneumonia/chest infections
   Chest injuries/deformities
5. *Current health*
   Current medications
   Allergies
   Immunizations
6. *Psychosocial history*
   Smoking
   Recreational drugs
   Occupation
   Hobbies
   Travel
7. *Family history*
   TB, asthma, allergic disorder
8. *Review of systems*
   General
   ENT
   Cardiac

on the last to direct you towards any abnormality so that by the time you use the stethoscope you will have a good idea of the location of any problem.

Usually the posterior chest is examined while the patient is sitting. Ask the patient to fold his or her arms across the chest with hands touching opposite shoulders. This serves to separate the scapula so that you avoid trying to listen through bone. If the patient cannot sit, ask someone to hold him or her in a sitting position or roll the patient to one side and then the other. The anterior chest can be examined with the patient sitting but many recommend a lying position, especially for a female patient because it is easier to move the breast during the examination.

INSPECTION

Observe the general state, height and weight of the person. The speed at which the person undresses may help you gauge the degree of respiratory impairment. Note the rate, rhythm and effort of breathing. Normally the rate is around 14 breaths/min. Rapid shallow breathing may be a sign of pleuritic pain and prolonged expiration may show airflow obstruction. In health the chest wall should move smoothly and symmetrically. Inspiration involves the external intercostal muscles and diaphragm while expiration is passive and dependent on the elastic recoil of the lungs. Women use more intercostal breathing than men and infants.

Look for use of accessory muscles such as the sternocleidomastoids, scaleni and trapezii. This indicates increased effort in breathing. If the person is breathing using mainly intercostal muscles there may be something interfering with the diaphragm, e.g. abdominal distension, ascites or pregnancy. If he or she is breathing using more abdominal muscles, consider pleural pain, ankylosing spondylitis or intercostal paralysis. Retraction of interspaces during respiration can indicate rib fracture.

Check for breathlessness, audible wheezing, cough or sputum. If the patient coughs, note the frequency during examination and if it is productive or dry. Observe the colour and amount of sputum. It is useful to have a specimen container available to collect an expectorated sample.

Observe skin colour for pallor or cyanosis as seen in chronic bronchitis or emphysema. Look for any skin rashes, nodules or scars. Check for neck vein distension. An increase in jugular venous pressure may indicate heart failure secondary to lung disease (p. 103). In COPD there may be distension of veins on expiration and collapse of veins on inspiration. The expiratory distension is caused by positive pressure in the chest from the effort of breathing. Look for clubbing and/or nicotine stains on the fingertips.

Check the extremities for peripheral oedema, which may be linked with right ventricular failure.

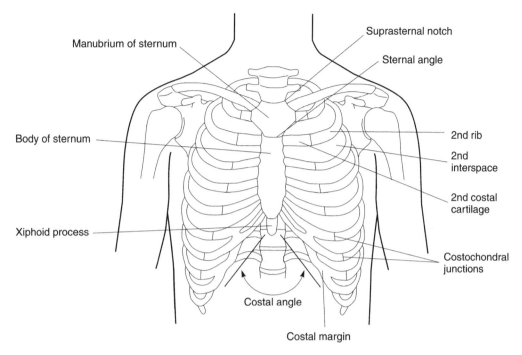

Figure 8.2 Anatomical landmarks of the chest.

Facial puffiness is seen in supraventricular obstruction, which often indicates bronchial carcinoma.

Identify anatomical reference points on the patient to help pinpoint the location of an abnormal finding and observe the shape of the chest, looking for any deformities such as pectus carcinatum (pigeon chest) or pectus excavatum (funnel chest). Assess the anterior-posterior diameter and compare to the lateral diameter. The normal ratio is 1:2. In emphysema this may increase to 1:1 and this is known as barrel chest.

PALPATION

You should always feel any areas of reported tenderness. Palpate the lymph nodes, particularly cervical, supraclavicular and axillary. With the patient's chin in the midline position and neck slightly flexed, check that the trachea is midline. Chest expansion can be checked by asking the patient to sit upright, then, from behind, placing your thumbs at the level of the 10th rib (posteriorly). The thumbs should be nearly touching with a loose fold of skin in between. Ask the patient to inhale deeply and observe the degree and symmetry of expansion. Tactile fremitus may also be assessed (Seidel et al 2003).

PERCUSSION

Percussion is the technique of tapping the body to produce sounds (Table 8.3) which indicate if the underlying structures are air-filled, fluid-filled or solid. A resonant note is produced over normal air-filled tissue. A large air-filled space such as a pneumothorax may produce a hyper-resonant note. Increased resonance is also found in emphysema. When lung tissue is fluid-filled or thickened it may have a dull percussion note. Percussion is usually carried out on the intercostal spaces; the exception is the clavicle where percussion may detect lesions in the upper lobes.

The technique involves placing the left hand over the region to be percussed and pressing firmly downwards with the second phalanx of the middle finger. This part of the left middle finger is then struck by the end of the right middle finger, rather like a hammer and anvil. The movement should come from the right wrist and not involve the arm. The exam should be conducted in an orderly

Table 8.3 Percussion notes and their significance

Note	Abnormal finding
Resonant	(Normal lung)
Hyper-resonant	Pneumothorax
Tympanitic	Hollow, air-filled space
	Large pneumothorax
Dull	Pulmonary consolidation
	(e.g. pneumonia) or collapse
Flat	Pleural effusion

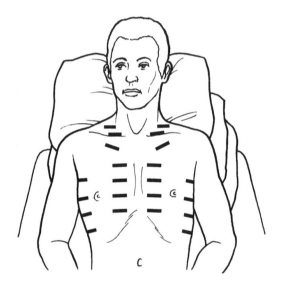

Figure 8.3 Anterior and lateral chest wall sites for percussion.

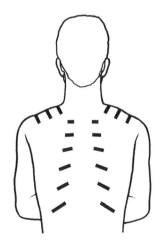

Figure 8.4 Posterior chest wall sites for percussion.

manner comparing left and right sides. In health there should be a symmetrical distribution of sounds. The areas to be compared are shown in Figures 8.3 and 8.4.

- Anterior chest wall:
  clavicle
  infraclavicular area
  second to sixth intercostal spaces
- Lateral chest wall:
  fourth to seventh intercostal spaces
- Posterior chest wall:
  trapezius
  above level of scapula
  every 4–5 cm from scapula to 11th rib.

AUSCULTATION

Stethoscopes

The modern stethoscope contains a diaphragm, a bell-shaped funnel, tubing, headset and ear tips. The open bell conducts sound well and is used to hear low-pitched sounds such as extra heart sounds or murmurs. The diaphragm screens out lower-pitched sounds and allows higher-pitched sounds to be heard more easily. The ear tips should closely fit the ear canal and incline towards the nose, matching the angle of the ear canal to block out outside noise.

Assessment of lung sounds

Breath sounds have frequencies which are hard for the human ear to hear. It is therefore important to listen to respiratory sounds in a quiet room with little external stimulation. It is helpful to listen with eyes closed to focus attention on the sound.

Breath sounds originate with the turbulent flow of air through the larynx during breathing. This causes vibration of the vocal cords and these sounds are transmitted to the chest wall via the trachea, bronchi and then normal lung tissue. It is the normal spongy structure of the lungs, due to the alveoli, that modifies these sounds until they have a rustling sound. These are the sounds normally heard with a stethoscope at the chest wall and they are described as vesicular breath sounds. The sound on inspiration lasts longer than expiration. Usually breath sounds are soft in the lower lobes and at the lung bases and they appear of shorter duration than in the upper airways.

If, however, the area of lung has lost the small air sacs that are normally present (alveoli) due to consolidation or fibrosis, and the main bronchus is still patent, this alters sound conduction so that the sounds detected are much more like the original sounds produced in the larynx. These are known as bronchial breath sounds and, apart from having a different quality to vesicular sounds, the sound on breathing out is of equal volume and duration as inspiration. Bronchial breath sounds can be heard by the manubrium in the normal person. It is important therefore to be able to distinguish between vesicular and bronchial breath sounds as the latter indicates significant lung pathology such as an area of consolidation associated with pneumonia.

Adventitious sounds

Two main categories of abnormal sounds can be heard in addition to the usual breath sounds: crackles (crepitations) and wheezes (Jarvis 2000). Crackles are intermittent, non-musical sounds such as the sound produced by rubbing hair next to your ear. If they are clearly heard on inspiration it is thought that this is due to the sudden reopening of collapsed airways that have become occluded during expiration. They may also be produced by air bubbling through secretions, as in pulmonary oedema. Crackles that clear with coughing are usually benign. Early inspiratory crackles may be heard with bronchitis.

Wheezes (rhonchi) are continuous musical sounds caused when air is forced through narrowed airways and usually heard on expiration. Spasm of the airway and mucosal oedema are the usual causes of narrowing and wheezes. If the sound is constant and low-pitched this may indicate a partial obstruction of a major bronchus by an inhaled foreign body or a tumour. Polyphonic wheezes (made up of several different notes) on expiration are heard in asthma, chronic obstructive airway disease and emphysema. There may be a relationship between the degree of bronchial obstruction and the presence of wheezes. There does not seem to be a relationship between the loudness or pitch of a wheeze and lung function.

A pleural rub is described as a leathery or creaking sound and is caused by movement of the visceral pleura over the parietal pleura when both surfaces have become roughened with a fibrinous exudate and are in contact. It is best heard at the end of inspiration and beginning of expiration and indicates pleurisy.

Transmitted voice sounds

When speaking, the sound of the patient's voice undergoes significant alteration as it passes through the lungs. Consequently, voice sounds heard with a stethoscope placed on the chest wall can give useful information on lung pathology. The following terms are commonly used.

Egophony describes change in sound caused by consolidation in the lung. This may be tested for by asking the patient to say 'ee'. In normal tissue the sound is a muffled 'ee', but when the stethoscope is located above abnormal tissue, such as in pneumonia, it sounds like 'ay'.

Whispered pectoriloquy: whispered sounds are not usually heard through a normal chest, but through consolidated tissue the high-pitched sounds are transmitted and the whispering can be heard loud and clear.

Bronchophony: normal speech is usually muffled as high-frequency sounds are screened out by healthy lung tissue. In an area of consolidation the sound becomes louder and clearer than normal. This may be tested for by asking the patient to say '99'

Using a stethoscope for auscultation

In examining the respiratory system the bell end will give the best results. Place the stethoscope on the chest wall in the same positions used in percussion (see Figs 8.3 and 8.4). Each position is matched symmetrically with the same location on the opposite side so that the examiner can compare sounds in both lungs. The examiner listens at each position for a complete breath (both inspiration and expiration) and evaluates the sounds produced by breathing and any additional abnormal sounds. If there are abnormal sounds the additional technique of using the patient's voice to transmit sound through the tissues is used. You should compare areas of normal with abnormal sound transmission to allow you to localize the problem area.

It is usually necessary to demonstrate how you want the patient to breathe and coach him or her through the examination. If breath sounds are faint, ask the person to breathe more deeply. Listen to a full breath in each location and pace the auscultation according to patient comfort, watching for hyperventilation. Concentrate on listening to inspiration, its length and any abnormal sounds, and then when you are clear about the sounds that go with inspiration, focus on expiration. Note the pitch, intensity

Table 8.4 Examination of the respiratory system

General	
Vital signs	Pulse, blood pressure, respiratory rate, temperature
Hands, fingers and nails	Clubbing
	Peripheral cyanosis
	Nicotine stains
Head and neck	Jugular venous pressure
	Horner's syndrome (carcinoma of the bronchus)
	Hoarseness
Lymph nodes	Cervical and axillary nodes
Chest	
Inspection	Scars, prominent veins
	Pattern of breathing
	Shape of chest
Palpation	Tracheal deviation
	Chest expansion
Percussion	Resonant, hyper-resonant
Auscultation	Breath sounds
	Adventitious sounds
	Vocal resonance

and duration of inspiratory and expiratory sounds. Sometimes chest hair can cause extra crackles. Wetting the hair may help reduce this sound. Also make sure that the stethoscope tubing does not touch anything else, such as clothing, or you may hear extra sounds. Never listen through clothing as breath sounds are difficult enough to hear without going through an extra layer.

Examination of the respiratory system may be summarized as shown in Table 8.4.

DIAGNOSTIC TESTS

Sputum

During physical examination of the chest the patient with a productive cough may produce a specimen of sputum. Always have a specimen pot available. Observe colour, consistency and odour. The ideal time to collect a sputum specimen is the first expectorated sputum on waking. Sputum can also be induced by inhalation of saline mist, which induces coughing.

Sputum samples can be sent for examination under the microscope after Gram stain, culture and sensitivity to identify bacteria and appropriate sen-

sitivity to antibiotics, staining for acid-fast bacilli (TB) or cytology (e.g. for *Pneumocystis carinii*).

Pulmonary function tests

Most tests depend on the patient's best effort so if the patient is too ill or unable to make a good attempt, the test results may not be valid.

Peak expiratory flow

A peak flow meter simply measures the rate at which a patient can forcefully exhale and has the advantage of being simple and portable so patients can use it to monitor symptoms at home. Serial peak flow measurements are useful to diagnose and monitor asthma control. They are especially useful to detect occupational asthma, noting if peak flows improve during times away from work. However, to diagnose occupational asthma they ideally should be recorded every 2 hours during the day. It must be recognized that peak flow is effort-related so measurement should be assessed in relation to the clinical picture.

Spirometry

Spirometry provides a more objective measure of lung function and where peak flow effort is questionable it may be preferable to diagnose asthma on FEV_1 reversibility using spirometry. Spirometry measures airflow and lung volumes:

- The forced vital capacity (FVC) is the total volume of air that can be exhaled with maximum force, starting from maximum inhalation and continuing to maximum exhalation.
- The forced expiratory volume in 1 second (FEV_1) is the amount of air that can be exhaled in the first second of forced blow from maximum inhalation.
- FVC and FEV are expressed in volume (litres) as a percentage of that predicted for age, height, gender and ethnicity. The ration of FEV_1 to FVC (FEV_1 /FVC ratio) is expressed as a percentage. Values of less than 70% indicate airflow obstruction.
- The volume/time trace must be smooth, upward and free of irregularities. The graph must reach a plateau demonstrating that the patient has blown to FVC.

Training in the use of the spirometer and interpreting the results (Table 8.5) is essential. Spirometers

Table 8.5 Values for FEV$_1$, FVC and FEV$_1$/FVC ratio

	Normal	Obstructive	Restrictive	Combined
FVC	> 80% predicted	> 80% predicted	< 80% predicted	< 80% predicted
FEV$_1$	> 80% predicted	< 80% predicted	< 80% predicted	< 80% predicted
FEV$_1$/FVC	> 70%	< 70%	> 70%	< 70%

Results must be interpreted in consideration of the clinical picture.

should produce a hard copy print out of the traces and results.

Pulse oximetry

A pulse oximeter measures oxygen saturation. It is a non-invasive technique that is quick and accurate at saturation levels above 70%. A plastic clip is attached to the patient's index finger (or earlobe). The top arm of the clip sends red and infrared light out to a photodetector in the other arm of the clip. The instrument measures the 'redness' of the transmitted light and is calibrated to convert this into a measure of oxygen saturation. It is important to remember that the relationship between saturation and partial pressure of oxygen is not linear. The clinical accuracy is reduced in conditions of anaemia, abnormal haemoglobin (e.g. carboxyhaemoglobin found in carbon monoxide poisoning), decreased flow in the vascular bed (in cases of hypovolaemic shock) or if the patient is wearing nail polish. A saturation level (SaO$_2$) of 95–97% is considered normal and reflects a partial pressure of oxygen in the arterial system of 10–14 kPa. A SaO$_2$ of 90–92% is abnormal and at this level the arterial partial pressure of oxygen is likely to be less than 8kPa, i.e. significant hypoxia.

MANAGEMENT OF COMMON CONDITIONS

THE COMMON COLD

Most people treat colds by themselves at home but it is important to recognize the symptoms, be familiar with the common non-prescription remedies and know how to advise those who seek help with their condition.

The best advice to prevent colds is to avoid others with a cold and wash hands frequently. High-dose vitamin C and zinc, although popular, have not been proven in clinical trials to prevent colds. Millions of pounds are spent on cold remedies which are often combination analgesics and decongestant, some at subtherapeutic levels. Decongestants may be helpful in relieving symptoms and also in preventing sinusitis or eustachian tube obstruction. Sympathomimetic agents are often used as decongestants. They work quickly to relieve nasal congestion and improve sinus drainage. They stimulate the alpha-receptors, causing vasoconstriction which reduces the formation of mucus but have the side-effect of increasing blood pressure. They are often used in the form of nasal sprays which are effective but should only be used in the short term due to the hazard of rebound congestion leading to an increase in use and dependence. Expectorants are of little value, although they are widely used. It is better to increase hydration by warm fluids while steam inhalations are also useful. Antihistamines are often in combination cold remedies but may only benefit because of their sedating effect. They may act as an irritant as they tend to dry mucous membranes.

The most important patient education is to explain that colds are viral infections that will not respond to antibiotics. Relief from symptoms seems to be brought about by resting, increasing fluids, particularly water, with steam inhalations and treating the discomforts of temperature, headache and muscle aches with aspirin or paracetamol.

ACUTE BRONCHITIS OR PNEUMONIA

It is best to refrain from treating acute bronchitis with antibiotics as it is usually self-limiting. The patient should be told to increase fluids and report if symptoms do not resolve.

Antibiotic therapy is essential for pneumonia but often has to be started before the causative organism can be identified from sputum samples. Local protocols may determine the drugs used but, whatever the choice, the antibiotic must be effective against *Streptococcus pneumoniae* as this is by far the most likely cause of the infection. Amoxicillin is the standard treatment with the addition of flucloxacillin if a *Staphylococcus* infection is suspected. Erythromycin should be used if the patient is allergic to penicillin. Cefuroxime combined with erythromycin is recommended for hospital-acquired infection (BNF 2003).

With early diagnosis and appropriate treatment, many patients can be managed at home. They should be encouraged to rest – not by lying in bed but sitting in an upright position which encourages maximal lung expansion. Deep breathing and coughing are important to clear secretions. Fluid intake should be increased. A humidifier in the room may help loosen secretions and soothe irritated airways. It is generally best not to suppress coughs but if the person is exhausted from coughing, codeine can be used to calm the cough. Aspirin or nonsteroidal anti-inflammatory agents may be useful to ease chest pain – taken with great caution if the patient has asthma, any history of peptic ulceration or is a child.

Patient education plays a key role in treatment. Rest should be encouraged and the importance of deep breathing and coughing to clear airways discussed. Patients should be taught to monitor their temperature at home. The importance of increasing fluid intake and stopping smoking should also be discussed.

Vaccination will prevent infection and should be considered for high-risk groups. The pneumoccocal vaccine contains purified polysaccharide from 23 of the commonest strains of *Streptococcus pneumoniae*. Antibody production after immunization depends on the immune function. After injection there is local erythema in 50% of patients and some tenderness. It is only recommended once in a lifetime for most people. However, repeat vaccination is recommended after 5–10 years in people who have had a splenectomy or who have nephrotic syndrome as their antibody levels decline more rapidly than other people.

Influenza vaccination may also be considered here. The influenza viruses A and B change every year, consequently the World Health Organization recommends each year which strains should be included in the vaccine. These are made ready to be given in the autumn, prior to the flu season from the end of November to mid-February. Only those at high risk are vaccinated, i.e. those with chronic conditions, those over 65 or residents of residential homes. It is not thought necessary to vaccinate staff unless they have a medical condition.

TUBERCULOSIS

Diagnosis is usually made by sputum examination for evidence of acid-fast bacillus on smear and the culture is positive for *Mycobacterium tuberculosis*. Most cases also show a positive reaction to TB skin tests (Mantoux or Heaf) and chest x-ray shows pulmonary infiltrates. People with active pulmonary TB are contagious but relatively few organisms are air-borne, so it is usually a household member or someone with close contact over a prolonged period who is at risk rather than a brief encounter.

Treatment is usually with a combination of three to four antibiotics for 6–9 months. The simplest regime is rifampicin, isoniazid and pyrazinamide for 2 months followed by rifampian and isoniazid for 4 months (Gleissberg 1997). After 2 weeks of treatment, patients are not considered to be an infection risk to others.

Skin tests are used to identify people who have been exposed to TB but who do not have active disease. The Heaf and Mantoux tests are placed subdermally and read in 72 hours. A grade 3–4 Heaf test and greater than 10 mm diameter wheal (not erythema) indicates exposure to TB. To prevent activation of TB, isoniazid is given for 6 months or isoniazid and rifampicin for 3 months.

Vaccination with BCG (bacille Calmette-Guérin) is recommended for all children aged 10–14 years in the UK to prevent TB. Also it is offered to high-risk neonates.

ASTHMA

In treating asthma the focus is firmly on prevention of acute attacks and managing the condition so that it has the minimum possible impact upon normal everyday life. It is particularly important to work with patients as partners in care as successful treatment depends on effective self-care by the patient. Patient education is important to ensure each understands and complies with the medication regime. Home peak flow monitoring and symptom awareness allow the patient to recognize any deterioration in asthma control and adjust the medication to prevent an acute attack.

Using inhalers takes some mastery and inadequate technique is often implicated in flare-ups of the disease. Spacer devices have been developed for those patients who find it difficult to coordinate breathing with hand movement (to press and activate the inhaler). The nurse practitioner must keep up-to-date in the rapidly changing field of inhaler device and spacer technology.

The importance of self-management is demonstrated by the fact that many people admitted to hospital with severe asthma have usually misjudged the severity of their asthma and made errors in their treatment. In a group of people admitted to hospital with severe asthma Kole et al (1998) found that there was a high frequency of psychological influences, especially anxiety and major socioeconomic disadvantage. These factors have powerful effects on learning about asthma and understanding behaviours necessary to manage asthma successfully. This is consistent with the work of Harrison (1998), who found in a review of the literature that those most likely not to follow a treatment plan were younger, depressed and worried about the side-effects of steroids or addiction to medications. Deprivation, life crises, family conflict, social isolation, substance abuse, unemployment, bereavement and emotional disturbance all place people with asthma at increased risk of premature death. It highlights the need for a full psychosocial assessment and patient-centred treatment – themes central to the nurse practitioner approach.

The British guidelines on the management of asthma (BTS/SIGN 2003) should be used – they provide an evidence-based approach to diagnosis and management. They also offer guidance on patient education and self-management, uncontrolled asthma, special situations such as pregnancy and occupational asthma and organization of care and audit.

The aims of pharmacological management are:

- control of daytime symptoms
- control of night-time symptoms
- control of exercise-induced symptoms
- prevention of exacerbations
- achievement of best possible pulmonary function
- minimal side effects.

Patients should be started at the pharmacological step appropriate to the severity of presentation. Inhaled corticosteroids are the mainstay of therapy with the addition of long-acting beta2 agonists or leukotriene receptor antagonists if symptoms are not controlled on low-dose inhaled steroids alone. Newer combination inhaled steroid and long-acting beta2 devices may help compliance if both these drugs are required. Figure 8.5 summarizes the main steps to take depending on the patient's condition, and care should be based on this protocol at all times.

The patient with an acute attack of asthma presents as a potentially life-threatening emergency. Every effort must be made to transfer the patient to an A&E department by ambulance as quickly as possible if his or her condition indicates while local care protocols are followed.

CHRONIC OBSTRUCTIVE PULMONARY DISEASE

The classic patient with COPD has a history of smoking, probably for more than 20 years. The main symptoms are breathlessness and productive cough with grey, white or yellow sputum. Most patients generally feel unwell and have difficulty with strenuous activity. They have frequent respiratory infections. Anorexia with weight loss may occur, or there may be weight gain due to oedema. The breathing pattern shows prolonged expiration with pursed-lip breathing and tachypnoea (rapid respiration). A barrel-shaped chest with increased resonance on percussion is common.

The most objective test for COPD is spirometry to measure forced expiratory volume and FEV_1/FVC ratio. Hypoxaemia occurs in advanced disease and would be shown by a low oxygen saturation. Arterial blood gas may be helpful in severe bronchitis when there is low PaO_2 but may show no abnormality in the early stages of COPD.

Sputum culture may reveal secondary infection with organisms such as *Streptococcus pneumoniae*, *Haemophilus influenzae* or *H. pneumoniae*, or *Moraxella catarrhalis*. Chest x-ray may show hyperinflation, barrel chest or a flat diaphragm. Sometimes enlarged air spaces (bullae) are seen with emphysema and blunting of the costophrenic angle on posterior-anterior view. A chest x-ray is also helpful in detecting complications such as heart failure, pneumonia or a pneumothorax.

The National Clinical Guidance of COPD (NICE 2004) offers an evidence-based approach to diagnosis and management of COPD and should be

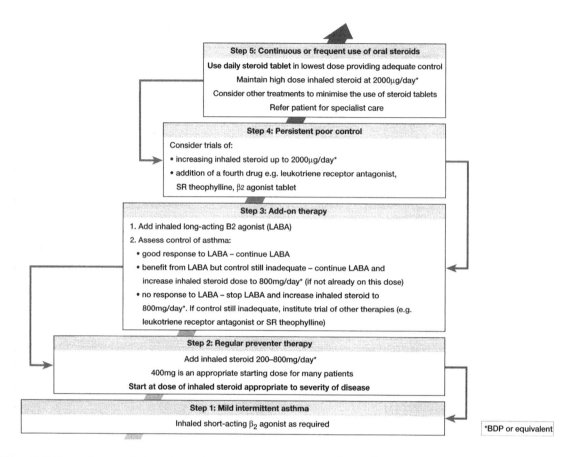

Step 5: Continuous or frequent use of oral steroids

Use daily steroid tablet in lowest dose providing adequate control

Maintain high dose inhaled steroid at 2000μg/day*

Consider other treatments to minimise the use of steroid tablets

Refer patient for specialist care

Step 4: Persistent poor control

Consider trials of:

• increasing inhaled steroid up to 2000μg/day*

• addition of a fourth drug e.g. leukotriene receptor antagonist,

SR theophylline, β2 agonist tablet

Step 3: Add-on therapy

1. Add inhaled long-acting B2 agonist (LABA)

2. Assess control of asthma:

• good response to LABA – continue LABA

• benefit from LABA but control still inadequate – continue LABA and

increase inhaled steroid dose to 800mg/day* (if not already on this dose)

• no response to LABA – stop LABA and increase inhaled steroid to

800mg/day*. If control still inadequate, institute trial of other therapies (e.g.

leukotriene receptor antagonist or SR theophylline)

Step 2: Regular preventer therapy

Add inhaled steroid 200–800mg/day*

400mg is an appropriate starting dose for many patients

Start at dose of inhaled steroid appropriate to severity of disease

Step 1: Mild intermittent asthma

Inhaled short-acting β2 agonist as required

*BDP or equivalent

Figure 8.5 The main steps for treating asthma. From: Thorax 2003 58(suppl.1):1–92. Copyright BMJ Publishing Group. Reproduced with permission.

referred to by nurse practitioners working in Britain.

Managing stable COPD:

• Smoking cessation advice to all COPD patients still smoking regardless of age or disease severity.

• Short-acting beta2 agonists and anticholinergics either as needed or regular use.

• Long-acting bronchodilators to control symptoms in patients who continue to experience symptoms despite the use of short-acting agents. Salmeterol and eformoterol are long-acting beta2 agonists and tiotropium is a once daily long-acting anticholinergic.

• Long-acting bronchodilators should also be considered in patients who have two or more exacerbations a year.

• Oral theophyllines may be considered only after a trial of short-acting and long-acting bronchodilators or in patients unable to use inhaled therapy.

• Inhaled corticosteroids should be prescribed for patients with an $FEV_1 \leq 50\%$ predicted who are having two or more exacerbations a year. The aim of treatment is to reduce exacerbation rates and slow the decline in health status and not to improve lung function per se.

• Maintenance use of oral steroids is not normally recommended but may be unavoidable in severe disease. All patients on oral steroids should be offered appropriate prophylaxis for osteoporosis.

• If patients remain symptomatic on monotherapy, their treatment should be intensified by combining therapies from different drug classes e.g. beta2 agonist with anticholinergic, long-acting beta2 with inhaled steroid.

- Pulmonary rehabilitation is a multidisciplinary programme of care involving both exercise and education. It should be made available to all appropriate patients with COPD. Programmes should be held in places easily accessible to patients.
- Pneumococcal vaccination and annual influenza vaccination should be offered to all patients with COPD.
- Long-term oxygen therapy (LTOT) is indicated in patients with PaO_2 less than 7.3 kPa when stable, or 7.3–8 kPa when stable and one of secondary polycythaemia, nocturnal hypoxaemia, peripheral oedema or pulmonary hypertension.
- Ambulatory oxygen should be prescribed for patients already on LTOT who want to continue with therapy outside home. Short-burst oxygen therapy should only be considered for episodes of severe breathlessness not relieved by other treatments.

Psychosocial support is an essential part of COPD management. As with any chronic illness, patients need to be involved in decision-making concerning their care, developing a personalized plan that addresses their problems. Involving the rest of the family is usually helpful. Although COPD is a chronic and progressive disease, patients can still have some choice and control over their illness.

Cigarette smoking is a major cause of disease in the UK and stopping smoking, even for elderly long-term smokers, is beneficial. In treating any respiratory complaint it is important to inform smokers of the hazards of smoking and suggest that they stop. Smoking is a complex habit which often starts in adolescence and is linked to peer pressure and parental influence. Once smoking becomes a habit it is difficult to change.

To promote health the nurse practitioner needs to develop expertise in strategies to help patients stop smoking. There are many techniques available and knowing how and when to use them is important. Often nurses become frustrated because they invest a lot of time in counselling, only to find that patients continue without any change in their habit. It is always important to ask patients if they would like to stop smoking as it is a waste of time attempting a smoking cessation programme with someone who has no intention of giving up the habit. There is evidence to suggest that only a brief intervention by a health professional can have a positive effect

(Black & Hawks 2004). The Agency for Health Care Policy and Research offers the following smoking cessation guidelines. It suggests:

- Everyone who smokes should be offered smoking cessation at every visit
- Clinicians should ask for and record the tobacco use status of every patient
- Cessation treatments – even as brief as 3 minutes – are effective
- More intense treatment is effective in producing long-term abstinence from tobacco
- Nicotine replacement therapy (patches or gum), clinician-delivered social support and skills training are particularly effective components of smoking cessation.

Change is complex and it may be years later that the person is ready and the message remembered. It is also important that relapse is an important phenomenon in any change of habit. Relapse should be viewed as part of learning to change and not as total failure for either patient or nurse. It is often 6–9 months after stopping that patients relapse because of life events or a stressful period, when old habits are associated with comfort and the familiar. It is helpful to warn patients of the possibility of relapse and develop strategies to avoid it. Also keep an open door so that if someone starts smoking again they can return quickly for guidance if desired. Most people who stop smoking are able to do so by themselves without outside help.

Summary

The broader approach used by nurse practitioners, taking into account psychosocial influences and patient preferences, contributes greatly to the successful management of many respiratory conditions. Health education plays a major part in the management of respiratory illnesses. Recent improvements in the management of asthma demonstrate what can be achieved when nurses and doctors work together with patients as equal partners. There remains a great deal to do in the promotion of respiratory health, especially given the worrying rise in the numbers of youngsters taking up smoking and the possible harmful effects of air pollution.

References

Black J, Hawks J 2004 Medical surgical nursing, 7th edn. Elsevier Saunders, St Louis

BNF 2003 British National Formulary 45. BMA/RPS, London

BTS/SIGN 2003 British Thoracic Society, Scottish Intercollegiate Guidelines Network. British guidelines on the management of asthma. Thorax 58:Supplement 1

Cross S 1997 The management of acute asthma. Professional Nurse 12(7):495–497

Custovic A, Green R, Taggart S C O et al 1996 Domestic allergens in public places II. Clinical and Experimental Allergy 26:1246–1252

Custovic A, Simpson A, Chapman M, Woodcock A 1998 Allergen avoidance in the treatment of asthma and atopic disorders. Thorax 53:63–72

Fletcher C M (Chairman) 1960 Standardisation questionnaire on respiratory symptoms: a statement prepared and approved by the MRC Committee on the aetiology of chronic bronchitis (MRD Dyspnoea Score). British Medical Journal 2:1665

Gleissberg G 1997 A shadow of the past: tuberculosis today. RCN nursing update 3, unit 067. Nursing Standard 11(1)

Global Initiative for Chronic Obstructive Lung Disease (GOLD Guidelines) www.goldcopd.com

Harrison B 1998 Psychosocial aspects of asthma in adults. Thorax 53:519–525

Haslett C, Chilvers E, Boon N, Colledge N 2003 Davidson's principles and practice of medicine, 19th edn. Churchill Livingstone, Edinburgh

Health Protection Agency 2004 Annual Report on Tuberculosis. Cases reported in 2001 in England, Wales and Northern Ireland. HPA, London

Jarvis C 2000 Physical examination and health assessment, 3rd edn. W B Saunders, Philadelphia

Kole J, Vamos M, Fergusson W, Eikind G 1998 Determinants of management errors in acute severe asthma. Thorax 53:14–20

LAIA 1999 Prevalence of asthma treated in general practice. Lung and Asthma Information Agency, London

NICE 2004 National Institute for Clinical Excellence. Management of chronic obstructive pulmonary disease in adults in primary and secondary care. February 2004. NICE, London

Nowak T, Handford G 2004 Pathophysiology; concepts and applications for health care professionals, 3rd edn. McGraw Hill, Boston

Phillips J, Murray P, Kirk P 2001 The biology of disease. Blackwell Science, Oxford

Russell G 2001 Epidemiology of asthma. www2.netdoctor.co.uk

Seidel H, Ball J, Dains J, Benedict G 2003 Mosby's guide to physical examination, 5th edn. Mosby, St Louis

Simpson A, Custovic A 2004 Exposure to domestic pets: effect on sensitisation and asthma. Airways Journal 2(1):39–42

Snider G L, Kleinerman J, Thurlbeck W M 1985 The definition of emphysema. Report of the National Heart and Blood Institute, Division of Lung Diseases Workshop. American Review of Respiratory Disease 132:182–185

Underwood J 2000 General and systematic pathology. Churchill Livingstone, Edinburgh

Chapter 9

Abdominal disorders

Mike Walsh

INTRODUCTION

The abdomen extends from the diaphragm to the pelvis. The major system associated with the abdomen is the gastrointestinal system and that is the focus of this chapter (including the liver, pancreas and gallbladder), together with the urinary system.

PATHOPHYSIOLOGY AND CLINICAL PRESENTATIONS

Patients may present with a variety of signs and symptoms which may lead you to carry out an abdominal examination. You may consider an examination of the abdomen, for example, in a patient who presents feeling tired all the time and has signs of jaundice or a person who complains of abnormal weight loss. The following clinical presentations are common complaints encountered in general practice or the hospital setting. The aim is to present these complaints in a logical order from mouth to anus and then consider other structures that lie outside the gastrointestinal tract.

DYSPHAGIA

Difficulty in swallowing may be a symptom of oesophageal disease or due to conditions which influence gut motility such as parkinsonism, multiple sclerosis and motor neurone disease. The most common causes of dysphagia include benign oesophageal stricture, carcinoma of the oesophagus, achalasia of the cardia and old age (presbyoesophagus).

GASTRO–OESOPHAGEAL REFLUX OR HEARTBURN

This is a common condition that can be encountered in any setting. The patient may complain of a variety of symptoms including a burning sensation or 'pain in the stomach' which may move up to the mouth. The pain is usually intermittent, occurs after meals, gets worse on lying down and is relieved by antacids; some people complain of an unpleasant taste in the mouth. The patient's discomfort results from gastric acid, pepsin and bile refluxing from the stomach into the oesophagus. These substances attack the oesophageal mucosa as this lacks the protective mechanisms of the stomach and duodenum. Coffee, tea, cocoa, chocolate, tomato products, citrus fruits and milk are all potent stimulators of acid secretion or add to the acidity of the stomach contents.

Additionally, fatty foods, alcohol and smoking cause relaxation of the gastro-oesophageal sphincter (Tortora & Grabowski 2002). A night out at the pub involving smoking and drinking followed by a mug of coffee and a late night supper consisting of fried food (including onions) just before going to bed is common practice for many people. It is hard to imagine a mix of activities better designed to induce heartburn! Increase in pressure in the abdominal cavity (e.g. from pregnancy or obesity) can also cause oesophageal reflux. Herniation of the stomach into the thoracic cavity is known as hiatus hernia and may be associated with reflux oesophagitis.

DYSPEPSIA AND INDIGESTION

The terms indigestion, heartburn and dyspepsia are often used interchangeably and there is clearly some confusion and overlap. The terms dyspepsia or indigestion refer to a sensation of fullness in the epigastrium which is frequently accompanied by belching, nausea or heartburn. The symptom is often caused by disorders of the upper gastrointestinal tract (GIT) such as peptic ulceration or gastritis. However, it can be associated with conditions affecting the pancreas or liver, renal failure, alcohol abuse or present as a side effect of a range of medications such as the non-steroidal anti-inflammatory drugs (NSAIDs) or corticosteroids.

One of the most common causes of dyspepsia is peptic ulceration. Peptic ulcers (PU) arise throughout the lower oesophagus, stomach and small intestine. According to Haslett et al (2003) some 10% of the adult population of western countries will be affected by PU, with the majority of cases occurring amongst males. For many years conventional wisdom had it that the acid environment of the stomach meant no bacteria could survive there. This has proved to be a mistaken belief and it is now known that the main causative factor is the *Helicobacter pylori* organism. This organism can penetrate the protective mucus layer of the stomach and live near the epithelium. It further defends itself against the highly acidic environment of the stomach by secreting an enzyme called urease which converts urea into ammonia and so raises the pH in the immediate vicinity of the organism.

H. pylori can initiate an inflammatory reaction on the stomach wall and interfere with the normal negative feedback mechanism which controls the function of those cells responsible for secreting the hormone gastrin – eventually leading to elevated levels of hydrochloric acid in the stomach. The combination of these two factors causes gastric ulceration. The mode of spread of *H. pylori* is unknown but worldwide the most likely explanation is either by oral–oral or the oral–fecal routes (CDC 2003).

Although less than 10% of the UK population aged under 40 are infected, this figure rises dramatically to 50% by age 50 (Bandolier 2004). However, only a small proportion of those infected develop PU disease – but 90% of duodenal ulcer (DU) and 70% of gastric ulcer (GU) patients test positive for *H. pylori*. It is thought that the other 30% of gastric ulcers are caused by NSAIDs (Haslett et al 2003). Why only a small proportion of those infected develop GU disease remains unclear. The link with DU is also very convincing, though the direct causative mechanism remains to be identified. Bandolier (2004) also notes that there is a strong link between *H. pylori* infection and an increased risk of gastric cancer. International studies cited by Bandolier indicate that if a population is 100% infected this increases the risk of gastric cancer to six times that of a population with zero infection. Gastric cancer accounts for 10% of all UK deaths from malignant disease.

NAUSEA, VOMITING AND HAEMATEMESIS

Nausea and vomiting result from a complex process involving the vomiting centre in the brain. The vomiting centre receives input from the gastrointestinal tract, the vestibular apparatus, the chemoreceptor trigger zone in the medulla oblongata and the cortex of the brain. The ingestion of toxins leads to stimulation of the vomiting centre which communicates with the gastrointestinal tract via the vagus nerve; the vestibular apparatus

responds to motion; the chemoreceptor trigger zone responds to toxins in the blood and inputs from the cortex result from disagreeable sights and sounds. Whatever the source, when the vomiting centre receives stimuli which exceed a certain threshold, nausea, retching and vomiting follow.

The characteristics of the vomit are important factors in assessment of the patient. Of particular importance is the presence of blood in the vomit (haematemesis). Vomiting blood indicates bleeding from the stomach, duodenum or oesophagus. The blood may be bright red or dark brown depending on the amount of time it has been in contact with gastric acid. Causes of gastrointestinal bleeding include gastric cancer, duodenal ulcer, gastritis, oesophagitis or oesophageal ulcer, duodenitis, varices, tumours or Mallory-Weiss tear (a tear which occurs at the gastro-oesophageal junction). In infants and small children, vomiting that is forceful (projectile) or bile-stained indicates intestinal obstruction and indicates the need for an immediate surgical referral (Barnes 2003).

ABDOMINAL PAIN

There are many causes of abdominal pain. The history-taking process and physical examination are essential in differentiating between a number of potentially life-threatening diagnoses. It is helpful to understand the difference between visceral, parietal and referred pain. The peritoneum is a serous membrane system in the abdominal cavity – the parietal layer lines the inner walls of the cavity

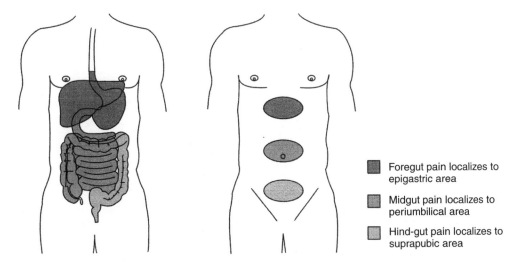

Figure 9.1 The location of visceral pain on the abdominal surface (adapted from Epstein et al 2003, with permission).

and the visceral layer is adherent to the surfaces of the organs. Visceral pain is pain caused by stretching or inflammation of a hollow organ and it is often associated with visceral symptoms such as anorexia, sweating, nausea and pallor. This pain is often described as a dull ache and tends to occur near the midline. Movement does not aggravate visceral pain so the patient may writhe or double up in response to it. The parietal layer of the peritoneum is innervated with pain-sensitive fibres and therefore the sensation is well localized; movement or stretching aggravates the discomfort. Patients describe parietal pain as sharp or stabbing and find palpation extremely painful; the pain is exacerbated when the palpating hand is released (rebound tenderness). Figure 9.1 outlines the location of visceral pain on the abdominal surface related to the structure within the abdominal cavity.

Epstein et al (2003) state that appendicitis is an excellent example of the difference between visceral and parietal pain. Acute appendicitis starts with a dull ache around the periumbilical area and the patient often complains of nausea. As the appendicitis develops, the inflammation advances through the visceral layer to the parietal peritoneum. The pain then shifts to the right lower quadrant, typically at a place which is named McBurney's point (the mid-point between the symphysis pubis and the right iliac crest) and the character of the pain changes from dull to sharp. Palpation becomes extremely painful and the patient displays reflex guarding with contracted abdominal muscles and rebound tenderness.

Inflammation in the abdominal organs can result in referred pain to other parts of the body. For example, inflammation in the gallbladder may be experienced as pain over the scapula and diaphragmatic pain may be felt as pain in the shoulder. Table 9.1 is adapted from Seidel et al (2003) and outlines the potential differential diagnoses of abdominal pain according to location on the abdomen.

It is worthwhile entertaining a number of potential differential diagnoses for patients who present with abdominal pain. The locations shown in Table 9.1 provide a general guide for your problem-solving process; however, unusual presentations occur and are particularly common in the elderly. As the incidence of cancer increases with age so does the possibility that the cause of abdominal pain may be malignant disease.

At the other end of the age spectrum, periumbilical pain in children can indicate conditions such

Table 9.1 Location of abdominal pain*

Diffuse pain
Peritonitis, pancreatitis, leukaemia, sickle cell crisis, early appendicitis, mesenteric adenitis, mesenteric thrombosis, gastroenteritis, aneurysm, colitis, intestinal obstruction, metabolic, toxic and bacterial causes

Right upper quadrant	Left upper quadrant
Cholecystitis	Gastritis, gastric ulcer
Hepatitis	Pancreatitis
Hepatic abscess	Splenic enlargement, rupture, infarction, aneurysm
Hepatomegaly	Renal pain
Peptic ulcer	Herpes-zoster
Pancreatitis	Myocardial ischaemia
Renal pain	Pneumonia
Herpes-zoster	Aortic aneurysm
Myocardial ischaemia	
Pericarditis	
Pneumonia	

Periumbilical
Intestinal obstruction
Acute pancreatitis
Early appendicitis
Mesenteric thrombosis
Aortic aneurysm
Diverticulitis

Right lower quadrant	Left lower quadrant
Diverticulitis	Diverticulitis
Intestinal obstruction	Intestinal obstruction
Appendicitis	Appendicitis
Leaking aneurysm	Leaking aneurysm
Ectopic pregnancy	Ectopic pregnancy
Ovarian cyst or torsion	Ovarian cyst or torsion
Salpingitis	Salpingitis
Endometriosis	Endometriosis
Ureteral calculi	Ureteral calculi
Renal pain	Renal pain
Seminal vesiculitis	Seminal vesiculitis
Regional enteritis	Strangulated hernia
Cholecystitis	Ulcerative colitis
Perforated ulcer	
Strangulated hernia	

*Adapted from Seidel et al (2003).

as lactose intolerance, gastroenteritis or diabetic ketoacidosis. Generalized abdominal pain may be psychogenic in origin indicating significant psychological and social problems are present. The possibility of an ectopic pregnancy or pelvic inflammatory disease secondary to a sexually transmitted infection should also be considered in girls who have achieved menarche, as well as adult women (Engel 2002). Another common presentation in children is known as acute non-specific abdominal pain (ANSAP) in which the child may be admitted for 24 hours observation but no significant pathology is found – ANSAP is therefore a diagnosis of exclusion. There is often a history of an upper respiratory tract infection in the preceding week (Barnes 2003). Urinary tract infections may also present as abdominal pain in children.

WIND

Flatulence (excessive belching) and flatus (the passage of wind through the anus) can cause considerable distress and patients often feel helpless and unsure about managing their symptoms. It is always worth exploring dietary causes for flatus, such as the excessive consumption of legumes or recent changes in dietary habits. Flatulence is usually caused by swallowing air during eating (aerophagy) and often occurs in patients who have a hiatus hernia, peptic ulcer or chronic gallbladder disease.

CHANGES IN BOWEL HABIT

Changes in bowel habits can take several forms – the patient may experience constipation, diarrhoea or a change in the type of stool being produced. A change in bowel habit can be a subtle first sign of serious disease and therefore it is essential to explore this area in detail with the patient.

Constipation

Constipation can be caused by organic disease such as hypothyroidism, strictures in the colon or electrolyte imbalance. A motility disorder or physical immobility can cause constipation and a variety of drugs such as the opiates and antidepressants have the same effect in reducing the motility of the gastrointestinal tract. A low-residue diet will also slow peristalsis. Depression or dementia can cause constipation. The fear of pain associated with passing stools when a patient has haemorrhoids is a further cause.

Diarrhoea

Diarrhoea means increased faecal fluidity. It is caused by increased fluid volume in the colon which pro-

duces distension and activates the defecation reflex. Three processes result in fluid gathering in the intestine – secretion, osmosis and impaired water absorption. Secretion of water into the lumen of the intestine is a response to irritation which may be caused by bacterial toxins. Intestinal secretion can also be caused by certain gastrointestinal tumours, laxatives or unabsorbed fatty acids. Problems with digestion can result in an increase in the osmotic pressure in the intestinal lumen. This is caused by several mechanisms, including lack of bile or enzymes necessary to break the food macromolecules into smaller subunits, a diet that has a high indigestible content such as legumes or carbohydrates, or bacterial growth within the lumen. The osmotic pressure rises and water is drawn into the lumen from the intestinal wall, resulting in an increase in the fluidity of the stool. The small intestine and colon absorb approximately 8600 ml/day and therefore any condition that impairs the absorption of this fluid will result in diarrhoea. Coeliac disease and Crohn's disease are examples of malabsorption conditions that impair absorption of water in the intestine, resulting in increased frequency and fluidity of the stool.

Alcohol and certain medications such as antibiotics can also produce diarrhoea by interfering with fluid absorption or promoting fluid secretion due to irritation of the intestine. Whatever the cause of the diarrhoea, the consequences can be severe, particularly in elderly or very young patients. Increased fluid loss may result in dehydration and acidosis as alkaline bicarbonate ions are expelled from the system.

An acute onset of diarrhoea in a previously healthy individual with no signs of other organ involvement is most likely to be food poisoning. A recent history of eating out or living closely with other people – as in an old people's home, for example – increases this possibility (Epstein et al 2003). Differential diagnoses for diarrhoea can be divided into acute and chronic. In a patient who presents with acute diarrhoea, consider a viral or bacterial cause, toxin-mediated (such as *Clostridium* or *Staphylococcus*), use of laxatives, antibiotics or other drugs or dysentery syndrome. Also consider rotavirus, *Salmonella* and *Shigella* – all of which occur more commonly in children than in adults. Chronic diarrhoea can be caused by irritable bowel syndrome, diabetes, giardiasis, inflammatory bowel disease (Crohn's or ulcerative colitis, for example) or lactase deficiency in infants or adults of African or Mediterranean descent.

Rectal bleeding

Polyps, diverticular disease, inflammatory bowel disease, carcinoma, haemorrhoids, anorectal lesions and ischaemia of the intestine can all produce rectal bleeding. The patient's description of the blood loss will help you gain some idea of the origin of the bleeding – although a diagnosis should be made with caution as bleeding from benign haemorrhoids can mask the signs of bleeding from a more serious disease which originates further up the intestinal tract. Sixty per cent of rectal bleeding is caused by haemorrhoids, however, as the patient's age increases your level of concern relating to the possibility of malignancy should also increase.

Rectal bleeding can present as bright red, plum or maroon, black and sticky or microscopic (occult) blood. Bright red blood loss tends to originate from the anus or rectum and plum or maroon coloured from the colon. Blood loss which presents as black and sticky originates from higher up the gastrointestinal tract, for example the stomach or oesophagus. Blood which has been denatured by gastric acid and enzymes develops a characteristic smell and the consistency of tar, which is known as melaena. Chronic gastrointestinal blood loss is a possible cause of iron-deficiency anaemia.

DIVERTICULAR DISEASE

Diverticula are pouch-like sacs which occur in the intestinal mucous membrane and bulge out through the wall of the large intestine. It is widely thought that low-residue diets have a part to play in their formation. The dry small stools that result from low-residue diets require greater colonic contraction to force them along the colon. This raises pressures in the wall of the colon and promotes formation of diverticula at areas of weakness in the walls. The presence of diverticula is described as diverticulosis. In many cases this condition is asymptomatic; however in a few people it can cause mild to severe bleeding into the lumen of the colon or may result in cramping pain and constipation. Irritation and bacterial damage may produce inflammation in the diverticula known as diverticulitis. This results in left lower abdominal pain, fever, diarrhoea or constipation and can cause a great deal of discomfort.

OBESITY

No discussion of the GIT can be complete without reference to the current epidemic of obesity which is causing serious health problems in advanced industrialized countries such as the UK. The commonest way of defining obesity is through body mass index (BMI) measurement:

$$BMI = (\text{weight in kg}) / (\text{height in metres})^2$$

Mortality and co-morbidity show an increase with a BMI over 25 and become very pronounced over 30 (WHO1998). As a result, overweight is defined as a BMI in the range 25–29.9, obese 30–39.9 and extremely obese is a BMI of 40 or more. The BMI statistic needs to be adjusted for age in children and also may be an unreliable guide to obesity in adults who have developed extensive muscle mass, such as professional sportsmen.

It is therefore very worrying to note that the House of Commons Select Committee Report (2004) finds 75% of the adult population of the UK are overweight or obese while 22% are officially classed as obese. Childhood obesity has trebled since 1974 and England has the fastest-growing obesity rate in Europe. The Report goes on to estimate the annual cost of obesity to the nation as £7.4 billion (and rising) and comments that this will be the first generation in which children die before their parents as a result of obesity.

It is not difficult to find the major causes of this major public health problem; declining levels of physical activity and increasing consumption of energy-dense food. Parsons (2002) identifies particular risk groups as being those from socially deprived backgrounds and those from south Asian or Afro-Caribbean ethnic populations. Smokers who quit will put on weight as smoking has an appetite depressant effect, while quitting smoking seems to reduce activity. The result is an average weight gain of 2.8kg in males and 3.8kg in females. However, a person would have to gain 11kg to cancel out the beneficial effects of quitting smoking 20 per day (Haslett et al 2003). Children with at least one obese parent are more likely to become obese and grow into obese adults. Prevention of adult obesity begins therefore in childhood.

LIVER DISEASE AND BILIARY OBSTRUCTION

The liver can be damaged in two ways – damage to the liver cells (hepatocellular disease) or biliary tree obstruction (intrahepatic or extrahepatic cholestasis). When hepatocytes are damaged, enzymes leak into the blood, where they can be detected in the plasma. In cirrhosis there is extensive damage to the liver which results in obstruction of the blood flow and one of the consequences is portal hypertension. The early symptoms of liver damage include malaise, fatigue, anorexia and nausea. The signs include darkening of the urine, lightening of stool colour (due to the lack of conjugated bilirubin entering the bowel in bile) and the gradual development of jaundice.

Brain function is depressed in patients who have severe liver damage due to the reduced ability of the liver to detoxify potentially neurotoxic products from the gut. In the case of a person who has developed portal hypertension, the blood bypasses the liver and the brain becomes exposed to toxic substances, resulting in changes in sleep patterns and, in some cases, personality changes. As the damage to the liver progresses, the patient may develop hepatic encephalopathy. A further complication of liver disease is ascites. This is an accumulation of fluid in the abdominal cavity and resulting from high portal pressure and low serum albumin levels, causing noticeable weight gain and increasing girth.

When sufficient hepatocyte damage occurs, glycogen storage and glucose secretion become impaired and bilirubin excretion fails, resulting in jaundice as the bile pigment accumulates in the tissues. Epstein et al (2003) divide the causes of jaundice into prehepatic, hepatocellular, intrahepatic cholestasis and extrahepatic cholestasis. Prehepatic relates usually to haemolytic anaemia. Hepatocellular disease includes viral hepatitis (A–E), alcoholic hepatitis, autoimmune hepatitis, drug hepatitis and decompensated cirrhosis. Intrahepatic cholestasis disorders include drugs, primary biliary cirrhosis and primary sclerosing cholangitis. Extrahepatic cholestasis includes bile duct stricture, common duct stone and cancer of the head of the pancreas.

PANCREATIC DISEASE

Pancreatitis is an autodigestive process whereby inflammation and damage occurs to the exocrine tissue of the pancreas. Pancreatic enzymes which are normally activated in the small intestine to digest protein become activated within the pancreas itself due to obstruction of pancreatic juice outflow. The main causes are obstruction by gallstones or heavy alcohol intake. Alcohol is thought to cause protein precipitates to form within the pancreatic ductules which act to obstruct outflow. In either case the enzymes then become activated within the pancreas and attack the pancreatic tissue. This may lead to a severe acute episode or repeated less severe episodes leading to chronic pancreatitis (Hughes 2004).

Patients who have undergone an ERCP procedure are another major risk group for acute pancreatitis. Acute pancreatitis commonly presents with severe epigastric or left upper quadrant pain which may radiate to the back. Intense attacks are associated with pancreatic necrosis, and vascular shock, renal failure and adult respiratory distress syndrome may threaten the patient's life. Successive episodes result in the formation of scar tissue in the pancreas and diabetes mellitus can occur as the islets of Langerhans are destroyed. People most at risk of chronic pancreatitis are those who have severe persistent cholelithiasis and those who continue to indulge in alcohol after an initial alcohol-related attack.

KIDNEY AND BLADDER DISEASE

A variety of diseases occur in the kidneys, ureters and bladder. The result of any disease process in these organs is usually a change in the frequency and volume of urination and pain or discomfort for the patient. Epstein et al (2003) list the variety of symptoms which can be found in the renal system and their possible causes (Table 9.2).

Disorders of the renal system can be divided into prerenal, postrenal and renal disease. Prerenal disease is caused by renal ischaemia resulting in inadequate glomerular filtration; postrenal disease is caused by urinary obstruction, creating back-pressure in the kidney and a destruction of kidney tissue. Renal disease results from changes within the kidney itself – an example of this is glomerular nephritis. Acute renal failure is of sudden onset, most commonly associated with shock, whilst chronic renal failure has an insidious onset with increased volumes of dilute urine being formed in the early stages before urine output declines as the disease process develops. There are many disorders of the renal system and you are advised to consult a specialist text on the subject if you need greater detail.

Table 9.2 Renal symptoms and signs and their causes*

Symptoms and signs	Causes
Frequency	Irritable bladder (infection, inflammation, chemical irritation)
	Reduced compliance (fibrosis or tumour)
	Bladder outlet obstruction (prostatism, detrusor muscle failure)
Polyuria	Chronic renal failure
	Diabetes mellitus
	Diabetes insipidus
	Diuretic treatments
Dysuria	Bacterial infection of the bladder
	Inflammation of the urethra
	Infection or inflammation of the prostate
Incontinence	Sphincter damage or weakness after childbirth
	Sphincter weakness in old age
	Prostate cancer
	Benign prostatic hypertrophy
	Spinal cord disease, paraplegia
Oliguria or anuria	Hypovolaemia
	Acute renal failure (acute glomerulonephritis)
	Bilateral ureteric obstruction
	Detrusor muscle failure
Haematuria	*Painful*
	Kidney stones
	Urinary tract infection
	Papillary necrosis
	Painless
	Infection
	Cancer of the urinary tract
	Acute glomerulonephritis
	Contamination during menstruation

*Adapted from Seller (1993) and Epstein et al (1997).

OTHERS

The male and female reproductive systems are found within the abdominal cavity. An assessment of the abdomen would not be complete without considering the prostate, the male genitalia (including the inguinal region), the uterus, fallopian tubes, ovaries and the female genitalia. Each of these systems is dealt with in Chapters 10 and 11.

Abdominal problems commonly present as non-specific symptoms and it is important that you consider possibilities outside the obvious GIT system, such as the renal or reproductive systems, as the possible source of the patient's problem. When the patient first presents, it is likely that you will have several differential diagnoses to consider. A thorough history-taking process will enhance the potential accuracy of your diagnosis and will help to narrow your differential diagnoses and guide your physical examination. The following is a guide to specific questions which might be useful when a patient presents to you with identifiable complaints. The history-taking process outlined in Chapter 2 is useful as a general guide to your approach.

DYSPHAGIA

Dysphagia caused by oesophageal carcinoma usually progresses quickly over 6–10 weeks (as opposed to that caused by a benign stricture) and is worse for solids than liquid. Less common causes include diseases of the swallowing centre in the brain (e.g. pseudobulbar palsy) or damage to the vagus nerve (e.g. bulbar palsy caused by myasthenia gravis) (Epstein et al 2003). It is therefore worthwhile asking questions which focus on the duration, precipitating factors and associated factors such as pain, cough or weight loss in patients who present with dysphagia. Other questions might include:

- At what level does the food stick?
- Has the symptom been intermittent or progressive?
- Are both food and drink equally difficult to swallow?
- Is there a history of reflux symptoms?

HEARTBURN

The pain of heartburn is described as burning or scalding and may radiate to the throat. The patient's description may be accompanied by a gesture with the hand, showing the upward movement of the retrosternal pain. An acid or bitter taste may develop in the mouth, resulting in reflex salivation, known as water brash. The PQRST tool will greatly assist analysis of heartburn as a symptom. It is also useful to ask the patient to describe his or her

Table 9.3 Differentiating between the pain of reflux dyspepsia and myocardial ischaemia*

	Position	Character	Associated features	Aggravating factors	Relieving factors
Reflux	Radiates towards the chest from the epigastrium	Burning, scalding	Water brash	Bending, lying down, eating	Antacids
Myocardial ischaemia	Radiates across the chest into the jaw and down to the left arm	Gripping, vice-like pressure	Nausea, shortness of breath	Exercise	Ceasing exercise, nitrates

*Adapted from Epstein et al (1997).

bowel pattern and whether it has changed recently. A description of black tarry stools might lead you to consider an upper gastrointestinal bleed or a malignancy of some kind.

A major concern of most nurse practitioners is the differentiation between heartburn and myocardial infarction. Epstein et al (2003) provide an overview of the distinguishing features of reflux and myocardial ischaemic pain (Table 9.3).

WEIGHT LOSS AND ANOREXIA

Weight loss and anorexia are both non-specific symptoms that may accompany acute or chronic conditions. Enquire about appetite, eating habits, average daily diet and any discomfort caused by eating or swallowing (odynophagia). Weight loss may be caused by a metabolic disorder such as thyrotoxicosis or diabetes mellitus or it may indicate other serious disorders such as malignancy. Some useful questions to ask when a patient presents with weight loss include the following (Epstein et al 2003):

- Is your appetite increased or decreased?
- Over what time span has the weight been lost?
- Do you enjoy your meals?
- Describe your average daily intake
- Do you experience nausea, abdominal discomfort or pain?
- Describe your bowel motions
- Have you experienced a fever?
- Do you pass excessive volumes of urine?
- Have you noticed a change in how you tolerate the weather?

DYSPEPSIA AND INDIGESTION

Ask the patient if the discomfort is associated with belching, nausea, vomiting, haematemesis, change in bowel habits or interruption in sleep. The timing of the dyspepsia is particularly useful in determining its association with food and fluid intake. It is useful to enquire if the patient has been diagnosed with *H. pylori* in a previous episode of dyspepsia as the course of treatment will change if the patient has received eradication therapy (see p. 156).

NAUSEA, VOMITING AND HAEMATEMESIS

There are a variety of causes of nausea, vomiting and haematemesis and the history-taking process will help you differentiate between those causes. Some key questions include:

- Is the vomiting worse in the morning?
- Does it occur in relation to meals?
- Is there associated abdominal pain?
- Is the vomit blood- or bile-stained?
- Is there recognizable food or coffee grounds in the vomit?
- What drugs are being taken?

The patient's responses to these questions will provide clues for diagnosis. For example, a woman complaining of nausea in the mornings could possibly be experiencing hyperemesis. If there is knowledge or evidence of liver disease, it is worth considering oesophageal varices in the case of a person who has complained of haematemesis. Weight loss associated with haematemesis suggests gastric cancer. Digoxin, morphine, NSAIDs and anticancer drugs are just some of the medications that cause nausea and vomiting as side effects. The history must always therefore include asking about medication, both over the counter and prescription.

ABDOMINAL PAIN

An assessment of abdominal pain should include the usual structured history-taking process associated with all forms of pain (PQRST), as described in Chapter 2. In particular it is worth exploring with the patient how long s/he has been experiencing pain, whether it is constant or intermittent and what relieves or aggravates the discomfort. If you consider the pathophysiology associated with visceral and parietal pain it is worth asking the patient to describe the type of pain and whether movement aggravates or relieves the pain. Associated symptoms such as vomiting, nausea, sweating and weight loss may provide a clue that the pain is visceral in nature.

It is also worthwhile including in the history-taking process an exploration of the patient's bowel habits and if there have been any recent changes. The exact location of the pain will help you determine if the patient is experiencing the diffuse discomfort of visceral pain or the specific discomfort associated with parietal pain. Always ask whether there is any sensation of pain elsewhere in the body, as referred pain to the shoulders or scapula could indicate problems within the abdominal cavity.

As with all history-taking, it is important to ask about medication, not only what the patient is currently taking but also what s/he has taken in the past. A history of NSAIDs, for example, might provide a clue to potential damage to the stomach and duodenum.

CHANGES IN BOWEL HABITS

Always begin by asking what the patient's normal bowel habit is.

Constipation

There is a great deal of individual variation in the frequency with which people defecate, therefore it is difficult to have a precise definition of constipation (Springhouse 2000). Straining to defecate is, however, abnormal and if only small amounts of

hard stool are passed, this may be considered as constipation (Epstein et al 2003).

If the history suggests constipation, you should also ask the patient if there is any associated nausea, abdominal pain, distension, nausea or vomiting. Ask about use of medication and particularly whether the patient has used constipating drugs such as opiates or codeine.

Diarrhoea

Important points in the history of a person who complains of diarrhoea include the duration of the problem and the number of motions per day. Ask the patient to describe the stools, including signs such as the presence of blood or mucus, colour and consistency of the stools, fatty streaking or greasiness and any aroma. Ask whether the patient is taking any medication, if s/he is awoken from sleep with the diarrhoea and if there is any recent history of travel abroad. If the patient states that it has been necessary to get out of bed at night to empty the bowels, this is a significant finding. Functional diarrhoea almost never occurs at night and rarely wakens the patient. It is also worth considering other medical conditions such as diabetes mellitus. Diabetes is associated with neurological dysfunction, which can also result in diarrhoea.

It is always necessary to extend the history-taking process to include the patient's family in the case of diarrhoea. Complaints of family members with the same symptoms may provide a clue to the infectious nature of the disease. Ask if the patient has recently ingested seafood. Shellfish poisoning can present within 30 minutes of ingestion of the contaminated food, causing abdominal pain, nausea, vomiting and diarrhoea which may last for more than 8 hours (Scoging & Bahl 1998). If the patient describes symptoms which may be caused by a bacterium or virus, it is also extremely important to enquire about occupation and possible transmission to other people in the food trade.

Acute gastroenteritis (AGE) in children is a serious problem and frequently presents as vomiting and diarrhoea, although there are many other possible differentials which are summarized in Table 9.4. Of particular concern is the risk of dehydration that may rapidly develop in a child. A good history from a parent is essential as AGE is readily managed in most children by re-feeding and rehydration; however, it is essential to have ruled out the differentials presented in Table 9.4 first.

Table 9.4 Causes of vomiting and/or diarrhoea*

Medical conditions		Surgical conditions
Toxic ingestion	Respiratory tract infection	Pyloric stenosis
Acute gastroenteritis (viral, bacterial, protozoal)	Otitis media	Intussusception
Septicaemia	Hepatitis A	Acute appendicitis
Haemolytic uraemic syndrome	Urinary tract infection	Necrotizing enterocolitis
Coeliac disease	Diabetic ketoacidosis	Hirschprung's disease
Cows' milk protein allergy	Reye's syndrome	
Adrenal insufficiency	Antibiotic use	
Meningitis		

*Adapted from Barnes (2003).

Rectal bleeding

This symptom could indicate a wide range of serious disorders including colorectal cancer. Ask the patient to describe the blood loss in terms of colour, smell, frequency and duration. As a general guide, a complaint of a smear of blood on the toilet tissue may increase your suspicion of haemorrhoids, a squirt of blood may be due to an anorectal lesion, complaints of blood on the surface of the stools or clots originate from the rectum or descending colon, plum or maroon-coloured blood is due to colonic bleeding which may be linked to diverticula or a malignant tumour, tarry stools result from bleeding in the upper gastrointestinal tract and green or black stools are a side effect of treatment with iron. If pain is associated with the bleeding this is significant, as haemorrhoids are often uncomfortable but rarely painful. A complaint of pain therefore should make you consider other causes for the patient's problems.

Remember that there is sensory innervation in the anal canal and lesions in this area will cause the patient some degree of pain. Indeed, symptoms vary according to the origin of the tumour and subtle differences can be noted between tumours arising in the caecum, sigmoid colon and the rectum. Tumours that form in the caecum can present with chronic bleeding or anaemia, however, tumours in this area are commonly large before the patient experiences any symptoms at all. The sensory innervation to the sigmoid colon results in the patient experiencing pain, there is noticeable bleeding and often patients report a change in bowel habits. Tumours that arise in the rectum can cause the patient to report a sensation of incomplete evacuation (tenesmus) and, as in the case of the sigmoid colon, the sensory innervation to the rectum results in reports of pain from the patient.

OBESITY

Taking a history from an obese person requires tact and diplomacy. However, the NP needs to know both the quantity and quality of diet and daily exercise levels together with other lifestyle information such as alcohol consumption, smoking and the weight of other close family members. The patient's own perceptions are extremely important – if they do not see their weight as a problem, little progress will be made in weight reduction.

LIVER DISEASE AND BILIARY OBSTRUCTION

Alcohol consumption is a key factor in the history. Foreign travel, the use of intravenous drugs, sexual orientation in men, and past exposure to blood products are important factors in the patient's history as exposure to viral hepatitis should be considered. One of the key questions in the history-taking process is whether the patient has developed a painless jaundice or whether there is any associated abdominal discomfort. Painless jaundice suggests chronic obstruction of the common bile duct which may have been caused by cancer of the bile duct or the head of the pancreas. If the patient complains of severe epigastric and right hypochondrial pain accompanied by fever, this suggests a gallstone in the common bile duct.

Consider the physical consequences of hepatic disease and focus your questions on these possible symptoms. As the bile acids build up in the patient's system it is common for a pruritus to develop, followed by the signs of biliary obstruction such as dark urine, pale stools, steatorrhoea and weight loss. The patient may have thought that these symptoms were of no consequence and may not offer the information unless you ask for it in a direct manner.

PANCREATIC DISEASE

The pain of acute pancreatitis is often severe and accompanied by nausea and vomiting. Again, alcohol consumption is a key question. If a patient has recurrent bouts of pancreatitis, symptoms and signs of jaundice should be checked. Apart from the risk of cirrhosis of the liver, the common bile duct may become obstructed by a stricture as it passes through the diseased pancreas. In later disease ask the patient about the symptoms of diabetes mellitus such as excessive thirst and polyuria.

KIDNEY AND BLADDER DISEASE

If a person presents with a history suggestive of renal system disease it is important to enquire about past medical history and the medications, which may be nephrotoxic. Cover the patient's normal fluid intake and ask him or her to describe their normal pattern of micturition. Areas to cover in the history-taking process include hesitancy, frequency, dribbling, urgency, sense of incomplete emptying of the bladder, flank pain or discomfort on passing urine.

MEDICATIONS

It is essential in the history-taking process to enquire specifically about the use of medications. Many drugs are associated with side effects involving the gastrointestinal tract and the renal system and it is always worth checking the current British National Formulary for side effects of those medications.

PHYSICAL EXAMINATION

As with all examinations, it is unlikely that you will be able to focus on one discrete area to provide you with the clues for diagnosis and management.

Patients may present complaining of left-sided upper abdominal pain which is of cardiac origin; alternatively, a person may present with leg oedema caused by a problem in the abdomen such as a pelvic mass or renal disease (Table 9.5).

Having considered the signs and symptoms occurring in systems beyond the abdominal cavity, we will now focus on physical examination of the abdomen. As with all physical examinations, you need to ensure that your patient is comfortable,

Table 9.5 Signs and symptoms that occur outside the abdominal systems and that are relevant in the abdominal examination*

Sign or symptom	Possible pathological condition
Shock or orthostatic hypotension	Acute pancreatitis, obstruction, ruptured tubal pregnancy, hypovolaemia due to fluid loss
Mental status deficit	Haemorrhage, duodenal ulcer
Hypertension	Aortic dissection, abdominal aortic aneurysm, renal infarction, glomerulonephritis
Pulse deficit	Aortic dissection, aortic aneurysm or thrombosis
Bruits	Aortic dissection, aortic aneurysm, dissection or aneurysm of splenic renal or iliac arteries
Atrial fibrillation	Ischaemia of the mesentery
Pleural effusion	Oesophageal rupture, pancreatitis, ovarian tumour
Flank tenderness	Renal inflammation, stone, infarct and thrombosis
Leg oedema	Iliac obstruction, pelvic mass, renal disease
Lymphadenopathy	Hepatitis, lymphoma, mononucleosis
Jaundice	Excessive haemolysis, liver, biliary disease
Dark yellow/ brown urine	Blood as a result of a stone, infarct, pyelonephritis or glomerulonephritis, liver, biliary disease
Fever and chills	Peritonitis, pelvic infection, cholangitis, pyelonephritis

*Adapted from Barkauskas et al (1998).

warm and relaxed. The patient can feel extremely vulnerable when exposing his or her abdomen, particularly where the patient has abdominal pain, as he or she may be afraid that you will exacerbate the pain. Therefore a careful and thorough explanation should be offered before carrying out the exam. In some cases you may need to ask patients to help you by using their hands for palpation – this will be explained in more detail below.

A further consideration before performing the abdominal examination is that the patient should be allowed to empty the bladder as a full bladder will interfere with the exam. This is a good opportunity to perform a dip-stick urine screen. The patient should be placed in a supine position with arms resting on the couch and should be allowed to cover areas of the body which do not need to be exposed for the examination. Ensure you have a good source of light and approach the patient in a calm, gentle manner. If the patient has been experiencing pain, ask him or her to point to the area of tenderness and make a mental note of its location. You will find that it is beneficial to examine painful areas last as the discomfort caused by palpating over an area of tenderness will result in a patient who is anxious and no longer relaxed.

In order to report your findings and to provide you with a structure for the abdominal examination, it is helpful to divide the abdomen into sections. The two commonest methods are quadrants and nine regions (Fig. 9.2). The quadrants are left upper quadrant, right upper quadrant, left lower quadrant and right lower quadrant. It is worthwhile becoming familiar with both systems as you will find that with certain conditions one system enables you to describe the area more specifically than the other. Both systems allow you to consider which organs lie beneath each region and therefore help you to link areas of tenderness with specific organs in some situations. A description of the organs which lie beneath each region can be found in Tables 9.6 and 9.7.

INSPECTION

Inspect the abdomen from a variety of positions. Sitting beside the patient and then standing above him or her will allow you to review the contour of the abdomen and to notice any lack of symmetry. Ascites will result in a taut glistening appearance over the abdomen. Seidel et al (2003) have outlined

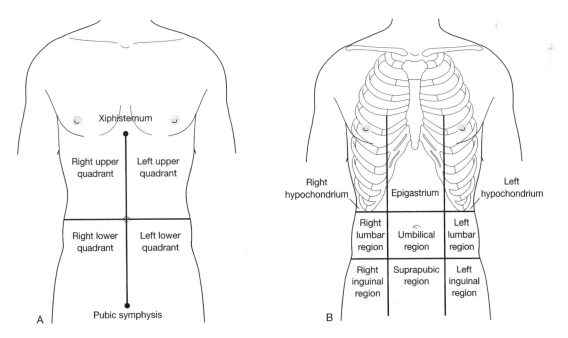

Figure 9.2 Abdominal examination: (a) the four abdominal quadrants, (b) the nine segments of the abdomen (adapted from Epstein et al 2003).

Table 9.6 Anatomical correlates of the abdomen

Right upper quadrant	Left upper quadrant
Liver and gallbladder	Left lobe of liver
Pylorus	Spleen
Duodenum	Stomach
Head of pancreas	Body of pancreas
Right adrenal gland	Left adrenal gland
Portion of right kidney	Portion of left kidney
Hepatic flexure of colon	Splenic flexure of colon
Portions of ascending and transverse colon	Portions of transverse and descending colon
Right lower quadrant	**Left lower quadrant**
Lower pole of right kidney	Lower pole of left kidney
Caecum and appendix	Sigmoid colon
Portion of ascending colon	Portion of descending colon
Bladder (if distended)	Bladder (if distended)
Ovary and salpinx	Ovary and salpinx
Uterus (if enlarged)	Uterus (if enlarged)
Right spermatic cord	Left spermatic cord
Right ureter	Left ureter

an easy way to remember the causes of abdominal distension – the Fs of abdominal distension:

- Fat
- Fluid
- Flatus
- Fetus
- Faeces
- Fibroid
- Full bladder
- False pregnancy
- Fatal tumour.

If you ask the patient gently to breathe in and out you should notice the abdomen move symmetrically and smoothly during the manoeuvre. If you ask the patient to lift his or her head off the table, you may find that a previously unnoticed mass appears as the diaphragm compresses the contents of the abdominal wall within the abdominal cavity. You may notice peristaltic movement during inspection, this is most often associated with an obstruction. You may also notice pulsations in the midline which are quite normal in thin adults; if they become marked they may be related to the increased pulse pressure of an abdominal aortic aneurysm. During inspection you are also looking for any discoloration and scars.

Table 9.7 Anatomical correlates of the abdomen

Right hypochondriac	Epigastric	Left hypochondriac
Right lobe of liver	Pyloric end of stomach	Stomach
Gallbladder	Duodenum	Spleen
Portion of duodenum	Pancreas	Tail of pancreas
Hepatic flexure of colon	Portion of liver	Splenic flexure of colon
Portion of right kidney		Upper pole of left kidney
Suprarenal gland		Suprarenal gland
Right lumbar	**Umbilical**	**Left lumbar**
Ascending colon	Omentum	Descending colon
Lower half of right kidney	Mesentery	Lower half of left kidney
Portion of duodenum and jejunum	Lower part of duodenum	Portions of jejunum and ileum
Jejunum and ileum		
Right inguinal	**Hypogastric (pubic)**	**Left inguinal**
Caecum	Ileum	Sigmoid colon
Appendix	Bladder	Left ureter
Lower end of ileum	Uterus (in pregnancy)	Left spermatic cord
Right ureter		Left ovary
Right spermatic cord		
Right ovary		

If renal disease is suspected, it is essential to check for any signs of oedema such as the facial oedema characteristic of nephrotic syndrome. Chronic loss of plasma proteins in the urine disturbs the normal osmotic pressures within the body, leading to an accumulation of tissue fluid as oedema.

Children with a history of diarrhoea and vomiting may become dehydrated. Inspection involves checking for clinical signs of moderate dehydration such as irritability, lethargy, decreased tissue turgor, dry mucus membranes, tachycardia, sunken eyes, decreased urine output and depressed anterior fontanelle. More serious dehydration results in hypotension and a weak thready pulse, tenting of greater than 2 seconds when testing for tissue turgor, as well as the above signs being even more pronounced (Barnes 2003).

AUSCULTATION

Auscultation is carried out before percussion and palpation in the examination of the abdomen as percussion and palpation may alter the bowel sounds. All four quadrants of the abdomen should be covered. Use a warm stethoscope and place the diaphragm gently on the abdomen in the desired location. The frequency and character of the bowel sounds should be noted. Clicks and gurgles which occur in a range of 5–35 per minute are quite normal. Increased bowel sounds may occur with gastroenteritis, hunger or intestinal obstruction and decreased sounds may occur with peritonitis or paralytic ileus. High-pitched

tinkling sounds may suggest early obstruction. At least 30 seconds of continual listening is necessary before you can assume reduction or absence of bowel sounds (Epstein et al 2003).

It is also possible to listen for vascular sounds during the abdominal examination. Using the bell of the stethoscope placed over seven different locations (Fig. 9.3), it is possible to listen for bruits. Friction rubs over the spleen and liver are rare but can be heard with respiration if there is a tumour or some other source of inflammation over the peritoneal surface of these specific organs.

PERCUSSION

Percussion is used to detect the presence of air, fluid or solid masses. You need to develop a structured approach to percussion, ensuring that you cover all regions of the abdomen in a logical order. The main sound you should hear is tympany – a high-pitched musical note. Dullness is heard over organs and solid masses, this is a short, high-pitched note. Resonance is a sustained sound of moderate pitch which can be heard over lung tissue and sometimes over the abdomen. You may hear hyper-resonance, which is a pitch lying between tympany and resonance.

Percussion can be used to estimate the location and size of the liver. Locate the mid-clavicular line on the patient's right side and percuss along this line from an area of resonance in the lung downwards to an area of dullness. Note this point and repeat the procedure from an area of tympany in the abdominal mid-clavicular line to an area of dullness. It is always useful to percuss towards the area of dullness as it is easier to hear the change in the sound rather than from a dull area to an area of resonance or tympany. When you measure the distance between the two points located through percussion you should find that the liver measures approximately 6–12 cm. It should lie approximately 2–3 cm below the costal margin and should appear no higher than the fifth intercostal space. If the liver lies outside any of these dimensions it may be enlarged, atrophied or displaced by lung tissue in pulmonary disease or abdominal fluid or masses.

PALPATION

You may need to enlist the patient's assistance in palpation. Patients who are ticklish or particularly frightened of you touching their abdomen such as

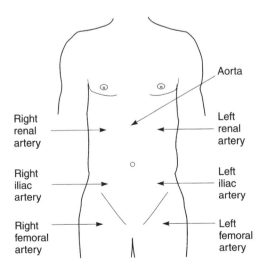

Figure 9.3 Sites to auscultate for bruits.

children may find the procedure more acceptable if you ask them to place their own hand on their abdomen and you place yours on top of theirs. You can palpate gently and slowly together and eventually the patient will allow you to palpate without his or her own hand being in place.

Begin with light palpation, using a systematic approach over the four quadrants, initially avoiding painful areas. Use the palmar surface of your hand to depress gently and smoothly over the abdominal surface at a depth of approximately 1 cm. A patient who is in pain will watch your every move and may guard certain areas; a more relaxed patient may lie on the couch with eyes closed. Continue palpating and gradually increase the depth of the pressure you apply. In thin adults you may be able to locate several of the abdominal organs; in some abdominal examinations you may find it difficult to feel anything at all.

EXAMINING THE GROINS

The abdominal examination is not complete without an examination of the groins for femoral or inguinal herniae. This has been covered in more detail in Chapters 10 and 11.

LIVER

To feel for the liver, rest your hand against the bottom of the right ribcage. Ask the patient to breathe in and you may be able to feel the smooth edge of the liver move under your hand. You can carry out the same manoeuvre by standing towards the patient's head, grasping the lower edge of the right ribcage by hooking your fingers over the costal margin and again asking the patient to take a deep breath.

SPLEEN

A similar procedure can be used to palpate for the spleen. Place your left hand behind the patient's left ribs and your right hand at the lower edge of the left ribs. Ask the patient to take a deep breath and push slightly forward with the left hand and down with the right. This pushes the spleen slightly forward to enable you to palpate it; it is unusual to be able to feel the spleen as it has to be approximately three times its normal size before you can feel anything (Walker 1995).

GALLBLADDER

A healthy gallbladder is not palpable. One which is palpable and tender indicates cholecystitis, whereas non-tender enlargement indicates common bile duct obstruction. If you are considering cholecystitis as a potential diagnosis you can demonstrate the presence of an inflamed gallbladder by eliciting a response called Murphy's sign. To demonstrate Murphy's sign, place your hand over the lower right rib margin with your fingers facing towards the centre and during deep palpation ask the patient to take a deep breath. As the inflamed gallbladder moves against your examining fingers, the patient will experience pain and will momentarily halt breathing.

KIDNEYS

The kidneys are not usually palpable; however, it is important to practise the technique to ensure that you find an enlarged kidney when one is present. The technique is similar to the assessment of the spleen. For the right kidney, place your left hand behind the patient just below the 12th rib and lift, trying to displace the kidney anteriorly. Place your right hand in the right upper quadrant and ask the patient to take a deep breath in. At the peak of inspiration, press your right hand into the right upper quadrant and try to capture the kidney. Ask the patient to exhale and feel for the kidney's return to its expiratory position. It is occasionally possible to palpate the right kidney, in thin women in particular. The same procedure is carried out on the left side to palpate for the left kidney.

The kidneys can also be assessed for tenderness by placing the ball of one hand in the costovertebral angle. You then strike your hand with the ulnar surface of the fist of your other hand. You need to use sufficient force to cause a thud. This should be a painless exercise. If the pressure from this manoeuvre causes pain, this suggests the possibility of kidney infection or possibly a musculoskeletal problem.

BLADDER

The bladder is not usually palpable unless it is distended with urine. If the bladder is distended it is possible to palpate a smooth rounded mass in the midline. It is possible to percuss a distended bladder and this will produce a lower percussion note than the surrounding air-filled intestines.

REFLEXES

The abdominal reflexes can be tested by lightly but briskly stroking each side of the abdomen above and below the umbilicus. Above the umbilicus tests the superficial reflexes of T8, T9 and T10 and below the umbilicus tests the reflexes of T10, T11 and T12. You should note the contraction of the abdominal muscles and the deviation of the umbilicus toward the stimulus. If the abdominal reflexes are absent there may be a central or peripheral nervous system disorder or a patient's obesity may obscure the response. In this case, place your finger on the patient's umbilicus, pulling slightly away from the side to be stimulated and you should be able to feel the response as the muscles contract during the reflex action.

THE ANUS AND RECTUM

It may be necessary to carry out an examination of the rectum and anus. Patients should be reassured that it should not be a painful experience, although it is certainly uncomfortable and may stimulate a feeling of rectal fullness. Position the patient in the left lateral position with the hips and knees well flexed. It is important to make sure that the patient is as relaxed and comfortable as possible, as tension and anxiety will make the examination impossible. Gently separate the buttocks and inspect the anus – describe what you see by viewing the area as a clockface. Twelve o'clock is the anterior position and six o'clock the posterior position (Fig. 9.4).

Lubricate your index finger, place it at the 6 o'clock position and slide it into the anal canal and then into the rectum, directing your finger posteriorly. Explore the posterior and posterolateral walls of the rectum by sweeping your finger around 180° in both directions. The normal rectum should feel smooth and pliable. A palpable mass in the anterior position is possibly the prostate in a man and may be the cervix in women who have a retroverted uterus. You may wish to ask the patient to contract the muscles of the anus around your finger. In doing this you can assess the tone of the anal muscles. When you withdraw your finger, check your gloved hand for stool. Blood, melaena or mucus

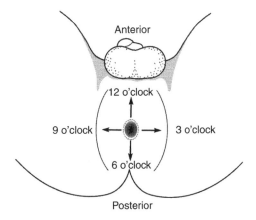

Figure 9.4 Clockface positions around the anus.

may be present and all of these signs will help you in your problem-solving process. Always ensure you have tissues available at this stage to wipe the patient and that you have easy access to a disposal system for your glove.

MANAGEMENT AND INVESTIGATION OF COMMON PRESENTATIONS

Disorders affecting the genitourinary system are discussed in chapters 10 and 11.

DIARRHOEA

It is important to take this condition seriously, particularly in children and the elderly. It is usually self-limiting and the focus should be on fluid intake and monitoring for signs of dehydration rather than treating the diarrhoea. Sachets of oral rehydration salts (ORS) are essential for patients showing signs of dehydration but do not taste very appetizing. Blackcurrant juice is effective at disguising the taste. The fluid should be taken little and often; in young children sips of the fluid every 10 minutes are useful even in the presence of vomiting. Mild dehydration in children can be corrected by aiming to give 50 ml/kg of ORS plus 10 ml/kg for each loose stool or vomit over a 4-hour period (Barnes 2003). Anti-diarrhoeal medication has no role in the treatment of children (BNF 2003).

Signs of moderate to severe dehydration indicate hospital admission is needed for re-hydration as IV therapy may be necessary, together with monitoring of blood biochemistry. As viruses are the usual causative agents in diarrhoea the use of antibiotics is usually unhelpful. Treatment with antibiotics should be considered, however, in cases of infection with specific organisms such as *Shigella*, *Campylobacter jejuni*, *Salmonella* or *Giardia* (BNF 2003), stool samples are only indicated if the condition persists beyond 7 days, if there is blood or there is persistent fever.

OESOPHAGITIS (HEARTBURN)

Patients should be assessed for lifestyle factors, food consumption and medications which may be contributing to the causes of their heartburn and should then be advised accordingly. Some useful tips for patients include avoiding caffeine, fatty foods, tomato, milk and citrus products. Small regular meals are preferable to large ones and the patient should be encouraged to eat slowly and sit in an upright position when eating. The evening meal should be consumed at least 3 hours before going to bed and it may help to be slightly elevated in bed. The patient should be encouraged to stop smoking, reduce alcohol consumption, wear loose-fitting clothing and, if overweight, lose weight. Drink water after eating to clear the oesophagus. Many of these suggestions require major changes to the patient's lifestyle and this may only be achieved with consistent empathic advice over several consultations.

Heartburn may be managed with antacids and alginates such as Gaviscon which form a 'raft' to protect the oesophageal mucosa. Proton pump inhibitors are significantly better than H_2 receptor agonists in healing oesophagitis and relieving symptoms, making them the treatment of choice if the above approaches fail to work.

It is important for the nurse practitioner to be aware of the need to refer on to a colleague if the patient presents with anything other than straightforward heartburn. Indications for referral are:

- If the symptoms are not relieved or have worsened even after initiation of medication
- If there is associated weight loss, anaemia, melaena, vomiting, anorexia or dysphagia
- If the patient is over 45 years of age and this is the first presentation with heartburn.

A high level of suspicion for other causes of the discomfort must be maintained with all patients but particularly in older people as the incidence of malignancy increases with age.

PAIN ASSOCIATED WITH PEPTIC ULCERATION

Initially treatment as for heartburn may be sufficient to relieve symptoms. If symptoms persist, investigations include endoscopy and/or screening for *H. pylori*, according to local protocols.

Screening for *H. pylori* may be done either by serology (testing for antibodies) or breath test. The latter depends upon the *H. pylori* enzyme urease metabolizing urea which is given to the patient first in a drink. The urea contains a radioactive carbon isotope, the breath test then tests for radioactive carbon in the CO_2 exhaled subsequently, indicating the presence of urease and hence *H. pylori*.

Patients may buy H_2 receptor agonist medication such as cimetadine over the counter to achieve short-term relief. However if *H. pylori* infection is present, the desired long-term treatment is eradication therapy with a one-week triple therapy regime of a proton pump inhibitor, amoxicillin and either clarithromycin or metronidazole which is effective in 90% of cases (BNF 2003). The link between *H. pylori* infection and gastric cancer is such that careful investigation and eradication therapy is preferable to symptomatic treatment.

COLORECTAL CANCER

The management of this serious condition obviously rests with the surgical team. However as this condition is responsible for 16 000 deaths per year, yet if detected early enough has a 90% cure rate (Fursland 2004), early detection by an alert nurse practitioner could make a great deal of difference to the outcome. From a health education point of view, eating a diet low in red meat and fat but high in fibre, fruit and vegetables considerably reduces the risk. Some forms of colorectal cancer are genetically determined and therefore a good family history going back at least two generations is essential to help identify people at risk.

IRRITABLE BOWEL SYNDROME

Irritable bowel syndrome is a common stress-related disorder occurring more frequently in women but with no anatomical abnormality or evidence of bowel inflammation (Springhouse 2000). It is characterized by pain, irregular bowel habits (constipation or diarrhoea) and abdominal bloating with flatulence.

There is therefore a disorder of function but with no structural alteration to the bowel. The patient may complain of pain as the intestines go into spasm; symptoms are usually intermittent and may last for days or weeks at a time. The diagnosis is made by excluding other possible disorders such as lactose intolerance, thyrotoxicosis, ulcerative colitis or Crohn's disease.

Once the diagnosis has been confirmed, the nurse practitioner can reassure the patient that irritable bowel syndrome is simply the abnormal movements of essentially healthy normal bowels. The condition is not fatal and can be managed with lifestyle adjustments and a change in diet. It is useful to explain to the patient that antibiotics, gastroenteritis, food intolerance, stress, anxiety, menstruation and smoking are all aggravating factors for irritable bowel syndrome and in some cases this may explain the timing of the patient's problems.

Pharmacological management of irritable bowel syndrome may be necessary in a few individuals and there is evidence that tricyclic antidepressant therapy is effective in patients whose main symptoms are pain and diarrhoea (Haslett et al 2003).

It is important to refer patients on if they present with the symptoms of irritable bowel syndrome, are over 40 years of age, have experienced a recent change in bowel habit, have noticed weight loss or rectal bleeding or have been woken from sleep with the pain.

OBESITY

Despite the massive dieting and slimming industry, obesity is a growing problem. The basic twin approaches of low calorie diet and increased levels of exercise are more effective in losing weight than either on their own, but require significant periods of time and a great deal of commitment and motivation to produce results. There are no quick fixes. Anti-obesity drugs (Orlistat and Sibutramine) are recommended for use by NICE only after patients have already lost some weight by conventional means – and then only for use in combination with a calorie control and exercise programme. Reducing television watching and taking a whole family approach seem to help secure weight loss in children (Parsons 2002). Adherents of the Atkins diet do lose weight and it seems that this may be the result of the diet's appetite suppressant effect, however long-term use of such an unbalanced diet may lead to a whole range of health problems.

References

Bandolier 2004 Online: www.jr2.ox.ac.uk/bandolier
Barnes K 2003 Paediatrics. Butterworth-Heinemann, Oxford
BNF 2003 British National Formulary. British Medical Association/Royal Pharmaceutical Society of Great Britain, London
CDC 2003 Center for Disease Control and Prevention. Online: www.cdc.gov/ulcer
Engel J 2002 Pediatric assessment. Mosby, St Louis
Epstein O, Perkin G D, deBono D P, Cookson J 2003 Clinical examination, 3rd edn. Mosby, London
Fursland E 2004 No nonsense approach. Nursing Standard 18:16–17, 29
Haslett C, Chilvers E, Boon N, Colledge N 2003 Davidson's principles and practice of medicine, 19th edn. Churchill Livingstone, Edinburgh
House of Commons Select Committee on Health 2004 Report on obesity. HMSO, London

Hughes E 2004 Understanding the care of patients with acute pancreatitis. Nursing Standard 18(18):45–52
Scoging A, Bahl M 1998 Diarrhetic shellfish poisoning in the UK. Lancet 352: 117
Parsons T 2002 Weight management for health. Primary Health Care 12(6):39–48
Seidel H M, Ball J W, Dains J E, Benedict G W 2003 Mosby's guide to physical examination, 6th edn. Mosby, St Louis
Springhouse 2000 Handbook of pathophysiology. Springhouse Corp, Springhouse, PA
Tortora G, Grabowski S 2003 Principles of anatomy and physiology, 10th edn. John Wiley, New York
Walker R 1995 Examination of the abdomen. Practice Nursing 6(15):19–20
WHO 1998 Obesity: preventing and managing the global epidemic. Report of World Health Organization Consultation. WHO/NUT/98.1. WHO, Geneva

Chapter 10

The male reproductive system

Mike Walsh

INTRODUCTION

Disorders of the reproductive system, by their very personal nature, tend to cause a great deal of embarrassment. This may be exacerbated if the nurse practitioner is female while the patient is male. A great deal of tact and diplomacy is therefore required in dealing with male reproductive system disorders. Men may present in a variety of ways, such as seeking treatment for an acute problem in the A&E department or at the health centre. In such circumstances they will probably be anxious and/or distressed. Alternatively there may be a chance finding on a routine examination such as a preoperative assessment. It is also possible that the initial contact may be made with the patient's partner, usually female, who might see the nurse practitioner for a range of reasons. In the course of the consultation it may become apparent that the source of her problem is her partner and advice to help him is needed. As ever, in dealing with disorders of the male reproductive system, good communication skills will always lie at the heart of a successful patient consultation.

PATHOPHYSIOLOGY

THE PENIS

As the penis is primarily a sexual organ, it is not surprising that many problems affecting this organ arise as a result of sexual activity. These include a range of sexually transmitted infections (STI) and also trauma.

Trauma may be due to catching the foreskin in a zip, biting in over-vigorous oral sex, or damage to the glans, urethra or foreskin as a result of sado-masochistic practices. An emergency condition which may be seen in young males is paraphimosis, where the foreskin has become retracted behind the glans and cannot be pulled back into its normal position. This causes discomfort, oedema and a great deal of embarrassment. Phimosis describes the situation whereby the foreskin cannot be retracted at all to reveal the glans. A congenital abnormality which occasionally occurs is hypospadias, in which the urethral orifice is located on the ventral surface of the penile shaft.

Sexually transmitted infections that produce obvious lesions include genital herpes, genital warts (condyloma acuminatum) and syphilis. Cancer of the penis may also produce a lesion, commonly under the foreskin. Frequently, however, an STI does not produce an obvious external lesion; the main presenting symptom may be a urethral discharge, soreness and discomfort. Recent years have seen a dramatic increase in the incidence of STI as shown in Table 10.1.

Of particular note, in view of the HIV/AIDS threat, is that between 2002 and 2003 there has been an increase of 22% in cases of homosexually acquired Chlamydia (compared to 9% in the overall population) and 11% in homosexually acquired gonorrhoea (compared to an actual *reduction* of 2% in the total population). Overall there has been an increase in all diagnoses during 1995–2003 of 77% in gay men compared to 57% in the whole population. These

figures indicate growing amounts of casual, unprotected sex which is affecting the gay community more than the whole population. There is therefore much health education work to do – but we must remember HIV/AIDS is also a heterosexually contracted disease. However, these statistics give a particularly worrying indication of the need for more work amongst the gay community in particular, if HIV/AIDS is to be prevented.

THE TESTES AND SCROTUM

Testicular cancer is the commonest cancer in young men aged 20–34 with 2000 new cases being diagnosed every year, of whom 50% will be under 35 – although some 14% may be over 50 (Cancer Research UK 2004). Most cancers arise from the germ cells associated with spermatogenesis, the most common being in the seminiferous tubules (seminomas). These account for approximately 50% of all testicular tumours and fortunately are the least aggressive. Early detection and treatment are especially important, as the tumour is very responsive to chemotherapy, with a good prognosis if treated early enough. Testicular tumours are four times more common in Caucasians and if a man has a first-degree relative with testicular cancer this increases the risk by a factor of 6. The biggest risk factor, though, is an undescended testicle as a child, which increases the risk by a factor of 10. Evidence is now emerging of an inherited genetic defect on the X chromosome (maternal) which may account for some 20% of testicular cancers (Cancer Research UK 2004)

Benign swellings may also occur in the scrotum, such as a hydrocele (an accumulation of fluid in the tunica vaginalis), while a spermatocele is a fluid-filled cyst occurring in the epididymis. A distorted knot of veins around the spermatic cord may produce a painful mass known as a varicocele, commonly seen in young men and adolescents.

An inguinal hernia presents as a protrusion of abdominal viscera into the inguinal canal. This may reach as far as the testes in what is known as an indirect inguinal hernia, which usually affects young men. Here the abdominal viscera have slipped through the inguinal ring and followed the spermatic cord. Older men suffer a direct inguinal hernia which results from a weakness in the fascial floor of the inguinal canal. This does not reach the testes. The hernia may be irreducible (incarcerated)

Table 10.1 Common STI in 2003 (England, Wales and Northern Ireland only)*

Infection	Male	Female
Chlamydia	39977	49841
(homosexually acquired)	1793	
Gonorrhoea	16841	7468
(homosexually acquired)	3757	
Herpes	6698	11292
(homosexually acquired)	474	
Warts	37458	33425
(homosexually acquired)	2184	
Syphilis	1394	181
(homosexually acquired)	783	
All diagnoses	330229	377854
(homosexually acquired)	22943	

*Source: Health Protection Agency www.hpa.org.uk.

or become strangulated. This latter situation is a surgical emergency as part of the intestine has become entangled in the hernia and may have its blood supply cut off, leading to necrosis and intestinal obstruction.

Inflammation of the epididymis (epididymitis) is a very painful condition leading to a swollen and painful scrotum with possible systemic symptoms of infection such as fever and malaise. It usually occurs secondary to an STI or a urinary tract infection. If not properly treated it can lead to infertility as scarring occludes the epididymis. Orchitis or inflammation of the testes may develop from epididymitis or as a consequence of an adult developing mumps. It frequently affects only one testicle.

A particularly urgent emergency presentation occurs when a testicle rotates upon the spermatic cord (torsion testes), impairing the blood supply. This occurs most commonly in neonates or around puberty and the teenage years. The result is severe pain, nausea, swelling and discoloration of the scrotum with irreversible ischaemic damage occurring within a few hours. This condition is a surgical emergency requiring immediate referral to hospital.

Various skin conditions may involve the scrotum and surrounding areas, including the penis. Psoriasis or dermatitis can present with familiar scaly lesions in this area; there will often be evidence of the problem elsewhere on the body, although in the case of a contact dermatitis the lesions may be localized to the genital area. Fungal infections are also possible; tinea cruris is a common example and may be localized to the groin area, producing an irritating, scaly, erythematous rash which has a well-delineated border. In all these cases the man may be anxious and upset, convinced that he has caught an STI.

THE PROSTATE GLAND

Benign prostatic hyperplasia (BPH) affects most men over 60 and causes obstruction to normal urinary outflow from the bladder, resulting in urinary problems. The cause is thought to be a hormonal imbalance associated with ageing. There is a decrease in testosterone and an increase in oestrogen production associated with higher levels of dihydrotestosterone, the main androgen found in the prostate (Springhouse 2002). The course of the disease seems very variable, with some men improving over time, while others may experience severe problems including retention with overflow, ascending urinary

tract infections involving the kidneys, and even the distress of acute urinary retention. Evidence available on Bandolier (2000a) suggests that in a 2-year period, 5% of men with moderate symptoms of BPH and a urine flow rate of less than 15 ml/second will experience at least one episode of acute urinary retention; over 4 years this rises to 7.5%. The best predictor of who would be effected was a prostate specific antigen (PSA) of over 3.3 ng/ml. Many men with BPH may not initially seek help, fatalistically accepting urinary problems as part of growing old.

Prostatic cancer is the second commonest cause of cancer-related death in men, after lung cancer, in both Europe and the USA. Every year in the UK there are 20 000 new diagnoses of prostate cancer and approximately 9500 men die as a result of the disease. These figures are showing a steady increase and prostate cancer may soon overtake lung cancer as the number one cause of cancer-related death in men. This upward trend may just reflect increased longevity amongst the general population as cancer of the prostate is an age-related disease (Templeton 2003). Over a lifetime, 73 men out of every 1000 will develop prostate cancer and 50% of all cases are diagnosed in men over 75 (Cancer Research UK 2004).

It appears that there are two types of prostate cancer. The type just referred to is clinically obvious and produces metastases affecting mostly bone, liver and lung. There is, however, a far more common form in which multiple microscopic foci are present, affecting about 80% of men over 75, but only 30% of these men will have any clinically significant disease even 10 years later (Underwood 2000). Many more men therefore die *with* cancer of the prostate than *of* cancer of the prostate. However, 20–30% of men on diagnosis will have metastatic deposits (Cancer Help UK 2003). No obvious causes are known although there is an increased risk if there is a family history. The initial symptoms are similar to BPH but as the disease metastasizes, the skeleton in particular is prone to secondary deposits, leading to bony pain and pathological fractures. The course of the disease is variable and poorly understood at present, with little evidence to suggest that any treatment option makes any significant improvement to the outcome.

Inflammation of the prostate (prostatitis) occurs in younger men aged most frequently between 30 and 50. The cause is frequently coliform bacteria and the condition may be acute or chronic. Prostatitis is recognized as sometimes being non-bacterial in origin and various explanations such as autoimmune problems and allergic reactions have been proposed (Donovan & Nicholas 1997).

HIV/AIDS

In June 2003 the Health Protection Agency reported that of the 25 148 male cases of HIV infection in the UK, 16 660 were homosexually acquired, 5212 heterosexually acquired and a further 1510 were intravenous drug users (IDUs). A further 3523 men were living with full AIDS and, in total, 8761 men had died of AIDS (HPA 2004). It should be noted that the HPA also recorded 8632 women with sexually acquired HIV infection and a further 769 with HIV as a result of IDU. A total of 1371 women had sexually acquired AIDS. The HIV problem is not confined to homosexual males – both sexes are involved and the disease is spreading by heterosexual activity and amongst IDUs. The rapid growth of homosexually acquired STIs revealed in Table 10.1 has major implications for the possible spread of HIV amongst homosexual males. It indicates a lack of safer sex practices such as condom use.

The period between HIV infection and the development of AIDS is normally between 8 and 10 years, although this period is much shorter in children, typically 17 months (Springhouse 2002). The normal pattern of the disease starts with a mild acute infection producing general symptoms of feeling unwell, although in many cases the person may not notice any signs as they are so mild and short-lived. Antibodies usually develop in 2–6 weeks, although in some cases seroconversion may take longer. A chronic infection develops, of which the patient is often unaware. As the disease progresses, generalized symptoms such as fever, night sweats and weight loss appear, together with opportunistic infections. Deterioration in the patient's condition occurs over time with the appearance of various infectious diseases, some rarely occurring in patients who do not have AIDS, as the body's immune system fails. Tuberculosis is a major AIDS-related infection, along with protozoal infections such as *Pneumocystis carinii* pneumonia and *Cryptosporidiosis*, viral infections such as herpes simplex and herpes zoster, and fungal infections such as candidiasis and cryptococcosis. Malignant lymphomas and Kaposi's sarcoma are two examples of malignant disease that may develop whilst women are developing cervical neoplasms as they survive longer. As there is no cure at present, the long-term prognosis is bleak.

ERECTILE DYSFUNCTION (ED)

This problem may range in severity from being unable to maintain an erection long enough for orgasm through to a situation where a man may get some degree of erection but not enough for full penetration of his partner. Total flaccidity of the penis is therefore only one extreme of a wide range of problems associated with ED. The basic pathology involves a failure of the normal neurovascular function which ensures there is sufficient vasodilatation to achieve tumescence of the penis due to engorgement with blood upon sexual arousal. There are a wide range of physical causes such as diabetes, hypertension, neurological disorder and renal failure. ED may also arise as a result of drug abuse, including smoking and heavy alcohol intake, or as a side effect of medication such as anti-hypertensives or cimetidine. It is a well-recognized problem after prostatic surgery. Psychological problems such as depression and anxiety may also underlie ED. It could be a sign of major relationship difficulties or some psychosexual disorder. A physical cause is more likely but inevitably there will be some psychological overlay due to the effects on the man of losing the ability to perform sexually.

INFERTILITY

Infertility in men has historically been much less of an issue than in women, yet the probability of a man alone being the cause of an infertile couple is around 35% – the same as a woman. In the remaining cases it is either a joint problem or no cause can be found. Most men who have erectile dysfunction (ED) problems are however still fertile, so while ED can prevent a woman conceiving naturally, it does not mean that the man is sterile. There are a range of causes of infertility, such as damage to the testicle (e.g. orchitis), hormonal imbalance, undescended testicles and congenital malformations. In most cases, there is no known cause.

SEXUALITY

A possible cause of consultation is the young man who realizes he is homosexual. This may be associated with a great deal of confusion and anxiety and it is possible that the (female) nurse practitioner in primary health care may be seen as someone the young man can talk to about his concerns rather than a male figure such as his father, for example. Feelings of transsexuality (gender dysphoria) may also bring a confused and embarrassed male patient seeking advice from the nurse practitioner, particularly if she is female and seen possibly as more understanding than a male. Transsexuality represents one end of a continuum; there are other men who desire to live partly in a female role and partly male whilst others derive pleasure from dressing in women's clothing whilst remaining completely heterosexual in their orientation and having no desire to be considered female. This end of the spectrum is often labelled transvestite and shades off into various degrees of fetishistic behaviour relating usually to specific items of female clothing, especially underwear.

HOLISM AND MALE SEXUAL HEALTH

The conditions discussed above affect the whole person, not just the genital area. Some diseases become systemic (e.g. syphilis, AIDS) whilst cancers can metastasize to affect distant organs. Other localized disorders can have a profound psychological effect (e.g. ED, infertility, BPH), whilst confusion over sexuality and gender identity can be associated with serious anxiety and depression. As chapter 20 will show, suicide is another major male health hazard, underlining the need to think holistically. The holistic perspective that characterizes nursing is therefore essential in assessing and managing male sexual problems. Good therapeutic communication skills are essential for helping both male and female patients deal with sexual health problems.

HISTORY-TAKING

Absolute privacy is essential to obtain an accurate history. Even then, the patient may be embarrassed and reluctant to talk about his problem. An open and welcoming attitude, showing unconditional regard for the individual, is essential. If the man has had a limited education, expression may be even more difficult and may involve the use of terms you may consider crude; however they may be the only words the man knows and he may be equally embarrassed at having to use them.

Encourage the patient to tell his story in his own words and give him the time and space to explain the problem fully. Beware making jokes to try and lighten the atmosphere as these could go badly wrong in such a sensitive area. The non-verbal aspect of communication is equally important, with special reference to facial expression and body posture on both the part of the nurse practitioner and patient. At all times avoid being judgemental.

Complaints of urethral discharge or lesions on the penis suggest a STI as the most likely cause. A detailed sexual history is required, covering the following points:

- Details of all sexual partners in last 4 weeks
- Gender of partners
- Use of condoms
- Sexual practices, i.e. oral, anal, etc
- Overseas contacts.

In addition, find out how long the complaint has been present and whether it can be related to a specific incident in the sexual history, such as a casual, unprotected sexual encounter. Ask the patient to describe the nature and quantity of any urethral discharge. A small amount of fluid under the foreskin is normal; however, it should not be sufficient to stain underwear – a pathological sign – nor should there be any smell. Enquire about pain, burning or any itching sensation. Previous STIs should be enquired about, together with medication – including attempts at localized self-medication. This will allow you to assess the probability of an STI before examination. Intravenous drug use is a key issue if HIV infection is suspected.

In the case of genital trauma, an accurate account is essential, including mechanism and timing of injury, however embarrassing this may be. The patient may be reluctant to disclose the nature of the practices involved but correct treatment requires knowledge of the cause of injury. A bite involving the foreskin, rather than a zip injury, for example, is extremely infective and antibiotic therapy is essential. A bite should not normally be sutured – except on the face where the excellent blood supply usually ensures healing without infection. Rectal trauma could have major implications if associated with unprotected anal intercourse, a high-risk behaviour for HIV. If it was caused by the insertion of objects such as dildos and no body fluids were involved, the HIV risk is greatly reduced. Health education advice about safer sex requires an accurate history of whatever the patient has been doing in order that advice about, for example, the use of lubricants, condoms and latex gloves (where full-fist insertion is practised) in anal sex can be given. As a final example, the presence of a retained rectal foreign body must be disclosed, before definitive treatment to remove it can begin. These examples show the importance of obtaining an accurate history from the patient, however difficult this may be.

If the patient is complaining of pain in the scrotum, the PQRST system can be used to analyse the symptom. Torsion of the testis produces a sudden onset of pain, the timing of which must be accurately determined given the urgent need for treatment. Epididymitis produces a more gradual onset of pain and the history should go on to explore the possibility of an STI. The pain of testicular cancer may be referred to the pelvic region if metastasis has occurred. Referral of pain into the loins suggests renal pathology (e.g. a stone) as the cause of the pain.

If the patient presents with a mass in the scrotum it is essential to find out when he first noticed this mass. Enquire about pain (testicular cancer initially presents as a small painless lump the size of a pea located to the front or side of the testis), any sensation of heaviness, changes in size of the testis and whether it feels normal or if changes such as irreg-ularities in contour have occurred. Childhood history with regard to undescended testes should be explored. A history of weight loss, coughing, lethargy and fatigue unfortunately suggests advanced malignant disease. If a scrotal swelling is intermittent and can be reduced, this suggests an inguinal hernia as the likely cause, especially if associated with lifting and heavy manual work.

The history suggestive of prostatic disease is usually focused on urinary symptoms. The patient with prostatic cancer will also present with a history similar to BPH. The enlarging prostate causes hesitancy and dribbling on passing urine. The patient may also complain of frequency in wanting to pass urine but of being unable to manage an adequate stream. He may report urgency and, in some cases, urge incontinence. It is important to take the history carefully in order that the patient's urinary problems may be distinguished from incontinence due to other causes. A useful means of assessing the impact of the disorder on the patient's life is to use the International Prostate Symptom Score (Table 10.2). This tool gives an objective baseline score and can be used to measure therapeutic response and progress over time.

The younger man presenting with some prostatic symptoms but also complaining of generally feeling unwell, having a temperature with lumbar or

Table 10.2 International Prostate Symptom Score*

Symptom	Not at all	< 1 time in 5	< half the time	Half the time	> half the time	Almost always	Your score
Straining	0	1	2	3	4	5	
Weak stream	0	1	2	3	4	5	
Intermittency	0	1	2	3	4	5	
Incomplete emptying	0	1	2	3	4	5	
Frequency	0	1	2	3	4	5	
Urgency	0	1	2	3	4	5	
Nocturia (times per night)	0	1	2	3	4	5	

Total scores: 0–7 mild symptoms; 8–19 moderate; 20–35 severe

Quality of life scale:

Delighted	0
Pleased	1
Satisfied	2
Mixed	3
Dissatisfied	4
Unhappy	5
Terrible	6

*From Barry et al (1992).

suprapubic pain and/or perineal discomfort is more likely to have prostatitis.

If the patient presents with a history of ED, the following questions can help determine whether the problem is physical or psychological in origin:

- How quickly has the problem developed? (Sudden onset suggests psychological origin, slow onset an organic cause.)
- Is it situational and/or partner related? (Yes suggests psychological origins.)
- Can you obtain a spontaneous erection at another time such as on wakening? (Yes indicates a psychological problem.)

In the case of infertility, the following areas should be explored:

- Previous children by other women
- Length of time attempting pregnancy, frequency of intercourse and knowledge of the female reproductive cycle
- Are there factors raising scrotal temperature above normal, such as the work environment?
- Medications
- History of undescended testes or any other relevant medical history
- Investigations undertaken on the female partner and her medical history.

The man who presents with problems relating to his sexuality should be encouraged to talk about how long he has had these feelings and whether he has felt able to share them with others. The patient's level of knowledge and experience should be carefully explored, as appropriate referral and advice can only be given when you have a clear view of his feelings, relevant knowledge, family and social networks.

PHYSICAL EXAMINATION

Discretion and a private area are necessary to carry out a physical exam, which should be conducted in as thorough and professional a manner as any other. In order to examine the male genitalia, you should ensure that there is a good light source and you are wearing gloves. It is easier to sit and have the patient stand in front of you.

A logical sequence should always be followed, starting away from the genitals and working inwards. The groin area should first be gently palpated to check for any abnormalities such as

a hernia or enlarged lymph nodes. The standing position makes any hernia more obvious, as does asking the patient to cough if a suspicious swelling is felt. If a hernia is identified, see if it can be reduced by gently pushing it and the results noted as reducible/irreducible. An irreducible hernia has the potential to become strangulated, leading to a bowel obstruction. The distribution of pubic hair should also be observed and noted; it is normally absent on the shaft of the penis and scant on the scrotum. Testicular malfunction may lead to a more female pattern of pubic hair distribution. Scratch marks around the pubic area suggests pubic lice infestation.

The penis should be examined next, checking first whether there are any lesions along the shaft (e.g. genital herpes) and if it has been circumcised. The glans must be examined; this requires retraction of the foreskin in an uncircumcised male. The patient should be asked to do this but it is essential to check that it has been fully retracted. If it is necessary for you to perform this manoeuvre, it should be done gently. If the foreskin cannot be retracted in an adult (phimosis), this suggests recurrent infections or inflammation of the glans; this condition is often seen in poorly-controlled diabetics. The glans should consist of smooth pink tissue with no lesions present; a small amount of fluid (smegma) is a normal finding in an uncircumcised male, it is normally dry in a circumcised male. No odour should be present. Any signs of trauma to the penis should be noted and if nothing has been mentioned in the history, tactful questioning should follow to determine the cause.

In uncircumcised boys the foreskin is normally adherent to the glans up to the age of 3 years therefore retraction should not be attempted until the child is at least 3 (Engel 2002).

The external urinary meatus should be examined, first to ensure that no congenital abnormalities are present (e.g. hypospadias) and second, to check whether there is any urethral discharge. Asking the patient to press his penis between the finger and thumb behind the glans will open the meatus and also express any discharge.

The final logical step is to examine the scrotum. The skin is normally darker than the rest of the body and the left testicle is normally lower than the right. In a small boy an absent testis may indicate that either he has a true undescended testis or that the problem is one of a retractile testis that has temporarily ascended into the pelvic cavity. In the latter case it will normally descend and fix itself eventually, however a medical referral should be made if an undescended testis is suspected due to the risk of testicular cancer in later life.

Swelling and bruising of the scrotum can reach alarming proportions after trauma but will resolve with the aid of ice packs. An inflammatory condition or a torsion testes will lead to the scrotum appearing redder than normal, being oedematous and tender to palpation. After observation, the next step is gentle palpation of each testicle between the thumb and first two fingers. The patient's facial expression should be checked for discomfort during this part of the exam. The testicles should feel equally smooth and have a soft rubbery texture. Any irregularity to the front or side of the testis is abnormal along with any other swelling or mass felt in the scrotum. If it is possible to feel above a scrotal swelling then that suggests it is confined to the scrotum and not a hernia. A cyst full of fluid (hydrocele) is fluctuant when gently compressed and can be transilluminated by holding a pen torch against the scrotum in a darkened room. A dense mass such as a tumour will not allow light to pass through it and therefore appears opaque as well as feeling solid.

If the history suggests a prostatic problem, then a digital rectal examination is necessary. The patient should lie in the left lateral position with his knees drawn up to his chest. Care should be taken to ensure he does not roll off the couch; an assistant may therefore be necessary who can also act as a chaperone. A careful explanation is needed before a well-lubricated index finger is inserted through the anus, checking for a normal external appearance first. Some initial spasm of the anal sphincter is normal but usually, after relaxation, the index finger can be eased into the rectum. The patient should be asked to contract his anus around the sphincter as a check for normal muscle tone. The walls of the rectum should feel smooth and even.

The prostate gland may be palpated through the anterior rectal wall and normally protrudes about 1 cm into the rectum (Seidal et al 2003). It should feel firm and smooth. Irregularities are an abnormal finding and a hard nodular feel suggests malignant changes. A protrusion that feels in excess of 1 cm indicates an enlarged prostate, typically feeling soft or boggy in BPH. The findings should be carefully noted. Secretions may be forced out of the urinary meatus by digital rectal examination. This should be explained to the patient as a normal side effect and any such secretions wiped away. The patient with prostatitis has an enlarged, indurated and tender prostate, therefore the exam should be carried out with particular gentleness if the history is suggestive of this condition. The glove should be routinely examined for any abnormal finding such as blood when the procedure is complete.

INVESTIGATIONS

A patient may have more than one STI present at the same time. Accurate diagnosis therefore requires a range of laboratory tests such as serology for syphilis, swab for chlamydia and Gram stain smear and culture for gonococci. As genitourinary medicine (GUM) clinics have found it more difficult to cope with the rapidly increasing number of patients, the traditional approach of referring all suspected STI patients to the clinic has started to become impractical in certain areas. It is essential therefore to know what local protocols are in place for the investigation and treatment of STI patients. If a referral is to be made, the patient should be advised to abstain from sexual activity with a partner until he has been to the clinic. Advise the patient that, in addition to blood samples, swabs of any discharge will also be taken at the clinic for diagnostic purposes, therefore he should abstain from any attempts at self-medication.

A child may present with evidence of an STI or trauma to the genital or anal area. This is a serious child protection issue as it probably indicates sexual abuse. It is also possible in older children that they have contracted the infection as a result of voluntary sexual activity which raises other serious issues relating to both health and the legality of such activity.

If a patient presents anxious that he may have contracted HIV and requesting an HIV test, counselling is necessary before the test. The test can only be performed when sufficient time has elapsed from possible exposure for seroconversion to occur, usually at least a month. Both these points need careful explanation before referring the man to the GUM clinic. Counselling is essential before the test so that the man may be helped to work out how to respond to a positive result, as well as to ensure that he understands the basic facts about HIV infection.

There has been a great deal of controversy regarding the use of a screening test for the prostate specific antigen (PSA), elevated levels of which can diagnose prostatic cancer well before any clinical symptoms appear. The problem is that as a screening test PSA lacks both sensitivity and specificity as up to 20% of men with clinically significant prostate cancer will not have a raised PSA and about 66% of men with a raised PSA level will not have prostate cancer (Watson et al 2002). Diagnosis depends upon biopsy, an uncomfortable procedure which carries risks of its own and even then may miss a cancer in a small percentage of cases. Consequently, Selley et al (1997) recommended that there is no evidence to support the widespread use of PSA testing or population screening at present. There has been no evidence since this report to alter their recommendation that: 'there is no justification for the routine use of PSA testing in primary care. GPs should be actively discouraged from using PSA tests for the purpose of early detection'. Biopsy provides more accurate data and prostate cancers are staged and then graded by being given a Gleason Score from 1–10 (assessed from microscopic examination of the tumour cells) with the higher scores indicating more aggressive, rapidly growing tumours.

DIFFERENTIAL DIAGNOSIS

In men who present with lesions of the penis it is important to differentiate between an STI and other causes such as cancer of the penis. The sexual history will usually make it clear which is the most likely cause.

Testicular torsion can be differentiated from other causes of scrotal pain by the rapidity of onset and the common association of vomiting and loss of appetite. The patient is typically a teenager. Scrotal pain of gradual onset associated with a testicular lump indicates a tumour, while signs of inflammation clearly indicate that an inflammatory process such as epididymitis or orchitis is the problem.

It is important to distinguish between urinary incontinence and a prostatic problem in elderly male patients presenting with urinary problems. Sometimes this may not be possible, as BPH may be one contributory factor amongst others in urinary incontinence. The history, a 'dipstick' urine test, culture and sensitivity of a sterile urine sample to check for a urinary tract infection and a digital rectal examination will all assist in assessing the importance of the prostate in causing urinary problems. Digital rectal examination is notoriously unreliable when it comes to distinguishing between BPH and a prostatic cancer. Referral for specialist medical opinion is urgently needed in such cases.

TREATMENT

Local protocols should be followed if you suspect an STI. Traditionally patients were referred to a GUM clinic for investigation, diagnosis and treatment. There are obvious reasons for this policy, such as the need for contact tracing and the possible need for specialist counselling, especially in the case of a confirmed HIV infection. Demand on services is leading to changes in this traditional approach so local protocols should be followed if you suspect an STI. It is particularly important to avoid inappropriate antibiotic therapy leading to more resistant bacterial strains.

Conditions such as epididymitis or prostatitis may be secondary to an STI and their management should reflect this. Before referring a patient to the clinic he should be advised to abstain from sex with a partner, with a careful explanation why. If he refuses, he should be urged to use a condom.

Trauma to the penis, such as a zip injury, can provoke a great deal of fear and anxiety. The rich blood supply ensures that any small wound bleeds profusely, increasing the patient's anxiety. Direct pressure will control bleeding and ice packs will reduce swelling. Depending on the location of the wound, i.e. if it is on the shaft, steristrips may suffice to close it. Referral to a hospital A&E department for assessment and treatment is advised if such simple measures are not effective as suture under local anaesthetic may be required. The highly infective nature of a human bite is such that referral is essential in such cases. If the foreskin has become retracted, it may be possible to manoeuvre it back into position after using ice packs to reduce the swelling and with a generous application of lidocaine (lignocaine) gel as a lubricant. Otherwise, referral to hospital is needed.

A significant number of conditions affecting the contents of the scrotum have potentially serious consequences, therefore an urgent medical opinion is required when such conditions are suspected. A patient with suspected torsion testes needs an immediate surgical referral as an emergency admission.

The nurse practitioner has a valuable role to play in educating men about testicular self-examination. Many men display depressing ignorance about their genitals and you should be prepared for initial resistance in undertaking health education in this field. Reactions may vary from embarrassment to defence mechanisms such as denial and trivialization of the whole issue. However, persevere, as eventually the message will get through to many patients. This is particularly important given the high success rates achieved by treatment when an early diagnosis is made. Basic guidelines for testicular self-examination are as follows:

- Self-examination should be carried out monthly, preferably after a bath, as the scrotal sac is more relaxed.
- Initially the man should aim to become familiar with the normal feel and weight of his testicles. (Taboos about 'playing with yourself' and masturbation may need to be overcome at this juncture.)
- Roll each testicle between the thumb and forefinger to ensure there is a smooth feel with no irregularities or bumps.
- Check for the normal feel of the epididymis, which lies posterior to the testicle, in order that this is not confused with any new growth.

If anything abnormal is detected, he should report to the surgery at once.

BPH is commonly managed by surgical referral and transurethral resection of the prostate (TURP). Many men have mild symptoms which can be managed without surgery, using a combination of medication, health education and community support to achieve lifestyle modification. Alpha-blocking agents improve symptoms in BPH by relaxing smooth muscle, improving flow rates and reducing obstruction. Examples include alfuzosin, indoramin, prazosin and terazosin (BNF 2004). An alternative approach is provided by the drug finasteride, which has been shown to produce significant improvements in symptoms by inhibiting the conversion of testosterone to dihydrotestosterone and thereby reducing the size of the prostate. An alternative therapy which has been shown in clinical trials to be equally effective as finasteride in mild to moderate cases of BPH involves taking Saw Palmetto extract, which is available in most health food shops (Bandolier 2000b).

The course of the disease is uncertain and significant numbers of men experience substantial improvements in their urinary symptoms and even complete remission. The regular use of the IPSS (p. 163) allows progress to be monitored. This watchful waiting approach may be the most cost-effective option for many men with mild to moderate symptoms, whilst surgical intervention is reserved for those with more serious symptoms. The nurse practitioner has a key role as the ideal person to manage the patient with mild symptoms in the community. Should symptoms become worse, it is important that the patient makes an informed decision about whether to opt for surgery, given the general risks of hospitalization in an elderly person and the specific risks of this surgery, such as ED. You have a key role in assisting the patient to make an informed choice about surgical treatment by spending time explaining the different procedures available and the risks and benefits associated with each. In this way the patient will be better equipped to discuss treatment with the surgical team at the hospital.

Whilst the benefits of surgery in moderate to severe cases of BPH are well proven, the same cannot be said of cancer of the prostate. The course of the disease is poorly understood and uncertain. There is no evidence that any one treatment confers an advantage over any other. In choosing options therefore, informed patient choice should be a major consideration, which is where the nurse practitioner can play a major role.

If acute prostatitis is suspected, rapid medical referral is needed as intravenous antibiotic therapy is required. Treating chronic prostatitis is difficult as the drugs (such as penicillin) which will be effective against the usual pathogens involved, penetrate prostatic tissue poorly. There is also considerable debate about the treatment of non-bacterial prostatitis – all of which makes this a condition which is perhaps best referred for a medical opinion, whatever form is suspected.

The adolescent or young man who has problems associated with sexuality may need specialist counselling to help him deal with potentially complex issues. Give the man time and space to talk about his feelings, remembering that this may be the first time he has felt able to do so. Homophobic bullying at school or in other predominantly male environments is a particular concern. Young men need reassurance that there is nothing wrong in being gay and that there are many gay men and women in society. There are obvious issues of sexual health to be discussed and the young man should be made aware of the risks of contracting a STI, of which HIV is only one. The nurse practitioner may be the only professional source of information to which a youngster can turn.

A key area to explore is how the young man's family may react to the news that their son is gay, as family acceptance can significantly improve his quality of life. Confidentiality should be ensured at all times, however. This is particularly important in small communities away from large urban areas where attitudes towards gays are less tolerant and where people know much more about their neighbours' business.

It may be that the chance to confide in a trusted person coupled with reassurance is all the young man needs. It would be helpful if you had the phone number of the local gay switchboard or self-help group to pass on. If there are problems with bullying at school, you should seek his permission to take the matter further, preferably involving the family and school nursing service, as well as the school. The potential for a ruined life ending in suicide is all too real.

The issues of transsexuality and transvestism are complex and their long-term solution clearly lies beyond the scope of a single nurse practitioner consultation. If a man does present with such problems, as is possible, you should have a strategy to try and help. Many of the points made in the discussion about a youngster with emerging gay sexuality are equally valid, such as a non-judgemental approach, awareness of fear and embarrassment, and confidentiality. However, many transvestites are not gay and transsexuals see themselves as fundamentally of the wrong gender, which is not the same as being gay either. Transsexuals and transvestites are individuals with complex problems who should not be stereotyped. Reassurance that he is not the only person in the world to feel like this and that there is nothing inherently wrong about such feelings may help the man feel a little better about himself. Practical help ranges from referral to a counsellor specializing in such problems through to the phone number or address of a self-help group, of which there are many in the UK – The Northern Concorde, PO Box 258, Manchester M60 1LN is one such group. The Gendys Network is a group of care providers, academics and service users who have considerable expertise in this area and may be contacted at their web site www.gender.org.uk/gendys.

Summary

Women's health has received a great deal of attention in recent years, but men's health is equally important. The attitude that many men have towards health is unhelpful and must change if the trend for men to die younger than women is ever to be reversed. You have a major role to play in promoting health amongst men in many areas not covered in this chapter, such as risk-taking behaviour, aggression management and healthy lifestyles. Sadly, many men know more about the workings of the offside trap than they do about their own genitalia, and find discussing football a lot less embarrassing. These barriers need to be overcome with tact, diplomacy and perseverance if we are to improve the overall health of half our population.

Many problems must be referred promptly to a medical practitioner for treatment, such as testicular cancer or torsion testes, but you can fulfil a valuable role in prompt diagnosis and referral. A great deal of health education work can take place, whether in the context of safer sexual practices or testicular self-examination, whilst a common chronic disease such as BPH is eminently suitable for nurse practitioner management in the community. The use of therapeutic communication skills with men having problems of sexuality can be beneficial.

References

Bandolier 2000a Predictors of acute urinary retention in Men. Online: www.jr2.ox.ac.uk/bandolier/band96

Bandolier 2000b Saw Palmetto and prostatic hypertrophy. Online: www.jr2.ox.ac.uk/bandolier/band73

Barry M J, Fowler F J, O'Leary M P 1992 The American Urological Association symptom index for benign prostatic hyperplasia. Journal of Urology 148:1549–1557

BNF 2004 British National Formulary. British Medical Association/Royal Pharmaceutical Society of Great Britain, London

CancerHelp UK 2003 Online: www.cancerhelp.org.uk

Cancer Research UK 2004 Online: www.cancerhelp.org.uk

Donovan D, Nicholas P 1997 Prostatitis: diagnosis and treatment in primary care. Nurse Practitioner 22(4):144–156

Engel J 2002 Pediatric assessment, 4th edn. Mosby, St Louis

Health Protection Agency 2004 Online: www.hpa.org.uk

Seidal H, Ball J, Dains J, Benedict G 2003 Mosby's guide to clinical examination, 5th edn. Mosby, St Louis

Selley S, Donovan J, Faulkner A, Coast J, Gillatt D 1997 Diagnosis, management and screening of early localised prostate cancer. Health Technology Assessment 1(2)

Springhouse 2002 Pathophysiology made incredibly easy, 2nd edn. Springhouse Corp, Springhouse, PA

Templeton H 2003 The management of prostate cancer. Nursing Standard 17(21):45–53

Underwood J 2000 General and systematic pathology. Churchill Livingstone, Edinburgh

Watson E, Jenkins L, Bukach C, Austoker J 2002 The PSA test and prostate cancer. Cancer Research UK, London

Chapter 11

The female reproductive system

Lesley Kyle

INTRODUCTION

In many clinical settings nurse practitioners have been introduced to enhance the diversity of health care services available to the local population. Whilst not all nurse practitioners are female, there has often been an underlying added advantage to introducing a female into a practice or clinical setting, as it has enhanced women's choice in who they might consult with to discuss issues of women's health. In the first UK nurse practitioner pilot scheme led by Barbara Stilwell, 71.6% of her patients were women with the majority being under the age of 40 (Stilwell 1985). More recently, Reveley (1998) reported that the nurse practitioner in her study recorded 71.7% consultations with women compared with the general practitioner's 64.2%.

Further studies have been completed in relation to consulting patterns and workloads in primary care. According to Horrocks et al (2002) nurse practitioners complement the primary care team and provide a high standard of care with improved patient satisfaction. It is clear that women consult frequently with nurse practitioners and it is therefore necessary to have an in-depth understanding of the major issues relating to women's health. Whilst it is clear that it is not possible to cover the whole gamut of women's health problems in one chapter, this chapter aims to cover the major types of clinical presentation of women's health problems in practice, the important aspects in taking a focused history from women who present with clinical problems and the essentials of physical examination related to the female reproductive system. The management and patient education relating to a selection of women's health problems will be covered to offer guidance for nurse practitioners who are dealing with women in their practice setting.

This chapter will also include brief discussion regarding the introduction and impact of extended and supplementary nurse prescribing in the UK for those nurse practitioners who have completed the relevant academic course (Courtenay & Butler 2002). This further enhances their role in the management of women's health in primary care as the extended formulary allows nurses to prescribe from a specific list of prescription-only medicines. This currently includes pre-conceptual care, contraception (both routine and emergency) and medicines to treat dysmenorrhoea, candidiasis, bacterial vaginosis, chlamydia, trichomonas vaginalis, menopausal vaginal atrophy and uncomplicated urinary tract infection. This list will be reviewed and extended by the Department of Health (Nurse Prescribers' Extended Formulary 2004). Supplementary prescribers are now able to issue repeat prescriptions for other drugs such as HRT if there is a clinical management plan that has been agreed and signed by an independent prescriber (usually the general practitioner), patient and nurse prescriber. This not only aids the nurse's autonomy in managing consultations effectively but may also improve patient satisfaction and relieve the workload of the general practitioner.

PATHOPHYSIOLOGY AND CLINICAL PRESENTATIONS

A woman may choose to consult with a nurse practitioner because a clinical problem has developed, because she needs advice on a completely normal process in her life or she may present for screening. The normal development of puberty, the menstrual cycle and the menopause will be discussed here, followed by clinical presentations of breast disease and of genital tract disease.

PUBERTY

The transformation from childhood to adolescence is known as puberty and this occurs between 8 and 13 years for girls; the average age of the menarche is 12.5 years (Epstein et al 2003). At this time there is a rapid growth spurt and development of sexual characteristics and sexual arousal. Puberty involves growth in a number of body systems and development in one part of the body may not necessarily coincide with development in another part. Development can be assessed using Tanner's staging (Tanner 1973; Figures 11.1 and 11.2). Pubertal milestones such as the presence of breast buds and the appearance and growth of pubic hair have been divided into five stages by Tanner and provide a useful guide for assessing development.

The developmental changes that occur during puberty are the product of hormonal influences. Gonadotrophin-releasing hormone (GnRH) is a small polypeptide produced by the hypothalamus. GnRH secretion is inhibited until puberty. GnRH release causes the release of luteinizing hormone (LH) and follicle-stimulating hormone (FSH) in the pituitary gland, which in turn stimulates the gonads. The hormonal influence of the gonads results in the development of the reproductive system, the development of secondary sexual characteristics and the menstrual cycle becoming established. It is usual

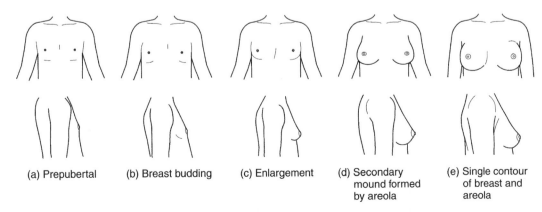

(a) Prepubertal   (b) Breast budding   (c) Enlargement   (d) Secondary mound formed by areola   (e) Single contour of breast and areola

Figure 11.1 Tanner's stages of breast development in puberty.

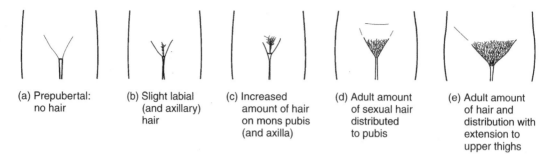

(a) Prepubertal:
no hair

(b) Slight labial
(and axillary)
hair

(c) Increased
amount of hair
on mons pubis
(and axilla)

(d) Adult amount
of sexual hair
distributed
to pubis

(e) Adult amount
of hair and
distribution with
extension to
upper thighs

Figure 11.2 Tanner's stages of pubic hair development.

for the female's first menarche to be anovulatory. The first ovulation may be up to 2 years after the first menstruation. Eventually the endocrine system and the brain mature so that the LH surge is sufficient to cause the first ovulation.

MENSTRUAL CYCLE

In order to understand some of the problems of menstruation it is important first to review the normal menstrual cycle. The purpose of the menstrual cycle is to release a single egg from the ovary and prepare the uterus to receive an embryo after fertilization occurs. When fertilization does not occur, the lining of the uterus degenerates and is expelled from the body at menstruation. Currently this process occurs in women who are on average between the ages of 13 and 51 years (Thomas & Rock 1997) and the length of cycles averages between 25 and 35 days. However, only 10–15% of menstrual cycles are exactly the length of a lunar month and younger women tend to have longer cycles than older women.

The physiology of the menstrual cycle is summarized in Figure 11.3. GnRH is produced by the hypothalamus and its release is controlled by neurotransmitters and by feedback of oestrogen and progesterone from the ovary. GnRH flows through the hypophyseal portal system to the anterior pituitary and stimulates the secretion of LH and FSH. LH and FSH stimulate the formation of a few selected dormant follicles in the ovary. Only one follicle usually matures to the point of ovulation (Epstein et al 2003). Under the influence of LH and FSH, the follicle secretes increasing amounts of oestrogen and grows to a preovulatory size of approximately 2–3 cm. In mid-cycle there is a surge of LH and FSH which is thought to trigger the follicle to rupture and expel the ovum from the ovary.

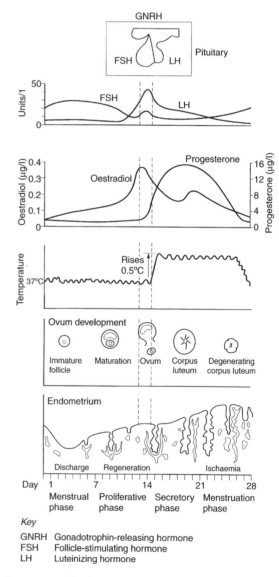

Key

GNRH Gonadotrophin-releasing hormone
FSH   Follicle-stimulating hormone
LH   Luteinizing hormone

Figure 11.3 Physiology of the menstrual cycle (adapted from Epstein et al 2003, with permission).

The ruptured follicle changes into the corpus luteum which secretes progesterone. By about the 23rd day of the cycle, if no pregnancy has occurred the corpus luteum begins to degenerate, progesterone levels fall, allowing FSH to start to rise again and, following vasospasm in the arterioles which feed the superficial layers of the endometrium, the lining of the uterus becomes necrotic and is finally expelled from the uterus through the vagina.

The menstrual cycle is divided into three phases: the menstrual, proliferative and secretory phases. The cycle begins with the onset of menses and the degeneration of the endometrial lining (Martini 2004a). In the proliferative phase the epithelial cells of the uterine glands multiply and spread across the endometrial surface. This occurs at the same time as the follicles in the ovary enlarge and is also known as the preovulatory or follicular phase of the cycle. This phase is stimulated and sustained by oestrogen secreted by the developing follicles. At ovulation the corpus luteum secretes progesterone and this, in combination with the continuing effects of oestrogen, is responsible for the secretory phase.

During the secretory phase the endometrial glands enlarge and the arteries elongate. This is also known as the postovulatory or luteal phase of the menstrual cycle. The granulosa cells of the corpus luteum have receptors for LH which are also capable of binding with human chorionic gonadotrophin (hCG). HCG is secreted by fetal tissue and therefore in the absence of fertilization, hCG does not appear, the corpus luteum begins to atrophy, progesterone levels fall and a new cycle begins with the onset of menses. The secretory phase usually lasts for 14 days and therefore the date of ovulation can be estimated by counting backwards 14 days from the first day of menses.

CLIMACTERIC AND THE MENOPAUSE

The menstrual cycle continues until approximately 45–51 years of age. It is common for women who have problems with menopausal symptoms or who are anticipating the onset of the menopause to seek help and advice from the nurse practitioner. The climacteric begins when the number of functional oocytes in the ovary has fallen to the point where the synthesis of sex hormones is reduced. FSH levels initially increase in an attempt to stimulate follicular ripening and gradually the cycles become more irregular and anovulatory. As the ovarian follicles become less sensitive to circulating hormones, the follicular phase shortens and it is not uncommon for women to experience shortening of the menstrual cycle to 18–24 days before the cycle lengthens, with gaps of amenorrhoea and finally cessation of menstruation. The final cessation of menstruation is due to the loss of the hormonal feedback system and this results in measurably high serum levels of FSH and LH. At the menopause oestrogen production decreases and this results in atrophy of the breasts, genital organs and bone.

Symptoms of the menopause

The symptoms of the menopause can be split into physical and psychological symptoms. Physical symptoms include flushes, sweats, dizziness, palpitations, migraine headaches, atrophic vaginitis, urethral symptoms, joint pain, stiffness and dyspareunia. Psychological symptoms include loss of libido, mood changes, depression, panic attacks, agoraphobia, poor concentration, tiredness and loss of self-esteem (Tortora & Grabowski 2003). The flushes associated with the menopause are associated with vasodilation of the blood vessels of the face, neck and hands. Hot flushes may occur as often as every 10 minutes and result from a more active sympathetic nervous system. Coope (1997) states that depression at the menopause is caused by many factors. It is important to measure the depth of the depression using an appropriate scale such as the Beck Depression Inventory (France & Robson 1986) and to refer suicidal patients appropriately. Coope (1997) also reports that perimenopausal patients respond better to oestrogen treatment than postmenopausal women; this may be due to the large swings in hormone levels which occur during the transition stage.

CLINICAL PRESENTATIONS OF BREAST DISEASE

Breast cancer is the commonest form of cancer in women in the UK. In 2000 there were 33 829 new registrations of breast cancer in women in England. One in 9 women will develop breast cancer at some time in their life – in 2001 11 574 women died from breast cancer in England and Wales (NHS cancer screening programmes 2004). The risk of developing breast cancer increases with age. The estimated risk of developing it in women who are 85 years of age and over is one in 10 (NHS cancer screening programmes 2004). Although risk factors have been identified the cause in most women is unknown (Dixon et al 2000). In recent years increased awareness and media coverage of breast cancer have heightened women's anxiety who have then felt the need to seek help and reassurance from health care professionals. Most consultations regarding breast symptoms in primary care are for benign breast disease. The nurse practitioner may encounter many women in planned consultations as well as opportunistically and therefore a detailed understanding of breast disease is vital.

The main role for the nurse practitioner is to encourage women to be breast-aware by informing and educating them, as well as stressing the importance of the National Breast Screening Programme for women aged 50–64, which commenced in the UK in 1988. This screening programme uses mammography, which is the only effective method to detect and screen breast tumours – this has been supported by various randomized controlled trials (Underwood 2000). However, some women may be anxious about exposure to radiation in mammographic screening although the potential benefit far outweighs the risk of exposure to radiation. Breast self-examination carried out as a monthly routine is now regarded as ineffectual as several studies have shown that it does not affect breast cancer mortality (Austoker et al 1997).

Health professionals used a variety of techniques and methods to encourage women to carry out breast self-examination. This caused confusion and anxiety in some women, who then felt reluctant to touch and examine their own breasts, as they were worried about using an incorrect technique. Breast awareness for women in all age groups is now being encouraged. This involves teaching women what is normal and abnormal, educating them to recognize changes in their breasts and encouraging them to report changes at the earliest possible opportunity. This hopefully results in more appropriate referral to specialist breast services.

Women who are experiencing breast problems consult with health professionals, as they need a clear diagnosis and the reassurance, if possible, that they do not have cancer. For the purpose of this section there will be a brief overview of the physiology of the breast with discussion of breast lumps, breast pain and nipple discharge.

THE FEMALE BREAST

The female breast is composed of glandular tissue arranged in lobes around the nipple, supportive fibrous tissue and fat, which surround the breast. Cooper's suspensory ligaments are fibrous and link the skin with fascia under the breast. It is the glandular tissue that produces milk following a pregnancy; a lactiferous duct opening out on to the nipple drains each lobe. The proportions of glandular tissue, fibrous tissue and fat vary with age, pregnancy, nutritional status, use of hormones such as hormone replacement treatment (HRT) or oral contraceptives, as well as other factors. Figure 11.4 shows the normal breast.

For descriptive purposes the breast may be divided into four quadrants - the upper outer, the upper inner, the lower outer and the lower inner – and the tail of Spence, which extends towards and into the axilla (Epstein et al 2003) (Fig. 11.5).

Lymphatic drainage is important as breast cancer can spread to regional lymph nodes. Of particular note is the fact that the internal mammary chain drains towards the opposite breast and abdomen (Fig. 11.6). The axillary nodes are arranged in five groups to drain the outer breast and the internal mammary chain, which drains the inner breast (Fig. 11.7).

BREAST LUMP

The commonest cause of breast lumps in women is one or more of the following: cyst, abscess, fibroadenoma, fibroadenosis, lipoma or carcinoma of the breast.

Cysts

Cysts are inflamed lobules or fluid-filled sacs found in the glandular tissue, which develop and enlarge over a short period of time. The commonest age of presentation is 40–50 years. They are usually found in the upper outer quadrant and 50% of women present with multiple cysts. Cysts are usually round and mobile, clearly defined from other tissues and feel soft or firm. They may appear in one or both breasts and may be tender due to leakage of fluid into the surrounding tissues. The pain associated with a cyst is unrelated to the menstrual cycle and there is normally no retraction of the nipple or tethering of the skin (Austoker et al 1997).

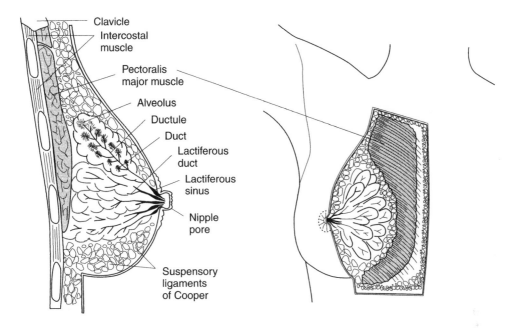

Figure 11.4 Anatomy of a normal breast.

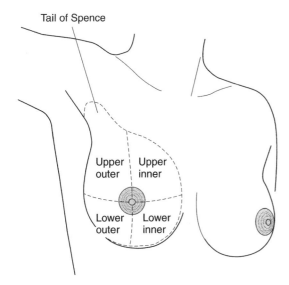

Figure 11.5 Four quadrants of the breast and tail of Spence.

Abscesses

Abscesses most commonly occur as mastitis during breast-feeding when one of the ducts becomes blocked. The skin is inflamed, red and may be hot to touch as well as extremely painful. The most common causative organism is *Staphylococcus aureus*. Treatment involves antibiotics and emptying the breast by expression to reduce the overall pressure on the tissue of the breast. An additional reason for carrying out expression of milk with these women is to help them maintain lactation. A small number of women will not respond to this treatment and will require surgical drainage of the abscess.

Fibroadenoma

Fibroadenomas are benign tumours, which are more common in puberty and younger women between the ages of 18 and 30. They may be round, disc-shaped or lobular, in one or both breasts and feel firm or rubbery. They are usually extremely mobile and non-tender with no retraction of the nipple or tethering of the skin. They may grow slowly in size but most regress with age as they are uncommon in women over the age of 30. Diagnosis is normally via referral to the specialist breast clinic where clinical examination, ultrasound and fine-needle aspiration will confirm the benign nature of the disease. Some women prefer to have the lump excised and this can be performed under local anaesthetic. Fibroadenosis, or 'lumpy breasts', is often bilateral and related to the hormonal influences of the menstrual cycle, causing pain during the pre-menstrual and menstrual phases. A lipoma may occur in the breast and, like its occurrence in other parts of the body, it tends to be benign and fatty.

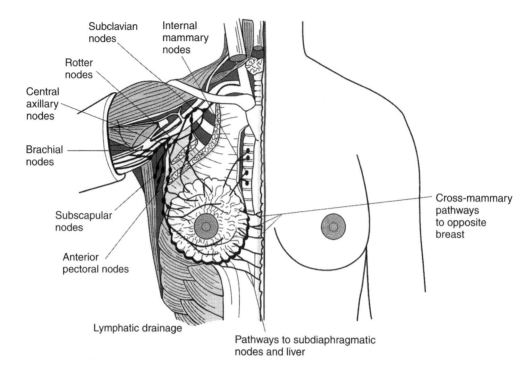

Figure 11.6 Lymphatic drainage.

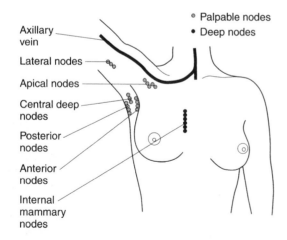

Figure 11.7 The axillary node positions.

A pseudolipoma may occasionally be the earliest sign of ductal carcinoma (Baum 1996).

Cancer

Cancer of the breast is often due to a primary tumour and most commonly affects women over the age of 40, and this continues to be a problem for women in the later years. Despite early diagnosis it may not be possible to confine the disease within the breast as there may already be lymph node involvement. However, this is less likely when the lump or cancer is 2 cm or less. Early detection and diagnosis are important as this influences the survival rate. A lump associated with breast cancer is often hard, irregular and painless but is more likely to be fixed to underlying tissues or skin. This may cause dimpling or puckering of the skin due to pectoral contraction when the lump is attached to the skin and fascia. This may be diagnosed during the physical examination when the woman raises her arms or places them on her hips. The lump may be single, although there may be other nodules present and it is more commonly found in the upper outer quadrant of the breast.

Some women may have always had retracted nipples and this should be established during the history-taking process. Recent retraction of the nipple and areola may suggest an underlying cancer which is near the centre of the breast. It is essential to ensure that you examine the breast thoroughly over this area. All women with suspected breast cancer must be referred urgently according to local guidelines to the specialist breast clinic for assessment and treatment.

> **Box 11.1 Risk factors for breast cancer**
>
> Genetic history
> Previous breast cancer
> Previous ovarian, colon, thyroid or endometrial cancer
> Early menarche (before age 12)
> First pregnancy over the age of 35
> Nulliparous
> Late menopause (over the age of 55)
> Increasing age
> Ionizing radiation

Risk factors for breast cancer are varied and some remain controversial. An assessment of family history is important and should be assisted by completing a genogram to help distinguish between familial and hereditary breast cancer. Familial breast cancer can be defined by two or more family members who have had breast cancer; hereditary is associated with the autosomal dominant transmission of the disease and is found in women who have the disease before the age of 45 years (McCance & Jorde 1998). The National Institute of Clinical Excellence (NICE) guidelines for familial breast cancer (2004) provide a standardized and structured approach with key priorities in the care and management of women with a family history. Several factors are associated with the development of breast cancer and therefore the aetiology of this disease is complicated. Box 11.1 summarizes the most common risk factors.

NIPPLE DISCHARGE

In women who have never been pregnant any discharge is regarded as abnormal. This presents more commonly with a lump but may be spontaneous. The discharge can be milk, blood-stained or coloured.

Milk

The most common discharge is milk, either after pregnancy or in endocrine abnormalities, causing a rise in prolactin level. This is known as galactorrhoea and may be due to a pituitary tumour or, more commonly, as a side effect of medication such as phenothiazines or metoclopramide.

Bloodstained fluid

Bloodstained fluid may be associated with benign or malignant disease. The cause should always be investigated. Possible diagnoses are duct papilloma, epithelial proliferation or cancer (Baum 1996).

Coloured discharge

Duct ectasia is a benign but painful condition in which the terminal lactiferous ducts become dilated and the surrounding tissues are inflamed. It is most common in postmenopausal women and often presents as a thick multicoloured discharge from multiple ducts. This is due to cellular debris from the epithelial lining forming in the ducts. A hard indurated lump may then be felt close to the areola and hopefully this resolves within a few weeks. Cystic disease may cause a green or yellow discharge, which can be swabbed for culture and sensitivity. Pus is usually associated with acute mastitis, which is accompanied by inflammation or abscess.

BREAST PAIN

Hormonal influences are the commonest cause of breast pain. Other causes include pregnancy, cracked nipple, cyst, abscess, trauma, anxiety state, angina and herpes zoster. Cyclical breast pain with or without nodularity is usually bilateral and most commonly occurs in the week preceding the woman's period. For most women this is not a problem as it resolves following menstruation. For some women the pain is more prolonged and severe during the luteal or secretory phase of their cycle, which can lead to anxiety and insomnia. This may be due to prolactin causing a hypersensitive reaction in the duct epithelium or an abnormality in the secretion of gonadotrophins (Austoker et al 1997). The oral contraceptive pill and HRT preparations may also be related to breast pain due to the hormonal influences of these medications. Non-cyclical pain is unrelated to the menstrual cycle, is often localized in one breast and is most common in women over the age of 40. Symptoms often resolve without treatment.

If a woman presents with a breast lump, nipple discharge or breast pain she should be fully assessed for the presence of all three symptoms as they are often related and one symptom may obscure the presence of another.

CLINICAL PRESENTATIONS OF GENITAL TRACT DISEASE

ADNEXAE

The adnexae include the fallopian tubes, ovaries and the pelvic fascia and ligaments. There are a variety of problems associated with these structures, including salpingitis, pelvic inflammatory disease, ectopic pregnancy, ovarian cysts and prolapse. Figure 11.8 shows the normal female pelvic anatomy.

Salpingitis and pelvic inflammatory disease

Several sexually transmitted infections and other organisms such as *Streptococcus*, *Staphylococcus* or *Escherichia* can invade the uterus and eventually the

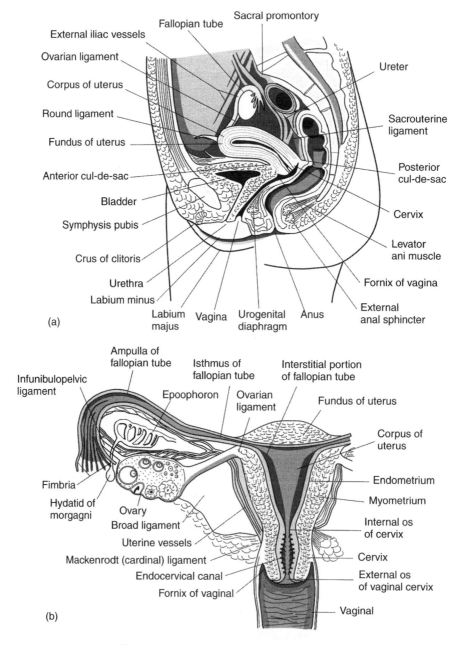

(a)

(b)

Figure 11.8 Normal female pelvic anatomy.

fallopian tubes, resulting in salpingitis. This inflammation may cause lower abdominal pain, fever and vomiting in the patient and may result in scarring, which may eventually be the cause of an ectopic pregnancy. If the infection spreads beyond the fallopian tubes, the pelvic organs may become involved, resulting in pelvic inflammatory disease, which can be a serious and life-threatening condition. Pelvic inflammatory disease can be acute or chronic. The acute presentation produces tender bilateral adnexal areas, the patient may guard on palpation and often cannot tolerate bimanual examination. Chronic pelvic inflammatory disease tends to produce irregular tender areas.

Ectopic pregnancy

Ectopic pregnancy is more common in women who have been sterilized, women who have had a previous abortion, multiparous or older women, or those women who have experienced pelvic inflammatory disease or endometriosis. In a normal pregnancy implantation occurs on the posterior wall of the uterus. The pregnancy is termed ectopic if implantation occurs outside the uterus. This most often occurs in the fallopian tubes and is extremely dangerous, as the embryo is growing in a restricted area, exerting pressure on the thin vascular walls of the tubes. The patient presents with lower abdominal pain and, if the condition has been allowed to develop unchecked, the woman will eventually haemorrhage, resulting in a serious risk to life. A woman who presents with unilateral tenderness and an adnexal mass should be assessed for tachycardia and shock as ruptured ectopic pregnancy is an emergency and must be treated surgically.

Ovarian cysts

There are two major kinds of ovarian cysts – cystic follicles which are large, fluid-filled sacs formed from unovulated follicles and luteinized cysts, which are solid masses filled with luteal cells. Both are common and can disappear spontaneously. In some cases the cysts persist and secrete abnormal amounts of steroid hormones, resulting in complications with fertility. These cysts must be removed surgically. In some women the ovaries may contain many cysts – a condition known as polycystic ovarian syndrome. A ruptured ovarian cyst can mimic the symptoms of tubal pregnancy; intact cysts tend not to be tender. On palpation, a cyst is smooth and sometimes compressible, whereas

tumours feel more solid and nodular (Seidel et al 2003).

Prolapse

The ligaments of the pelvis span laterally, connecting the cervix and upper vagina to the bony pelvis. These are known as the cardinal ligaments. The uterosacral ligaments pass posteriorly and backwards from the posterolateral cervix to the sacrum. If the pelvic ligaments become lax and the muscular floor of the pelvis weakens, the pelvic organs may drop and prolapse (Epstein et al 2003). There are several causes of genitourinary prolapse (Jackson & Smith 1997). Those associated with childbirth include large babies, long labours, assisted delivery and poor postnatal exercise regimes. Other causes of prolapse include hysterectomy, increased intra-abdominal pressure associated with obesity, chronic respiratory disease and pelvic masses which may have the same effect, and connective tissue disease which may also weaken the supporting structures of the pelvis. The patient may present with a variety of clinical problems associated with prolapse (Box 11.2).

Box 11.2 Presenting symptoms of genitourinary prolapse

Cystourethrocele
Urinary stress incontinence, urinary retention, recurrent urinary tract infection

Uterine prolapse
Backache, difficulty inserting and keeping tampons in, ulceration if procedentia

Rectocele
Constipation

Any prolapse
Lump coming down, difficulties with sexual intercourse

UTERUS

Abnormal patterns of uterine bleeding

Problems with uterine bleeding may present as oligomenorrhoea, amenorrhoea or dysfunctional uterine bleeding, including intermenstrual or postmenopausal uterine bleeding.

Oligomenorrhoea and amenorrhoea

Oligomenorrhoea is the term used to describe infrequent or scanty menstrual periods. Dealy (1998) defines oligomenorrhoea as irregular bleeding episodes that occur at intervals of more than 42 days. This pattern may be a normal feature of the climacteric or of menarche before a regular menstrual pattern develops. In some women this pattern persists for life and it is therefore worthwhile taking a thorough history of the woman's experience of menstruation to determine how abnormal this pattern is for her. If this pattern presents as a definite change from the woman's normal experience of menstruation then it should be treated in the same way as amenorrhoea, as the causes are generally the same (Rees 1997).

Amenorrhoea can cause great distress to a woman as the absence of the normal pattern of menstruation has implications for her femininity and her overall general health and wellbeing. Tothill (1998) states that all women who present with amenorrhoea should be considered pregnant until proven otherwise and that they should all be advised to continue with a reliable form of con-

traception as amenorrhoea does not necessarily indicate subfertility. There are numerous causes of secondary amenorrhoea and oligomenorrhoea, which are summarized in Box 11.3. Primary amenorrhoea results from genetic disturbances such as Turner's syndrome, when the woman will never menstruate and the reproductive tract never matures fully.

Dysfunctional uterine bleeding

Dysfunctional uterine bleeding can be defined as painless irregular vaginal bleeding which originates from the endometrium and may be excessive, prolonged or irregular. Dealy (1998) defines five terms related to abnormal uterine bleeding:

- Hypomenorrhoea: decreased uterine bleeding that occurs at regular intervals
- Intermenstrual bleeding: episodes of uterine bleeding between regular menstrual periods
- Menorrhagia: uterine bleeding at the usual time of menses that is excessive in either duration or flow
- Menometrorrhagia: frequent irregular bleeding that may be excessive in amount or of prolonged duration
- Metrorrhagia: uterine bleeding that occurs at regular intervals and may range from spotting to a menses-like flow.

The unusual pattern of bleeding can be related to an underlying systemic or local lesion but most often in young women it is related to anovulation. Dysfunctional uterine bleeding can be divided into three categories: cyclical abnormal uterine bleeding, cyclical bleeding superimposed with abnormal uterine bleeding, and non-cyclical. These categories can help the nurse practitioner make decisions about the probable causes of the bleeding pattern and make appropriate treatment and management decisions. For example, cyclical bleeding superimposed with abnormal uterine bleeding may have an organic pathology such as trauma, uterine polyps, congenital malformations, cervical haemangiomas or infections (Dealy 1998). The list of potential diagnoses for women who present with dysfunctional bleeding is extremely lengthy. Some possible causes are listed in Box 11.4.

Intermenstrual and postmenopausal bleeding require a special mention here as it is particularly important to maintain a high level of suspicion with these women and to take a thorough history

---

Box 11.3 Causes of secondary amenorrhoea and oligomenorrhoea

Ovarian, uterine and vaginal disorders
Polycystic ovarian disease
Ovarian failure
Ovarian tumour
Severe acute illness
Chronic infections or illness
Autoimmune disease

Hormonal disorders
Thyroid hormone deficiency or excess
Pituitary tumours
Adrenal tumours
Post oral contraceptive pill

Psychological
Anorexia nervosa
Depression
Fear of pregnancy
Stress or anxiety

Physiological
Pregnancy
Lactation

Box 11.4 Possible causes of abnormal bleeding

Vaginal/cervical
Cervical polyps
Cervical erosions
Cervical cancer
Infection, *Chlamydia*, trichomoniasis, gonorrhoea
Vaginal trauma
Atrophic vaginitis

Ovarian/uterine
Intrauterine devices
Endometrial polyps
Retained tampon
Uterine fibroids
Ovarian cancer
Uterine cancer

Hormonal
Ovulation
Oral contraceptive pill
Hormonal replacement therapy

Pregnancy complications
Incomplete or missed abortion
Threatened abortion
Molar pregnancy
Ectopic pregnancy

Medications
Phenytoin
Warfarin
Hormonal contraceptives
Phenobarbitone

Blood dyscrasias
Leukemia
Pernicious anaemia

Hypothalamic anovulation
Stress
Eating disorders
Chronic disease, for example hypothyroidism, diabetes mellitus
Excessive exercise

followed by a thorough physical examination with investigations to rule out the possibility of malignant causes of the problem. Diseases of the uterus and cervix may present in this way, so it is worth considering disorders of the mucosa, such as endometritis, carcinoma or endometrial polyps, or submucosa, such as fibroids or submucosal leiomy-omas. Post-coital bleeding usually indicates local cervical or uterine disease such as cervical polyp, cervicitis, or erosion; it may also indicate carcinoma.

Dysmenorrhoea

Painful menstruation may be classified as primary or secondary dysmenorrhoea and is a common reason for missing school, work or leisure activities. Primary dysmenorrhoea appears 6–12 months after the menarche and in general is not associated with pelvic pathology. Secondary dysmenorrhoea can present at any time and may be associated with other pelvic disease. In primary dysmenorrhoea the patient may complain of discomfort in the first 2 days of menstruation. The pain may be described as lower abdominal cramps and backache and this may be associated with diarrhoea and vomiting. Dysmenorrhoea has been found to be associated with uterine hypercontractility resulting in ischaemia as the contractions reduce endometrial blood flow and produce colicky-type pain (Rees 1997). It has been found that this hypercontractility is related to increased prostaglandin production and raised vasopressin levels, although the stimulus for their production remains unknown.

Secondary dysmenorrhoea is associated with endometriosis, pelvic inflammatory disease, endometrial polyps, the use of an intrauterine device and adenomyosis. The patient may present with a change in intensity or timing of pain; it may be associated with discomfort before the bleeding begins and may last for the whole of the menstruation. Any such changes or presentations, which occur several years after the onset of menstruation, should be thoroughly investigated to rule out possible pelvic pathology.

Dyspareunia

Dyspareunia is pain occurring during sexual intercourse. The pain may be superficial and localized or deep and experienced as a sensation of discomfort deep inside the pelvis. The history-taking process and symptom analysis using PQRST (as described in Chapter 2) is extremely useful in this situation as it will help differentiate between the various causes of dyspareunia. If the patient describes a sensation of pain at the entrance to the vagina, this may be due to vaginismus (vaginal spasm), failure of the vagina to lubricate, irritation or damage to the clitoris, inflammation of Bartholin's glands or a vaginal infection. If the pain is described as dull and deep it may be due to lack of arousal and consequent absence of ballooning in the inner vagina, which results in the cervix being buffeted during sexual intercourse and produces an uncomfortable sensation in the pelvis. Deep pain can also be related to a retroverted, displaced or prolapsed uterus or other pelvic pathology such as chronic salpingitis, fibroids or endometriosis.

In an older postmenopausal woman it may be necessary to consider atrophic vaginitis as the vulva and vagina become dry after the menopause, resulting in discomfort on intercourse. Whatever the cause of the pain, it is likely to be associated with a great deal of anxiety and therefore it is essential that the woman is treated with sensitivity and care. It may be that she simply needs advice about lubrication, sexual arousal or positioning during intercourse to help reduce discomfort or in the case of pelvic pathology it will be necessary to investigate the problems further.

VAGINA

Vaginitis is a common presenting problem. There are a number of causes, including bacterial vaginosis, candidiasis and trichomoniasis.

Bacterial vaginosis

Bacterial vaginosis results from high concentrations of anaerobic bacteria such as *Gardnerella vaginalis*. Contributory factors in the development of this disease include retention of a diaphragm or tampon, recent intrauterine device placement, administration of antibiotics and multiple sexual partners.

Candidiasis

Candidiasis tends to present as vaginal itching and burning. Predisposing factors for the development of Candida include diabetes mellitus, pregnancy, vaginal trauma, antibiotics and tight-fitting synthetic underwear.

Trichomoniasis

Trichomoniasis is the third commonest cause of vaginitis and a common sexually transmitted infection. Symptoms vary enormously between patients. In about 15% of women there are no symptoms while in others there may be acute inflammatory disease. Most commonly there is a copious yellow-grey or green malodorous discharge and vulvovaginal

---

Box 11.5 Causes of abnormal vaginal discharge

Vaginal causes
Candida
Trichomoniasis
Gardnerella
Genital warts
Genital herpes
Atrophic vaginitis
Bacterial infection caused by retained tampon
Irritants and allergic reactions

Cervical causes
Gonorrhoea
Cervical polyp
Cervical erosion
Herpes
Intrauterine contraceptive device

---

irritation. The condition is caused by the organism *Trichomonas vaginalis* and diagnosis is confirmed with a fresh wet slide for mobile flagellated organisms. Occasionally diagnosis may be established as a result of a report following a cervical smear.

Each of these three conditions may cause the woman great discomfort and irritation. However, the NP who is able to prescribe can now treat all three of these conditions when confirmed by laboratory testing (NPEF 2004).

There are several other causes of vaginal discharge, summarized in Box 11.5.

Genital herpes

Genital herpes may be caused by herpes simplex virus 1 (HSV1) or 2 (HSV2). Infection with HSV1 is the same virus responsible for cold sores on the mouth. In all, 80–90% of genital herpes cases are caused by an infection with HSV2 (Martini 2004b). The presentation of this condition is extremely painful. Itchy, ulcerated lesions appear on the external genitalia and may also appear on the cervix. Sometimes these lesions produce a serous discharge, which may be swabbed for viral cultures. The ulcers gradually heal in 2–3 weeks. The initial infection is extensive but recurrent infection tends to be localized on the vulva, vagina, perineum or cervix. This condition is sexually transmitted and recent research has indicated that transmission may occur during acute episodes and even in the latent phase of the disease (Patel et al 1997).

Chlamydia

Chlamydia is the commonest bacterial sexually transmitted infection in this country and the prevalence is highest in younger age groups. However, as the majority of those infected are asymptomatic many cases remain undiagnosed (Low & Cowan 2000). Several pilot studies have been set up in an attempt to address this issue and identify a national programme for chlamydia screening. If left untreated it may persist in women for up to 15 months and cause scarring of the fallopian tubes and pelvic inflammatory disease, leading to infertility. If symptoms are present the discharge is mucopurulent and originates from the cervical os; there may also be intermenstrual postcoital spotting and a discharge from the Bartholin's glands. An area of the cervix may appear hypertrophic, oedematous and friable and the patient may have asymptomatic urethritis. Swabs must be taken from the endocervical canal of the cervix. In some areas the new urine-screening test using the Beckton Dickinson Probetec assay is available for both women and men to screen for chlamydia in a less invasive way. This test uses amplified DNA technology to improve sensitivity and specificity of the test.

VULVA

Women may present with complaints of vulval swelling, itching, discomfort or pain, soreness, bleeding or purulent discharge from the vulva. It is not uncommon for women to be unaware of problems in this area of their body and the nurse practitioner may notice a lesion during a routine examination for a smear or for other pelvic problems. The vulva is a common site of thrush, boils, genital warts and cysts and it may also be the site of a carcinoma. A vaginal discharge due to *Candida* or *Trichomonas* can result in excoriation of the vulva or may result in *Candida* spreading to the labia and upper thighs. The patient may present with a painful swelling on the vulva which may be a furuncle (a deep staphylococcal follicular pustule). Cysts tend not to be tender on palpation and present as firm round, yellow lesions.

Genital warts

A crop of small painful perianal pustules and vesicles may suggest herpes infection. The patient may also present with multiple genital warts, which may extend into the vagina and posteriorly may extend on to the perineum. The warts may coalesce to form irregular tissue masses and most often are caused by the human papillomavirus. The presence of genital warts is linked to the development of cervical intraepithelial neoplasia and this should therefore heighten your suspicion for the possibility of a positive smear test.

Inflamed Bartholin's glands

A further cause of vulval discomfort is inflamed Bartholin's glands. This condition may present as an acute or chronic problem and is commonly but not always caused by gonococcal infection. The acute inflammation causes hot, red and tender swelling which may drain pus and the chronic condition may result in a non-tender cyst on the labium.

HISTORY-TAKING

It is essential during the history-taking process to build up a rapport with the woman as most often examination of the most intimate parts of the woman's body will follow and if the woman is relaxed the examination will proceed more smoothly. An anxious patient will have tense muscles and the examination will be traumatic for both patient and NP. It is therefore essential that you consider the history-taking process to be an integral part of the whole consultation and that one of the underlying purposes of the communication at this stage of the consultation is to relax the patient and to gain her confidence.

In many consultations with women for problems associated with the female reproductive system it will be important to enquire about family history. Incidence of genetic disorders in the family is important, as is the incidence of breast cancer. It is useful to enquire about the patient's mother and, if appropriate, sister's experience of the menarche and menopause as this is likely to have an impact on the patient's expectations. As systemic disorders such as diabetes and thyroid disease can have an effect on menstruation it is worth enquiring about the incidence of these problems in the family.

Past medical history is important to discover any incidence of surgery such as dilatation and curettage, cone biopsy, hysterectomy or a repair of prolapse, for example. It is also useful to ask the woman about previous pregnancies and methods of delivery as trauma at the birth such as prolonged labour or a large baby may account for the presenting symptoms of the current problem. Termination of pregnancy is an extremely sensitive issue, which should only be addressed with a woman if it is deemed to be an important aspect of the examination and history-taking process with regard to the presenting clinical problem.

Other generally important aspects of history taking include current medications, particularly those which might affect the menstrual cycle. It may be useful to ask about numbers of sexual partners and to what extent the presenting problem is affecting the patient's lifestyle. Methods of contraception in the past and at present should also be addressed.

A general history from any woman should also include her smear status. This will provide an excellent opportunity to follow up patients who have slipped through the screening net or those who may need encouragement and education relating to the process of screening for cervical cancer. It is almost always necessary to enquire about the woman's last menstrual cycle and whether she considers that this was a normal period or if it was different in some way. Enquiring about the timing of the last menstrual cycle is necessary before smear-taking, discussing contraception, assessing a woman in abdominal pain and many other likely presenting clinical problems associated with the female reproductive system.

FOCUSED HISTORY FOR PROBLEMS ASSOCIATED WITH THE BREAST

The most common symptoms will relate to breast lump, breast pain or nipple discharge. Some women may present with one, two or all three symptoms and the most useful starting point for the assessment is using the mnemonic PQRST, adapted according to the presenting problem (Chapter 2).

Box 11.6 is a summary of the questions you might choose to explore with the patient.

Past medical history

This should include any previous breast problems and investigations undertaken with dates and results, any gynaecological problems or investigations and previous pregnancies, including complications. The presence of chronic illness such as thyroid disease, diabetes or other endocrine abnormalities may also be relevant.

Box 11.6 History-taking for breast lumps, pain and nipple discharge

Breast lump
- Identify when the patient first became aware of the problem and how it was detected
- Was the onset sudden or gradual?
- Describe the quality and quantity of the lump(s)
- What size is the lump? Has it grown or changed in any way?
- Is it smooth, soft, hard, irregular, mobile, attached?
- In one breast or both?
- Single or multiple?
- Ask the patient to identify on a diagram the exact location
- Is it painful? How severe is the pain, using an appropriate scale?
- How often do you notice the lump? Is it present constantly or does it vary?
- Is the nipple retracted? Is this permanent or transient?

Breast pain
- What causes the pain? Does anything relieve or provoke it?
- Is it related to your menstrual cycle?
- How would you describe the pain?
- How often do you experience the pain?
- Where is the pain? Is it in both breasts?
- Is the pain localized of diffuse? Is there any radiation?
- How severe is the pain, using an appropriate scale?
- When did you first notice the pain?

Nipple discharge
- What provokes the discharge? What reduces it?
- Is it spontaneous? Does it need to be expressed?
- Is the discharge from single or multiple ducts?
- How much discharge is there? What colour is it?
- Is there an odour present?
- How often do you have the discharge? Is it constant?
- Are there any skin lesions or crusting around the nipple?
- Are both breasts affected or only one?
- Is it related to your menstrual cycle?
- Do you experience pain with the discharge?
- When did you first notice the discharge?

Family history

Genetic risk factors associated with breast cancer are discussed above (p. 117). It is essential to enquire about a family history of breast cancer.

Personal and social history

Occupation, including exposure to radiation, chemotherapy, heavy lifting or trauma to breasts, should be explored. It is important to discuss current medication, including oral contraceptive, HRT, antidepressants, opiates or tamoxifen. If the woman reports that she has recently experienced stress, this is an important issue to discuss further. It is also worthwhile exploring her values and beliefs in relation to breast disease.

FOCUSED HISTORY FOR PROBLEMS ASSOCIATED WITH THE GENITAL TRACT

Menstrual cycle

Important questions to ask a woman who presents with problems with the menstrual cycle include age of menarche and development during puberty. As a baseline it is important to establish the woman's normal pattern of menstruation, length of cycle, days of blood loss, number of tampons or pads used each day, presence of blood clots and any recent changes. Recent changes in appetite or weight and general health and psychological well-being will help identify the possibility of stress-related causes for change in menstruation. It is clearly important to discuss contraceptive methods used and any possibility of contraceptive failure resulting in pregnancy.

Dysfunctional uterine bleeding

Fisher & Glenn (1998) state that it is essential to ask the patient to describe what she thinks is a normal menstrual cycle and normal quantity of bleeding before eliciting a history relating to the current problem. Women vary enormously in their perception of what is normal and abnormal and it is therefore worth attempting to quantify the problem before making a judgement about its extent. The patient can be asked to report the number of tampons or pads used with each episode of bleeding and this will help you gain an idea of how heavy the blood loss is. Thomas & Rock (1997) state that the patient

can be asked if she floods the bed at night, as this is a good indicator of the amount of blood loss. Ask the patient how long it has been since her pattern of bleeding was normal, if she has had an episode of irregular bleeding before, and whether she has a history of sexually transmitted infection. It is also useful to ask the following:

- Do you experience premenstrual syndrome?
- Do you have any menopausal symptoms?
- Have you been sterilized?
- Have there been any episodes of dysmenorrhoea?
- What is your usual form of contraception?

In addition, it is worth exploring whether she has noticed any bruising or bleeding elsewhere on her body and if there is any history of other illness or family history of bleeding disorders.

Vaginal discharge

Ask the woman to describe the colour and consistency of the discharge, whether it is bloodstained and if it has an odour. It is useful to explore how long the discharge has been present and if there has been any associated itching or burning of the vulval area. Ask the woman to quantify the amount of discharge by describing if it is scanty and whether or not she needs to use protective pads.

PHYSICAL EXAMINATION

Examination of the female genitalia or breasts may occasionally cause embarrassment and anxiety. It is important to recognize these feelings and to make the environment as safe and relaxed as possible. In addition to the embarrassment of being exposed for the examination, some women may have psychological difficulties associated with past traumatic experiences or possibly sexual abuse. It is therefore important to appear calm and relaxed yourself, use a private room where no one else will be expected to interrupt during the examination and that you make every effort not to cause any discomfort or pain. A full explanation of what is about to take place during the examination should be given before the patient has undressed.

Ask the patient to empty her bladder and assist her into a comfortable position, with a blanket or sheet covering the areas of her body which do not need to be exposed. It is useful to ask the woman to lie in a supine position with her head and shoulders slightly elevated and arms resting beside her. This helps the woman relax and specifically helps to relax the abdominal muscles. Any instruments used should be warmed to the appropriate temperature and the patient should be kept informed of the progress throughout the examination so that she can equally inform you if the exam becomes uncomfortable in any way.

EXAMINATION OF THE BREASTS

It is essential to ensure that you are fully competent to carry out breast examination when required to do so. Breast examination should not form a routine part of a well-woman check but may be necessary if a woman consults with you because she is experiencing a problem with her breast or breasts. As with all physical examinations, it is essential to ensure that you are operating within the code of professional conduct (NMC 2002) and that you are working within local guidelines and protocols. A full explanation regarding the examination is necessary to reduce anxiety and embarrassment. The room should be warm and private as the woman will need to undress to the waist. There should be a good light source available.

Inspection

The patient should be sitting on the couch or in a chair with her arms by her side. Observe the breasts for size and symmetry. Look at the contour, lumps, skin changes and nipple retraction. Note redness, ulceration, oedema and an abnormal venous pattern. Have the patient raise her arms above her head to observe mobility. Ask her to place her hands on her hips and lean forwards to assess tethering to the serratus anterior muscles.

Palpation

Always examine the unaffected breast first if only one breast is involved. With the patient lying down flat on the couch, a pillow is inserted under the shoulder and the arm placed above the head on the side to be examined. This will help relax the pectoral muscles and allow the breast to 'float' on the chest wall.

The breast is palpated with your fingers flat against the breast, using a circular motion, applying gentle pressure and then firm pressure, compressing the tissues against the chest wall. Each quadrant is examined systematically, as well as the areola and tail of Spence well into the axilla. Alternatively, the breast can be assessed using a concentric circular pattern from the periphery, ensuring the axillary tail is included, inwards towards the nipple. The nipple and retroareolar tissue is palpated between the index finger and thumb. Further palpation will be necessary if an abnormality is detected. Bimanual palpation may be necessary if the breasts are pendulous.

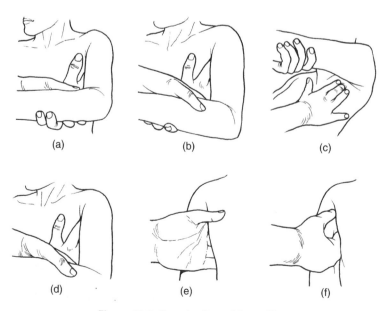

(a) (b) (c)

(d) (e) (f)

Figure 11.9 Examination of the axilla.

Examining the axilla is part of the examination of the breasts and the patient should be asked to sit up for this. To examine the left axilla you will need to support the weight of the patient's left arm in your left hand. Using your right hand, palpate the anterior lymph nodes by pressing against the muscles and fascia of the anterior wall (Fig. 11.9a and b). To palpate the apical and medial lymph nodes, cup your fingers and press upwards and inwards into the apex of the axilla and then move downwards over the medial wall, continuing to apply pressure (Fig. 11.9c and d). In order to examine the posterior and lateral nodes it is necessary to stand behind the patient (Fig. 11.9e and f). The procedure is then repeated for the right axilla using your left hand (Lumley & Bouloux 1994).

EXAMINATION OF THE FEMALE GENITAL TRACT

Before commencing with the specific examinations associated with the female reproductive tract, it is useful to carry out a general inspection of the patient. There may be signs of anaemia, which could be associated with menorrhagia. Signs of thyrotoxicosis, hypothyroidism, anorexia nervosa or other chronic diseases might be clues to presenting problems with the menstrual cycle. Signs of hirsutism or thinning hair may be a clue to a hormonal imbalance. As with all physical examinations, a general inspection is vital to inform your decision-making process and the rest of your examination.

If a woman presents in severe lower abdominal pain you should consider the differential diagnoses of salpingitis or ectopic pregnancy and the possible harmful effects of carrying out a physical examination. In some cases it may be necessary to scan the woman or to take swabs and send them for culture and sensitivity before carrying out an examination. The physical examination may cause discomfort and harm and yet it would be unlikely to have an impact upon your management plan. If a woman presents with lower abdominal pain it is important to consider referral to a medical colleague for advice and assistance.

In other presentations of problems with the genital tract a full abdominal examination should precede examination of the vulva and vagina. An overview of the abdominal examination can be found in Chapter 9. It may be possible to identify abnormalities associated with the uterus and adnexae just above the pubis. Ovarian tumours or cysts may fill the abdomen and an ectopic pregnancy or a normal pregnancy may appear as a large mass, which is dull to percussion. Ascites may be present; this tends to have a central resonance and dullness in the flanks on palpation. An added advantage of starting the examination of the external genitalia with the abdominal examination is that you have placed your hands on the patient and the subsequent examination of the vulva, vagina and cervix will appear a little less intrusive.

External genitalia

Inspect the mons pubis, labia and perineum. It is particularly useful to look for excoriations, and to observe the pattern of hair distribution which confirms the sexual maturity of the woman. Gently separate the labia with the fingers of your gloved hand and inspect the clitoris, urethral meatus, vaginal introitus and the labia minora (Fig. 11.10). Palpate the length of the labia majora, which should feel smooth and fleshy. If there are any noticeable lesions, palpate them, noting tenderness and any signs of ulceration or swelling. The Bartholin's glands can be checked by inserting your finger into the vagina near the posterior end of the introitus while the thumb palpates the outer surface of the labia majora posteriorly (Fig. 11.11). A normal Bartholin's gland is not palpable; however, these glands may become acutely or chronically infected, producing great discomfort and swelling.

If the patient has presented with a history which makes you suspect urethritis you can milk the urethra from inside out by placing your index finger into the vagina and gently palpating anteriorly and moving downwards. Note any discharge and collect a sample for culture and sensitivity.

EXAMINATION OF THE VAGINA

Separate the labia to expose the vestibule. Ask the patient to 'bear down' and observe the area for bulges and swellings. If the pelvic floor muscles are lax or damaged, it may be possible to see the posterior bladder wall prolapsing along the anterior vaginal wall (cystocele or urethrocele) or the rectum prolapsing into the posterior vaginal wall (rectocele). Examination of the vagina continues with the insertion of a speculum, allowing inspection of the walls of the vagina.

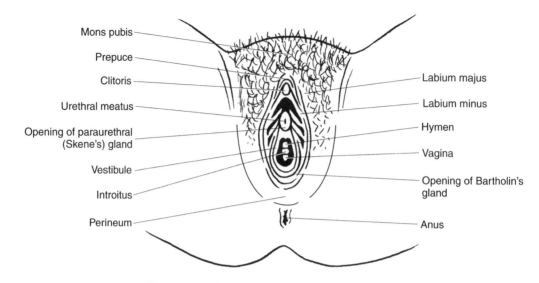

Mons pubis

Prepuce

Clitoris

Urethral meatus

Opening of paraurethral (Skene's) gland

Vestibule

Introitus

Perineum

Labium majus

Labium minus

Hymen

Vagina

Opening of Bartholin's gland

Anus

Figure 11.10 Examination of the external genitalia.

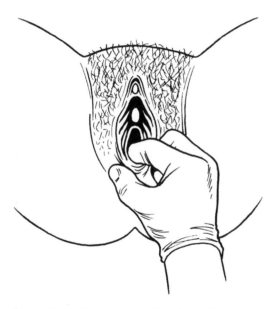

Figure 11.11 Examination of the Bartholin's gland.

Internal examination

A bivalve speculum (Cusco's) is the instrument most commonly used to inspect the vagina. Specula are available in a variety of sizes and can be obtained in either disposable plastic or reusable metal. Selection of an appropriate size for the woman is important and paediatric or virginal specula are available for women with small vaginal openings. Familiarize yourself with both types of specula and check the use of the thumbscrew and how to open and shut the blades.

Insertion of the speculum can be assisted with water to lubricate the instrument. Other lubricants should not be used as they might interfere with subsequent cytological studies or swabs for bacteriology or viral cultures. Inserting your index and middle fingers inside the vagina and applying a slight pressure downward assist insertion of the speculum. You can then feel when the muscles are relaxed and you can gently slide the speculum into the vaginal opening over your fingers at a 45° downward angle (Fig. 11.12a). Slide the speculum into the vagina, rotating it in a clockwise direction until the blades run along the length of the anterior and posterior vaginal walls (Fig. 11.12b). Remove your fingers and open the blades of the speculum by pressing on the thumb piece of the instrument. If you have directed the blades in the downward direction on insertion the cervix will come into view as you sweep the speculum slowly upward on opening the blades. Once the cervix is visualized, manipulate the speculum a little further so that the cervix is well exposed between the blades and lock the blades into place. If you are unable to find the cervix it may be necessary to withdraw the speculum and to reinsert it on a more horizontal angle. Ensure that you have a good source of light and then you can carry out a thorough inspection of the cervix.

Inspect the cervix for colour, size, position, discharge, size and shape of the os, presence of polyps and surface characteristics. In early pregnancy the

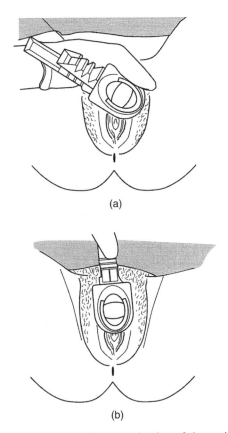

(a)

(b)

Figure 11.12 Speculum examination of the vagina.

cervix may be a bluish colour, which indicates increased vascularity; a pale cervix may indicate anaemia and erythema may be associated with exposed columnar epithelium from the cervical canal – commonly known as an ectropion. There are many causes of erythema on the cervix and this should always be considered as an abnormal finding until proven otherwise.

During the speculum examination you may wish to take a smear or swabs for culture and sensitivity. You should familiarize yourself with local guidelines on cervical screening and national standards for the methods of obtaining samples for cytology. If obtaining smears is part of your role in clinical practice you should ensure that you have received adequate training and regular updates on cervical cytology. The purpose of cytology is to detect premalignant cells to allow early detection and give a higher successful cure rate.

Before proceeding with the smear you should ensure that your equipment is prepared and that you have a labelled slide or container ready to

collect the sample. You may use an Aylesbury spatula or a Cervex brush for the collection of the specimen. The Aylesbury spatula and the Cervex brush are used to collect both ectocervical and endocervical cells at the same time. Liquid based cytology has now been introduced in to some areas of the UK and is proving to be more effective as there are less inadequate tests reported (NHS cervical screening programme 2004).

You should always carry out the smear test before taking any other swabs for culture. Place the tip of the Cervex brush or spatula in the cervical os and, whilst maintaining gentle pressure, rotate the brush or spatula by rolling the handle between the thumb and the forefinger three to five times to the left and to the right. It is essential that you cover the whole 360° surface of the cervix when collecting your specimen so that you do not miss any of the vital cells which may assist in the diagnosis of premalignant disease (Fig. 11.13). Withdraw the brush and transfer the specimen to a slide. With two single paint strokes, apply first one side of the spatula or brush and then the other. You need to be gentle but firm when applying the cells to ensure that the cells can be visualized in the laboratory and have not been damaged in the process of application to the slide. Apply fixative to the specimen immediately. In liquid based cytology the Cervex brush is placed directly into the container of preservative fluid or rinsed in the fluid according to local laboratory guidelines.

If you need to take further swabs, do so before withdrawing the speculum. If testing for chlamydia an endocervical swab will be needed. Unlock the

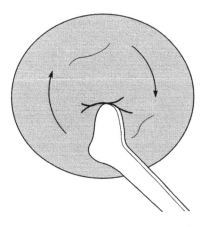

Figure 11.13 Cells are collected by rotating the spatula 360° around the cervix.

speculum and, as you withdraw the instrument, rotate it slowly and gently to inspect the vaginal walls. Note the colour, any lesions and any discharge. Always ensure that you dispose of the speculum appropriately and that reusable specula are sterilized adequately according to local control of infection procedures.

BIMANUAL PALPATION

You may now wish to carry out a bimanual examination of the woman's genital tract. However, this examination should only be undertaken by a fully trained health professional and not done as a routine screening examination (Austoker et al 1997).

Using gloved hands and plenty of lubricant, insert the index and middle finger into the vagina. The thumb should remain abducted and the ring and little finger should be flexed into the palm (Fig. 11.14). Pressure should be exerted posteriorly rather than anteriorly as this avoids causing discomfort by exerting pressure on the sensitive urethra. The flexed fingers should press inward towards the perineum as this causes little or no discomfort. It is useful to be in a standing position to perform this procedure. Palpate the vaginal walls, which should be supple, moist and slightly rugose. Note any nodularity or tenderness. Locate the cervix and note its position. Palpate it for regularity, shape and consistency. The cervix should normally be slightly mobile without causing the patient any discomfort. Pain on movement of the cervix is known as cervical excitation and, together with discomfort in the adnexae, may be due to pelvic inflammatory disease.

Place the palmar surface of your second hand on the abdomen about midway between the umbilicus and symphysis pubis. The fingers of the pelvic hand elevate the cervix and uterus and you attempt to capture the uterus by gently apposing the fingers of both hands (Fig. 11.15). This allows you to assess the size, shape and mobility of the uterus and to identify any tenderness or masses. Your pelvic hand can also be placed in the anterior fornix and this may allow you to palpate the anterior surface of the uterus with your pelvic hand; the posterior surface may be palpated by the hand on the abdominal wall. It is quite normal to feel nothing on bimanual palpation of the pelvis and only regular training and supervision will make you confident in your technique.

If you are checking for a prolapse it may be necessary to turn the woman on to her left side with her lower arm placed behind her in a similar location to the recovery position. Using a Sims speculum to inspect the vaginal walls, ask the woman to cough or bear down and observe for signs of a rectocele, cystocele or urethrocele.

When you have completed your examination, explain to the woman that she may experience some spotting associated with the disturbance of the cervix. You may wish to provide her with a small protective pad and to advise her that this is a completely normal occurrence, particularly after a smear test. Allow her the time and privacy to get dressed and then conclude your consultation with a report of your findings and your plan for follow-up and investigation. This may be the appropriate moment for you to offer education and advice on a

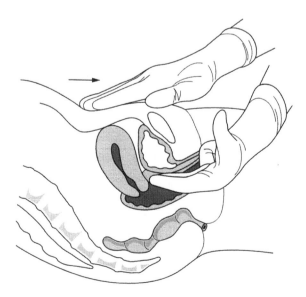

Figure 11.15 Examination of the anterior surface of the uterus.

Figure 11.14 The thumb and finger positions for a vaginal examination.

particular subject to help inform her of what to expect and how her particular problem may be managed.

PATIENT EDUCATION

Women may consult with nurse practitioners for a whole variety of reasons and will need education and management according to their presenting problem and individual needs. Refer to the specialized texts for more detailed advice. We have chosen to focus on the management of breast disorders here as there are clear national guidelines in operation to help guide your practice.

Breast care remains a sensitive area in women's health and is still the cause of considerable anxiety and embarrassment for some women. The psychological impact of discovering a breast lump and experiencing breast pain or nipple discharge can be very disturbing and should not be underestimated. Nurse practitioners will need to use their communication skills effectively to establish a safe and therapeutic environment to explore the woman's concerns. Social factors are important and should be discussed to establish if there is a family member or friend who can offer support should referral be necessary.

The NHS has issued guidelines for the referral of patients with breast problems (Austoker & Mansel 2003). The guidelines cover breast lumps, nipple discharge and breast pain.

BREAST LUMP

Cysts are usually managed in the specialist clinic by fine-needle aspiration by the nurse specialist or medical staff. If the fluid is bloodstained, then a sample will be sent for cytology but otherwise the woman should be advised that the cyst might refill or recur elsewhere in the breast (50% may recur) and to reconsult as necessary. See Figure 11.16 for NHS guidelines.

NIPPLE DISCHARGE

The woman should be assessed as described earlier in the history-taking section and then should be managed according to the guidelines shown in Figure 11.17.

BREAST PAIN

Figure 11.18 summarizes the NHS guidelines for the management of breast pain. After completion of

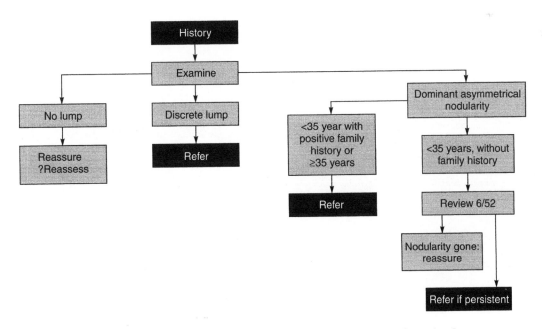

Figure 11.16 NHS breast lump guidelines (from Austoker & Mansel 2003 NHS Breast Screening Programmes; reproduced with permission).

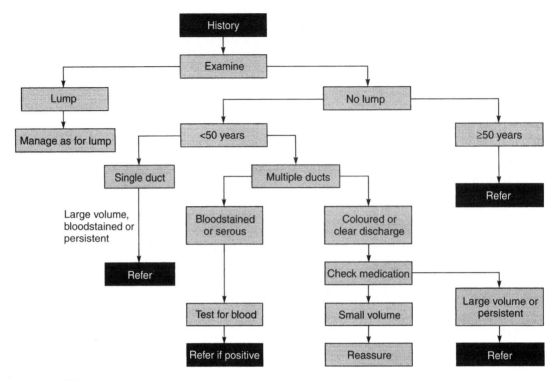

Figure 11.17 NHS nipple discharge guidelines (from Austoker & Mansel 2003 NHS Breast Screening Programmes; reproduced with permission).

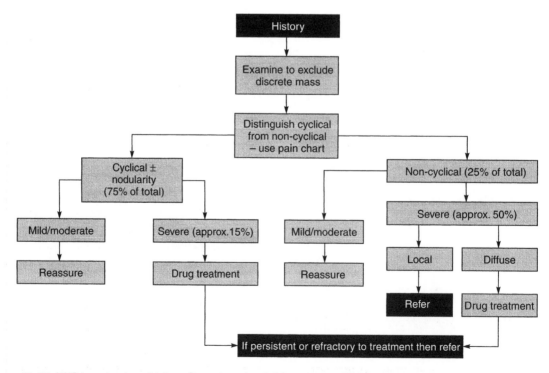

Figure 11.18 NHS breast pain guidelines (from Austoker & Mansel 2003 NHS Breast Screening Programmes; reproduced with permission).

a pain diary, cyclical pain can be managed with mild analgesics and reassurance that the pain is physiological rather than due to cancer. Women taking the oral contraceptive or HRT may need their medication altered to ensure that the lowest dose of oestrogen is used.

Referrals from nurse practitioners to a specialist breast clinic need to be negotiated locally with the hospital trust and primary care teams. According to the NHS guidelines (Austoker & Mansel 2003) 'urgent' referrals should only be made when symptoms are highly suspicious of breast cancer. This includes a discrete breast lump in the appropriate age group (see Fig. 11.16), ulceration, skin nodule or skin distortion. Ideally these women will be assessed within 2 weeks, although this may vary according to local policy. Any woman consulting for health checks and cytology should be educated in breast awareness and leaflets are available to reinforce this message.

Nurse practitioners have a great deal to offer women who consult with them. The NP who has completed the extended and supplementary prescribing course may be able to use the extended formulary to prescribe the drug of choice for women who consult with them regarding contraceptive choices. The supplementary prescribing system can be used to issue a repeat prescription for HRT according to an individual clinical management plan. The NP must ensure that any prescribing decision is based on an appropriate level of knowledge and in some cases the appropriate professional qualification. A prescription is not always necessary and so a discussion of alternative approaches that may be appropriate to the individual may also be useful. Women can be encouraged to access websites such as menopause matters (www.menopausematters.co.uk) for the latest information relating to the menopause and the use of HRT. This is an invaluable source of information regarding all aspects of the menopause founded by clinician Dr Heather Currie and is available for both women and health professionals.

The research shows that women consult more frequently with health care professionals than men (Horrocks et al 2002) and it is therefore worthwhile developing your skills of history-taking and physical examination for women. These skills, in conjunction with the more generic communication and holistic assessment skills of the NP, can help to provide a service that addresses the individual and unique needs of women.

References

Austoker J, McPherson A, Clarke J, Lucassen A 1997 Breast problems. In: McPherson A, Waller D (eds) Women's health, 4th edn. Oxford University Press, Oxford

Austoker J, Mansel R 2003 Guidelines for referral of patients with breast problems, 2nd edn (revised). NHS Breast Screening Programme, Sheffield

Baum M 1996 Breast lumps, breast pain, nipple abnormalities and nipple discharge. In: Bouchier I, Ellis H, Fleming P (eds) French's index of differential diagnosis, 13th edn. Butterworth-Heinemann, Oxford

Coope J 1997 The menopause. In: McPherson A, Waller D (eds) Women's health, 4th edn. Oxford University Press, Oxford

Courtenay M, Butler M 2002 Essential nurse prescribing. Greenwich Medical Media, London

Dealy M 1998 Dysfunctional uterine bleeding in adolescents. Nurse Practitioner 23(5):12–23

Dixon J M, Rodger A, Johnson S, Gregory K 2000 Breast cancer – non metastatic. In: Clinical Medicine, June 2001. BMJ Publishing Group, London

Epstein O, Perkin G D, deBono D P, Cookson J 2003 Clinical examination, 3rd edn. Churchill Livingstone, Edinburgh

Fisher P, Glenn K 1998 Intermenstrual bleeding. Practice Nursing 9(17):39–42

France R, Robson M 1986 Behaviour therapy in primary care: a practical guide. Croom Helm, Kent

Horrocks S, Anderson E, Salisbury C 2002 Systematic review of whether nurse practitioners working in primary care can provide equivalent care to doctors. British Medical Journal 324:819–823

Jackson S, Smith P 1997 Diagnosing and managing genitourinary prolapse. British Medical Journal 314:875–880

Low N, Cowan F 2000 Genital chlamydial infection. In: Clinical Medicine, June 2001. BMJ Publishing Group, London

Lumley J S P, Bouloux P M J 1994 Clinical examination of the patient. Butterworth-Heinemann, Oxford

Martini F 2004a Fundamentals of anatomy and physiology, 4th edn. Prentice-Hall, London

Martini F 2004b Fundamentals of anatomy and physiology. Applications manual, 4th edn. Prentice-Hall, London

McCance K L, Jorde L B 1998 Evaluating the genetic risk of breast cancer. Nurse Practitioner 23(8):14–27

Menopause Matters 2004 Online: www.menopausematters.co.uk

NHS Cervical screening programme May 2004 Online: http://www.cancerscreening.nhs.uk/cervical/index.html

NHS Cancer screening programmes November 2004 Online: http://www.cancerscreening.nhs.uk/breastscreen/breastcancer.html#incidence

NICE Clinical Guidelines for Familial Breast Cancer. May 2004 Online:
http://www.nice.org.uk/page.aspx?o=203189

NMC 2002 Nursing and Midwifery Council Code of Professional Conduct. NMC, London

NPEF 204 Nurse Prescribers' Extended Formulary 2004 British Medical Association and Royal Pharmaceutical Society of Great Britain, London

Patel R, Cowan F M, Barton S E 1997 Advising patients with genital herpes. British Medical Journal 314:85–86

Rees M C P 1997 Menstrual problems. In: McPherson A, Waller D (eds) Women's Health, 4th edn. Oxford University Press, Oxford

Reveley S 1998 The role of the triage nurse practitioner in general medical practice: an analysis of the role. Journal of Advanced Nursing 28(3):584–591

Seidel H M , Ball J W , Dains J E, Benedict G W 2003 Mosby's guide to physical examination, 5th edn. Mosby, St Louis

Stilwell B 1985 Opportunities in general practice. Nursing Mirror 161(19):30–31

Tanner J M 1973 Growth at adolescence, 2nd edn. Blackwell Scientific Publications, Oxford. Cited in: Jones R E 1991 Human reproductive biology. Academic Press, London

Thomas E J, Rock J 1997 Benign gynaecological disease. Health Press, Abingdon

Tortora G, Grabowski S 2003 Principles of anatomy and physiology, 10th edn. John Wiley and Sons, New Jersey

Tothill S 1998 Diagnosis and treatment of menstrual problems. Prescriber 19:91–95

Underwood J 2000 General and systematic pathology, 3rd edn. Churchill Livingstone, Edinburgh

Wright J 1998 Older women's experience of the menopause. Nursing Standard 12(47):46–48

Chapter 12

The musculoskeletal system

Mike Walsh

INTRODUCTION

Problems with the musculoskeletal system are most likely to manifest themselves as pain or a decrease in function. These are the type of symptoms that patients are least likely to ignore. The management of serious injuries clearly lies in the medical field and the nursing care of such patients can be found elsewhere. Consequently this chapter will focus on the kind of injury or condition that the nurse practitioner may reasonably be expected to manage.

PATHOPHYSIOLOGY

This section will initially consider some common orthopaedic conditions before reviewing the minor trauma that you may be involved in diagnosing and/or managing.

OSTEOARTHRITIS (OA)

Osteoarthritis is a complex pattern of joint failure involving degeneration of the articular cartilage and the proliferation of new bone, cartilage and connective tissue. Inflammation plays little part in this disorder. It is mostly found in older people as a primary disease process but can occur in younger persons where it is secondary to some other disease (e.g. Perthe's disease) or a fracture involving a joint. Primary osteoarthritis is more common in women and obesity is a major risk factor for disease affecting load-bearing joints such as the knee.

The disease affects synovial joints and involves loss of articular cartilage and a consequent reaction in the surrounding bone. After the breakdown in articular cartilage, irritation of the synovium occurs and attempts at repair lead to the formation of new bone, including fragments known as osteophytes. These tend to be located towards the edges of the joint and will limit joint movement. Eventually the joint surface may be eroded down to the bone, causing severe pain and stiffness. Callus formation in response to the trauma leads to the development of dense sclerotic bone, further deformity and eventual disorganization of the joint, producing severe disability (Springhouse 2000). Diagnosis by radiography is a reliable approach, although many patients whose radiographs show changes indicative of OA may not be complaining of any symptoms at that time. The disease is usually more advanced when pain and disability bring the patient to the health centre.

OSTEOPOROSIS

This term refers to a loss of bone mass which occurs when the rate of bone resorption exceeds the rate of deposition. It is associated with a decrease in sex hormone production and consequently is most common in postmenopausal women (lack of oestrogen) and eventually becomes a problem in older men as their testosterone production declines gradually with age. The result is a reduction in calcium and phosphate salts leading to porous, brittle bone which easily fractures (Springhouse 2000). Other risk factors include early menopause, low body weight, smoking, poor diet, alcoholism and being of European descent. Osteoporosis can also occur as a side effect of large doses of steroids or prolonged immobilization.

The obvious effect of osteoporosis is to make the person more prone to fractures. The most serious fractures involve the femoral neck area – this is likely to happen to one in four women living to the

age of 85, and carries a high mortality rate of around 25%. Weakening of the spinal vertebrae leads to chronic backache and the possibility of a vertebra collapsing (pathological fracture) producing the characteristic stoop of 'dowager's hump'. A fall on the outstretched hand which in earlier life would probably have produced nothing worse than a few bruises now leads to a fracture of the distal radius, often with significant posterior displacement (Colles fracture) or a fractured neck of humerus. The cost of osteoporosis to the NHS is estimated at £1.4 billion per annum with some 30% of women and 12% of men likely to suffer an osteoporotic fracture at some stage in their life (Haslett et al 2003). It is therefore a matter of high public health priority.

RHEUMATOID ARTHRITIS (RA)

This condition can occur at any age but is most common between 30 and 50 years, affecting three times as many women as men, particularly in the younger age groups. The ratio is 6:1 under 45 years of age (Haslett et al 2003). It is a painful, inflammatory condition which attacks several joints at once in a symmetrical pattern causing joint deformity and loss of function. It also has a range of systemic effects. Both genetic and environmental factors seem to be involved in what is essentially an autoimmune disease, leading to inflammation, granuloma formation and joint destruction. In addition to its disabling effects, rheumatoid arthritis is associated with fever and general malaise, anaemia, vasculitis, lung disease such as pericarditis, respiratory disease such as bronchiolitis, neurological problems such as spinal cord compression, peripheral neuropathy and a range of other disorders including ocular disease, bursitis, subcutaneous rheumatoid nodules and splenomegaly. The disease is associated with reduced life expectancy and accounts for 1.9 million GP consultations each year in the UK (Oliver 2004).

The disease usually has an insidious beginning, affecting peripheral joints first. Both small and larger joints may be involved simultaneously. Pain and signs of inflammation are present initially and if the disease is not controlled there may be serious joint damage and deformity such as the characteristic ulnar deviation that affects both hands. Tendons can also become involved, adding to the deformity and disability the patient suffers. The disease may have periods of remission followed by active flare-ups. Its severity is also very variable ranging from mild to severe resulting in joint destruction and reduction in life expectancy (Nowak & Handford 2004).

OTHER RHEUMATOID DISORDERS

There are several other rare rheumatoid diseases which occur in a handful of patients in each general practice. Polymyalgia rheumatica and giant cell arteritis are two closely related conditions which mostly affect the over-50s and women more than men. They present as a syndrome of pain and stiffness in the neck, shoulders and pelvis associated with generalized symptoms such as weight loss and tiredness. A low-grade pyrexia may be present and there is an increased erythrocyte sedimentation rate (ESR).

Another important but rare autoimmune condition is systemic lupus erythematosus. This is a complicated syndrome that is nine times more common in women than men and, similarly, nine times more common in Asians and Afro-Caribbeans than Europeans. The major features include generalized pain and stiffness in the joints, a characteristic butterfly rash on the face after exposure to the sun, hair loss and fatigue. Major organ involvement may occur, with a potentially fatal outcome.

MALIGNANT DISEASE

This is most likely to be due to secondary deposits from primary growths in the lung, breast or prostate. Primary tumours can occur, usually involving bone marrow (e.g. myeloma or Ewing's sarcoma) but fortunately are rare.

OTHER CONDITIONS

Many other diseases affect the skeleton. Metabolic disorders associated with vitamin D deficiency produce diseases such as rickets (in children) or osteomalacia (in adults). Paget's disease is the commonest of the diseases which disrupt bone architecture, mostly affecting older people. For reasons unknown, the person has periods of excessive bone resorption followed by periods of excessive bone repair – leading to the development of poorly organized, weak bone. Chronic pain and deformity eventually develop (Springhouse 2000). Osteochondritis is a term used to describe a range of diseases affecting the epiphyseal cartilages (growth plates) of children.

Avascular necrosis leads to loss of bone at the epiphysis which eventually regenerates as the blood supply is restored – but in the process significant deformity and pain may develop. Examples include Perthe's disease (femoral head) and Osgood-Schlatter's disease (tibial tuberosity).

DISORDERS AFFECTING THE SPINE

In addition to osteoporosis and OA, the spine may be affected by a range of other conditions. Abnormal spinal curvature may develop (Fig. 12.1) and the following are most likely to be encountered:

- Kyphosis: a rounded thoracic convexity due to the ageing process, especially amongst women
- Lordosis: where the normal lumbar curve is accentuated, usually to compensate for serious obesity or for pregnancy
- Scoliosis: lateral curvature of the spine. When the patient stands upright the gluteal cleft normally lies directly below the first thoracic vertebra. The spine may be seen to tilt to one side when the patient with a scoliosis stands upright. It is best seen when the patient bends forward, as in the vertical plane compensation may have occurred.
- Flattened lumbar curve suggests ankylosing spondylitis in men, although it may be due to a herniated lumbar disc

Low back pain is a chronic problem that affects many individuals but in only a very small minority does it indicate serious pathology, where it is characterized by constant pain not associated with movement or any mechanical forces. In such circumstances malignant disease of the pelvic or abdominal organs or a spinal cord lesion is the likely cause. Most presentations have a mechanical cause where the pain is related to activity and relieved by rest. The pain is confined to the lumbar/sacral region, buttocks or thigh. Psychological factors can play a part and the problem can become chronic.

Where the patient describes the pain as sharp, radiating down one leg and maybe associated with paraesthesia, this suggests a nerve root is involved and is known as radicular pain. The pain frequently is felt the length of the leg, below the knee. Movement may play little part in causing pain which can be triggered by something as trivial as sneezing or coughing. The cause is likely to be a prolapsed intervertebral disc, although chronic inflammation

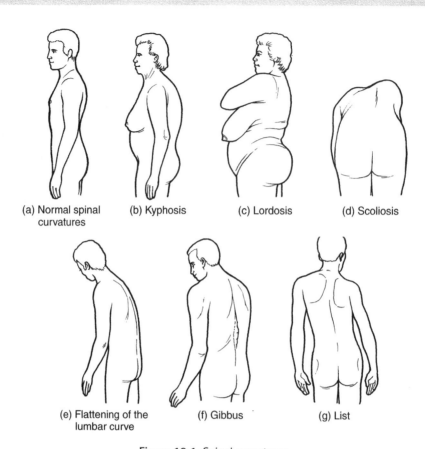

(a) Normal spinal curvatures   (b) Kyphosis   (c) Lordosis   (d) Scoliosis

(e) Flattening of the lumbar curve   (f) Gibbus   (g) List

Figure 12.1 Spinal curvatures.

of the nerve root sheaths (arachnoiditis) is also a possibility (Haslett et al 2003).

Spondylitis is an inflammatory painful condition of the spine affecting young adults. The age of onset is usually under 30 and the pain has a symmetrical distribution.

The lower part of the back is not the only region affected by disease. Disc problems can affect any part of the spine, including the cervical region, and compression of a cervical nerve root by a protruding disc may occur. Torticollis describes acute and often severe neck pain which is usually caused by muscle spasm, causing the patient to hold the neck rigid and often to one side. Care needs to be taken to exclude any more serious pathology such as an acute disc prolapse.

COMMON DISORDERS AFFECTING THE HAND AND WRIST

The tendons which connect the bones of the hand to the muscles of the forearm are prone to localized problems in the wrist region. Tenosynovitis refers to inflammation of tendons and most commonly occurs as a result of repeated twisting movements involving the extensor pollicis brevis and abductor pollicis longus tendons (involved in thumb movements) where they run adjacent to the radial styloid. Movement becomes painful as the inflamed tendons swell and a soft creaking sound may be heard on movement. Friction and inflammation can also affect the flexor profundus longus tendon leading to trigger finger (or thumb), a condition in which the finger becomes locked in the flexed position for several hours until the soft-tissue swelling subsides, allowing normal tendon movement to be resumed.

Carpal tunnel syndrome is caused by compression of the median nerve as it enters the hand through the restricted space of the carpal tunnel. Overuse of the wrist is the most likely cause of compression, although fluid retention associated with pregnancy can also cause this condition. The effect is paraesthesia in the median nerve distribution (see below) which may even disturb sleep. In time pain and even numbness may develop.

Both the radial and ulnar nerves may suffer from compression in the arm. Radial nerve compression is most commonly caused by sustained pressure on the inner aspect of the upper arm where the radial nerve winds over the surface of the humerus. The result is the development of wrist drop – due to motor nerve damage the person cannot extend the wrist properly. The ulnar nerve is closely involved in the anatomy of the elbow and therefore susceptible to damage in this region, especially when the elbow is flexed and therefore stretching the nerve over the medial epicondyle of the humerus. The symptoms of numbness and tingling will be confined to the ulnar nerve distribution of the hand (Fig. 12.2).

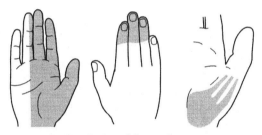

(a) Distribution of the median nerve

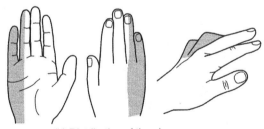

(b) Distribution of the ulnar nerve

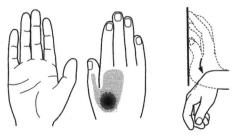

(c) Distribution of the radial nerve

Figure 12.2 Peripheral nerve distributions in the hand.

CONDITIONS AFFECTING THE ELBOW AND SHOULDER

Damage can occur to the muscle or tendon which inserts into the lateral epicondyle of the humerus as a result of sharp flexion of the wrist. Although called tennis elbow, this disorder can occur as a result of other activities such as gardening and lifting. The patient usually presents with a painful elbow exacerbated by gripping or twisting movements. Tenderness is found over the lateral epicondyle – if the patient attempts to extend the wrist against resistance this will produce pain.

Inflammation of the olecranon bursa (olecranon bursitis) can lead to a hot and painful elbow with restricted movement. The cause may be infection but it may also be associated with rheumatoid arthritis, gout or minor trauma.

The tendons of the shoulder joint can become inflamed. Several tendons combine to form the rotator cuff, one of which is the supraspinatus tendon. This is prone to inflammation, giving rise to the painful arc syndrome (Fig. 12.3). In this situation the supraspinatus tendon becomes inflamed where it crosses the humeral head, leading to swelling just below the acromion (Fig. 12.4). As the arm is abducted, this swelling comes into contact with the acromion but, when the arm reaches more than 60° of abduction, it slips out from below the acromion. The result is little pain when the arm is at rest against the side of the body or abducted out beyond about 60° but in the arc between 30° and 60° of abduction, the patient experiences considerable pain; hence the name painful arc syndrome.

One other common condition is frozen shoulder (adhesive capsulitis). The patient finds it painful and difficult to rotate the arm externally at the shoulder joint, consequently s/he cannot comb the hair at the back of the head. Typically the patient at first finds it painful and difficult to move the shoulder in all directions. Several months later the pain disappears but the stiffness remains and it may be over a year before a large degree of normal movement returns. The cause of this problem remains unknown.

DISORDERS OF THE FOOT AND ANKLE

The big toe is the source of many foot problems. A frequent complaint is that of a bunion. This term is often used loosely to refer to any bump or lump on

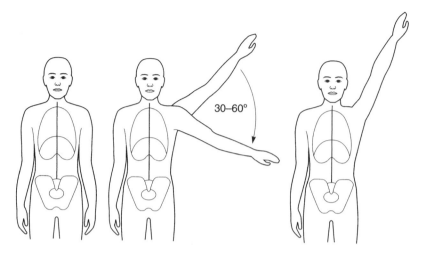

Figure 12.3 Painful arc syndrome.

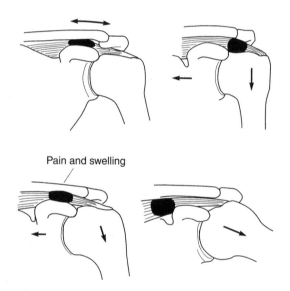

Pain and swelling

Figure 12.4 Painful arc syndrome. Note how inflamed supraspinatus tendon is released from below the acromion at 60° of abduction and hence the pain is relieved.

the foot. It is more accurate to restrict the term to describe a bursa occurring over the first metatarsal head. This may become infected and involve the metatarsophalangeal joint. The first metatarsophalangeal joint is also the classic site for gout. This condition involves the deposition of urate crystals in and around the joint. It can occur at any age and the result may be exquisitely painful. Pseudogout is similar but the deposits consist of crystals of calcium pyrophosphate.

The big toe is notorious for developing as an ingrowing toenail. This is because toenails are curved and consequently the medial edge can dig into the soft tissue of the toe, leading to a painful lesion which in turn may become infected.

Hallux valgus is the final problem associated with the big toe. This deformity leads to the big toe pointing laterally and consequently the second toe underlies or overlies the big toe. Dislocation of the second metatarsophalangeal joint may occur as a result of this deformity and an inflamed bursa develops over the protuberance at the first metatarsal head.

CONDITIONS AFFECTING THE KNEE

The prepatellar bursa may become inflamed, infected or injured as a result of minor trauma leading to the accumulation of fluid within the bursa. This is the classic 'housemaid's knee' of old, although today it is other groups such as carpet-fitters who spend a great deal of time kneeling, who are prone to the disorder.

Adolescent girls are prone to recurrent dislocation of the patella due to laxity of the ligaments holding it in place and a smaller bone structure compared to boys. A twisting mechanism is sufficient to cause the problem – ice-skating and playing netball are frequent causes (Purcell 2003). Anterior knee pain is a common problem in adolescent girls but usually no obvious cause is found and the problem resolves with time. It may well be associated with the growth spurt found in adolescence and the mechanical strains this puts on the lower limbs.

TRAUMA

This chapter is only concerned with patients who have minor injuries which the nurse practitioner might be expected to manage.

THE SPINE

The problem of low back pain has already been discussed. The other type of spinal injury you may encounter is commonly known as whiplash or post-traumatic neck injury. The patient is sitting in a car when it is hit from behind, causing an extension-flexion injury to the neck. Often symptoms do not appear for 6–12 hours after the accident. When they do, the patient typically complains of pain and stiffness in the neck and shoulders, and sometimes dysphagia and transient neurological symptoms such as numbness and tingling. Unfortunately many patients continue to suffer symptoms for lengthy periods after the accident, even though there are no obvious accompanying physical signs.

THE HAND AND WRIST

The hand is prone to injuries for obvious reasons and, as it has a good nerve supply, not only are injuries painful but they may involve damage to the nerve fibres themselves. The hand is usually in a dependent position, therefore gravity will exacerbate any soft-tissue swelling occurring as a result of injury. Finally, such is the peripheral nature of the hand that the blood supply can easily be compromised in trauma. These obvious fundamentals should be borne in mind whatever injury to the hand is involved.

Crush injuries to the tip of the finger are common and painful. These may involve fracture of the distal phalanx; however, the soft-tissue injury is more important than the fracture and the focus should be on successfully healing the wound without infection. Closed fractures of fingers are painful but usually involve little or no displacement. If the hand is immobilized for any period of time, stiffness rapidly becomes a major problem as joint contractures and muscle problems develop. The recommended position for immobilization which causes minimum stiffness is the 'Edinburgh position' with the metocarpophalangeal joints (MCPJs) flexed to 80°, the interphalangeal joints (IPJs) only slightly flexed and the thumb in abduction.

Dislocation of an IPJ in the finger is a common problem, especially in sporting injuries. It is usually caused by forced hyperextension and may have already been reduced at the scene of the accident by a sharp pull. Chronic strain of the IPJ capsule may occur due to forced lateral movement of the joint. This can cause pain lasting for several weeks, even though no bony injury has occurred. The patient may present with the tip of their finger flexed and unable to straighten it. This is known as mallet finger and is due to a rupture of the extensor tendon where it inserts into the distal phalanx or an avulsion fracture at the insertion of the tendon (Fig. 12.5). An avulsion fracture means that the tendon (or ligament) has pulled a small piece of bone off the bone to which it normally attaches.

Fractures of the metacarpals are usually confined to the fifth metacarpal, just below the head. This is known as a boxer's fracture (perhaps a weekend fracture might be a more appropriate term given the usual time such individuals present) and is usually caused by punching. There may be significant angulation of the fracture and, if in excess of 30°, this requires manipulation by an orthopaedic surgeon.

Injuries involving the thumb are particularly serious as, without the thumb, a large part of the function of the hand is lost. A fracture may run across the base of the first metacarpal or, in the case of a Bennet's fracture, run through the base of the first metacarpal and involve the joint (Fig. 12.6). As we have already seen, fractures involving joints are significant due to the long-term possibility of OA caused by disruption of the normal joint structure.

The eight carpal bones of the wrist are all at risk of fracture due to a fall on the outstretched hand, however 71% of all carpal fractures involve just one of them, the scaphoid, an injury which is notorious for being undiagnosed due to difficulty in recognizing the fracture on radiographs (McNally & Gillespie 2004). Complications arising from an untreated scaphoid fracture include delayed union, malunion, avascular necrosis of the scaphoid and osteoarthritic changes in the wrist.

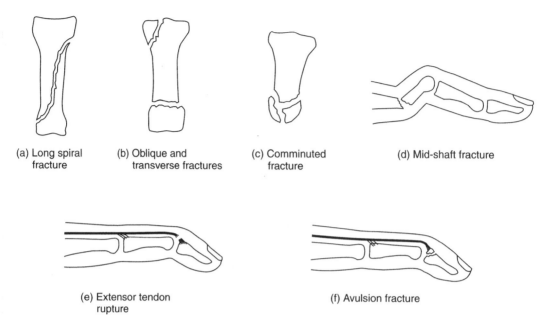

(a) Long spiral fracture

(b) Oblique and transverse fractures

(c) Comminuted fracture

(d) Mid-shaft fracture

(e) Extensor tendon rupture

(f) Avulsion fracture

Figure 12.5 Fractures affecting the phalanges.

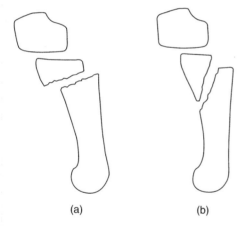

(a) (b)

Figure 12.6 Fractures of the first metacarpal: (a) through the base of the metacarpal, and (b) involving the carpal-metacarpal joint (Bennet's fracture).

INJURIES AFFECTING THE ARM

A fracture of the distal 2–3 cm of the radius is a common injury after a fall on the outstretched hand and in the classic Colles' fracture involves a posterior displacement of the lower fragment. The fracture may also be impacted and typically occurs amongst late middle-aged and elderly patients. There are several complications of a Colles fracture, including median nerve compression due to the swelling involved, subluxation of the inferior radioulnar joint and rupture of extensor pollicus longus 4–8 weeks after the injury which leaves the patient unable to extend the thumb at the IPJ. The reverse injury – anterior displacement of the lower fragment – is called Smith's fracture and results from a fall on a clenched hand such as might happen to a cyclist. This injury is notoriously unstable and prone to displace in a simple cast.

Young children falling on an outstretched arm can also fracture the distal radius, frequently involving the epiphysis, which has potentially serious implications for fracture healing as deformity may result unless the fracture is correctly managed by orthopaedic surgeons. A considerable degree of violence is needed to sustain a fracture of the shaft of the radius and ulna, so much so that if one bone is fractured, either the other will also be fractured or there will be disruption of the superior or inferior radioulnar joint. A fracture of the radial head may occur after a fall on an outstretched hand in a younger adult. The injury usually consists of a longitudinal crack running into the elbow joint with bleeding into the joint (haemarthrosis) which is painful and restricts the movement of the elbow.

Injuries involving the elbow can range from a simple fracture of the olecranon caused by a fall onto the point of the elbow to childhood injuries, usually associated with falling off walls or out of trees. A supracondylar fracture of the humerus is a likely result of such a fall and involves the lower fragment being displaced and tilted backwards as the person falls on an outstretched hand. It is therefore an extension injury and is probably the most common fracture involving the elbow in children, especially between 4 and 8 years of age (Platt 2004). A range of serious complications may ensue from this injury, including median nerve damage and brachial artery occlusion in the immediate short term and deformity and loss of function in the long term associated with epiphyseal damage. The child may also fracture the lateral epicondyle of the humerus – an injury which may not be visible on x-ray due to the immature state of the child's skeleton and the involvement of epiphyseal cartilage. This too can lead to long-term deformity if not managed properly.

Fractures of the shaft of the humerus may be pathological in origin due to metastatic deposits or occur as a result of high-energy trauma. A more likely scenario that the nurse practitioner will encounter is the elderly person who has fallen and suffered a fracture of the neck of humerus. Osteoporosis plays a major part in this injury, which may be a day or more old by the time you see the patient. This delay may be partly due to social factors and also may be attributed to the fact that a significant number of these fractures are impacted so that the arm may still move as one unit. Such old injuries have a characteristic pattern of bruising over the outer part of the upper arm below the fracture site.

Reference has already been made to chronic shoulder problems; acute injuries are common. Dislocation of the shoulder usually occurs as a result of a fall and is most frequently an anterior dislocation – the head of the humerus is displaced forwards and downwards through a tear in the joint capsule. The shoulder appears flattened and angular, having lost the normal rounded contour which is due to the head of the humerus. Damage to the axillary nerve can occur. Posterior dislocation is rare but can happen due to a severe epileptic fit, an electric shock or a violent force driving the humeral head backwards (Wyatt et al 1999). The shoulder does not have the angular appearance seen in an anterior dislocation but the key sign is that the patient has to support the weight of their arm and cannot externally rotate the arm, even to a neutral position.

Violence to the shoulder such as a heavy fall can cause a subluxation (partial dislocation) or disloca-tion of the acromioclavicular joint. A fracture of the clavicle may result from a heavy fall, but usually this is an indirect injury as the person has managed to break the fall with an outstretched hand. A fracture of the scapula may occur due to direct violence but this is a rare injury.

INJURIES AFFECTING THE LEG AND FOOT

Foot trauma usually involves the toes and is frequently a crush injury or the result of a longitudinal force (stubbed toe). Fractures of the metatarsal bones are usually due to heavy objects being dropped on them. Although painful, they are usually stable injuries and require little active intervention to promote healing.

An extremely common problem you will encounter is the sprained ankle. A sprain is simply a tear in some of the ligament fibres holding the joint together followed by an inflammatory response, hence the pain and swelling. The ankle joint has four sets of ligaments: anterior, posterior, medial and lateral – any of which can be damaged depending upon the mechanism of the injury. The most common injury, accounting for some 85% of presentations (Loveridge 2002), involves inversion (adduction) which the patient describes as 'going over on my ankle', and this results in pain and swelling on the lateral aspect of the ankle. Lateral ankle sprains are graded from one to three in increasing order of severity. A grade three injury involves disruption of the ligaments, instability, bruising and severe swelling whilst a grade one injury is stable with only microscopic tears in some ligament fibres and mild swelling (Loveridge 2002).

As injury severity increases so does the possibility of an avulsion fracture as the stretched ligament pulls a fragment of bone away from the lateral malleolus (Fig. 12.7). It is possible in a high-energy accident for the ankle to be dislocated, with the possibility of coexisting fractures of the lateral and medial malleoli. The lateral malleolus can also be fractured by a direct blow. Disruption of the ankle joint carries with it the risk of neurovascular impairment. More serious accidents such as these tend to occur as a result of road traffic, agricultural and industrial accidents.

The distal tibia and fibula articulate with the talus to make the ankle a hinge joint. The entire weight of the body is therefore passed through the

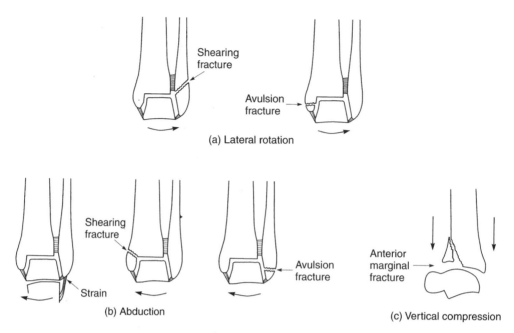

Figure 12.7 Fractures involving the ankle joint.

talus and loaded onto the other tarsal bones, making this area also prone to injury. Patients who fall a distance of up to a few metres but land on their feet may suffer a compression fracture of the calcaneum. In falls from a greater height, the whole ankle joint may be disrupted. Alternatively, the patient may suffer a compression fracture of a spinal vertebra.

A potentially very serious injury affecting particularly the lower leg is compartment syndrome. This may result from blunt trauma causing extensive soft tissue injury with or without a fracture (Edwards 2004). Leg muscle is grouped into four compartments each surrounded by tissue known as fascia which is relatively inelastic. Within each compartment are vital neurovascular structures. Tissue trauma will initiate an inflammatory response causing swelling to develop within the compartments, however the surrounding fascial tissue is relatively inelastic. The problem is compounded if the leg is in its normal dependent position as gravity prevents drainage of accumulating tissue fluid. The result is a rapid rise in intracompartmental pressure which can occlude the arterial blood supply and cause serious nerve damage. Tissue becomes non-viable and death of muscle tissue sets in chain another set of events as the protein myoglobin is released. In large enough quantities this causes renal failure. A cascade of events involving death of a large volume of tissue, renal failure, sepsis, limb amputation and even death can rapidly ensue without a break in the skin or a bone being broken.

The knee is prone to a complex array of possible injuries. Dislocation of the knee itself is a serious high-energy injury that should never be confused with dislocation of the patella. The patella may however be fractured by a direct blow.

A tear of the meniscus in the knee joint (semilunar cartilage) occurs as a result of a twisting injury with the knee flexed. This is a typical sporting injury, especially in football. The medial meniscus is much more commonly injured than the lateral. It is accompanied by an effusion of synovial fluid. The individual finds it impossible to extend the knee fully and carry on with activity. The knee is painful and within 24 hours has become swollen. Subsequently the patient has further episodes of locking when s/he cannot fully extend the knee.

Knee ligaments can also be damaged. The injury may be a partial tear (sprain) or a complete rupture in more severe cases. It is usually the medial ligament which is sprained as a result of a force which abducts the tibia under the femur; the reverse injury produces a sprain of the lateral ligament. The joint is stable as the ligaments are grossly intact but, like the ankle, there will be localized pain and swelling. If violence is sufficient to rupture a medial or lateral ligament, leading to a haemarthrosis, it may also tear the cruciate ligaments. A severe force pushing the tibia backwards relative to the femur may rupture the posterior cruciate ligament. A force acting in the opposite direction, hyperextension of the knee joint or the effects on the weight-bearing knee of suddenly changing direction (typically a sporting injury) can rupture the anterior cruciate ligament.

A less dramatic knee injury is known as jogger's knee and is due to a combination of natural degeneration of the articular cartilage within the knee due to ageing and the repeated stress of jogging and road running. Not surprisingly, this affects people over 30 who do a lot of running on hard surfaces. A similar presentation in younger people is known as patellofemoral syndrome and its main cause is overuse (excess road running for example) combined with slight abnormalities in the alignment of the patella to the rest of the knee joint (Austermuehle 2001).

Tendons and muscles are prone to injury as a result of sporting activity. The Achilles tendon may rupture as a result of a sudden dorsiflexion of the ankle, making it a common injury in racket sports such as squash. There is a sudden sensation of being kicked in the back of the leg followed by pain. This injury is more common in men than women (M:F ratio 3:1) and typically occurs in the late 30s to early 40s age group (Levi 1997). The quadriceps tendon can be ruptured just above the patella by a forced flexion injury of the knee, such as falling on to a flexed knee. Muscles may also be damaged. Usually there is a tearing injury with the possibility of haematoma formation within the damaged muscle. Swelling and tenderness quickly occur and bruising becomes apparent after 24 hours. A common tearing injury involves the gastrocnemius muscle in the calf.

TAKING A FOCUSED HISTORY

The patient's initial description of the presenting condition should in most cases make it clear whether this is a traumatic or non-traumatic problem. Occasionally the patient may complain of an injury aggravating a problem s/he has had for some time. Where the patient presents with a non-traumatic condition, it is usually possible to focus on whether the problem involves joints, muscles or bones and, in cases of trauma, the patient will be able to indicate which structures are involved.

The following simple screening questions are particularly useful in ascertaining whether a patient has a musculoskeletal problem:

- Has the patient any significant pain or stiffness in their muscles, joints or back?
- Does the person have any difficulty in dressing or undressing?
- Does the person have any difficulty walking up and down stairs?

If the patient answers no to all three questions, it is unlikely that they have any significant musculoskeletal problems (Epstein at al 2003).

If the patient is complaining of a non-traumatic joint problem, the history should try and ascertain exactly which joints are involved as the pattern of joint involvement can be a key finding (e.g. in rheumatoid arthritis). How the condition affects the joints should be ascertained next. Important symptoms include pain, stiffness, swelling, redness and the effects on activities of daily living. The PQRST symptom analysis tool provides a useful framework and the list below shows some typical questions which could be asked about any joint symptom the patient mentions:

- Provocation/palliation: Does anything bring on the symptom, especially movement? What relieves the symptom (rest, heat, ice packs, elevation)? OA tends to produce pain which is constant even at rest.
- Quality: Is there redness, swelling or inflammation around the joint? How easy is it to stand up from a sitting position? Describe the sensation, is it tingling, numb, pins and needles?
- Radiation/region: Exactly which joints are affected and where does it hurt most? Does the pain radiate anywhere else such as into the lower leg? Does the funny sensation you describe in your wrist affect your fingers or go up your arm? If so, exactly where?
- Severity: How severe is the pain on a scale of 0–5? You must also assess how much limitation in function there is ranging from ability to dress, walk and manage stairs. It is also important to discover if the pain affects the ability to sleep.
- Time: How long have you had the problem? Does the pain/stiffness vary through the day such as being worse in the morning or evening? How long does it take for the symptom to wear off?

Joint stiffness is found in both inflammatory and degenerative joint disease, while swelling around a joint strongly suggests an inflammatory disease process. Inflammatory disease such as rheumatoid arthritis is associated with a marked daily variation in symptoms which are worst first thing in the morning and last thing at night. A localized inflammatory lesion such as gout also produces severe throbbing pain which can prevent sleep and interfere with joint movement as a result of protective muscle spasm. Degenerative diseases such as OA do not show the classic diurnal pattern of rheumatoid arthritis. The pain and stiffness may be worst early in the morning, but they are present all day, even at rest, and so will disturb sleep. Function gradually deteriorates over time.

A similar approach can be used if the patient is complaining of a more general skeletal problem such as backache. Pain associated with spinal nerve root disorder may be felt over a wide area of the body and the distribution should be carefully checked. For example, cervical lesions involving the C6 and C7 nerve roots typically result in pain affecting the whole chest wall. The patient should be asked to describe the distribution of low back pain. The onset of back pain is a key indicator as acute herniation of a disc produces pain of sudden onset. OA and degenerative disc disease pain develop gradually over time while mechanical back pain can usually be linked to recent activity such as gardening or DIY.

The patient should be asked whether there are any problems with walking, pain on movement, unusual sensations or if any changes in body shape and contour have been noted. In the case of a woman, she should be asked whether she is postmenopausal in order to assess the risk of osteoporosis.

Muscle weakness is a less common presenting symptom but could be indicative of serious disease. It is important to check whether the weakness is secondary to a painful limb as may happen in OA where localized muscle wasting can develop. It is essential to explore which areas of the body are affected by muscle weakness as a more proximal distribution suggests a primary muscular disorder (myopathy). Muscular dystrophy is a term which covers a group of diseases characterized by progressive degeneration of groups of muscles, starting typically around 10 years of age. Proximal groups are affected first, especially of the upper arms and legs in Duchenne's muscular dystrophy. A distal distribution suggests a neurological cause such as

motor neurone disease. If the weakness develops as the day wears on this suggests myasthenia gravis (Epstein et al 2003).

General questions about whether the presenting problem is confined to a joint(s) or is skeletal in nature include:

- Current medication: drugs such as steroids and hormone replacement therapy have a direct bearing on musculoskeletal problems, together with other non-steroidal anti-inflammatory drugs (NSAIDs) that the patient may be taking without a prescription. Diuretic therapy can also precipitate gout.
- Past medical history: key points include known orthopaedic disease such as osteoporosis or OA, previous trauma and skeletal deformities.
- Family history: the presence of conditions such as rheumatoid arthritis, OA and ankylosing spondylitis in the family should be established.
- Social history: occupational hazards can predispose to certain conditions such as back pain (poor posture, lifting) whilst sporting activities may predispose to others (e.g. jogger's knee). Diet, weight and exercise levels should be checked, together with tobacco and alcohol use. These areas are particularly important when dealing with OA and osteoporosis.

It is possible that the history presents a bizarre picture of generalized joint and back pains which are constant or rapidly changing, do not fit any logical pattern and are unassociated with other objective signs such as joint stiffness and swelling. This raises the possibility of psychological problems rather than organic disease.

In traumatic conditions it is important to obtain a clear history of the mechanism of the injury (e.g. twisting or extension) and the magnitude and direction of the forces involved, as well as the time since the injury. This gives valuable clues about the possible nature and severity of the injury. For example, someone walking along the pavement and stumbling over an uneven paving stone is likely to have sustained much less of an injury to the ankle than a footballer running headlong into a crunching tackle. It may require a little coaxing to obtain this history and possibly the assistance of an eye-witness, as the accident will probably have happened suddenly and when the patient's attention was on other things. It is important not to ask leading questions which the patient may readily agree with when actually they are unsure (Loveridge 2002).

Patients with ankle injuries will sometimes mention hearing or feeling a crack at the time of the accident. A report of hearing a cracking sound is of no significance in taking the history from a patient with a low energy injury of the ankle.

Pain and swelling are common features and the patient should be carefully questioned concerning these symptoms, together with others such as alteration in sensation which might suggest peripheral nerve involvement. This is particularly true if the injury is not fresh. The PQRST approach will be useful, as this tool directs you to find out what caused the injury and what has been done by way of first aid and subsequent symptom relief. The nature of the pain/swelling, the affected area, severity (including impact upon the patient in areas such as function) and time since the accident naturally follow on in this sequence. It is important to relate this to function before the accident to gain a clear picture of the impact of the injury. This is especially important in older people.

The history should include significant medical history, including allergies, and note any medication. This is essential – for example, advice about analgesia for minor injuries must take into account the risks of taking NSAIDs if the patient is asthmatic or has a history of peptic ulceration. If the patient happens to be an insulin-dependent diabetic, this should be taken into consideration in the care provided, whilst any allergies to Elastoplast should be determined before the patient with a finger injury has the fingers strapped together!

Social and occupational history should also be noted as treatment may present significant problems. A cast for a Colles fracture may make walking with a Zimmer frame difficult for an elderly patient, whilst a single mother with a young child may find a non-weight-bearing backslab causes major social problems. These potential difficulties will be immediately apparent with a comprehensive social history.

PHYSICAL EXAMINATION

GENERAL SCREENING

The GALS screening tool (Doherty et al 1992) is a validated tool which allows a patient to be assessed for musculoskeletal disability. The full screen is particularly effective in assessing patients with disorders such as OA or RA or as part of a comprehensive assessment of an older person. You will also find parts of the tool of use when assessing a localized problem. It is presented in Figure 12.8.

GENERAL PRINCIPLES

The examination begins when the patient is first met. Observe the patient's posture, manner and gait for any obvious clues. Although the patient history may focus on one particular joint or limb, such is the generalized nature of many conditions that you should ensure a thorough physical examination has taken place. The assessment should include inspection and palpation, testing range of joint movements and carrying out other procedures to test the functioning of associated structures such as ligaments, nerves and tendons. Always examine the unaffected limb first, this acts as a standard against which you can compare the affected limb.

In cases of trauma, injuries elsewhere to the body must also be excluded once the injured limb has been examined. In non-traumatic conditions, the examination should assess whether there are any other systemic effects of the disease process, checking for example whether the patient is feverish or has circulatory problems. When carrying out the exam you should remember that many orthopaedic conditions and injuries are extremely painful. Palpation, range of movement assessment and other tests should therefore be carried out with great care.

Inspection should reveal whether there are any swellings, signs of inflammation, deformities, skin changes, nodules, scars from previous surgery/injury or other abnormalities. Palpation helps to identify swelling which may be hard(bony)-tissue or soft-tissue related. A warm feel to the skin suggests localized inflammation, best detected with the back of the hand. Palpation will also pinpoint areas of tenderness. Localized bony tenderness is the cardinal sign of a fracture and, if present, should be assumed to indicate a fracture until proved otherwise. Range of movement should be assessed when performed first actively by the patient and then passively by the nurse practitioner.

A goniometer is useful for accurate measurements and movements should be recorded from the neutral positions described in the classical anatomical position, except that the hands should rest by

(1) Inspection of gait

Symmetry, smoothness
of movement
Normal stride length
Normal heel-strike, stance,
toe-off, swing-through
Able to turn quickly

(2) Inspection of patient
standing from behind

Straight spine
Muscle bulk/symmetry of paraspinal,
shoulder and gluteal muscles
6 Level iliac crests
No popliteal swelling
No hindfoot swelling or deformity

(3) Press over each
mid-supraspinatus

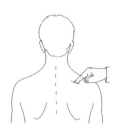

?Hyperalgesia
of fibromyalgia

(4) Inspection from the
side

Normal cervical and
lumbar lordosis
Normal thoracic kyphosis

(5) 'Touch your toes'

Normal lumbar spine
(and hip) flexion

(6) Inspection from the
front

Full elbow extension
Shoulder and quadriceps
muscle bulk, symmetry
No knee swelling or deformity
No forefoot or midfoot deformity

(7) 'Hands behind head,
elbows right back'

Full shoulder abduction,
external rotation
Normal acromioclavicular
and sternoclavicular
movement

(8) 'Place ear on shoulder'

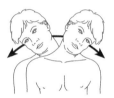

Normal pain-free cervical
lateral flexion

(9) 'Open jaw, move
side to side'

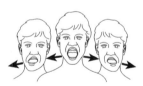

Normal temporo-mandibular
movement

(10) 'Hands in front, palms
down'

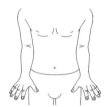

No swelling or deformity of
hands/wrists
Able to extend fingers

(11) 'Turn hands over'

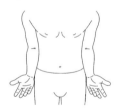

Normal supination
(wrist, distal radio-ulnar joint)
Normal palms

(12) 'Make a fist'

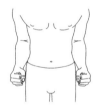

Strong power grip

(13) 'Place tip of finger on
tip of thumb'

Fine precision pinch

(14) Metacarpal squeeze

?Metacarpophalangeal
joint tenderness

(15) Examination on couch
'Put your heel on your
bottom' (flex knee and
hip, holding knee)

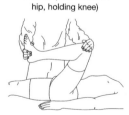

Full knee and hip flexion
No knee crepitus

(16) Internal rotation of hip
in flexion

No pain or restriction of hip
movement

Figure 12.8 The GALS screening tool (adapted from Doherty et al Annals of the Rheumatic Diseases 1992,
with permission from the BMJ Publishing Group)

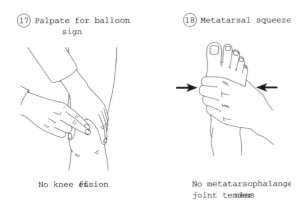

(17) Palpate for balloon sign

No knee effusion

(18) Metatarsal squeeze

No metatarsophalangeal joint tenderness

(19) Inspect soles

No callus or adventitious burstitis

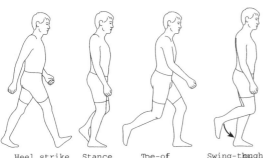

| Heel strike | Stance | Toe-of | Swing-through |

Recording results	
A normal screen	Example of an abnormal screen

	A normal screen			Example of an abnormal screen		
G	✓	A	M	G ✗	A	M
L	✓	✓		L	✓	✓
A	✓	✓		A	✗	✗
S	✓	✓		S	✓	✓

(A = appearance
M = movement)

Antalgic gait
Right knee
arus
↓   Flexion
ep€tru's
fusdon

Diagnosis osteoarthritis right

Figure 12.8 (Continued.)

the side with the palms against the thigh and the feet firmly placed on the ground at 90° to the leg. If any joints have a restricted range of movement, gentle passive movements may be performed whilst palpating the joint for any unusual sensations or evidence of crepitus, which usually indicates roughened articular cartilage (OA) or, if felt over tendons, inflamed tendon sheaths.

Palpation may reveal the presence of osteophytes around a joint as a hard swelling. A soft, warm, generalized swelling indicates synovitis and a synovial effusion within the joint capsule may coexist with the inflamed synovial membrane. If palpation elicits tenderness, try and be as specific as possible in placing the tenderness as this indicates which structures are involved – a bursa, tendons, intra-articular structures or the bone itself, indicating osteomyelitis (infection of the bone) or a fracture.

If a joint capsule or ligament has been sprained it will be painful to both active and passive joint movements which stretch the damaged ligaments and movement will be restricted by the pain. Tenderness will be found over the swollen area and a joint effusion is likely if the joint capsule is intact. A dislocated joint due to trauma will be painful and have little movement. You should also check for signs of muscle wasting on the affected limb, indicative of a long-term disabling joint problem.

If the tendon sheath is involved (tenosynovitis), the inflammation and swelling will cause limitation of active movement and possibly crepitus over the sheath. Passive movement will still be possible. Rupture of a tendon (e.g. Achilles) will mean that the patient cannot carry out active movement, although passive movement remains possible.

Muscle power should be assessed using the Medical Research Council classification in Box 12.1 (Epstein et al 2003).

Box 12.1 MRC classification of muscle power
0   Total paralysis
1   Flicker of contraction
2   Movement with gravity eliminated (i.e. limb supported)
3   Movement against gravity (i.e. upwards)
4   Some movement possible against resistance
5   Normal power

You may notice spontaneous contractions of muscle (the patient might comment upon 'twitching' in the history) which are known as fasciculation. This can be intermittent, subtle and not very obvious. It is a sign of either upper or motor neurone disease, assuming shivering has been eliminated as a possible cause. Muscle bulk should be assessed for signs of wasting (see p. 209). Increased muscle bulk is usually due to bodybuilding and should lead to a suspicion of steroid abuse, however it may be associated with muscle weakness and fatty infiltration, as in Duchenne's muscular dystrophy. In muscle injuries, any contraction of the muscle, with or without movement, causes pain.

REGIONAL EXAMINATION

The spine

Ask the patient to remove all clothing from the upper half of the body and trousers or skirt to permit a full examination of the spine. Privacy is essential. See the spinal exam in GALS screening on p. 208 whilst reading this section. Inspect the back for scars and other skin lesions before spinal posture and alignment are assessed with the patient upright and then bending forward, attempting to touch the toes. Asking the patient to bend forward not only allows assessment of flexion but makes a scoliosis more apparent. Range of movement in the neck can be tested by asking the patient to look right and left (rotation) then to tilt the head forward, trying to touch chin on chest and then tilt backwards while finally moving the head from side to side to test lateral movement. Loss of lateral movement is most likely to occur in cervical disease and may indicate degenerative changes such as OA. Sit behind the patient, stabilizing the hips with your hands and ask the patient to bend sideways to left and right (lateral movement), then backwards (extension) and finally to rotate about the hips by twisting first the left and then the right shoulder forwards. OA and ankylosing spondylitis are most likely to cause a reduction in the range of movement of the spine.

The spinous processes and bony contours of the spine should then be palpated with the thumb, checking for tenderness and abnormal protrusions. If none are detected, the spine may be percussed by gently thumping with the ulnar aspect of the fist. This may identify tenderness associated with osteoporosis or malignancy not apparent on palpation.

This should be followed by palpating the paravertebral muscles. If palpation identifies tenderness between L4 and L5 or L5 and S1, this suggests a herniated intervertebral disc, while tenderness over the sacroiliac area is associated with ankylosing spondylitis.

If the history involves low back pain, the patient's ability to straight-leg raise should then be tested (Fig. 12.9). S/he should lie on a couch and raise each leg in turn as far as it will comfortably go. If the patient experiences sharp pain as the leg is raised this indicates nerve root problems at the level of L4 or below as this manoeuvre puts tension on the nerve roots. Dorsiflexing the foot increases the pain as the tension is increased further. If the foot is put into the neutral position and the knee flexed to 90° the pain is then relieved as this relaxes the tension on the nerve root; however, extending the knee further brings the pain back. The femoral stretch test will reveal problems at a higher level in the lumbar spine (Fig.12.10). The patient lies prone and you should gently flex the knee to see if this triggers pain – if not, extend the leg at the hip to see if this is painful. A positive, painful response indicates nerve root irritation up to the level of L2.

If there is L5 and S1 nerve root irritation, a range of neurological signs will be present. These include inability to walk on the heels (L5) and loss of ankle jerks plus inability to walk on tiptoe (S1). These may be tested for if nerve root irritation is suspected as a cause of low back pain. It should be remembered that for many patients with a history of back pain no obvious cause can be found on examination.

The upper limb

The patient's history should act as a guide to ensure that the examination is concise and relevant. The basic stages of inspection, palpation and assessing movement apply whichever area of the upper limb is involved.

Inspection of the hand and wrist should be guided by the history and presenting complaint. It should also document the MCPJ and IPJ, noting any abnormalities such as ulnar deviation of the fingers or swan-neck deformity (flexion of the MCPJ, extension of the proximal IPJ and flexion of the distal IPJ) found classically in rheumatoid arthritis. Any areas of redness, swelling or abnormal alignment of the fingers should be noted (e.g. mallet finger). The swelling and deformity of a dis-

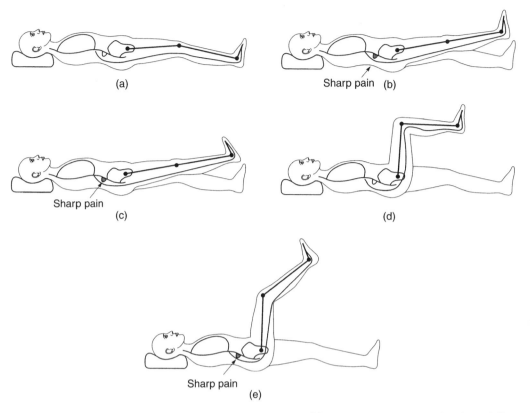

Figure 12.9 Stretch tests for sciatic nerve roots. Straight leg raising (b) restricted by pressure of prolapsed disc on nerve root, made worse by dorsiflexion of foot (c). Flexion of knee (d) relieves pressure but subsequent extension (e) increases pressure causing pain radiating to back.

placed fracture of the distal radius are obvious but there may be little to see with a scaphoid fracture.

Palpation will demonstrate the hard, small bony fragments (osteophytes) characteristic of OA which are found at the interphalangeal joints or the soft, rubbery joint swelling that indicates synovitis. Tenosynovitis frequently produces palpable swelling over the affected area. The carpal bones and distal radius should be carefully palpated for localized bony tenderness if the patient's history indicates a fall on an outstretched hand. The scaphoid can be palpated in the anatomical snuff box – the hollow at the base of the thumb just distal to the end of the radius. McNally & Gillespie (2004) cite extensive evidence indicating that the most reliable indications for a scaphoid fracture are a history of a fall with a hyperextension injury and tenderness in the anatomical snuff box. Extending the thumb or wrist whilst palpating this region may make the tenderness more apparent according to these authors. The whole wrist area should be carefully palpated as a fracture of a carpal bone other than the scaphoid is possible. The ulnar styloid should also be palpated where a distal fracture of the radius is suspected, as this may also be involved.

The ability to reach 90° of flexion or extension of the wrist joint may be assessed by asking the patient to place the backs of the hands together and then raise the arms or the palms of the hands together and lower the arms respectively. Gross finger movement can be assessed by asking the patient to make a tight fist and then open out the hand, fanning out the fingers and thumb. Arthritis, tenosynovitis or Dupuytren's contracture (fibrosis of the palmar fascia) all prevent the patient from being able to make these movements. When asked to hold out the fingers, the patient may show a pronounced droop of the ring and little fingers, indicating rupture of the respective extensor tendons. This is a complication of rheumatoid arthritis.

The median nerve is prone to compression, due to its passage through the narrow carpal tunnel

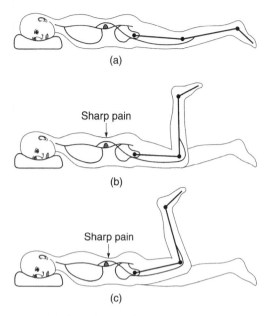

(a)

Sharp pain

(b)

Sharp pain

(c)

Figure 12.10 Stretch tests for the femoral nerve. Flexion of the knee (b) or flexion of the knee and extension of the hip (c) cause pain as the femoral nerve roots are tightened.

(carpal tunnel syndrome). If the history is suggestive of carpal tunnel syndrome, the patient should be asked to press the backs of the hands together (flexing the wrists to 90°) and hold this position (Phalen's test). This compresses the median nerve and is positive if numbness and tingling develop over the distribution of the median nerve.

The motor branch of the median nerve supplies the thenar muscles, allowing abduction of the thumb, while the ulnar nerve permits adduction. The effectiveness of the motor branch of the median nerve can be tested by asking the patient to place the thumb across the palm of the hand and then abduct it against resistance (compare with the unaffected hand). The motor branch of the ulnar nerve can be tested by asking the patient to hold a card between the thumb and the radial side of the second fingers. In the normal hand the thumb will be held straight but in the abnormal hand the thumb will flex at the MCP and IP joints due to weakness of the adductor muscle. The ability to elevate the thumb into the hitchhiking position depends on having a patent extensor pollicus longus tendon. Inability to perform this manoeuvre suggests a problem with this tendon. Rupture occurs as a later complication of a Colles fracture or rheumatoid arthritis.

The sensory distribution of the median, radial and ulnar nerves in the hand is described on p. 199. Any suggestion of numbness or tingling associated with an injury to the wrist or arm should be checked by assessing pinprick sensation in both hands with the patient's eyes closed. The motor branch of the radial nerve permits wrist extension, therefore a wrist drop would suggest damage to this nerve. The ulnar and median nerves have been discussed above.

Examination of the elbow should pay particular attention to the olecranon, noting whether there is any swelling suggestive of olecranon bursitis or signs of inflammation. The arms should be examined from behind with both the elbows fully extended as this will reveal any deformity in the elbow joint. Palpation may reveal tenderness over one of the epicondyles, suggesting tennis elbow or synovitis and a joint effusion within the elbow, depending on the history. It may also detect any nodules within an olecranon bursa, other irregularities associated with the joint, or the localized bony tenderness indicative of a fracture. The radial head in particular should be carefully palpated after a story of falling on an outstretched hand as it may be fractured.

The normal elbow may show slight hyperextension beyond the neutral position and should be capable of 150° of flexion. The patient should then be asked to hold the elbows by the sides flexed at 90° and then required to demonstrate full pronation and supination of the forearm. Restricted movement indicates probable arthritic changes within the joint.

Serious injuries of the elbow should always be assessed for evidence of neurovascular compromise before referral on for medical management. Assess sensation in the ulnar, median and radial nerve distributions and check that there is a good radial pulse.

The shoulder is a complex joint and inspection should include comparison of both shoulders to assist detection of any visible abnormality. There may be muscle wasting caused by lack of use due to arthritis or frozen shoulder syndrome or, conversely, the shoulder may appear enlarged as a result of swelling associated with synovitis and joint effusion. Anterior dislocation alters the contour of the shoulder, leading to a flattened appearance (p. 203). Bruising after a fractured neck of humerus may become obvious some 24 hours later and track down the upper arm over the next few days.

Palpation should include the acromioclavicular and sternoclavicular joints. It may reveal a soft, boggy tender area characteristic of synovitis or the hard irregularities of OA (osteophytes). Supraspinatus tendinitis (leading to painful arc syndrome) causes localized tenderness over the shoulder tip and in the subacromial space. If the axillary nerve is damaged in a dislocation, it will produce a paralysis of the deltoid muscle and a small area of anaesthesia on the outer part of the upper arm. This area should always be checked for sensation in suspected dislocations.

The shoulder is capable of a wide range of movements so a structured approach is necessary to test range of movement. Initially ask the patient to raise the arms from the sides, straight above the head, then lower them to touch the back of the head; then drop the arms to the sides and touch the back between the shoulder blades. During the first part of this manoeuvre you should anchor the scapula to ensure that the first 90° of abduction involves only the external rotation of the humerus within the glenoid of the shoulder joint rather than being due to movement of the scapula across the thorax.

If this is pain-free the patient may be asked to hold the arm by the side with the elbow flexed at 90° and rotate the upper arm outwards to test rotation within the shoulder joint. Failure to get beyond half the normal range of rotation indicates a frozen shoulder. The patient should be able to swing the arm forward parallel to the body up to at least 90°. Osteoarthritic changes will restrict movement, particularly in this latter direction, and also in abduction. Painful arc syndrome has already been discussed (p. 199) and will be apparent when the patient attempts to abduct the arm away from the side of the body (see Fig. 12.3). If the patient is unable to initiate abduction at all, this indicates complete rupture of the supraspinatus tendon. This may be confirmed if the arm is passively elevated to about 45° from the side as, from this position, due to the mechanics of the shoulder, the patient will be able to continue abduction unaided.

The lower limb

The patient's gait, observed as s/he walks into the consulting room, may reveal significant information (see GALS screening tool, p. 208). Two common abnormalities due to musculoskeletal problems are:

- Pain-relieving hip gait, usually seen in OA: the patient only takes short steps when weight-bearing on the affected side and leans the body over to that side in order to reduce the load on the painful hip.
- Trendelenburg gait: this rolling gait is caused by either an unstable hip joint or inadequate abductor muscles. The Trendelenburg test will be positive at every step (p. 217).

There are other abnormal gaits, such as the scissor gait of cerebral palsy where the abductor spasm makes the legs cross over each other. Dropfoot gait is due to a nerve palsy or a lumbar root lesion causing the toes to point downwards – the person therefore has to raise the knee unusually high to compensate. The nurse practitioner will be familiar with the gaits of individuals who are hemiplegic or who have Parkinsonism.

After observing the gait for any abnormalities, the feet and ankles should first be inspected for deformities, lesions such as bunions or signs of localized pressure indicated by callus formation. Attention should be focused on the toes and metatarsal heads in particular. Palpation over the metatarsophalangeal joints may demonstrate tenderness, indicating synovitis (tenderness on compression of the metatarsophalangeal joints is an early sign of rheumatoid arthritis) whilst a tender, inflamed area over the first metatarsal head indicates gout. Palpation of the injured ankle should attempt to distinguish between a tender swollen area indicative of a sprain and the localized bony tenderness of a fracture, usually involving the medial or lateral malleolus. If there is extensive swelling, this may be difficult. The history will act as a guide towards the possibility of a fracture, depending on how much force was involved, together with the weight and age of the patient. The Ottawa ankle rules are a useful guide in deciding whether radiography is indicated after clinical examination and are discussed on p. 219.

The active and passive range of movements of the ankle (tibiotalar joint) should be noted (normally dorsiflexion 20° and plantar flexion 45°) (Fig. 12.11). The subtalar joint should also be tested by stabilizing the ankle with one hand (hold firmly the lateral and medial malleoli) whilst inverting and everting the foot by moving the heel with the other hand. Restricted and/or painful movement in any of these four directions will indicate which part of the joint is damaged. For example, sprained lateral ligaments cause pain on inversion as the injured ligaments are stretched but are pain-free on eversion

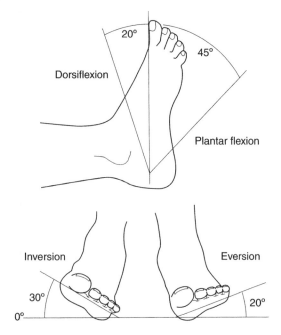

Figure 12.11 Range of ankle movements for the normal ankle.

as they are relaxed in this position. An arthritic ankle joint will be painful whatever direction it is moved in. The joints of the midfoot can be tested by stabilizing the heel with one hand and moving the rest of the foot by holding the metatarsophalangeal joints with the other.

The calf-squeeze test is a reliable method of diagnosing a ruptured Achilles tendon. Ask the patient to kneel and squeeze the calf just distal to its maximum circumference. Plantar flexion of the foot should occur in response; if it does not, the tendon is ruptured. If this test does produce plantar flexion of the foot accompanied by localized tenderness in the calf, this suggests injury to the gastrocnemius muscle (avulsion of the medial head) rather than the Achilles tendon.

If the patient has suffered blunt trauma to the lower limb, you should be aware of the possibility of compartment syndrome (p. 204). The most sensitive sign is sensory deficit, particularly the loss of two-point discrimination (p. 76). Other key findings are paraesthesia and severe pain. Loss of the pedal pulse is a late sign, indicating seriously raised intracompartmental pressure (Edwards 2004).

The knees should initially be inspected with the patient standing looking for evidence of deformity such as genu valgum (knock knee) or genu varum (bow leg). The patient should then be asked to

lie down (supine) and inspected for evidence of quadriceps muscle wasting or swelling, as revealed by loss of the normal hollows that surround the patella. Swelling adjacent to the patella is likely to indicate an effusion in the joint or thickening of the synovium whilst tenderness and redness suggest synovitis. OA tends to be associated with a non-tender swelling whilst prepatellar bursitis leads to a more localized swelling in front of the patella. A dislocated patella is obvious as the bone is displaced laterally and the knee is usually held in flexion.

Palpation of the knee must be performed carefully to detect one of several possible problems. Initially place a hand some 10 cm above the patella, spanning the leg with the thumb on one side and the second and third fingers on the other, gently compressing the leg and feeling the soft tissue. Gradually moving towards and over the patella will allow palpation of the suprapatellar pouch which should be checked for tenderness, softness or excess warmth, all of which indicate synovitis. A loose body may be detected at this stage of the examination; localized tenderness along the joint line of the knee suggests intra-articular pathology.

Palpate the tibiofemoral joint with the knee flexed at 90° and the patient's foot on the examining table. Palpation is best done by pressing with both thumbs along the tibial margin, starting at the patellar tendon and working outwards and around the joint. Tenderness within the joint indicates intra-articular pathology. The menisci are most likely to be damaged. Tenderness over the collateral ligaments suggests that one or the other has been injured. The patella should also be palpated.

Excess fluid in the knee joint (an effusion) may be obvious but a smaller effusion requires careful testing to be detected. Ballotment (patella tap) is a useful procedure and involves using the left hand to push fluid out of the suprapatellar pouch under the patella and then using the second and third fingers of the right hand to press down on the patella. If there is a significant effusion the patella will rebound back off the fluid that has been swept under it. Smaller effusions may be revealed by testing for the bulge sign. This involves forcing any fluid out of the suprapatellar pouch but then anchoring the patella with the index finger of the same hand used for this technique. You should then gently stroke first one side and then the other of the patella in the groove between the patella and the femoral condyle. Any fluid will appear as a bulge

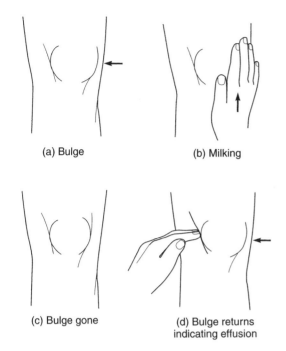

(a) Bulge

(b) Milking

(c) Bulge gone

(d) Bulge returns indicating effusion

Figure 12.12 Bulge sign indicating an effusion in the knee joint.

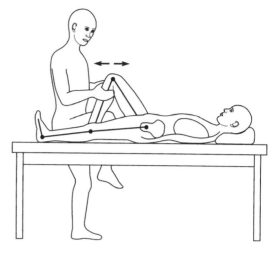

Figure 12.13 Testing cruciate ligaments. The examiner sits on the patient's right foot and draws the tibia forward (anterior cruciate) then attempts to push the tibia backwards (posterior cruciate). Compare the degree of movement of both knees. Hamstrings need to be relaxed for a valid test.

on the opposite side of the patella to the one you are stroking (Fig. 12.12).

The range of movement in both knees should be assessed; normal is 0–150°. Quadriceps weakness may prevent the patient from fully extending the knee actively, indicating a long-term knee problem. If there is a block to full extension (flexion deformity), this suggests an intra-articular problem such as a torn cartilage. Even full passive extension can be blocked in such a situation if the torn cartilage becomes displaced.

After the general knee examination described above, any of the following tests may be carried out if the history indicates they are necessary.

The Apley test should be carried out if damage to a semi-lunar cartilage (meniscus) is suspected. The history will indicate knee locking and/or injury associated with twisting on a flexed knee. The patient lies prone and you should flex the knee to 90°. Press down on the sole of the foot firmly, rotating the lower leg externally and internally – being careful to stop if there is pain. Any locking or clicking is a positive sign indicating meniscal damage. This test is simpler to perform than the traditional McMurray test. Here the patient should lie on the couch with the hip and knee both flexed

to 90°. If right-handed, you should stand on the right side of the couch and grasp the heel with the right hand whilst steadying the knee with the left. The tibia should be externally rotated and the knee gradually extended whilst the left hand palpates the joint line. Repeat this with the tibia in internal rotation. If there is a damaged meniscus the patient will experience some pain and a clunking sensation will be felt with the left hand as the cartilage is suddenly displaced. The patient should be warned in advance that this may be painful, as s/he should for the next two tests, described below.

Two other important tests for knee stability will examine the cruciate and collateral ligaments. The first is the drawer test for damaged cruciates (Fig. 12.13). A history of a sudden change of direction on a weight-bearing knee, which is a common sporting injury, suggests anterior cruciate damage. Other structures such as the medial meniscus or medial collateral ligament may be involved and an avulsion fracture is possible. The test involves the patient lying down flat with the knee flexed and the examiner sitting on the patient's foot to anchor it to the couch. Check that the hamstrings are relaxed and then attempt to draw the tibia forward from the femur – this will test the anterior cruciate – and then push it backwards to check the posterior cruciate. No significant movement should be possible in either direction in a normal knee. Both knees should be compared in this way. Any abnormal laxity suggests damage to the anterior or posterior cruciate.

The collateral ligaments may be tested by lying the patient flat on the couch and wedging his or her ankle between your elbow and side (Fig. 12.14). With one hand just below the knee and the other just above (on opposite sides of the leg), you should then attempt to abduct and adduct the femur by a sideways movement. Both legs should be tested and little or no movement should be possible. Laxity indicates damage to the appropriate ligament. Both the drawer test and the collateral ligament test should be painless, but if there has been injury to the ligaments, these manipulations can be painful. The nurse practitioner should therefore be careful when carrying them out and note the site of any pain reported by the patient.

One final test which should be used if the history is suggestive of patellar instability involves laying the patient flat and applying a gentle but firm pressure against the medial edge of the patella. The knee should then be gently flexed up to about 30° while maintaining pressure. If there is patellar instability, abnormal laxity will be felt at the start of flexion. The patient's facial expression will indicate discomfort and a sensation that it is about to dislocate again. For this reason this is known as the patella apprehension test!

Inspection of the hip joint rarely shows anything of significance about the joint, although one leg may look shorter than the other. Measurement of limb length is essential as shortening may be apparent due to hip deformity rather than actual loss of

length. The distance from the anterior superior iliac spine to the medial malleolus is defined as the true length. A fracture of the proximal femur usually produces shortening by about 2 cm and external rotation of the limb. Palpation will reveal tenderness associated with the fracture, although it may be the pelvis that has fractured rather than the neck of femur. The classic shortening and external rotation will not then be present.

If the person has normal hips, s/he should be able to pull each knee (flexed) up to the chest wall to demonstrate normal hip flexion. Restricted internal rotation of the hip is a strong indicator of OA and may be tested by asking the patient while lying on the back to flex both hip and knee joints to 90°. You should hold the leg firmly just above the knee and grasp the ankle with the other hand. By swinging the lower leg medially, this tests external rotation of the hip, while swinging it laterally tests internal rotation (Fig. 12.15). Abduction and adduction should be tested as these will also be restricted by OA. This is best done with the patient lying flat and the pelvis immobilized by holding down the opposite iliac crest to the one being tested. Abduction of 45° is normal and some 20° of adduction beyond the midline should be possible.

If OA is present the hip may have developed a fixed flexion deformity. This may not be apparent when lying the patient flat as s/he will compensate by arching the back (lumbar lordosis) to make the

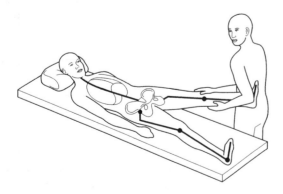

Figure 12.14 Testing collateral ligaments. Attempt abduction and adduction of the femur while keeping the knee straight.

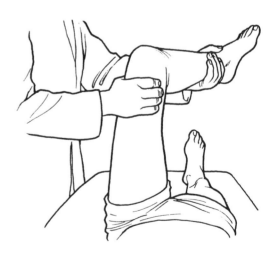

Figure 12.15 Testing external rotation of the hip. The lower leg is swung medially while the thigh is held still. Reverse the test for internal rotation. Restricted movement indicates hip disease, especially arthritis.

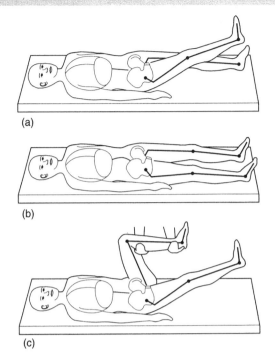

(a)

(b)

(c)

Figure 12.16 Flexion deformity of the right hip. Lordosis of the lumbar spine may hide this (b) but full flexion of the left hip (c) makes this apparent as the lordosis is corrected.

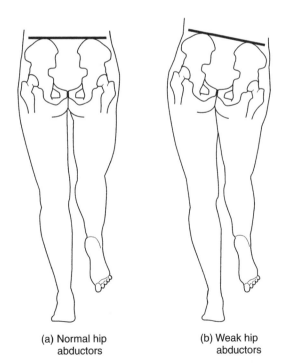

(a) Normal hip abductors

(b) Weak hip abductors

Figure 12.17 Trendelenburg's sign. Weak hip abductors mean that when the patient stands on one leg, the pelvis tilts down on the non-weight-bearing side.

position more comfortable. This will conceal the hip flexion deformity. If the opposite hip is fully flexed this will eliminate the compensatory lordosis, making the flexion deformity of the arthritic hip apparent (Fig. 12.16). This is Thomas' test and will work even if both hips are affected. Thomas' test should be carried out if the history indicates OA of the hip.

Trendelenburg's test is a general assessment of hip function. Ask the patient to stand unsupported on one leg. This is only possible if the hip on the side off the ground is stable and has normal muscles surrounding it. Drooping of the pelvis on the side off the ground, which is apparent from the rear, indicates joint instability and/or muscle wasting (Fig. 12.17).

DIFFERENTIAL DIAGNOSES

A common problem is a patient complaining of a painful joint or joints. To differentiate between OA and rheumatoid arthritis, the guide shown in Table 12.1 will be useful.

Back pain is another common problem that may have several different causes. It will be helpful to differentiate between a mechanical cause and other organic causes.

A mechanical origin for the pain will be characterized by a history of sudden onset, linkage to activity such as digging the garden, previous recurrent episodes and generalized unilateral distribution of symptoms – the pain will usually be eased by rest. Nerve root problems will produce neurological symptoms in the distribution of the affected lumbar nerve root.

Postural back pain tends to be more chronic with no obvious sudden onset and no neurological signs or symptoms. The history will give clues to poor posture.

Ankylosing spondylitis tends to be found in young men aged 15–30. The patient complains of back stiffness and pain that is worse first thing in the morning and it may be reported as moving from side to side. Chest expansion is restricted to less than 5 cm.

Continuous severe back pain suggests malignant disease with secondary deposits affecting the spine – therefore in addition to generalized symptoms such as malaise and weight loss there may be evidence of a primary tumour affecting an organ such as the breast or prostate.

Table 12.1 Differential diagnosis of rheumatoid arthritis and osteoarthritis

Rheumatoid arthritis	Osteoarthritis
Usually affects younger patients under 40	Patient likely to be over 50
Affects multiple joints, usually in a symmetrical pattern, starting with swelling, stiffness and pain in the small joints of the hands and feet	Asymmetrical; larger joints affected
Joint shows signs of inflammation and is tender and boggy	Joint usually cool; osteophytes may be palpated (bony enlargements) and crepitus may be present
No relationship between weight and onset of disease	Obesity is a major risk factor for osteoarthritis of the lower limb
Stiffness and pain worse in the morning.	No obvious relationship with time of day
Pain present at night and at rest	Use causes pain in weight-bearing lower limbs; rest reduces pain. Affected upper limb is relatively free from pain as non-weight-bearing
ESR* may be elevated	ESR usually normal
Constitutional symptoms such as fatigue, malaise and anorexia	No constitutional symptoms

ESR = Erythrocyte sedimentation rate

One other important differential diagnosis lies between gout and an infection such as septic arthritis as their appearance is similar. In either case the patient may be pyrexial and have a raised erythrocyte sedimentation rate as part of the generalized inflammatory response. A history of trauma, especially a penetrating injury such as a thorn or nail, tends to suggest infection as the diagnosis, whereas gout can be confirmed by microscopy of synovial fluid or tissue which will reveal the presence of urate crystals.

INVESTIGATIONS

BLOODS

A patient suspected of having rheumatoid arthritis can have bloods taken for a range of tests, including rheumatoid factors (anti-immunoglobulins). However, approximately 20% of patients with clinical disease are seronegative. The inflammatory nature of the disease leads to an elevated erythrocyte sedimentation rate in 85–90% of patients. Anaemia is a common finding. Synovial fluid analysis usually shows a picture of turbidity together with an increase in both volume and white cell count (Springhouse 2000).

In patients with suspected osteoporosis, bloods should be taken for serum calcium, phosphate and alkaline phosphatase and creatinine. Bone density measurement using dual energy x-ray absorptiometry (DEXA scan) is the gold standard for diagnosis. There has to be bone mass loss of at least 30% before conventional x-rays show evidence of osteoporosis whereas DEXA scanning gives a much earlier diagnosis (Doheny et al 2003).

RADIOGRAPHY

Radiographic examination is a major component of the diagnosis in OA, rheumatoid arthritis and, together with bone densitometry, in osteoporosis. The hospital orthopaedic clinic will usually be responsible for these investigations.

Radiography is highly important in the diagnosis of fractures and joint injuries. In order to avoid unnecessary delays in treatment and also unnecessary radiographs, most Trusts have developed local protocols which should be followed, but the presence of localized bony tenderness as the cardinal sign of a fracture should underpin decision-making in this field. This is illustrated by the introduction of the Ottawa ankle rules (Fig. 12.18). Similar protocols can be developed for other common injuries.

Before requesting the radiograph

A comprehensive clinical examination of the patient and a detailed history are the first stages in the process. This information is then relayed to the radiographer undertaking the examination via the clinical indications section of the x-ray request card. The radiographer will then have all the facts needed in order to adapt the radiographic tech-

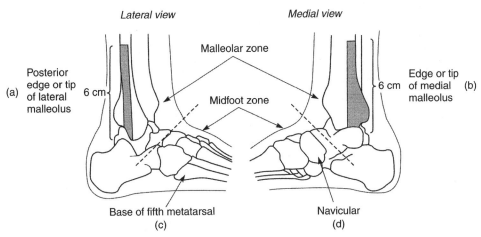

Figure 12.18 Ottawa ankle rules. Ankle x-rays are needed only if there is pain in the malleolar zone and any of the following: bone tenderness at (a) or (b); inability to bear weight both immediately and in A&E. Foot x-rays are needed only if there is pain in the mid-foot region and any of the following: bone tenderness at (c) or (d); inability to bear weight both immediately and in A&E.

niques to suit the particular situation. For example, examination of a patient with a badly injured elbow can vary enormously. A procedure designed to demonstrate a supracondylar fracture will be inappropriate if a fractured radial head is suspected. Incorrect technique can easily result in injuries being overlooked. The importance of effective communication between the individual requesting the examination and the radiographer, via the x-ray request form, cannot be overstated.

Examining the radiograph

The first consideration to be made relates to the adequacy of the image and whether or not it fulfils the criteria for diagnosis. This will involve the following stages:

- Check you have the correct radiographs for your patient by referring to the name marker on the image. The date should also be checked as multiple images of the same body part may exist.
- Check the left/right-side marker on the image to ensure that this tallies with the anatomy demonstrated and the site of injury.
- Ensure all the region of interest has been included within the image. Ambiguous clinical indications on the request card may lead to some important anatomy being excluded from the image.

- Note if the film density is sufficient to demonstrate all the anatomy to a diagnostic standard within the region of interest.

Once you are satisfied the technical factors used to produce the image are adequate you can proceed to search for a pathology. A systematic approach is of vital importance. A surprising number of images contain more than one pathology. The eye will be immediately drawn to the more obvious abnormality. Other less obvious pathologies may therefore be missed as you will be content to have detected the abnormality. If a rigorous and systematic search strategy is employed, the likelihood of missing important injuries will be reduced. Examples of such strategies are given below.

Lateral cervical spine

- Check the alignment of the vertebra. Figure 12.19 shows a number of lines used for this purpose. Trace a line coincident with the anterior and posterior margins of the vertebral bodies (lines A and B). The lines should be smooth and without deviation. Any steps or slippages of greater than a few millimetres could indicate a fracture or dislocation.
- Examine the line formed by the facet joints (line C). The inferior articular processes of one vertebra should line up with the superior

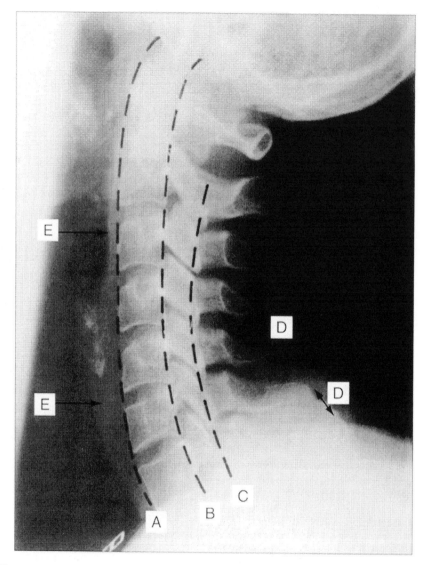

Figure 12.19 Lines used for assessing pathology on lateral cervical spine radiographs.

process of the vertebra below. If it does not, a facetal dislocation may have occurred.

- Check the distance between the spinous process (D). If the distance between two spinous processes is significantly greater than the others, ligamentous damage may have occurred.
- Trace the outline of each vertebra to look for fractures. Each body should trace a uniform box shape. Look out for wedge or compression fractures.
- Examine the soft tissues immediately anterior to the vertebral bodies (E). An abnormal

swelling may have been produced by haematoma formation resulting from a fracture. Remember that the prevertebral soft tissues normally widen below C4.

The chest radiograph

The chest radiograph is a real challenge, owing to the wide range of pathologies potentially visible. This search strategy represents the simplest method:

- Technical factors: the appearance of the radiograph can vary greatly depending on how the image was obtained. If the examination was performed supine, fluid levels will disappear and the size of the mediastinum will alter. A small degree of rotation may cause structures which are normally obscured by the heart to become visible. The vena cava is a good example. It will become evident as a line on the right side of the mediastinum if the patient is rotated to the left. The degree of rotation may be assessed by comparing the distance from the medial end of each clavicle to the midline. The phase of respiration will also have a profound effect on normal appearances, especially in the lower regions. The presence of six anterior ribs above the diaphragm indicates that the image was taken on inspiration.

- The mediastinum: the diameter of the heart should be less than half the diameter of the chest at the widest point. The outline of the mediastinum should be smooth. A dark line running adjacent to the heart may indicate a pneumomediastinum. The whole mediastinum should be central within the chest, although the heart is situated with two-thirds of its diameter to the right of the midline as you view the image.
- The lungs: the lungs should be of equal density. An increase in density, either generally or associated with one of the fissures, is indicative of a pathology such as infection. The blood vessels within the chest should be visible from the lung hilum to the chest wall. Absence of these vessels may indicate a pneumothorax. Pay particular attention to the lung apices if a pneumothorax is suspected.
- Diaphragms: these should be smooth with clear costophrenic and cardiophrenic angles. Fluid may collect here as a result of an effusion.
- The thoracic skeleton: ribs should be checked for fractures, beginning with the first rib and progressing downward. Start where the rib is joined to the thoracic spine and follow the whole of the rib to its anterior end. Do not forget the clavicles and scapulae.
- Other areas: note any artefacts, e.g. buttons. The soft tissues may also demonstrate pathology such as surgical emphysema.

Hip radiographs

Shenton's line is defined by the anatomy of the pelvic region and is a useful reference line. It is used

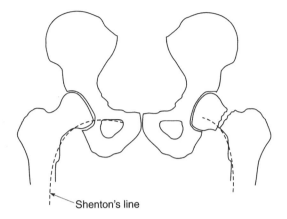

Figure 12.20 Shenton's line can be followed through to the obturator foramen in the right hip. This is not the case in the left hip, which is fractured.

as part of a pelvic evaluation routine and to detect femoral neck fractures (Fig. 12.20). In the normal hip a line defining the medial border of the femur may be followed continuously round to that defining the upper border of the obturator foramen. If this line cannot be followed, the femoral neck should be scrutinized for a fracture.

Recognizing the normal

Before attempting to make diagnoses from radiographs it is imperative to have a good knowledge of bony anatomy and normal radiographic appearances. This should be combined with an understanding of how anatomy can change on the radiograph when the patient is positioned using a non-standard projection. This can radically alter the resultant image and may affect the final diagnosis. There are many variants of normal anatomy which can fool the unwary observer. A few examples are described here; extensive detailed descriptions are given in the recommended texts.

Nutrient arteries

These are channels or pathways that allow the passage of blood vessels into the bone (Fig. 12.21). They appear as dark lines within the bone or disruptions visible on its outer margin. They are often confused with fractures but can be quite easily distinguished as they always have smooth edges, whereas fractures will have sharply defined edges. Nutrient arteries are commonly visible within the skull or in long bones.

Figure 12.21 The nutrient artery is often mistaken for a fracture – it can be distinguished by its smooth edges.

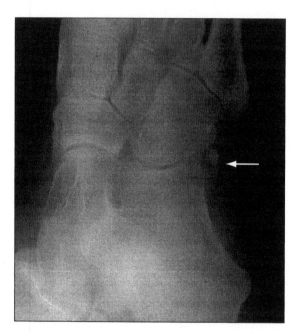

Figure 12.22 Example of an accessory bone in the foot.

Accessory bones

Accessory bones are small ossicles that develop close to joints (Fig. 12.22). They may be confused with fragments of bone from a fracture. Again they can easily be set apart by their smooth, well-defined edges while bone fragments will have sharp edges. They are often found in the foot, ankle and hand. The os trigonum, found behind the talus, is often mistaken for a fracture.

Epiphyses

The dark lines caused by epiphyses are often mistaken for fractures, especially when they begin to fuse. It is important to be aware where these structures are and note the patient's age when viewing a film. The epiphysis at the base of the metacarpal is frequently mistaken for a fracture. It is quite easy to differentiate as this epiphysis will run in a longitudinal direction whereas a fracture nearly always runs transversely across the bone (see avulsion fractures, below).

Recognizing fractures and the abnormal

The following sections will focus on the diagnosis of fractures and dislocations; some other acute pathologies will also be mentioned. There is a wide variety of fracture types and each has a characteristic appearance or combination of appearances.

Simple fractures with minimal displacement

The search for a fracture will involve a number of stages. First, the whole of the dense margin on the outside of the bone (the cortex) should be examined for any sharp steps, breaks or disruptions. These can often be subtle and may easily be overlooked. A fracture of the radial head is a good example of a commonly occurring fracture that will only manifest itself with a cortical abnormality. Figure 12.23 shows an example of a torus fracture in a child; this occurs when a longitudinal force is applied to an immature bone. The relatively soft bones of children often do not completely fracture but will bend or partially break, rather like bending a cardboard tube. The torus fracture will often appear as a slight buckle or raising of the outer bone cortex. Tibial plateau fractures may only be evident as a small defect in the cortex or a small flake of bone raised above the surrounding cortex.

The hunt for a fracture will continue with an examination of the intricate honeycomb pattern that constitutes the centre of a bone (the trabeculae). This should be scrutinized since disruptions in the continuity of the trabecular pattern or areas of increased film density (radiolucency) would be indicative of a fracture. In the case of a radiolucency the x-rays are able to pass through the space within the bone caused by a slight displacement of the fracture. They are then free to pass through to the film, thus causing an increase in blackening compared to the surrounding bone. When a fracture occurs, bone fragments may be forced together and could overlap. This will provide an additional barrier to the x-rays. Thus fewer will reach the film

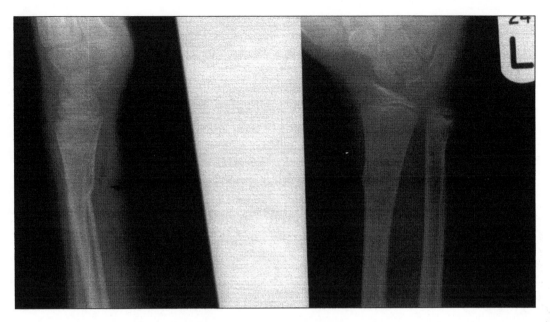

Figure 12.23 Torus fracture of distal radius.

compared to those from areas immediately adjacent to the fracture. A lighter area defined by sharp edges will then be observable within the normal trabecular pattern. Good examples of these appearances may be found as a result of an impacted fracture of the hip or a depressed skull fracture (Fig. 12.24).

Compression and comminuted fractures

An injury that results in a compressive force being applied to a bone may result in a comminuted fracture in which the bone is shattered into a number of pieces. Many of these fractures will be easily identified but some are less obvious.

A compressive force applied to the top of the head may cause a total disruption of C1. This is referred to as a Jefferson fracture and can be identified by the increased distance between the odontoid peg and the lateral masses of C1. The articular surfaces between C1 and C2 will not be in alignment (Fig. 12.25). Compression fractures are common elsewhere within the spine. A hyperflexion injury may result in the collapse of the anterior portion of the vertebral body, causing the characteristic wedge deformity (Fig. 12.26). This may be dramatic or subtle and hardly visible. The shape of each vertebral

body should therefore be carefully examined and compared to its neighbours.

Avulsion fractures

An avulsion fracture results from a force being transmitted along a tendon or ligament, resulting in a piece of bone being pulled off at its attachment. This often occurs at the greater tuberosity of the humerus where the tendons of the supraspinatus, infraspinatus and teres minor muscles are attached (Fig. 12.27). The base of the fifth metatarsal is also prone to avulsion fractures. The peroneus brevis tendon will be responsible for a transverse fracture across the base of the metatarsal following an inversion injury to the ankle (Fig. 12.28).

Epiphyseal injuries

A range of injuries may occur at any growth plate. These may be quite subtle and only involve the smallest displacement of the epiphysis, or could involve fractures with epiphyseal separation. If the injury involves an impaction of the epiphysis there may be no separation, which makes diagnosis difficult. Figure 12.29 shows slippage of the upper femoral epiphysis. This is often encountered in

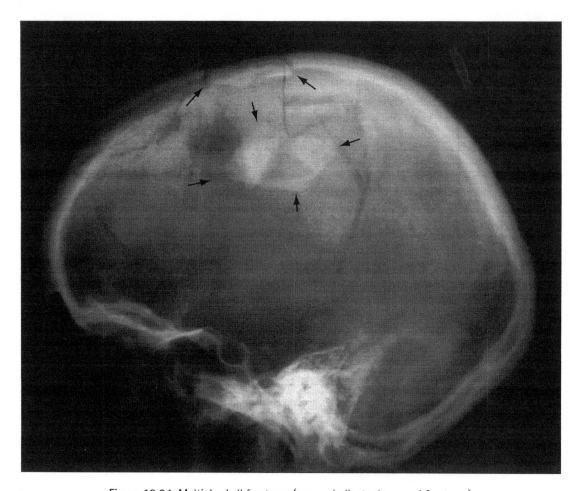

Figure 12.24 Multiple skull fractures (arrows indicate depressed fractures).

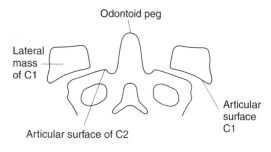

Line drawing of 'open mouth' projection of C1/2.

Figure 12.25 Jefferson fracture of C1. Note how the lateral masses of C1 have been displaced outwards and the articular surfaces are no longer in alignment.

overweight boys and may not be evident on an AP hip projection. A second 'frog-leg' lateral will be required in such cases.

Contrecoup fractures

These injuries occur where the force causing a fracture in a bony ring is transmitted to the other side of the ring, causing another fracture. It is rather like trying to break a biscuit with a hole in the middle. You will have difficulty in causing a break in one place only; you always end up with two or more breaks. Common sites for these fractures include the skull, mandible and the tibia and fibula. An injury to the medial malleolus of the ankle may be accompanied by fracture at the upper end of the fibula just below the knee. This is often overlooked both clinically and radiographically.

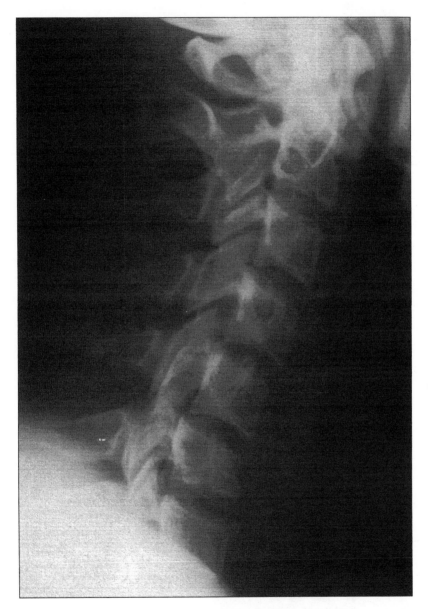

Figure 12.26 Wedge fracture of C6 with a teardrop fracture, to the body of C7.

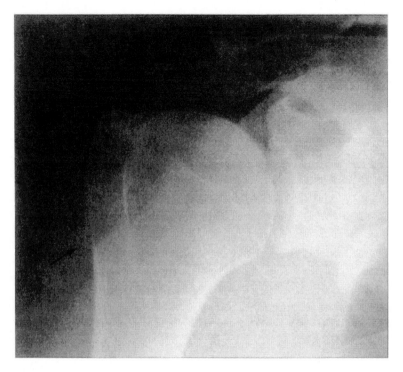

Figure 12.27 Avulsion fracture at the greater tuberosity of the humerus.

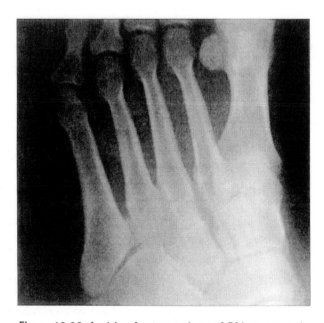

Figure 12.28 Avulsion fracture to base of fifth metatarsal.

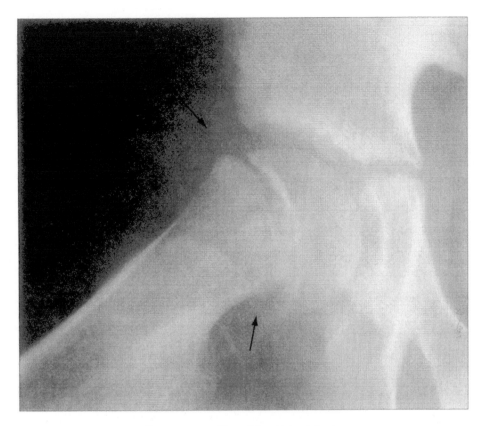

Figure 12.29 Slipped femoral epiphysis.

Dislocations

A dislocation will involve the articular surface in one component of a joint being completely separated from the other articular component. They are most often encountered in the shoulder, although other sites such as the hip or IPJs are not uncommon. An anterior dislocation of the glenohumeral joint will involve a considerable amount of forward and inferior displacement of the humerus. Posterior dislocations are quite rare but difficult to diagnose. The degree of displacement is much less and will take place in a posterior direction. An AP shoulder radiograph may not appear significantly abnormal due to the direction of the displacement. A second projection of the shoulder is always required if an obvious anterior dislocation is not evident. The acromioclavicular joint is also prone to dislocations or subluxation (partial dislocations) and should merit special attention when assessing the shoulder radiograph.

Other pathologies

Soft-tissue injuries and evidence of bleeding are sometimes evident on radiographs. A classic example is the elbow effusion (Fig. 12.30). A build-up of fluid in the elbow joint capsule following an injury will cause the fat pads in the capsule wall to be displaced outwards. These can be identified as two sail-like radiolucent areas found anteriorly and posteriorly to the joint. If the fat pad sign is noted then careful analysis of the joint should follow, as a fracture is likely to be present.

Bleeding may also occur in the maxillary sinuses following a fracture to the facial bones (Fig. 12.31). As before, a careful inspection of the bones should follow; sinusitis may also result in a fluid build-up within the sinuses.

Infection in a bone or joint may be difficult to identify. The joint space may become slightly wider as a result of fluid build-up in the joint. The bone periosteum may lift slightly or the sharp cortical

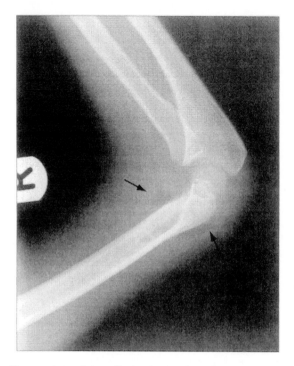

Figure 12.30 Joint effusion in the elbow from supracondylar fracture (arrows indicate raised fat pads).

outline of the bone may become indistinct when infection is present. Chronic bone infection will result in the gradual destruction of bone.

TREATMENT

RHEUMATOID ARTHRITIS AND OTHER INFLAMMATORY CONDITIONS

If RA or some other inflammatory rheumatoid condition such as ankylosing spondylitis is suspected, a rapid medical referral should be made. A multidisciplinary approach is essential for the management of patients with these conditions and clinical nurse specialists in rheumatology have made a major contribution towards such teams (O'Donovan 2004).

Although the patient is usually managed by hospital-based specialists, the primary care NP has a key role to play in supporting the patient, especially in monitoring for drug side effects involving the powerful medications that are prescribed by hospital specialists for the management of RA. These disease-modifying antirheumatic drugs (DMARDs)

are not curing the patient but give substantial relief and improve the quality of life. The NSAIDs can be used on a short-term basis to help manage pain but attention should be paid to the possible side effects, especially involving gastric irritation. These side effects are greatly reduced by use of the cyclo-oxygenase-2 selective inhibitors such as etodolac and rofecoxib, however NICE recommends this group of drugs should not be routinely used for management of RA and should only be used where there is a high risk of gastric complications due to the risk of other side effects and interactions (BNF 2003). The DMARDS can have serious side effects and the newer ones such as the tumour necrosis factor inhibitors (etanercept and infliximab) are also very expensive, costing in the region of £8 000–10 000 per year to treat a single patient. There are therefore strict guidelines from NICE about their use (BNF 2003) and also issues around so called 'postcode prescribing' which mean that some patients who could benefit from these new drugs are not doing so.

This disorder has far reaching implications for all aspects of the person's life and frequently leads to reduced self-esteem and depression (Oliver 2004). Factors such as these should be borne in mind when seeing a patient with RA, whatever the reason for the consultation. Every effort should always be made to reinforce the work of the multidisciplinary team as there is far more to RA than the pathology and the medical approach to dealing with that pathology, however important that may be.

Gout is extremely painful, so treatment with NSAIDs (naproxen or indometacin) is required. The side effects must be reviewed carefully with the patient – particularly gastric complications. In older people, gout may be diuretic-induced so a review of the cardiovascular system and medication is necessary. Obesity exacerbates gout – lifestyle advice concerning diet and exercise is needed. Reducing beer consumption will assist weight loss and help with the problem of hyperuricaemia. If necessary a drug such as allopurinol may be used to lower uric acid levels.

Shoulder problems associated with rotator cuff disorders such as painful arc syndrome usually respond to rest and NSAIDs. If necessary, a mixture of local anaesthetic and corticosteroids can be injected into the subacromial bursa by a medical practitioner to achieve symptom relief. The same approach can be used with elbow problems such as tennis elbow. Frozen shoulder will usually respond to NSAIDs during the painful phase but a course of

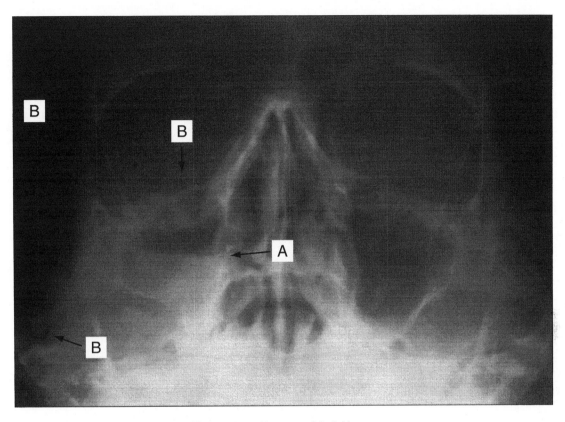

Figure 12.31 Fracture of facial bones.

oral steroids may be needed if the pain is severe. Gradual mobilization and exercise will help recover function subsequently when stiffness is a major problem.

OSTEOARTHRITIS

This is another condition where a medical referral is required if you suspect its presence in a patient. Even after referral for surgery, the patient may experience considerable pain and disability while awaiting operation. The health education role of the nurse practitioner comes to the fore as every effort should be made to get the patient in the best possible condition for surgery and to relieve symptoms as far as possible while on the waiting list. Pain management with paracetamol is preferable to NSAIDs as there are fewer side effects and OA has little inflammatory component. Weight loss and improved fitness are obvious targets in the obese as this will reduce wear and tear on all lower limb joints and also improve postoperative recovery.

Smoking cessation will be beneficial while waiting for surgery.

The psychosocial dimensions of care are important as isolation and depression are common problems. Efforts should be made to arrange for social support and to stress the positive side of things to the patient. Nurse practitioners are developing in the specialist field of orthopaedics and they can have a major beneficial impact upon patients with OA, especially in preparing them for surgery.

OSTEOPOROSIS

Treatment should always begin with prevention. Although it may not be easy to persuade a teenage girl to relate to a health problem that may not affect her for 40 years, there are real benefits to be gained from health education aimed at this age group. General health-promoting activities such as a healthy diet rich in calcium and vitamin D, weight-bearing exercise, avoiding smoking and discouraging an unhealthy obsession with weight loss and dieting will all help build up a stronger skeletal structure which will protect against osteoporosis in later life.

Lifestyle advice concerning smoking cessation, reducing alcohol intake, healthy diet and exercise will all benefit, as will calcium supplements. The bisphonate group of drugs (such as alendronate or etidronate) are beneficial in more advanced cases as they will kill osteoclasts and so inhibit bone resorption – leading to an increase in bone mass of 5–10%. Steps should also be taken to avoid falls which could easily lead to fractures in an osteoporotic patient. The NP should work with the patient and their family to reduce risks in the environment, such as ensuring good footwear and avoiding obstacles such as rugs which could be tripped over. Physical assessment should also investigate organic risks such as poorly controlled blood sugar levels and hypertension, which may lead to dizziness and falls. Vision, balance and walking ability should be checked.

A major treatment to prevent osteoporosis has been hormone replacement therapy (HRT), however the almost simultaneous publication of results from the Million Women Study (Beral et al 2003) and the US Women's Health Initiative (Biomedcentral 2003) caused a great deal of controversy about the safety of HRT. The WHI study reported increased risks of death from various causes including breast cancer and cardiovascular disease in women on HRT. Beral et al (2003) found that HRT increased the risk of both breast cancer and dying from breast cancer, especially when combinations of oestrogen and progestagen were used. One headline that was extensively reported was that the risk of dying from breast cancer increased by 22% in HRT users. This alarming statistic is correct, however, it is misleading in that it is a relative risk, the actual risk is small. There were 637 breast cancer deaths from amongst the total of 1 084 110 women studied, with 6 deaths per 10 000.

The death rate amongst the current users was 0.00066 compared to 0.00060 in those who had never used of HRT. This should be compared with the risks of dying from other diseases, including osteoporosis-related fractures of the hip, an injury which has an incidence of around 30/1000 in women aged 65–74. The study also found that the use of oestrogen-only HRT produced 1.5 extra cases of breast cancer per 1000 women whilst the combined HRT produced 6 extra cases per 1000. These

are small increases and the cause of death in these extra cases may be completely unrelated to breast cancer. The WHI study has been criticized on the grounds that the average age at which women entered the study was 63, well past menopause, and at an age when serious pathology was already likely to be advanced. Critics argue the whole point is to see whether HRT *at menopause* can bring significant health benefits to women, therefore this WHI study misses the point (Powledge 2004).

The NP therefore needs to understand the research in order that s/he can spend time with women discussing the options. There are real benefits to be gained from HRT but there are also slightly increased risks. Ultimately the woman will decide for herself and that is how it should be. However, the tendency of the media to sensationalize health scare stories is to be deplored, as is their lack of social responsibility.

BACK PAIN

If there is evidence of neurological involvement, serious spinal pathology or a suspicion that the cause may be systemic, a medical referral should be made immediately. Simple backache with no obvious physical signs should be managed by advising the use of simple analgesics (paracetamol) or NSAIDs and heat or cold for pain relief. Bed rest should be avoided as evidence indicates that bed rest for 2–7 days is worse than placebo or ordinary activity (Waddell et al 1996). The only demonstrated effective treatment is exercise and patient education as in most cases of back pain no organic cause is ever found (Phillips et al 2003). Advise the patient that activity is not harmful and will help to reduce pain, so early activity is encouraged. Discuss key activities such as lifting, sitting, sleeping and walking and offer health education advice. Prolonged absence from work reduces the probability of that person ever returning to work, consequently advise the patient to return to work as soon as possible. Physiotherapy should only be contemplated if this simple advice fails to improve the situation after a week or two.

Simple analgesics and a soft collar for neck support together with advice about the need for early mobilization will help most patients with whiplash injury. The minority who suffer long-term problems, like those patients with chronic low back pain, experience significant social disruption and psychological distress. Avoid the temptation to label or stigmatize such individuals and remember the importance of the psychosocial aspects of care, particularly with respect to avoiding isolation and inactivity.

TRAUMA

It is worth noting some general principles that apply to all injuries, starting with the fact that a minor injury can be painful and therefore by no means minor as far as the patient is concerned.

It is essential always to think beyond the front door of your minor injuries unit or health centre. Consider how, in the light of their injury and your treatment, the patient will manage to get home, how s/he will cope at home and what follow-up arrangements are needed. Discussing these matters with patients before they leave is essential in order to ensure that they will cope and that your treatment will stay in place and be effective, rather than disregarded as soon as the person gets home simply because it is not practical. A further point is to remember that it is not what is taught that counts, but what is learnt. You may feel you have given a comprehensive teaching session about the need to keep fingers mobile, but has the patient learnt what you have taught? You should check learning with one or two key questions and have a series of pre-printed advice slips to give to patients to take away and refer to later, as they may well forget what you have taught them. Finally, follow-up arrangements should always be given in writing to patients to be sure they do not make a wasted trip if confused about when they are coming back for a check-up or to see a doctor.

Hand injuries

A key principle in treating hand injuries is to concentrate on mobility rather than immobilization. This is because fingers can become stiff quickly and then require a great deal of physiotherapy to return to normal.

In crush injuries of the fingertip, attention should be paid to healing the wound rather than dealing with any comminuted fracture of the distal phalanx. Little can be done for the bony injury, but preventing infection in the fingertip is essential, hence this priority. A fingertip dressing with silver sulphadiazine cream (Flamazine) and a tubular bandage for the affected finger is recommended. These wounds should not be sutured due to the swelling and infection risk.

Undisplaced fractures of a phalanx can best be managed by simple analgesia and strapping the injured finger to its neighbour to act as a splint. Any rings should first be removed as these could act as a constriction around the injured finger if swelling occurs. The strapping must leave the joints free and there should be a piece of gauze between the fingers to avoid potential problems where the two areas of skin would be in prolonged contact. If Elastoplast is to be used as strapping, check first whether the patient is allergic. The patient should be encouraged to keep the finger as mobile as possible and dispense with the strapping when the finger is no longer painful. Mallet fingers should be referred for a medical opinion as if an avulsion fracture is present, an operative reduction and wiring will be needed.

If x-ray reveals that the fracture is displaced or it involves joint surfaces, a medical opinion is needed as manipulation may be necessary. The finger should be gently strapped to its neighbour as support, any rings removed and the hand placed in a high arm sling to reduce swelling as an interim measure while a same-day medical opinion is sought, usually from an A&E department. A simple dislocation of an interphalangeal joint needs reduction as soon as possible and gentle but firm longitudinal traction whilst pressing the base of the displaced phalanx is usually all that is needed. Entonox gas should provide sufficient pain relief for this to be accomplished. A check x-ray will confirm reduction and the patient should then be encouraged to mobilize the finger as much as possible. Whether the nurse practitioner carries out such a procedure is a matter for local determination. Dislocations of the MCPJs are potentially more complex and probably best left for medical management.

Fractures involving the metacarpals, once diagnosed, should be referred to A&E for medical management. If there is likely to be a significant delay before the patient attends A&E, a fracture through the base of the first metacarpal may be best managed by applying a plaster of Paris backslab to immobilize the thumb and wrist. This is particularly important if the fracture involves the first MCPJ (Bennet's fracture). The other likely fracture is of the fifth metacarpal – temporary immobilization and support with a padded crêpe bandage should be carried out in the Edinburgh position (see p. 201). This position minimizes problems with immobility and may be attained with either a wad of cotton wool or a rolled bandage applied to the palm and then bandaged in place. In either injury a high arm sling should be applied to reduce swelling and the patient given sufficient NSAID analgesia, such as diclofenac sodium (Voltarol), until an A&E visit.

Fractures involving the carpal bones or distal radius and ulnar should be referred on to the A&E department for management. If there is likely to be a delay in treatment, a plaster of Paris backslab should be applied to immobilize the wrist as this will give considerable pain relief, together with analgesia as described above and a broad arm sling. Patient teaching should emphasize the importance of maintaining finger movement and elevation and watching for any sign of neurovascular compromise. A printed set of plaster instructions explaining these points should be given to the patient. Traditionally, patients with a fracture of the distal radius and ulnar have been starved in case they need manipulation under anaesthesia. This practice is unnecessary where intravenous regional anaesthesia is used (Bier's block) and, as this is the technique of choice, keeping patients nil-by-mouth should no longer occur (O'Sullivan et al 1996).

Forearm, elbow, upper arm and shoulder injuries

Fractures and/or dislocations involving the forearm, elbow, upper arm and shoulder should be referred on immediately to the A&E department. The patient will be greatly helped if every step is taken to immobilize and support the injured limb in the best possible position. Rings and any other constrictions should be removed. A clear account of the injury should be telephoned ahead to the A&E department so that they know what to expect and, if any x-rays have been taken, they should accompany the patient. You will have to make a judgement as to whether an ambulance or private transport is best to transfer the patient. The neurovascular state of the arm should be carefully assessed to ensure there is no nerve or arterial damage and, if this is suspected, the patient's transfer to A&E should then become an emergency undertaken by ambulance. There is a case for a fasting policy where injuries are above the wrist if manipulation or operative surgery will possibly be required, as they are

less suitable for the Bier's block technique. This is especially true in the case of children.

Foot injuries

Trauma affecting the foot frequently involves heavy objects dropped on to the toes. A simple fracture of a toe can be managed as an undisplaced finger fracture, by strapping to its neighbour. Elevation to reduce swelling and pain is just as important; this involves the patient resting with the foot at least at the same level as the heart. Blunt trauma to the metatarsals which produces bruising but no fracture should also be managed by rest, elevation and analgesics. Recovery will be helped by the application of ice in the initial stages to reduce swelling. If a metatarsal is fractured, a medical referral is needed. Immobilization in a cast is more for pain relief than to assist fracture healing.

Ankle injuries

If an ankle injury involves a fracture and/or dislocation, then A&E referral is necessary. Support, immobilization and elevation in the interim are essential to reduce swelling and pain. A plaster of Paris backslab may be needed if there is likely to be a delay in transfer. This can be quickly removed in the A&E department once the patient arrives. An alternative is to use a vacuum splint to immobilize the ankle, providing it is possible to have the splint returned to the minor injuries unit. The nurse practitioner should always check colour, sensation and the presence of a pedal pulse in the foot once immobilization is complete. It may help to mark the exact location of the pulse with a skin marker pen to assist future monitoring.

The large majority of ankle injuries will have no fracture and be diagnosed as a sprain. Smith (2003) has undertaken a review of the literature which indicates that the early application of ice immediately after the injury for up to 20 minutes is beneficial in reducing swelling, histamine release and oxygen demand. Elevation in the acute phase also reduces swelling and pain but the key to a rapid recovery seems to be early mobilization and weight bearing as soon as possible. The use of NSAIDs is beneficial in relieving pain, especially diclofenac, but there is no evidence that supportive bandages such as the familiar tubigrip or Elastoplast strapping improve patient outcomes (Sexton 2002). Crutches should be discouraged as they tend to delay weight bearing and require careful use if further problems are not to occur. They are also expensive and difficult to recover from the patient. It is possible that some patients may find that the ankle is too painful for weight bearing even after a day or two. In such cases they should be checked by the local A&E department to ensure that no fracture has been missed and the ankle may require a few days of immobilization in a walking cast before the person can resume normal activity. This may be particularly important for social and economic reasons.

If a soft tissue injury is suspected of developing into compartment syndrome, urgent medical referral is required. In the meanwhile the limb should be elevated and any constrictions removed. Surgical intervention (fasciotomy) may be required to relieve the pressure within the compartment and save the limb.

Knee injuries

Knee injuries which upon examination demonstrate significant signs of ligament or meniscal damage such as inability to bear weight, laxity, effusion, haemarthrosis, or limited movement on testing should be referred for a medical opinion. Overuse problems respond to rest and NSAIDs but management should be negotiated on an individual basis with the patient as they may be very reluctant to take time off from their training schedule (Austermuehle 2001). It is important to ascertain how important training and sport is to the person if a management strategy is to be agreed which the patient will adhere to. In the absence of obvious signs and assuming the patient is weight bearing even with a minor effusion, double tubigrip, analgesia and advice about rest and mobilization is usually sufficient treatment. The patient should be encouraged to return if the knee is not improving. Adams (2004) points out that physiotherapy will often help the patient's recovery and urges NPs to refer promptly where required.

Prevention

A further important strategy in the management of trauma and low back pain is prevention. The nurse practitioner should lose no opportunity to explore the causes of accidents with patients and how they could have been prevented. Many injuries happen at work and could have been prevented by, for example:

- Wearing shoes with reinforced toecaps when working with heavy objects
- Keeping floors clear and dry to avoid trips and slips
- Training in good lifting technique
- Use of lifting aids
- Correct seating and work surface heights
- Good lighting conditions
- Use of protective guards on machinery
- Wearing protective equipment.

The waiting room is a good area to convey messages to patients while they are waiting for treatment, whether by posters, leaflets or the use of videos. Whilst larger companies have occupational health departments, nurse practitioners might usefully target small businesses where this is not the case and organize an accident prevention campaign with the local Chamber of Commerce or branch of the National Farmer's Union/Young Farmers Club (NFU/YFC). For example, the nurse practitioner could help in the production of much-needed literature that is relevant and in language that is easy to understand. S/he could also attend local Chamber of Commerce NFU/YFC meetings to discuss accident prevention and basic first aid.

Summary

The nurse practitioner has a major part to play in the triage and management of musculoskeletal conditions, whether traumatic or otherwise. The nursing approach to the problem should ensure that treatment takes into account the person's psychosocial wellbeing as well as the physical disease and/or trauma. Furthermore, the strong health education tradition within nursing means that the nurse practitioner is well placed to tackle the whole preventive area. This is particularly the case in preventing osteoporosis, which is an issue that is relevant to women of all ages. A community-based accident prevention programme would be another area where s/he could make a significant difference, particularly in high-risk groups such as children (cyclists, roller-bladers), young men (work and sporting accidents) and the elderly (domestic accidents). The nurse practitioner can bring to the field of trauma an extra dimension that has been lacking from traditional A&E medical practice – accident prevention.

References

Adams N 2004 Knee injuries. Emergency Nurse 11(10):19–27

Austermuehle P 2001 Common knee injuries in primary care. The Nurse Practitioner 26(10):26–45

Beral V et al 2003 Breast cancer and hormone replacement therapy in the Million Women Study. Lancet 362:419–427

Biomedcentral 2003 Online: www.biomedcentral.com/news/

BNF 2003 British National Formulary 45. British Medical Association/Royal Pharmaceutical Society of Great Britain, London

Doheny M, Sedlack C, Estok P, Poiner V 2003 DXA valuable for bone mineral density testing. The Nurse Practitioner 28(11):44–49

Doherty M, Dacre J, Dieppe P, Snaith M 1992 The GALS locomotor screen. Annals of Rheumatology and Disease 51:1165–1169

Edwards S 2004 Acute compartment syndrome. Emergency Nurse 12(3):32–38

Epstein O, Perkin D, Cookson J, deBono D 2003 Clinical examination. Mosby, London

Haslett C, Chilvers E, Boon N, Colledge N 2003 Davidson's principles and practice of medicine, 19th edn. Churchill Livingstone, Edinburgh

Levi N 1997 Incidence of Achilles tendon rupture in Copenhagen. Injury 28(4):311–313

Loveridge N 2002 Lateral ankle sprains. Emergency Nurse 10(2):29–33

McNally C, Gillespie M 2004 Scaphoid fractures. Emergency Nurse 12(1):21–25

Nowak T, Handford A 2004 Pathophysiology: concepts and applications for health care professionals. McGraw Hill, Boston

O'Donovan J 2004 Managing rheumatoid arthritis. Primary Health Care 14(4):31–32

Oliver S 2004 Social and psychological issues in rheumatoid arthritis. Primary Health Care 14(4):2528

O'Sullivan I, Brooks S, Maryosh J 1996 Is fasting necessary before prilocaine Bier's block? Journal of Accident and Emergency Medicine 13:105–107

Phillips K, Ch'ien A, Norwood B, Smith C 2003 Chronic low back pain management in primary care. The Nurse Practitioner 28(8):26–28

Platt B 2004 Supracondylar fractures of the humerus. Emergency Nurse 12(2):22–31

Powledge T 2004 Hormone researchers revolt. Gendys Journal 26(Summer):23–26

Purcell D 2003 Minor injuries: a clinical guide for nurses. Churchill Livingstone, Edinburgh

Sexton J 2002 Managing soft tissue injuries. Emergency Nurse 10(1):11–17

Smith M 2003 Ankle sprain: a literature search. Emergency Nurse 11(3):12–17

Springhouse 2000 Handbook of pathophysiology. Springhouse Corporation, Springhouse, PA

Waddell G, Feder G, McIntosh A 1996 Low back pain evidence review. Royal College of General Practitioners, London

Wyatt J et al 1999 Oxford handbook of accident and emergency medicine. Oxford University Press, Oxford

Chapter 13

Blood disorders

Mike Walsh

INTRODUCTION

Many blood disorders are either very rare and/or potentially life threatening in their severity. Consequently their management is in the hands of hospital specialists. This chapter will therefore focus on the early detection and diagnosis of such disorders, which will allow the nurse practitioner (NP) to refer the patient as soon as possible for medical treatment. We will also explore the therapeutic interventions that a NP can make mainly in a primary care setting.

PATHOLOGY

ANAEMIA

A simple way to think of anaemia is that a person's red blood cells (erythrocytes) have inadequate oxygen carrying capacity. Oxygen carrying capacity is ultimately determined by the number of haemoglobin (Hb) molecules present and the normal Hb values are: male 130–180 g/l, female 115–165 g/l. The root of the problem will usually be that there are inadequate numbers of erythrocytes (normal male red cell count $4.5–6.5 \times 10^{12}$, female $3.8–5.8 \times 10^{12}$) or the cells that do exist are abnormal in some way. This situation arises from inadequate production of erythrocytes, excessive destruction of erythrocytes or blood loss. The main causes of anaemia can be summarized as follows.

Iron deficiency anaemia

This condition is the most common and accounts for approximately half of all cases. Iron is a key element in the haemoglobin molecule. The average sized male has 4 g of iron within his body, of which 75% is locked up in haemoglobin (Pallister 1999). If a person's diet fails to meet the demand for iron then iron deficiency anaemia will ensue. This is usually due to inadequate iron intake, malabsorption or excessive loss of iron and haemoglobin in chronic bleeding. Absorption of iron from the diet depends upon hydrochloric acid; consequently a patient who has had gastric surgery or who is on long-term proton pump inhibitor therapy is at particular risk of developing anaemia. The lack of iron means that the red cells formed are smaller than normal. This is reflected in the measurement known as mean cell volume (MCV), which measures the size of red cells, being below normal.

The main effects of iron deficiency anaemia are due to the lack of oxygen carrying capacity in the blood, producing fatigue, breathlessness and palpitations on exertion. Pallor is the other obvious sign. However the lack of iron also produces other signs as it is an essential component of various enzymes, such as cytochromes, which are most active in epithelial tissue (Pallister 1999). Consequently iron efficiency anaemia leads to:

- glossitis – a smooth inflamed tongue lacking normal papillae
- angular stomatitis – cracks at the corner of the mouth
- koilonychia – spooning of the nails.

Additionally the tissue lining the stomach may become inflamed, leading to atrophic gastritis and ultimately achlorhydria.

Megaloblastic anaemias

This term refers to a group of disorders whose origin lies in a lack of vitamin B_{12} or folic acid. The diet of vegans makes them particularly at risk of this disorder as it is lacking in vitamin B_{12}. In the rest of the population the diet usually contains adequate amounts of vitamin B_{12} but the problem arises from malabsorption due to lack of the intrinsic factor in the stomach. The autoimmune condition known as pernicious anaemia is usually responsible. It has a mean age of onset of 60 and leads to a gastric mucosa which is atrophic and unable to secrete intrinsic factor (Nowak & Handford 2004). Some drugs can impair absorption of vitamin B_{12}, notably alcohol and phenytoin. The main cause of folic acid deficiency is poor diet or malabsorption due to

coeliac or Crohn's disease. The problem can also develop during pregnancy, being compounded by iron deficiency anaemia as the increased demands of pregnancy outstrip the resources of the woman. Cytotoxic chemotherapy can also produce a megaloblastic anaemia as the drugs interfere with cellular metabolism.

Haemolytic anaemias

This range of conditions all have in common the fact that erythrocytes are being destroyed faster than they can be replaced. The erythrocytes are, however, normal in size so the term normocytic anaemia can be applied to this group of disorders. Normally, worn-out red blood cells are destroyed in the reticuloendothelial cells in the liver and spleen. In haemolytic anaemias, this is also the usual site of the excess erythrocyte destruction. If the process occurs within the vascular system itself then free haemoglobin, which is toxic to cells, will be found in the plasma. Protective proteins bind to the haemoglobin to prevent damage occurring but if this defence system is inadequate, damage to renal tubular cells occurs and the urine may be darkened in colour as haemoglobin is excreted in the urine.

There are several congenital haemolytic anaemias which become apparent during childhood. Hereditary spherocytosis derives its name from a defect in the cell membrane making the erythrocytes spherical rather than biconcave in shape. The cells are prone to spontaneous lysis (disintegration) leading to a major crisis but many patients are asymptomatic while others just have a moderate anaemia and associated splenomegaly. Splenectomy may be performed to help relieve symptoms, usually when the child is over 8 years of age (Candy et al 2001). Disorders of the enzyme systems within the erythrocytes give rise to conditions such as glucose-6-phosphate dehydrogenase deficiency, which commonly affects people of Mediterranean, Asian and African descent. Acute episodes can be precipitated by eating fava beans or drugs such as vitamin K and antipyretics.

Haemolysis can also occur as a result of external factors such as:

- toxic substances e.g. copper, arsenic, gas
- drugs such as sulfasalazine
- Falciparum malaria
- trauma such as burns.

Anaemia may also be seen in patients with chronic disease or in the elderly as a wide range of disorders can lead to a reduction in erythrocyte pro-duction or increased rates of destruction. Malignant disease which does not involve the bone marrow seems able to suppress the bone marrow and so cause anaemia. Collectively these disorders are known as anaemia of chronic disease (Nowak & Handford 2004).

Haemoglobinopathies

Abnormal haemoglobin can also cause anaemia; the most common disorders include:

- β-Thalassaemia – a congenital disorder affecting mostly people of Mediterranean origin, resulting in an inability to synthesize a specific part of the globin chain. The disease can vary from mild to severe when it is termed 'major' (usually if both parents have the defective gene). The haemoglobin formed is unstable and haemoglobin A may be completely lacking. The bone marrow hypertrophies to compensate for the disorder, leading to facial and skeletal changes. The child may present in infancy with a sallow appearance and splenomegaly (Candy et al 2001).
- α-Thalassaemia is found in south-east Asia, especially amongst people of Chinese origin. Its impact can vary from a mild anaemia to stillbirth, depending upon the extent of the genetic defect that is inherited from the parents.
- Sickle cell disease is an autosomal recessive disorder. If the person inherits the abnormal gene from both parents their haemoglobin is abnormal and when deoxygenated it is prone to form abnormal structures known as tactoids. These distort the membrane of the erythrocyte to form the sickle shape which gives the disorder its name. Normally when the haemoglobin is reoxygenated this process is reversed, however it may not be and the cell is then said to be irreversibly sickled. Such cells can block up the microcirculation and also have a much shorter survival time. Sickling is triggered by hypoxia, dehydration or infection and can lead to widespread serious disorder as the microcirculation of various body organs becomes blocked. This is known as a sickle cell crisis and can be life threatening, especially as it is superimposed upon a chronic state of anaemia due to the shortened lifespan of the erythrocytes (Black & Hawks 2004).

LEUKAEMIA

This term describes a group of disorders involving the tissue responsible for the manufacture of all the different types of blood cells (haematopoietic tissue). There is a malignant proliferation of white cells with adverse effects on erythrocytes and thromboblasts, leading to anaemia and bleeding disorders in addition to the main manifestations of the disease. Haslett et al (2003) estimate the incidence of all types of leukaemia is 10/100 000 of the population, evenly divided between acute and chronic forms of the disease – with males more affected than females.

Acute leukaemia is characterized by a failure of white cells to mature and its sudden onset and aggressive course. The white cells that are produced are dysfunctional and readily detected in the blood. As a result of their excessive production, normal production of erythrocytes and thromboblasts suffers. Vital organs may have their normal function compromised by the large numbers of immature white cells impairing the microcirculation (brain, lungs or eyes) and systemic disturbances may develop leading to metabolic imbalance. Acute leukaemias are divided into either lymphoid or myeloid depending upon which type of white cell predominates (lymphoblasts or myeloblasts).

Acute leukaemia commonly leads to the following symptoms (Springhouse 2000):

- rapid onset of fever
- abnormal bleeding
- weakness, weight loss, lassitude and signs of anaemia
- recurrent infections
- bone pain due to leukaemic infiltration
- neurological symptoms due to leukaemic infiltration
- enlargement of the liver, spleen and lymph nodes due to leukaemic infiltration.

Chronic leukaemia tends to develop in older people and is again divided into lymphoid or myeloid. The disease process is the same as imma-ture white blood cells are over-produced at the expense of normal white cells, making the patient gradually more prone to infection, bleeding and anaemic. The less aggressive nature of the disease means that its discovery is sometimes a chance finding when bloods have been taken for some other reason such as a presentation for anaemia. Chronic myeloid leukaemia usually accelerates in intensity over time, however, and can end with a fatal blast crisis. Chronic lymphocytic leukaemia is the most common of all the leukaemias and more gradual in its progression.

Chronic leukaemia typically produces:

- slow development of weight loss, fatigue and anaemia
- splenomegaly due to large numbers of destroyed red blood cells
- enlargement of the liver and lymph nodes from leukaemic infiltration
- increased bleeding tendency
- increased incidence of infections.

LYMPHOMAS

This type of malignant disease affects lymphoid tissue and is divided into Hodgkin's and Non-Hodgkin's lymphoma. There are around 1400 new cases of Hodgkin's lymphoma diagnosed each year in the UK, most commonly in early adulthood and in the over-50s. The disease occurs when normal lymphocytes become abnormal and cell division occurs, resulting in the presence of what is known as Reed-Sternberg cells – malignant derivatives of B lymphocytes. The malignant cells are concentrated in the lymph nodes but they can infiltrate and destroy normal tissue such as lymphatic tissue and bone marrow (Cole & Dunne 2004). The patient usually presents with enlarged but painless lymph nodes, most frequently in the cervical region. As the disease progresses, infiltration produces enlargement of the spleen or liver. Systemic symptoms such as fever, night sweats, fatigue and weight loss develop. Non-Hodgkin's lymphoma affects T and B lymphocytes and is more widely distributed throughout the body than Hodgkin's, involving organs such as the brain, gut and testis. Patients present with a similar set of generalized symptoms but may have other symptoms depending upon which organs are being most affected.

BLEEDING DISORDERS

Disorders of platelet function

A person may have a normal platelet (thrombocyte) count but if the platelets are abnormal, bleeding disorder occurs. A range of drugs inhibit platelet function and may cause bleeding as a side effect such as aspirin and the NSAIDs, as well as, rarely, some antibiotics such as the penicillins and cephalosporins.

A reduced platelet count is known as thrombocytopenia and can be secondary to marrow disorders such as leukaemia, drug-induced as in the use of cytotoxics or caused by a deficiency of vitamin B_{12} or folic acid. Other conditions can lead to thrombocytopenia by destroying thrombocytes faster than the body can replace them. Examples include disseminated intravascular coagulation, hypersplenism and serious bacterial or viral infections.

Coagulation disorders

The following disorders are congenital and therefore affect children as well as adults.

- Haemophilia A is the most common congenital coagulation disorder and is due to a reduction in factor VIII. In the UK, haemophilia is classed as severe when the Factor VIII level is less than 1% of normal – at this level there can be spontaneous disabling bleeds into joints and muscles. Levels between 1% and 5% of normal are classed as moderate – even slight trauma can cause extensive bruising. Levels between 5% and 40% of normal are classed as mild and can lead to serious bleeds if surgery or trauma are experienced. Approximately 60% of cases are classed as severe in the USA (Black & Hawkes 2004). The gene responsible is on the X chromosome, making haemophilia a sex-linked disease. Any son of a female carrier therefore has a 50% chance of the disease. The first problems tend to occur when a baby is about 6 months old.
- Haemophilia B (Christmas Disease) is associated with deficiency of Factor IX. It is also an X-linked disorder but is said to be clinically indistinguishable from haemophilia A.
- Von Willebrand's Disease is another genetic disorder but the defect is linked to chromosome 12 so it is not sex-linked. Inheritance follows an autosomal dominant pattern but the severity of the disease is much less than haemophilia. The patient tends to have excessive nose bleeds, menorrhagia when old enough and lengthy bleeds from minor lacerations.

VENOUS THROMBOSIS

Thrombus formation results from one or a combination of the following factors:

- injury to the blood vessel wall
- reduced rate of blood flow
- abnormal blood coagulability.

A thrombus may occur in an artery such as a coronary artery (see p. 99) or in a vein. A venous thrombosis is known as a red thrombosis as it contains a high proportion of erythrocytes and is dangerous because a fragment that breaks away will follow the circulation back to the heart and eventually lodge in a pulmonary artery, with potentially fatal consequences if the artery is big enough.

Patient risk factors are as follows:

- age over 40
- varicose veins
- immobility
- obesity
- dehydration
- pregnancy
- oral contraceptive use
- previous history of deep venous thrombosis (DVT)
- medical conditions such as myocardial infarction, nephrotic syndrome, inflammatory bowel disease
- surgery.

The formation of a DVT often leads to swelling and pain in the affected leg which may also feel warmer and look redder due to distension of peripheral veins. Post-thrombotic syndrome describes a condition that develops after a DVT involving chronic pain, swelling and skin changes. It is estimated that 33% of DVT patients will develop this problem within 5 years (Kolbach et al 2004).

HISTORY TAKING

Disorders of the blood are less likely to produce well-defined symptoms than other systems of the body such as pain, stiffness or alteration in normal habits such as defecation and micturition. The presentation is more likely be to a vague complaint of feeling 'tired and under the weather', 'lacking energy' or breathlessness. You therefore have to be constantly aware of the possibility of anaemia or one of the other rare disorders such as leukaemia when the patient is telling you this kind of story.

From the brief review of the major blood disorders above, the following key questions need to be asked:

- Do you get breathless or experience palpitations on exertion? Yes suggests anaemia.
- Do you have any soreness in and around the mouth? Yes suggests iron deficiency anaemia.
- Any history of weight loss? Yes, suggests, amongst other things, leukaemia.

- Has the onset of symptoms been rapid or gradual? This will indicate whether you are dealing with acute or chronic disease.
- Have you had more infectious illnesses than normal recently? Yes suggests a disorder affecting white blood cells.
- Have you noticed unusual bruising or bleeding? Yes suggests a disorder affecting thrombocytes or another bleeding disorder.
- Is any pain associated with your symptoms? Yes indicates the possibility of tissue infiltration as found in leukaemia or lymphoma.
- Have you noticed any unusual swellings? Yes also suggests leukaemia or Hodgkin's.

This history should pay particular attention to diet as information obtained here may indicate anaemia as a likely cause. Medication should be checked including over-the-counter medicines as the use of NSAIDs may point towards iron deficiency anaemia due to the medication causing chronic gastric bleeds. Other possible sources of chronic bleeding should be checked such as menorrhagia. The family history is very important due to the congenital nature of many blood disorders. Alcohol intake should always be assessed, particularly as excessive consumption may be contributing towards anaemia by causing malabsorption of vitamin B_{12}. A previous medical history and final review of systems is important as this may lead to evidence of a chronic bleed or malabsorption (due for example to inflammatory bowel disease) which could be causing anaemia. It may also give rise to suspicions of other organs being involved as happens in diseases such as leukaemia or lymphoma. The risk factors for DVT are well known and should be carefully checked with the patient if appropriate, including recent long-haul flights.

EXAMINATION

When examining a patient who presents with a history of tiredness and lethargy, the following signs of anaemia should be checked for:

- Pallor. In severe anaemia this may be apparent from just looking at the patient. It can be checked by gently everting the lower eyelid to check the colour of the palpebral conjunctiva whilst asking the patient to look upwards. Experience will teach you the normal red colour of the conjunctiva so that the paler pink of anaemia will be easily recognized.

- Glossitis and stomatitis indicate iron deficiency anaemia.
- Examination of the nail bed and palmar creases will also reveal abnormal pallor. Spooning or flattening of the nails indicates iron deficiency anaemia.
- Respiratory rate and pulse may be elevated.

The usefulness of conjunctival pallor as a sign of anaemia has been confirmed by a study carried out by Sheth et al (1997). They had three clinicians independently examine the conjunctival colour of 302 patients and indeed found that reporting the presence of the clinical sign correlated closely with a Hb < 110 g/l (lower limits of normal 115 g/l for women and 130 g/l for men). Their data gave this sign a likelihood ratio of 16, which can be interpreted as saying that if a patient has anaemia, they are 16 times more likely to show conjunctival pallor than if they have normal Hb levels.

If the history is suggestive of lymphoma or leukaemia an abdominal exam is necessary to check for evidence of an enlarged spleen or liver. Lymph nodes should be carefully checked, especially the cervical nodes. An accurate temperature should also be recorded. The skin should be carefully examined for evidence of bruising, indicating an increased bleeding tendency.

A DVT may produce obvious signs in the affected leg but sometimes swelling may be minimal. It is also true that other conditions can produce unilateral calf swelling such as cellulitis, a haematoma due to trauma or a ruptured Baker's cyst.

INVESTIGATIONS

A full blood count will greatly help in arriving at a diagnosis. Local pathology services will usually provide standard values of the various parameters being measured which will reveal whether the patient's values on a full blood count are within normal limits. Local protocols may limit the investigations that the NP may be able to request. The most powerful investigation for iron deficiency anaemia involves measuring serum ferritin (ferritin is a protein that plays a key role in storing iron within the body) which will be depressed in iron deficiency anaemia but normal in anaemia caused by chronic disease (Montoya et al 2002).

The MCV will also be reported – this indicates whether the red cells are smaller (microcytic) or larger (macrocytic) than normal. Generally a low MCV indicates iron deficiency anaemia or thalassaemia, normal MCV (normocytic) suggests anaemia due to an acute blood loss or chronic disease, whilst a high MCV suggests vitamin B_{12} or folate deficiency (Haslett et al 2003). There are several different types of white cells. The total white cell count may be normal yet the count of one particular type of white cell may be elevated, indicating significant pathology. A differential white cell count is therefore needed which gives the numbers of the five different types of white cells – neutrophils, eosinophils, basophils, monocytes and lymphocytes. The first three are known together as granulocytes and the latter two as mononuclear leukocytes. The normal differential white cell count is given in Box 13.1.

Box 13.1 Differential white cell count: normal values	
Total WCC	$4.0–11.0 \times 10^9/l$
Neutrophils	$2.0–7.5 \times 10^9/l$
Lymphocytes	$1.5–4.0 \times 10^9/l$
Monocytes	$0.2–0.8 \times 10^9/l$
Eosinophils	$0.04–0.4 \times 10^9/l$
Basophils	$0.01–0.1 \times 10^9/l$

In acute leukaemia the total white cell count can be as high as $500 \times 10^9/l$ and the patient has an accompanying anaemia. White cell counts in chronic myeloid leukaemia average around $220 \times 10^9/l$ and in chronic lymphocytic leukaemia range between $50–200 \times 10^9/l$. The lab report will usually comment on the maturity of the white cells as well as their differential count.

Platelets normally range between $150–400 \times 10^9/l$. A low platelet count is known as thrombocytopenia. If platelet function has not been affected by drugs such as aspirin, spontaneous bleeding may occur when levels drop to $30 \times 10^9/l$. The main coagulation screening test involves measuring the prothrombin time (PT) which should be between 12 and 15 seconds. This reveals deficiencies in factors II, V, VII or X. The international normalized ratio (INR) is the ratio of the patient's PT to an internationally agreed normal control and is used to control anticoagulant treatment. Patients on warfarin therapy should have an INR of between 2 and 4 (Casey 2003). An elevated INR suggests liver disease, vitamin K deficiency or salicylate intoxication (Springhouse 2000), although INR should not be used as a screening test.

A suspected DVT needs to be investigated for a definitive diagnosis with either ultrasound or, most accurately, by venography.

TREATMENT

Many of the conditions discussed so far must be referred on to expert medical investigation and treatment. However, iron deficiency anaemia is a common condition that can be readily managed in primary care. The standard treatment is ferrous sulphate 200 mg 8-hourly – over a period of months this will gradually restore the patient's Hb levels to normal. However the patient needs to be educated about the possible side effects such as epigastric pain, nausea, diarrhoea and dark stools. You should spend time discussing a healthy diet containing iron-rich foods, which, apart from red meat, includes spinach, raisins and dried beans, none of which are expensive (Black & Hawks 2004). It is also essential to deal with any problem causing chronic bleeding such as the use of NSAIDs or menorrhagia. Intramuscular injections of iron are a last resort for those who cannot tolerate oral iron supplementation as the injections are painful and cause skin staining.

Megaloblastic anaemia (vitamin B_{12} or folate deficiency) may also be managed in primary care, although it is essential to know first what is causing the problem and whether the deficiency is primarily vitamin B_{12} or folate. Hydroxocobalamin injection, 1 mg 3 times weekly for 2 weeks followed by a top up of 1 mg every 3 months is the recommended treatment for vitamin B_{12} deficiency (BNF 2003). Folic acid 5 mg daily for 4 months with a maintenance dose of 5 mg between 1 and 7 times per week is recommended for folic acid deficiency anaemias. Advice about healthy eating should also be offered for long-term health promotion reasons.

Where patients are known to be heavy drinkers, the alcohol problem has to be addressed as alcohol shortens the life span of erythrocytes and damages red bone marrow, precursor cells and also mature blood cells (Henderson 2000). It is likely that a heavy drinker will also be eating an inadequate diet. This combination of factors leads to anaemia being a chronic problem for alcoholics, the solution of which lies in dealing with their alcoholism, rather than a quick fix with medication.

A DVT is treated by administering low molecular weight heparin (LMWH) and then warfarin to prevent the extension of the clot (Casey 2003). These drugs will not dissolve the clot however – this is best left to normal physiological processes as fibrinolysis is too dangerous. The patient is usually given LMWH for the first 5–7 days with oral warfarin at the same time. The INR must be checked daily at this stage (Nadeau & Varrone 2003) with the aim being to keep it in the range 2–3 as this produces fewer bleeds than the slightly higher range of 3–4 (Haslet et al 2003). Long-term therapy with an oral anticoagulant can then be continued for up to 6 months.

Careful patient education is necessary as warfarin has potentially serious interactions with a range of common drugs including antiepileptics, oral contraceptives, antibacterials, the statins and analgesics, as well as alcohol. Patient education can also tackle lifestyle risk factors such as obesity and smoking. Other key elements to include in patient education (Nadeau & Varrone 2003) are:

- symptoms that indicate a recurrence
- signs of bleeding
- safety precautions such as avoiding contact sports
- limb elevation and use of compression stockings
- correct administration of medication.

There is significant evidence from a large systematic review that home treatment of DVT with LMWH is as safe as hospital treatment in terms of complications, more cost effective and preferred by patients (Schraibman et al 2004). Compression stockings have been shown to be very effective in reducing the incidence of post-thrombotic syndrome and should be used post-DVT (Kolbach et al 2004).

Summary

The initial presentation of a blood disorder can often be with nonspecific symptoms of tiredness and general malaise. It is therefore an important differential diagnosis that needs to be carefully ruled out in many patients, as failure to diagnose the condition could lead to serious and possibly life-threatening disease being missed. Although the medical management of many of these conditions lies with hospital specialists, a great many patients with anaemia can be successfully managed in a primary care setting. The nurse practitioner has a wide range of health education skills to help such patients. There are a wide range of lifestyle issues which need to be tackled in dealing with anaemia – medication such as ferrous sulphate is only one part of the treatment.

References

Black J, Hawks J 2004 Medical surgical nursing, 7th edn. Elsevier Saunders, St Louis

BNF 2003 British National Formulary 45. British Medical Association/Royal Pharmaceutical Society of Great Britain, London

Candy D, Davies G, Ross E 2001 Clinical paediatrics and child health. W B Saunders, London

Casey G 2003 Haemostasis, anticoagulants and fibrinolysis. Nursing Standard 18(7):45–51

Cole S, Dunne K 2004 Hodgkin's lymphoma. Nursing Standard 18(19):46–52

Haslett C, Chilvers E, Boon N, Colledge N 2003 Davidson's principles and practice of medicine, 19th edn. Churchill Livingstone, Edinburgh

Henderson C 2000 Natural compounds protect red blood cells from alcohol induced damage. Blood Weekly 3(16):4-6

Kolbach D, Sandbrink M, Hamulyak K, Neumann H, Prins M 2004 Non-pharmaceutical measures for prevention of post-thrombotic syndrome. Cochrane Library, Issue 3

Montoya V, Wink D, Sole M 2002 Adult anaemia; determining clinical significance. The Nurse Practitioner 27(3):38–53

Nadeau C, Varrone J 2003 Treat DVT with low molecular weight heparin. The Nurse Practitioner 28(10):22–29

Nowak T Handford A 2004 Pathophysiology concepts and applications for health care professionals, 3rd edn. McGraw Hill, Boston

Pallister C J 1999 Haematology. Butterworth-Heinemann, Oxford

Schraibman I, Milne A, Royle E 2004 Home versus in-patient treatment for deep vein thrombosis. Cochrane Library, Issue 3

Sheth T, Choudry N, Bowes M, Detsky C 1997 The relation of conjunctival pallor to the presence of anaemia. Journal of General Internal Medicine 12:102–106

Springhouse 2000 The nurse practitioner's clinical companion. Springhouse Corp, Springhouse, PA

Chapter 14

The endocrine system

Wendy Fairhurst-Winstanley

INTRODUCTION

This chapter will focus on the two diseases which the nurse practitioner is most likely to encounter – diabetes mellitus and thyroid disorder. However, a brief overview of the less common endocrine problems will be included. Male and female sex hormones are discussed in Chapters 10 and 11 respectively.

The endocrine system consists of glands that produce hormones (chemical messengers) which pass into the blood stream to target tissues. Most diseases of the endocrine system involve an over- or under-production of hormones, a process which is normally controlled by neural and chemical feedback mechanisms. Some hormones are produced by glands which are dedicated only to their production. These are endocrine glands and include:

- pituitary
- adrenal
- thyroid
- parathyroid.

Other hormones are produced by groups of endocrine cells within organs. Examples include:

- pancreas
- ovary
- testis.

Many endocrine diseases are caused by autoimmune disorders. It should be noted that patients who develop one autoimmune disease appear to be at risk of other autoimmune disorders such as type 1 diabetes, Addison's disease and SLE (Devendra et al 2004), thus annual screening for these conditions is important if any one of them is present.

DIABETES MELLITUS

Diabetes mellitus, whilst classified in this chapter as a disease of the endocrine system, could equally be categorized as a cardiovascular disease. Increasingly connections between the two diseases are being uncovered to the extent that conversely, cardiovascular disease may indeed be regarded as a disease of the endocrine system. These issues will be discussed further in this chapter.

Traditionally, diabetes has been classified as two distinct types – type 1 and type 2. However as research continues into the area, other sub-groups of diabetes are being identified (e.g. maturity onset diabetes of the young – MODY). Types of diabetes can no longer be classified in terms of the treatment they receive – type 2 patients with diabetes are frequently treated with insulin, thus negating the previous classification of non-insulin dependent diabetes mellitus (NIDDM).

INCIDENCE

Diabetes is a condition which affects between 4% and 8% of the population according to demographic differences such as age, ethnicity and affluence. People of Asian and Afro-Caribbean origin and, to a lesser extent, those of a Chinese origin, have an increased risk of developing type 2 diabetes. There is a greater incidence in less affluent populations (DOH 2001).

INSULIN

Insulin is synthesized within the beta cells of the islets of Langerhans. The islets are endocrine cells scattered throughout the exocrine gland of the pancreas. Insulin is released from the pancreas in response to a rise in blood glucose and the release of hormones from the gut after eating. Insulin has many functions, one of which is to allow the transport of glucose into the cells of the body. This is commonly described as a lock and key mechanism – with insulin being the key to allow entry of glucose into cells.

Insulin prompts the liver to store excess blood glucose as glycogen (for short-term energy storage) or to use it to produce fatty acids (which become triglycerides).

Insulin resistance is the body's inability to utilize effectively the insulin produced. Ninety-two percent of people with type 2 diabetes have insulin resistance.

Insulin resistance leads to low cellular glucose levels and raised blood glucose, thus glucose remains in the blood stream rather than being utilized for energy. A negative feedback mechanism causes the pancreas to produce more insulin in response to high blood glucose levels, leading to *hyperinsulinaemia*. This eventually results in beta cell degeneration and a corresponding loss of insulin production. Type 2 patients at this point will need additional insulin.

Increased insulin levels increase sodium retention by the kidneys, resulting in increased blood pressure. Additionally hyperinsulinaemia appears to be correlated to low HDL cholesterol and raised triglycerides (Marchesni et al 2004). Insulin causes free fatty acids to be released from adipose tissue into the bloodstream. The liver responds by increasing triglycerides. High density lipoprotein (HDL) excretion is increased, therefore lowering HDL. LDL changes to a more atherogenic form. This is shown below:

Cellular insulin resistance
↓
↑Circulating insulin
↓
↑fatty acids
↓
↑triglycerides and ↓HDL

TYPE 1 DIABETES

Type 1 diabetes is thought to be an autoimmune disease with the presence of islet cell antibodies. It is postulated that the autoimmune response may be triggered in susceptible individuals (those with HLA-DR3-4 genotypes) in the presence of environmental factors (e.g. viruses or stress) (Atkinson & Eisenbard 2001).

Type 1 diabetes usually occurs in people under the age of 40 years and is often associated with the presence of ketonuria on diagnosis. As a rule of thumb, the presence of more than a small amount of ketones in the urine is an indication for referral to a specialist team on diagnosis in order to rule out the possibility of type 1 diabetes and prevent ketoacidosis.

Type 1 diabetes usually has a rapid onset following the absolute failure of the beta cells in the islet of Langerhans in the pancreas to produce the hormone insulin. Glucose therefore does not move from the blood stream into cells leading to a dramatic rise in circulating blood glucose – *hyperglycaemia*. Blood glucose remaining in the blood stream is therefore not being used for energy production thus resulting in *lethargy*. The body needs to create energy and thus utilizes fat stores, the breakdown product of which are *ketone bodies* which are excreted in the urine. A continued rise in these leads to *ketoacidosis*, a life-threatening condition which may lead to coma. Patients may also present with diarrhoea and vomiting, caused by autonomic neuropathy, which exacerbates the dehydration. Increased circulating blood glucose results in increased concentration of glucose in the glomerular filtrate, which increases the osmotic pressure of the filtrate with the result that water is not reabsorbed but excessive amounts are excreted (*polyuria*). The renal tubules are unable to reabsorb the increased sugar and this is also excreted in the urine (*glycosuria*). This leads to cellular dehydration, resulting in increased thirst (*polydipsia*).

TYPE 2 DIABETES

Type 2 diabetes is thought to have a polygenic cause. Polygenic diseases result from a number of scattered genes. Genetic make-up produces a predisposition to the disease with environment acting as the trigger (Stevens & Lowe 1995).

In this condition the pancreas continues to produce insulin. It is thought that the main problem is one of insulin resistance. This process is important in understanding the logic behind current treatments for type 2 diabetes. Type 2 diabetes usually occurs in people over the age of 40 and is not usually associated with the presence of ketonuria on diagnosis (although this may indeed be present if the patient has been vomiting or not eating as a result of feeling unwell).

Whilst many of the presenting features of type 2 diabetes are the same as type 1 diabetes (polyuria, polydipsia, lethargy, glycosuria, hyperglycaemia), the onset is usually slower and insidious, indeed at the point of diagnosis many patients may have had the condition for a number of years and may already have complications. The main distinguishing factors are that blood glucose may be relatively lower, symptoms may be less acute and there is usually an absence of ketonuria – and therefore no risk of ketoacidosis.

METABOLIC SYNDROME

Metabolic syndrome – otherwise known as Syndrome X or insulin resistance syndrome (Reaven 1988) – is a cluster of factors which have been shown to increase the risk of cardiovascular disease. The true prevalence of the disease is unknown, however, the incidence of this syndrome and of type 2 diabetes is rising globally – possibly as a result of increased obesity and physical inactivity. Additionally we may be identifying more people earlier through improved screening and earlier diagnosis. In the UK up to 25% of the population show signs of the disease and in the US it has been estimated that 47 million may have the syndrome (Tonkin 2003). Insulin resistance is heavily implicated in metabolic syndrome (hence one of the alternative names), however the cellular and molecular mechanisms are complex and not fully understood.

In the literature there appear to be three main definitions of metabolic syndrome – those of the World Health Organization (WHO) (Tonkin 1993), the European Group for the study of Insulin Resistance (EGIR) (Balkau & Charles 1999) and the National Cholesterol Education Programme Adult Treatment panel 11 (NCEP 2001). All definitions have the following factors in common:

1 Fasting plasma glucose > 6.1 (WHO definition specifies actual presence of type 2 diabetes = fasting glucose > 6.9 mmols, EGIR specifies insulin resistance or hyperinsulinaemia) plus 2 of the following

2 Central obesity (excessive fat distribution around the abdomen, small hip / waist ratio – people with this propensity are sometimes referred to as being apple shaped). Central obesity is strongly associated with the presence of metabolic syndrome and the presence of CHD (Marchesini et al 2004)
3 Raised triglycerides
4 Low HDL cholesterol
5 Raised blood pressure
6 Microalbinuria (WHO definition only).

Additionally, blood markers of inflammation (C reactive protein – CRP) have been implicated in the syndrome.

Minimum criteria for the metabolic syndrome are met in most patients with type 2 diabetes (Marchesini et al 2004).

GESTATIONAL DIABETES

Gestational diabetes develops because a mother's body in pregnancy may not be able to produce enough insulin. The exact causes remain unknown, although it is thought that hormones produced in pregnancy may block the action of insulin. It usually begins in the second trimester of pregnancy and frequently disappears after the baby is born, although women known to have gestational diabetes are subsequently at a higher risk of going on to develop diabetes. Women are at a higher risk of developing gestational diabetes if they:

- have a family history of type 2 diabetes
- are > age 35
- are obese
- have had a previously large baby
- have previously given birth to a baby with an abnormality
- have previously had a stillbirth.

Effects on the baby

As a result of the mother having a high blood sugar the baby may grow larger, which can result in a difficult birth. The baby may develop hypoglycaemia after birth because in utero the pancreas will have been producing more insulin in response to the mother's high blood glucose. Babies are more likely to develop jaundice and there is an increased risk of congenital abnormalities and stillbirth. In later life

the individual may be at more risk of being overweight or developing type 2 diabetes.

SCREENING

Type 1 diabetes commonly has a fast onset and patients will usually present acutely, therefore the issue of screening for diabetes relates mainly to type 2 diabetes.

There is some evidence that changes in lifestyle amongst at risk subjects can prevent the onset of type 2 diabetes. In the Finnish Diabetes Prevention Study, Tuomilehto et al (2001) studied overweight subjects with impaired glucose tolerance. They concluded that weight loss through increased exercise and diet could reduce the incidence of the development of diabetes by 58%. The diabetes strategy recommends targeted screening for diabetes rather than a whole population approach.

An understanding of metabolic syndrome is a good starting place to discuss the types of people who should be targeted for screening for type 2 diabetes. Given the fact that there is a close correlation between obesity, hyperlipidaemia, hypertension and the development of ischaemic heart disease, these groups should clearly be targeted.

Groups for targeted screening can be separated into those who should be screened on a regular basis and those who it is appropriate to screen annually and routinely. Those with hypertension, hyperlipidaemia and ischaemic heart disease should be having annual blood tests as part of their management plans for these diseases (British Hypertension Society, National Service Framework). It is therefore appropriate to test their fasting blood glucose on an annual basis. Additionally those requiring an annual fasting blood glucose include women with a history of gestational diabetes or polycystic ovaries and people with an impaired glucose tolerance.

Opportunistic screening for diabetes should therefore include those with a BMI > 35, people > 40 years with a close family history of diabetes (because of the genetic predisposition) and those who have incidentally been found to have borderline blood glucose. Because of the slow onset, type 2 diabetes can go undiagnosed for years, therefore those presenting with symptoms associated with diabetes (thirst, tiredness, polyuria, boils, poor healing of infections, vulvovaginitis, balanitis, intermittent claudication, erectile dysfunction, problems with eyesight) should be screened for diabetes.

Table 14.1 Diagnosis or exclusion of diabetes

Blood sugar results		Action
Fasting	*Random*	
> 6.9	or > 11	Diabetes – repeat test to confirm if no symptoms
6.1–6.9	or 7.9–11	Needs glucose tolerance test
4.6–6.0	or 5.6–7.8	– may need GTT but only if risk factors for diabetes are strongly present – may need annual fasting glucose
<4.6	and <5.6	excludes diabetes

Table 14.2 Glycaemic index of common foods

Low GI index, < 55	Medium GI index, 55–69	High GI index, 70–100
Apples, oranges pears peaches	Honey, jam	Glucose
Beans and lentils	Shredded Wheat	White and wholemeal bread
Pasta	Weetabix	Brown rice
Sweet potato	Ice cream	White rice
Sweetcorn	New potatoes (peeled)	Cornflakes
Porridge	White basmati rice	Baked potato
Custard	Pitta bread	Mashed potato
Noodles	Couscous	
All Bran		
Special K		
Sultana Bran		

DIAGNOSIS

Diabetes is now defined as a fasting blood sugar > 6.9 mmols or a random blood sugar > 11 mmols (Table 14.1). Impaired glucose tolerance is an intermediate category between normal glucose tolerance and full-blown diabetes.

GLUCOSE INTOLERANCE

As it is thought that the development of overt type 2 diabetes can be prevented or delayed by modifying lifestyle such as diet, weight and exercise (Tuomilehto et al 2001, Steyn et al 2004) it is clearly important to give such advice as soon as the problem is identified. Nurse practitioners should give the same advice to these patients as they would to diabetic patients. This advice should be based around the principles of a low fat (monosaturated fat should be the main source of fat in the diet because of lower atherogenic potential), low sugar (rather than no sugar) and low glycaemic index diet (Connor et al 2003).

GLYCAEMIC INDEX (GI)

This is a way of categorizing carbohydrate foodstuffs according to how rapidly they increase blood glucose levels. Some are absorbed quickly and result in a rapid rise in blood glucose. Others are absorbed more slowly. Thus, blood glucose levels remain more stable avoiding rapid peaks in levels and maintaining a more steady insulin production. A low fat, low GI diet has been found to improve metabolism of fats and glucose (Wolever 2000). Low GI foods can help in weight loss as they tend to be more filling and help people to avoid snacking. However, some care needs to be exercised when giving advice as some low GI foods are low because they are high in fat (e.g. milk chocolate). Carbohydrates are ranked on a scale of 1–100, with glucose being 100 (Table 14.2).

HISTORY

As discussed previously, people may be diagnosed as having diabetes through the development of acute symptoms or following routine or opportunistic blood tests. Therefore the history-taking process may take place either before or after a diagnosis has been made. If presenting with acute symptoms the PQRST mnemonic will be useful to explore each symptom in turn thoroughly.

Secondary causes of diabetes should be excluded (e.g. pregnancy, pancreatitis, cancer of the pancreas, steroid-induced diabetes). Past medical history, family history, medication usage and current health status should also be explored in depth.

Many patients with type 2 diabetes present with complications already present. The patient should be assessed for evidence of these complications.

Family history

Because of the genetic predisposition (particularly in type 2 diabetes) many people will have some knowledge of family members with diabetes and their response to their diagnosis may well be coloured by this experience. Nurse practitioners may frequently be in the position of giving news of this diagnosis to their clients and should proceed carefully. It is important that patients understand why they are having blood tests and what could be found. Whenever possible, prior to having blood tests, the NP should establish the patient's understanding of diabetes. This enables you to assess beforehand what the patient's reaction might be to such news and to work with their knowledge and health beliefs.

COMPLICATIONS OF DIABETES

The assessment and screening for complications should be undertaken on diagnosis and thereafter at least annually (NICE 2002c).

Cardiovascular disease

Most people with type 2 diabetes fulfil the minimum criteria for metabolic syndrome which, with the combined effects of hypertension, hyperlipidaemia and obesity, puts them at a high risk of atherosclerosis and thus cardiovascular disease.

Angina

Patients should be questioned carefully about the presence of exercise-induced chest pain or breathlessness. The NP should bear in mind the possibility of silent angina in type 2 diabetics (this is as a result of peripheral neuropathy). The patient will not describe chest pain on exertion but may say that they become breathless or experience fatigue on exertion. Patients demonstrating any evidence of these symptoms should be referred to a cardiologist or rapid access chest pain clinic according to local referral pathways.

Intermittent claudication

Intermittent claudication is caused by atherosclerotic peripheral vascular disease and affects diabetics more than any other risk group (Stevens & Lowe 1995). The most commonly affected arteries are the iliofemoral and popliteal arteries. Atherosclerosis causes reduced blood flow and hypoxia of calf muscles when demand is increased. Typically, cramp-like pain occurs in the calves on exercise and

goes away at rest. Physical changes as a result of reduced blood flow include smooth, shiny, hairless skin which is slow to heal if damage occurs. Gangrene is a further complication caused by more severe blockage and leads to necrosis, which in turn can lead to the possibility of septicaemia and amputation. If intermittent claudication is suspected patients should be referred to a vascular surgeon and advised to stop smoking if appropriate.

Transient ischaemic attacks

These are episodes of non-traumatic focal loss of cerebral or visual function lasting no more than 24 hours. These are evidence of significant atherosclerotic cerebrovascular disease and as for the above diseases, secondary prevention measures should be adopted.

Erectile dysfunction

Men may be reluctant to discuss sexual problems, particularly on initial diagnosis (however this may be the most significant way in which their diabetes has been affecting them). You are in a good position to build up a trusting relationship with patients in order to encourage them to air such concerns. Erectile dysfunction may be as a result of genital, vascular and neurological pathophysiology and may also be caused by medications such as digoxin, beta-blockers, thiazide diuretics and tricyclic antidepressants. History and examination should seek to determine likely causes and men should be referred for further urological or cardiological investigations as appropriate. However, in the absence of urological or cardiovascular problems, erectile dysfunction can be treated by phosphodiesterase type 5 inhibitors and men with diabetes are eligible for NHS treatment with these preparations. However, they should be used with caution in people with cardiovascular disease and are contraindicated in people taking nitrates (BNF 2004). Many men with diabetes will fall into this category.

Peripheral neuropathy

Neurological dysfunction in both peripheral and autonomic systems occurs as a result of diabetes. Pathologically it is principally an axonopathy caused by toxic and metabolic damage to nerve cells.

Symptoms resulting from damage to the autonomic system include: dizziness on standing due to postural hypotension, constipation due to alterations in gastrointestinal motility, decreased bladder control as a result of effects on genitourinary function and erectile dysfunction. Sensory problems will include the possibilities of silent angina/silent myocardial infarction, numbness in the feet. Problems with the feet are particularly common due to the combination of neuropathic and cardiovascular problems. People with diabetes may not feel injuries to the feet and wounds may be slow to heal. Careful inspection of the feet is therefore essential during any physical examination procedure.

Deterioration of vision

Diabetic eye disease is the biggest single cause of blindness amongst working people in the UK (Evans 1992). Within 20 years of onset more than 60% of people with type 2 diabetes will have diabetic retinopathy (NICE 2002a). Eyesight may deteriorate as a result of a number of disease processes:

- Background retinopathy (patients will not normally notice any visual changes) small vessel abnormalities in the retina leading to hard exudates, haemorrhages and micro-aneurysms.
- Proliferative retinopathy is caused by new small vessel proliferation in the retina. These small vessels may bleed and retinal detachment may occur. Sudden deterioration in vision can occur.
- Maculopathy (reduction in visual acuity occurs) is caused by hard exudates, oedema and retinal ischaemia.
- Cataract formation is increased in people with diabetes.
- Glaucoma is increased in people with diabetes and is caused by neovascularization of the iris.

Renal/genitourinary problems

It is unlikely that renal problems will be identified through history taking but they will be identified through investigations. People with diabetes frequently present with polyuria and are likely to develop a number of genitourinary problems such as increased incidence of urinary tract infections, candido-vaginitis and ballanitis.

PHYSICAL EXAMINATION

Height, weight and body mass index (BMI) should be recorded. Careful inspection of the lower limbs and feet is essential.

Blood pressure

Blood pressure control is equally as important as blood sugar control in the prevention of diabetic complications (UKPDS 38 1998). Targets are shown in Box 14.1. There is currently some discrepancy between the guidelines provided by NICE and The British Hypertension Society (BHS). The BHS recommend that the target blood pressure for all patients with diabetes should be 130/80 (Williams et al 2004). Box 14.2 provides a summary of blood pressure management in diabetes.

Eye examination

This is covered in depth in Chapter 6. The patient should be referred for fundoscopy through dilated pupils. This is regarded as a specialist skill and should not be attempted by those who have not been specially trained or who do not have access to specialized equipment. Nowadays many trusts have arrangements for retinal photography which is performed on an annual basis for diabetic patients.

Box 14.1 Targets for blood pressure control

- <130/75   Diabetics with renal failure and/or proteinuria/microalbuminuria Patients with existing CHD/CVD
- <135/85   Acceptable for type 1 diabetes
- <140/80   Acceptable for type 2 diabetes without proteinuria/microalbuminuria

Source: NICE 2002d, 2004

Box 14.2 Summary of blood pressure management in diabetes

Type 2 Diabetes or high risk of diabetes

- Angiotensin converting enzyme inhibitor (ACEI) or angiotensin receptor blocker (ARB) if ACEI not tolerated (first line if microalbinuria present)
- Thiazide-type or beta blocker
- Add calcium channel blocker
- Add alpha-blocker

Source: NICE 2002d, 2004

Patients should also be encouraged to have an annual eye examination by an optometrist (NICE 2002a).

Cardiovascular examination

This should be carried out as outlined in Chapter 7. However, the NP should bear in mind the high incidence of cardiovascular disease, the possibility of silent myocardial infarction or angina and consequently the presence of undiagnosed heart failure.

INVESTIGATIONS

Urinalysis

Urine should be tested for the presence of glucose, ketones and microalbinuria.

Glucose

Glucose may or may not be present on initial diagnosis. Blood sugars need to be > 11mols in order for glucose to be present in the urine. Urinalysis, therefore is not a very useful diagnostic or screening test.

Ketones

Ketones are a result of fatty acid catabolism. Excessive production of these occurs when no carbohydrates are available for catabolism. This occurs in type 1 diabetes because insulin is not available to stimulate glycogenesis and glucose transport into cells. This results in the excretion of excess ketones into the urine. The presence of more than ++ ketones on urinalysis is a sign that the patient's condition is deteriorating and may result in ketoacidosis and ultimately coma.

Microalbinuria

Microalbinuria is the earliest indicator of diabetic renal disease (NICE 2002b). Microalbinuria relates to values of albumin in the urine which, although small, are above normal ranges. It is reversible if blood pressure is strictly controlled. In addition to being a marker for the development of renal disease the presence of microalbinuria also predicts total mortality, cardiovascular mortality and cardiovascular morbidity. In short, if microalbinuria is present the patient is at risk of developing other complications of diabetes. In order to test for microalbinuria an early morning urine sample is necessary. This can

either be sent to the laboratory or patient testing strips are available. If microalbinuria or proteinuria is present urine should be repeated twice more within 1 month (NICE 2002b). Serum creatinine should be measured concurrently. Results will indicate the albumin/creatinine ratio (abnormal: > 2.5 mg/mmol for men and > 3.5 mg/mmol for women).

Blood tests

These blood tests should be performed on diagnosis and at least annually for monitoring purposes. The haemoglobin molecule gradually accumulates glucose and other sugars at a rate that depends upon the overall blood glucose level; this is measured as glycated haemoglobin (HbA1c). This measurement gives a good picture of average blood glucose levels over time and should be performed more frequently (2–6 monthly) for type 1 patients and for type 2 patients whose control is less than optimum (NICE 2002c).

Urea and electrolytes

The most significant of these results relating to diabetes will be *creatinine* levels. A raised creatinine indicates the presence of some stage of renal disease. If creatinine is persistently raised at > 150 mmols metformin should be stopped (in the presence of renal disease the patient is at risk of developing lactic acidosis if taking metformin) and the patient should be referred to a renal physician (NICE 2002b).

Additionally, urea and electrolytes are measured in order to get a baseline level of renal function in case of the necessity of commencing treatment with ACE inhibitors.

HbA1c (glycated haemoglobin)

Haemoglobin A (HbA) is 97% haemoglobin; 5–9% of HbA has glucose molecules attached. The process of this attachment is called glycation of haemoglobin A1. HbA1 is formed over 120 days which is the life span of red blood cells: HbA1 is composed of three haemoglobin molecules: HbA1a, HbA1b, HbA1c (LeFever Kee 1999).

Haemoglobin A1c is therefore a test which indicates how well controlled the blood glucose has been over about a 3-month period. Acceptable levels can vary according to the type of assay used in laboratories, therefore it is important to check local guidelines for acceptable control. However, as a rule of thumb, acceptable control is usually between 6.5% and 7.5% (NICE 2002c).

Fasting lipids

As many type 2 diabetics will have metabolic syndrome – and therefore raised lipids – it is crucial to screen for and monitor hyperlipidaemia. As obesity is implicated in the development of metabolic syndrome and diabetes, weight loss and increased physical activity should be the first intervention. A low fat, low glycaemic index diet should be recommended (see p. 247). If weight loss is difficult, treatment with orlistat can be used in diabetic patients (BNF 2004). In many areas, exercise on prescription programmes can be accessed to help people to increase physical activity.

Fasting lipids should be measured as a high carbohydrate/high fat diet and alcohol can elevate the serum levels. Patients should fast for 12 hours before the test. They should be advised that they can drink clear fluids. A request for fasting lipids will result in investigations for:

Total cholesterol

Cholesterol is a blood lipid synthesized by the liver and used by the body for many things including the formation of bile salts and for the formation of some hormones. High levels cause plaque deposits in the arteries. The aim of treatment should be to achieve a total cholesterol of < 5.0 (NSF for CHD).

High density lipoproteins (HDL – 'good' or 'protective' cholesterol)

HDL is composed of 50% protein which aids in decreasing fat deposits in blood vessels (LeFever Kee 1999). The treatment target is > 1.0 mmol/l.

Low density lipoproteins (LDL – 'bad' cholesterol)

LDL cholesterol is the major cholesterol particle in plasma. High levels of LDL contribute significantly to the risk of cardiovascular disease (McGee 2000). The treatment target is < 3.0 mmol/l.

Triglycerides

These are carried by serum lipoproteins. They are processed from dietary fat in the intestine and are also manufactured by the liver. Triglycerides are also implicated in cardiovascular disease. Alcohol can cause an elevated level. Treatment target: < 2.2 mmol/l.

Liver function tests

These tests should be performed mainly in order to get a baseline level in case of the need for the commencement of statins for hyperlipidaemia.

Thyroid function tests

As diabetes mellitus is an autoimmune disease, patients are at an increased risk of developing other autoimmune diseases such as thyroid disease (Devendra & Eisenbarth 2003).

TREATMENT

Treatment is based on the principles of tight blood glucose and blood pressure control, and control of lipids – all of which should be initially addressed with lifestyle advice.

Lifestyle advice

Patient-centred care involves empowering the patient through education – enabling them to take an equal part in decisions. In order to be able to make informed decisions about their lifestyle and treatment patients need to be given detailed information about their disease (see Chapter 18). Advice regarding the prevention and management of cardiovascular disease is extremely important. This should include advice on diet, the benefits of increasing exercise and smoking cessation.

Smoking and diabetes

There is increasing evidence that smoking is an independent risk factor for the development of diabetes (Haire-Joshu et al 1999, Rimm et al 1993, 1995). In addition, smoking significantly enhances the risk of cardiovascular disease, neuropathy and nephropathy (Haire-Joshu et al 1999). Interestingly in Haire-Joshu's review of the literature, only half of diabetics who smoked were advised to stop by health care professionals.

Other information

The following is a list of topics specific to diabetes which need to be discussed:

- What diabetes is
- Diagnostic criteria
- Annual review

- Blood glucose monitoring
- Signs and symptoms and treatment of diabetic emergencies
- Erectile dysfunction
- Care during illness
- Foot care
- Eye screening
- Alcohol
- Driving and informing insurance companies and the DVLC.

Blood glucose control

Type 1 diabetes

The Diabetes Control and Complications Trial demonstrated that tight control of blood glucose is closely associated with the reduction of complications such as the development of retinopathy, microalbinuria, proteinuria and neuropathy (DCCT Research Group 1993). Outcomes were measured over a 7-year period. Intensive therapy was not related to increased mortality or decreased quality of life. Thus the aim of blood glucose control for most patients with type 1 diabetes should be to achieve as near to normal blood sugars (HbA1c < 7 mmol/l).Exceptions to this may include patients with hypoglycaemia unawareness and terminally ill patients.

In the absence of insulin production, patients with type 1 diabetes require insulin replacement therapy in the form of subcutaneous insulin injections/pump. Short, intermediate and long-acting insulins are available. Recombinant human insulin has now, for the most part, replaced pork and beef insulins.

Most people will need a split/mixed insulin regime. This may range from a combined short/long acting mix twice daily to a long-acting bolus with multiple short-acting injections or an insulin pump with superimposed short-acting insulin. These will be chosen according to the patient's lifestyle, wishes and physical ability.

A new development is the use of metformin alongside insulin for type 1 patients. Recent studies suggest that this may benefit patients who are overweight or receiving large doses of insulin (Devendra et al 2004). The patient will usually be referred to a diabetes specialist team who will work with the patient to find the most suitable regime.

Future research is focussing on prevention of diabetes and 'cure' involving islet transplantation (Devendra et al 2004). Stem cell research will have to follow the ethically difficult route of studying embryonic stem cells due to the discovery by Douglas Melton that the insulin-forming beta cells divide by simple division of mature cells rather than descending from an adult stem cell progenitor (SciAm 2004). Research into adult stem cells will therefore not lead to a solution that can withstand the body's immune system.

Type 2 diabetes

For patients with type 2 diabetes, similarly, tight blood glucose control has been shown to be crucial in the prevention of diabetic complications (UKPDS 38 1998). Reduction in microvascular complications was seen regardless of how this was achieved. There was some risk reduction of macrovascular complications. In order to achieve this a combination of diet and oral medication or diet and insulin injections is needed. This is frequently managed in primary care. The following is a description of the major classes of oral anti-diabetic drugs.

Biguanides (e.g. Metformin)

Metformin decreases gluconeogenesis and increases peripheral utilization of glucose. It acts only in the presence of endogenous insulin. As it addresses the problem of insulin resistance it should be the first drug of choice for type 2 diabetes patients, particularly for those who are overweight.

Contraindications: Creatinine > 150 µmol/l, ALT more than twice the upper limit of normal, severe heart failure, severe peripheral vascular disease, severe alcohol abuse, past history of pancreatitis, dehydration, pregnancy, breast-feeding.

Side effects: anorexia, nausea, vomiting, diarrhoea, abdominal pain, metallic taste, lactic acidosis, decreased vitamin B_{12} absorption, erythema.

Sulphonylureas (e.g. gliclazide, tolbutamide)

These drugs act by increasing insulin secretion and are effective only when there is some residual insulin production. They may cause hypoglycaemia (particularly the longer-acting products), although this is uncommon. As weight gain can occur they should be used carefully in patients who are overweight.

Contraindications: severe hepatic and renal impairment, porphyria, breast-feeding and pregnancy, ketoacidosis.

Side effects: nausea, vomiting, diarrhoea, constipation, weight gain.

Thiazolidinediones – commonly referred to as Glitazones (e.g. Rosilglitazone, Pioglitazone)

These drugs reduce peripheral insulin resistance by attaching to insulin receptors on cells, causing cells to become more sensitive to insulin. This leads to a reduction in blood glucose concentration. They may be used either on their own or in combination with metformin or a sulphonylurea. Its use in combination with metformin may be advisable for obese patients. It should be noted that they have a slower onset of action than metformin or the sulphonylureas (2–3 months for maximum benefit). Liver function tests should be monitored every 2 months for 12 months (BNF 2004).

Contraindications: hepatic impairment, history of heart failure, combination with insulin, pregnancy, breast-feeding.

Side effects: gastrointestinal disturbances, headache, anaemia, altered blood lipids, weight gain, oedema, hypoglycaemia, fatigue, parasthesia, alopecia, dyspnoea, rarely pulmonary oedema, angiodema, urticaria.

Other drugs less commonly used include:

Acarbose. Delays the digestion and absorption of starch and sucrose and is used most effectively in combination with metformin or sulphonylureas. Its use has decreased over recent years due to poor tolerance because of the side effect of flatulence.

Nateglinide and Repaglinide. These drugs stimulate insulin release and have a short duration of action and rapid onset. They are taken immediately before a meal. These drugs may be useful in overweight patients as weight gain is reduced or for patients who have non-routine lifestyles. Nateglinide is only licensed for use with metformin.

Blood pressure control

Treatment of hypertension (Box 14.3) depends upon the presence or absence of microalbuminuria or renal failure (NICE 2002d). However, there may be local variations, particularly regarding the issue of whether patients with type 2 diabetes should receive primary or secondary prevention.

Blood lipid control

Again treatment is based upon coronary heart disease risk assessment. The major principles include treatment with statins for patients with a total cholesterol > 5.0 mmols or triglycerides > 2.3 mmols with a CHD risk > 15%. The National Institute for

---

Box 14.3 Treatment of hypertension

- >134/74 Diabetics with renal failure and/or proteinuria/microalbuminuria. Offer lifestyle advice and pharmacological treatment
- <140/80 (without CHD and risk <15%). Offer lifestyle advice and monitor at least 6-monthly
- >140/80 (with existing CHD or risk >15%). Offer lifestyle advice and pharmacological treatment
- >160/100 Offer lifestyle advice and pharmacological treatment. Aim for 140/80

Diabetes or high risk of diabetes
- ACEI or ARB if ACEI not tolerated
- Thiazide-type
- Add calcium channel blocker
- Add beta-blocker
- Add alpha-blocker

NB: check all contraindications before commencing on any of these drugs. When starting patients on ACE inhibitors, serum creatinine should be measured 1 week after initiation and after each increase in dose.

Source: NICE 2002d

Clinical Excellence (NICE 2002d) guidelines provide further details. Statins may be beneficial for all diabetics, regardless of CHD risk.

DIABETIC EMERGENCIES

Hypoglycaemia

This may occur in patients with type 1 or type 2 diabetes who are being treated with insulin or oral hypoglycaemic agents as a result of excessive medication, missing a meal or doing more exercise than normal or a combination of all of these.

Symptoms

Hypoglycaemia causes the body to release adrenaline which causes the following symptoms: sweating, trembling, pounding heart, anxiety, weakness, hunger and nausea. Eventually, the brain becomes deprived of glucose – carbohydrate storage in the brain is limited therefore a continuous supply of glucose is needed for adequate functioning. A depleted supply of glucose therefore causes symptoms such as mental confusion, drowsiness, speech difficulty, irritability, lack of co-ordination, loss of consciousness, seizure and coma.

Treatment

Initial treatment, if the patient is alert and able to swallow, involves giving 10–20 g of glucose orally. This may take the form of either 2–4 teaspoons of sugar, 3 sugar lumps or 90 ml of non-diet cola. This may be repeated after 10–15 minutes. If the patient is drowsy, Hypostop gel squeezed into the inside lip or cheek may be used.

Unconsciousness constitutes an emergency. Glucagon, a hormone produced by the alpha cells of the islets of Langerhans, increases plasma glucose concentrations by mobilizing stored glycogen from the liver – 1mg may be injected by any route and patients and relatives may be given this to keep at home in case of emergencies. Glucose should be given intravenously if glucagon is not effective in 10 minutes.

If the patient is being treated in acute care, trusts may have their own local guidelines or protocols which you should follow.

Diabetic ketoacidosis (DKA)

This occurs in a state of absolute or relative lack of insulin, possibly if diabetes is undiagnosed, out of control or if the patient is ill. Glucose, unable to be utilized by the cells, stays in the bloodstream and the fat is broken down to provide energy, producing excess ketone bodies (acetoactic acid, B hydoxybutyric acid and acetone) which accumulate in the blood. Blood pH is initially maintained by buffer systems but eventually alkali reserves become depleted and the pH falls, resulting in acidosis. Increased osmotic pressures result in dehydration and depletion of electrolytes.

Symptoms

Symptoms begin with those associated with hyperglycaemia (polyuria, polydipsia, tiredness) and lead to signs of dehydration, with dry skin and mucous membranes. The accumulation of ketones result in nausea, vomiting, anorexia, rapid breathing, drowsiness, abdominal pain and muscle cramps. Eventually the blood pressure falls because of severe dehydration and the patient will become comatose.

Urinalysis will show high levels of glucose and ketones. Blood chemistry will reveal a high blood glucose, urea and eventually raised potassium (initially this may be low because of nausea and vomiting). Sodium and chloride levels, pH and carbon dioxide will be reduced.

Treatment

It is important to gain adequate plasma insulin concentrations and this may be achieved by the administration of soluble insulin through an infusion pump. Blood glucose should reduce by 5 mmols per hour to a concentration of 10 mmols per litre. Intravenous replacement of fluids and electrolytes is crucial. A sodium chloride solution is commenced with potassium chloride added according to the patient's potassium levels. In severe cases sodium bicarbonate infusion may be needed in order to rectify the acid–base balance.

Hyperglycaemic hyperosmolar non–ketotic syndrome (HHNK or HONK)

Patients with type 2 diabetes may develop HHNK. This syndrome is characterized by a hyperglycaemic (frequently very high blood sugars) and a hyperosmolar state in the absence of ketonuria. Increased osmolarity pulls water out of cells. Thromboembolic events may occur as a result. The patient becomes dehydrated, develops polydipsia and neurological signs, and may progress to coma. The onset is insidious and the prognosis is much poorer than for DKA with a 58% death rate (DOH 2001).

Box 14.4 outlines a glucose management regime for patients with type 2 diabetes.

PITUITARY GLAND

Many of the functions of the pituitary gland are controlled by stimuli from the hypothalamus, leading to secondary abnormalities in pituitary function. The pituitary gland is divided into the anterior and posterior pituitary.

ANTERIOR PITUITARY

The anterior pituitary produces growth hormone, prolactin, follicle stimulating hormone, luteinizing hormone, adrenocorticotrophic hormone (ACTH), thyroid stimulating hormone and melanocyte hormone. The hypothalamus communicates with the anterior pituitary via the hypophyseal portal system, a specialized blood network.

An excess of one of the anterior pituitary hormones suggests the presence of an adenoma. These are categorized as either functioning or non-functioning adenomas and are benign (they do not metastasize), although they can be life threatening because of the position and because of the excess production of hormone.

Functioning adenomas usually present earlier than non-functioning and although small may produce significant abnormalities. Most commonly they produce prolactin, growth hormone or ACTH:

- Prolactin – producing menstrual disturbances and infertility in women
- Growth hormone – gigantism/acromegaly
- ACTH – Cushing's disease.

Non-functioning adenomas enlarge progressively in an upward direction and compress the optic chiasma, leading to bitemporal hemianopia. They produce signs and symptoms of hypopituitarism. Pituitary tumours may also produce symptoms due to the mass effect (mainly with large tumours). These symptoms include disturbances in vision, visual field headaches and cranial nerve palsies. Panhypopituitarism, a reduction of anterior pituitary hormone, is extremely rare but may be caused by surgical removal of a pituitary tumour, ischaemic necrosis as a result of haemorrhage, inflammation or brain tumour affecting the hypothalamus.

POSTERIOR PITUITARY

Two key hormones are synthesized in the hypothalamus and stored in the posterior pituitary for subsequent release. They are antidiuretic hormone and oxytocin. Disorders of the posterior pituitary are extremely rare, with the most common being *diabetes insipidus* caused by a deficiency of antidiuretic hormone. Symptoms of this are polydipsia and polyuria. There are many possible causes such as anterior lobe adenomas, metastatic cancer, meningitis, tuberculosis, sarcoidosis, surgical or radiation damage, severe head injuries or idiopathic causes.

THYROID DISEASE

Thyroid disease is eight times more likely to occur in women than in men. In some women it occurs during or after pregnancy. The thyroid gland is located at the base of the neck in front of the trachea. It has two lobes and is shaped like a butterfly.

PATHOPHYSIOLOGY

Thyroid disease manifests itself either as an overproduction or an underproduction of the thyroid hormones. The thyroid gland produces two types of hormone – tri-iodothyronine (T3) and thyroxine (T4). Both hormones have widespread effects on the body including regulating overall basal metabolic rate. Production is controlled by thyroid stimulating hormone (TSH) produced by the anterior pituitary in response to thyrotropin releasing hormone (TRH) released by the hypothalamus. This is regulated via a negative feedback mechanism. If levels of circulating T4 and T3 are low, then the hypothalamus responds by increasing output of TRH, which in turn causes the anterior pituitary to increase production of TSH in order to increase T3 and T4 levels. Contrarily, if levels of circulating T3/T4 levels are high, then TRH production is reduced, leading to a reduction in TSH and ultimately T3 and T4.

HYPERTHYROIDISM

The most common cause for hyperthyroidism (thyrotoxicosis) is Graves' disease – a form of autoimmune thyroiditis associated with HLA-DR3 antigen. An IgG antibody (long-acting thyroid stimulator antibody – LATS) inadvertently stimulates thyroid follicle cells to secrete T3/T4 continuously outside of the control of TSH. Patients present with symptoms of thyrotoxicosis, diffuse, soft enlargement of the thyroid gland, and exophthalmus (protruding eyes resulting from excess retro-orbital adipose tissue). Eventually patients can become hypothyroid.

DIFFUSE (SIMPLE) AND MULTINODULAR GOITRE

This is a result of excessive replication of epithelial cells leading to the generation of nodules of various sizes. Eventually this can lead to multinodularity. Historically this form of goitre was seen in areas of iodine deficiency (iodine is essential in the production of thyroid hormone). TSH levels rise and induce growth of the gland. However, since iodine has been added to salt this cause has almost disappeared. If the goitre is long-standing, hyperthyroidism occurs.

THYROID ADENOMA

These are benign tumours representing about 80% of solitary nodules and are more common in the elderly. They are spherical, completely encapsulated and usually < 5 cm in diameter. However, on palpation it is difficult to differentiate them from carcinomas and further investigations will need to be carried out.

MALIGNANT TUMOURS OF THE THYROID

These are relatively uncommon with a prevalence of 2.5 per 100 000 of the population. Most swellings are of benign origin. However, women are 2–3 times more likely to be affected than men.

Well–differentiated tumours (papillary and follicular)

Papillary tumours constitute 60–70% of all thyroid cancers; follicular tumours make up 20%. They are found most frequently in young or middle-aged adults and metastasize to nodes in the neck (papillary) and bone (follicular – may present with fractures). They are strongly associated with exposure to radiation.

Anaplastic carcinoma

These constitute 10–15% of thyroid tumours and affect the elderly (age > 60 years). They grow rapidly, and metastasize widely into the trachea and tissues of the neck. They are felt as a bulky mass. They are highly malignant and have a very poor prognosis, almost always causing death within 2 years.

Malignant lymphoma

These also affect the thyroid in the elderly but are more responsive to treatment (Stevens & Lowe 1995).

HYPOTHYROIDISM

As in type 2 diabetes, this may occur as a result of a deficiency in the hormone or peripheral resistance to the hormone. There are three main causes of hypothyroidism:

- surgical reduction or removal of the gland as treatment for Graves' disease or thyroid cancer
- Hashimoto's thyroiditis
- autoimmune origin resulting from the formation of anti-bodies that block TSH receptors.

Hypothyroidism in children (previously known as cretinism)

This is a rare congenital disorder with an incidence of 1 in 3000. Routine screening 5–7 days after birth will detect the problem and hormone replacement treatment can begin almost at once. Severe retardation in both mental and physical development will occur without treatment.

Hypothyroidism in adults (myxoedema)

Myxoedema is usually preceded by a period of thyrotoxicosis and may be caused by:

Hashimoto's disease (the most common cause of hypothyroidism) is a destructive form of autoimmune thyroiditis which is organ-specific and is associated with the HLA DR5 antigen. Physical examination would reveal diffuse, symmetrical firm enlargement of the thyroid. Hashimoto's disease progresses by initially producing a hyperthyroid state, destroying thyroid cells and resulting in eventual *hypothyroidism*. Many patients will present when they have reached this latter state.

Subacute thyroiditis. This is an inflammatory disease, possibly caused by a virus. It is self-limiting, and the thyroid is enlarged asymmetrically. Initially thyrotoxicosis may occur, eventually developing into a hypothyroid state.

Chronic painless thyroiditis

This is more common in women and often occurs post-partum. The thyroid may be mildly enlarged and is not painful. Thyrotoxicosis may occur. This usually passes within a year, however a number of patients subsequently develop hypothyroidism.

HISTORY

Thyroid disease should always be suspected in patients presenting with any of the symptoms listed in Table 14.3 and patients will usually present with more than one symptom.

As thyroid disease affects many systems, thorough history taking and physical examination is crucial. The PQRST mnemonic may be useful in exploring symptoms further and help in the formation of differential diagnosis. A particularly useful assessment tool is the Wayne Index for Hyperthyroidism (McGee 2001) which consists of a point scoring system for various signs (Table 14.4) on the basis of which a probable diagnosis of hyperthyroidism can be made.

A Wayne index score of 20 or more gives a sensitivity of between 66% and 88% (the probability that a person has a hyperthyroid condition) whereas a score of less than 11 equates to a sensitivity of between 1 and 6% only. Application of a tool such as this as a first level screening test can avoid unnecessary and expensive laboratory investigations (see below).

It is important to note that many of the symptoms of hypothyroidism may be present in women who are experiencing the menopause and in women over 45 years this should be an important differential diagnosis. Depression is another important differential.

Table 14.3 Symptoms of thyroid disease

Thyrotoxicosis	Myxoedema
Caused by excessive secretion of thyroid hormone (TH) and results in symptoms which are related to an increased metabolic rate such as: – weight loss in spite of increased appetite – sweating and heat intolerance – diarrhoea	Caused by a reduction in the amount of thyroid hormone being produced and therefore results in symptoms related to a reduced metabolic rate such as: – weight gain – feeling cold – constipation
– tachycardia, palpitations, atrial fibrillation, cardiac failure	– reduced cardiac output, bradycardia, heart enlargement
– breathlessness – menstrual changes	– pleural effusions – increased menstrual flow
– emotional lability, restlessness – tremors and loss of strength	– lethargy, apparent depression – stupor, eventually coma

However, particular care should be taken in patients presenting with emotional lability as physical causes for this may be overlooked. In these patients it is always important to probe about the presence of physical symptoms. Patients themselves may be unlikely to have made these connections. However, the disease will only be confirmed by blood assays.

Additionally, young people presenting with a thyroid nodule should be questioned about previous radiation exposure to the head and neck – this greatly increases the risk of malignancy.

PHYSICAL EXAMINATION

As all systems may be affected by thyrotoxicosis or myxoedema, a full physical examination should be performed including examination of the cardiovascular, respiratory, neurological and gastrointestinal systems (see the relevant chapters).

The NP should observe for signs of *exophthalmus* and should examine the thyroid gland for the presence of *goitre*, an enlargement of the thyroid gland which manifests itself as a palpable and sometimes visible swelling in the front of the neck.

Table 14.4 Wayne Diagnostic Index for Hyperthyroidism

Symptoms of recent onset or ↑ severity	Present	
Dyspnoea on effort	+1	
Palpitations	+2	
Tiredness	+2	
Preference for heat	-5	
Preference for cold	+5	
Excess sweating	+3	
Nervousness	+2	
Appetite ↑	+3	
Appetite ↓	-3	
Weight ↑	-3	
Weight ↓	+3	
Signs	Present	Absent
Palpable thyroid	+3	-3
Bruit over thyroid	+2	-2
Exophthalmos	+2	
Lid retraction	+2	
Lid lag	+1	
Hyperkinetic movements	+4	-2
Hands		
Hot	+2	-2
Moist	+1	-1
Pulse		
Atrial fibrillation	+4	
< 80, regular	-3	
80–90, regular	0	
> 90, regular	+3	

It may be nodular or smooth and may involve either all or part of the thyroid.

The neck should first be *inspected* for enlargement of the thyroid gland. As the gland moves up and down with the larynx on swallowing, the patient should be asked to swallow in order to observe (it may be useful to give them a glass of water). The thyroid gland may be difficult to *palpate*. In order to achieve this, stand behind the patient and palpate both sides of the gland at the same time. The patient should be warned of this as it can feel as though they are about to be strangled! Note whether the gland is enlarged unilaterally or bilaterally, uniform or nodular, multinodular or only a single nodule, hard or soft. The gland should be *auscultated* – a bruit heard over the gland suggests that it might be overactive.

Examination should also include palpation of the lymph nodes of the head and neck as outlined on page 59.

INVESTIGATIONS

Thyroid profile

Thyroid disease will normally be diagnosed through blood tests. As thyroid profile is included in annual screening tests for patients with diabetes and ischaemic heart disease, it may be an incidental finding. It should be noted that raised T4 can occur during pregnancy, liver disease and porphyria or if patients are taking oestrogen, amiodarone, propanolol, amphetamines or heparin. Lowered T4 can occur in nephrotic syndrome, hepatic failure, renal failure, Cushing's syndrome, hypopituitarism and if patients are taking phenytoin or non-steroidal anti-inflammatory drugs (McGee 2000). It is therefore the full thyroid profile (Box 14.5) which is truly diagnostic of thyroid disease.

Additional blood tests

- Thyrotrophin antibody test (raised in 50–80% of patients with Graves' disease)
- Haemagglutination tests for thyroid antibodies – levels are very high in Hashimoto's disease and raised in Graves' disease and myxoedema

---

Box 14.5 Full thyroid profile

Thyroid profile normal values

T4 (total thyroxine):	60–135 nmol/l
T3 (tri–iodothyronine):	1.1–2.8 nmol/l
TSH (thyroid stimulating hormone):	0.5–5.5 mIU/l.
Serum free T4:	9.4–25 pmol/l
Thyroid perioxidase antibodies:	< 36 kU/l
Serum free T3:	3.0–8.6 pmol/l
Thyroxine-binding globulin (TBG):	8–15 mg/l
T4/TBG ratio:	6:12

Hyperthyroidism

Raised T4, raised T3 and low TSH suggests thyrotoxicosis

Low TSH suggest over-treatment with thyroxine

Hypothyroidism

Elevated TSH, low T4, lowered T4/TBG ratio

- Antimicrosomal thyroid antibody is positive in Hashimoto's disease and sometimes in Graves' disease.

If the cause is not obviously autoimmune, patients may be referred for the following tests:

- Ultrasound sonography (evaluates size) – a radioactive scan or ultrasound may be needed to determine whether overactive thyroid nodules are the cause of the hyperthyroidism
- Radionuclide imaging (evaluates function)
- Fine-needle aspiration, surgical biopsy or excision
- RAIU (Radioactive Iodine Uptake Test) – this determines the metabolic activity of the thyroid gland and can be useful for differentiating between Graves' disease and an overactive adenoma.

TREATMENT

Clearly treatment will depend on the cause and severity of the problem.

Thyrotoxicosis

Anti-thyroid drugs

Carbimazole is most commonly used in the UK, or propylthiouracil if the patient is sensitive to carbimazole (BNF 2004). Carbimazole may cause bone marrow suppression – patients should report symptoms of infections early and a white cell count should be taken. The drug should be stopped immediately if there is any evidence of neutropenia. Doses of these drugs should be titrated according to patient response. The drugs should be continued for at least a year; after this time many patients will go into remission.

Beta-blockers

Usually propanolol may be used to counteract tachycardia, feelings of anxiety and tremors.

Surgery

Partial thyroidectomy may be carried out in patients with a large goitre, or if anti-thyroid drugs have failed, particularly in people of child-bearing age in whom radioactive iodine treatment would be contraindicated. Resultant hypothyroidism, damage to the recurrent laryngeal nerve and damage to the parathyroid gland resulting in hypoparathyroidism are the major complications of surgery.

Radioactive iodine

As the thyroid gland absorbs nearly all the iodine in the blood, radioactive iodine is used in patients of post-child-bearing age in order to ablate the thyroid gland. This may also be used to treat thyroid cancers.

Hypothyroidism

Thyroxine (levothyroxine sodium)

This is used as a replacement therapy. The initial dose should not exceed 100 mcg daily before breakfast. The elderly and people with cardiac disease should commence on 25–50 mcg. The dose should then be titrated according to response at intervals of at least 4 weeks (BNF 2004).

PARATHYROID DISEASE

The parathyroid glands consist of between four and eight small glands located to the right and left of the upper and lower aspects of the thyroid gland. Their only function is to secrete parathormone which is mainly involved in maintaining calcium, magnesium and phosphate balance by:

- stimulating reabsorption of mineralized bone by osteoclasts, thus releasing Ca^+ phosphates into the bloodstream
- stimulating reabsorption of calcium and magnesium from the urine in the renal tubules
- stimulating loss of phosphates from blood to the urine
- stimulating kidneys to form calcitrol, the active form of vitamin D which increases absorption of calcium, magnesium and phosphates from the gut.

PATHOPHYSIOLOGY

Diseases result in either hypercalcaemia or hypocalcaemia, confirmed by serum calcium levels. Hypercalcaemia may be episodic and thus a series of tests may be needed to confirm its presence. Taking blood with a tourniquet may elevate calcium levels artificially.

Hyperparathyroidism

The main cause of primary hyperparathyroidism is a parathyroid adenoma. These are not usually palpable and patients usually present with signs and symptoms of hypercalcaemia. Malignant tumours are rare. Secondary hyperparathyroidism is caused by chronic renal failure, osteomalacia, malabsorption and rickets.

Symptoms

These include: weakness, loss of appetite, nausea, vomiting, constipation, drowsiness and confusion, occasionally pancreatitis, backache, pseudogout and hypertension.

Differential diagnoses

Differential diagnoses of hypercalcaemia include metastatic tumour, multiple myeloma and oat cell carcinoma of the bronchus.

Hypoparathyroidism

This is rare and has a number of causes, most commonly surgical removal or damage of the parathyroid glands. Autoimmune disease (particularly in patients with other autoimmune diseases) may also be a cause.

Symptoms

Tetany: caused by excitability of peripheral nerves due to reduced plasma concentrations of calcium. This leads to carpal spasm, stridor, and tingling in the hands and feet and around the mouth.

Differential diagnoses

Differential diagnoses of hypocalcaemia include: chronic renal failure (may lead to compensatory hyperparathyroidism) and vitamin D deficiency.

DISEASES OF THE ADRENAL GLAND

The adrenal glands are positioned on the top of each kidney and are divided into the adrenal cortex and the adrenal medulla.

ADRENAL CORTEX

The main hormones secreted from the adrenal cortex are cortisol, androgens and aldosterone. Adrenocorticotrophic hormone (ACTH) from the pituitary governs the secretion of cortisol (glucocorticoids) and androgens, whilst aldosterone (mineralocorticoid) is controlled by renin-angiotensin mechanisms.

Glucocorticoids raise the blood sugar by converting amino acids from protein breakdown into glucose (gluconeogenesis). They also suppress inflammatory responses.

Aldosterone is involved in the retention of sodium and excretion of potassium. Hyperaldosteronism leads to raised aldosterone levels and therefore increased excretion of potassium.

Cushing's syndrome

This most commonly occurs in middle age and is four times more common in women. It occurs when corticosteroid levels are raised. The most common causes are:

- excess ACTH production resulting from a pituitary adenoma
- the therapeutic long-term use of corticosteroids
- tumours of the adrenal cortex
- secretion of ACTH from non-endocrine tumours.

Most systems are affected and the patient develops the typical moon face, hirsutism, thinning of the skin, osteoporosis, hypertension, diabetes, peptic ulceration, myopathy and mood disturbances.

Addison's disease

Addison's disease is caused by adrenal cortex insufficiency. The most common cause of destruction of the adrenal cortex is autoimmune. Other causes include adrenal tuberculosis. The disease results in a lack of corticosteroids leading to dehydration, postural hypotension, lethargy, vomiting and brown pigmentation of the skin and buccal mucosa.

ADRENAL MEDULLA

Phaeochromocytoma (a tumour of the adrenal medulla) causes excessive production of adrenaline and noradrenaline, resulting in paroxysmal hypertension, palpitations, sweating, epigastric pain, chest discomfort, severe headaches and unexplained cardiac failure. It can result in hypertensive crisis.

References

Atkinson M A, Eisenbard G S 2001 Type 1A diabetes: new perspectives on disease pathogenesis and treatment. Lancet 358:221–229

Balkau B, Charles M A 1999 The European Group for the Study of Insulin Resistance (EGIR): Comment on the provisional report from the WHO consultation. Diabetic Medicine 16:442–443

BNF 2004 British National Formulary. British Medical Association and Royal Pharmaceutical Society of Great Britain, London

Connor H, Annan F, Bunn E et al 2003 The implementation of nutritional advice for people with diabetes. Diabetic Medicine 20(10):786–807

DOH 2001 Department of Health. National Service Framework for Diabetes. DOH, London

DCCT Research Group 1993 The Diabetes Control and Complications Trial. The effect of intensive treatment of diabetes on the development and progression of long-term complications in insulin-dependent diabetes mellitus. New England Journal of Medicine 329: 683–689

Devendra D, Eisenbarth G S 2003 Immunological endocrine disorders. Journal of Allergy and Clinical Immunology 111:624–636

Devendra D, Liu G, Eisenbarth S 2004 Type 1 diabetes: recent developments. British Medical Journal 328:750–754

Evans J 1992 Causes of blindness and partial sight in England and Wales 1990–91. HMSO, London

Haire Joshu D, Glasgow R, Tibbs T 1999 Smoking and diabetes. Diabetes Care 22(11):1887–1898

Joint British Societies Coronary Risk Prediction 1998 Heart 80:S1–S29

LeFever Kee J 1999 Laboratory diagnostic tests with nursing implications, 5th edn. Appleton and Lange, Connecticut

Marchesini F, Forlani G, Cerrelli F et al 2004 WHO and ATPIII proposals for the definition of the metabolic syndrome in patients with Type 2 diabetes. Diabetic Medicine 21:383–387

McGee S 2000 A guide to laboratory investigations, 3rd edn. Radcliffe Medical Press, Oxford

McGee S 2001 Evidence based physical diagnosis. W B Saunders, Philadelphia

NCEP 2001 Expert panel on detection, evaluation and treatment of high blood cholesterol in adults. JAMA 285:2486–2497

NICE 2002a Clinical guidance E. Management of type 2 diabetes, retinopathy – screening and early management. NICE, London

NICE 2002b Clinical guidance F. Management of type 2 diabetes, renal disease – prevention and early management. NICE, London

NICE 2002c Clinical guidance G. Management of Type 2 diabetes, management of blood glucose. NICE, London

NICE 2002d Clinical guidance H. Management of Type 2 diabetes, management of blood pressure and blood lipids. NICE, London

NICE 2004 Clinical guideline 15. Type 1 diabetes: diagnosis and management of type 1 diabetes in adults. NICE, London

Reaven G M 1988 Banting lecture: the role of insulin resistance in human disease. Diabetes 37(12):1595–1607

Rimm E B, Chan T, Stampfer M, Colditz G, Willett W 1995 Prospective study of cigarette smoking, alcohol use and the risk of diabetes in men. British Medical Journal 310:555–559

Rimm E B, Manson J, Stampfer M 1993 Cigarette smoking and the risk of diabetes in women. American Journal of Public Health 83(2):211–214

SciAm 2004 Douglas A Melton, Policy Leader of the Year. Scientific American December 2004:36

Stevens A, Lowe J 1995 Pathology, 1st edn. Mosby, St Louis

Steyn N P, Mann J, Bennett P H et al 2004 Diet, Nutrition and the prevention of Type 2 diabetes (review). Public Health Nutrition 7(1A):147–165

Tonkin R 2003 The X Factor: obesity and the metabolic syndrome. The Science and Public Affairs Forum. Report of a WHO consultation: definition of metabolic syndrome in definition, diagnosis and classification of diabetes mellitus and its complications. 1. Diagnosis and classification of diabetes mellitus. WHO, Geneva

Tuomilehto J, Lindstrom J, Eriksson J G, Valle T T, Hamalainen H, Ilanne-Parikka P 2001 Prevention of type 2 diabetes mellitus by changes in lifestyle among subjects with impaired glucose tolerance. New England Journal of Medicine 344:1343–1350

UKPDS 38 1998 Tight blood pressure control and risk of macrovascular and microvascular complications in type 2 diabetes. British Medical Journal 317:703–713

Wolever T M 2000 Dietary carbohydrates and insulin action in humans. British Journal of Nutrition 83(Suppl 1):S97–102

Williams B, Poulter N R, Brown M J et al 2004 Guidelines for the management of hypertension: report of the fourth working party of the British Hypertension Society. Journal of Human Hypertension 18:139–185

Chapter 15

Common paediatric problems

Sally Panter-Brick and Mike Walsh

CHAPTER CONTENTS

INTRODUCTION

Many nurses and nurse practitioners working in primary care do not hold registration as paediatric nurses, however a large part of their workload includes children. This anomaly underlines the need for all NPs to work hard at improving their knowledge of common paediatric presentations. The most important point for all health care staff who are not paediatric trained is to realize that children are not little adults. This crucial point is underlined in the recently published National Service Framework for Children, Young People and

Maternity Services (DoH 2004). As Agnew (2004) points out the mistakes highlighted by the Bristol cardiac surgery scandal and tragic cases such as that of Victoria Climbie must never be repeated again. We all must recognize the special needs of children and ensure they are met (BRI Inquiry 2001).

The British government's NSF has set out 11 standards which the health and social services must endeavour to achieve. These standards are equally valid internationally and are presented in Box 15.1.

Box 15.1 Summary of the UK National Service Framework Standards

1. A coordinated approach to promoting health and wellbeing, identifying needs and *intervening early*

2. Supporting parents and carers to achieve optimum results for their children

3. Child and family centred services: care must be coordinated and focussed on the needs of the child and their family and take into account their views.

4. Growing up into adulthood requires older children to have access to age-appropriate services

5. Safeguarding and promoting the welfare of children and young people means all agencies working together to prevent harm coming to children

6. Children and young people who are ill must have their health, social, emotional and educational needs met

7. Children in hospital must have high quality, evidence-based care delivered in *appropriate* settings

8. Disabled children and young people with complex needs must receive individualized care that promotes social inclusion for them and their families

9. The mental health of children and young people must be cared for by appropriate multidisciplinary services with good access

10. Medicines for children and young people should be prescribed on best available evidence and users must have access to full information about risks and benefits

11. Maternity services must be available to women which are of high quality and designed around their individual needs

---

All NPs, whether they are paediatric specialists or not, should be aware of these standards in their day-to-day care of children as the NSF expects all staff caring for children to demonstrate core knowledge, skills and competencies in relation to child development, communication and safeguarding the welfare of children (Smith 2004).

The paediatric nurse practitioner (PNP) role has been well established in North America for many years. We now see UK nurses developing PNP roles in acute hospital care while NPs working in primary care and A&E units will also see many children in daily practice. This chapter will try to cover the most commonly seen paediatric conditions and their management. It will also enable the nurse practitioner to recognize when a child is seriously ill – essential if speedy expert intervention is to be provided.

It is also essential for NPs to realize that adolescents may be sexually active and that they are at increased risk of acquiring a sexually transmitted infection (STI) compared to other age groups (Metcalfe 2004). The NP needs to be able to communicate effectively about the risks of STIs with adolescents if effective care is to be provided. This is frequently in the face of lurid tabloid headlines. Nurse practitioners are in an ideal position to:

> 'actively engage with clients in ways that can lead to the promotion of optimum sexual health well being, devoid of stigma, discrimination and the imposition of personal morals ... which are detrimental to client care'

to quote Evans' (2004) review of the need for nurses to promote the sexual health of adolescents.

Mental health problems are also common in this age group. Indeed, there is increasing evidence that adults with severe psychotic disorders show symptoms while still at school and that the sooner these are recognized and treatment begun, the better the long-term prognosis (Etheridge 2004). The issues of mental and sexual health are addressed in some depth in Chapters 11, 16 and 20 and the reader should look further at these chapters.

KEY DIFFERENCES BETWEEN YOUNG CHILDREN AND ADULTS

HEALTH ASSESSMENT

The principle that the child is not a small adult has profound implications for both history-taking and the physical examination. These skills are covered in depth by authors such as Barnes (2003) and Engel (2003) but the following is a brief summary of some of the key points to bear in mind during assessment:

- Consider the child's developmental status and attention span at all times.
- Involve the parent fully and in young children, learn how to examine on the parent's knee.
- Try and make the physical exam a game wherever possible; have plenty of toys available and use them. Let children familiarize themselves with equipment such as an otoscope by playing with it.
- Make the decoration of the consultation space age-specific if possible.
- Ask parents whether they have noticed any changes in their child's behaviour.
- Take your time, work slowly and avoid sudden movements; seek eye contact.
- Sequence the assessment so the most uncomfortable things are done last.
- Spend time watching the child before you try to do anything; observe their general manner and behaviour.
- Be prepared to demonstrate any technique on the parent first.
- Non-verbal communication can be just as important as verbal, especially in younger children.
- Remember, young children may take what you say literally, including the well-meaning joke about sawing off the child's leg! Be careful what you say and always recognize the child's developmental age and cognitive skills.
- Be sensitive to different cultural and ethnic norms.

PHYSICAL DIFFERENCES

There is not space to undertake a systematic review here of developmental anatomy and physiology. There are, however, several key differences between infants, older children and adults which we must mention. An infant or toddler's respiratory tract is much shorter, therefore inhaled infectious agents can more readily be transmitted into the lungs, increasing the susceptibility to chest infections. The Eustachian tubes are more vulnerable, giving rise to an increased risk of middle ear infection. A child's airway is narrower and therefore more likely to become blocked by inflammatory exudates or oedema. This narrowness makes bronchospasm (as

in asthma) even more of a problem than in adults The muscles are less toned and are therefore less efficient, with the young child being dependent on the function of the diaphragm rather than the inter-costal muscles for breathing (Barnes 2003).

Though all the neurological structures, cranial nerves and cord reflexes are present at birth, fine motor control is not fully developed and the autonomic nervous system is immature. At 1 year the brain is approximately 66% of adult size and 80% by the age of 2. Infants can lose heat quickly as they have a large surface area – infants aged less than 6 months are unable to shiver to generate heat. Immaturity of the heat-regulating mechanisms means that body temperature is less stable in the first year or so of life. In the first 2–3 years of life temperature is normally above 37°C, with 37.5°C considered not abnormal in a 1-year-old according to Engel (2003), although by the age of 3 the normal adult temperature of 37°C should have been settled on.

Infants have an under-developed immune system state and when maternal stores of antibodies become depleted at between 2 and 5 months, the infant is most susceptible to infections. Different antibodies are produced at different rates as the immune system develops so that by the age of 9 months the infant will have reached adult levels of IgM but at the age of 1 year will only have 40% adult levels of IgG. It is not until between the ages of 4 and 7 years that the child fully develops adult levels of immunoglobulins.

RECOGNITION OF THE SERIOUSLY ILL CHILD

MENTAL STATUS

The early signs of poor perfusion of the brain are agitation, confusion and drowsiness. Irritability can therefore indicate an infection which may be causing cerebral hypoxia or it could indicate meningitis. There are other possibilities in an infant or toddler including accidental poisoning, metabolic disturbances or some other neurological problem such as a seizure disorder (Londhe et al 2002). A baby may be irritable but drowsy with a weak or high-pitched cry. The child will become increasingly drowsy until they become unconscious. Critically ill infants will not maintain eye contact.

A toddler will normally be suspicious of strangers but if ill, will become irritable and only want their parents. If their condition deteriorates they will become lethargic and unresponsive. A simple measure of mental state is:

- A = **A**lert
- V = responds to **V**oice (may respond better to parent/carer)
- P = responds to **P**ainful stimuli
- U = **U**nresponsive.

HEART RATE

Heart rates in young children are naturally faster than older children and adults and in the first 3 months of life can normally range between 100 and 220 when awake (Engel 2003). Tachycardia can be found for many reasons including pyrexia, anxiety, hypoxia or hypovolaemia. In shock it is caused by an attempt to maintain cardiac output. Bradycardia can be caused by hypoxia and acidosis and is a pre-terminal sign.

SKIN PERFUSION

This is a useful early sign of shock. Slow capillary refill of more than 2 seconds after a blanching pressure of 5 seconds is evidence of reduced skin perfusion. Mottling, pallor and peripheral cyanosis can also show poor perfusion but this may be difficult to assess if the child has been exposed to cold.

RESPIRATIONS

The child may have rapid deep breathing due to acidosis as in diabetic ketoacidosis. The child may be tachypnoeic due to a respiratory illness. Breathing may be noisy with inspiratory or expiratory wheeze in conditions such as croup and asthma. The child may be using accessory muscles to aid the work of breathing.

EXAMINATION OF INFANTS AND CHILDREN

Observation of children is going to be most important – before you approach them just spend a little time watching. Are they crying and irritable or listless and floppy? As Barnes (2003, p. 15) succinctly puts it: 'a sick kid looks sick'. Interaction with the parents or carer should be closely observed and the ease with which the child becomes interested in toys is another important sign. An apathetic child will not be interested, suggesting a significant health problem.

Observation can be combined with obtaining the history. The history will also need to include extra information to that obtained during an adult history taking:

- Who is giving the information – parents, grandparents, a teacher, or the child?
- Birth history including gestation, type of delivery, mother's health during pregnancy, birth weight and if the infant was admitted to a SCBU with details of this. This information is of relevance in all infants and any young child with neurological or respiratory symptoms.
- Developmental history – is the child meeting milestones?
- Immunization history.
- Social history – who lives at home, what the parents' jobs are (which may have relevance to admission, for example children of farmers who present with gastroenteritis). Does anyone smoke at home? Also, whether they have access to transport and a telephone as this may influence your management if you wish to review the child later or send them into hospital for admission.
- The parents' views of what the problem might be should always be ascertained.

EXAMINATION

For the examination, infants and young children should be undressed apart from a nappy and can be examined on the parent's lap, as this will upset them less than being examined on the bed. Examination of infants and young children is largely opportunistic depending on how co-operative they are, but as a general rule, leave the examination of ears and throat until last as this will probably be the most upsetting.

- Monitor and record vital signs.
- Vital signs differ in children from adults and Table 15.1 is an approximate guide to what may be found normally.
- Measure weight and height plus head circumference in infants. Blood pressure may be checked but this is often distressing to younger children.

Table 15.1 Normal vital signs in infants and children

Age	Heart rate	Respiratory rate	Systolic blood pressure
< 1 Year	110–160	30–40	70–90
2–5 Years	95–140	25–30	80–100
5–12 Years	80–120	20–25	90–110
> 12 Years	60–100	15–20	100–120

- General appearance, colour, any obvious deformities, general observation.
- Chest and heart. Auscultate for breath sounds and heart sounds in all areas and also bowel sounds. The chest can be examined and any signs of respiratory distress noted. Infants and small children may have subcostal and intercostal recession as well as tracheal tug in a respiratory illness as the cartilage of the ribs enables more movement than with adults. Palpate for apex beat and any fremitus or thrills. Check capillary refill.
- Abdomen. Observe for any distension or hernias. Check skin turgor. Palpate abdomen for liver, spleen, bladder, kidneys and any masses. The liver edge may be felt up to 2 cm below the costal margin in infants and young children. Palpate femoral arteries and for inguinal lymph nodes. Percuss all quadrants. Inspect genitalia, palpating the scrotum for testes in boys.
- Neurological examination. In infants this is assessed mainly by observation of their movements and tone. Cranial nerve testing is usually difficult to do below the age of about 4 years. Toys can be used in young children to aid examination, for example using a soft toy to check visual fields or to check power in each hand and seeing if the child will reach with either hand for a toy. Modified testing of cranial nerves in infants can be carried out by shining a light in the eyes and obtaining blink reflex, eyes following a movement and if they look at your face or a close object (cranial nerves 2, 3, 4 and 6). Check for rooting reflex and if they can suck (cranial nerve 5). Watch while they are crying or smiling to assess whether the facial movements are symmetrical (cranial nerve 7). Check if the infant blinks when hearing a loud hand clap from about 12 inches away from the head (cranial nerve 8). Check for swallowing and gag reflex and if the infant can co-ordinate sucking and swallowing (cranial nerves 9 and 10). If you pinch the infant's nose gently their mouth should open and their tongue rise in the midline (cranial nerve 12).
- Musculoskeletal examination. This is similar to adults.
- Head and neck. Palpate fontanelles in infants to see if they are sunken or bulging. Palpate for cervical lymph nodes. Inspect the nose and eyes, checking for discharge. Inspect the ears and examine using auroscope with the parent or carer holding the child to the side with one arm across the head and one across the arms. Examine the throat with the child sitting facing you with the parent or carer having one arm across the head and one holding the arms across the body – look for any thrush or ulceration and using a tongue depressor examine the back of the throat and tonsils for signs of infection. If you suspect tonsillitis a throat swab should be taken now to avoid upsetting the child again by looking again in the mouth.

RESPIRATORY DISORDERS

ASTHMA (see also p. 122)

Asthma in children is usually associated with an atopic genetic predisposition and is precipitated by environmental factors such as parents who smoke and house dust mite. It causes narrowing of the airways, as there is oedema, bronchospasm and excess mucus production. There is increased cough, particularly at night as fluid accumulates in the airways, and breathlessness. The classic wheeze on expiration is present but there are many other reasons, such as bronchiolitis or some other type of chest infection, why a child may have a wheeze or a cough. Labelling a child as asthmatic after their first episode is unhelpful and Valman (2000) recommends waiting to see if a child has three episodes within a year before using 'asthma' as a diagnosis.

History

The PQRST approach provides a useful framework as this allows you to:

- explore possible environmental triggers (Provocation)
- ask whether an inhaler has been used to relieve the symptoms (Palliation)
- ask what it feels like to the child and whether this involves shortness of breath, wheezing, tightness or coughing (Quality)
- check where the sense of tightness seems to be (Region)
- ask how it is affecting the child (Severity)
- ask when the attack began (Timing)
- additionally, it is important to know if this is the first episode (and if it is, whether s/he could have inhaled anything), whether or not the child needed admission to hospital before with a similar episode and, if so, how many times, and when the last time was.

Examination

- Look for signs of respiratory distress such as recession and tachypnoea.
- Is there an audible wheeze?
- Check peak flow if the child is over 5 years old, adjusted for height of the child. An improvement in peak flow upon administration of a bronchodilator is a strong indication of asthma.
- Measure oxygen saturations.
- Auscultate, listening for wheeze and any crepitations. If there is a silent chest this will show that there is no airflow and this is a paediatric emergency.

Management of acute exacerbation

This should be according to BTS guidelines (p. 135). In acute situations – where the child shows signs of respiratory distress and is too breathless to talk or feed – give oxygen, a salbutamol nebulizer and commence prednisolone before transferring to hospital for further management.

Long-term management

The long-term aims of management are to ensure the child can take part in all the normal activities that a child of this age would, such as play, taking part in sport and attending school fully. The child should be symptom-free and demonstrate normal growth and development. More specifically, effective treatment means that a bronchodilator is being used less than three times per week (Valman 2000). This requires both parents and child, together with key agencies such as the school, to have a full understanding of the disorder and its treatment, especially the difference between preventive and symptomatic treatment.

CROUP

This is caused by a viral infection that causes inflammation, oedema, swelling and obstruction of the upper airways mostly in young children. There is stridor, a noise heard on inspiration and a cough that sounds like a barking seal. They will sound hoarse due to inflammation of the vocal cords. It is usually worse at night and commonly follows an upper respiratory tract infection. The most common cause is parainfluenza virus and the most usual age to have croup is at around 2 years (Londhe et al 2002).

History

Key areas to explore in the history include whether the child has had an upper respiratory tract infection recently which has got worse. This is a common precursor to croup. Any changes in the child's voice should be noted and whether anything like this has happened before. If so, were they admitted to hospital?

Examination

- Look for signs of respiratory distress.
- Monitor vital signs including oxygen saturations.
- Listen for stridor on auscultation.

Do not upset the child as this will aggravate symptoms – and do not examine the throat as an important differential diagnosis is epiglottitis (see below). Such an examination should only be performed by a skilled medical specialist with appropriate resuscitation equipment to hand as laryngospasm may be provoked if the epiglottis is inflamed. Londhe et al (2002) consider that if the child is comfortable while lying supine, non-toxic looking and does not appear particularly distressed, it is much less likely to be epiglottitis.

Management

This will depend on severity. If the symptoms are only mild and the child settles at rest with no stridor or signs of respiratory distress, then the child can be managed at home. If there are any doubts then the child should be referred to hospital for further management, which may include oral dexamethasone and nebulized budesonide and nebulized adrenaline.

EPIGLOTTITIS

- **This is a paediatric emergency**.

Epiglottitis is usually caused by *Haemophilus influenzae* type b, though it is more uncommon now since the introduction of the Hib vaccine. There is a risk of laryngospasm and complete airway obstruction, leading to death. The child will look ill and will be febrile. They will be unable to speak or swallow and will be drooling. The child will also have signs of respiratory distress.

The child must be referred immediately to hospital. It is important to keep the child calm. Contact the local A&E department as well as the paediatrician on call. They will then notify the consultant anaesthetist and consultant ENT surgeon to make them aware of the admission. The child is usually intubated before any investigations are done or treatment started.

BRONCHIOLITIS

This is a common viral respiratory infection in infants. The most common cause is respiratory syncytial virus (RSV) and it occurs in seasonal outbreaks through the winter. It is most severe in infants who were premature, have bronchopulmonary dysplasia or have congenital heart disease. The infant can develop a secondary bacterial infection. It is diagnosed by laboratory analysis of nasopharyngeal aspirate. The infant usually recovers within a couple of weeks but may have a recurrent cough and wheeze which can last for 2 or 3 years.

History

Apart from a general history and then focusing on the cough, you should check whether the infant is feeding normally. Respiratory distress in a young infant can seriously hamper feeding in many cases.

Examination

Check vital signs including oxygen saturations. Of particular importance is whether the infant is tachypnoeic and showing signs of respiratory distress with recession and a high-pitched wheeze.

Management

This is symptomatic depending on the severity of the illness. The illness usually reaches its peak at 5 days. If the infant is at risk they will need hospital admission and supportive treatment. This may include oxygen therapy, tube feeding and, in severe cases, intravenous fluids. Ribavarin may be given to high-risk infants.

PNEUMONIA

Streptococcus pneumoniae is the most common bacterial cause of pneumonia, but viruses such as RSV or parainfluenza can be the cause. Alternatively *Mycoplasma pneumoniae* or a fungus such as *Pneumocystis carinii* may be to blame. In infants, bacterial pneumonia is frequently a widespread bronchopneumonia; in older children it is more likely to be lobar in nature. In neonates the most common causative organism is Group B streptococcus, which comes from the mother. There has usually been a preceding upper respiratory tract infection followed by a sudden deterioration in the child's condition as they develop fever, tachypnoea, rigors, an initially unproductive cough and restlessness alternating with drowsiness (Candy et al 2001). Cyanosis may develop in infants and they may also show abdominal distension due to swallowing air as they struggle for breath.

History

Key areas to explore include the history of any upper respiratory tract infection or cough. Feeding and fluid intake must be assessed as dehydration can develop very quickly in a young child with pneumonia as they are anorexic and may reduce fluid intake significantly. Chest or abdominal pain should be checked.

Examination

- Monitor vital signs including oxygen saturations.
- Check for respiratory effort and signs of respiratory distress.

- Are there decreased breath sounds on auscultation and is air entry equal? Check for adventitious sounds such as crackles.
- On percussion are there areas of consolidation or dullness?
- Check the child's overall appearance and whether there are any signs of cyanosis.

Barnes (2003) reminds us that when confronted by a child in respiratory distress, there are several important differential diagnoses that need to be considered including asthma, inhaled foreign body, tuberculosis, caustic ingestion, trauma or sickle cell disease (acute chest syndrome). This should be borne in mind when considering the possibility of pneumonia in a child with respiratory distress.

Management

If the child's symptoms are severe they will need hospital admission. They will need a chest x-ray to check for any consolidation. In hospital, blood will be taken for full blood count and culture. They will have oral antibiotics and, if the infection is severe, will need intravenous antibiotics according to local protocol. Intravenous fluids and oxygen may be necessary. Physiotherapy may also be useful. Less severe cases in older children may be managed at home.

ABDOMINAL PAIN

There is a need to differentiate between a surgical cause and medical cause for abdominal pain. In young children lower lobe pneumonia may present with abdominal pain. Surgical causes include appendicitis and intussusception, while most common medical causes include mesenteric adenitis, urinary tract infection and constipation. In teenage, sexually active girls the possibility of ectopic pregnancy or pelvic inflammatory disease needs to be considered. The possibility of sexual abuse should also be thought about.

HISTORY

The familiar PQRST tool will help explore the symptom of abdominal pain:

- Does anything make the pain better or worse? (P)
- What do you think may have caused the pain? (P)
- Can they describe the type of pain? (Q)

- Does it come and go or is it constant? (Q)
- Where is the pain? (R)
- Estimate the severity of the pain? (S) (using a standard paediatric pain assessment tool)
- When did it start? (T)
- Is the pain getting worse? (T)

Other key areas to explore are vomiting and nausea; the nature and frequency of the vomit should be checked. Box 15.2 provides useful information on vomiting.

Box 15.2 Emesis and importance of description	
Undigested milk, formula feed or food	Probably expelled from stomach very soon after ingestion as no digestion has occurred
Yellow vomit, may smell 'acidic'	Contents originated in stomach
Dark green vomit, bile stained	Originated below ampulla of Vater
Dark brown vomit, foul odour	Due to intestinal obstruction
Bright red	Fresh blood
Dark red/coffee grounds	Old blood or altered by gastric acid
Source: Engel 2003	

It is necessary to check for urinary symptoms and whether there has been any diarrhoea. Recent upper respiratory tract infection should be checked. Previous episodes of abdominal pain should be checked together with previous medical history. Recent family medical history is important due to the risk of an infectious agent causing gastroenteritis. Similarly, check whether there are any illnesses going around nursery or school. If appropriate you should also check both menstrual and sexual history.

EXAMINATION

Observe the child as they walk into the room and the ease with which they can climb onto the examination couch, as this will be an indication of the severity of the pain. Monitor temperature and pulse. Carry out a general examination before a specific abdominal one. The examination is the same as that carried out for adults. It is important to try and have the child as relaxed as possible using distraction therapy with toys for young children or talking about school, music, television, sport or films with older children.

APPENDICITIS

History

There is usually a history of a sudden onset of central abdominal pain, which localizes to the right iliac fossa. However, Valman (2000) indicates that in about 25% of children the pain starts in the right iliac fossa. The pain can be colicky or a continual dull ache. Nausea and vomiting develop soon after the onset of pain. A low-grade pyrexia, usually less than 38°C, is common. The child tends to lie still as movement aggravates the pain.

Management

You need to exclude other causes such as a urinary tract infection or a respiratory tract infection, which can produce abdominal pain in children. The patient will need referral for a surgical opinion when blood tests will be carried out, and if there is uncertainty over the diagnosis, an ultrasound scan may be performed.

INTUSSUSCEPTION

This is the telescoping of one piece of bowel into another. It is most common in infants below the age of 1 year and in boys. There is typically intermittent colicky pain with the knees being drawn up. The infant will usually be pale, distressed and crying. There will be vomiting which is often bile-stained. On rectal examination there will be blood-stained mucus. There is frequently a sausage shaped mass in the right hypochondrium or epigastrium, which may be palpable unless the child is particularly upset.

Management

This is by referral to hospital for further management. The treatment is usually by air enema under radiographic control, though in some cases surgery may be necessary if there are signs of perforation or peritonitis or if the bowel cannot be reduced by the enema.

MESENTERIC ADENITIS

This is a cause of abdominal pain, which can mimic appendicitis. It is thought to be an inflammation of the mesenteric lymph nodes, though the only way to prove this would be surgery to identify it. There is usually a preceding upper respiratory tract infection. The abdominal pain associated with mesenteric adenitis is more generalized than that of appendicitis.

History

Apart from a detailed PQRST symptom analysis it is important to assess whether the child has had a cough, cold or sore throat recently, nausea or vomiting, or whether there have been any urinary symptoms.

Examination

In addition to a full physical and abdominal exam, you should observe the ease of the child's movements and ensure an ENT examination has been carried out to check for evidence of tonsillitis.

Management

- Refer for medical opinion if symptoms persist.
- Throat swab if necessary.
- Urine culture to exclude a urinary tract infection.
- Analgesia.

URINARY TRACT INFECTION

This is an important condition to diagnose – if a child has vesicoureteric reflux (i.e. reflux of urine back into the ureter and kidney), renal scarring will develop which can lead to hypertension and chronic renal failure in early adult life. The most common cause of a urinary tract infection is *E. coli* from the child's bowel.

History

In an infant this may be very non-specific with the infant presenting as febrile, not feeding and irritable. In children there are more specific urinary symptoms. Key questions to ask are:

- Does the child have frequency?
- Is passing urine painful?
- Has a previously continent child started wetting themselves?

- Are they now wetting the bed at night?
- Has the child had previous urinary tract infections?
- Is there a family history of urinary tract abnormalities?

Any pain should be carefully assessed (e.g. PQRST).

Examination

- Check vital signs.
- Collect urine for culture and dipstick using a clean catch if possible, otherwise a urine collection pad.
- Abdominal examination.

Management

This is by appropriate antibiotics once the urine specimen has been collected and sent for culture. If possible, carry out a microscope analysis of the urine specimen immediately – if you find a colony count of more than 100 000 of a single organism commence antibiotics. If there is a mixed growth then a repeat specimen will be needed as this indicates contamination of the specimen.

A child with vesicoureteric reflux can develop renal scarring within 3 days. Infants younger than 1 year will need a renal ultrasound scan, DMSA (dimercaptosuccinic acid) scan and a micturating cystourethrogram; 1–4-year-olds will require a DMSA scan and renal ultrasound scan; those aged over 4 years will require a DMSA scan and a renal ultrasound scan.

The ultrasound scan will show any anatomical abnormality. The DMSA scan uses a radioactive substance which will identify areas of renal scarring. The micturating cystourethrogram will show if there is any reflux. If a dilated urinary tract is shown then a MAG 3(mercaptoacetyl-triglycine) scan may be used.

The child will need prophylactic antibiotics, usually trimethoprim, taken at night while results are assimilated – then a plan for further management will be organized by a consultant paediatrician.

ACUTE GASTROENTERITIS

Acute gastroenteritis is one of the most common medical conditions in childhood. It can be defined as a sudden onset of diarrhoea with or without vomiting. Viral infections such as rotavirus and adenovirus are the most common causes, with rotavirus accounting for 60% of cases of gastroenteritis in winter in children aged less than 2 years old. Bacterial infections are less common and are more likely to occur during the summer months. Pathogenic organisms can cause changes in the lining of the small intestine which decrease absorption or provoke increased secretions. Either way the result is diarrhoea.

Medical causes of vomiting and diarrhoea include septicaemia, meningitis, respiratory tract infection, otitis media, hepatitis A, urinary tract infection, diabetic ketoacidosis, haemolytic uraemic syndrome, coeliac disease, cow's milk protein allergy, adrenal insufficiency and Reye syndrome.

Surgical causes of vomiting and diarrhoea include pyloric stenosis, intussusception, acute appendicitis, necrotizing enterocolitis and Hirschsprung disease.

History

Once again the PQRST tool can be used to explore the symptom of diarrhoea. When enquiring about the nature of the diarrhoea (Q for 'Quality') it is important to check how watery it is and whether it contains blood or mucus. Severity (S) requires asking how many stools have been passed today. Check whether:

- any other family members are affected with similar symptoms
- there is any history of recent foreign travel
- there have been visits to farms or animal sanctuaries
- there were any preceding symptoms of upper respiratory tract or urinary tract infection
- there is any abdominal pain
- there are any skin rashes
- there has been any change in appetite and drinking.

Examination

Assessment of the child's general appearance and behaviour should be followed by vital signs. The extent of dehydration may be assessed clinically (Barnes 2003) from the signs shown in Table 15.2. An accurate weight measurement is essential for rehydration therapy. Weight can give an idea of level of dehydration if there is a recent weight for comparison. The physical exam should assess carefully whether and to what extent the signs listed above are present. Auscultation of the abdomen would be expected to reveal increased bowel

Table 15.2 Clinical assessment of dehydration

Clinical signs	Mild (< 5%)	Moderate (< 10%)	Severe (10–15%)
Appearance	Miserable, irritable	Irritable or lethargic	Drowsy, unresponsive
Tissue turgor	Normal to minimally decreased	Noticeably decreased	Obviously decreased (tenting > 2 secs)
Mucous membranes	Dry	Dry	Very dry
Capillary refill	Normal	Normal/prolonged	Prolonged (> 2 sec)
Pulse	Normal	Rapid	Rapid, thready
Blood pressure	Normal	Normal/low	Low/unrecordable
Urine output	Decreased	Decreased	Oliguria
Eyes	Normal	Sunken	Very sunken
Anterior fontanelle	Normal	Depressed	Very depressed

sounds. There should be no distension or significant abdominal tenderness or hepatosplenomegaly as these will point to a different diagnosis, which will need referral.

Management

Acute gastroenteritis with mild to moderate dehydration can be managed at home with the correct advice for parents. For mild dehydration the child should be given oral rehydration solution (ORS) with the aim being to correct dehydration over a 4-hour period when the situation should be reassessed. The child requires 50 ml/kg of ORS plus a replacement of 10 ml/kg for each loose stool. It may be necessary to give ORS one teaspoon at a time if the child is still vomiting (Barnes 2003). Once vomiting has stopped normal, diet can be introduced. If the child is breast-feeding this should continue.

Early refeeding of children during oral rehydration therapy is important with children able to eat as normally as possible. Food should initially not be too fatty as this may aggravate the condition but generally children should be able to have what they like. Oral rehydration therapy tastes unpalatable, so disguise the flavour with juice or make flavoured ice-lollies (popsicles) with it, which might make it more acceptable to the child. Fluids should contain sugar to aid absorption and should be given little and often.

Moderate levels of dehydration can be corrected with 100 ml/kg over a 6-hour period, with an extra 10 ml/kg for each loose stool or vomit. It may be best for the child to be admitted as a nasogastric tube may be needed. If vomiting persists intravenous rehydration will be required, with close monitoring

of blood electrolytes. The home circumstances need to be taken into account in making such a decision.

Parents need to be reassured that there is no need to give any medication to alleviate the symptoms of diarrhoea and vomiting. They are generally ineffective and may prolong the excretion of bacteria from the stools. However antibiotics may be used in specific infections such as shigella, cholera and giardia.

The child will need referral to hospital for further management if there is severe dehydration or a suspected surgical cause. If oliguria persists the child must be investigated for haemolytic uraemic syndrome caused by E. coli 0157. This serious condition can lead to renal failure.

The child can return to school or nursery when they have had no diarrhoea for 24 hours. Occasionally diarrhoea persists, as there may be an associated secondary intolerance to lactose. There could be intolerance to cow's milk, disaccharides or gluten.

Parents should be warned that if the cause for their child's gastroenteritis is notifiable then officials from public health would visit them. A follow-up visit by the health visitor or community paediatric nurse may be helpful in reinforcing information given about prevention of gastroenteritis.

CONSTIPATION

This is a common problem, which occasionally can become so severe that it requires admission to hospital for treatment. A vicious cycle begins after a period of constipation which may be due to having had a febrile illness, being unwell and eating or drinking less than usual – or there may be changes socially such as starting school or a change in diet. A large stool develops and water continues to be drawn from the colon so the stool enlarges and becomes harder, making it more difficult to pass. This may lead to pain on passing the stool and an anal fissure may also occur, aggravating the pain. The child may then develop soiling through overflow (encopresis) which also makes school attendance more difficult and could lead to bullying. Significant emotional and family problems are often involved either as a major contributing cause of the problem or secondary to the disordered bowel function (Valman 2000).

History

The history should focus on how long the child has had problems with constipation. Check how frequently the child has their bowels opened, and whether there is any soiling, and assess the child's diet. Ask whether there were any illnesses or significant events that preceded the constipation. Family history is important as this may indicate poor diet affecting the whole family or a genetic susceptibility. The family should also be assessed carefully as there may be major family problems which are contributing to the problem or that are being exacerbated by it.

Examination

On palpation of the abdomen the faeces will be felt. The abdomen may also be distended. Inspect the anal area for stool and to see if there is an anal fissure. Neurological examination of the lower limbs should be carried out to rule out hypotonia as a cause. Check the spine for any sacral dimple to exclude spina bifida occulta (Barnes 2003).

Management

If Hirschsprung disease or a neurological cause is suspected then the child will need referral to hospital. It may be necessary to use an enema or glycerin suppositories to empty the bowel before commencing laxatives such as lactulose, which will help soften the stool. Other laxatives that can be used in older children include sodium picosulphate, sodium docusate and senna.

Education of parents so they understand how the treatments work and how constipation happens is essential. Education on diet and the need for an adequate fluid intake will also assist. In young children using praise and aids such as star charts to encourage the child helps motivate the child to learn correct bowel habits. Issues within the family such as matrimonial disharmony need to be explored, as well as the impact of the problem upon the child's schooling.

In severe cases the child may need referral to hospital to see a consultant paediatrician and admission for treatment to clear the bowel of faeces. Referral to a child psychologist may also be needed.

ENT CONDITIONS

ACUTE OTITIS MEDIA

This is a painful infection of the middle ear as opposed to otitis externa, which affects the outer ear. It is more common in infants as the Eustachian tube is more horizontal and allows easy access for the passage of pathogens from the nose to reach the middle ear. Recurrent ear infections can lead to chronic secretory otitis media, which is the most common cause of conductive hearing loss in children.

History

Acute otitis media is usually secondary to an upper respiratory tract infection – therefore after taking a history focussed on the pain, which is always present and can be very distressing, recent medical history should be checked. It is also important to ascertain if the child is eating and drinking normally as appetite may suffer. Sleep may be disturbed by the pain. A key sign to check, especially in toddlers, is whether the child has been pulling at their ears, as this suggests pain and discomfort within the ear. Any changes in hearing acuity should be noted.

Examination

The general assessment of the child's behaviour and appearance should be accompanied by vital signs as temperature is often elevated. Otoscopic examination of a distressed toddler or young child with a painful otitis media is not easy. They should be securely held by their parent and sitting on the parent's lap. It is a good idea to let the child play with the otoscope first to allay some of the fears. The technique for adults explained in Chapter 4 will be satisfactory for older children. However in children under 3 it is better to pull the earlobe gently downwards and out before placing the speculum in the auditory canal and then directing the speculum upwards as you insert it (Engel 2003). In otitis media the eardrum is swollen, opaque and red and the normal landmarks are obscured. Fluid may be visible through the tympanic membrane.

Management

An important differential diagnosis to consider is a foreign body impacted in the ear, although otoscopic examination will usually reveal this problem. Some infections are viral and will resolve without treatment. The use of antibiotics for bacterial infections is controversial and you should follow your local protocols. If a child has three episodes within 6 months or four within a year, this is defined as recurrent otitis media and prophylactic antibiotics may be considered (Barnes 2003). Paracetamol can be given for pain.

TONSILLITIS

There is inflammation of the tonsils with exudate present. The most common organisms are Group A haemolytic *Streptococci* and Epstein-Barr virus. In young children under 3 years the most common signs are fever and a refusal to eat. A febrile convulsion may also occur. Older children complain of a sore throat and may have obvious enlarged cervical lymph nodes. It is not possible to distinguish clinically between a bacterial or viral cause as a purulent exudate may be present in either case (Valman 2000).

History

Key aspects of the history should focus on whether the child has had an upper respiratory tract infection recently and whether they are eating and drinking normally. Check for vomiting, headache and whether they have pain when they swallow.

Examination

The throat is inflamed with enlarged tonsils and white exudates. There will be cervical lymphadenopathy.

Management

Though tonsillitis is often caused by a virus, antibiotics such as penicillin or erythromycin are often prescribed. A throat swab ideally should be taken prior to commencing antibiotics as this will determine the micro-organisms responsible. As ever, you should follow local protocols. If there is a Group A haemolytic streptococcal infection then a 10-day course of oral penicillin is necessary in order to prevent rheumatic fever.

NEUROLOGICAL CONDITIONS

There are many neurological conditions which can affect children – however, the frequently seen presentation in primary care/A&E is seizure. Infants and children may present with seizures for a variety of reasons. They may be febrile or non-febrile. Loss of consciousness in children also has many causes besides seizures, including head injury, hypoglycaemia, diabetic ketoacidosis, poisoning, drug abuse, encephalitis, meningitis, a tumour or intracranial bleed.

FEBRILE CONVULSIONS

These are extremely alarming for the parents. They occur between the ages of 6 months and 6 years and are associated with a rising body temperature. There is often a genetic predisposition, with close relatives having had similar episodes. The seizure is usually short-lasting and is generalized. According to Candy et al (2001) about 66% of children who have a febrile convulsion do not have another. However 2–5% go on to develop epilepsy, particularly if the episode consisted of more than one seizure and lasted for more than 15 minutes, or if it occurred in the first year of life.

History

It will usually be necessary to calm and reassure the parents before taking a history as they may be very distressed. Key questions to ask are:

- How long did the fit last?
- What limbs were affected?
- Was there a post-ictal (drowsy/confused) phase?
- Has the child been unwell recently?
- Has the child had a raised temperature or looked hot and flushed?
- Is there a family history of febrile seizures?

Examination

Temperature needs to be measured along with other vital signs. The child will often be wrapped in blankets by the parents and so tactful unwrapping is needed to help prevent further temperature rise. A careful examination is necessary to identify the cause of the fever, paying particular attention to the neurological examination in order to exclude meningitis or other neurological causes such as raised intracranial pressure.

Management

In primary care the child should be referred to hospital for further management and investigations. The child will usually be observed in hospital overnight. Parents need reassurance about the cause of the seizure as there is a frequent (usually mistaken) assumption that this means the child will suffer from epilepsy. Advice on managing future illnesses, such as keeping the child cool and giving anti-pyretic medication, is essential. Rectal diazepam may be prescribed for use at home.

NON-FEBRILE SEIZURES

These are best classified as primary seizures (cause unknown) or secondary where a cause is known. If the seizure affects the whole body this is a generalized seizure, whereas if it affects a part of the body it is a partial seizure. Consciousness may still be lost in a partial seizure (complex partial) or the child may remain awake (simple partial). This nomenclature is simple and self-explanatory and helps get away from terms such as 'grand mal epilepsy' and all the associated anxiety-producing stigmatization associated with those terms (Candy et al 2001).

History

It is essential to ascertain that the person being interviewed did actually witness the seizure firsthand and is therefore a reliable witness. Key questions to ask include:

- What was the child doing when the seizure occurred? Photosensitive seizures occur in children associated with flashing lights such as video/computer games.
- Was there any aura such as a strange smell or flashing lights?
- Is there any raised temperature, headache or neck stiffness?
- Was the child hungry (and therefore possibly hypoglycaemic)?
- Is there any family history of seizures?

- Birth history – were there any problems with the baby or mother?
- Developmental history – are milestones being met?
- Was there a loss of consciousness?
- Could the child speak?
- What limbs were affected?
- Was there a period when the child did not appear to breathe?
- Does the child remember anything about what happened?
- How long did it take before the child was back to normal?
- Was there any incontinence?
- How long did the fit last?

These questions are organized in line with the PQRST approach.

Examination

- General appearance – is the child awake and orientated now?
- Check vital signs, Glasgow Coma Score and pupil reactions.
- Neurological examination is mandatory and you should check carefully for signs of meningitis or head injury which may be secondary to the seizure.
- Note whether there has been any incontinence.

Management

Refer to hospital for investigations and further management.

Differential diagnoses for seizures include:

- Breath-holding attacks which commonly occur between the ages of 6 months and 3 years.
- Tourette's syndrome, which can look like a partial seizure with twitches and blinks.
- Shuddering in a shivering infant with no loss of consciousness.
- Vasovagal syncope (faint) where the child may fall slowly and look pale and may then appear to have a seizure.

MENINGITIS

This may occur at any age but is most common in the age range 6–12 months (Valman 2000). In children under 3 years of age the early signs are particularly difficult to detect, but fever, irritability, vomiting, convulsions and a high-pitched cry are strongly suggestive of this diagnosis. Drowsiness and a refusal to feed are very serious signs. In addition, unusual behaviour and headaches may become apparent in older children. Neck stiffness in a young child should be tested for by trying to make a game of following an object. Of particular concern is the appearance of a non-blanching purpuric rash (see p. 67), indicating possible meningococcal septicaemia. This is fortunately rare but the child will be very ill. The rash may start anywhere on the body. **Any child who is febrile and develops a purpuric rash requires administration of intramuscular penicillin and immediate referral to hospital**. Valman (2000) recommends 300 mg for children under 1 year, 500 mg if aged 1–9, and 1200 mg if 10 or older.

MUSCULOSKELETAL CONDITIONS

Chapter 12 contains a review of the common types of injury and musculoskeletal disorder that the NP will encounter, this section will therefore focus on key aspects which make their presentation in children different.

TRAUMA

Children are frequent attenders in A&E with a range of injuries. The key difference is the immaturity of a child's skeletal system. A child's bones contain a higher proportion of organic material than an adult's bones, and therefore less inorganic material such as calcium phosphate. As a result they are less rigid and so tend to buckle or only partly break ('greenstick fracture') leaving some degree of cortical continuity. A child's bones are in a state of continual growth, lengthwise, due to the deposition of new bone at the epiphyseal cartilages which are located at either extremity of each long bone. New bone is also being deposited to enable the width of the bone to keep in proportion to the length whilst remodelling is continually widening the medullary canal at the same rate. The implications of these developmental changes are as follows:

- Any fracture involving the epiphyseal cartilage needs careful management as deformity may develop due to destruction of the epiphyseal cartilage or malalignment of the epiphyses.
- Fractures in young children require more violence than normally is the case in older adults.

- X-ray interpretation is more difficult as areas of cartilage do not show up on the radiograph.
- Fractures in children tend to heal more rapidly.
- Internal fixation can only be a temporary measure.
- Fractures are just as painful to a child as they are to an adult.

CHILD ABUSE

Child abuse can take many forms and violence directed against the child has to be placed alongside sexual abuse, psychological abuse and neglect. What constitutes neglect is very difficult to define as it is a socially constructed issue; what is neglectful in one society may not be considered so in another (Truman 2004). Neglect is a different form of child abuse as it involves the failure to act rather than purposeful actions such as violence or sexual interference. Certain factors are known to increase the risk of neglect such as a family history of neglect (victim/offender cycle), drug and alcohol abuse, poverty, domestic violence and maternal depression. However the NP should avoid falling into the traps of either assuming that the absence of any evidence indicating these factors means neglect cannot happen or that their presence means neglect will definitely happen. It is much more complicated than that and every child and family must be assessed individually.

There is a range of well known signs which should raise the suspicion of non-accidental injury. Despite this fact, tragedies still occur. *A continual state of alertness and a willingness to act are essential for any health professional who comes into contact with children* – particularly a NP given the high degree of autonomy usually associated with the role. Signs which should alert the NP may be summarized (Engel 2003, Londhe et al 2002) as follows:

- The injuries/condition do not match the history.
- Presence of old injuries ranging from multiple bruises of varying age through to old fractures on x-ray. Spiral fractures are almost certainly due to abuse, indicating severe twisting of the child's limb.
- Injuries are inconsistent with the child's age and developmental status (especially true of infants).
- Unexplained burn marks (may be due to a cigarette).

- Delay in seeking attention.
- Unexplained illness or poisoning.
- Poor standards of hygiene, dress and cleanliness.
- Fear or unusual wariness of adults coupled with withdrawn behaviour demonstrating unwillingness to interact with their environment.
- A pattern of repeated attendance for various injuries.
- Failure to keep other medical appointments.
- Hunger.

Common features in the family background include (Engel 2003):

- Parental history of neglect and abuse leading to the victim-as-offender cycle.
- Parental age at birth of child under 18.
- Domestic violence involving partner or parental separation.
- Unstable domestic arrangements.
- Single mother.
- Parental drug/alcohol abuse.
- Prematurity of infant.
- Lack of parental knowledge concerning child development and parenting skills.

It is crucial that every NP knows what their practice or unit procedure should be in a case of suspected child abuse and acts immediately in the child's best interests. You are accountable as a registered nurse for your actions at all times and a lack of enthusiasm for action on the part of other health professionals is no excuse for you failing to act, even if this may make you unpopular.

NON-TRAUMATIC PRESENTATIONS

Most commonly seen is a child complaining of a painful hip, knee or presenting with a limp. This could be due to several causes but the most likely are:

- Toxic synovitis, which usually occurs between the ages of 18 months to 12 years and is more common in boys. There is usually a preceding upper respiratory infection. On examination, there is limited hip abduction and rotation.
- Osteochondritis, which involves an avascular necrosis of specific bones for reasons which are still unclear. Perthes disease is due to ischaemia of the femoral epiphysis leading to avascular necrosis. This usually occurs between the ages

of 4 and 9 years and is found predominantly in boys. On examination there is limited hip abduction. Osgood-Schlatter disease affects the knee in adolescents and is exercise related. It more commonly affects boys and leads to tender swelling around the anterior aspect of the tibial tuberosity.
- Septic arthritis, which usually occurs in children under the age of 2 years and equally in boys and girls. They will be febrile and may have had an upper respiratory infection. Examination shows that the hip is held flexed and abducted.
- Slipped upper femoral epiphysis, which is most common between the ages of 8 and 16 years, affecting boys more than girls. The child is usually obese. The child will have Trendelenburg gait with a hip that rotates externally with flexion (p. 217).
- Osteomyelitis refers to a bacterial infection of bone and occurs most commonly in boys under 1 and in the mid-childhood years. *Staph. aureus* is the most common cause. It appears that the infection originates elsewhere in the body and localizes at the metaphysis where the epiphyseal plate joins the main shaft of the bone (diaphysis). This area has low levels of phagocytic activity, which probably explains this as the common site (Candy et al 2001).

History

A full history is necessary with particular focus on both the pain and the extent of the limp. The PQRST model will allow the NP to arrive at a good summary of both symptoms. Any possible history of trauma, including whether the child could have stood on a sharp object, should be explored. It is particularly important to assess whether there have been problems in other joints or if the pain is confined to one joint only.

Examination

A full musculoskeletal exam should be performed as for an adult (p. 207). Examination of the soles of the feet for signs of a foreign body is essential and you should check vital signs, especially temperature, to eliminate any active infection.

Management

Once trauma has been eliminated as a possible cause, referral to hospital for investigations and further management by an orthopaedic surgeon is required.

COMMON SKIN COMPLAINTS

Rashes are very common reasons for a parent seeking a consultation with the NP. The rash could be anything from a sign of a serious systemic disease to a localized irritation. It could indicate an infection or an allergy or indicate a developing dermatological condition such as eczema. In Chapter 3 the main skin disorders were discussed and the reader is referred to that chapter for a further discussion. A rash is frequently a sign of one of several common childhood infections. The different types of rash will therefore be discussed below, together with their associated disorder.

PURPURA

Purpura are caused by haemorrhages in the skin and they do not disappear with pressure. They indicate serious pathology such as meningococcal septicaemia or leukaemia. Purpura also appear in Henoch-Schönlein syndrome and they are most notable on the extensor surface of the limbs together with oedema. This disorder is characterized by an acute inflammatory reaction, suggesting an immune response, affecting small blood vessels, the cause of which is unknown. There is a purpuric rash which typically is found on the buttocks, and extensor surfaces of the arms and legs. The rash is made up of palpable lesions which range between 2 and 10 mm in diameter. It is most common between the ages of 3 and 10 years with boys being more commonly affected. There may have been a preceding upper respiratory tract infection and the child may be febrile. As well as the purpuric rash the children may have arthralgia, abdominal pain and glomerulonephritis. The average duration of the acute illness is between 2 and 4 weeks with a likelihood of recurrence. The child will need referral to hospital for diagnosis and management.

MACULES

Macules are discrete red/pink lesions that fade under pressure (blanch) while papules project proud of the skin. Macules are characteristic of

rubella, which has an incubation period of 14–21 days. They appear on day one of the illness and there may also be a slight fever. Roseola is caused by one of two strains of the human herpes virus and causes infants to become irritable and have a high fever (a common cause of febrile convulsions). As the condition resolves a faint macular rash appears on the trunk. A blanching macula rash affecting the trunk and neck is also associated with scarlet fever. This has an incubation period of 2–4 days before fever, headache and tonsillitis become apparent. The rash lasts for 6 days. Oral penicillin is necessary to deal with the causative organism, which is a strain of the group A haemolytic streptococci.

MACULOPAPULAR RASH

A maculopapular rash is a mix of both types of lesion and is classically seen in measles (rubeola). The incubation period is 8–14 days and on day 1–2 of the illness the child looks as though they are developing a bad cold but will have a cough and fever together with Koplik spots – white spots scattered on the buccal membranes opposite the first and second molars (Seidal et al 2003). The rash appears on days 3–4 and starts at the hairline before spreading downwards across the body. Secondary bacterial infections may occur leading to otitis media, pneumonia or conjunctivitis while in one or two cases per thousand, post-infectious encephalitis develops. All NPs will be aware that measles is a serious disease and this must be impressed upon parents in view of the immunization crisis which has been produced by irresponsible reporting of the MMR vaccine debate. Glandular fever (infectious mononucleosis) may also produce a maculopapular rash. The disease has an incubation period of 14–21 days and produces pharyngitis, fever and cervical adenopathy. In 15% of cases it produces a primary rash but almost invariably after treatment with amoxicillin a maculopapular rash develops.

VESICLES

Vesicles consist of raised lesions filled with fluid and in chickenpox (varicella) the skin lesions quickly pass through the stages of being macules and papules before becoming vesicles and eventually pustules (filled with pus). Chickenpox is caused by the varicella zoster virus and has an incubation period of 10–21 days. The child is unwell, has a runny nose and fever and the rash begins to develop within the first day or two. The child becomes non-infectious once the skin lesions become dry (post-pustular phase). Vesicles may also erupt after an infant's first exposure to herpes zoster, particularly in the mouth. The infant will be distressed, in pain and reluctant to feed.

OTHER INFECTIONS

Skin disorders in children can also be associated with fungal infections. In newborn infants *Candida albicans* can cause infection of the mouth or napkin area. The *Trichophyton* and *Microsporidium* species of fungi can infect the skin and are commonly known as ringworm. Infection of the scalp is known as tinea capitas, the body tinea corporis, the feet tinea pedis ('athlete's foot') and the nails, tinea unguum. Direct or indirect contact with other infected humans or animals can spread the disease. Clotrimazole or miconazole are effective against tinea pedis but systemic treatment with griseofulvin is needed in other infections.

Other viral infections can also produce dermatological symptoms. The parvovirus produces a raised temperature and a mild systemic illness. Classically the child has an intensely red 'slapped cheek' rash on the face (so called because of its appearance) and a symmetrical maculopapular rash on the arms which moves downwards to affect the rest of the body. There is no specific treatment. The incubation period is between 4 and 14 days. Hand, foot and mouth disease is caused by the Coxsackie virus and presents usually in summer as vesicles on the hands and feet and in the mouth. The child will have a raised temperature There is no specific treatment. The incubation period is 4 to 6 days. This should not be confused with the animal foot and mouth disease which caused massive damage to UK agriculture recently.

HISTORY

The specific questions that need to be asked when seeing a child with a rash which is thought to be associated with one of the common childhood infectious diseases are as follows:

- How long has the child had the rash?
- What is the distribution?
- Does anything make it better or worse?
- Is it itchy?
- Has the child a raised temperature?
- Has the child had any possible contact with an infectious disease – and if so, when?
- What has the child's general health been like in the last few days?
- If the child has siblings, how have they been?

EXAMINATION

Your initial observation of the child should assess whether they are happy and playing or irritable and unwell. The child needs to be stripped off so a full examination can be carried out. Check for location of the lesions, their distribution, and size and describe them. The child's vital signs should be recorded.

MENINGOCOCCAL SEPTICAEMIA

This is rare. The child will be very ill with a non-blanching purpuric rash. The rash may start anywhere on the body. Any child who is febrile and develops a purpuric rash requires administration of intramuscular penicillin and immediate referral to hospital (p. 275).

IDIOPATHIC THROMBOCYTOPENIC PURPURA

This is caused by the development of platelet antibodies and subsequent destruction of platelets. It usually affects children aged between 2 and 10 years and is often seen after a viral illness. The child develops bruising and a purpuric rash. In most children the disease is self-limiting and no treatment is needed. Some children will need steroids or immunoglobulins if bleeding is a problem. The child will need referral to hospital for diagnosis and initial management. The child will need to avoid contact sports and will have platelet levels checked to show if the illness is resolving. Complications include intracranial bleeds or gastrointestinal bleeds. The duration of the illness can be for several months.

References

Agnew T 2004 Blueprint for children. Nursing Standard 19(2):12

Barnes K 2003 Paediatrics: a clinical guide for nurse practitioners. Butterworth-Heinemann, Edinburgh

BRI Inquiry 2001 The Report of the Public Inquiry into Children's Heart Surgery at the Bristol Royal Infirmary 1984–95. HMSO, London

Candy D, Davies G, Ross E 2001 Clinical paediatrics and child health. W B Saunders, London

DOH 2004 Department of Health. The children's national service framework for children, young people and maternity services. Department of Health, London

Engel J 2003 Pediatric assessment, 4th edn. Mosby, St Louis

Etheridge K 2004 Recognising and responding to adolescents with mental illness. Primary Health Care 14(9):36–41

Evans D 2004 Behind the headlines: sexual health implications for nursing ethics and practice. Primary Health Care 14(8):40–49

Londhe V, Marmor A, Dandekar A, Caughey A 2002 Clinical cases in pediatrics. Blackwell Science, Malden, MA

Metcalfe T 2004 Sexual health: meeting adolescent's needs. Nursing Standard 18(26):40–43

Seidal H, Ball J, Dains J, Benedict G 2003 Mosby's guide to physical examination, 5th edn. Mosby, St Louis

Smith F 2004 The NSF for children: key issues for primary care. Primary Health Care 14(9):16–17

Truman P 2004 Problems in identifying cases of child neglect. Nursing Standard 18(29):33–36

Valman B 2000 The ABC of one to seven. BMJ Publishing, London

Chapter 16

Child health and the role of the nurse practitioner

Fiona Smart

INTRODUCTION

In 2002 the Royal College of Nursing (RCN) revised its definition of the nurse practitioner (NP) role and in so doing provided a benchmark for emerging practice. Embedded within the list of role expectations are statements that readily associate with the work of the NP, most notably perhaps the one which reads 'receives patients with undifferentiated and undiagnosed problems'. However, the RCN (2002) makes it clear that its expectations of the NP extend well beyond the focus of illness, into that which embraces screening, health education and leadership.

This chapter picks up these wider expectations and examines them in the context of child health. It is appreciated that this focus might appear narrow to the NP who works primarily with adults, however, as the chapter unfolds its relevance to all NPs, regardless of their place of work and speciality, will become apparent. The health of children is a public concern and should be a matter of professional interest across the range of settings in which NPs practise. Before moving on to outline the plan for the chapter, it would be useful to define the word 'child'.

A much-debated construct – for example, see Alderson & Montgomery (1996) – the term 'child' is used in this context to mean a person under the age of 18 years. It is appreciated that this may seem out of step with the fact that in England and Wales the child aged 16 years and over has the statutory right to give consent to treatment and to access their medical records (Dimond 1996). However, as Dimond (1996) explains, in the event of a dispute between the parent(s) and the child aged 16 years and over, case law has established that the child does not have an unqualified or absolute right to refuse treatment. As Alderson & Montgomery (1996) note, it is the right of the child to dissent to treatment which is especially vulnerable up to the age of 18 years. Consequently, despite the fact the readers might be working in settings outside of England and Wales, for the purposes of this chapter the term 'child' is used to define a person under the age of 18 years.

The chapter is divided into four sections. Each intends to be informative and challenging. It begins by presenting statistics which highlight key global data as they concern child health prior to centring on the UK – where it will become apparent that there is a tremendous variation of experience for children within and across social groups.

The second section will overview recent government-led initiatives that can be understood as attempting to 'level the playing field', so as to minimize inequalities. The effects of the new GMS contract and the reduction in doctors' working hours combined with changes in medical education will be drawn into the debate. Government-supported change of health roles will feature here and will be examined in brief in terms of the extent to which they can support new ways of working. The role of the NP will feature at this point, alongside the need for interdisciplinary working.

The third section examines two particular child health issues (diet/obesity and mental health/wellbeing) drawing two constructs into focus – culture and health promotion. The fourth section centres on the potential of the role of the NP to promote health in partnership with children and their families, in collaboration with fellow health care providers and other agencies. It will employ Kelly et al's (1993) thinking to organize its reflection on the possibilities that already have or might be realized. It will be evident that isolated action limits the possibility of change which can alter children's lives and release their potential – now and into adulthood.

GLOBAL PERSPECTIVE: A BRIEF INSIGHT

Currently it is estimated that the world's population is 6.3 billion (Global Issues 2004). Of this number it is predicted that 80 million children and mothers will die unnecessarily before the year 2015 (Save the Children 2003). Preventable diseases,

such as measles and gastroenteritis, will account for many of these deaths (Save the Children 2003). AIDS will take its toll. Recent data suggest that some 2.5 million children were living with HIV at the end of 2003 (UNAIDS 2003). And then there are the growing numbers of AIDS orphans (Blair et al 2003). The threat to child and adult health worldwide becomes easier to understand when it is explained that 800 million people lack access to health services and 10 million children do not receive primary education (Kmietowicz 2001) – a sad reflection on the hope that underpinned the UN Convention on the Rights of the Child (1989) (Box 16.1)

Box 16.1 The United Nations Convention on the Rights of the Child

Every child has the right to:

- have a name and be guaranteed a nationality
- live with parents unless this is deemed incompatible with the child's best interests
- express opinions and have them taken into account
- information
- freedom of thought, conscience and religion
- expect freedom from neglect and abuse
- education, with primary education being free and compulsory
- the highest level of health care possible
- enjoy and practise his/her own culture, language and religion
- leisure, play and participation in cultural and aesthetic activities
- protection under the law

For 158 million children aged less than 5 years to be malnourished (see Kmietowicz 2001) says something about us, our values and the massive differences in experience across the world. Starvation and obesity are global bedfellows.

Given all this, it might be timely to write about child health and the role of the NP from a global perspective. And yet to do so would focus attention away from the UK where, despite government-led initiatives, child health is an issue in need of thoughtful action which commits us to the empowerment of the child, their family and their community. However as Aynsley-Green (2003, p. 202–203), the first Director of the Children's Taskforce observes, this can only be achieved if health and social care providers evacuate professional bunkers which keep separate groups in individual silos and so limit their combined ability to provide 'child-centred services that are needs-based and developed around the child and (his/her) journey through the health and social care system.'

So just as the global population needs to take the health of its children seriously, so too the people of the UK appear charged with a responsibility: to live with the status quo or pledge to change the way things are by employing strategies which appreciate and seek to work with factors that can disarm and so disempower the youngest, and arguably the most vulnerable, of our population. The reader might think that given the UK's developed nation status, the problems faced by children in the UK pale in significance compared to those elsewhere. Well, it depends – evidence points to marked inequalities within the UK which some commentators are convinced are widening (Blair et al 2003).

THE UK SCENE: SOCIAL CHANGE, PREVAILING INEQUALITY

In mid-2001, an estimated 59 0505 800 people lived in the UK (National Statistics 2002). This represented an increase of 2.7 million people on 1981 data, a rise accounted for by the proportion of births over deaths; less than 25% of the total gain was explained by civilian migration (National Statistics 2002). Wales accounted for less than 5% of the total population (4.9%); England the most (83.7%) (National Statistics 2002).

Drawing upon the 2001 census data and National Statistics (2002), dependent children comprised 11.7 million of the national total – a figure that exceeds the total population size of, for example, Sweden, Belgium, Greece and Portugal. Of the total child population in the UK, almost 23% were living in lone-parent families, 92% of which were headed by women, more than 10% lived in step-families, whilst 65% lived with both natural parents. Over 45 000 children under the age of 16 years lived in communal establishments, while 150 000 children under 18 years of age were identified as unpaid carers within the family unit – a figure which is widely thought to be an underestimate. Box 16.2 highlights other key census data.

Box 16.2 Data from the UK 2001 census

Workless households
Over 2 million children live in households where there are no adults in work (approximately 16%); 33% of Muslim households are defined as 'workless'

Overcrowding
Muslim children experience more overcrowding than their peers (41.7% compared with 12.3%); 1 in 8 Muslim children live in households with no central heating compared with 1 in 16 of their peers

High-rise living
58,000 children under 2 years live in homes two or more storeys above ground level; 11 000 on the 5th floor or above

Source: National Statistics 2002

In terms of poverty, Kmietowiccz (2001) reports that the number of children affected by poverty has fallen by 33.3% in the past 2 years, a gratifying statistic for a government committed to the eradication of this scourge on wellbeing. Yet as Kmietowicz (2001) admits such hopeful data belie some children's reality of going without warmth, waterproof coats and shoes that fit. Given that the UK is the fourth largest economy in the world, it seems scandalous that a third of its children live in poverty (Save the Children 2004).

Recently we have been reminded that poverty statistics are far from benign artefacts. Plans in the UK to change the formula for calculating poverty will effectively wipe 1 million children from the total number and so make it easier for the government to reach its target of halving child poverty by 2010 (End Child Poverty 2004). To avoid the charge of moving the goalposts, Stearn (2004) suggests that the government should include housing costs in all top line figures on child poverty. Whilst such a step would put the UK out of step with its European partners, it would recognize that housing costs tend to be higher in the UK, especially in the Greater London area (End Child Poverty 2004).

Whether we choose to accept a figure that puts child poverty at 3.8 million (1 in 3), or 2.7 million, it is necessary to acknowledge societal inequalities which disadvantage some children more than others. The experience of poverty is damaging and is accompanied by difficulties in accessing good quality services, including health care (Save the Children 2004).

Other factors can co-exist with poverty to disadvantage some children in the UK still further. Take as an example the children of asylum seekers who, as HARP (Health for Asylum Seekers and Refugees) (2004) explains, arrive in the UK having lost their homes, friends and some family members. They may have witnessed horrific events; they might have been in hiding; they may even have been tortured (HARP 2004). There are perhaps 80 000 of these children in the UK, 68% in the Greater London area (where living costs are especially high), with smaller pockets in Manchester and Glasgow, and sprinklings in coastal towns (Clark & McGregor 2002). It is not uncommon for the children of asylum seekers to have to wait months for a school place, only to find themselves the target of bullies when they get there (Clark & McGregor 2002). It cannot be assumed that the communities in which they live are any more peaceful and accepting. Accessing services is likely to be complicated by language barriers and the indigenous people's beliefs about the rightful place of these children and their families in the UK. A recent government Green Paper threatens to create even more difficult conditions for a particular sub-section of children of asylum seekers (Save the Children 2003). Families who have been refused refugee status face separation from their children, a proposal which Blackwood (2003) is convinced is designed to encourage them to leave the UK and should be understood as another 'disgraceful attempt to isolate refugee children'.

But perhaps focusing on the children of asylum seekers was a poor choice in this chapter, given that they are not UK citizens, and possibly may never be. Maybe their lives are not our concern. So what about the children of UK-born gypsies/travellers? Lloyd (2000) explains that because they are part of a non-mainstream cultural group, these children experience daily difficulties which impact on their health and wellbeing. Problems include access to water and refuse collection, access to education, access to primary health care and racial harassment (Lloyd 2000). Yet perhaps this is another bad choice. It can be argued that because they choose to live on society's margins, gypsies and travellers should not expect to enjoy the privileges that accompany fully paid up membership of mainstream life. However this begs the question of whether or not the children of gypsies and travellers are free to decide their way of living? It also invites us to consider the extent to which the intolerance of difference can marginalize particular groups still further and so keep them at the edge of society.

Having acknowledged the well-recognized link between poverty and ill health, Dutt & Phillips (2000) go on to explain that black and minority ethnic people experience poorer health than their white counterparts. Citing Nazroo (1997), they add that within-group differences are notable, with Pakistanis and Bangladeshis reporting the poorest health. Correlating with these self-report data are infant mortality statistics which show an increased prevalence in families from Bangladesh, Pakistan and the Caribbean (Smaje 1999). These data are in part explained by socioeconomic conditions:

> 'Ethnic minority groups are more likely than the rest of the population to live in poor areas, be unemployed, have low incomes, live in poor housing, have poor health and be the victims of crime'

> (Social Exclusion Unit 1998)

Interestingly, whilst Dutt & Phillips (2000) acknowledge that there is no difference in the cognitive or educational capacity of black children as compared to their white counterparts, they explain that children of African-Caribbean origin are four times more likely to face permanent exclusion from school. Unlike excluded children generally, Kundnani (1998) found that African-Caribbean children who had been excluded from school tend:

- to have higher than average ability
- to exhibit less evidence of deep-seated trauma
- to have been less disruptive from early on in their school career.

The link between educational achievement and future health prospects means that we should be concerned by this information. The question is whether or not we are. And if we are, how does our concern translate into practice? Of note is the fact that in 1999 the Royal College of General Practitioners (RCGP) did not break down consultation data to reveal patterns by ethnicity, although social class was employed as an explanatory variable. Despite this oversight, which might be remedied in the future, the RCGP (1999) report makes particularly interesting reading when considered against the detail of the chapter thus far. For example, patients under 15 years comprise 20% of the average general practitioner's list with the under-4s being the most frequent users of the service (RCGP 1999). The most common reason for visiting the GP was for upper and lower respiratory tract conditions. The health of children from the lower social classes was acknowledged as being less robust – influencing their need to access provision more frequently (RCGP 1999). One wonders what the picture would be like if the children of asylum seekers, gypsies and travellers were able to access health care provision with ease and if ethnicity was accounted for in the statistics?

INITIATING CHANGE: GOVERNMENT SPONSORED SCHEMES

Up to this point in the chapter, the portrayal of children's lives in the UK whilst not wholly bleak, is less rosy then might have been imagined given the articles set out in the UN Convention (1991) and the government's espoused commitment to uphold them (Cook 2001). Yet it is all too easy to concentrate on what is wrong, rather than on positive measures designed to promote social change and improve health. As Kmietowicz (2001) concedes, simply by acknowledging the reality of poverty for some children, the government is taking action that might be viewed as beginning the process by which the playing field will be levelled.

Other steps have been taken too. A Children's Taskforce and National Service Framework (NSF) have been set up to improve the health and lives of children and young people (Carlisle 2003; DOH 2002; DOH 2004). Moreover, the Taskforce's director is charged with the responsibility of ensuring that the standards set out in the NSF connect with initiatives in other government departments (Carlisle 2003). The worthy aspiration of joined up thinking and working might just become a reality. In fact, perhaps it is already happening in one area of activity – Sure Start. As Healy (2003) explains, Sure Start aims to work with parents-to-be, parents and children to promote:

'the physical, intellectual and social development of babies and young children – particularly those who are disadvantaged – so they can flourish at home and when they get to school, and thereby break the cycle of disadvantage for the current generation of young children'

Yet Sure Start is neither a quick fix solution, nor is it a 'one size fits all' in its approach. Each of the 500 programmes is local in its orientation, seeking to listen to the local community, involving its members in making it work (Healy 2003). Resourced with an annual budget of £500 million, it brings together health workers, early-years providers and voluntary agencies to deliver accessible, necessary services in community venues and on a peripatetic basis (Healy 2003). As an initiative, Sure Start appears to have the potential to enable change, by tackling poverty and disrupting cycles of disadvantage – however each of the programmes requires long-term evaluation in order to demonstrate that benefits outweigh costs. For now, Sure Start represents both an exemplar of cross-silo working and a model of best practice because of its intention to listen to local communities and individual people, a theme picked up and actioned by the Department of Health (2002) in its Listening, Hearing and Responding document.

Having acknowledged the commitment of all government departments to give children and young people 'a real say and real choices about Government policies and services that affect them', *Listening, Hearing and Responding* (DOH 2002) sets out the Department's vision as it concerns the arena of health. It promises to make sure that 'children, young people and their parents, carers and families form an integral part of their programme' and explains that in order to improve the patient's overall experience, the following themes will be looked at (DOH 2002):

- Making the overall environment safe, comfortable and friendly
- Better information and choices
- Reduced waiting times
- Creating baseline standards
- Better communication with children, young people and parents
- Parents fully engaged in decisions about their child's treatment and care.

It would be churlish to argue the spirit of the Department of Health's (2002) vision. The pursuit of each theme is laudable. The commitment to work with and not for children and young people is exemplary, not least because it indicates a concern for a sector of the population which does not have the right to vote and can therefore be seen to lack power. And yet, careful reading of the document suggests a narrowness of focus within which health and wellbeing are attached to health service provision, rather than being understood as twin pillars that facilitate the enjoyment of life, wherever children and young people engage with life.

It is also less than clear the extent to which health care providers are to be prepared for a re-orientation of service delivery that 'puts patients at the heart of everything it does' (DOH 2002). True, but it is the case that the sentiments of the Department's vision agree with those presented in the *NHS Plan* (DOH 2000), *Liberating the Talents* (DOH 2002) and the *National Service Framework for Children, Young People and Maternity Services* (DOH 2004). There too the rhetoric speaks of patient-centredness. Lobbied from all quarters, as each new government-sanctioned directive appears, perhaps the expectation is that the cultural change mentioned as being necessary in *Listening, Hearing and Responding* (DOH 2002) will evolve, so that health care providers will no longer need to learn new ways of thinking and working. Rather they will be inlaid into their collective psyche. Maybe one day, children and their families will be the primary motivator for action without having to think about it.

Primary care focused as it is, *Liberating the Talents* (DOH 2002) is noteworthy across the community of nursing and midwifery because its goals can readily be extrapolated. Having recognized that nurses, midwives and health visitors together constitute the largest workforce in the NHS, and acknowledged their importance in patient's journeys 'across sickness and health, home and hospital, birth and death' (DOH 2002), it explains (p. 34): 'our objective is to liberate the talents and skills of all the workforce so that every patient gets the right care in the right place at the right time'.

It goes on to note that necessary changes in service delivery present nurses, midwives and health visitors with challenges and opportunities and suggests that three core functions should be provided:

1. First contact/acute assessment, diagnosis, care, treatment and referral.
2. Continuing care, rehabilitation, chronic disease management and delivering NSFs.
3. Public health/health protection and promotion programmes that improve health and reduce inequalities.

Just as was the case in the *NHS Plan* (DOH 2000), it is evident in Liberating the Talents that the government has faith in the capacity of nurses, midwives and health visitors to facilitate change. Yet an analysis of the Chief Nursing Officer's interpretation of role development as set out in the *NHS Plan* (2000) can be interpreted as essentially task-focused. Thus whilst the rhetoric might speak of the primacy of the patient, as any nurse who lived the tradition of task centred care will know, it is easy to lose sight of the person in the pursuit of task acquisition and delivery. It is also possible that a series of tasks can connect together so as to be patient-centred, smoothing the patient's journey through their experience of health care. The *NHS Plan* (DOH 2000) and *Liberating the Talents* (DOH 2002) looked towards the introduction of the new GMS contract, the reduction in doctors' hours and changes in medical education. The role development envisaged for nurses can indeed liberate their potential, but more importantly, benefit patients.

If new ways of working are to be found, as the Department of Health (DOH 2003) is convinced is necessary, then there are templates for nurses keen to expand their practice. One template is that of the nurse practitioner. Against a 40-year history with ample evidence from both sides of the Atlantic to persuade doubters of its promise, the role of the nurse practitioner is well placed to address known and impending problems and to advance the practice of nursing. Despite criticisms of its limitations – which centre on the mistaken belief that it is a role which simply substitutes for medicine – the breadth of possibilities set out by the RCN (2002) clarifies its potential (see Chapter 21). The issues of childhood obesity and mental health in children will be considered next as exemplars to illustrate the contribution NPs can make to child health.

THE NURSE PRACTITIONER'S ROLE IN CHILD HEALTH

CHILDHOOD OBESITY: AN EVOLVING EPIDEMIC?

Children have high energy requirements because they are growing. However, as BUPA (2004) explains, like adults, if they take in more energy in the form of food than they use, the extra energy will be stored as fat. Recent estimates suggest that 1 in 12 6-year-olds can be classified as obese (Buckland 2003). Lee's (2004) assessment adds to the concern.

He suggests that 19% of 5-year-olds and 33% of 15-year-olds are overweight. According to the BMJ (2001) obesity in children in the UK is on the increase but it is not just confined to school-aged children and teenagers. Citing research in which weight, height, sex and age data were used to calculate the body mass index (BMI) of 2–4-year-olds, it reported that more preschool children were obese and overweight in 1998 than in 1989 (Disability UK 2004). Between 1989 and 1998, the percentage of overweight preschool children rose from 14% to 23% (Disability UK 2004). During the same time frame there was no increase in the weight and height of the target group.

The trend is not confined to the UK. Black (2004) reports that in China obesity levels have risen by 20% and in the USA they have doubled. Startlingly, in Brazil figures have trebled (Black 2004). Given these data, it should not be surprising to find that the subject of childhood obesity is 'hot' in the press, across public and professional publications. Explanations and remedies abound. Brazil's epidemic, for example, is explained by the country's rising gross domestic product and greatly increased television use (Black 2004). Interestingly, although Drummond (2003) is convinced that the causes of obesity are multifactorial, she argues that high fat diets and low levels of physical exercise cannot be ignored. BUPA (2004) agrees, noting that very few children are overweight because of an underlying medical problem. Rather it is their life style which is implicated, an experience that they are likely to share with their parents and siblings – which explains why children are more likely to be overweight if their parents are obese (BUPA 2004). Lee (2004) subscribes to the same view, noting that 'for the majority of children, a combination of diet, environment and lifestyle is to blame'.

In sharp contrast, drawing on data from the Avon Longitudinal Study of Parents and Children, Emmett (2002) explains that: 'children's diets are influenced by the educational level of their mother and that groups with the least educated mothers had higher levels of obesity.' Emmett (2002) continues, arguing that: 'our findings show that it is important that health professionals have a role especially in encouraging the less educated mothers to follow best practice'.

Followed to its logical conclusion, Emmett's (2002) argument would blame health professionals who do not get the message through to mothers and on mothers who are less educated and who do not listen to what they have been told. It also risks alienation and an exacerbation of the problem. The experience of less education is associated with lower incomes (Blair et al 2003). Lower incomes can marginalize sub-groups in society and create disaffected communities who disengage from positive health messages. Perhaps there are other ways of interpreting Emmett's (2002) evidence.

For Kelly (2003), obesity is a health inequality issue. Evidence links children from poorer backgrounds with weight problems. High fat, high salt foods including confectionery are abundant, relatively cheap and targeted at children (BUPA 2004, Carlisle 2002, Wright 2002). Other factors which make it harder for low income families to eat healthily include reduced access to cheaper shopping facilities (Piachaud & Webb 1996), especially in rural areas (Caraher et al 1998), and a reluctance to try new foods for fear of wastage, combined with limited knowledge and cooking skills (Caraher et al 1998). Viewed in this way, childhood obesity in lower income groups becomes a more complex issue to address. It would be far more convenient to attribute the problem and the ensuing solution to maternal education, citing it as the single explanatory variable.

Interestingly although the association between childhood obesity and low income features in the literature, little appears to be written about the rise in obesity across the social class gradient as a whole. As a phenomenon it is constructed either as a particular group's problem or as everyone's. But perhaps it is wise to see everyone as being at risk because the health consequences are substantial. Before moving to outline the risks, it is necessary to clarify terms.

Body mass index is a measure of body fatness (Disability UK 2004), however whereas in adults it is calculated with ease using two measures (height and weight), in children, age, growth spurts and rates of development need to be accounted for (Lee 2004). Even so, the SIGN (2003) guidelines maintain the validity of BMI as a measure of obesity and explain that clinically obese children are those with a BMI > 98th centile (UK 1990 reference chart for age and sex). For epidemiological purposes, SIGN guidelines note that overweight is defined as > 85th centile and obesity as > 90th centile.

The SIGN guidelines go on to recommend that the prevention and treatment of obesity needs to be initiated in childhood, a view that is in marked contrast to that of Hume (2003), who suggests that recent responses to obesity in childhood are unnecessarily alarmist. And yet Hume concedes that illnesses associated with obesity are on the rise. Lee (2004) summarizes the health risks, noting that 'the biggest health worry for overweight children is heart disease caused by high cholesterol and high blood pressure.' BUPA (2004) is equally clear in its identification of the health problems directly attributable to childhood obesity. It too writes about cardiovascular problems – heart attacks, strokes and high blood pressure. It also warns about bowel cancer and orthopaedic problems, and in addition recognizes the psychological distress that excess weight can cause resulting in lower self-confidence and self-esteem, which can lead to isolation and depression.

Currently one particular potential outcome of obesity is attracting significant interest – the rise of type 2 diabetes, defined by Lyons (2002) as diabetes mellitus which results from a relative deficiency of, or insensitivity to, insulin. In contrast to type 1 diabetes which results from an absolute deficiency of insulin (Lyons 2002), type 2 diabetes was once considered rare in children (Engelgau 2003, Shield 2002). However, there is evidence of an epidemic of type 2 diabetes in the USA with Fagot-Campagna & Narayan (2001) reporting that between 8% and 45% of children recently diagnosed with diabetes have it and not type 1. Variations in incidence are explained by the fact that type 2 diabetes is more common in females and in individuals of non-European descent (Fagot-Campagna & Narayan 2001). Cases have been reported in the UK too (Shield 2002). Worryingly, Fagot-Campagna & Narayan (2001) are convinced that the rise of type 2 diabetes in both the adult and child populations is underestimated. Given the health risks that accompany its incidence, and the costs that ensue at a personal and societal level, it should not be surprising to find that Fagot-Campagna & Narayan (2001), amongst others, ask that obesity be treated as a public health issue.

Importantly, employing the evidence that is available, SIGN (2003) guidelines suggest that attempts to prevent obesity need to adopt interventions which target the family, the school and society. Simplistic solutions to a complex problem that eludes unidimensional explanation are to be avoided. So too it seems the desire to blame – children for not exercising, parents for buying high fat, high salt foods, families for having low incomes, local education authorities for selling school playing fields, the computer industry for marketing games that create sedentary hobbies, television adverts designed to generate 'pester power', undermining parents' intentions to buy healthier products, and so on. If obesity is to be addressed, there is a need to move on from 'finger pointing' to collaborative, multi-targeted action that values people, respects culture and does not expect immediate results. More of this shortly, first however, the chapter picks up the second health topic – childhood mental health/illness.

CHILDREN'S MENTAL HEALTH AND WELLBEING

Reviewing the literature, it is curious to see that articles which focus upon children's mental health and wellbeing are actually concerned with mental illness. It is as if mental health can be understood via what is presented as its converse. However, given the overall figures and manifestations of mental ill health in children, it is not surprising that individuals and groups want to draw attention to the problems children can and do experience.

FOCUS, a UK-based group set up in 1997 with the intention of promoting clinical and organizational effectiveness in child and adolescent mental health services, observes the rise in the incidence of mental disorders in young people since World War II (FOCUS 2004). Behavioural problems, substance abuse, eating disorders, depression and suicide are listed (FOCUS 2004). In line with data from other developed countries, FOCUS (2004) estimates that between 10% and 20% of young people have a mental disorder severe enough to cause significant impairment in functioning and to warrant treatment. Data from 2001 provides more detail in respect of one particular dimension of mental ill health – self harm (National Statistics 2001).

Defined as 'deliberately self-damaging behaviour that is not intended to be life threatening' (Bywaters & Fleet 2002), survey data identified that 1 in 17 11–15-year-olds had tried to self harm (National Statistics 2001). An unstated proportion of this number had also attempted suicide. The average age at which children begin to self harm is 13 years (Bywaters & Fleet 2002). When asked what triggered their self harm, the responses included unwanted pregnancy, being bullied at school, not getting on with their parents, parental divorce, physical abuse, bereavement and going into care (Bywaters & Fleet 2002). Methods of self harm varied and there were gender differences. For example, although 25% of all self harm involved cutting, and it was the method of choice for females, males were more likely to pick/scratch (Bywaters & Fleet 2002).

Gender differences in the experience of mental ill health are recognized by Lloyd (2003) too. His analysis focuses on males and their particular vulnerability to suicidal behaviours because they are less likely to talk to others about their problems. Citing Bennett, Lloyd (2003) urges those who work with children with mental health problems to account for gender when they develop, review and redesign services. As a result of 'thinking gender', Lloyd (2003) reports the decision taken in Dorset to move the Child and Adolescent Mental Health Services (CAMHS) out of a clinic setting into the community with the intention of enhancing access by males. Lloyd (2003) also notes that 'thinking gender' has increased service providers alertness to the issues of aggression, drug misuse and schizophrenia in the male population.

If gender needs to be accounted for in recognizing risks to mental health and wellbeing, then, so too do other sub-groups of the child population. For example, as Richardson & Joughin (2000) recognize, children in the care system have a much higher incidence of mental health problems than those in the general population. They note that mental health problems in looked-after children can lead to placement difficulties, so exacerbating the situation for individuals who find themselves back in group care facilities. Richardson & Joughin (2000) advocate the need to be proactive in order to minimize the risks to the mental health and well being of children. However, as they appreciate, to be proactive requires an alertness to the reality of mental health problems in children. Thinking this through, this would mean that rather than simply attributing 'bad' or non-conformist behaviours to their status as a child, especially if they are in their teenage years, the possibility of a problem might be considered. Depression is a case in point.

As Flach (2002) appreciates, children are as vulnerable to depression as adults and yet, it is frequently unrecognized (Flach 2002, Son & Kirchner 2000). Indeed Flach (2002) is convinced that children are more vulnerable to depression because they have had less opportunity to build up a repertoire of strengths that can enable stressors to be managed.

Son & Kirchner (2000) advise that, as is the case with adults, childhood depression can encompass a spectrum of symptoms ranging from normal responses of sadness and disappointment to severe impairment caused by clinical depression that may or may not include evidence of mania. Flach (2002) explains that depression becomes clinical depression when it occurs without obvious reason, when it is dangerously intense (as with suicide attempts), if it recurs often or persists for a long time, if it is associated with disturbing signs and symptoms or if it has a damaging effect on the child's overall adjustment at school and at home.

Risk factors include a family history of depression and poor school performance (Son & Kirchner 2000). Gender plays a part too. As Marcotte et al (2002) note, although boys are equally, if not slightly more likely to experience depression in their pre-adolescent years, girls are more vulnerable in their teenage years – a trend attributed to the stress of puberty and their (in)ability to manage it. Citing several studies conducted during the 1980s and 1990s, Jackson et al (2003) suggest that family characteristics can offer protection against stress and so limit the risk of depression. These characteristics include having positive relationships with family members, opportunities for personal growth within the family unit and the provision of a structure which includes negotiated rules.

If the possibility of depression in children is something that society needs to be alert to, then Flach's (2002) identification of possible signs and potential triggers is helpful (Box 16.3).

Depression needs to be understood in a context. It is also evident that the existence of one sign does not mean that the child is depressed. It is about pattern recognition. And it is necessary to look beyond the child to other factors that might impact on mental health.

Young Minds (2004) acknowledges that although children's mental health needs should be prioritized, they tend not to be. As it explains, of the children aged 5–15 years with a mental disorder, only 27% are in contact with specialist health services (Young Minds 2004). Young Minds (2004) reports that 50% of 26-year-olds with mental health problems first experienced problems in their childhood. Had treatment been secured at that time, it argues that problems might have been eliminated or reduced in terms of their severity. Young Minds (2004) goes on to estimate that there needs to be a four-fold increase

Box 16.3 Possible signs and potential triggers of depression in children

Possible signs
- Sad face in contrast to previously more or less happy one
- Normally talkative child becomes much less communicative
- More time spent alone
- Aimlessness and loss of interest in usual activities
- Tearfulness
- Irritability and temper outbursts in a child who has previously been affable
- Not wanting to go to school or mix with friends
- Doing poorly at school in contrast to previous performance
- Discipline problems in a child who was previously generally well behaved

Potential triggers
- Death of a family member or close family friend
- Serious open or covert conflict between the parents
- Major communication difficulties in the family unit
- Parental infidelities, separation, divorce
- Failure to perform adequately at school in studies, interpersonal adjustments or special ambitions e.g. sport
- Disabling illness
- Illness directly linked to depression e.g. thyroid disease
- Victim of physical and/or sexual abuse

in the amount of money currently invested if needs are to be met. Bolstering its case, Young Minds (2004) explains that currently the total spending is £240 million, a figure which comprises 2% of the crime budget and 7% of the adult mental health budget. It adds the following statistics to its case:

- Children with a mental health problem are 10 times more likely to get into trouble with the police
- 95% of young offenders have a mental health problem

- Children with a conduct disorder at age 10 will cost the criminal justice system £42 000 by the time they are 28 years old
- Of regular smokers aged 11–15 years, 41% have a mental health problem.

Clearly the topic of children's mental health cannot afford to be ignored by central and local government, schools, social care settings and health care providers, including nurse practitioners. However, as was evident in the exploration of childhood obesity, there are no easy answers. To promote reflection on the possibilities, this chapter employs the health promotion framework offered by Kelly et al (1993). First, however, it is necessary to define the meaning of health promotion.

DEFINING HEALTH PROMOTION

Chapter 17 presents a general discussion of this topic – here we will focus just on children. Unlike *health education* which Hall (1991) explains focuses on facilitating health related learning, Downie et al's (1990) interpretation of *health promotion* is that whilst it embraces health education it extends beyond it to enhance positive health and prevent illness via three overlapping spheres of activity – identified as health education, prevention and protection. Whereas the remit of health education is to facilitate learning, McQuaid et al (1995) explain that health promotion has three components:

- *primary* prevention, which prevents disease or injury occurring
- *secondary* prevention, which aims to stop disease/problems developing by means of early detection via organized screening programmes
- *tertiary* prevention, which seeks to prevent deterioration, if possible, and to impede progress of a disease or disability by means of appropriate treatment, rehabilitation or palliative care.

In contrast to both health education and (ill) health prevention, *health protection* is 'concerned with legal and fiscal measures, regulations and policies and voluntary codes of practice' (McQuaid et al 1995). Together, these spheres of activity combine to enable the goal of health promotion which Downie et al (1990) see as: 'The balanced enhancement of physical, mental and social positive health, coupled with the prevention of physical, mental and social ill health.'

It is a goal which seeks to reduce health inequalities and to improve the quality of life for children and their families (McQuaid et al 1995). Important aspirations, no doubt, but readers might recall that the RCN's (2002) definition of the nurse practitioner role spoke of health education, not health promotion and the intent of health education has been much critiqued. Not only is it seen to focus on the prevention of medically-defined disease, it is also perceived to be negative in its message – you should not smoke, you should not have unprotected sex, you should not eat an unhealthy diet. By concentrating on correcting the behaviour of the individual, it ignores the influence of political, cultural and societal factors that impact on children, their families and their communities and which can prove to disable the best of intentions (McQuaid et al 1995). Consequently one wonders the extent to which health education, if narrowly defined, if focused purely on behavioural change in isolation from other variables that might impact upon health, is an appropriate goal for nurse practitioners. A wider perspective – that of health promotion – might prove liberating for the role, and empowering for children, their families and the communities in which they live.

Kelly et al's (1993) model which identifies four levels of health promotion is an example of an integrated approach which has the potential to embrace initiatives that sit within the overlapping spheres of health education, (ill) health prevention and health promotion (Downie et al 1990). Consequently it has the ability to shift thinking so that it is at least as focused on what is happening 'upstream' (the causes of ill health) as it is on what happens 'downstream' (the reality of ill health) (Ashton & Seymour 1996).

To explore the possibilities afforded by Kelly et al's (1993) model, the chapter will now examine each of the four levels of health promotion (Box 16.4), suggesting opportunities for collaborative action as they link with the topics of childhood obesity and mental health and wellbeing. It will quickly become apparent that isolated initiatives are neither sought nor possible. To achieve change within the different levels of health promotion, NPs will need to connect with other agencies, including the voluntary sector, fellow health care providers and most important of all, children, their families and their worlds.

Box 16.4 Kelly et al's (1993) integrated approach to health promotion

The environmental level
The environment matters. It may be damaging. The quality of the environment directly impacts on the opportunity to enjoy health. It also provides the background within which health promotion activities take place.

The social level
Social structures provide the framework within which individuals live and behave. Communities influence the ways in which events and initiatives are perceived. Parents, families, peers, friends and the media are part of social structures.

The organizational level
Health promotion is not often the primary function of the organizations which touch and shape children's lives. For example, the school is committed to the education of the child, not health promotion. The same argument might be made about the children's ward in the district general hospital or the oncology unit in the tertiary referral centre. There the need to focus on ill health and its redress captures attention. The culture of the organization matters too.

The individual level
The importance of recognizing the child as an individual, rather than as a member of an age band, or a cultural group, or family group, is well documented, but challenging. The interests, beliefs, values, concerns, etc. of the individual can get lost because the child is situated within their family, their school, their community, their context. Subscribing to the belief that one size will not fit all might prevent the reduction of the individual into a group and the neglect of them as a person.

THE ENVIRONMENTAL LEVEL

In comparison to their peers in some parts of the world, children in the UK have a better chance of enjoying health. Immunization against childhood disease is provided without direct charge; the same is true of health care generally. Water is available on tap; housing, whether owned or rented, has to comply with set standards. Basic sanitation is an expectation rather than a surprise. And yet there is deprivation, there is evidence of disease and there is despondency (Blair et al 2003). Type 2 diabetes has been identified within the child population and despite the desire to construe it as a disease of opulence, there is evidence that it is associated with low income. One in 10 or maybe even 1 in 5 children have a mental health problem that is limiting their lives and could well impact on their adulthood.

Known links between smoking behaviours and the incidence of mental health problems almost beg for health education intervention – until it is appreciated that attempts to address what is a recognized life limiter will be worthless unless the reasons as to why the two phenomena are associated are understood. Equally it is argued that measures to protect health by increasing the taxation on tobacco will not succeed and might actually exacerbate social problems by promoting crime to pay for cigarettes – or by drawing children into health damaging behaviours involving other abused substances. Either way the environment does not improve and might degenerate. Is change possible? The literature suggests examples which assuage the risk of hopelessness.

White (2003) reports the findings of a study designed to explore the barriers to eating 'five-a-day' fruit and vegetables. Employing a focus group method, White (2003), talked with low income families living in rural settings about their perceptions of the challenge to purchase items which would then enable the recommended number of items per day to be consumed. Barriers identified included lack of availability, low income and transport problems. Solutions were suggested but interestingly did not identify the potential of a food co-operative, an option which Milner & Winspear (2004) working with children and parents in a rural school explain make it 'easier and more appealing to eat at least five portions of fruit and vegetables per day'. Most notable in the press report of the food co-op was the lack of reference to health professionals. Even so, it is argued that there is a place for the nurse practitioner in the possibility of provoking environmental change.

Reflective Exercise 1

The next time you find yourself asking someone about what they eat (and don't), find out what the barriers are for them. It is so easy to assume every one has a car and ready access to products that don't degenerate within hours. What do you know about food co-ops in your area? If there aren't any, who might you talk to in order to identify/reinforce the need for improved options?

42nd Street is a Manchester-based project established over 20 years ago. It seeks to alter the environment within which young people find themselves and to find 'creative, innovative and accessible forms of therapeutic support that reduce young people's experiences of stigma' (Lloyd 2003). Collectively funded by health, social and voluntary agencies, 42nd Street aims to create an environment within an environment in which there is space to be and accept difference.

Reflective Exercise 2

What is happening where you work? Are there mental health and wellbeing initiatives which are working to adapt the environment? Who 'owns' them? How do you inform the children and families that you meet in walk-in centres, A&Es and outpatient departments about them? If a parent talked with you, worried about their child, how would you respond? How do the initiatives you've identified make you feel? If you've looked around and seen little happening, who are you going to talk with and with what goal?

THE SOCIAL LEVEL

To belong to something, to be part of a structure and adhere to its values and order is important. The sense of belonging nestles readily alongside predictability. And yet, although social groups might create identity, they don't necessarily confer advantage. There is a hierarchy. Position is interpreted and some children, families and their communities fare less well than others. For example, despite attempts to be liberal, as the child enters the playgroup or joins the table tennis class, the fact that they are the first of four children in the family unit, each with different fathers, and of mixed race, can matter. Despite the best of intentions, it is hard not to be judgemental, a reality which can exacerbate existing divides. Sometimes it is really difficult to appreciate why pathways to health and wellbeing are not pursued. Page (2002) provides an example.

Picking up the theme of childhood obesity, Page (2002) reports an association between a reduction in television viewing and a significant decrease in the amount of fatty tissue in the child population. She goes on to talk about the need to adjust dietary intake and increase physical exercise. The onus of responsibility appears to fall on parents. The importance of parental control as regards television watching is further underlined in research undertaken by Sustain (2001) – the alliance for better food and farming – which noted that food and soft drink adverts dominate children's peak viewing times.

As Carlisle (2002) accepts, the best intentions of parents in respect of healthy eating can be undermined by TV adverts. And yet, for a raft of reasons, including parents' perceptions of unsafe environments which lead them to limit their child's physical activity outside the home, children watch TV and play computer games. However as Carlisle (2002) realizes, the negative construction of computers can be debunked. As she explains, sites promoting healthy-eating projects are accessible via the internet. One – Food Dudes (www.fooddudes.co.uk) – is specifically aimed at primary school children and uses the techniques employed by advertisers to influence their thinking – peer modelling and rewards. Now available on video, Food Dudes presents six episodes which feature the 'heroes' battling successfully with General Junk and the Junk Punks using special powers afforded by eating fruit and vegetables (Carlisle 2003). TV viewing and internet access may not be as bad as we imagine!

Reflective Exercise 3

In the area in which you practise, how easy is it for parents to provide a social setting wherein their children are encouraged to adopt a pattern of healthy eating? Do cultural beliefs sometimes make it harder? If so, why? Have you checked out the internet to see the sites that promote positive health messages? If you work predominantly with adults, to what extent are you enabling them to talk about their children and society's expectations as it concerns their children's wellbeing? The responsibilities they experience can be health damaging for them as individuals and as a family unit and so need to be appreciated.

If parents have the potential to safeguard physical health, Jackson et al (2003) would argue that they have a key role in enabling positive mental health. Again the onus is clear and potentially burdensome. Halliday (2001) reports an initiative designed to share the load. She reports on a school-based project centred in a multi-ethnic working class, high unemployment area set up in response to a realization that an increasing number of the 400 pupils aged 4–11 years were experiencing confusion in their personal lives. Funded for 1 year, the project sought to improve the self-esteem, confidence and relationships of the pupils (Halliday 2001). It also extended its focus to provide parenting skills courses for parents that evaluated positively in respect of behavioural change on their part and so enabled their relationships with their children to be enhanced. Examples cited included listening more, letting their child solve their own problems, using praise and positive approaches, demonstrating reason and the ability to compromise (Halliday 2001).

Reflective Exercise 4

Whatever your role, wherever you work, in what ways are you working to support the parent/child relationship to promote mental health and wellbeing? What about getting involved in a project like that reported by Halliday (2001)? There is evidence that a multi-agency approach enhances outcomes.

THE ORGANIZATIONAL LEVEL

Barriers and trenches create divides. They might also provide comfort because they appear to delineate roles and responsibilities and allow people to think that what sits outside their particular silo is not theirs to worry about. If it was possible to do it, it would be fascinating to know how many non-paediatric NPs are still reading this chapter. Child health, its assessment and the factors that impinge on it cannot be everyone's concern, surely? Arguably it must be, if only because children become adults. Cultural divides that separate the work of the NP from that of the school nurse, educational welfare officer, youth worker, voluntary play scheme leader, minister and the police officer, to name a few, have to be unhelpful. Child health has to be the concern of the fire fighter and housing officer, just as it should matter to the practice nurse. If health is 'out there' and some one else's business, conversations are being closed down before they even open up.

Reflective Exercise 5

Maintaining the focus on childhood obesity and mental health/illness, in the past 6 months, when have you stepped outside your particular silo to connect with other individuals/agencies who might work with you to promote child health? Or perhaps the approach was made to you in that you were invited to work with individuals/agencies outside of your 'normal' sphere of reference? Think about the barriers and trenches you have found on these journeys into other territories. Can they be addressed and if so, how?

THE INDIVIDUAL LEVEL

The individuality of the child is perhaps a central theme of modern day western culture. If so, then it would be reasonable to expect that their individual interests, beliefs, values and concerns are recognized and accounted for by those who work with them. The need to connect with, to listen and respond seems obvious. Interpretative research might provide the avenue. With this in mind, the findings of a research project, organized by the Institute of

Grocery Distributors are informative. In essence, the IGD found that children from the age of 7 years understand the need for a balanced diet, yet, like their adult counterparts they saw eating fruit and vegetables as a 'trade-off' for eating foods they perceived to be less healthy. Children reported that free gifts and other incentives would be the best way to encourage them to try a new healthy food. Interestingly, the report's author noted that 'children are a very important group of consumers ... with purchasing power in their own right' (Hutchins 2002).

Reflective Exercise 6

Like adults, children might respond to incentives. Reflecting on your area of work, how do you or could you work with the notion of individual gain to create the potential for change? What might disable your ideas? How is success accounted for in the initiatives that you have identified?

If children tell stories of individual experience, and the narratives they share as they concern mental stress this cannot be ignored. Dated now, but still instructive, Salmon et al (1998) report the effect of bullying on self-reported anxiety, depression and self-esteem in the secondary school population. Bywaters & Fleet (2002) focused on self-harm and young people's interpretation of events. Their report does not make for comfortable reading. One respondent said 'I'd rather deal with the physical pain than I would feeling really hurt and upset'. Reading what Bywaters & Fleet (2002) report, it is evident that distress wears many guises and might so easily be missed, not least if physical problems appear to be most apparent.

Reflective Exercise 7

If mental anguish can be silent in the child population, how are you ensuring that you hear and are able to respond to the distress that is experienced by children, their families and their communities?

CLOSING THOUGHTS

At heart this chapter sought to be provocative, but not in a combative way. The aim was to trigger thinking, with a view to enabling change. As it closes, readers are asked to reflect on three things. First, inequalities prevail and are worsening in the UK. Child health and wellbeing is a casualty of the divide between those who have and those who have not. Second, the role of the NP is one of many which can operate to effect change that can benefit children's lives, but to achieve such an outcome requires an open mind which embraces the concept that child health is everyone's business. Third and

finally, individual action, although laudable, is likely to be ineffective and frustrating. Collaboration across artificial divides is far more likely to reap results – but to do so NPs will need to have conversations with colleagues located in the world of health care provision, with partners in both the statutory and voluntary sectors, and of course with children, their families and their communities. In the busyness of everyday practice it is so easy to miss what is already happening 'out-there' and to appreciate what it is that matters to others. If we listen perhaps we might start to build alliances that maximize possibilities. If we do not, the risk is that we will continue to tinker on the margins to little avail. The choice is ours.

References

Alderson P, Montgomery J 1996 Health care choices: making decisions with children. Institute for Public Health Policy, London

Ashton J, Seymour M 1996 The new public health. Open University Press, Buckingham

Aynsley-Green A 2003 In: Carlisle D (2003) Building the framework. Community Practitioner 76(6):202–203

Black R 2004 Child obesity 'surging'. Online: news.bbc.co.uk/2/hi/health 10 Feb 20004

Blackwood R 2003 In: Punishing the Innocent. Save the Children. Online: www.savethechildren.org 10 Feb 2004

Blair M, Stewart-Brown S, Waterston T, Crowther R 2003 Child public health. Oxford University Press, Oxford

British Medical Journal March 3rd Online via: www.findarticles.com 10 Feb 2004

Buckland Y 2003 Six year olds facing obese future. Online: news.bbc.co.uk/1/hi/health 10 Feb 2004

BUPA 2002 Now children develop adult diabetes. Online: www.bupa.co.uk/health_information/html/ health_news/210202kidsdiabetes 10 Feb 2004

BUPA 2004 Avoiding childhood obesity. Online: hcd2.bupa.co.uk/fact_sheets/html/child_obesity 10 Feb 2004

Bristol University 2002 Issues and action in childhood obesity: media release. Online: www.bris.ac.uk/news/2002/obesity 10 Feb 2004

Bywaters P, Fleet A 2002 Self help or self harm? Mental Health Today November, 20–23

Caraher M, Dixon P, Lang T, Carr-Hill R 1998 Access to health foods: Part 1. Barriers to accessing health foods: differentials by gender, social class, income and mode of transport. Health Education Journal 57:191–201

Carlisle D 2002 Pester power. Community Practitioner 75(6):202–203

Carlisle D 2003 Building the framework. Community Practitioner 76(6):202–203

Clark C, McGregor L 2002 Learning together. Online: education.guardian.co.uk/schools/story 10 Feb 2004

Cook P 2001 Cultivating health and the UN Convention on the Rights of the Child. In: MacLachan M (ed) Cultivating health: cultural perspectives on promoting health. Wiley, London

Department of Health 2000 The NHS Plan: a plan for investment, a plan for reform. HMSO, London

Department of Health 2002 Liberating the talents. Department of Health, London

Department of Health 2002 Listening, hearing and responding. Department of Health Action Plan: core principles for the involvement of children and young people. Department of Health, London

Department of Health 2003 Getting the right start: the NSF for children, young people and maternity services – standards for hospital services. Department of Health, London

Department of Health 2004 The national service framework for children, young people and maternity services. Department of Health, London

Dimond B 1996 The legal aspects of child health care. Mosby, London

Disability UK 2004 Overweight and obese children. Online: www.disabilityuk.com/health/obesity/health 24 Aug 2004

Downie R S, Fyfe C, Tannahill A 1990 Health promotion: models and values. Oxford University Press, Oxford

Drummond S 2003 Obesity in the UK. Community Practitioner 76(3):79–80

Dutt R, Phillips M 1996 Report of the National Commission of inquiry into the Prevention of Child Abuse, Volume 2 Background Papers. HMSO, London

Emmett P 2002 Issues and action in childhood obesity: media release. Online: www.bris.ac.uk/news/2002/obesity 10 Feb 2004

End Child Poverty 2004 Plans to wipe 1 million children from poverty stats should be scrapped. Online: www.ecpc.org.uk 24 Aug 2004

Engelgau M M 2003 Epidemiology of type 2 diabetes in childhood and adolescents in North America: Possible lessons for the UK. Online: www.endocrine-abstracts.org/ea 10 Feb 2004

Fagot-Campagna A, Narayan K M V 2001 Type 2 diabetes in children: exemplifies the growing problem of chronic diseases. British Medical Journal Feb 17th Online via: www.findarticles.com 10 Feb 2004

Flach F 2002 Recognize and manage normal depression and depressive disorders in children. Healthcare Review Nov 26th Online via: www.findarticles.com 10 Feb 2004

FOCUS 2004 Child and adolescent mental health. Online: www.nelmh.org/home_child.asp 24 Aug 2004

Global Issues 2004 Understanding global issues. Online: www.global-issues.co.uk 24 Aug 2004

Hall D 1991 Health for all children, 2nd edn. Oxford Medical, Oxford

Halliday M 2001 Circles of support. Mental Health Today November,18–21

Health for Asylum Seekers and Refugees Portal (HARP) 2004 Child Info. Online: www.harpweb.org.uk 24 Aug 2004

Healy P 2003 Getting off to a sure start. Community Practitioner 76(6):204–206

Hume M 2003 A weighty worry. Online: www.timesonline.co.uk/article 24 Aug 2004

Hutchins R 2002 Children endorse health diets. Online: news.bbc.co.uk/2/hi/health 24 Aug 2004

Institute of Grocers 2002 Children endorse health diets. Online: news.bbc.co.uk/2/hi/health accessed 24 Aug 2004

Jackson Y, Sifers S K, Warreb J S, Velasquez D 2003 Family protective factors and behavioural outcome: the role of appraisal in family life events. Journal of Emotional and Behavioural Disorders. (Summer) Online via: www.findarticles.com 10 Feb 2004

Kelly M 2003 Six year olds facing obese future. Online: news.bbc.co.uk/1/health 10 Feb 2004

Kelly M P, Charlton B G, Hanlon P 1993 The four levels of health promotion: an integrated approach. Public Health 107(5):319–326

Kmietowicz Z 2001 UK sets up fund to improve child health in Commonwealth.

Kundnani H 1998 The sanction of last resort. Voluntary Voice 129. Voluntary Services Council, London

Lee H 2004 Obesity in children – a growing problem. Online: www.ivillage.co.uk/parenting/school/schealth/articles 24 Aug 2004

Lloyd M 2000 Response to the Equal Opportunities Committee Inquiry into Travelling People and Public Sector Policies. Save the Children, London

Lloyd T 2003 Big boys don't cry. Mental Health Today February,20–23

Lyons C 2002 Diabetes and young people. Community Practitioner 75(2):48–49

Marcotte D, Fortin L, Potvin P, Papillon M 2002 Gender differences in depressive symptoms during adolescence. Journal of Emotional and Behavioural Disorders (Spring) Online via: www.findarticles.com 10 Feb 2004

McQuaid L, Huband S, Parker E 1995 Children's nursing. Churchill Livingstone, Edinburgh

Milner S, Winspear L 2004 School scores top marks for healthy eating. Cumberland and Westmorland Herald

National Statistics 2001 Children: 11.7 million dependent children in England and Wales. Online: www.statistics.gov.uk.cci.nugget.asp 23 Feb 2004

National Statistics 2002 Population estimates. Online: www.statistics.gov.uk.cci/nugget.asp 23 Feb 2004

Nazroo J Y 1997 The health of Britain's ethnic minorities: findings from a national survey. Policy Studies Institute, London

Page A 2002 Issues and action in childhood obesity: media release. Online: www.bris.ac.uk/news/2002/obesity 10 Feb 2004

Pichaud D, Webb J 1996 Cited in White J 2003 Barriers to eating 'five-a-day' fruit and vegetables. Community Practitioner 76(10):377–380

Richardson J, Joughin C 2000 The mental health needs of looked after children. The Royal College of Psychiatrists, London

Royal College of General Practitioners 1999 Children and general practice. Information Sheet 13. RCGP, London

Royal College of Nursing 2002 Nurse practitioners: an RCN guide to the nurse practitioner role, competencies and programme accreditation. RCN, London

Salmon G, James A, Smith D M 1998 Bullying in schools: self reported anxiety, depression and self esteem in secondary school children. British Medical Journal Oct 3rd Online via: www.findarticles.com 10 Feb 2004

Save the Children 2004 Where we work/ England. Online: www.savethechildren.org.uk 24 Aug 2004

Save the Children 2003 Punishing the Innocent. Online: www.savethechildren.org.uk 24 Aug 2004

Scottish Intercollegiate Guidelines Network (SIGN) 2003 Management of obesity in children and young people: a national clinical guideline. SIGN, Edinburgh

Shield J 2002 Now children develop adult diabetes. Online: www.bupa.co.uk/health_information/html/health_news/210202kidsdiabetes 24 Aug 2004

Smaje C 1999 Health, race and ethnicity: making sense of the evidence. Kings Fund Institute, London

Social Exclusion Unit 1998 Bringing Britain Together: a national strategy for neighbourhood renewal. HMSO, London

Son S E, Kirchner J T 2000 Depression in children and adolescents. American Family Physician November 15th Online via: www.findarticles.com 10 Feb 2004

Stearn J 2004 Plans to wipe 1 million children from poverty stats should be scrapped. Online: www.ecpc.org.uk 24 Aug 2004

Sustain 2001 Cited in Carlisle D 2002 Pester power. Community Practitioner 75(6):202–203

United Nations 1989 United Nations Convention on the Rights of the Child. United Nations, Geneva

UNAIDS 2003 United Nations HIV and AIDS Statistics. Online: www.avert.org 10 Feb 2004

White J 2003 Barriers to eating 'five-a-day' fruit and vegetables. Community Practitioner 76(10):377–380

Wright C 2002 Hungry for success. Community Practitioner 75(11):412–413

Young Minds 2003 Briefings for politicians and government decision makers: One million children have a mental disorder. Online: www.youngminds.org.uk 26 Aug 2004

Chapter 17

Promoting health

Alison Crumbie

INTRODUCTION

Much of the work of the nurse practitioner is involved in the promotion of health. Amelia Mangay Maglacas (1991) states that the role of the nurse practitioner is to carry out a wide range of health-care services, including nursing, medical care, preventive care and health promotion. Schofield (1991) lists one of the attributes of nurse practitioners as the ability to focus on health promotion and whole-person care and Barbara Stilwell (1991) records that nurse practitioner consultations include health teaching and the exploration of clients' attitudes to follow-up and treatment. The practice of nurse practitioners encompasses the principles of health promotion; indeed, every consultation can be seen as a health-promoting opportunity.

There is much debate about the definition of health promotion and health education. Downie et al's (1996) perspective is that health education is:

*'communication activity aimed at enhancing
positive health and preventing or diminishing
ill health in individuals and groups through
influencing the beliefs, attitudes and behaviour of
those with power and of the community at large'.*

Health promotion is defined as:

*'efforts to enhance positive health and reduce the risk
of ill health through the overlapping spheres of
health education, prevention and health protection'.*

Clearly, nurse practitioners have a role to play at a variety of levels of health promotion, however, during individual consultations, the activity of nursing intervention will tend to be focused upon health education at an individual level. The purpose of this chapter is to examine a variety of approaches to promoting the health of all clients in the practice setting. Chapter 16 provides a more detailed perspective on promoting the health of one extremely important group in society, children.

HEALTH

In a survey of 9000 adults in England, Scotland and Wales, Cox et al (1987) discovered that 30% of the respondents defined health as 'not ill' or 'no disease'. Whilst it is important to remain cognizant of the perspectives of the general population, many authors have defined health as a concept which incorporates a sense of wellbeing and is not merely the absence of disease. The World Health Organization (WHO) in 1948 defined health as 'a state of complete physical, mental and social wellbeing', and in 1984 a WHO working group on health promotion defined health as: 'the extent to which an individual or group is able, on the one hand to realize aspirations and satisfy needs and on the other hand to change or cope with the environment'. Health is therefore seen as a resource for everyday life, not the objective of living – it is a positive concept emphasizing social and personal resources as well as physical capabilities. This definition has been heavily criticized for being too unrealistic and idealistic and also for implying that an individual's health status is static. Ewles & Simnett (2001) point out that life is anything but static and they suggest that health is more appropriately associated with the ability to adapt to a changing environment and with the ability to adapt to constantly changing demands, expectations and stimuli.

David Seedhouse (2001) has developed a similarly dynamic perspective on health. He states that a single uncontroversial definition of health is not waiting to be discovered. What is required is a theory of health which incorporates the multitude of possible definitions and provides us with a meaningful resource to guide our practice. In an attempt to clarify the fuzzy limits of health, Seedhouse uses an analogy which helps to clarify the objective of health-promoting interventions – the key is that work for health is work on building a solid stage, and keeping that stage in good condition. The roles that people perform, and how they choose to perform these roles upon that stage, is up to the individuals – provided that the platform is sound. This is the philosophical basis of the 'foundations theory of health' (Seedhouse 2001).

Seedhouse suggests that the most important issue is that we work to clarify the priorities of other people without imposing our own. We need to ask ourselves questions such as: 'Does this person want what I regard as health?' 'How can I find out what this person wants?' 'What am I trying to do when I work towards health promotion with this client?' In this way we avoid imposing our own values and beliefs on other people. A common understanding between the patient and the nurse practitioner can lead to clarification of the goals for health-promoting interventions.

FACTORS AFFECTING HEALTH

It is clear that ill health does not happen by chance. There are many factors which affect a person's health status. Naidoo & Wills (2000) list the main influences upon health as genetic and biological, lifestyle, environmental and social factors. The nation's health promotion activity can therefore be focused on any or all of these factors. Genetic factors used to be considered as the one area healthcare professionals could do nothing about; however, research into the human genome is creating possibilities for health promotion even at a genetic level and society will have to address the implications and the ethics of such activity. It is important to remain aware of the multiplicity of factors affecting an individual's health and therefore to consider the range of influences upon the person including family, employment, learned behaviour, health beliefs, politics, housing and available health services.

HEALTH PROMOTION

It is clear that there are a variety of definitions of health and that each client will bring his or her own definition to the consultation. Working towards an understanding of the meaning of health for the individual will help the nurse practitioner to determine the goals of nursing interventions. If we consider that health is something greater than the absence of disease, the concept of health promotion becomes an area of activity with limitless boundaries. If a client is unable to administer preventive steroid inhalers for uncontrolled asthma because s/he is unable to pay for the prescription, the focus of health promotion could be seen to be working towards an improvement in that patient's financial security. If a child attends a casualty department with injuries sustained in a car accident where she was not wearing her seat belt, the focus of health promotion could be aimed at changing the laws of our country to ensure that no child ever travels in the back of a car without a seat belt. Clearly there are several levels of health promotion activity.

The WHO has defined health promotion as 'the process of enabling people to increase control over and to improve their health' (WHO 1986). Implicit in this statement is the need to address not only individuals' specific needs but also environmental influences upon a person's health status. Health promotion according to the WHO definition is an action, and it includes activity at an individual level as well as at a national level. Health promotion is defined by Tones (1993) as the product of healthy public policy and health education, with the major function of health education being empowerment.

IMPLEMENTING HEALTH PROMOTION IN PRACTICE

HEALTH PROMOTION IN ACUTE SETTINGS

Traditionally the focus of health promotion has been seen as an activity which occurs in primary care. Nurse practitioners can also be located in hospital settings where time and resources are frequently cited as reasons for not putting health promotion into practice (Wilson-Barnett & Latter 1993). Latter (2001) points out that there is a dearth of literature relating to the role of health education and health promotion in hospital settings, and yet, the health promotion message is just as important in acute care as it is in primary care. Indeed, the patient may be having a life-changing experience during the hospital stay or in the A&E department and the nurse practitioner should be prepared to offer the health promotion message at the appropriate moment for the patient.

Latter (1993) found that nurses in acute-care settings tended to follow the traditional medical approach to health promotion. The activity of the nurses was focused on disease processes and tended to ignore the social aspects of health. Jones (1993) analyzed transcripts of taped conversations between nurses and patients and found that there

seemed to be little spontaneous health education in the acute-care setting. Jones points to the need for improvement in communication skills for nurses and that nurses themselves need to feel empowered before they are able to empower others. Wilson-Barnett & Latter (1993) came to a similar conclusion; their findings suggest that the organization of the acute-care setting should offer continuity, autonomy and responsibility and should maximize empowerment for nurses. The nurses' level of knowledge was an essential component in the process of health promotion.

Nurse practitioners who are educated to an advanced level will clearly address many of the difficulties outlined in the research above. Nurse practitioners have a level of autonomy and responsibility beyond the level of the ward-based nurses addressed in Wilson-Barnett & Latter's research and consequently should experience a greater level of empowerment. As Jones (1993) points out, to empower others it is essential for the nurse to feel empowered. Nurse practitioners should therefore work towards an organizational structure which supports not only themselves but also their nurse colleagues and other members of the health-care team.

HEALTH PROMOTION IN PRIMARY CARE

In 1978 the WHO held an international conference which resulted in the Alma Ata declaration exhorting governments to strengthen primary health care (WHO 1978). There are a variety of definitions of primary health care; most agree that it represents the first contact for community-based health care, provides open access to generalist services and takes a patient-centred, holistic approach (Coulter 1996). Nurse practitioners can often be the first point of contact for patients in primary care. Patients in this setting often present with undifferentiated undiagnosed problems. The nurse practitioner's role is to assess, diagnose, treat and discharge or refer. The nurse practitioner consultation therefore may be the patient's only interaction with the health service. It is essential then that every opportunity is taken to reinforce health promotion messages and to work towards the self-empowerment of each individual who chooses to consult with the nurse practitioner.

Primary care in the UK is dominated by general practice. Orme & Wright (1996) point out that this could potentially lead to a medical model of health promotion in the primary health-care setting. The introduction of the 1990 GP contract led to a system of remuneration for the number of health promotion clinic sessions held in the GP surgery. This approach emphasized a task-oriented style and fits neatly with the medical approach to health promotion. A diabetic clinic would be held for people with diabetes, an asthmatic clinic for people with asthma and a weight reduction or lifestyle clinic for people who need to reduce weight. This type of clinic does not provide the foundation for a holistic approach to health care and health promotion. The latest General Medical Services (GMS) contract (Department of Health 2003) for general practice services in England no longer rewards practices for the number of chronic disease clinics they hold. Instead practices are remunerated for reaching measurable targets. How they reach those targets can be determined at local level and this paves the way for nurse-led clinics that focus on the patient holistically, dealing with more than one medical condition at a time when necessary.

There is incredible potential for the practise of health promotion in each nurse practitioner consultation, whether it is in a chronic disease clinic or dealing with patients who have presented with acute problems. If a nurse practitioner views the individual client as a presenting problem then health promotion will be conducted in the traditional medical approach – which tends to address the problem in isolation from the multitude of influencing forces upon the individual. Viewed from the perspective of the individual's health beliefs and lifestyle, and as a product of genetic factors, family influences and the society in which he or she lives, the nurse practitioner will gain an understanding of the person which will help to direct the focus of health-promoting activities.

APPROACHES TO HEALTH PROMOTION

In order to work with individuals who have a wide variety of definitions of health and have numerous influences upon their health status, it is necessary to consider the range of approaches to health promotion. This will equip the nurse practitioner with a breadth of resources to draw on when working with clients in practice. Naidoo & Wills (2000) outline five approaches to health promotion: medical, behavioural, educational, empowerment and social change. Empowerment is a concept that is seen as central to the activity of health promotion by Tones (Tones 1993, Tones & Tilford 2001).

Medical approach

The medical approach to health promotion uses scientific methods to address the problems of disease and ill health. Preventive measures include immunizations and screening to allow for prevention and the early detection of medically defined illnesses. This approach relies heavily upon a national infrastructure to deliver the service and on individual compliance. The medical approach to health promotion will evaluate the level of success by the incidence and prevalence of disease.

Behavioural approach

The behavioural approach seeks to encourage individuals to adopt healthy behaviours. The individual who engages with the behavioural approach should then be at a decreased risk of developing diseases which are associated with high-risk behaviours such as smoking, consumption of alcohol, excessive consumption of fatty foods or, in some cases, sexual intercourse with no barrier protection. Health education is often focused on behaviour change and relies heavily upon the individual's willingness to adopt a healthier lifestyle. The result of the behaviour change approach should be that the individual no longer indulges in high-risk activities and ultimately that the potential diseases associated with those activities do not develop. The danger of sending out too many negative messages is, however, discussed in Chapter 17.

Educational approach

The educational approach aims to provide individuals with the knowledge and understanding necessary to make an informed choice about their health. This approach does not set out to persuade an individual to change in a certain direction; rather, the aim is to provide the individual with the information necessary to make an appropriate decision. Clearly an individual may choose not to make any lifestyle changes having understood the information provided and weighed up the pros and cons of change. This result is acceptable within the educational model as it respects the individual's right of free choice and the health educator has fulfilled his or her responsibility of providing the necessary educational content to ensure that the individual can make an informed choice.

Client–centred approach

The client-centred approach helps the client to identify concerns and priorities. The role of the health educator is to provide the client with the necessary tools and skills to set the agenda and to act upon the identified concerns. This approach sets the client firmly at the centre of the activity; the client is an equal partner in the health education process and the health promoter simply addresses the areas of concern to the client. Tones (1993) points out that it is beneficial for individuals to believe that they have some control over their lives. This sense of control can be seen as self-empowerment. Tones states that there are four factors which are central to the dynamics of self-empowerment: the environment, level of individual competency, sense of belief in control and emotional state. An individual who is empowered will be able to challenge the world and the social reality of life. The role of the health promoter is to help the individual identify areas of concern and to provide the necessary tools for the individual to make change.

Social change

Social change is directed at the environment within which a person lives. Political action is focused upon changing the social, physical or economic environment and thereby making it possible, or more likely, for individuals to make healthy lifestyle choices. An example of this top-down approach might be an organization choosing to make its premises a non-smoking area or the government introducing a greater level of taxation on cigarettes. As smoking becomes increasingly socially unacceptable, it could be suggested that individuals will be more likely to make the decision to stop smoking.

Implementing health education in practice

Preconceptual care is an area of practice which clearly involves a number of health education messages. It is possible to consider preconceptual care by linking it to each of the five different health education approaches listed above. The medical approach would be to consider the administration of folic acid to prevent the development of neural tube defects in the infant before commencing with the

pregnancy. The educational approach would involve making sure that the woman and her partner were fully aware of all the information available for people considering pregnancy. They could then make their own informed choices about lifestyle change and the adoption of healthy lifestyle behaviours based on the knowledge they have gained from the nurse practitioner. The behavioural approach would address high-risk behaviours and aim to change those behaviours, for example smoking in pregnancy or consumption of high levels of alcohol. The client-centred or self-empowerment approach would aim to identify the agenda of the woman and her partner, recognizing the importance of their own values and ideas around pregnancy. The social approach would consider community and societal influences upon the couple. Health promotion might address issues around societal expectations of smoking in pregnancy or the demands upon a woman to drink alcohol when in fact she is trying to abstain.

The approach to health promotion adopted by the nurse practitioner will be determined by the needs of the individual or, in other situations, the client group. A variety of approaches can be utilized to address any one particular issue and in some situations several approaches will be necessary to produce the desired outcome. Nurse practitioners will be involved in each approach to a varying degree. In addition to considering the variety of approaches available, it is also worth considering models of health promotion to help analyse clinical practice and evaluate outcomes.

MODELS OF HEALTH PROMOTION

A model of health promotion helps to provide a framework to analyse and guide practice. There are many models of health promotion and an individual practitioner may find one model suits the style of activity with certain clients or client groups more than another. Tones (2001) states that health promotion should primarily be concerned with helping people to gain control over their lives and health. Therefore the purpose of healthy public policy and health education should be to empower individuals and communities. A framework depicting the reciprocal relationship between community and individual empowerment can be found in Figure 17.1. Tones suggests that an individual's level of

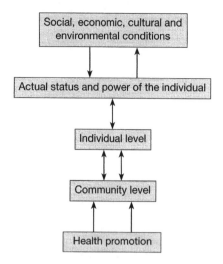

Figure 17.1 The relationship between health promotion and empowerment (adapted from Tones 2001.), reproduced with permission of Palgrave MacMillan.

empowerment is linked to their life skills, self-esteem and personal beliefs about control. Community empowerment is linked to active community participation and sense of community membership. Many nurse practitioners have worked at both the community and individual levels, for example Barbara Stilwell in her work with people who were homeless (Smith 1992), Dee Howkins, who worked with the farming community (Walsh & Howkins 2002), and Lance Gardner, who was one of the first nurse practitioners in the UK to take on a general practice that was struggling to recruit a doctor (Kenny 1997).

It is clear then that health education forms only one part of a health promotion strategy. If nurse practitioners are to be successful in working towards acceptable levels of health for each individual it is essential to consider the variety of levels of activity required to achieve the goal of optimum wellbeing. Most frequently nurse practitioners will be focusing nursing interventions on health education, self-empowerment, personal counselling and health persuasion and will less frequently be involved in the creation of legislation or public health policy. The following are examples of models which can be applied to practice and can be utilized within each nurse practitioner consultation.

THE HEALTH BELIEF MODEL

The health belief model (Becker 1984) focuses on the role of health beliefs in determining an individual's actions. This model is based on the assumption that, in order to engage in behaviour which will prevent illness and/or promote health and wellbeing, the individual must believe that:

- he or she is susceptible to the disease
- the disease is serious
- the preventive behaviour or activity will be beneficial
- the benefits of the behaviour or action will outweigh the costs.

Each person will consider the costs and benefits of a particular behaviour and engage in health actions accordingly. According to Becker (1984) an additional influence on the individual's behaviour is the presence of cues or triggers. A cue is a reminder to engage in certain behaviours.

Nurse practitioners regularly consult with patients who are overtly weighing up the pros and cons of a particular action or behaviour. The health belief model can help to refine the approach taken in the consultation and assist the nurse practitioner in understanding why some individuals may choose not to adopt a behaviour which may prevent illness or promote their general wellbeing. For example, consider a man who presents to the A&E department with an acute myocardial infarction. At this stage he will have a clear understanding that he is susceptible to heart disease; he will be experiencing the pain of infarction which emphasizes the seriousness of the problem; he will be aware that his smoking habits could be linked to his present problem and during the acute phase he could well be weighing up the advantages and disadvantages of smoking cessation. As the patient recovers from the acute phase of the illness the trigger of the pain will subside. As the memory of the crushing chest pain fades, his perception of the seriousness of his illness may also change. He may no longer believe that he is susceptible to heart disease and as time passes he may decide that his illness is not too serious. He may tell himself that the smoking probably was not linked to the infarction as he has an aunt who is in her 80s and who has smoked all her life, and after a few days at home that irresistible urge to smoke overcomes his temporarily changed beliefs during his time in hospital.

The nurse practitioner could utilize the framework of the health belief model to enhance the possibility of the patient in the above scenario engaging in health-promoting activities. The patient could be encouraged to join a cardiac rehabilitation programme which would continue to educate him about his susceptibility to the disease, the seriousness of the illness and the benefits of changing his behaviour. The patient's family could be involved in providing cues such as congratulating the patient on the number of days without smoking or working together on exercise and healthy eating. The nurse practitioner might also explain to the patient the need to monitor lipid levels, blood pressure and weight and may also explain that he should receive an annual influenza vaccination. Each of these activities would emphasize the seriousness of the disease and, according to the health belief model, this will have an influence on the patient's behaviour.

THEORY OF REASONED ACTION

Ajzen & Fishbein's (1980) theory of reasoned action is another model which can help the nurse practitioner to understand the behaviour of patients and the reasons why some choose to adopt healthy lifestyle actions and others do not (Fig. 17.2). The authors argue that behaviour is influenced by an individual's attitudes towards a certain behaviour and also by subjective norms. An individual's attitude is comprised of a belief and the strength of feeling towards this belief. For example, an individual may believe that excessive alcohol consumption causes liver damage but it does not happen often. In this example the individual holds the belief but the strength of that belief is weak. Subjective norms are the individual's perceptions of what others might think of their behaviour. If the individual's peer group believes that smoking marijuana helps to reduce stress and helps everyone

have a good time the subjective norms of the group will influence the individual's lifestyle choices. The individual's attitude and the individual's subjective norms form the two major influences creating an intention to behave in a certain manner. The intention is closely linked to the behaviour itself, although people do not always behave consistently with their intentions.

Ajzen & Fishbein (1980) separated beliefs from attitude and emphasized the importance of significant others in influencing health behaviour (Tones & Tilford 2001). This is a particularly useful model in helping to understand the behaviours of people who choose to engage in risky actions even when they have all the information and a full understanding of the implications of their behaviour. Young people who have type 1 diabetes are often labelled as non-compliant when they choose to stop their insulin injections and to go out on the town with their friends. In this example the overwhelming pressure of subjective norms outweighs the attitude toward the behaviour and, even though the intention might be to maintain the blood glucose levels, the behaviour is an overindulgence in alcohol. This results in an admission to the A&E unit with health-care professionals and parents left scratching their heads in wonderment at the futility of the behaviour.

The theory of reasoned action can be used by nurse practitioners to consider the possible outside influences which have an impact on the patient's behaviour. It may be that a woman has the belief that smoking is harmful. She may have a fairly weak strength of feeling about the harm of smoking and therefore when she is socializing with her friends who smoke regularly she will indulge in smoking behaviour. If the theory of reasoned action is applied to this situation, the patient might be advised to find an alternative to the social circle who provide the subjective norms and clearly affect her intentions. The nurse might provide literature for the patient in an attempt to enhance the strength of feeling related to the harmful effects of smoking behaviour. The theory of reasoned action provides a framework for nurse practitioners to engage in more effective health education with clients.

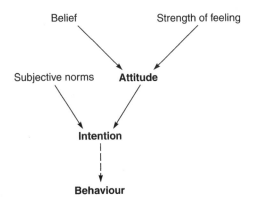

Figure 17.2 Theory of reasoned action.

HELPING PEOPLE CHANGE

It is clearly of great concern to any health-care professional involved in health promotion that if

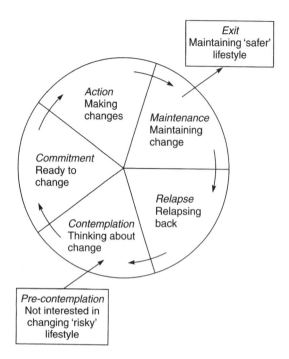

Figure 17.3 Prochaska & DiClemente's stages model of behaviour acquisition (adapted from Ewles & Simnett 2001).

changes are made towards a healthier lifestyle, those changes should be permanent. Prochaska & DiClemente (1984) developed a model of behaviour acquisition which outlines the stages involved in changing behaviour (Fig. 17.3).

In the precontemplation stage the individual has not yet become aware of the need to change. The health professional has a role here in bringing healthy lifestyle issues to the attention of the individual so that the contemplation stage can begin. The nurse practitioner could plan to provide the patient with information or could choose to confront the patient with their high-risk behaviours. The approach taken will be guided by the individual circumstances of the patient and a judgement call on the part of the nurse practitioner as to the best possible course of action with this particular client.

After precontemplation, the individual moves on to contemplation. In this stage the individual is aware of the benefits of change but may be thinking about the change and awaiting further information. S/he then becomes ready to change and may require some extra support at this stage to move on to make the change. It is possible for an individual

to take weeks or even years over any stage and s/he may move back and forth between stages until they are ready to move on. After making the change the individual may relapse and then return to the precontemplation stage. If relapse does not occur the individual has maintained the healthy lifestyle and the new behaviour is sustained. The important message for health-care professionals is that relapse may be part of the cycle and is not necessarily a sign of failure.

The stages model of health promotion, which has been widely used in primary health care, is particularly relevant in the management and support of people who are overweight and attempting to change their dietary habits. In the precontemplation stage individuals have not become aware that their weight is a potential risk to health; indeed they may even see their size as healthy. Discussing a weight-reducing diet at this stage would be a waste of time for both patient and nurse practitioner as the patient is not interested in making a change and has no awareness of the need to change. Patients may move into the contemplation stage for a variety of reasons, including objective changes in their own health such as the development of hypertension or diabetes mellitus or health problems in their friends and family. In the contemplation stage the patient has entered the cycle and has enough motivation to consider seriously changing dietary or exercise habits.

During the contemplation stage the nurse practitioner could provide the patient with dietary information to help in the decision-making process. If the patient continues to progress through the stages, the next stage is a commitment to change. At this stage the patient requires support and encouragement and may benefit from regular meetings, either with a group of other patients who have made the same decision or on an individual basis with the nurse practitioner. The patient's subsequent actions should be supported by clear goals and a realistic plan. Rewards help to promote the patient's actions at this stage; obvious rewards in the case of diabetes mellitus are the fact that the patient begins to feel better as the blood glucose falls.

Maintaining a reduction in weight can cause a great deal of anxiety and patients have to adopt coping strategies to deal with the change in their dietary habits. It is not uncommon for relapse to occur and for a previously highly motivated patient to begin to put on weight after several weeks or months of weight reduction. It is essential that the patient is made aware that this is simply one of the stages in the cycle of change and that it is common to go through several revolutions of the cycle before adopting a permanent change to lifestyle behaviours. (Indeed, Ewles & Simnett (2001) point out that on average, successful former smokers take three revolutions of change before they finally stop smoking.) At the exit stage the patient undertaking weight reduction will have made permanent alterations to dietary habits and exercise routines and will be able to maintain an acceptable body mass index without the anxiety of relapse and the struggle to maintain the behaviour changes.

The stages model of health promotion can help the nurse practitioner to support and understand the patient as they work through the change process. The problem arises when the patient is in the precontemplative stage, is unaware of the risky behaviour and is not motivated to do anything about it. Naidoo & Wills (2000) point out that there are several prerequisites to change which are worth considering when faced with a patient who refuses or is unable to change. It is important that the change is self-initiated. Telling patients that their behaviour is a risk to their health and that they must stop smoking will probably result in an angry, highly demotivated patient. It is also important that the risky behaviour becomes salient. A patient who shares a house with four student friends, all of whom smoke, will reappraise her smoking behaviour when she moves into a new house with her non-smoking partner. The smoking activity which was previously automatic and habitual has become problematic as she is now more aware of her habit; this leads to a reappraisal of her behaviour and a greater chance of moving into the contemplative stage. If the behaviour is a coping mechanism for the patient it will be extremely difficult to change. In this case the patient needs to consider alternative coping strategies. It is not always easy to find alternatives to smoking; however, some people find that chewing gum at times when they would have smoked or engaging in diversions such as exercise or other activities can help.

Naidoo & Wills (2000) point out that there is a limit to an individual's ability to change. Lifestyle change is stressful and if life is problematic and uncertain then the capacity to cope with change is limited. Social support is essential to reinforce the need for behaviour change and to maintain the change. Nurse practitioners need to consider all the prerequisites for change and to ensure that the patient has adequate support. Only then can success be achieved in the form of reduction of risky lifestyle behaviours and the promotion of health.

EVALUATION

Nurse practitioners who engage in health promotion activities either as individual practitioners or as a member of a health-care team must be aware that evaluation of their practice is essential. Evaluation helps to demonstrate whether a particular programme has achieved its stated aims. It is often extremely difficult to determine whether the number of clients who received advice about exercise and coronary heart disease actually remained free of heart disease. There are so many other potential factors to consider that absolute proof is often elusive. Attempts must be made to develop overall aims and objectives of a particular health-promoting activity and then to measure outcomes against measurable objectives. For example, a practice might decide that the primary health-care team will target the prevention of heart disease as a specific programme of activity. The aims and objectives of the programme might be developed by the team before a plan of activity is developed:

Aim
- To reduce the incidence of coronary heart disease in the practice population

Objectives
- To enhance awareness of the risk factors for heart disease
- To reduce the number of people who smoke in the practice population
- To reduce the number of people with a body mass index over 25

Measures
- The incidence of heart disease in the practice will be monitored and reduced
- Patients will be able to describe what the risk factors for heart disease are when asked
- Numbers of people who smoke in the practice can be recorded and reduced
- Numbers of people with a body mass index over 25 can be recorded and reduced.

It is clear that it may take a decade of sustained health promotion to produce any recordable results relating to the aim of the programme; however, other objectives such as number of people with a body mass index over 25 in the practice population can easily be recorded and the number before the programme was initiated can be compared with the number of people after 12 months of targeted health promotion. Evaluation of health promotion programmes is a complex process, yet without evidence it is difficult to be sure of the value of activities carried out in practice.

This chapter has provided an overview of the meaning of health and illness, health promotion and health education. Several approaches to health education and models of health promotion have been presented to provide a framework to help guide activity in practice. Whilst it is clear that health promotion is a multidisciplinary, multilevel activity many clients require continued individualized support to work towards a healthy lifestyle. Nurse practitioners working in both the primary health care and hospital setting are ideally placed to offer that support.

References

Ajzen I, Fishbein M 1980 Understanding attitudes and predicting behaviour. Prentice-Hall, Englewood Cliffs, New Jersey

Becker M H (ed) 1984 The health belief model and personal behaviour. Charles B Sack, Thorofare, New Jersey

Coulter A 1996 Why should health services be primary care-led? Journal of Health Service Research Policy 1(2):122–124

Cox B D et al 1987 The health and lifestyle survey: preliminary report. The health promotion trust. Cited in: Katz J, Peberdy A 1997 Promoting health knowledge and practice. The Open University/Macmillan, Basingstoke

Department of Health 2003 General Medical Services Contract. The Stationary Office, London

Downie R S, Tannahill C, Tannahill A 1996 Health promotion models and values, 2nd edn. Oxford University Press, Oxford

Ewles L, Simnett I 2001 Promoting health. A practical guide, 5th edn. Balliére Tindall, Edinburgh

Jones K 1993 Opportunities for health education: an analysis of nurse-client interactions in acute areas. In: Wilson-Barnett J, Macleod J (eds) Research in health promotion and nursing. Macmillan, London

Kenny C 1997 Fighter pilots. Nursing Standard 93(45):14–15

Latter S 1993 Health education and health promotion in acute settings: nurses, perceptions and practice. In: Wilson-Barnett J, Macleod J (eds) Research in health promotion and nursing. Macmillan, London

Latter S 2001 The potential for health promotion in hospital nursing practice. In: Scriven A, Orme J (eds) Health promotion professional perspectives, 2nd edn. Palgrave, New York

Mangay Maglacas A 1991 A global perspective. In: Salvage J (ed) Nurse practitioners working for change in primary health care nursing. Kings Fund, London

Naidoo J, Wills J 2000 Health promotion. Foundations for practice, 2nd edn. Balliére Tindall, London

Orme J, Wright C 1996 Health promotion in primary health care. In: Scriven A, Orme J (eds) Health promotion professional perspectives. Macmillan, London

Prochaska J O, DiClemente C 1984 The transtheoretical approach: crossing traditional foundations of change. Harnewood, Illinois

Schofield T 1991 Commentary. In: Salvage J (ed) Nurse practitioners working for change in primary health care nursing. Kings Fund, London

Seedhouse D 2001 Health. The foundations for achievement, 2nd edn. John Wiley, Chichester

Smith S 1992 The rise of the nurse practitioner. Community Outlook November/December:16–17

Stilwell B 1991 An ideal consultation. In: Salvage J (ed) Nurse practitioners working for change in primary health care nursing. Kings Fund, London

Tones K 1993 The theory of health promotion: implications for nursing. In: Wilson-Barnett J, Macleod Clark J (eds) Research in health promotion and nursing. Macmillan, London

Tones K 2001 Health promotion: the empowerment imperative. In: Scriven A, Orme J (eds) Health promotion professional perspectives, 2nd edn. Palgrave, New York

Tones K, Tilford S 2001 Health education effectiveness, efficiency and equity, 3rd edn. Nelson Thornes, Cheltenham

Walsh M, Howkins D 2002 Lessons from a farmers' health service. Nursing Standard 16(16):33–40

Wilson-Barnett J, Latter S 1993 Factors influencing nurses, health education and health promotion practice in acute ward areas. In: Wilson-Barnett J, Macleod J (eds) Research in health promotion and nursing. Macmillan, London

World Health Organization 1948 Preamble of the constitution of the World Health Organization. Cited in: Katz J, Peberdy A 1997 Promoting health knowledge and practice. Macmillan, Basingstoke

World Health Organization 1978 Alma Ata declaration. Cited in: Katz J, Peberdy A 1997 Promoting health knowledge and practice. Macmillan, Basingstoke

World Health Organization 1984 Report of the working group on concepts and principles of health promotion. Cited in: Katz J, Peberdy A 1997 Promoting health knowledge and practice. Macmillan, Basingstoke

World Health Organization 1986 Ottawa charter for health promotion. Cited in: Katz J, Peberdy A 1997 Promoting health knowledge and practice. Macmillan, Basingstoke

Chapter 18

Assessment and management of the patient with chronic health problems

Alison Crumbie

INTRODUCTION

Whether based in a hospital or a primary health-care setting, nurse practitioners will be constantly interacting with people who live with chronic conditions. Longevity and the impact of medical progress and social reform upon people who previously might have died from their disorder or would have faced a life in care have resulted in chronicity becoming an ordinary feature of family life (Cole & Reiss 1993). Some nurse practitioners may find that a major focus of their role involves taking responsibility for people who are chronically ill. Other nurse practitioners may not specifically be involved in the management of the condition but they will still have to consider the effect of the chronic condition on the presenting complaint. The aim of this chapter is to consider the meaning of chronicity and its impact upon the care of people who consult with nurse practitioners. Issues at both an individual and organizational level will be considered.

CHRONIC CONDITIONS

People who live with a chronic condition live with a permanent alteration in their way of existing in the world. Most people live with rather than die from a chronic condition (Verbrugge & Jette 1994). There are a variety of definitions of chronicity. Lyons et al (1995) state that a chronic illness is not a singular event, rather it signifies a set of complex processes that develop and endure over time. Cameron & Gregor (1987) argue that chronic illness is a lived experience which involves a permanent deviation from the norm caused by unalterable pathological changes. Bleeker & Mulderij (1992) speak of the body losing its silence and Morse et al (1994) describe a body in dis-ease. Clearly chronicity involves a heightened awareness of the physical self which permeates the whole being.

PHYSICAL IMPLICATIONS

The body changes in chronic illness and can be seen as letting the person down (Kelly & Field 1996). Many chronic conditions, such as thyroid disorders, diabetes, cardiovascular diseases and inflammatory disorders, affect the whole body. The high blood glucose levels found in diabetes mellitus, for example, affect the macrovascular system, the microvascular system, the nerves and each individual cell and hence it has an effect on the whole body. The person living with a chronic condition therefore has to deal with a complexity of effects resulting from the one disease process.

In addition to the multiple physical implications of living with a chronic condition, the patient is also likely to have to deal with the physical effects of treatment regimes. People with diabetes for example have to learn to monitor their blood glucose levels and therefore have to learn to use finger pricking devices and blood glucose monitors. They may also have to learn to inject themselves with insulin and therefore have to cope with the difficulties of injecting in public, or carrying equipment on planes and remembering to administer the medications at the right time, in the right location and in the right quantity. Other people with chronic illnesses have to learn to manage complex medication regimes such as the numerous inhalers used in chronic obstructive airways disease or the moisturizers and steroid creams used in eczema. The physical impact of living with a chronic condition can affect a patient on many levels and certainly adds to the complexity and stress associated with the patient's life.

SELF-CONCEPT AND PERSONAL RELATIONSHIPS

The patient who lives with a chronic problem experiences a change in self-concept associated with the physical changes which occur in the body. Jerret (1994) states that a chronic condition results in a reappraisal of functioning and health, while Price (1996) makes an interesting connection between the patient's case notes and the experience of chronic illness. He states that 'as the case notes get fatter so does the catalogue of experiences and with each successive passing year the redefinitions of what happiness and hope means'. The changes in self-concept, reappraisal of life and redefinitions of hope and happiness clearly impact upon the person's relationship with family, friends, health-care professionals and the world. Lyons et al (1995) state that health challenges can threaten the stability of close relationships. Roles and responsibilities alter and changes in autonomy can cause additional stressors within the relationship. Lyons describes illness as removing the window dressing of everyday life, leading to the exposure of elements in a relationship which are of central importance. This can ultimately strengthen and improve a relationship or the subsequent emotional distress may compromise the links between individuals.

Relationships are under threat from chronic conditions. However, a relationship can also be a source of strength and support for the person who has the chronic condition and can be an additional beneficial tool in the nurse practitioner's interventions aimed at promoting coping strategies. While there is no comprehensive model detailing strategies for relationship-focused coping, Lyons et al (1995) suggest that the re-evaluation of self and relationships, the containment of the impact of illness on relationships, network modelling, relationship adaptation, relationship reciprocity and communal coping, provide a viable framework for relationship coping.

The nurse practitioner can help individuals and their families to cope more effectively by considering the issues raised in Lyons et al's framework. Recognizing the importance of significant others and therefore involving them in the process of education at the point of diagnosis can be helpful. It can also be helpful to acknowledge the likely impact of a diagnosis on relationships and therefore the nurse practitioner can introduce this as a topic of conversation with patients – thereby providing them with the opportunity to explore these issues and be more alert to the potential problems that could occur in their relationships. It can be helpful to think of the diagnosis of a chronic condition as a diagnosis for the family rather than simply for the individual patient.

SPIRITUALITY

Having considered the physical effects of chronic illness, the social impact and the effect it might have upon family relationships, the nurse practitioner might also consider the spirituality of the person who lives with a chronic condition. In Heriot's discussion about spirituality and ageing (1992) she states that:

'Even though physical functions decline with ageing, the spiritual dimension of life does not succumb to the ageing process even in the presence of debilitating physical and mental illness.'

This statement has interesting connotations for people who live with a chronic condition. In the presence of debilitating illness a person can still achieve a sense of wellness. Pilch (1988) states that wellness spirituality is:

'a way of living, a lifestyle that views and lives life as purposeful and pleasurable, that seeks out life sustaining and life enriching options to be chosen freely at every opportunity and that sinks its roots deeply into spiritual values or specific religious beliefs.'

The nurse practitioner therefore should not only consider the physical manifestations of the chronic illness but should also focus attention on the individual's sense of meaning and purpose in life. By focusing upon spiritual wellbeing a person can feel well even in the presence of disability and ill health.

ASSESSMENT OF PEOPLE WHO LIVE WITH CHRONIC CONDITIONS

Chronicity then has an enduring quality; it permeates a person's whole being and affects relationships. Chronic illness is a condition with which a person has to learn to live; it represents a permanent alteration and affects the physical, mental, social and spiritual wellbeing of the person. Examples of chronic conditions are asthma, epilepsy, cardiovascular disease, arthritis, diabetes mellitus, psoriasis, cancer, multiple sclerosis, Parkinson's disease, AIDS/HIV, thyroid disease, chronic back pain, a bipolar disorder of mental health and stroke, to name but a few.

It is clear from this list of conditions that the impact of the illness will vary enormously according to the perceived level of intrusion of the illness into the person's life. A person with type I diabetes constantly has to inject with insulin – indeed, their life depends upon it – and the individual's sense of self will become intricately tied into the routines associated with the management of blood glucose levels.

However, the nurse practitioner cannot presume that the patient will necessarily view the management of the insulin regime as intrusive. Some patients may have lived with diabetes for so many years that they find the management of the condition less intrusive than one might expect. They learn to live with their condition and the injections simply become a part of everyday life. A person with acne, however, (whose treatment regime is less complicated and physically intrusive than that of the person with diabetes) may feel that their condition is obvious to the world and this can have an overwhelming impact upon their wellbeing.

The care of people who have a chronic condition represents an exciting challenge for nursing. Not only do they require medical interventions to improve their physical functioning, they also require the skills of nursing to be sensitive to their needs, offer appropriate levels of assistance, include the person as a partner in care and provide a flexibility that acknowledges the individuality of each person who presents with the condition. McBride (1993) states that the care of people who have a chronic condition is central to the mission of nursing and Funk et al (1993) describe it as being at the heart of nursing. Nolan & Nolan (1995) state that the medical model is appropriate when cure is the aim and yet so often in the management of chronic conditions cure is not the aim. Nurse practitioners have the skills and a variety of models of care which can be utilized to address the various levels of need for people who live with chronic conditions.

Kelly & Field (1996) state that the management of physical problems in chronic illness is at the epicentre of the coping experience. Social coping, family relationships and spiritual wellbeing all depend on ability to cope with the physical body. Conversely, it could be argued that spiritual wellbeing can have a positive impact on the individual's ability to cope with the physical manifestations of the disease process. Indeed, Leetun (1996) points out that no amount of body healing will work if the spirit is not also healed. In a study of women with advanced breast cancer, Coward found that self-transcendence directly affected emotional wellbeing and that emotional wellbeing led to a reduction in illness distress (Coward 1991). The following framework for assessing people who live with chronic conditions will take a holistic approach considering physical wellbeing, social coping, family relationships and spiritual health, recognizing the impact of each upon the other.

HISTORY-TAKING FOR PEOPLE WHO LIVE WITH A CHRONIC CONDITION

History-taking has been addressed in Chapter 2. History-taking in people who live with a chronic condition should follow the same structured format as for any person in the health-care setting. It is vitally important that the nurse practitioner creates the space for individuals to tell their story. People who live with chronic conditions will have had many interactions with people in the health service and are often more expert in the assessment and management of their condition than the myriad of health-care professionals with whom they interact.

CHIEF COMPLAINT

The nurse practitioner must consider if the chief complaint is associated with the underlying condition and if not, what its impact might be upon the chronic condition. It is important to ensure that an awareness of the chief complaint does not cloud the judgement in making a clinical assessment. It is equally important that the nurse practitioner does not forget to consider the possible impact of the condition upon the chief complaint. This becomes particularly complex in the management of people who have more than one chronic condition, such as people who have diabetes mellitus and coronary heart disease or people who have hypertension and chronic obstructive airways disease.

In answer to the question 'what brought you here?' the patient may immediately identify the chronic condition as the source of the presenting problem when it may not necessarily be so. Conversely, the patient may not have made the connection between the chief complaint and the chronic condition. For example, a patient who presents with a sore throat and who has hypothyroidism may have a throat infection or may be experiencing a sore throat due to the presence of a goitre. The nurse practitioner must be alert for all possibilities and therefore a structured and thorough history-taking approach is essential in making an accurate diagnosis.

PRESENT PROBLEM

A detailed analysis of the presenting problem will begin to help differentiate between the chronic condition and the presenting problem or may link them together. Exploring issues around current health status and health status before the presenting problem became an issue will provide clear clues about the impact of the chronic condition on the presenting problem and/or the impact of the presenting problem on the chronic condition. The PQRST framework (p. 18) is a useful tool for this purpose.

Palliation

It is important to explore with the patient what interventions have been tried to improve the condition, what medications have been used and what impact they have had. People who live with chronic conditions may have tried altering their own medications before seeking help – for example, just taking a few extra thyroxine tablets to help arrest weight increase or increasing antihypertensive agents if the person experiences headaches. Patients have their own rational decision-making process for trying such interventions and the nurse practitioner must be alert to this to ensure that alterations in medications are properly evaluated.

Provocation

Exploring the issues of provoking factors with the individual can help the nurse practitioner identify links between the problem and the chronic condition. Individuals may have their own ideas about the cause of the problem and this should be explored with them to give them a clear message that the nurse practitioner values their input to the assessment process.

Quality or quantity

Asking patients to describe the problem in their own words will help the nurse practitioner to assess the patient's level of concern. This is particularly important in people who live with chronic conditions as the patient can often learn to live with extraordinary levels of discomfort. The onset of symptoms may be gradual and insidious and it is therefore essential to carry out an accurate assessment.

Region or radiation

Asking the patient to locate the source of discomfort and what region of the body it radiates to is particularly helpful in differentiating between sources of pain. This is an important aspect of the assessment in people who suffer from a skin disorder. The nurse practitioner should consider the whole body and ask appropriate questions to determine if the patient is experiencing symptoms in areas beyond the immediately obvious.

Severity scale

An accurate assessment of the type and level of severity of the presenting problem is essential in obtaining a clear picture of the progression or regression of problems for people who have chronic illnesses. This is particularly important in the management of chronic pain and an assessment tool should be utilized to help provide a subjective and objective measurement of the level of discomfort.

Timing

Exploration of the timing of the presenting problem is valuable in the assessment of any problem for a person who has a chronic condition. Timing can relate to time of year. This is particularly important in the assessment of people who have allergic conditions. Timing in the week can help make links between environmental triggers in asthma, for example, or occupational hazards leading to repetitive strain injuries. Timing in the day will be particularly valuable when considering the impact of medications upon the presenting problem. For example, night-time restlessness or diaphoresis in people with type I diabetes mellitus may lead the nurse practitioner to consider the timing and dosage of insulin injections.

PAST MEDICAL HISTORY

This is of particular importance in the assessment of people who have a chronic condition. The patient may have experienced the presenting problem before and may have a clear idea of how to treat it. Exploring the patient's past medical history will help to piece together the complex picture of his or her current health status. Past illnesses, immunizations, allergies, surgery, medications and mental health status all contribute towards the patient's ability to cope with the presenting complaint and will also have an impact upon his or her perception of the complaint.

FAMILY HISTORY

In taking a history from someone with a chronic condition it is important to enquire about other family members and their health status. A person who has been diagnosed with ischaemic heart disease may have a high level of anxiety if other family members have experienced debilitating illness associated with heart disease and may logically assume that the same will happen to them. However, a person who has been diagnosed with diabetes mellitus may have family members who have had no ill effects from their diabetes and have continued to eat whatever they like. Clearly this will have an effect upon the patient's perception of their problem and this issue should be explored in order to address any anxieties or concerns. Some patients may be concerned about the implications of their diagnosis for their children and grandchildren. Knowledge about familial tendency or the potential for the genetic inheritance of a particular disorder is essential if the nurse practitioner is going to advise patients appropriately. In diabetes, for example, there is a familial tendency which is particularly associated with the development of type 2 diabetes. The patient can then be advised to encourage their children to be tested for diabetes regularly – then if the disorder does develop in the patient's offspring they could benefit from an early diagnosis and rapid intervention at the onset of the disease.

PERSONAL AND SOCIAL HISTORY

The patient's culture, financial situation, personal values and beliefs, occupation, home environment, religion, spiritual beliefs, general life satisfaction and support networks are all important to help determine the impact of the complaint upon the wellbeing of the individual. Spirituality is a particularly important aspect of the personal assessment as it assists the nurse practitioner in determining the level of personal distress an individual may be experiencing.

Leetun (1996) suggests that an assessment of wellness spirituality can be carried out by utilizing a wellness spirituality protocol. The protocol includes an assessment of clinical presentation and an evaluation of self-actualization activities, connectedness activities, healing and new life activities and religious or humanistic activities. A person who lives with a chronic condition should be assessed for spiritual wellbeing as many of the problems which may emerge in an assessment of personal and social history could be addressed by creating a treatment plan which is focused on reducing the spiritual distress of the individual. For example, a patient may state that s/he feels out of touch with the world and that the chronic condition has resulted in a withdrawal from society. The nurse practitioner may be able to suggest support groups or voluntary organizations to improve connectedness. A person who states that finances are the main concern could be offered benefits counselling from the appropriate source. A tool such as the wellness spirituality protocol can be utilized at an appropriate moment or the nurse practitioner can use it as a mental framework throughout the history-taking process.

REVIEW OF SYSTEMS

A review of the systems will be guided by the presenting complaint and/or the chronic condition. Chronic conditions tend to affect several body systems or, in some cases, all body systems. The review of the systems is particularly appropriate in this situation. Of particular importance is an assessment of mental health. The nurse practitioner should ask about mood changes, sleep disturbances, depression and ability to concentrate. Living with a chronic condition, particularly chronic pain, can lead to alterations in mental health status. Callaghan & Williams (1994) state that living with a chronic illness affects the psychosocial aspects of a person's life. Psychosocial effects include anxiety, feelings of fear, uncertainty and decreased self-esteem. Any of these outcomes will adversely affect other treatment plans and therefore taking a focused history from a person who lives with a chronic condition will not be complete without a full review of systems.

SEXUAL HISTORY

A sexual history is an important consideration in many nurse practitioner consultations. In the management of people with chronic conditions it is particularly important. Many chronic conditions adversely affect a person's ability to achieve an optimum level of sexual health. The nurse practitioner should be sensitive to this issue and create a safe and open therapeutic environment so that the patient feels able to discuss such sensitive issues. The question: 'in what way has your condition affected your sexual relationships?' is open and may pave the way for a discussion around sexual

health and sexuality. This is clearly an important consideration in consultations with men who live with diabetes mellitus as erectile dysfunction is a common complication. The same is true for people who live with skin disorders as their bodily appearance can be a source of great damage to their self-esteem and identity and hence their sexual health.

COMPLIANCE AND CONCORDANCE

Members of an expert nurse advisory group responded to the findings of a study into diabetes nurse specialists' views of changes in the NHS, by stating that compliance is almost an obsession in chronic disease management (Healey 2000). Nurses can spend a great deal of time and energy persuading patients to be compliant with the treatment regime for their particular condition and the suggestion is that there may be more appropriate ways of working with people who live with chronic illnesses. Wichowski & Kubsch (1997) report, however, that non-compliance is a major concern in the management of people with chronic conditions; Kyngas et al (1998) quote a series of studies which estimate that approximately 50% of young diabetic people do not comply with treatment regimes. Haynes et al (2000) estimated that the rates of non-compliance with prescribed medications are 50% and Simons (1992) estimated non-compliance rates range from 10% to 94%. The value of pursuing patient compliance therefore has to be questioned.

Compliance is often defined as the extent to which a patient follows medical advice, however, this unidimensional view has no place in the management of people who live with chronic illness. Hentinen (1988) views compliance as an active responsible process of care in which the person works to maintain his or her health in close collaboration with health-care professionals. More recently, an editorial in the British Medical Journal (1997) stated that the concept of concordance, which suggests a frank exchange of information, negotiation and a spirit of co-operation, probably more accurately reflects the desired approach in prescribing treatment regimes for patients. Collaboration and partnership are important considerations in the treatment of people who have chronic conditions. The individual has to live with the condition and therefore must be allowed to own the management plan and to feel that there is some control over treatment. When making decisions about the treatment regime and being involved in the organization of services, nurse practitioners as leaders and clinicians can help people become involved with the treatment regime of their choice.

Figure 18.1 provides an overview of some of the issues that should be considered when working in concordance with patients. The first step is for the health-care professional to make every effort to understand the patient. This includes learning about the patients' health-care beliefs, values, expectations and lifestyle preferences. The patient's internal factors will have an impact on the way the patient views the condition. Internal factors will also play a part in determining the resources available to the patient in managing the condition. The

nurse practitioner should also consider factors that are external to the patient such as, relationships with family and friends, social activities and relationships with other health-care professionals. Some patients, for example, strike up extremely close relationships with their consultants, others like to rely on the support of nurse specialists and in some cases the patient will turn to the nurse practitioner to build an ongoing relationship – the important issue is that the nurse practitioner recognizes how these relationships affect the patient's perspective.

In addition to understanding the patient and the external and internal factors that have an impact upon this particular individual, it is important for

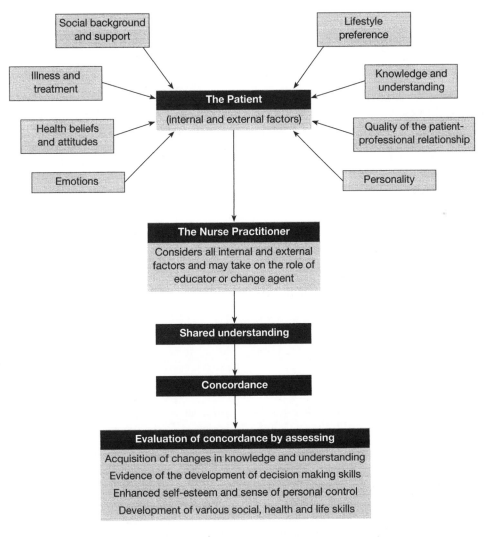

Figure 18.1 Concordance (adapted from Crumbie 2002).

the nurse practitioner to consider how his or her own values and beliefs might effect the view of the patient. If, for example a nurse practitioner has personal family experience of dealing with a chronic condition, this experience could colour the nurse practitioner's view of the patient. A reaction such as 'well my sister did not respond that way' or 'my father always cheated with his diet so I expect this person will too' should be checked and reviewed. Such reactions are examples of bias and preconceived ideas. Getting to understand the patient through a consideration of the external and internal factors will help to guard against bias and preconceptions.

Once the nurse practitioner has truly understood where the patient is coming from and has considered the disease and the likely course of treatment for the disease, the patient and the nurse practitioner can reach a level of shared understanding. This is a solid foundation from which to work towards concordance. The aim of concordance may not be to make sure that the patient complies to the prescribed treatment regime, however, in many situations there is some value in the patient following an agreed treatment pathway. The nurse practitioner can adopt certain strategies to enhance the likelihood of patients choosing to engage with treatment plans. In a review of the literature Yoos (1981) identified six classes of variables associated with compliance to treatment regimes: sociodemographics, the nature of the disease, the patient's beliefs and values, the nature of the treatment regime, factors associated with the organization and delivery of care and the quality of the caregiver–patient interaction. Nurse practitioners can acknowledge the first three and positively impact the latter three. The first three variables represent the internal and external factors as described in Figure 18.1. The second three are amenable to intervention from nurse practitioners.

TREATMENT REGIMES

The treatment regimes for people who live with a chronic condition will vary according to the condition and also according to the individual concerned. Issues common to all people living with a chronic condition are the feeling of uncertainty, loss of control over their body, negative self-concept, concern with the management of treatment regimes and alterations in the balance of family relationships. Callaghan & Williams (1994) suggest that people adopt a variety of coping strategies for living with

diabetes. However, in an effort to make their lives as normal as possible, some people attempt to limit the effect of the condition on their lives by not attending for hospital appointments, not taking their medications or choosing not to monitor their condition. It is important for the nurse practitioner to provide the patient with as much control as is wanted or is possible so that they can optimize their individual treatment plan.

In many chronic conditions there are numerous treatment options and these options can be discussed with patients to determine what the right course of action is for them. In asthma, for example, there is a whole variety of inhaler devices that patients can choose between and their choice will be based upon what works best for them. In diabetes, metformin can be administered at a dose of 500 mg three times a day or a reasonably equivalent dose of 850 mg twice a day. Patients may choose to take the tablets three times a day because they would prefer to avoid side effects that might be associated with higher dose tablets; others may choose to take the tablets twice a day to make sure that they do not miss a dose. Frequency of dosing is also an important consideration for schoolchildren who sometimes find it difficult to take a tablet or ask for an inhaler in the school playground. People who work on night shifts also have particular individual needs when it comes to treatment regimes. It is therefore essential for the nurse practitioner to be aware not only of the patient's lifestyle factors and wishes but also to be knowledgeable about the condition so that they are able to discuss with the patient all the available options.

ORGANIZATION AND DELIVERY OF CARE

Many nurse practitioners are in a position to influence the provision of health-care services at both an individual and organizational level. It is essential to consider what might work best from the patient's perspective. Diabetes clinics that run through school hours and involve long waiting times when the clinics run late, are not going to be well attended by young people. Similarly, clinics for hypertension that are offered on one morning a week will be poorly attended by people who have working lives.

It is also important to consider patients who have multiple conditions and to offer services so that they make as much sense to the patient as possible. Calling a patient to a clinic for their heart disease one week, for their diabetes the next, and their hypertension the week after, is likely to alienate the patient and result in non-attendance and non-compliance. Instead every effort must be made to consider how services will best work for patients from their perspective. The organization then needs to attempt to offer services to the patients in the most appropriate way possible given the available resources and personnel. Indeed services that are organized around the needs of patients are often the most effective and economical as the number of unfilled appointments is kept to a minimum and clinicians can discuss treatments for a variety of conditions (many of which are interrelated) during the one visit.

One method of reviewing the services provided to people with chronic conditions is through the use of audit. Audit results are valuable tools when the nurse practitioner wants to develop a proposal for the improvement of clinical services. Audits can help to reveal important gaps in services and can also be used to demonstrate areas of good practice. An overview of the audit cycle can be found in Figure 18.2. The development of the electronic record has resulted in a great deal of patient information being available to clinicians at the touch of a button. For example, the number of people with diabetes who have had their blood pressure

checked in the last 12 months can be calculated in a matter of a few seconds and the number of people with thyroid disease who have had their thyroid function tests carried out in the preceding year are just as simple to find. The important issue, however, is acting on the information once it is available. The audit cycle can help the nurse practitioner to follow through with actions based on information gained from the electronic record. The following example will help to illuminate how the cycle can be used in practice.

Assess need and choose a topic

It is estimated that in the UK asthma effects 1 in 25 adults (over the age of 16 years) and 1 in 7 children (aged 2–15 years) (National Asthma Campaign 1999). Asthma is therefore a widespread condition. Asthma is also an important condition as death from asthma accounted for 0.25% of all deaths in 1997 representing a total of 1584 people (Office of National Statistics 1997). There is therefore a great need to provide a well-organized service for patients with asthma to ensure that their asthma is as well managed as it possibly can be. The nurse practitioner would need to consider whether such a topic was important within his or her organization. In most primary health-care teams the management

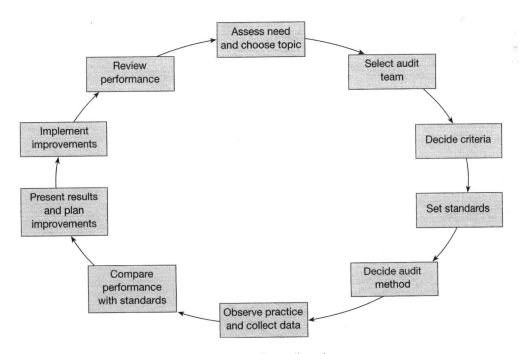

Figure 18.2 The audit cycle.

of asthma will be important – not only to help to address the morbidity associated with living with the condition but also because asthma forms an important component of the quality and outcomes framework in general practice. Therefore it would be entirely reasonable for a nurse practitioner to choose asthma as an important area for audit within a practice.

Select audit team

An audit can be carried out as a lone affair with an individual who is interested in a particular area forging ahead on their own and producing a summary for colleagues. If the aim of an audit is to alter organizational behaviour, then the greater number of people involved in the process the better. It is important for all relevant members of the primary health care team to be involved at the outset, not only to help engage as many people as possible in the process but also to gain a variety of views on problem areas and areas of good practice. It is particularly valuable in some situations to seek the help of a patient as they will be able to provide yet another perspective and can help to identify gaps and problems with the service.

Decide criteria

A criterion is an item of care or some other aspect of clinical practice that can be used to assess quality. Each criterion should be recorded in a statement. An example of this might be 'Every patient who has asthma should attend an annual review clinic once a year'. It is possible that there may not be general agreement about this statement and refinement may be necessary after discussion with the audit team. It is probably reasonable to suggest that if a patient has not had an inhaler for 2 years they are probably not having too many problems with their asthma. It would be possible then to refine the criteria to state 'Every patient who has asthma should attend an annual review clinic once a year if they have required treatment for their asthma within the preceding 2 years'.

A second criteria that might be relevant to this subject could be 'All patients with asthma (who have required treatment for their asthma within the preceding two years) should receive an influenza vaccination each year'. Criteria can be found in numerous places such as the national service frameworks, national guidelines and the wide range of articles in professional journals. It is valuable for the nurse practitioner to regularly engage in reading journals to ensure that ideas for audits remain relevant and current.

Set standards

A standard is a statement of the proportion of occasions or patients that must fulfil the criteria. Hence once the criteria have been set the team need to decide a reasonable level of achievement for that criteria. It might be reasonable to expect that 80% of all people with asthma should attend an annual review clinic once a year if they have required treatment for their asthma within the preceding 2 years, and that 90% of patients with asthma (who have required treatment for their asthma within the preceding 2 years) should receive an influenza vaccination each year. It is important to set realistic standards and yet at the same time to ensure that the standards reflect good practice.

Decide audit method

Once the criteria and standards have been set, a method of collecting the data will have to be agreed. In the asthma examples given above, it would be reasonably straightforward to use the computer to calculate how many people had attended an annual review clinic and how many people had received an influenza vaccination. This may not be so easy if records have been kept on paper or if various clinicians are using different codes to record the data in the electronic record. The team therefore needs to determine what the best method is going to be for their particular circumstances. If the audit is going to require people trailing through paper notes, it is reasonable to select a random sample of the target population. A decision can be made to sample 10% of the population and to make some assumption that this sample is representative of the whole. When teams are dealing with large numbers of patients and with a huge task of data collection, use of a random sample is appropriate and efficient.

Observe practice and collect data

Some audit topics might require a person to actually observe what is happening in practice. An audit that looked at how many times a patient who lives with a chronic condition is consulted on their views about treatment regimes might require observers to sit in on consultations and to look for instances of such activity. In many cases, however, the electronic record makes the data collection quite simple. This step of the audit cycle can often be achieved in a matter of seconds.

Compare performance with standards

Once the data have been collected the results can be compared with the standards that the audit team set at the outset. If they fall short of the standards the team then have to analyse the results to look for explanations. If they meet the standards the team can be congratulated. It is important to realize that the cycle does not stop there, however, even when the standards have been met, the team may want to increase the level of the standards and repeat the audit, making the targets more difficult to achieve.

Present results and plan improvements

Once all the data are collected in and the standards achieved have been calculated, the team will then want to share the results with anyone who has an involvement in the topic area. Collectively then ideas for change can be presented and a plan of action developed. In the case of asthma, for example, the team might find that only 60% of patients are attending for an annual review. On closer inspection of the service they may discover that clinics are offered at 1pm to 3pm on three weekdays. A large proportion of the population with troublesome asthma are likely to be schoolchildren who will have problems getting out of school at these times. Therefore proposals for a change in the time of the clinic might help to address the shortfalls. If the team also found they were not meeting their targets for influenza vaccination, they might want to consider how they have informed the younger population of asthma sufferers about the need for protection. Young people might not be aware that they need to have influenza vaccination, thinking that it is only necessary for people over the age of 65. The primary health-care team can then look at how they advertise the vaccination and again, take a look at the timing of the clinics.

Implement improvements

Whatever suggestions have been made, the team needs to ensure that they act on their plans and implement the changes. This can be the most difficult step in the whole audit process and will be dependent upon good working relationships, a preparedness to change and strong leadership. Seeing this step through can have real rewards and can have a great impact on patient care.

Review performance

The audit cycle never ends. Once changes have been implemented, the audit should be carried out again to compare the standards. Audit should be an integral component of the practice of all nurse practitioners, assisting them in reflecting on their care and alerting them to services that fall short of acceptable standards. The use of audit when nurse practitioners are working with people who live with chronic conditions is particularly valuable because so much of the work with this group of people is dependent upon the efficient organization of the services that are offered to them. People with chronic conditions interface with health-care services over many years and this makes them very appropriately placed to contribute to the audit cycle and to benefit from the improvements in service over time.

QUALITY OF THE PATIENT–CARE-GIVER INTERACTION

Yoos (1981) identified the quality of the patient–care-giver interaction as an important aspect of working with people toward compliance and concordance. Nurse practitioners carry out comprehensive history-taking and physical examination and they communicate therapeutically to arrive at a diagnosis and plan of treatment in partnership with the patient. Nurse practitioners are therefore equipped with the skills to achieve the highest possible quality patient–nurse practitioner interaction. Utilizing these skills effectively will enhance the health and wellbeing of people who live with chronic conditions.

This chapter has explored some of the issues that arise for patients who live with chronic conditions when they interact with health-care services. Nurse practitioners can have an impact on the experience of this group of patients at both an individual and an organizational level. The words of Thorne & Paterson (1998) capture the fundamental values which have provided the framework for this chapter:

'Let us learn when our patients want to be treated as partners, but let us also learn when they want to be in control of our actions and when they want us to assume complete control. Only then will we be able to offer the full range of support the chronically ill tell us they need to live their lives as productively and as fully as is possible within the limits of their illness.'

References

Bleeker H, Mulderij K 1992 The experience of motor disability. Phenomenology and Pedagogy 10:1–18. Cited in: Price B 1996 Illness careers: the chronic illness experience. Journal of Advanced Nursing 24:275–279

British Medical Journal 1997 Editorial: Compliance becomes concordance. British Medical Journal 314:691–692

Callaghan D, Williams A 1994 Living with diabetes: issues for nursing practice. Journal of Advanced Nursing 20:132–139

Cameron K, Gregor F 1987 Chronic illness and compliance. Journal of Advanced Nursing 12:671–676

Cole R E, Reiss D (eds) 1993 How do families cope with chronic illness? Lawrence Erlbaum, Hove

Coward D D 1991 Self-transcendence and emotional well being in women with advanced breast cancer. Oncology Nursing Forum 18(5):857–863

Crumbie A 2002 Patient–professional relationships. In: Crumbie A, Lawrence J (eds) Living with a chronic condition. A practitioner's guide to providing care. Butterworth-Heinemann, Oxford

Funk S G, Tornquist E M, Champagne M T, Wiese R A (eds) 1993 Key aspects of caring for the chronically ill: hospital and home. Springer, New York

Haynes R B, Montague P, Oliver P, McKibbon K A, Brouwer M C, Kanani R 2000 Interventions for helping patients to follow prescriptions for medication. The Cochrane Database of Systematic Reviews Issue 1. Update Software, Oxford

Healy P 2000 Let patients with diabetes make their own decisions. Nursing Standard 14(27):8

Hentinen M 1988 Hoitoon sitoutuminen hoitotyon nakokulmasta. Sairaanhoitaja 4:5–7. Cited in: Kyngas H, Hentinen M, Barlow J H 1998 Adolescents, perceptions of physicians, nurses, parents and friends: help or hindrance in compliance with diabetes self-care? Journal of Advanced Nursing 27:760–769

Heriot C S 1992 Spirituality and ageing. Holistic Nursing Practice 7(1):22–31

Jerret M 1994 Parent's experience of coming to know the care of a chronically ill child. Journal of Advanced Nursing 19:1050–1056

Kelly M P, Field D 1996 Medical sociology, chronic illness and the body. Sociology of Health and Illness 18:241–257

Kyngas H, Hentinen M, Barlow J H 1998 Adolescents perceptions of physicians, nurses, parents and friends: help or hindrance in compliance with diabetes self-care? Journal of Advanced Nursing 27:760–769

Leetun M C 1996 Wellness spirituality in the older adult. Nurse Practitioner 21(8):60–70

Lyons R F , Sullivan M J L, Ritvo P G, Coyne J C 1995 Relationships in chronic illness and disability. Sage, California

McBride A B 1993 Managing chronicity: the heart of nursing care. In: Funk S G, Tornquist E M., Champagne M T , Wiese R A (eds) Key aspects of caring for the chronically ill: hospital and home. Springer, New York

Morse J, Borttorff J, Hutchinson S 1994 The phenomenology of comfort. Journal of Advanced Nursing 20:189–195

National Asthma Campaign 1999 National Asthma Audit. National Asthma Campaign, London

Nolan M, Nolan J 1995 Responding to the challenge of chronic illness. British Journal of Nursing 4(3):145–147

Office of National Statistics 1997 Mortality statistics: cause 1997. Series DH2 No. 24. Office of National Statistics, London

Pilch J 1988 Wellness: wellness spirituality. Health Values 12(3):28–31

Price B 1996 Illness careers: the chronic illness experience. Journal of Advanced Nursing 24:275–279

Simons M R 1992 Interventions related to compliance. Nursing Clinics of North America 27(2):477–484

Thorne S, Paterson B 1999 Shifting images of chronic illness. Journal of Nursing Scholarship 30(2):173–178

Verbrugge L M, Jette A M 1994 The disablement process. Social Science and Medicine 38(1):1–14

Wichowski H C, Kubsch S M 1997 The relationship of self perception of illness and compliance with health care regimes. Journal of Advanced Nursing 25(3):548–553

Yoos L 1981 Compliance: philosophical and ethical complications. The nurse practitioner. American Journal of Primary Health Care 6(4):27–34

Chapter 19

The patient as partner in care

Alison Crumbie

INTRODUCTION

As the boundaries between medicine and nursing become increasingly blurred, nurse practitioners must not lose sight of one of the main advantages of the delivery of health services by a nurse – the ability to work with the patient as partner. Brearley (1990) states that patient participation is seen as a positive part of the nurse's role whereas participation can be construed as a potential threat to the autonomy of medicine.

> *'If they ask me what's wrong with them, I say to them, that's my business. Do as I tell you and take your medicine and you'll get better': Dr John Pickles at the turn of the century*
>
> (Livesey 1986, p. 8)

Few patients today would accept such an approach from any health-care professional. As nurse practitioners take on many of the tasks of medicine, however, there is a risk that patients will perceive the nurse in a different way and may be less willing to enter into a partnership. It is essential therefore to consider why we want to encourage partnerships with patients and how we might go about enhancing such a relationship. This chapter aims to explore the nature of partnerships with patients from an ethical, sociological, psychological and political perspective. Models of nursing and the skills that can be used to enhance partnerships with patients will be explored, with a particular focus on the consultation process.

PARTNERSHIPS

Participation means getting involved or being allowed to become involved in a decision-making process of the delivery of a service or the evaluation of a service – or even simply to become one of a number of people consulted on an issue or matter (Brownlea 1987).

A partnership is a relationship between parties working towards a joint venture. At its most basic level, this partnership is between the nurse and an individual patient during the consultation process. The relationship is commonly more complex than this and can include any or all of the following: the patient's family, other groups of patients, the local community and the population of the nation. Similarly, the nurse practitioner can be influenced by other members of the health-care team, the organization within which s/he works, the local primary care organization, the NHS and even the government (Fig. 19.1).

The one-to-one relationship is the most frequently occurring partnership in the everyday practice of nurse practitioners and therefore this chapter will focus most attention at this level. Brearley (1990) states that individual patient participation can be viewed as a continuum with complete passivity at one end and complete activity at the other. The completely passive patient is moribund on arrival in the A&E department or an unconscious patient on a ward. This patient requires health-care providers to make all the decisions and actively to carry out all aspects of care. The completely active patient cares for his or her own health-care needs without any input from the health-care professional.

Brearley goes on to state that the activity of the health-care professional is inversely proportional to the activity of the patient. As the patient becomes more active, the health-care provider can become less active. The level of activity of the patient depends on the nature of the problem and also on the willingness of the health-care professional to allow the patient to be an active participant in the process. There is inequality in the relationship between the patient and the health-care professional as the power lies with the clinician – this clearly influences the nature of the partnership. It could be suggested that in order to enhance a patient's level of activity the nurse practitioner needs to increase his or her level of activity to form a dynamic active relationship with the patient (Fig. 19.2). If the health-care professional remains passive, the two parties could slip into the traditional roles of submissive patient and dominant physician or nurse.

Toop (1998) describes three models which have been used to describe the types of relationship between clinicians and patients originally developed by Szasz & Hollender almost 30 years ago (Szasz & Hollender 1976). The activity–passivity approach outlined above is based on a parent–infant model, the guidance–co-operation model is based on a parent–child approach and the mutual participation approach is based on adult–adult interaction. Toop (1998) states that none of these models is claimed to be better than the other as any of the three approaches may be appropriate in certain situations. Mutual participation (the basis of patient-centred care) has been gaining popularity over recent years.

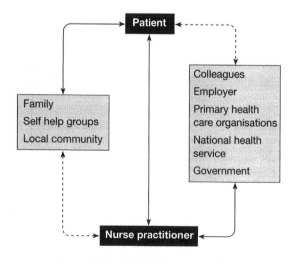

Figure 19.1 The links in partnerships.

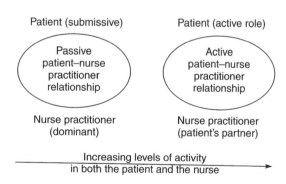

Figure 19.2 Passive–active partnerships.

In primary health care the relationship between the nurse practitioner and the patient often develops over a period of time. The US Institute of Medicine (Donaldson et al 1994) has recognized this enduring relationship and developed the concept of sustained partnerships. Leopold et al (1996) have developed a model of sustained partnership and state that the defining features include the following:

- Focus on the whole person
- Clinician's knowledge of the person
- Caring and empathic approach
- The patient has trust in the clinician
- The care offered to the patient must be appropriately adapted to the patient's goals
- The patient participates in the decision-making process.

Health-care professionals have tended to discourage patients from taking sole responsibility for their health and wellbeing for a variety of reasons. In the past many ailments were treated without referral to the health services and the individual would rely upon acquired knowledge, the family or other members of the community to manage the problems of ill health. Downie et al (1997) point out that sleeplessness is an example of a problem which used to be treated by individuals as it was seen as a normal condition which could be managed effectively at home. Grief or anxiety are further examples of normal experiences which would have been managed quite effectively by visiting a member of the clergy or a supportive friend or neighbour. We now turn to the health services for all our problems and we expect an expert and a cure. This has been encouraged by people in the health service who warn against delays in diagnosis and the possible lethal consequences of missing those early warning signs in meningitis, malignancies or heart disease, for example. As a result the public have lost confidence in their ability to diagnose and treat minor conditions (Downie et al 1997) and consequently the expectation is that the health service is responsible for curing all the problems facing each individual and the broader community.

Other risks associated with patients playing an active role in their health care include the possibility of misusing treatments, exposure to the ill effects of self-medication and diagnosis without expert advice. It is difficult for nurses to accept any level of risk when dealing with an individual's health. Nurses who work as nurse practitioners, however, have to accept uncertainty and risk management as part of everyday practice. The advantages of patient participation therefore must outweigh the disadvantages if it is to be encouraged.

Tudor Hart (1988) points out that the active, intelligent contribution of the patient to the diagnostic process becomes obvious when one considers the difficulty faced by clinicians when a patient is unable to communicate due to cultural or language barriers. When the patient is unable to provide a history for the nurse, the diagnosis relies upon other methods of detection such as the physical examination or other investigations. Tudor Hart states that, in 80 newly referred medical outpatients, the final diagnosis could be reached after reading the GP's letter of referral and taking a history in 82% of patients, a further 7% could be diagnosed after physical examination and 9% after technical examinations. This emphasizes the importance of patient participation in the diagnostic process. Livesey (1986) adds that participating patients will save time in the long run as their greater level of knowledge will enhance satisfaction and reduce the number of return visits in the search for reassurance and understanding.

The accuracy of diagnosis associated with patient participation can also have advantages at a community level. According to Brearley (1990), the advantages of patient participation include not only increased patient responsibility and commitment to health and health-promoting behaviours and activities but also the contribution to the health system of new community-based resources. Consumer demand can lead to the development of new health services and improved integration of existing health services combined with better utilization of those services. Patient participation can therefore have a positive effect at both individual and community level.

Clearly partnerships with patients are complex relationships which may or may not involve a wider community. Waterworth & Luker (1990) raised the point that some patients may not wish to be involved in the decision-making process about their health care. Their research found that some patients comply with active involvement as it is a means of 'toeing the line'. Collaboration can be seen as a duty rather than a desirable approach to care and Waterworth & Luker question whether the encouragement of active involvement respects the rights of human beings.

Nurse practitioners therefore must consider the issue of partnerships whilst remaining mindful of the individuality of each patient. Taking the risk of encouraging the patient to play an active role in health care could potentially enhance patient satisfaction. In order to implement the concept of partnership in your practice you need a clear understanding of the principles which underpin your actions. The principles which govern the nurse practitioner's practice can be examined from ethical, sociological, psychological and political perspectives.

THE ETHICAL PERSPECTIVE

The involvement of the patient with the health-care process involves a number of complex ethical decisions. The issues of autonomy, paternalism, beneficence and non-maleficence and justice are worth considering, as each can help to inform decisions about the level of passivity or activity a patient should have in the health-care relationship.

AUTONOMY

Autonomy refers to individuals' capacity to choose freely for themselves and to direct their own life. Autonomy in its pure form is not attainable and therefore should not be thought of as an absolute – rather it is something which can be gained to a greater or lesser degree. Respecting autonomy involves respecting another person's rights as a human being. The rights relating to health care include the right to information, the right to privacy and confidentiality, and the right to appropriate care and treatment (Naidoo & Wills 1994). If the nurse practitioner utilizes the ethical principle of autonomy to consider the patient as a partner then each patient has a right to information relating to his or her diagnosis and treatment and this information should be provided for the patient in an appropriate and understandable way.

PATERNALISM

Paternalism refers to an action taken by one person in the best interests of another without the latter's consent (Childress 1979). Thomasma (1983) distinguishes between strong and weak paternalism. Weak paternalism is an action taken in the absence of consent when a person does not have the ability to give consent. Strong paternalism is a decision

which has been taken against the wishes of another. The provision of health care has tended to be based on a paternalistic framework. For example, health-care professionals who made decisions for the patient because they thought that they knew what was best were behaving in a paternalistic manner. Paternalism does not respect the rights of the human being and results in the patient taking a passive role in health care.

BENEFICENCE AND NON-MALEFICENCE

Beneficence and non-maleficence relate to promoting good and doing no harm. Patients should be informed that the course of action aims to promote their wellbeing and do them no harm in the process. A patient who is participating in the process of health care therefore needs to be fully informed of the consequences of treatment decisions. Possible harmful side effects should be discussed so that a decision can be made about the advantages and disadvantages of a particular treatment. Livesey (1986) states that where there is some debate about treatment plans, a patient who is fully informed about the pros and cons of the treatment is most likely to choose not to proceed with the prescription. This saves health service resources and saves the patient from possible iatrogenic effects of a medication, which may not have been necessary.

JUSTICE

Justice refers to the fair distribution of scarce resources, respect for individual and group rights and following morally acceptable laws (Naidoo & Wills 1994). This is a particularly important concept when the nurse practitioner considers the patient's voice in the planning and evaluation of health-care services. Patients' views can be sought by forming patient advisory groups. Pritchard & Pritchard (1994) state that one of the major benefits of patient advisory groups is that the patient becomes a member of the health-care team at an organizational level. It is hoped that the patient's voice will help to inform decisions about health-care services and to provide a more equitable and fair system for all patients in the community. Patient participation in advisory groups does not necessarily guarantee a fair system; however, it is one method of enhancing the possibility of justice.

The issues considered above help nurse practitioners to include patients in the decision-making process by respecting each individual as a human being and providing full and appropriate information to ensure that they are fully informed. Ethical principles dictate that patients should be treated as active partners in their care and that the nurse practitioner has a duty to engage the patient in this way.

THE SOCIOLOGICAL PERSPECTIVE

A sociological perspective on the issue of patients as partners considers the issue of the roles people play in society. Strong (1979) explored the ceremonial order of the clinic by analysing over 1000 observations of the parents of children who were consulting with doctors. Strong found that even though there were a whole variety of circumstances for the meetings the ceremonial order of the occasion was the same. He argued that medical consultations have a distinct social form and pointed out that the imbalance of power within this bureaucratic format was most striking. Parents might be partners but it was certainly not an equal partnership. The parents were cast in a role that was subordinate to the doctor. The doctors had more rights than the parents and largely controlled the sequence of events. For example, it was acceptable for the doctor to leave the room without explanation and to turn and speak with students or nurses during the consultation but it would not have been acceptable if the parents had engaged in such behaviour.

A further exploration of the roles people play during the consultation process can be informed by Talcot Parson's concept of the sick role (Parsons 1951). Parsons viewed health and illness as being intimately involved with the social system. Illness is seen as sociologically deviant behaviour – a negative and undesirable state. The effective performance of social roles is diminished by ill health. Once a person is in a state of ill health s/he is obliged to reverse this situation, as it is a state of being which threatens the normal equilibrium of society. This leads us to the four fundamental responsibilities and obligations of a person who is an occupant of the sick role: the person becomes exempt from normal responsibility, is not responsible for his or her own condition, is obliged to get well and must seek competent help. The sick role then requires sanctioning from other members of

society – it places clinicians in a powerful position and patients in a dependent position. If we consider the patient as a partner in care, Parson's sick role certainly requires that the patient actively seeks competent help and should get well and therefore should play an active role in the health-care process; however, medical dominance is present in the power to legitimize the illness by providing a label or diagnosis for the patient.

Both Strong (1979) and Parsons (1951) outlined roles that health-care professionals and patients play in the health-care setting. It is useful for nurse practitioners to be aware of the social meaning of the roles we adopt in each consultation with a patient. If we adopt the trappings of the medical profession with consulting-room desks, large chairs, white coats, stethoscopes and prescription pads, we too may exhibit the power which was uncovered in the study by Strong. We should then question the value of this power, the lack of equality in our relationship with our patients and the effect it might have on the outcome of our interventions. If we analyse our consultations from the perspective of the sick role, it could be perceived that once again the relationship between the nurse practitioner and the patient is unequal. It would be possible to address some of the inequality by utilizing the patient's need to actively seek help and to get well and engage them in the diagnosis and treatment planning process.

THE PSYCHOLOGICAL PERSPECTIVE

The contention that an increase in patient participation in health care will prove beneficial to patients has been supported by psychological theory, albeit with some reservations (Brearley 1990). A variety of personal characteristics, including hardiness, learned helplessness, self-efficacy and locus of control can be examined within a psychological framework and linked to the patient's willingness or ability to participate in health care.

HARDINESS

Kobasa et al (1981) described hardiness as a group of characteristics that function as a resistance to stressful life events, including commitment, control and challenge. Commitment is the tendency to be actively involved in whatever you are doing, control is the tendency to feel and act as though you have influence over your life and challenge is the belief that change rather than stability is normal in life. Lee (1983) conducted a review of the literature relating to hardiness and found that endurance, strength, boldness and power to control were all related to hardiness. People who have a high level of hardiness have been found to engage in good self-care behaviours (Payne & Walker 1996). This has strong implications for nurses who wish to engage patients as partners in their care. If the nurse practitioner can recognize hardiness in a patient then it might be possible to anticipate their reaction to the illness experience. A hardy person may need to take more control over the course of his or her treatment once in the health-care system and therefore be more participatory. If nurse practitioners can recognize hardiness and utilize this quality in individual patients then it may be possible to judge more accurately those patients who may respond to being offered the opportunity to take a more active role in self-management.

LEARNED HELPLESSNESS

Learned helplessness means learning that one's own actions have no influence upon outcomes (Seligman 1975). Seligman demonstrated the concept of learned helplessness in the laboratory by administering a series of minor electric shocks to two dogs. One dog was provided with the means to stop the shock and the other was not. When the dogs were transferred to another setting the dog that had learned to stop the shocks soon learnt to jump over a small barrier to escape whereas the second dog made no attempt to move, failed to recognize the escape routes and appeared very miserable. The difference in the behaviour of the two dogs was attributed to the learned behaviour in the first situation. Payne & Walker (1996) relate these findings to human depression, suggesting that it is necessary to help depressed people relearn that they are capable of doing something positive to gain control over their lives.

People who have experienced a lack of control over their surroundings have fewer personal resources to allow them to become partners in health care. Learned helplessness can result in a person who has poor motivation, an emotional deficit and a cognitive deficit, rather like the second dog in Seligman's experiments. It is not sufficient simply to tell a person that s/he can regain control. The nurse practitioner should focus on assisting the

person to identify his or her personal skills, which can be utilized to help them act in a positive way to influence their lives.

SELF-EFFICACY

Self-efficacy is a sense of self-competence or self-mastery, which leads to a sense of self-esteem or self-worth (Payne & Walker 1996). This sense of self is derived from beliefs about oneself which are generated from life experiences and feedback from others, from successes and failures in life and from humiliations (Burns 1980). This collection of experiences results in the construction of a self-picture and the person behaves according to this picture, which in turn generates feedback from others. This is a vicious cycle and results in a person believing and therefore behaving in a certain manner – and this in turn is reinforced by others.

Self-esteem is a value judgement based on the sense of self. Self-efficacy is the conviction that it is possible to carry out a behaviour to achieve a desired outcome. People avoid activities that they believe are beyond their capabilities and will engage in behaviours that they judge they are able to perform (Payne & Walker 1996). Nurse practitioners can use these principles to influence a person's behaviour. By providing information and education for a patient the person can begin to believe that he or she does have the ability to achieve whatever the behaviour is that is expected of him. By making the activity seem achievable to the client and by understanding the client's sense of self-efficacy, the nurse practitioner can tailor health-care advice and information to the client's needs to optimize the self-care behaviour.

LOCUS OF CONTROL

Learned helplessness, hardiness and self-efficacy all involve the issue of personal control. A person's locus of control is the degree to which the person believes that the events which happen to him or her occur as a result of his or her own behaviour or as a result of luck or fate (Strickland 1978). It has been found that people who have an internal locus of control are more likely to engage in screening and other health-care behaviours as they feel that this behaviour might in some way make a difference (Payne & Walker 1996). People who have an external locus of control have a sense that they are con-

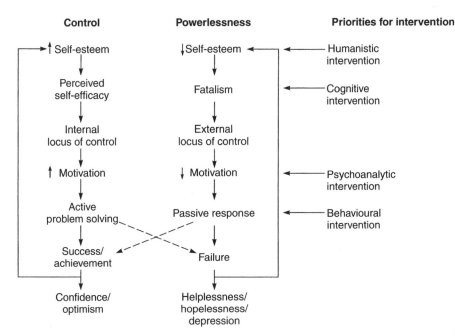

Figure 19.3 Hypothetical model of the dynamic relationships between control-related concepts and outcomes (adapted from Payne & Walker 1997.), with permission of McGraw-Hill Education.

trolled by external forces and therefore there is little point in carrying out any health-care behaviour as it will not have any impact on the outcome of events. It has been suggested that a person's locus of control is generated from past experiences (Brearley 1990) and therefore it may change with current and future experiences (Payne & Walker 1996).

Nurse practitioners can intervene on a variety of levels to enhance a person's self-esteem, self-efficacy, internal locus of control, motivation, active problem-solving, level of success and achievement and overall confidence and optimism. Payne & Walker (1996) link each of these concepts and suggest a variety of therapeutic interventions to improve a patient's level of control over his or her problem situation (Fig. 19.3).

A desire for control over health care is aimed at coping (Brearley 1990). Nurse practitioners can help patients to gain a sense of control over their situation by providing information, educating patients about their rights and recognizing the fallibility of health-care professionals.

POLITICAL CONTEXT

The current political climate in the UK has helped to enhance awareness of patients' rights and the value of engaging patients as partners in care. The health service has not always been so attuned to the views of patients and in 1974 community health councils were set up throughout England and Wales (there are similar bodies in Scotland and Northern Ireland) in response to evidence that the NHS was not sufficiently patient-centred (Tschudin 1995). Community health councils represented the patient's voice in the health service and they had rights to visit health-care premises, to inspect them and to make reports on their findings.

The Association for Community Health Councils in England and Wales (ACHCEW) published its own *Patient's Charter* in 1986 (ACHCEW 1986) outlining a list of 17 rights for all who may need to access health services. This list included such issues as the right to be fully informed, the right to refuse treatment, the right to be treated with respect at all times and the right for a second opinion. The National Consumer Council issued a similar document in 1983 which outlined the patient's rights in relation to choice and consent, information, the rights of children and the right to complain. These documents set the stage for *Working for Patients* (Department of Health 1989) and *The Patient's Charter* (Department of Health 1991). *Working for Patients* outlined several key government proposals, including the patient's right to information, explanation and rapid notification of results, which clearly emphasized the value of the provision of information for patients. If the patient had been considered equal in his or her relationship with the health service, however, the document might have been more appropriately titled Working with Patients.

The Patient's Charter was said to be 'a big disappointment' by ACHCEW, 'rather flabby' by the Patient's Association and 'something of a middle class charter' by the Director of the King's Fund Centre (Stocking 1991). The charge that *The Patient's Charter* did not represent the rights of people who are in ethnic minorities or people who are homeless, for example, was countered by others who felt that it was a step in the right direction (Millar 1991). Many of the rights identified in *The Patient's Charter* are a repeat of previous rights for all citizens in relation to the health care service, however, *The Patient's Charter* re-emphasized these established rights, introduced new rights and promoted the public's awareness of them.

The white paper *The New NHS: Modern, Dependable* was published in 1997 and recognized quite clearly that people certainly do expect more from the health service (Department of Health 1997). Six key principles are identified in this document, including the need to get the NHS to work in partnerships and that by breaking down organizational barriers and forging stronger links with local health authorities the needs of the patient will be put at the centre of the care process.

The white paper was followed in 2000 by *The NHS Plan* (NHS Executive 2000). The *NHS Plan* set out the government's plans to abolish the community health councils and to replace them with a system of patient and public involvement in England known as PALS (Patient Advice and Liaison Service) and PPIFs (Patient and Public Involvement Forums). The new system was to be implemented by 2002 and it was thought that it would enhance the level of patient and public involvement in the NHS. A member of the PPFI will act as a non-executive board member on the Trust boards from 2004 onwards. Included in the PALS core functions is the provision of on-the-spot help to negotiate resolutions to problems and the provision of accurate information to patients and their families. Hence PALS acts as an advocate for patients who have concerns or complaints and PPIFs seek the views of patients and make recommendations to Trust management. In this way they both act as a catalyst for change within the NHS by providing feedback to the Trusts and to staff.

The Department of Health published its new arrangement for patient and public involvement in 2003 and the opening line in this document is 'The NHS should put the patient at the centre of everything it does' (Department of Health 2003) emphasizing the need for the whole system to work in partnership with patients. Recognizing the value of patients, involvement in their care empowers them and tends to encourage more active partnership in health-care provision.

METHODS OF ENHANCING PARTNERSHIPS

THE CONSULTATION

The skills required to promote the active involvement of patients in their health care will be employed by nurse practitioners during the consultation process with their patients. Balint (1957) stated that by far the most frequently used drug in general practice was the doctor himself (or herself) which, by analogy, clearly emphasizes the importance of the nurse–patient relationship during the consultation process. Balint also stated that 'no guidance whatever is contained in any textbook as to the dosage in which the doctor should prescribe himself, in what form, how frequently, what his curative and maintenance doses should be and so on'.

Livesey (1986) points out that for many doctors the outcomes of their consultations are regularly examined during medical school but the consultation process itself is rarely questioned. Nurse practitioners, however, are being examined on their history-taking process and their communication style during their courses. Patient participation can assist you in diagnostic reasoning and in making decisions relating to interventions. Tudor Hart (1988, p. 183) quotes Jean-Martin Charcot from the 19th century, who said: 'Listen to the patient, he is telling you the diagnosis'. Allowing patients the time and space to tell their story respects their autonomy and actively engages them in their health care.

Livesey (1986) suggests that we should consider the following points in consultations with patients:

- expectations
- welcome
- patient's story

- partners in care
- physical examination
- examination of the emotions
- personalities and problems
- simple explanations
- the farewell.

The patient in Livesey's consultation process is clearly an active participant in the problem-solving process. Livesey points out that the patient's problem can be dealt with more effectively if the clinician has built up a clear idea of the patient's expectations and thoughts about the matter. If a thorough understanding of the patient's perspective has not been gathered during the consultation advice, medications and resources can all be misdirected. This failure, according to Livesey, is most commonly due to a communication breakdown between the patient and the clinician.

Anthony Clare (1991) provided a guide to help develop communication and interviewing skills for the consultation process. Clare suggests that clinicians should have a rough plan of the interview before meeting with the patient; persuade the patient to talk; control and guide him or her with encouragement and appropriate questioning; record salient features of the interview; arrive at a diagnosis and summarize and make decisions on treatment. Throughout the process the clinician should be aiming to elicit the patient's feelings and should be aware of the social, cultural and linguistic barriers to communication. Communication and interviewing skills can be developed with practise. A further discussion of communication and the therapeutic relationship can be found in Chapter 20.

A FRAMEWORK FOR PRACTICE

Much of the research relating to the consultation process has been carried out with doctors in the role of health-care professional. Nurse practitioners are now consulting with patients in a similar way and many of the lessons from medicine can be applied to our own practice. As with all nurse practitioner practice, it is essential that nurses do not lose sight of the benefits to the patient in delivering their care within a nursing framework. There are several nurse theorists who have considered the value of partnerships in care. Depending upon your area of practice and your own nursing philosophy you may find that a nursing model can provide a framework for your work.

One such nursing model is Dorothea Orem's self-care model for nursing (Orem 1985). The most fundamental belief, which underpins Orem's model, is that a need for self-care exists in each individual (Pearson & Vaughan 1986). Self-care is the personal care that human beings require each day and that may be modified by ill health, environmental conditions, the effects of medical care and other factors (Orem 1985). Ideally the person has the ability to meet this self-care need but sometimes the demand for self-care is greater than the individual's ability to meet it – this results in a self-care deficit. The inability to maintain a therapeutic level of self-care is the condition that validates the existence of nursing and this is how nursing relates to individuals. The goals of nursing are:

- to reduce the self-care demand
- to increase the self-care ability
- to enable relatives to give dependent care when self-care is impossible
- when none of these can be achieved, the nurse may meet the self-care needs.

The focus of the model is to help individuals view themselves as self-care agents. As individuals come to understand themselves in this way a process of personalization occurs (Orem 1985). Personalization is the potential fulfilment of wholeness, the health of body and mind and the experience of wellbeing. Nurse practitioners could utilize Orem's model of nursing to structure the assessment process and to focus interventions towards enhancing self-care activities and in this way a partnership in care can be developed. For a more detailed explanation of the assessment process and self-care requisites see Dorothea Orem's text *Nursing: Concepts of Practice* (1985).

Other nurse theorists who respect and encourage the active involvement of patients in their care include Sister Callista Roy, who made the client visible in the health-care process (Roy 1980, Meleis 1985), Imogene King, who identified a role of nursing as setting mutual goals with clients (King 1981) and Henderson, who identified the nursing role as complementary to and supplementing the patient's own knowledge (Henderson 1978). There are many more; frameworks such as the health belief model can also be utilized to involve the patient as a partner in health care (see p. 302). The value in turning to nurse theorists and health promotion models to underpin the work of the nurse practitioner is that it can guard against the dominance of the medical model. The medical model aims for biological homeostasis in patients and this can be achieved by diagnosing the cause of the disturbance and treating it. There are many occasions where this approach is necessary and appropriate, however, the individual patient plays a limited and mostly passive role within this framework. Nurse practitioners who adopt this approach will be providing a one-dimensional service. It would therefore be difficult to suggest that nurse practitioners who simply adopt the medical model would be offering anything more than a substitute medical service. The whole purpose of implementing the role of the nurse practitioner should be to enhance the service we are currently offering our clients.

QUALITY ASSURANCE AND SERVICE PLANNING

If nurse practitioners are to suggest that offering patients health-care services within a nursing framework will promote partnerships in care and will enhance the quality of care we provide, how do we prove that these claims can be made and how do we ensure that the patient's voice is heard in the process? Many authors have pointed out the importance of actively involving patients in quality improvement programmes (National Association of Health Authorities and Trusts 1995) and identifying patients as major stakeholders in the provision of health-care services (Ham & Shapiro 1996). Toop (1998) states that there is not yet any solid evidence to prove that patient-centred care improves health outcomes. As patient participation is central to the current changes in delivery of health-care services in the UK, this is an area of practice that should be firmly on the research agenda.

Nurse practitioners can choose to research or audit their work in a variety of ways. The Dynamic Standard Setting System (DySSSy) is one method of setting standards of care and monitoring those standards (Royal College of Nursing 1990). This system is not only a method of evaluating the results of your work in practice but it also recognizes the value of engaging the patient in the standard-setting process. The DySSSy system is based on six key principles, which were originally developed by a group of nurses in Oxford (Kitson 1989):

- Ownership: the standards are written by the practitioners delivering the care
- Participation: the practitioners must be involved with the process

- Patient-focused: the patient should be at the heart of the initiative
- Situation-based: it must be clear who the standards are for
- Setting achievable standards: the standards must be practical and realistic
- Multidisciplinary standard: the standards must transfer across disciplines.

The patient is placed firmly in the centre of this process and the aim is always to improve quality from the patient's point of view (Poulton 1994). This requires active involvement from patients and willingness on the part of health-care professionals to work with patients to achieve quality. The DySSSy system is presented in three phases – defining, auditing and monitoring, and taking action. Patients have an active role to play in defining the standards and it is in this phase that patients' views should be sought. There is evidence to suggest that the participative approach to improving quality which is exemplified by the DySSSy system improves patient outcomes and changes nursing practice (National Institute for Nursing 1994).

In practice, the DySSSy system can provide nurse practitioners with a framework to measure the quality of health care delivered to patients. Involving patients in the standard-setting process is a method of representing the patient's voice. This process ensures that the patient is not only a partner during individual consultations at the bedside or in the consulting room but also a partner in the planning and delivery of health-care services to the local population.

CONCLUSION

If you consider the concept of patient participation in your work as a nurse practitioner, you will broaden your perspective of the patient. You may find that some patients do not wish to be actively involved in the decision-making process or the management of their condition and you will need to be flexible to adopt the appropriate approach in each situation. It is without question, however, that your nurse practitioner role will always be an active one. Your energies will be directed towards assessing the patient's expectations and responding to them in a manner which respects the individuality of each human being in every consultation with your clients.

References

ACHCEW 1986 Association for Community Health Councils in England and Wales. Patient's Charter – Guidelines for Good Practice. ACHCEW, London

Balint M 1957 The doctor, his patient and the illness. Pitman, London

Brearley S 1990 Patient participation: the literature. Scutari Press, London

Brownlea A 1987 Participation: myths, realities and prognosis. Social Science and Medicine 25(6):605–614

Burns R B 1980 Essential psychology. MT Press, London

Childress J F 1979 Paternalism and health care. In: Robinson W L, Pritchard M S (eds) Medical responsibility. Human Press, Clifton, New Jersey

Clare A 1991 Developing communication and interviewing skills. In: Corney R (ed) Developing communication and counselling skills in medicine. Routledge, London

Department of Health 1989 Working for patients: the health service caring for the 1990s. HMSO, London

Department of Health 1991 The patient's charter. HMSO, London

Department of Health 1997 The new NHS: modern, dependable. HMSO, London

Department of Health 2003 Patient and public involvement (ppi): the new arrangements. HMSO, London. Online: http://www.dh.gov.uk/PolicyAndGuidance/Organisati onPolicy/PatientAndPublicInvolvement/InvolvingPatie ntsPublicHealthcare/InvolvingPatientsPublicHealthcare Article/fs/en?CONTENT_ID=4000457&chk=V44bEb

Donaldson M, Yordv K, Vanselow N (eds) for the Institute of Medicine 1994 Defining primary care: an interim report. National Academy Press, Washington, DC

Downie R S, Tannahill C, Tannahill A 1997 Health promotion models and values, 2nd edn. Oxford Medical Publications, Oxford

Ham C J, Shapiro J 1996 Learning curve. Health Service Journal January 18:24–25

Henderson V 1978 The concept of nursing. Journal of Advanced Nursing 5:245–260

King I 1981 A theory for nursing: systems, concepts and process. John Wiley, New York

Kitson A 1989 Framework for quality. Royal College of Nursing, London

Kobasa S C, Maddi S R, Courington S 1981 Personality and constitution as mediators in the stress–illness relationship, Journal of Health and Social Behaviour 22:368–378

Lee H J 1983 Analysis of a concept: hardiness. Oncology Nursing Forum 10(4):32–35

Leopold N, Cooper J, Clancy C 1996 Sustained partnership in primary care. Journal of Family Practice 42:129–137

Livesey P G 1986 Partners in care: the consultation in general practice. Heinemann, London

Meleis A 1985 Theoretical nursing: development and progress. J B Lippincott, Philadelphia

Millar B 1991 I have in my hand a piece of paper. Health Service Journal 101(5277):12

National Association of Health Authorities and Trusts (1995) Improving quality in health care – partnership agenda.

National Association of Health Authorities and Trusts, Association for Quality in Healthcare and British Medical Association, London

Naidoo J, Wills J 1994 Health promotion. Foundations for practice. Baillière Tindall, London

National Consumer Council (NCC) 1983 Patient's rights: a guide for NHS patients and doctors. HMSO, London

NHS Executive 2000 The NHS plan: a plan for investment, a plan for reform. HMSO, London. Online: www.nhs.uk/nhsplan

National Institute for Nursing 1994 The impact of the dynamic standard setting system (DySSSy) on nursing practice and patient outcomes (the DySSSy Project). National Institute for Nursing, Oxford

Orem D E 1985 Nursing: concepts of practice, 3rd edn. McGraw-Hill, New York

Parsons T 1951 The social system. Routledge and Kegan Paul, London

Payne S, Walker J 1996 Psychology for nurses and the caring professions. Open University Press, Buckingham

Pearson A, Vaughan B 1986 Nursing models for practice. Heinemann Nursing, Oxford

Poulton B 1994 Setting standards of care. Nursing Standard 8:51, RCN Nursing Update: 3–8

Pritchard P, Pritchard J 1994 Teamwork for primary and shared care: a practical workbook, 2nd edn. Oxford Medical Publications, Oxford

Roy C 1980 The Roy adaptation model. In: Riehl J P, Roy C (eds) Conceptual models for nursing practice, 2nd edn. Appleton Century Crofts, New York

Royal College of Nursing 1990 Quality patient care: the dynamic standard setting system. RCN, London

Seligman M F P 1975 Helplessness: on development, depression and death. Freeman, New York

Stocking B 1991 Patient's charter. British Medical Journal 303(6811):1148–1149

Strong P M 1979 The ceremonial order of the clinic. Routledge & Kegan Paul, London

Strickland B R 1978 Internal–external expectancies and health related behaviours. Journal of Consulting and Clinical Psychology 46(6):1192–1211

Szasz T S, Hollender M H 1976 The basic models of the doctor–patient relationship. Archives of Internal Medicine 97:585–589

Thomasma D C 1983 Beyond medical paternalism and patient autonomy: a model of physician conscience for the physician–patient relationship. Annals of Internal Medicine 98:243–248

Toop L 1998 Primary care: core values. Patient centred primary care. British Medical Journal 316:1882–1883

Tschudin V 1995 Ethics: the patient's charter. Scutari Press, London

Tudor Hart J 1988 A new kind of doctor: the general practitioner's part in the health of the community. Merlin Press, London

Waterworth S, Luker K A 1990 Reluctant collaborators: do patients want to be involved in decisions concerning care? Journal of Advanced Nursing 15:971–976

Chapter 20

Therapeutic communication and mental health problems

Mike Walsh

INTRODUCTION

Mental health problems are one of the most common presentations in primary care, accounting for approximately 25% of GP consultations (Craig & Boardman 1998). They also present in A&E departments and acute general wards, as well as in childhood and adolescence. Whilst helping people with serious mental illness is the role of the specialist mental health practitioner, the nurse practitioner has a key role to play in helping people with less serious mental health problems. In addition, many people experience serious emotional problems but are not suffering from mental illness. They may present in a host of ways, some of which are less obvious than others. Patients may be recently bereaved, the victim of domestic violence, under great stress as a result of social circumstances such as debt, or have a range of personality problems. S/he may simply be angry and frustrated at what is perceived to be inadequate treatment or feel desperately insecure and become very demanding as a result. Every patient has the potential to experience emotional difficulties such as these, which makes the health-care environment a potential minefield of uncertainty, psychological disruption and personal vulnerability. The crucial skills of therapeutic communication are therefore as essential as a stethoscope for the nurse practitioner.

COMMON MENTAL HEALTH PROBLEMS

DEPRESSION

Depression is the third most common reason for consultation in primary care (York CRD 2002) and up to 15% of the population experience depressive disorder, although many of them do not present for treatment and go unrecognized (Walters & Tylee 2003). The term depression covers a wide range of conditions from mild to severe. Mild depression represents a state of low mood which may simply be a normal reaction to adverse events such as losing a job or divorce. Such a low mood will spontaneously resolve. Chronic serious disease such as cancer, rheumatoid arthritis or renal failure will produce depressive symptoms of varying intensity. Some people experience only a single bout of depression while others have repeated episodes. Depression may present as a major depressive disorder which can totally disable a person and culminate in suicide. Many depressive episodes are now thought to be associated with brain biochemical disorders involving neurotransmitters such as serotonin and noradrenaline. Depression has a combination of physical (somatic) and psychological symptoms and can frequently occur in combination with anxiety. It also occurs across all cultures, even though many languages do not actually have a word equivalent to 'depression' (Armstrong 1995)

The common features of depression are a continual low mood state, lack of enjoyment of life, loss of interest and diminished activity associated with lack of energy. The following other symptoms may be present in varying degrees:

- Inability to concentrate
- Low self-esteem and lack of self confidence
- A sense of guilt
- A bleak pessimistic outlook on life
- Disturbed sleep and loss of appetite
- Suicidal thoughts or acts of deliberate self-harm.

The physical symptoms of depression include loss of appetite and weight, loss of libido and persistent early wakening. In severe depression there may also be hallucinations and delusions as the patient loses touch with reality, in which case the term 'psychosis' may be used by some authorities – indicating a lack of insight. Neurosis is a general term used to describe conditions where insight remains intact, although the word has acquired pejorative connotations and is best avoided. Although the prevalence of depression is rare in children, it reaches adult levels during adolescence.

ANXIETY

Anxiety is an essential human emotion for survival. If we were not worried or fearful we would be reckless and not live very long as a result. However in some people feelings of anxiety take over and dominate the person's whole life. The anxiety can be related to a specific object or situation, in which case it becomes a phobia and can be very disruptive. Alternatively the anxiety can be free floating with the person chronically anxious but not knowing why, possibly then becoming anxious about being anxious – a vicious circle that is difficult to break.

Such anxiety can lead to physical symptoms such as gastrointestinal pain, nausea, vomiting, palpitations, chronic fatigue and sweating – culminating in acute anxiety episodes which can be disabling and lead to collapse (Forster 1997). Anxiety can affect children where separation anxiety leading to refusal to go to school can become a problem. Social anxiety is a recognized problem in some children leading to the child finding it very difficult to socialize and make friends. Phobias usually have their origins in childhood with irrational fears (Roberts 1998).

SUBSTANCE MISUSE

Alcohol

The growing scale of this problem is revealed by the fact that 20–30% of all hospital admissions are alcohol-related and it is estimated there are 33 000 premature deaths each year in England and Wales due to the effects of alcohol. The destructive effects of alcohol lead to it contributing to 33% of all divorces and cases of child abuse, 80% of suicides, 50% of murders and 40% of road traffic accidents (Ashworth & Garada 1998). Since these statistics were compiled, a great deal of attention has recently been focussed on the problem of 'binge' drinking and its links to violence.

There are approximately 200 000 people in the UK who are alcohol-dependent. This is defined by the following signs (Haslet et al 2003):

- Drinking takes priority over other activities
- The range of alcoholic drinks becomes narrowed

- Increasing tolerance means that the person can drink more and more without becoming inebriated
- The person experiences withdrawal symptoms which are relieved by further alcohol intake
- The person feels compelled to drink; they have no control over this urge
- A repeated pattern of relapse after a period of abstinence.

Alcohol dependence or heavy drinking leads to the following physical health problems:

- Liver disease (cirrhosis, hepatitis)
- Pancreatitis
- Gastritis
- Hypertension, cardiac arrhythmias
- Cancers such as those affecting the mouth, oesophagus and liver
- Gout
- Neurological disorders such as blackouts, fits and neuropathy
- Erectile dysfunction.

In addition, anxiety, depression and personality changes are common. Withdrawal can lead to acute hallucinations and other features of delirium tremens.

There are important gender differences in the effects of alcohol. Becker & Walton-Moss (2001) remind us that as women have on average 14% less water in their bodies than men and as ethanol is a water-soluble molecule, women reach higher blood alcohol concentrations than men after drinking the same amount. This difference helps explain the lower 'safe limits' for weekly alcohol consumption in women compared to men. A further problem is that in women the rate of progression from being a heavy drinker to alcohol dependency is considerably quicker than men and female alcoholics have death rates 50–100% higher than men (Becker & Walton-Moss 2001). There is also the risk of damage to the fetus if a pregnant woman continues to drink. This is known as fetal alcohol syndrome and can lead to brain damage in the newborn infant.

Illegal substances

It is known that illegal drug use is a growing problem, but so too is the abuse of prescription medicines such as benzodiazepines, which is made easier by their widespread availability over the internet. Another aspect of this problem is anabolic steroid abuse which is prevalent amongst 20–40% of gym users and up to 50% of attenders at needle-exchange schemes are anabolic steroid users (Hampshire 2002). The following are some of the commonly used illegal drugs:

- Cocaine, which is a major and highly addictive stimulant especially when smoked as crack, the base form of cocaine. A high lasts for up to 15 minutes. Death in overdose is due to myocardial infarction, ventricular arrhythmia or hyperthermia.
- Opioids. Heroin is the drug of choice which can be sniffed or smoked as well as injected intravenously. Withdrawal symptoms begin after a few hours, peak at around 2–3 days and subside after a week (Gerada & Ashworth 1998). Death in overdose is usually from respiratory depression.
- Amphetamines are stimulants causing increased arousal and overactivity. Their effects last a few hours, after which the person becomes irritable, tired and depressed. Long-term use is associated with paranoid delusions and hallucinations.
- Ecstasy is a form of amphetamine whose euphoric and stimulant properties have made it very popular amongst young people on the club scene. Death can occur from hyperthermia and dehydration.
- Volatiles such as glue and lighter fuel are abused by groups of young boys, with similar effects to alcohol. Gerada & Ashworth (1998) estimate they produce 100 deaths per year in the UK.

MAJOR MENTAL DISORDER

The term psychosis has already been introduced, indicating the person has lost touch with reality. Severe depression can manifest itself with psychotic symptoms such as hallucinations in this way. Some patients exhibit dramatic mood swings and after recovering from a depressive episode may progress to a manic state. This psychotic condition is known as bipolar disorder (formerly known as manic depression). Other patients may just exhibit episodes of mania without the depressive component.

Schizophrenia is a major psychiatric disorder with an annual incidence of 10–15 per 100 000 (Turner 1998). There is thought to be a significant genetic component in this disease, which typically develops in early adulthood. The patient exhibits delusions (false irrational beliefs such as thoughts being tampered with, aliens controlling the person or secret messages broadcast on television), hallucinations (frequently auditory as they hear voices talking about themselves in the third person) and disordered thought patterns, which are expressed in speech, the sense of which is difficult to follow. Withdrawal from the surrounding world, lack of emotion and activity together with loss of initiative also develop. This is accompanied by neglect of personal appearance. It is quite common to have consultations with anxious parents worried about their son as his personality has changed markedly and he does not seem to care anymore. The parents may be seeking advice as they think he is on drugs. This could be the first indication of a developing schizophrenic illness. Turner (1998) estimates that some 20% of patients will require long-term intensive psychiatric care, about 50% can manage in the community with support, whilst the remaining 30% hold down jobs and function with a high level of independence.

DEMENTIA

The incidence of this problem is increasing with the ageing population. It refers to a gradual loss of intellectual or cognitive function which interferes with the person's everyday life. There is a wide range of diseases which can cause dementia. The two most common are Alzheimer's disease and disease affecting the vasculature of the brain. Dementia is a major problem in the elderly and may easily be confused with depression (Maynard 2003).

Dementia itself is a syndrome whose origins lie in a defect in the neuronal circuitry in the brain, whatever the cause. The manifestations of dementia are a decline in short- and long-term memory, orientation, knowledge and cognitive ability, reasoning, abstraction (the ability to generalize) and general use of language (Springhouse 2000). The early stages often present as memory loss, short-term memory loss being most obvious, and personality changes. As the degenerative process continues the person may become unsteady and clumsy, disoriented in time and space, no longer recognize people, incontinent and ultimately completely dependent upon others as their whole mental and physical functioning disintegrates.

SUICIDE AND DELIBERATE SELF-HARM (DSH)

Deliberate self-harm (DSH) can range from minor superficial scratches or taking a small quantity of tablets all the way to a completed suicide. Suicides account for approximately 5000 deaths in the UK each year (Hale 1998) and recent trends show an increase in young men committing suicide. It is estimated that 40–50% of suicides have a previous history of DSH and many suicides have seen their GP or some other caring agency in the period immediately before their suicide. Whilst the true number of DSH incidents is impossible to know, as many never reach hospital, a conservative estimate is 150 000 per year in the UK (York CRD 1998). DSH is a significant problem in adolescence with estimates as high as 13% of 15- and 16-year-olds engaging in DSH (Hawton 2002). For every completed adolescent suicide in the USA there are approximately 1000 non-fatal cases (Koplin & Agathen 2002).

McAlaney (2004), in reviewing this data, points out the lack of facilities for adolescents. The review also brings out the point that while a very high proportion of suicides have already presented with DSH or some other warning problem, the vast majority of people who do self-harm do not go on to suicide. This presents the NHS with the major problem of managing the large numbers of DSH patients, but also trying to identify the small minority of suicide risk patients amongst them.

EATING DISORDERS

Anorexia nervosa involves deliberate self-starvation leading to emaciation. It mostly affects females in adolescence and early adulthood. The key diagnostic criteria include a weight which is 25% or more below the norm for the person's age, height and sex or a Body Mass Index of below $17.5 \, \text{kg/m}^2$. Patients have an unreal and distorted body image – seeing themselves as obese no matter how emaciated they actually are. Amenorrhoea of at least 3 months duration is another feature. Anorexia has been described as a physical expression of severe emotional distress. At its heart lies the view that loss of weight will in some way lead to an improved life. The person typically has very low self-esteem and feelings of guilt (Murphy & Manning 2003). The alternate binge eating and extreme dieting of bulimia is also associated with lack of self-esteem and guilt but has a better prognosis than anorexia. Both conditions are associated with significant psychological co-morbidity (depression, anxiety) as well as serious physical health problems. A significant proportion of anorexic patients will die either as a result of their illness or suicide; Crisp & McClelland (1996) estimated that 12–20% of patients will have a fatal outcome.

HISTORY-TAKING

Taking a history from a patient with mental health or emotional problems can be as difficult as it is important. The development of basic communication skills will greatly facilitate this process and can take the heat out of potentially confrontational situations. In addition, it is important to know when simple counselling skills can help patients tell you their story and take responsibility for making decisions about their care. This can reduce problems of non-concordance. You also need to know when to refer patients for specialist counselling help. This chapter seeks to help you in these important aspects of your work and is aimed at finding communication strategies that can help you in your therapeutic response, laying the foundation for the development of a therapeutic relationship. Although we can suggest principles, it is what you do with these principles that determines the success of the intervention. Feedback and ongoing evaluation of personal performance in nurse–patient relationships is crucial to following these guidelines and selecting the right tools for the right situation. If one response does not work then there may be others.

As ever, in taking a history it is important to have a structure to guide you. Initially you will ask the patient to explain why they have come to see you and want them to give you an account of their problems. The patient may give a vague story of feeling tired or unwell rather than openly admitting they are having mental or emotional problems. Tact and awareness are therefore needed to guide the consultation into this area.

Assuming that the patient is eventually prepared to talk about their psychological problems, Jarvis (2000) makes an important point. She reminds us that you are always inferring a person's mental state from their behaviour whereas in a physical exam you are testing or measuring directly factors such

as blood pressure or reflexes. The following are the key aspects that Jarvis considers you should be assessing while the patient is telling you their story:

- Consciousness; awareness of self and surroundings
- Language; clarity of expression, speed and volume of speech
- Orientation; in time and place
- Attention; concentration
- Memory; long- and short-term
- Abstract meaning; going beyond the literal concrete meaning of words
- Thought processes; speed and logicality
- Thought content; what a person says and believes
- Perceptions; awareness through the five senses.

Any abnormality in these areas would suggest a mental health problem. A particularly useful tool that Jarvis (2000) suggests is the ABCT mnemonic. This incorporates the items listed above:

- **A**ppearance. Check posture, movement and other non-verbal communication. Assess whether the person is dressed appropriately and whether they are clean and well groomed or dishevelled and neglected.
- **B**ehaviour. Start by checking whether they are alert or confused, drowsy or lethargic. Facial expressions may be relaxed, smiling or tense and expressing anger. Speech may be slow or rapid, easy or difficult – indicating problems expressing themselves. It may be disjointed and make little sense, indicating seriously disorganized thought processes. A loud voice could indicate anger. The whole demeanour and behaviour of the person may tell you a great deal about their mood – be it sad, withdrawn, angry, distressed or agitated.
- **C**ognition. Key areas to explore here include orientation in time and space, memory and attention span. How realistic is the patient being in what they are saying?
- **T**hought processes. Do thoughts flow in a logical sequence or suddenly stop and jump on to something else quite unconnected? This is 'thought block', a classic sign of schizophrenia. The content of what they are saying should be logical and demonstrate insight, rather than evidence of delusions. Assess whether the person is in contact with the real world or whether there is evidence of hallucinations.

One final key issue is to check for suicidal thoughts. This is difficult but use questions such as:

- Have you ever felt so low that you have thought of harming yourself?
- Do you have a plan to harm yourself?
- Do you feel like harming yourself now?
- How do you think other people would react if you were dead?

This simple framework can be applied from the moment the patient walks into the consultation.

Having established the patient's perceptions of their mental and emotional problems, the history should review their previous medical history, including both physical and mental illness. Family history is particularly important, including marital status, dependent children and the patient's own parents. Any history of mental illness in the family should be carefully checked as both schizophrenia and bipolar disorders have a strong genetic component (Epstein et al 2003).

The patient's personal history takes on added importance, especially their childhood and their relationships with their own parents. Ascertain whether the patient considers they had a happy childhood and verify the answer by further probing as sometimes contradictions become apparent. Sexual development is important – ascertaining when a female reached menarche, her menstrual history and whether she is sexually active. An important point for male patients concerns their sexuality, in particular if they are gay, and how easy it was to discuss this at home. The personal history should include information about the state of the person's marriage or relationship with their partner as well as their occupational history. Domestic stresses should be explored as factors such as debt, an abusive partner, alcohol and drug abuse, and unemployment may all be contributing to serious emotional and mental health problems.

A useful approach to assessing alcohol and drug use is set out on p. 23 involving the CAGE screening tool. This tool is effective in revealing harmful drinking but less so in revealing hazardous levels of alcohol consumption (Alcohol Concern 2002). CAGE has been refined for use with women given the differences that exist in the effects of alcohol on men and women. The refined version is known as the 'TWEAK' questionnaire and is given in Box 20.1.

Box 20.1 TWEAK Screen for Alcohol Problems in Women

- Tolerance : How many drinks can you hold (>6 indicates tolerance) OR How many drinks does it take before you notice a difference in your mood? (>3 indicates tolerance)
- Worry: Have close friends or relatives worried or complained about your drinking in the last year?
- Eye-opener: Do you sometimes take a drink in the morning when you first get up?
- Amnesia : Has a friend or family member ever told you about things you said or did that you could not remember?
- Kut down: Do you sometimes feel the need to 'kut-down' your drinking?

Scoring: 2 points for a yes to the tolerance and worry questions, one point for the others. A total of 2 or more indicates a drinking problem

Source: Russell 1994

The Five Shot questionnaire (Box 20.2) has also been based on the CAGE tool and is aimed at detecting hazardous drinking habits before they become harmful (Seppa et al 1998).

Box 20.2 Five Shot Questionnaire

1. How often do you have a drink containing alcohol?
   - (0) Never
   - (0.5) monthly or less
   - (1.0) two or four times a month
   - (1.5) two or three times a week
   - (2.0) four or more times a week

2. How many drinks do you have on a typical day when you are drinking?
   - (0) 1 or 2
   - (0.5) 3 or 4
   - (1.0) 5 or 6
   - (1.5) 7–9
   - (2.0) 10 or more

3. Have people annoyed you by criticizing your drinking?
   - (0) No
   - (1) Yes

Box 20.2 Five Shot Questionnaire—*cont'd*

4. Have you ever felt bad or guilty about your drinking?
   - (0) No
   - (1) Yes

5. Have you ever had a drink first thing in the morning to steady your nerves or get rid of a hangover
   - (0) No
   - (1) Yes

Scoring: A score of 2.5 or more indicates possible alcohol misuse and the need for further investigation.

A range of similar screening tools has been designed to assess both depression and anxiety. A review by the York CRD (2002), however, reported that routine administration of such questionnaires had no impact upon the recognition and management of depression. However if scored by the practice nurse and then active feedback was given to clinicians if the results were above a diagnostic threshold, this increased detection rates of depression. Use of such tools therefore has to be more than a routine paper chore if they are to be of value in helping recognize depression. The key features of depression are outlined in Box 20.3 and key questions in the diagnosis of anxiety are given in Box 20.4.

Box 20.3 Key features in depression

Presenting complaints
May present initially with one or more physical symptoms (fatigue, pain). Further inquiries will reveal depression or loss of interest.

Diagnostic features
Associated symptoms are frequently present:

- disturbed sleep
- guilt or low self-worth
- fatigue or loss of energy
- poor concentration
- disturbed appetite
- suicidal thoughts or acts.

Movements and speech may be slowed, but may also appear agitated. Symptoms of anxiety or nervousness are frequently also present.

Box 20.3 Key features in depression—*cont'd*

Differential diagnosis
If hallucinations (hearing voices, seeing visions) or delusions (strange or unusual beliefs) are present consider acute psychotic disorder.

If a history of manic episode (excitement, elevated mood, rapid speech) is present consider bipolar disorder.

If heavy alcohol use is present consider alcohol use disorder and drug use disorder

Source: Freeman 1997

Box 20.4 Key questions to diagnose generalized anxiety

1. Have you felt keyed up / on edge?
2. Have you been worrying a lot?
3. Have you been irritable?
4. Have you had difficulty relaxing?

If the person answers 'yes' to 2 or more of those questions, proceed to ask:

5. Have you been sleeping poorly?
6. Have you had any of the following: trembling, tingling, dizzy spells, sweating, diarrhoea or frequency?
7. Have you been worried about your health?
8. Have you had difficulty falling asleep?

Score one point for each yes answer. Five or more points indicate a 50% probability of a clinically important disorder.

Source: Freeman 1997

DIFFERENTIAL DIAGNOSIS

Anxiety and depression are two common disorders that can be difficult to distinguish. According to Freeman (1997) the following symptoms are more typical of depressive rather than anxiety disorders and can help in making this differential:

- lowered mood
- loss of interest
- thoughts of guilt or worthlessness
- loss of energy and fatigue
- early morning wakening
- broken sleep

- indecision
- inability to concentrate
- somatic symptoms
- loss of appetite
- loss of libido
- suicidal ideas.

Another very important differential in older people is between depression and dementia. Maynard (2003) suggests that practitioners should work with the following six-step framework to improve their differential diagnostic skills in this area.

1. Assess and reflect upon your own assumptions about the ageing process. You may unwittingly be set up to favour a diagnosis of depression because you assume that growing old is a depressing experience or conversely you may assume cognitive deterioration is commonplace in ageing and so favour a diagnosis of dementia.

2. Rule out normal ageing. In normal ageing, a person's cognitive abilities are relatively stable, although there may be a slight decline in learning ability. An older person may forget where they put things but they do not normally forget birthdays or where they live.

3. Know the signs and symptoms of depression. Everybody, whatever their age, can have a bad day, but a prolonged sense of despair is abnormal.

4. Understand dementia and know its signs and symptoms.

5. Now you are ready to perform a thorough assessment involving a careful history and a physical exam which focuses on the neurological system. There are frequently no physical signs in early Alzheimer's disease, however.

6. Making the differential diagnosis from the information you have gathered (see Table 20.1).

PHYSICAL EXAMINATION AND INVESTIGATIONS

It is important that a physical examination is conducted to rule out any coexisting morbidity, especially as this might be contributing to the patient's mental health problem. Often a mental health problem will be a diagnosis of exclusion as the patient on presentation will have a physical complaint such as fatigue or sleeplessness. Investigations may be necessary to eliminate conditions such as anaemia. A plasma gamma-glutamyl transferase (GGT) measure can give important information

Table 20.1 Differential diagnosis of depression and dementia*

Characteristic	Depression	Dementia
Mental status	Able to follow instructions although may refuse to do so. Often answers 'don't know' to questions	Worsens as disease progresses. Denies memory problems, attempts to answer all questions. Confabulation common
Onset	Weeks to months	Insidious
Course	Self-limiting, recurring episodes but with periods of improvement	Slow continual decline
Affect	Pervasive sadness	Cognitive decline precedes depressive affect, no depression may present at all. Emotionally labile at first then apathetic. Suspicious at times
Behaviour	Apathetic, fatigued. Patient complains more than family	Agitated, aggressive or apathetic. Family more concerned than patient. Wandering
Sleep	Early morning wakening. Insomnia or excess sleep	Normal at first, then repeated wakening and finally day/night reversal
Memory	Slowed recall, often short-term memory deficits	Short-term memory loss in early stages then long-term memory loss later
Attention	Problem concentrating	Intact, may focus on one thing for a long time
Perception	Intact, although severe depression may be associated with hallucinations	Misperceives events/people as threatening
History	Often has previous psychiatric history with undiagnosed episodes of depression	Psychiatric history less common

*Source: Maynard (2003).

about the effects of heavy alcohol use on the liver as it will be elevated if damage is occurring.

TREATMENT

Serious mental illness is the province of mental health specialists and if detected by the nurse practitioner should be promptly referred in line with local protocols. Treatment of severe mental illness and complicated conditions such as substance abuse therefore lie outside the scope of this chapter. However the nurse practitioner can still help a large number of people with less severe mental health problems.

DEPRESSION AND ANXIETY

A key first step in treating depression in primary care is to discuss the options with the patient and work to a plan that is 'tailored' to their needs (Walters & Tylee 2003). This greatly increases the degree of concordance that can be expected and hence the chances of a positive outcome. A range of options is possible with several quite different types of drugs now available. Various 'talking therapies' may also be tried along with alternative therapies. Different patients will respond best to different packages of care.

A major systematic review (York CRD 2002) into the recognition and management of depression in primary care indicated that there was a real role for non-psychiatric primary care nurses. This review found that simple telephone support, monitoring of medication and the use of counselling skills such as those outlined below were clinically and cost effective. Practice nurses who had been given some extra training in management of depression were especially effective. It will be some time before nurse practitioners are able to prescribe antidepressant medication, but this remains the bedrock of therapy and is most effective in the most severely depressed – although talking therapy such as cognitive behaviour therapy is equally effective in the less severely depressed (Hale 1998). Ensuring that the patient takes their medication is critical and it is here that the primary care based NP can be very effective in supporting and encouraging the patient.

Selective serotonin reuptake inhibitors (SSRIs) are the most recent group of antidepressants to become available and they work by inhibiting the re-uptake of serotonin in the brain. They have significant side effects such as increasing the risk of gastric bleeds and should only be used cautiously if the patient also has epilepsy. They interact dangerously with the older monoamine-oxidase inhibitors (MOAIs) which are also used to treat depression, although a lot less frequently today. The third group of drugs is the tricyclic antidepressants, which have a wide range of side effects including cardiac arrhythmias such as heart block and the ability to interact dangerously with SSRIs and MAOIs (BNF 2003). It is important that the NP is fully aware of the side effects and interactions of these three major groups of drugs before offering support. It may take some time for their effects to become apparent to the patient so considerable encouragement is required in the early stage of treatment. There is also the danger of the patient stopping their medication without telling anybody as they feel well and then slowly slipping back into a depressive state.

There has been considerable interest in the use of St John's Wort as a natural alternative remedy for depression. Evidence indicates that it can have beneficial effects but it does have a range of interactions with conventional drugs such as anticonvulsants and antidepressants (Moore & McLaughlin 2003).

Brief interventions (counselling and structured problem-solving techniques) can help patients with anxiety-related problems (Hale 1998). These brief interventions are defined as behavioural counselling by a generalist clinician, lasting from a few minutes up to a maximum of 1 hour and restricted to a maximum of four sessions (Bien et al 1993). The counselling skills outlined in the following sections can be very beneficial in helping such patients. Minor tranquillizers may also be prescribed such as the benzodiazepines but there is a potential for dependence to develop. Moore & McLaughlin (2003) observe that many patients find their anxiety is helped by alternative therapies such as massage and touch. Brief interventions can also assist patients reduce their alcohol intake as long as they have not become alcohol dependent (Becker & Walton-Moss 2001).

DELIBERATE SELF-HARM

Treatment in this area is generally unsatisfactory. A major systematic review by Hawton (2004) analysed 23 trials of different interventions and found no clear evidence as to which approach was more effective than another. Those trials that did appear to give positive results were too small and had not been replicated. This repeats the findings of the York CRD (1998) whose systematic review concluded that there was insufficient evidence to recommend a specific clinical intervention to help people who self-harm. The best approach is therefore to utilize the skills outlined in the next section and refer on for a specialist assessment, given the known suicide risk.

HELPING SKILLS: EGAN'S MODEL OF HELPING

Egan's model offers a framework for working with the patient to achieve exploration, understanding and action on his or her problems. Originally geared towards the world of counselling, Egan (1986) argues that his model is applicable to any context in which people need help and as such can easily be translated to the health-care setting (Duxbury & Brown 1997). The approach is essentially a general framework for helping people to help themselves (Davis & Fallowfield 1994) and is suitable for nurse practitioners helping patients with complex personal problems over a period of time. It consists of three stages: problem clarification, setting goals and facilitating action.

Stage 1: problem clarification

In order to address problems effectively it is necessary to have a full picture of the individual's experience and needs. This requires exploration of how you as a nurse perceive the situation and also full exploration of the presenting problem from the client's viewpoint. Egan commonly refers to this as encouraging the person to 'tell their story' and the nurse practitioner will be familiar with the importance of this in history-taking. Allowing the individual to outline these feelings takes time and an ability on the part of the helper to establish a trusting and supportive atmosphere (Davis & Fallowfield 1994). This stage also involves the early initial phases of bonding.

How the practitioner manages this early stage will lay the foundations for future progress. In order to establish a fruitful therapeutic relationship, the following are needed – active listening skills, the use of reflection in portraying empathy, probing to explore certain areas more fully and the ability to respond appropriately ensuring consistency in both your verbal and non-verbal communications. Above all it is crucial that the individual feels valued by the helper, which requires a style that gives messages of respect, genuineness and trust. The ability to show your patients that you are interested in them, accepting of their needs and willing to help requires an effective combination of verbal and non-verbal communication skills. These qualities will be invaluable even if your consultation is with a straightforward patient who has a problem which is mainly physical (e.g. asthma). If your patient has multiple social and emotional difficulties then this model is even more beneficial. Your assessment and problem clarification work lead logically to the second and third stages, described below.

Stage 2: setting goals

We do not always recognize our own problems or the part we can play in solving them. Sometimes our view of what has happened is distorted, therefore the helper can enable clients to develop a more realistic understanding of their situation. This can be achieved because, as practitioners, we are able to stand outside a situation which may for the client be loaded with pain, anxiety or disappointment. We can also identify potential weaknesses and untapped resources, giving a much fuller picture of the individual's situation beyond his or her own subjective view.

Once a better understanding has been gained we can help the person decide what s/he would like to achieve by way of managing the problems identified. This in turn may involve setting a single goal or a series of sub-goals, leading to a final desired outcome for more complex problems. Goals must be clear, specific, measurable, realistic, achievable and owned by the individuals themselves. If goals are not set in this way then often the patient will have difficulty moving on to the third stage.

Stage 3: facilitating action

The aim of this final stage is to put into operation ways of achieving goals set in stage 2. This is a crucial stage and requires you to be a catalyst rather than a doer, which requires facilitation skills rather prescriptive and informative skills. Evaluation of client progress is essential as it leads to the beginning of a new cycle of therapeutic intervention.

Example

Mrs X weighed 100 kg but claimed that, despite following a 1000 cal/day diet rigorously and taking exercise, she could not lose any weight. The nurse practitioner realized that conventional patient teaching and information-giving techniques were not working and so began to explore the situation with Mrs X using Egan's framework. The first stage of exploration was used to analyse the patient's situation. With gentle probing she revealed that she did take a mug of Horlicks and a ginger biscuit before going to bed as this helped her sleep. Having shared this with the nurse practitioner, Mrs X immediately said, 'I suppose I could cut out the Horlicks and biscuits'. Attending and listening skills had helped the patient to start to solve her own problem. It transpired that since the death of her husband a year previously she had found sleeping difficult. This knowledge allowed the nurse practitioner and Mrs X to explore other strategies to help her sleep. Subsequent sessions revealed other digressions from the 1000-calorie diet that she had not mentioned at the first meeting and on each occasion it was Mrs X who came up with a solution which allowed her to adhere to the correct diet more consistently. The exploration, understanding and action stages of Egan's model were all in evidence in helping Mrs X.

Therapeutic communication skills

In order to use Egan's model, or simply to get the patient to tell you the full story during a history-taking session, there are certain skills which are invaluable. The most fundamental communication skill involves the ability to attend to patients fully and to listen actively. Patients rate the need to be listened to highly and these skills involve both verbal and non-verbal behaviour.

Attending skills

Attending skills involve being receptive to another person both verbally and non-verbally. This includes displaying non-verbal signals that show constant attention and being able to communicate the same to another by means of eye contact, head nods, facial expression and appropriate verbal encouraging clues.

Active listening

Active listening includes the process of attending but takes the concept of hearing and showing you are hearing to a much deeper level, and is essential for therapeutic communication. It is a dynamic process whereby one person hears a message, decides upon its meaning and conveys an understanding about the meaning to the sender. It includes the integration of factors such as non-verbal cues, tone of voice, intuition and previous conversations. Above all, in listening to a person, you must be sure that you really hear that person's voice rather than respond to a stereotype which may be quite discriminatory.

Passive listening requires far less time and energy and largely involves lying back and letting something happen. It is highlighted by non-attending and is often without response or with an inaccurate response.

The SOLER framework is well known as a guide for active listening. Although a basic recipe, it incorporates the crucial elements of attending effectively:

- S: sit squarely to your patient
- O: Adopt an open posture
- L: Lean slightly forward
- E: Maintain good eye contact
- R: Endeavour to portray a relaxed approach.

The key is to show concern and interest in an accepting and relaxed atmosphere. It is not about putting yourself into positions that feel unreal and unnatural to you, but about recognizing the importance of what you say and do in establishing a trusting relationship. SOLER largely emphasizes the non-verbal elements of actively listening, yet when you are listening, the intermittent verbal messages you give back to the patient must also be recognized and valued for their importance. Verbal skills will assist the active listening process and prompt patients to open up more, allowing you to listen more effectively. Nelson-Jones (1994) suggests the following combination of skills: openers, small rewards and open-ended questions. Each requires the use of only a few words as well as good and accurate voice and body messages.

Openers

Openers indicate 'I am interested and prepared to listen' such as 'You seem a bit down today, is there something on your mind?' Your tone of voice and body message must be congruent with your verbal messages in order to be effective. Some clients may find it difficult to talk straightaway, therefore an encouraging comment such as 'Take your time' might be useful. Setting the scene in any relationship is all-important and first impressions really do count. Persuading a patient to open up on that initial meeting, even though feeling vulnerable, is a crucial step forward.

Small rewards

These are brief verbal expressions of interest designed to encourage the speaker to continue once started. Examples are 'Go on' or 'And…'. Another form of small reward is to repeat the last word or last few words back to someone in the form of a question. So, for instance, if a patient said to you 'I feel so angry with him for what he did', you might want to turn this into a question – 'What he did?' This shows you are both listening attentively and interested and encourages the individual to expand upon something that is obviously painful.

Open-ended questions

These encourage individuals to elaborate their internal viewpoints or get them to expand into an area you feel is important. They cannot be answered by yes, no or a one-word response and usually begin with 'In what way…?' or 'Can you tell me…?' They are the how and why questions.

Empathy

Empathy in its most fundamental sense involves understanding the experience, behaviours and feelings of others as they experience them. The concept was developed by Rogers (1957) who defined empathy as the ability 'to sense the client's private world as if it were your own without ever losing the "as if" quality'. Empathy should not be confused with sympathy, which involves sharing the same feelings as another person as opposed to recognizing these feelings (Thompson 1996).

Empathy consists of natural basic empathy we all have and trained empathy which we can learn and use therapeutically (White 1997). A crucial point made by Baillie (1997) is that empathy is useless unless the nurse communicates back to the patient that s/he is empathizing with them – there has to be an external expression of empathy. This should not be a glib remark such as 'I know how you feel', when clearly a young female nurse practitioner aged 30 cannot know how a 70-year-old widower, who has just been discharged after major surgery for rectal cancer, really feels.

Entering into the other person's world is a difficult and challenging task, but it can be rewarding therapeutically. For instance, a client talks about his anger at his wife, but as he talks, the helper hears not just anger but also hurt. It may be that someone can talk with relative ease about anger but not about feelings of hurt. Empathetic listeners ask themselves questions such as 'What is this person only half saying?'.

A key skill involved in the process of empathy is reflection, which involves rewording the client's statements, reflecting feelings and the reasons that might lie behind them. Skilled helpers are very sharp at picking up clients' feelings. Reflecting feelings is built upon the ability to reword. Both reflecting feelings and rewording involve taking what the patient has said to you and rephrasing the gist of the meaning in your own words. It is not about parroting or just repeating.

Rewording alone has distinct limitations. The nurse practitioner must look beyond superficial words to find feelings and reasons. The client may say 'I'm OK' yet be speaking with tearful eyes. A good reflection of feelings picks up these messages and reflects them back to the client. A simple example of rewording might be:

Mother: "I told my kids to go to hell."

Nurse practitioner: "You were really angry with them."

A good rewording of verbal content can provide mirror reflections that are clearer than the original statements. Clients may show appreciation and feel that you are in tune with them and say something like, 'That's right'. A simple tip for rewording is to start your responses with 'You'.

Rewording is a basic technique used mainly to reflect verbal content. However, the language of feelings is not just words. Reflecting feelings is seeing a client's flow of emotions and being able to communicate this back to him or her. Inadequately distinguishing between thoughts and feelings can be a problem for both clients and helpers. The distinction is important both in reflecting feelings and also when helping clients to influence how they feel by altering how they think. Constant reflective responding which focuses on feelings runs the risk of encouraging clients to wallow in feelings rather than to move on to how best to deal with them.

A useful formula is: 'I think I hear what you're saying. It sounds like you … am I right?' Further clarification might still be needed, such as: 'I'm not altogether clear what you're saying to me.' This is the core skill of clarification and is an ongoing and integral part of reflection. When reflecting feelings there are two key stages:

- Decode the overall message accurately using any of the above techniques
- Formulate an emotionally expressive reflective response that communicates back the crux of the client's feelings.

A useful variation on reflective responding is to reflect both feelings and the reasons for them. This does not mean that you make your own interpretation or offer an explanation from your external viewpoint but instead use the client's reasons for a feeling.

Here the helper's 'You feel … because' response shows greater understanding. This helps clients tell their stories and reveals how the client's thinking contributes to unwanted feelings. The following tips are useful for improving the quality of empathy:

- Give yourself time to think – don't jump in!
- Use short responses – it is the client you want to engage in dialogue
- Gear your responses to the individual client – share emotional tone.

Advanced empathy is a term highlighted by Egan (1986) and involves giving expression to that which the client only implies. This is particularly in relation to finding feelings and meanings that are buried or beyond the immediate reach of the client. It is an ongoing process that involves piecing together relevant information and experience from the helping relationship. The nurse practitioner has to beware of putting words in the client's mouth, however. Advanced empathy can be communicated in a number of different ways:

- Expressing what is only implied once rapport has been established.
- Identifying themes – patterns of behaviour and/or emotion, e.g. poor self-image, helplessness.
- Connecting islands – building bridges and helping clients to make connections or fill the gaps between emotions and behaviours. It may be that you notice they become angry or upset at certain times or when discussing certain people or situations.
- From the less to the more – unclear issues are clarified and built upon. Greater understanding may be achieved as you explore issues with

them and ask for clarification or check out uncertainties. Do not be afraid to get the clearest possible picture you can. If you do not understand, say so. This also means that you role model good foundations, whereby the client will feel more able to ask questions when unsure.

Example of empathy in action

On New Year's Eve, a local publican presented at the health centre with a history of chest pain. Examination and an ECG were carried out leading to a provisional diagnosis of a myocardial infarction. Arrangements were made for admission to hospital. At this point the man became very distressed and asked if the admission could be delayed until after New Year. The nurse practitioner was aware that this was the busiest time of the year for a publican and checked her understanding of this fact with the patient by stating 'It seems you are feeling really worried about how your pub will cope without you over New Year'. The subsequent dialogue involved the patient expressing his disbelief that this was happening to him as well as his fears of what would happen to the business at this crucial time of the year in his absence. A critical component of actively empathizing with the patient is detachment and the nurse practitioner was careful to retain her own identity during the dialogue, which concluded with the patient agreeing to admission. Without this therapeutic communication, involving the nurse practitioner empathizing with the patient, it is possible he may have refused admission, with tragic consequences.

One final point is that we must lay our own feelings aside in order to achieve full empathic understanding. Identifying too closely with the patient or thinking this could never happen to me will prevent empathy.

DIFFICULT SITUATIONS: COPING WITH AGGRESSION AND CONFRONTATION

One issue which causes a great deal of concern in dealing with mental health problems is the risk of aggression and confrontation which could turn to violence, so we will finish this chapter with a discussion of this problem.

Aggression and violence are forms of confrontation and are more directly threatening than passivity, withdrawal or manipulation (Miller 1990). As such, they are the most feared form of behaviour experienced by nurses in all specialities. Although some areas such as A&E departments and mental health settings have a more widely reported incidence of violence, all nurses are at risk and report episodes of expressed patient anger that may escalate into something more violent (Duxbury 1999). Irrespective of place of work, nurses are increasingly likely to face confrontation from patients and their kin. Confrontation is usually caused by a combination of factors such as unrealistic expectations, stretched resources and increased waiting times, the effects of stress and lowered morale on staff, impaired communication, alcohol and other drugs.

Any person-centred activity can be a minefield of anxieties, complaints, fears and frustrations which can result in confrontation if not recognized and addressed. When dealing with confrontation, communication is largely both the problem and the solution. Questions regarding prognosis, waiting times, information about treatment and even questions which relate to the nurse's knowledge, skill and ability can appear challenging and confrontational. The need to communicate effectively and understand the difficulties of being a patient are essential steps in reducing the incidence of aggression and confrontation.

The confrontational patient poses a range of real and potential problems for the nurse practitioner, the biggest of which is the degree of threat that confrontation involves. Aggression is mostly the expression of anger with an implication of violence. Violence is the actual physical act against another, self or property which is intended to cause damage. Often it is simply not enough to feel an emotion, there is also the urge to express it in some form which is unknown until it happens. Past experience will influence our concern about an aggressive encounter with a patient while our responses will play a crucial part in determining the course of an aggressive outburst. The following key points will help reduce the risk of an aggressive person becoming violent:

- Do not raise your voice in response to shouting or give any other non-verbal cues to the individual which might provoke further confrontation (e.g. facial expressions, body posture).
- Avoid direct eye contact: this can be threatening and challenging in these circumstances.

- Stand slightly more than arm's length away from the individual. This avoids crowding his/her personal space and also reduces the risk of you being grabbed or punched suddenly.
- The ideal posture is slightly oblique to the individual (square-on is confrontational) with your weight on your dominant leg, which should be slightly behind you and your arms by your side. This is least threatening but gives you the best chance of taking defensive action in the event of a sudden attack.
- Try and find out what is causing the aggression and try to make the person understand that you want to help.
- If the person is with others, try and talk to him or her alone. Removing the group usually reduces the risk of violence, although if one individual is having a calming effect on the patient, try and retain that person's involvement.
- It is easier to repair damaged property than damaged staff, therefore if the person starts breaking things, do not physically intervene.

In many cases, speaking in an even tone, establishing what the problem is and that you are there to help will calm things down and allow for a successful outcome. If the situation does escalate out of control the police should be called and as a matter of policy assaults upon staff should result in prosecution.

Although the confrontational patient is feared for his or her potential to become aggressive, other forms of confrontational behaviour are possible. This may include:

- The lodging of a formal written complaint.
- A disagreement over care which may lead to non-concordance. Such confrontations are particularly common in mental health or in patients with chronic problems who may see no need for therapeutic interventions which have no immediate effect.
- Patients who refuse to co-operate when their values do not conform to those of the health professionals. This may range from the strong beliefs held by certain religious groups regarding various medical interventions to unhealthy or high-risk lifestyle choices. Patients may also not wish to follow traditional medical care but opt instead to follow a course of alternative therapy of no empirically demonstrated benefit.

- Assertive patients who make reasonable demands upon our service by requesting information may still be perceived as a threat to our authority.
- Patients who display emotive behaviours such as fear, sadness, anxiety and neediness. Many nurses find it difficult to cope with displays of emotion, be it their own or that of the patients they care for (Burnard & Morrison 1991).
- Patients who overstep the nurse–patient relationship boundaries. This may include patients who are sexually intrusive.

All these individuals may be viewed as emotionally disturbed clients. No one set of behaviours is more problematic or distressing for the nurse than another. Each will be rated and perceived by different nurses in different ways depending upon experience, personality, knowledge and confidence. What may be perceived as a threat one day may appear less troublesome in the light of a new day. Personal variables and situational context are important in our experience of emotional patients, whether withdrawn, passive, demanding, confrontational or generally uncooperative.

Emotionally disturbed patients will also experience a level of threat; therefore there must be joint exploration, discussion and negotiation about the way forward. In order to be most effective, the degree of non co-operation, the reasons behind it and the behaviour it leads to must be determined. It may be a deliberate act to block progress, a personal attack against an individual practitioner, a protective defence mechanism or a genuine lack of knowledge and awareness. Only when these issues are explored and determined can an effective therapeutic programme be initiated.

The most beneficial approach to ensuring that the needs of the emotionally disturbed patient are met is to focus on the positive challenge facing the nurse and the ultimate difference s/he can make. To view such patients in a solely negative light can only do harm and perpetuate the need. Nurses must try to put subjectivity to one side and objectively seek to intervene, on the understanding that here you have an individual in distress. Recognize the distress and the underlying thinking and feelings of the individual and a therapeutic connection may be possible.

Summary

The NP has a major role to play in the recognition and management of mental health problems in a range of settings and across the age spectrum. Patients with serious mental illness or who have become dependent on alcohol or other substances need specialist help but early recognition and referral may improve their outlook. Many other less serious emotional and mental health problems can however be successfully managed by the NP as part of the primary care team. On a more general note, the communication skills outlined in this chapter will enhance your history-taking in any situation, whilst the advice on dealing with aggression is also widely applicable.

References

Alcohol Concern 2002 Primary care alcohol information service; screening tools for health care settings. Alcohol Concern, London. Online: www.alcoholconcern.org.uk

Armstrong E 1995 Mental health issues in primary care. Macmillan, London

Ashworth, M Garada C 1998 Addiction and dependence; illicit drugs. In: Davies T, Craig T (eds) ABC of mental health. BMJ, London

Baillie L 1997 A phenomenological study of empathy. Journal of Advanced Nursing 24:1300–1308

Becker K, Walton-Moss B 2001 Detecting and addressing alcohol abuse in women. The Nurse Practitioner 26(10):13–23

BNF 2003 British National Formulary 45. BMA/RPSGB, London

Bien T, Miller, Tonigan J 1993 Brief interventions for alcohol problems; a review. Addiction 88:315–336

Burnard P, Morrison P 1991 Caring and communicating. Macmillan, London

Craig T, Boardman A 1998 Common mental health problems in primary care. In: Davies T, Craig T (eds) ABC of mental health. BMJ, London

Crisp A, McCelland L 1996 Guidelines for assessment and treatment in primary and secondary care. Psychology Press, Hove

Davis H, Fellowfield L 1994 Counselling and communication in health care. John Wiley, Chichester

Duxbury J, Brown A 1997 Day surgery – communicating and interviewing skills. British Journal of Theatre Nursing 7(4):10–15

Duxbury J 1999 An exploratory account of registered nurses' experience of patient aggression in both mental health and general nursing settings. Journal of Psychiatric and Mental Health Nursing 6(2):107–114

Egan G 1986 The skilled helper. Brooks/Cole Publishing, California

Epstein O, Perkin G, Cookson J, de Bono D 2003 Clinical examination, 3rd edn. Churchill Livingstone, Edinburgh

Forster S 1997 The A–Z of community mental health practice. Stanley Thornes, Cheltenham

Freeman R 1997 Depression and anxiety intervention guide. The Kings Fund, London

Hampshire M 2002 Muscle bound. Nursing Standard 16(38):14–15

Haslett C, Chilvers E, Boon N, Colledge N 2003 Davidson's principles and practice of medicine, 19th edn. Churchill Livingstone, Edinburgh

Hawton K 2004 Psychosocial and pharmacological treatment for deliberate self harm. Cochrane Library 3

Hawton K 2002 Deliberate self harm in adolescents; self report survey in schools in England. British Medical Journal 325:1207–1211

Hale A 1998 Depression. In: Davies T, Craig T (eds) ABC of mental health. BMJ, London

Jarvis C 2000 Physical examination and health assessment. W B Saunders, Philadelphia

Koplin B, Agathen J 2002 Suicidality in children and adolescents: a review. Current Opinions in Pediatrics 14:713–717

Maynard C 2003 Differentiate depression from dementia. The Nurse Practitioner 28(3):18–27

McAlaney J 2004 A specialist self harm service. Nursing Standard 18(17):33–38

Miller R 1990 Managing difficult patients. Faber and Faber, London

Murphy B, Manning Y 2003 An introduction to anorexia nervosa and bulimia nervosa. Nursing Standard 18(14):45–52

Moore K, McLaughlin D 2003 Depression; the challenge for all healthcare professionals. Nursing Standard 17(26):45–52

Nelson-Jones R 1994 Practical counselling and helping skills. Cassell, London

Roberts H 1998 Children and their families. In: Davies T, Craig T (eds) ABC of mental health. BMJ, London

Rogers C 1957 The necessary and sufficient conditions of therapeutic personality change. Journal of Consulting Psychology 21:95–103

Russell M 1994 Screening for pregnancy risk drinking. Alcoholism: Clinical and Experimental Research 18:1156–1161

Seppa S, Lepisto J, Sillanaukee P 1998 Five shot questionnaire on heavy drinking. Alcoholism: Clinical and Experimental Research 22:1788–1791

Springhouse 2000 Handbook of pathophysiology. Springhouse Corp, Springhouse PA

Thompson N 1996 People skills. Macmillan, London

Turner T 1998 Schizophrenia. In: Davies T, Craig T (eds) ABC of mental health. BMJ, London

Walters P, Tylee A 2003 Tailoring depression treatment to patient needs. Primary Health Care 13(5):27-31

White S 1997 A literature and concept analysis. Journal of Clinical Nursing 6:253–257

York CRD 2002 Improving the recognition and management of depression in primary care. Effective Health Care Bulletin 7:5. York University NHS Centre for Review and Dissemination, York

York CRD 1998 Management of deliberate self harm. Effective Health Care Bulletin 4:6. York University NHS Centre for Review and Dissemination, York

PART 2

Professional and legal issues

PART CONTENTS

Chapter 21

Development of the nurse practitioner role

Mike Walsh

A HISTORICAL PERSPECTIVE

The title nurse practitioner (NP) was first used in the USA in the 1960s to describe a level of advanced nursing practice in primary health care. The role was supported by a programme of education at the University of Colorado, pioneered by Loretta Ford, a nurse, and Henry Silver, a doctor. Since 1965 the title has been used extensively in the USA, and latterly in Canada, to describe an advanced nursing role in both primary care and hospital settings. The nurse practitioner movement developed rapidly with the establishment of a wide range of university-based courses during the 1970s under the umbrella of the National Organization of Nurse Practitioner Faculty (NONPF). This body has played a key role in establishing educational standards for NP practice in the USA.

In the UK, the concept was introduced and pioneered by Barbara Stilwell working in two general practices in Birmingham in the early 1980s, and Barbara Burke-Masters (1986) working with homeless people in London. The early impetus for the growth of the NP movement on both sides of the Atlantic was a shortfall in the provision of medical care (Fawcett-Henesy 1991). This was a major problem for the new Labour government which took office in the UK in 1997 with promises to dramatically improve the ailing British National Health Service. NPs offered a way to remove major bottlenecks in the NHS such as lengthy waiting times in A&E departments, waits of several days for a GP appointment and long waiting lists for surgery. They also offered a solution to the problems caused by the implementation of reduced working hours for junior doctors in hospital and a lack of GPs in primary care. A wide range of NP roles have therefore been developed in hospital as well as primary care.

The implementation of the new GP contract in 2004 further reduced the availability of medical manpower in primary care, especially in the provision of out-of-hours services. There has been a great demand for improved access to health-care services and for those services themselves to change, becoming more user friendly and patient sensitive. NPs have thrived in this environment of change and their role as essential providers of care has now become widely recognized as a result.

That the NP should become a feature of primary health care was forecast in the Report of the Community Nursing Review Team known as the Cumberlege Report which stated:

> 'We believe that community nurses who have, or acquire, the necessary skills in health promotion and the diagnosis and treatment of disease among people of all ages should have the opportunity to practise those skills in the setting of a clinic or neighbourhood'
> (Department of Health and Social Security 1986)

The review team's vision was that the NP would be managed by the neighbourhood nursing manager and assigned to a general practice where s/he would be accountable to the GP. The Tomlinson Report (1992) and the NHS Executive Committee (1993) further supported the concept of the NP in primary health care. A major factor resulting from changes to the GP contract in 1989 (Department of Health and the Welsh Office 1989) was the enormous rise in the number of practice nurses. Many primary care NPs come from the ranks of practice nurses.

NP development was given a huge stimulus when the United Kingdom Central Council (UKCC) published the Scope of Professional Practice document (UKCC 1992) which provided a coherent set of principles to allow expansion of nursing roles. The UK Nursing and Midwifery Council (NMC), which took over from the UKCC in 2001, incorporated the principles of the Scope of Professional Practice within its newly issued Code of Conduct (NMC 2001). These key professional developments have liberated nursing in the UK and fundamentally underpin NP development.

A great deal of water has flowed under the bridge since Tudor Hart (1984) called for doctors to rethink their role in primary care. He called for GPs to become proactively involved in the health of whole neighbourhoods, as well as reactively dealing with individual disease-related problems. The expanded primary care team would be involved in searching out health needs, screening for preventable disease, planning chronic disease management, and collecting morbidity and mortality statistics for the local population to use. This would also mean that patients/clients would be involved in decision-making and professionals would be more accountable to them. Such changes would utilize the skills of all team members and entail an active role for GPs instead of the passive 'shop-keeping inheritance' wherein they meet the public only in times of health breakdown (Tudor Hart 1984).

Primary care nurses would need to adopt a much more integrated approach under this system, rather than the traditional divisions of labour such as that between district nurse and health visitor. Since Tudor Hart made this clarion call for reform, primary care nursing has been further fragmented into the eight Community Nurse Specialist branches that we are familiar with. However, the English Chief Nurse in a consultation paper about the future of advanced practice has proposed bringing together these fragmented roles into a much more integrated primary care advanced nursing role (CNO 2004). Although she did not use the title nurse practitioner, what she is proposing looks rather similar!

There has been one further gradual change affecting nursing which has impacted on NP development and that concerns education. It is not feasible to consider preparation for the NP role in terms of the traditional nurse training of the 1970s. The relocation of nursing education into higher education has been accompanied by a general raising of educational standards with many nurses now being educated at honours degree level and a significant minority working at Masters and Doctoral level. Advanced clinical roles have to be supported by appropriate education and these changes have undoubtedly facilitated the growth of the NP role in the UK.

In summary, therefore, this brief historical overview suggests the following key factors have been involved in NP development in the UK:

- A serious shortfall in the provision of medical services
- Developments in the USA acting as a role model for the UK
- Professional changes such as Scope of Professional Practice

- Recognition of the need for major changes in primary care provision
- Political necessity
- Public demand
- Higher educational standards.

ADVANCED NURSING PRACTICE AND THE NURSE PRACTITIONER ROLE

The concept of advanced nursing practice is highly contentious and this has direct implications for the role and education of nurses. Although the literature on nurse practitioners sees the role as being an advanced nursing role, there are different definitions of advanced nursing which have come from sources other than nurse practitioners. The situation has been further confused by the way the UKCC muddled up the terms 'specialist' and 'advanced' in its report *Standards for Education and Practice Following Registration* (UKCC 1994) which became known as 'PREP' for short. The UKCC used the term specialist, which defines an area of practice, to define a level instead, whilst laying the term 'advanced' on top of specialist as another level. This conceptual confusion has caused many problems and is analysed by the 2004 CNO consultation on advanced practice, which neatly dissects the different meanings of these terms (CNO 2004).

A common theme that emerges from the literature in this area is that advanced practice is distinguished by a high degree of autonomy which is underpinned by accountability and authority. All three must coexist and be underpinned by appropriate education if a nurse is to practice in an advanced role. It is therefore not surprising that nurses in advanced practice roles in hospital care sometimes experience more frustration than those in primary care. The bureaucratic and traditional institutions which make up the culture of large hospitals find it harder to accommodate the fundamental changes that have to happen if an advanced practice nurse is to be allowed to function with autonomy and authority. This assertion is based upon the personal experience of providing nurse practitioner education since 1995.

The importance of these three issues to advanced practice is well illustrated by the development of prescriptive authority for nurses. This has crept forward at a glacial pace over the last decade. If NPs do not have the authority to prescribe, their autonomy of practice is limited and so are the potential advantages they could bring to patient care. Bodies such as the RCN have consistently argued that appropriately educated nurses should be allowed to prescribe from the British National Formulary and trusted as accountable professionals to only prescribe what they feel competent to prescribe. This is the way medicine works. However in nursing we find the process of extended and supplementary nurse prescribing allowing only a limited number of nurses a very limited and specified range of medications that they can prescribe. Patient group directives are a pragmatic attempt to work around these problems and they do help, but they are no substitute for prescriptive authority. Conversations with North American colleagues reveal they are very perplexed at this lack of trust which the British authorities seem to show in their nurses. Prescriptive authority does vary on a state-by-state basis in the US, but even in the most conservative states it does allow far more autonomy than UK nurses enjoy. We know that global warming is rapidly speeding up the rate of flow of glaciers worldwide – the NHS would benefit from such a thaw which would give NPs the authority to prescribe and therefore facilitate autonomous practice for which they would always be fully accountable.

The key definition of the nurse practitioner role in the UK is that offered by the Royal College of Nursing (2002) which draws heavily upon the work of NONPF (USA). The RCN defines a nurse practitioner as a RN who has undertaken a specific course of study of at least honours degree level and who:

- Makes professionally autonomous decisions for which s/he is accountable
- Receives patients with undifferentiated and undiagnosed problems, making an assessment of their health-care needs based on highly developed nursing knowledge and skills, including skills not normally exercised by nurses, such as physical examination
- Screens patients for risk factors and early signs of illness
- Makes differential diagnosis using clinical decision-making and problem-solving skills
- Develops with the patient a plan of care for health
- Orders investigations and provides treatment both individually and as part of a team
- Has a supportive role in helping people manage illness
- Provides counselling and health education

- Has the authority to admit, discharge and refer patients
- Works collaboratively with other health-care professionals
- Provides leadership and consultancy.

The RCN description goes on to describe seven major domains of practice within which the NP displays competency; they are:

- The management of patient health/illness status. This includes health promotion and disease prevention as well as the management of a current illness. The NP has to not only assess the patient but also use decision-making skills to plan and implement a programme of care that is fully acceptable to the patient.
- The nurse–patient relationship. This covers areas such as confidentiality, trust and mutual respect whilst challenging the nurse to reflect upon their own feelings towards the patient in line with the NMC code of conduct.
- The teaching and coaching function. The NP needs to discover what the patient's needs are, assist in providing the necessary patient education, negotiating with the patient over issues such as timing and content whilst providing practical coaching.
- The professional role. Development of the NP role is required together with the direction of care and provision of leadership.
- Managing and negotiating health-care delivery systems. This involves the organization of health-care delivery and liaising with all the other staff and agencies concerned.
- Monitoring and ensuring the quality of health-care practice. Maintaining and improving the standard of health care is an active process that requires both audit and action flowing from the audit process, when necessary.
- Cultural competence. The multicultural nature of society requires us to provide care that is sensitive to the needs of differing ethnic and religious groups.

There is a common mistaken belief that a registered nurse can become a nurse practitioner by learning new assessment skills such as physical examination techniques which are not taught in pre-registration nursing education, and how to take a structured medical history. This is not true. The NP does much more than that and is able to take the information derived from the assessment and use this as the basis for clinical decision-making. Differential diagnoses have to be worked out, investigations ordered and decisions made about the plan of care to be followed. In short, advanced assessment skills are a necessary condition for NP practice but not a sufficient condition. This process of clinical judgement involves bringing together general or abstract knowledge about health and illness with personal knowledge of the patient's story derived from the assessment (Crabtree 2000). In the meanwhile nursing in the UK would be well served if enhanced assessment skills which are currently taught to NPs were actually taught to all pre-registration nurse students. This would increase their fitness for purpose as RNs.

The issue of whether NPs are merely doctor substitutes has been around as long as NPs. Watson et al (1994) argued that a new ecological niche is appearing in the division of health labour that is located between doctors' and nurses' traditional work. This new role requires a level of education and skills that not all nurses will wish to obtain. They argued that: 'whatever this is called, some nurses in some areas will be recruited to it. If they do not colonize it for whatever reason, some other group will' (p. 63). This latter point is very telling as there is the danger that a government desperate to meet its promises to the electorate will be tempted to create yet more new categories of health-care worker to plug emerging gaps in health-care provision. North America has seen the rise of the physician's assistant role in precisely this way and now we are being promised 'First Contact Practitioners' as an ill thought out, quick fix that is one example of this approach by the Department of Health in England. Such initiatives will only confuse and complicate a health-care system that is in urgent need of simplification. Furthermore, they are unnecessary as investment in the advanced nurse practitioner role will resolve such problems.

The 'doctor substitute' argument is often conducted from the starting point that the gold standard for health care is the doctor. This is a fundamental assumption that is often unquestioned. Clearly this implies that NP-led health care cannot be any better and has to be scrutinized as it may be worse. This is of course a fallacious assumption as we know doctors make mistakes. We also know doctors are educated to deliver a particular kind of service to patients which, while it is often what is indeed required, sometimes it is not and patients are dissatisfied. Patients may require the different more holistic approach characteristic of nursing. Perhaps it is time some researchers started from the position that NP delivered care is the gold standard and compared medical services with that?

Leaving that discussion aside and moving on, there is overwhelming evidence that NPs deliver health care that is at least as good as conventional medical care and which produces better levels of patient satisfaction. Perhaps the definitive UK study was carried out by Horrocks et al (2002). This major piece of work was a systematic review of 11 randomized controlled trials and 23 observational studies. It concluded that patients were indeed more satisfied with NP-led care which tended to involve longer consultations. The review also found no evidence that 'doctor care' was in any way better than the health care provided by NPs. Numerous studies reach the same conclusions in the USA (Chase 2004). The NP consultation is longer because it is often a different type of consultation as the NP takes a more holistic approach. Comparing medical and NP consultations on the basis of time alone is therefore invalid as it is comparing two things that are intrinsically different when examined carefully. Chalk and cheese both look like solid white blocks but they are rather different as anybody who has tried to eat a chalk sandwich will testify!

The RCN definition makes clear that the NP remains rooted in nursing but is incorporating skills and knowledge from medicine to develop a new type of health-care service. Van Soeren (2004) has expanded upon this thesis, demolishing the idea that NPs are simply medical substitutes whether in acute hospitals or primary care. They are a new type of health-care practitioner able to provide an intrinsically different, more holistic type of service to the patient. Failure to use the NP in this way is not only a failure of imagination but is also failing the patient. The NP–patient relationship therefore has a wider focus than merely the treatment of disease. The NP becomes a partner working with families and patients, whether in hospital or primary care, to achieve improved health status (Chase 2004).

The situation can be summed up by saying that there are some patients whose health-care needs are best met by doctors, others for whom the NP is better and a third group where it does not matter whether they see a doctor or an NP. The important thing is that the right patient receives the right care from a practitioner who is appropriately qualified to deliver it.

During the 1990s, the UKCC was reluctant to affirm the nurse practitioner role as a legitimate role within nursing. As a result the title has remained unregulated, a matter of grave concern to the profession, not least from a patient protection point of view. It is therefore encouraging to note that as this book goes to press, the NMC are proposing to end this unhappy state of affairs and register the title of Advanced Nurse Practitioner. Consultation is underway as this book is being printed.

The NMC proposals taken together with the CNO consultation document also offer a way out of the rather sterile debate about the difference between clinical nurse specialists (a largely hospital term) and the nurse practitioner. This debate has raged in both North America and the UK and there is no simple answer. There are differences and there are similarities, and the extent to which the roles overlap varies from hospital to hospital. There has been some degree of merging between the roles and both are considered to be advanced practice roles (Chase 2004). There is certainly no reason why a nurse cannot be a nurse practitioner, as defined by the RCN, and work in a hospital environment in a specialist field such as orthopaedics or urology or with children as a paediatric nurse practitioner. There are too many barriers in health care already without erecting more, especially as there is no need. The consultations now taking place in the UK offer the chance to establish a single role, that of the Advanced Nurse Practitioner who can operate either in primary or hospital care with either a generalist or specialist focus. Such a development will simplify matters for the patient and also make for more cost-effective educational provision by avoiding duplication and overlap (Page & Arena 1994).

INTRODUCING THE ROLE

Introducing the NP role represents a major change which has to be skilfully handled. The author has discussed changing nursing roles at length elsewhere (Walsh 2000) but the following key principles can be applied to the challenge of introducing a new NP service.

It is often the perception of change that causes resistance rather than the reality, therefore effective and clear communication is essential in order that there are no misperceptions. The NP role is likely to be successfully introduced if there is good interpersonal communication between all involved, absolute clarity of boundaries and role definitions from the outset, and the NP role is fit for purpose in that it matches the needs of the population served. In order to introduce a nurse practitioner service, whether in primary health care or a hospital environment, the following points are essential:

- There should be a close match between the job description (which should be agreed in advance of making an appointment) and the health need of the target group.
- Ensure all staff clearly understand and agree where the boundaries of practice lie.
- Good communication between team members is essential.

In setting up the new role it is essential to look carefully at the client group involved and ask what authority the NP will need to deliver care. It is better to negotiate access to laboratory investigations, diagnostic radiography and referral rights before setting up the service than to try and do so when they have been refused after the service has commenced. Health services are very complex organizations and introducing an NP can affect a wide range of other staff and services. It is necessary to anticipate these effects and think widely if problems are to be avoided.

Change is not a precise science and things often get very complicated – with all manner of unexpected consequences flowing from introducing an NP service. The implications of this are that NPs must expect the unexpected, have a flexible approach and invest in rapid evaluation and feedback of their new service. The science of complexity has much to teach nurses about introducing NP-led services (Walsh 2000). A key concept is that the relationships between parts of the system are more important than the parts themselves (Plsek & Wilson 2001). Consequently, rather than focus on what the individual players do, such as the NP, RN, doctor or clerical staff, it is more productive to look at how they relate to each other. Job descriptions will only go so far, what matters is how the different team members work together and designing a system that facilitates their interaction.

Staff are more likely to accept change if they feel they are involved in the decision-making process, rather than having change forced upon them. It also is a great help if the individual can see benefits for themselves in change. The implications of these observations are that there should be a widespread discussion process involving everybody from the very beginning. All members of staff should feel they have had their point of view heard and valued.

The change leader should then demonstrate to staff what advantages there are in the new NP role for themselves, as well as improving patient care. Regular updates about progress with role implementation are essential to keep staff involved and avoid the risk of misperception.

It is possible that the biggest opposition to a new NP role will come not from medicine but from within nursing itself. After many years as an educator of NPs I have come to recognize the 'Who does she think she is?' syndrome which can adversely affect student NPs. The problem arises from other nurses who are resentful of change, perhaps feeling already undervalued, and now seeing one of their own sent off to do this high prestige course and receiving what looks like preferential treatment. The NP has to adapt to a new role which is not conventional nursing, and which may be perceived to have moved towards medicine, particularly if the NP dispenses with the traditional nursing uniform.

The NP does upset the traditional order. The sociologists Hall & Spencer-Hall (1982) offer us an insight into what happens as their work demonstrated that in established institutions, staff develop patterns and perceptions about systems that condition them not to question why things are the way they are, or consider alternatives. The NP is of course an alternative and s/he is negotiating new ways of doing things which will directly impact upon erstwhile nursing colleagues who have been doing things their way for many years. They may perceive this new approach as an implicit criticism of their own work. Seen like this, a 'Who does she think she is?' attitude is more understandable.

It is crucial that the NP keeps close links with the nursing community whilst working through a new and changing relationship with medical colleagues. Territorialism within nursing is rife and the NP must be aware of the sensitivities of groups such as mental health nurses, health visitors and of course the midwifery profession. This requires considerable diplomatic skills as the NP negotiates a new order or way of doing things.

THE ROYAL COLLEGE OF NURSING

No discussion of NP development would be complete without mention of the key role played by the Royal College of Nursing (RCN). The RCN has been in the vanguard of the NP movement and developed the first formal NP course in the UK.

The RCN also endorses its support of nurse practitioners by providing indemnity insurance cover against legal liability for members working in the NP role.

The formal course of preparation for nurse practitioners began as a diploma course run at the RCN Institute in 1990. Within 2 years, it was realized that the level of practice for NPs was more than diploma level and the course was developed into an honours degree programme. The RCN course has received much support throughout the country, and there are now nine institutes of higher education nationwide whose programmes are accredited by the RCN. The RCN's leadership has now brought these institutions together with other universities providing advanced practice courses to form the Association of Advanced Nursing Practice Educators (AANPE), which has just negotiated an affiliation with NONPF in the USA. This makes the AANPE the first non-US body to affiliate with NONPF and marks a major step forward in the development of the role. Similar negotiations are underway with Canadian NP educational providers.

The International Council of Nurses has established an Advanced Practice and Nurse Practitioner Network. The RCN represents the UK in this ICN Network and over 30 countries now belong. Nurse Practitioner recognition is taking place in countries such as the Republic of Ireland, the Netherlands, Sweden, Australia and New Zealand. The role is spreading from the USA, Canada and the UK, while the NP has great potential to improve the health care of the developing world.

References

Burke-Masters B 1986 The autonomous nurse practitioner: an answer to a chronic problem of primary care. Lancet i(8492):1266

Chase S 2004 Clinical judgement and communication in nurse practitioner practice. F A Davis, Philadelphia

Chief Nursing Officer England 2004 Post registration development; a consultation. Department of Health, London

Crabtree K 2000 Teaching clinical decision making in advanced nursing practice. NONPF, Washington DC

Department of Health and Social Security 1986 Neighbourhood nursing – a focus for care: report of the community nursing review team (Cumberlege Report). HMSO, London

Department of Health and the Welsh Office 1989 General practice in the National Health Service: a new contract. HMSO, London

Fawcett-Henesy A 1991 The British scene. In: Salvage J (ed) Nurse practitioners: working for change in primary health care nursing. Kings Fund, London

Hall P, Spencer-Hall D 1982 The social conditions of the negotiated order. Urban Life 11:328–349

Horrocks S, Anderson E, Salisbury C 2002 Systematic review of whether nurse practitioners working in primary care can provide equivalent care to doctors. BMJ 324:819–823

National Health Service Management Executive 1993 Nursing in primary health care: new world, new opportunities. HMSO, London

Nursing and Midwifery Council of the UK 2001 Code of professional conduct. NMC, London

Page N E, Arena D M 1994 Rethinking the merger of the clinical nurse specialist and the nurse practitioner roles. Image Journal of Nursing Scholarship 26:315–318

Plsek P, Wilson T 2001 Complexity, leadership and management in healthcare organisations. BMJ 323:746–749

Royal College of Nursing of the United Kingdom 2002 Nurse practitioners. Royal College of Nursing, London

Tomlinson B 1992 Report of the enquiry into London's health service, medical education and research. HMSO, London

Tudor Hart J 1984 A new kind of doctor. In: Black J (ed) Health and disease: a reader. Open University Press, Buckinghamshire

United Kingdom Central Council 1992 The scope of professional practice. United Kingdom Central Council, London

United Kingdom Central Council 1994 The future of professional practice: the Council's standards for education and practice following registration. United Kingdom Central Council, London

Van Soeren M 2004 Developing the nurse practitioner role. ICN Network NP/APN International Conference, Groningen, Netherlands

Walsh M 2000 Nursing frontiers; accountability and the boundaries of care. Butterworth-Heinemann, Oxford

Watson P, Hendey N, Dingwall R 1994 Role extension/expansion with particular reference to the nurse practitioner. School of Social Studies, University of Nottingham, Nottingham

Chapter 22

The professional and legal framework for the nurse practitioner

Claire Callaghan

INTRODUCTION

The nurse practitioner movement in the UK is developing in the midst of continual political, professional and legislative change. Nurse practitioners and their employers are concerned with the issues of accountability for practice and legal issues relating to this expanded nursing role. Nurse practitioners are pushing forward the boundaries of nursing practice and are in the front line of innovation, therefore they sometimes feel vulnerable and question their legal position. The RCN (2002) points out that NP roles are many and varied and therefore the Nursing and Midwifery Council (NMC) must set standards for education and practice, with the NP qualification becoming a part of the Register if both practitioner and patient alike are to be protected. Formal recognition and agreement on the role of nurse practitioners 'will go a long way toward minimizing feelings of insecurity' (RCN 2002, p. 7).

It is vital that nurse practitioners feel they have a secure base from which to practise, and this requires a strong foundation of knowledge derived from education and experience, together with a contract of employment and a good grasp of the professional/legal framework within which to function. This chapter is concerned with that legal and professional framework and, although these issues will be discussed under separate headings, of course the two are inextricably linked.

ACCOUNTABILITY

The NMC rightly insists on the personal accountability of nurses for their practice in the interests of public safety and professional development (NMC 2004). From 1977 practice at a level beyond that of initial registration was covered by what was known as the extended role of the nurse guidelines. In 1992 the Chief Nurses of the UK Health Departments withdrew previous guidance on the extended role, requesting instead that all nurses and managers act in accordance with *The Code of Professional Conduct* (UKCC 1992a) published by the then United Kingdom Central Council for Nursing, Midwifery and Health Visiting and *The Scope of Professional Practice* (UKCC 1992b). Accountability was the cornerstone of both these documents. This meant answering for one's actions and the opening statement in the booklet *Guidelines for Professional Practice* (UKCC 1996, p. 8) was as follows:

'*As a registered practitioner, you hold a position of responsibility and people rely on you. You are professionally accountable to the UKCC, as well as having a contractual responsibility to your employer and accountability to the law for your actions.*'

The latest NMC version of *The Code of Professional Conduct* (NMC 2004) also underlined each nurse's professional accountability:

'*As a registered nurse, midwife or public health nurse you must protect and act in such a way that justifies the trust and confidence the public have in you, support the health of individual patients and the wider community, uphold and enhance the good reputation of the professions.*'

Accountability simply means being able to give an account of your actions with rationales and reasons. It involves obligations and liabilities that arise from several areas of regulation:

- The professional code of conduct laid down by the NMC
- The law on civil wrongs to patients (a civil wrong is known as a tort)
- Employment law which covers the relationship between employer and employee.

Figure 22.1 illustrates how these different lines of accountability affect the nurse. Sometimes they can be pulling in different directions and set up real

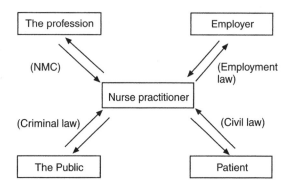

Figure 22.1 Patterns of accountability. The arrows show the two-way nature of accountability. The possible involvement of the law is shown in brackets. Nurse practitioners are also accountable through the process of critical reflection on practice and ultimately their own conscience.

conflicts, especially between accountability to your employer and the NMC. If accountability involves giving an account of your actions it means that you have to be prepared to justify your practice at all times. Accountability may be:

- Personal: the individual is accountable
- Goal-related and therefore measurable: a person cannot be held accountable unless there are written goals to be achieved (standards of care, critical pathways, for example). Clinical audit therefore has a key role in accountability
- About a two-way contract: the employer must make resources available and agree goals before holding the employee accountable
- Motivational for staff: success brings rewards but underperformance brings sanctions.

To be accountable the nurse practitioner needs to be in possession of all the facts and information (education and communication), and have the power (authority) to act as s/he sees fit with proper mechanisms for measuring outcomes in place (audit). Having the power to act is the link between accountability and autonomy. Freedom to act (autonomy) always means freedom to act within the boundaries of competence as well as other external constraints. Autonomy is therefore a relative concept, as nobody has complete autonomy. Even the most powerful medical consultant is constrained by factors such as the General Medical Council, NHS Trust management (e.g. expenditure limits) or limitations on drugs that can be prescribed on the NHS.

Responsibility is a word which is often and mistakenly used interchangeably with accountability. Responsibility means that a person is responsible for following orders, doing what s/he is told and acknowledging when s/he is out of his or her depth. A health-care assistant or pre-registration student is responsible in law and to his or her employer for the care given, but it is the registered nurse who is ultimately accountable. The nurse practitioner should therefore think carefully before delegating tasks to staff who do not hold a nursing registration as the NP will be held professionally accountable for the care received by that patient even though s/he did not carry it out.

EXTENDED AND EXPANDED ROLES

The publication of *The Scope of Professional Practice* document (UKCC 1992b) made clear an important difference between extended and expanded roles. Extension was acceptance of new tasks which were usually delegated by doctors, whilst expansion referred to the practitioner's decision as to which new roles or tasks to take on. Extension therefore implied dependence and expansion implied independence. This led Vaughan (1989, p. 54) to make an important distinction between the two terms: 'If expansion does not occur, the unique function of nursing will be lost'.

Historically, issues in expanding nursing roles were pointed out by Ralph (1991), previously Registrar of the UKCC. He accepted that informal adjustments to role boundaries change in response to patient need and agreed that working arrangements between nurses and doctors leading to improvements in treatment and practice were required. However, he warned of the consequences: 'when a nurse strays into territory formerly bounded by medical practice' (Ralph 1991, p. 123). He pointed out that amongst the consequences, the personal liability of the practitioner accepting the new element of practice and the liability of the practitioner who may have authorized the assumption of new responsibilities must be considered. At all times the best interests of the patient should be paramount.

Another consequence identified by Ralph was that there is always an unavoidable delay between the occurrence of developments and their formalization because developments in clinical practice and care usually happen in the clinical setting before policies and the curriculum can be revised. Ralph argued that this phase – the 'pioneering' phase – is when patient, client and practitioner are most vulnerable. This issue has been addressed by Sarah Mullaly in her final publication as Chief Nurse, England (CNO 2004). Here she outlines some long overdue reforms needed in the way nurses are preceptored after initial registration and then move towards an agreed single generic benchmark for advanced practice, underpinned by education at Masters level. This paper also acknowledges the conceptual confusion which the UKCC displayed in the way they got the terms 'Specialist' and 'Advanced' hopelessly muddled and which has handicapped the development of an advanced practice standard ever since. The CNO paper appears to take a high level of autonomous practice as a given for advanced practice.

The Scope of Professional Practice (UKCC 1992b) was an important document in helping doctors and nurses decide which activities were appropriate to share, and under what circumstances. It moved nursing on from tasks delegated by doctors for which an endless series of certificates of competence had to be obtained. However the political circumstances of the time cannot be ignored. West (1995) pointed out:

> *'that while nurses can expand their scope of practice they should not automatically take on the previous practice of the medical profession but rather work within clear parameters with good support mechanisms and appropriate education.'*

In summary, *The Scope of Professional Practice*:

- made nurses arbiters of their own competence to expand their role
- emphasized their personal accountability
- negated the need for certification for new roles and tasks
- required nurses to delegate appropriately
- insisted that expansion must not compromise existing practice
- offered the potential for expansion of practice in a professional way.

However, there were certain problems with this approach that the nurse practitioner needed to recognize, starting with the awkward question: how could nurses assess their own competence? In other words, how do you know what you do not know? The suspicion has remained ever since 1992 that it was merely a means of resolving medical staffing shortages which might have the paradoxical effect of stimulating conflicts with other professions such as radiography, let alone medicine. The key question of whether nurses can be held truly accountable when they have so little power and therefore autonomy remains. Nurse practitioners have been caught up in all these issues and need to be thinking through strategies with colleagues and employers to work around these problems.

AUTONOMOUS NURSING PRACTICE

The term autonomous has been criticized by some commentators in relation to nursing. For example Kendrick (1995) argued that the use of such terminology is useless in the face of medical dominance. He argued that terms such as 'autonomous' lack validity in view of the power of medicine. In this book we have already argued that autonomy is a relative term for all practitioners and nobody has total autonomy. However, doctors, unlike nurses, are trained to work on their own and to rely on their own independent judgement, consequently professional autonomy is a much more natural concept in medicine.

Nurse practitioners are aiming for higher degrees of autonomy than traditional nurses. It is clear that the more autonomy a nurse practitioner enjoys, the more authority she will have to determine practice and therefore the more accountable s/he may truly be said to be. The reverse is also true – and this calls into question the concept of accountability for many nurses as they have little authority over practice.

How easy is it for the NP to claim a high degree of autonomy? Data from the study by Reveley (1997) – which was carried out to evaluate the nurse practitioner role – is consistent with many studies in this area. The work was done in primary health care in a typical large group practice and involved interviews with patients, nurse and doctors on their perceptions of the NP role. The question of autonomy was a key issue. The nurse practitioner working in the practice herself felt she had a lot of autonomy:

'It (nurse practitioner role) has evolved into me seeing all the acute GP patients who need to be seen and assessing them and diagnosing them and deciding on treatment and deciding on the prescription and again it's how far do you go? I have a lot of freedom; a lot of responsibility. I have a lot of support and I think I'm very careful about where I stand legally … There's a lot of clinical issues that

come up that I ask the doctors about and they haven't got the answer to and there aren't protocols for them either. And again it's just making a clinical decision based on what you know and what the patients tell you.'

This study can be placed in the context of the large scale systematic review carried out by Horrocks et al (2002) which clearly demonstrated the effectiveness of NPs in primary care roles similar to that described by Reveley. Horrocks et al (2002) found NPs were as effective as GPs in dealing with common presentations and scored higher in terms of patient satisfaction.

There are commentators who are concerned about nurse practitioners working autonomously in this way as they lack the ability to deal with the full range of symptoms that may present. Inadequate education of nurse practitioners (such as in-house training or short courses) will limit their capacity to deal with diagnostic uncertainty and complexity. As a result they will be unable to reason from first principles and handle probabilistic reasoning. The limited exposure of nurses to these concepts is likely to find them unprepared for certain diagnostic and therapeutic tasks unless they have a rigorous educational preparation. Chase (2004) has stressed the need for complex problem-solving skills in the full management of patients that go beyond the boundaries of traditional nursing, but which are not coincidental with the boundaries of medicine. This is new territory for nurses and NPs may not always appreciate what it is they do not know.

Doctors are well aware of the medicolegal implications of the current ambiguous nature of the nurse practitioner role and most still see the buck stopping at their door. Doctors have learned to live with uncertainty and this is a new skill NPs have to acquire.

There is a major limitation in the autonomy of NPs however – the prescribing of medication. It is difficult to imagine how any group of nurses could be autonomous when they do not have the power to prescribe medicines but have to rely on another professional to sanction their treatment decisions. The Community Nursing Review first recommended that the Department of Health and Social Security should agree a limited list of items and simple agents which may be prescribed by nurses as part of a nursing care programme, and issue guidelines to enable nurses to control drug dosage in well-defined circumstances (Department of Health and Social Security 1986). In 1992, nurse prescribing became legal with the passing of the Medicinal Products: Prescription by Nurses etc. Act (1992). Nurse prescribing was originally permitted only to those nurses holding a recognized community nursing qualification, thus a nurse not holding such a qualification (including many practice nurses and nurse practitioners) was effectively barred from this professional activity. Commentators also wrote of the severe limitations of the formulary, which contained little more than dressings and minor drugs. Many would have wished the formulary to be extended and to see nurses having prescribing rights which extended to the full British National Formulary (Jones & Gough 1997).

The Health and Social Care Act 2001, Section 63, enabled the introduction of the two categories of independent and supplementary prescribers, thus granting nurses greater scope than ever before for the prescribing of medicines. However, independent prescribing has been limited to medicines on the Pharmacy and General Sales List and approximately 180 Prescription-Only Medicines to treat specified medical conditions; supplementary prescribers are able to prescribe from a wider range of medicines for a broader range of medical conditions but only within a Clinical Management Plan. Such a plan has to be drawn up in consultation with an independent prescriber and requires the patient's agreement (National Prescribing Centre 2003).

Review indicated the need to extend these boundaries still further. In April 2004, within the structure of independent and supplementary prescribers, new additions of medicines were proposed in order that 'patients can more easily access the treatment they need and are able to more fully benefit from the NHS' 'highly skilled workforce' (DoH 2004a,b). The additions included medicines which may be used in the treatment of urgent and life-threatening conditions. Thus the scope of nurse prescribing powers has been slowly extended over recent years. This piecemeal and glacial approach to extending prescriptive authority to nurses is still providing a major handicap to developing autonomy.

It can be seen that the question of the nurse practitioner's autonomy is a difficult one. With regard to seeing patients with undifferentiated conditions and making management decisions from a range of options, the nurse practitioner can be said to be working autonomously. As a qualified nurse s/he is also accountable for those decisions. Yet that autonomy is limited by the constraints of prescribing rights and also by the fact that others exert a large degree of control over the content of his/her work.

Furthermore, a question hangs over the relationship between autonomy for nurses and their role as patient advocate. Porter (1991) contended that the justification for nurses being a patient's advocate was that doctor–patient relationships are biased in favour of doctors so that nurses need to speak up for patients. This is founded on the idea that the nurse does for the patient what s/he would do for him/herself if s/he were well enough. As the NP takes on a more active and autonomous role in managing a patient's health problems and the doctor slips into the background, might not the patient need an advocate to intervene between NP and patient? Clearly the NP cannot advocate against him/herself on behalf of the patient. In mental health, lay practitioners have evolved to take on the advocacy role and NPs may well find the same problem in their evolving practice.

There is therefore a tension between nurses being partners in care with patients, acting as their advocate on the one hand, whilst being autonomous decision-makers on the other. Also, in their relationship with doctors and managers NPs cannot be truly autonomous any more than autonomous practitioners can work successfully as part of a multidisciplinary team. Government policies on teamwork and interagency collaboration further limit the notion of pure autonomy. The best that can be said is that autonomy for nurse practitioners, as for everyone else, is relative.

LEGAL ISSUES SURROUNDING THE NURSE PRACTITIONER ROLE

Within the legal system there are two main aspects – criminal and civil law. Criminal law refers to that system wherein offences are punished by the state and the action is brought by the Crown against a defendant. A case in criminal law is referred to as Regina versus (the defendant), usually written as R v. (the defendant's name), e.g. R v. Brown.

This section is largely concerned with civil law as legal issues surrounding nursing are usually related to civil rather than criminal law. The possible consequences of accountable expanded practice involving greater degrees of autonomy mean that in order to practise safely, the nurse practitioner must understand some of the basic principles which govern civil law. In civil law an action is brought by a person (the claimant in England, the pursuer in

Scotland) against another person or organization (the defendant/defender in Scotland). An action is usually brought because a person has suffered some harm or loss and is seeking compensation. The type of civil law action nurses are most likely to be involved in are claims for damages as a result of the tort of negligence (McHale et al 1998). A tort is a civil wrong and can refer to negligence or trespass to the person.

As well as being accountable to patients via the NMC Code of Professional Conduct (NMC 2002), nurses are also accountable in law, as are all other professionals. A nurse has a legal duty to act carefully towards patients. Failure to do so could lead to a civil action or, in the case of gross negligence resulting in death, could lead to criminal prosecution. A nurse who breaches this duty of care and thus causes harm to a patient may face a civil action in the tort of negligence. The standard legal definition of negligence dates from the 19th century and it is:

> 'The omission to do something which a reasonable man, guided upon these considerations which ordinarily relate the conduct of human affairs, would do, or doing something which a prudent and reasonable man would not do.'
>
> Blyth v. Birmingham Water Works (1856) 11 Exch 1047 per Alderson, B. at 1049

Put simply, therefore, negligence involves not doing something that you should have done, doing the right thing wrongly or doing completely the wrong thing. The tort of negligence has five elements:

1 There must be a duty of care owed to the person
2 The standard of care appropriate to that duty must be breached
3 That breach must cause the harm or damage complained about
4 That harm or damage must have been reasonably foreseeable
5 That harm or damage must be of a kind that the courts can recognize and compensate.

Only if all five elements are present will an action in negligence exist – the absence of any one element will prevent a claimant establishing negligence (*Donoghue v. Stevenson 1932*). The claimant normally has to prove his or her case on the balance of probabilities. A nurse practitioner who is alleged to be in breach of a duty of care would have his or her conduct viewed from the perspective of what is known as the Bolam test (see below) which can be summarized as what (that which) the 'ordinary skilled

nurse in his or her speciality would have done in the circumstances of the case'.

Thus lawyers would take advice from a clinician in the same speciality as the defendant and if the case went to trial, the judge would draw conclusions from expert evidence as to the standard of professional practice. The legal principles have their basis in the case of *Bolam v. Friern Hospital Management Committee [1957] 2 All ER 118* and this has become known as the Bolam test. The term nurse practitioner can be substituted for man in the definition below:

> 'The test is the standard of the ordinary skilled man exercising and professing to have that special skill. A man need not possess the highest expert skill; it is well established in law that it is sufficient if he exercises the ordinary skill of an ordinary competent man exercising that particular art'
>
> (per McNair J in Bolam v. Friern Hospital Management Committee [1957] 2 All ER 118.)

In practice this means that if there is expert opinion supporting a course of action, it is deemed reasonable. If there is expert opinion to the contrary, judges have not chosen between them, merely observing that there are sometimes differences of professional opinion. The support given by expert opinion means the action is reasonable even if arguments to the contrary are deployed.

The recent growth of the evidence-based practice movement has not gone unnoticed in law and has begun to change the Bolam principle. A key decision was handed down by Lord Slynn of Hadley in the *Bolitho v City and Hackney Health Authority* case in 1997. This case went all the way to the House of Lords and hinged upon whether the opinions of expert witnesses can override other considerations. In this case the judgement opened the door for the judiciary to set aside expert opinion by stating that the court, if it thinks a course of action is wrong and illogical, is not bound to hold that a defendant practitioner escapes liability just because he can produce expert opinion in his support. This means that if the judge is satisfied that expert opinion cannot be logically supported, he may set that opinion aside. Evidence-based practice may be used by those wishing to make just that point as they seek to destroy a practitioner's defence based on the Bolam test. The nurse practitioner will be on safer ground in justifying practice upon the basis of evidence which demonstrates clinical effectiveness rather than opinion as to what constitutes 'the ordinary skill'.

But what of nurses expanding their roles? Does the nurse practitioner taking on tasks that traditionally belong in the medical domain have to work to the same standard as the ordinary doctor? In *Wilsher v. Essex Area Health Authority* (1987), it was determined that 'the inexperienced doctor needs to realize his own incompetence and seek supervision'. In the case of *Nettleship v. Weston (1971)*, Lord Denning said that:

'The learner's incompetent best is not good enough. A junior doctor should have a minimum of competence necessary for the safety and proper treatment of the patient, regardless of his actual level of competence and experience.'

In determining competence the primary focus of the courts is not whether a task is carried out by a nurse or a doctor but what reasonable standard of care the patient should expect to receive. Therefore Dimond (2004, p. 551) explains that:

'when a clinical nurse specialist or consultant nurse takes on an expanded role they must provide the same standard of care which would have been provided by the health professional who would originally have performed that activity.'

Nurse practitioners taking on doctors' tasks need to remember that if doctors are used as the 'gold standard' by which to measure competence, the medical standard of care is the standard of a reasonably skilled and experienced doctor (Bolam test). This begs the question – reasonable by whose standards?

'In my view the law requires the trainee or learner to be judged by the same standard as his more experienced colleagues. If it did not, inexperience would frequently be urged as a defence to an action for professional negligence'
(Glidewell in the Court of Appeal Judgement, Wilsher v. Essex AHA 1986)

In other words, a nurse is likely to be judged by the professional standard of the post s/he is performing at that time, 'regardless of the innovative nature of the post', rather than by his or her own standards as a nurse (Dowling et al 1996, p. 1212). This leads logically to the view that:

'If a nurse undertakes a task for which s/he knows s/he has insufficient training, this in itself may constitute negligence, even if she is acting on the orders of a doctor … if a nurse takes on the doctor's

role s/he will be judged by the standards of the reasonable doctor.'
(Kloss 1988, p. 41–47)

To paraphrase Glidewell, the nurse practitioner, if called upon to perform a specialist skill, should as part of that skill seek the advice and help of someone more experienced. Glidewell was referring to junior doctors and said: 'If he does seek such help, he will often have satisfied that test, even though he may himself have made a mistake' (Kloss 1988, p. 43). Kloss adds that 'a nurse who accepts instruction from the doctor is not negligent unless the instructions are patently wrong, because it is usually reasonable to rely on someone more expert than oneself'. However, the liability of a doctor does not necessarily exclude the liability of the nurse.

This complex issue may be summarized as follows:

- The best legal advice to nurse practitioners is that whenever you are practising in an expanded role which was once medical territory, you have to be as competent as a reasonable doctor.
- All nurses are aware that it is no excuse to say: 'I only did what the doctor told me' when such instructions were obviously wrong, such as in a drug error. That principle also applies to nurse practitioners – such is the nature of accountable practice.

VICARIOUS LIABILITY

Earlier in this section we saw that the person responsible for the commission of a tort is the person held to be liable. It is possible, however, that another person who has not personally committed the tort may be held to be liable in addition to the person who did commit it. This is referred to as the doctrine of vicarious liability. In such a situation there has to be a clearly recognized relationship between these two individuals such that in law it can be accepted that one person has responsibility for the other person who committed the tort in question. Relationships of relevance in vicarious liability are:

- Master and servant relationship
- Principal and independent contractor relationship
- Principal and agent relationship
- Parent and child relationship.

A contract of service usually involves a close relationship between the parties whereby one can hire or fire the other and where he or she has greater control over the actions of the other person – the master and servant relationship. In more modern language this translates as employer (e.g. NHS trust or GP) and employee (nurse practitioner). The master and servant relationship is the one that most vicarious liability actions tend to involve. A legal maxim 'qui facit per alium facit per se' is applied – this translates into: 'he who does a thing through another does it himself'. The relationship that exists between master and servant is defined in the following rather arcane legal language:

- The master controls his servant
- The master chooses his servant
- The master and servant are a group
- The master profits from the servant's work for him.

Translating these terms into a modern health-care setting shows that the employer fulfils the criteria for vicarious liability for the nurse practitioner. There is a let-out for the employer, however; he is not liable if the nurse practitioner was working for his or her own personal gain when the incident occurred. As long as the nurse practitioner was working for the employer and not for personal gain, the employer remains liable, however inappropriate the employee's actions may have been. It is wise therefore to always be working within your job description and contract and where significant role expansion takes place, these should be re-negotiated. Situations where the employer may be liable on his own account include:

- The employer authorizes the act
- The employer is negligent him/herself
- The work involves certain serious risks of damage
- The employer is under a statutory or strict liability.

In summary, the employer is liable for the civil wrongs of the employee during the course of employment, providing those acts are not for personal gain.

The NMC Code of Professional Conduct (2004, para 6.3) states that:

'If an aspect of practice is beyond your level of competence or outside your area of registration, you must obtain help and supervision from a competent practitioner until you and your employer consider that you have acquired the requisite knowledge and skill'.

In order to fulfil their accountability to the patient and to the NMC, nurses 'must acknowledge the limits of your professional competence and only undertake practice and accept responsibilities for those activities in which you are competent' (NMC, 2004,para 6.2) before expanding their roles. In certain circumstances, Kloss (1988, p. 43) pointed out that 'in fact it may constitute gross misconduct justifying dismissal for a nurse to refuse to obey a doctor's instructions'. Obvious examples include a patient resuscitation attempt or refusal to help a patient as a result of some personal view held by the nurse. No nurse can pick and choose which patients s/he will or will not care for. The principle of professional accountability means each nurse is personally accountable; nobody else will take the blame.

All vicarious liability means is that lawyers for the claimant will always sue the employer as the employer can be held liable for the tort of negligence and higher damages can be recovered from the employer rather than an individual. Nurse practitioners have no need to join the Medical Defence Union (MDU) and could be placing themselves in an awkward position if things ever did go wrong. In such a situation, who would be the main priority for the MDU, the doctor or the NP? The Royal College of Nursing indemnity insurance scheme provides full cover for NPs as back-up to the principle of vicarious liability and ensures there is no conflict of interest with another professional group. Vicarious liability does not mean that doctors can cover nurses, although this notion may still be evident in some quarters. In the following quote (Reveley 1997) a practice nurse interviewed stated that:

'Well, you're always going to have the GP to back you, aren't you? You're never going to make a decision on your own. Someone's always going to have to check at some point, I always feel reassured when there's someone to back you and I guess it's the same for the nurse practitioner.'

This view is very naive. The problem is that it has not been the same for the nurse practitioner. If you are practising in a true NP role with a high degree of autonomy, you cannot ask the GP to check every decision. The need expressed in this quote to have all decisions verified by another profession really calls into question in a fundamental way nurse's aspirations to full professional status. Since this chapter was first published, the Code of Professional Conduct has been reissued and now states (NMC 2004) that:

'you are personally accountable for your practice. This means that you are answerable for your actions and omissions, regardless of advice or directions from another professional.'

TRESPASS

Trespass is a civil law concept and can apply to land, property or to the person. Trespass to the person has several aspects: assault is an attempt at, or threat of, unlawful force being applied to the person. Battery is the actual application of force to that person where physical contact occurs (Dimond 2004). Touching a patient without consent is battery and, unlike negligence, harm does not have to ensue for damages to be awarded. There is no trespass to the person however if there is no intention. Accidental contact is not battery (although it may be negligence!).

The major legal defence against the civil torts of assault and battery is consent. It follows that the nurse practitioner must be careful to gain consent to care whenever possible. Consent can be given in writing, orally or by co-operation (NMC 2004). Where investigations or treatments carry a special risk, written consent should be obtained and traditionally this has been the responsibility of the doctor. However, nowadays nurses are becoming involved increasingly in gaining written consent from patients. The nurse practitioner involved in gaining written consent from patients should act in accordance with local policy, the NMC Code of Professional Conduct and at all times be aware of the limits to his or her own competence.

A person can give a legally valid consent if s/he 'can understand and retain treatment information and can use it to make an informed choice' (NMC 2004). Consent is described (Dimond 2004) as: 'a process of communication between the patient and professional that may result in the patient signing a form which is evidence that the patient agrees to the proposed treatment'.

A difficult area concerns how much information constitutes a sufficient amount for consent to be informed. The view in the UK is that the doctor decides how much is sufficient, which means that the doctor is not obliged to discuss every possible complication, however remote the possibility. Not all patients wish for detailed information and the nurse practitioner must respect this, but it must be remembered that legal action may follow if the patient feels s/he was given incomplete information and harm ensued as a result. This is where a note communicating what the patient was informed of should be put on the patient's records as this will be crucial in any subsequent legal action.

Consent to touching by one person or profession does not act as consent to touching by any other person or profession (Dowling et al 1996). Without explaining to the patient that she is a nurse, the nurse practitioner may invalidate the patient's consent if the patient assumes by the nature of the task and the way the nurse practitioner 'held herself out' that she is a doctor.

In determining standard of care, the court will take account of a range of things, including the task and the way in which the nurse 'holds herself out'– her dress, language, name badge, and so on. According to Dowling et al (1996, p. 1212), if a task is usually performed by a doctor and the patient expects it to be performed by a doctor, the nurse practitioner must explain her status to the patient. In these circumstances, it is possible that the patient may not consent to the task being performed by a nurse. In her early pioneering days in the 1980s Stilwell approached the Medical Defence Union for insurance cover and, after much negotiation, a 10-point agreement was reached to safeguard patients. One of the points stated that:

'it is essential, both ethically and for the credibility of the project, that the patients realize that they are consulting a nurse, not a doctor, and there will be considerable emphasis on conveying this information.'

(Stilwell 1988, p. 86)

If the patient gives consent to a procedure and the nurse practitioner's title and role are carefully explained, there is no civil case to answer for assault, battery or trespass upon the person.

Criminal proceedings would only be likely in extreme cases, for example, where a patient died as a result of gross negligence – when a charge of manslaughter might be brought. For a criminal charge of assault leading to actual or grievous bodily harm, the prosecution has to prove intent to inflict harm on the part of the assailant. This explains why doctors or nurses are rarely prosecuted (despite one or two dramatic and rare cases such as Dr Harold Shipman) under this section of the criminal law as, however incompetent they may have been, to prove that harm was intentional is extremely unlikely. The Shipman case though does mean we all have to be alert and never assume that a health-care practitioner could not possibly deliberately harm a patient. One final point about the criminal law is that if the victim consents to having violence inflicted upon him or her, this does not constitute a defence for the accused.

RECORD-KEEPING

The Code of Professional Conduct states that 'health care records ... should provide clear evidence of the care planned, the decisions made, the care delivered and the information shared' (NMC 2004). Good record-keeping promotes good-quality patient care, safeguards the nurse in case of legal or disciplinary action and empowers nurses to practise to the highest standard of care.

Your records must stand up in a court of law or disciplinary hearing, and should be capable of use by another health professional in order that continuity of care is provided. In the event of a patient complaint about the care given by a nurse practitioner, the complaint could be heard in a number of places: a local investigation aimed at resolution, a NMC hearing, a Healthcare Commission investigation or a court of law. Legal action can be taken up to 3 years after an alleged incident, which means that unless the nurse practitioner has kept good records, s/he is unlikely to have any recollection of a patient subsequently bringing a complaint. In addition, 'the approach to record keeping that courts of law adopt tends to be that "if it is not recorded, it has not been done" ' (NMC 2004). The NMC states that there are a number of factors that contribute to effective record keeping – records should:

- be factual, consistent and accurate
- be written as soon as possible after an event has occurred, providing current information on the care and condition of the patient or client
- be accurately dated, timed and signed, with the signature printed alongside the first entry

- not include abbreviations, jargon, meaningless phrases, irrelevant speculation and offensive subjective statements.

CONFIDENTIALITY

Confidentiality is an important consideration in record-keeping, as in any other area of professional practice. Dimond (2004) states that there is a duty of confidentiality owed to the patient by every employee. The duty of confidentiality owed by a nurse practitioner would arise from the duty of care in negligence, implied duties in the contract of employment, from the statutory duties required by the Data Protection Act (1998) and the European Convention on Human Rights (Dimond 2004). In addition, the case of *A v B plc [2002] EWCA Civ 337* establishes that:

> *'in the great majority of situations where the protection of privacy was justified, an action for breach of confidence would provide the necessary protection ... a duty of confidence would arise whenever the party subject to the duty was in a situation where he either knew or ought to know that the other party could reasonably expect his privacy to be protected.'*
>
> (per Lord Woolf, CJ)

It is now thought that the Human Rights Act will lead to an increase in litigation for claims that confidentiality has not been respected (Dimond 2004). A patient who suffers damage 'due to an unauthorized disclosure' is entitled to compensation (DoH 2000).

The Code of Professional Conduct states that the nurse must 'treat information about patients and clients as confidential and use it only for the purposes for which it was given' (NMC 2004). Disclosure should be made only with the patient's consent, where required by law or the order of a court, or where your disclosure can be justified in the wider public interest.

The Data Protection Act 1998 grants the right to patients to access personal information held as written and computer records. Request for access may be made in writing, and following payment of the required fee and verification of the patient's identity, the information must be provided. Information may be withheld in accordance with specified exemptions to the right of access (Dimond 2004). If it is believed that the data is erroneous, the patient can ask for these to be amended. If a patient is incapable due to mental disorder or incapacity, a request can be made on his or her behalf. Children can request to see their records if they are deemed to be mature enough to do so.

The Data Protection Act (1998) requires personal data to be:

- obtained fairly and lawfully
- obtained only for one or more specified and lawful purposes
- adequate, relevant and not excessive for these purposes
- accurate and where necessary kept up-to-date
- not kept for longer than is necessary for the specified purpose
- made available to data subjects on request
- properly protected against loss or disclosure.

The doctor may refuse to divulge any or all personal health data if requested by a patient on the grounds that:

- it may be possibly harmful to the patient's physical or mental health
- where the request is made by another, and where the subject had supplied that information in the expectation that it would not be disclosed
- where disclosure of the personal data would reveal information which relates to and identifies another person.

KEEPING UP-TO-DATE

The law expects that professionals keep up-to-date with current practice (*Gascoine v Ian Sheridan, 1994*). This does not mean that if a nurse practitioner fails to read one article or use equipment that is newly invented and not widely available s/he will be held to be negligent. But it does mean that where new information is widely available the nurse practitioner should read it and act on it. Clinical guidelines such as those from the National Institute for Health and Clinical Excellence (NICE) are increasingly available. They are intended to promote good practice but may be used as part of the evidence in a claim in negligence (*Bolitho v City and Hackney Health Authority, 1997*). Employers also have a responsibility in this regard, particularly in relation to health and safety, such as moving and handling techniques.

The National Patient Safety Agency (NPSA) issues bulletins regarding a variety of products and equipment which the employer would be advised to observe and to direct its employees also to observe.

The nurse practitioner therefore has a legal and professional duty to update his or her knowledge: ignorance is no defence in law. Health-care workers should 'at the very least be prepared to demonstrate a personal systematic updating regime' (Tingle 2002). Nurses 'have a responsibility to deliver care based on current evidence, best practice and where applicable, validated research when it is available' (NMC 2004, para 6.5).

DELEGATING TO OTHERS

A more senior nurse or manager can be negligent in delegation. This leaves him or her liable in the event of a claim in negligence and also accountable to the NMC (if a nurse) for misconduct. Before delegating any tasks, a nurse practitioner therefore should satisfy him/herself on the following:

- The extent of the nurse's knowledge
- How skilful the nurse is at the delegated task – a verbal check may be sufficient
- Supervision of the nurse while s/he carries out the delegated function. This should take place over time and follow teaching of knowledge and skill as appropriate to compensate for any deficiencies. This is important in the case of an unregistered nurse – supervision should be ongoing (Young 1994, p. 58).

In nursing there is a hierarchy of authority which may be reinforced in job descriptions and grading criteria. Thus, a postholder may be expected to supervise junior staff and teach qualified or unqualified staff. A student nurse is responsible for giving good-quality care, but it is the registered nurse who remains accountable to the NMC (NMC 2004).

The General Medical Council's guidance *Good Medical Practice* (1995) permits the delegation of medical care to nurses if they are certain the nurse is competent to undertake the work. However, the doctor remains responsible for managing the patient's care. When accepting a task the nurse must be sure s/he is competent to perform it. Negligent delegation and negligent acceptance of a task are both liable for any resultant harm to the patient (Kloss 1988).

Summary

This chapter has outlined the legal and professional position of the emerging nurse practitioner role. As a result of the newness of the role, we have had to extrapolate from existing principles to offer a discussion of the likely situation. It is in the nature of the civil law that precedents have to be set before principles become firmly laid down in law, therefore important changes to the guidance offered in this chapter may occur in the future. The fundamentals for safe practice remain those of personal accountability, the basic tests surrounding the tort of negligence, and the advice that if you cannot do something as well as a reasonable doctor, you should not be doing it at all. Above all, keep the patient informed of who you are and what you are about to do. Good communication will eliminate many potential problems.

References

Blyth v. Birmingham Water Works (1856) 11 Exch 1047

Bolam v. Friern Hospital Management Committee (1957) 2 All ER 118

Chase S 2004 Clinical judgement and communication in nurse practitioner practice. F A Davis, Philadelphia

CNO 2004 Chief Nursing Officer. Post Registration Development. Department of Health, London

Department of Health and Social Security 1986 Neighbourhood nursing – a focus for care: report of the community nursing review (Cumberlege Report). HMSO, London

Department of Health 2000 Data Protection Act 1998. Online: http://www.dh.gov.uk/PolicyAndGuidance/Organisation Policy/RecordsManagement [Accessed 19:11:04].

Department of Health 2004a Nurses' prescribing powers to be expanded even further. Online: http://www.dh.gov.uk/PolicyAndStatistics/ PressReleasesNotices/fs/en [Accessed 17:11:04].

Department of Health 2004b Supplementary prescribing FAQ. Online: http://www.dh.gov.uk/PolicyAndGuidance/Medicines PharmacyAndIndustry/Prescriptions/Supplementary Prescribing/fs/en [Accessed 17:11:04].

Dimond B 2004 Legal aspects of nursing. Pearson Education, Harlow, Essex

Donoghue v. Stevenson [1932] AC 562

Dowling S, Martin R, Skidmore P et al 1996 Nurses taking on junior doctors' work: a confusion of accountability. British Medical Journal 312:1211–1214

General Medical Council 1995 Good medical practice. GMC, London

Horrocks S, Anderson A, Salisbury C 2002 Systematic review of whether nurse practitioners working in primary care can provide equivalent care to doctors. British Medical Journal 324:819–823

Jones M, Gough P 1997 Nurse prescribing – why has it taken so long? Nursing Standard 11(20):39–42

Kendrick K 1995 Codes of professional conduct and the dilemmas of professional practice. In: Soothill K, Mackay L, Webb C (eds) Interprofessional relations in health care. Edward Arnold, London

Kloss D 1988 Demarcation in medical practice: the extended role of the nurse. Professional Negligence, March/April

McHale J, Tingle J, Peysner J 1998 Law and nursing. Butterworth-Heinemann, Oxford

National Health Service Training Directorate 1996 Keeping the record straight: a guide to record keeping for nurses, midwives and health visitors. Department of Health, London

National Prescribing Centre 2003 Supplementary prescribing: a resource to help healthcare professionals to understand the framework and opportunities. National Prescribing Centre, Liverpool. Online: http:www.npc.co.uk_pres.htm [Accessed 19:11:04]

Nettleship v. Weston (1971) 2QB 691. (Cited in: Dowling et al 1996)

NMC 2004 Nursing and Midwifery Council. Code of professional conduct: standards for conduct, performance and ethics, Nursing and Midwifery Council, London

Porter S 1991 The poverty of professionalisation: a critical analysis of strategies for the occupational advancement of nursing. Journal of Advanced Nursing 17:720–726

Ralph C 1991 The role of the regulatory body. In: Savage J (ed) Nurse practitioners: working for change in primary health care nursing. King's Fund, London

Reveley S 1997 Introducing a nurse practitioner into general medical practice; the Maryport experience. A report for North Cumbria Health Authority in association with Celiste College. St Martin's College, Carlisle

RCN 2002 Nurse practitioners – an RCN guide to the nurse practitioner role, competencies and programme accreditation. Royal College of Nursing, London

Stilwell B 1988 Patient attitudes to a highly developed role – the nurse practitioner. Recent Advances in Nursing 12:82–100

Tingle J 2002 Clinical negligence and the need to keep professionally updated. British Journal of Nursing 11(20):1304–1307

UKCC 1992a The code of professional conduct for nurses, midwives and health visitors. United Kingdom Central Council for Nurses, Midwives and Health Visitors, London

UKCC 1992b The scope of professional practice. United Kingdom Central Council for Nurses, Midwives and Health Visitors, London

UKCC 1996 Guidelines for professional practice. United Kingdom Central Council for Nurses, Midwives and Health Visitors, London.

Vaughan B 1989 Autonomy and accountability. Nursing Times 85(3):54–55

West B J M 1995 Health service developments and the scope of professional nursing practice: a review of the pertinent literature. National Nursing Midwifery and Health Visiting Advisory Committee, Edinburgh

Wilsher v. Essex Health Authority (1986) 3AII ER 80

Young A P 1994 Law and professional conduct in nursing. Scutari Press, London

Index

Page numbers in *italics* refer to boxes, figures and tables.